Globalization and Economic and Financial Instability

The Globalization of the World Economy

Series Editor: Mark Casson
Professor of Economics
University of Reading, UK

Future titles will include:

Global Supply Chain Management
Masaaki Kotabe and Michael J. Mol

Critical Perspectives on Globalization
Marina Della Giusta, Uma S. Kambhampati and Robert Hunter Wade

Wherever possible, the articles in these volumes have been reproduced as originally published using facsimile reproduction, inclusive of footnotes and pagination to facilitate ease of reference.

For a list of all Edward Elgar published titles visit our site on the World Wide Web at
www.e-elgar.com

Globalization and Economic and Financial Instability

Edited by

H. Peter Gray

*Emeritus Professor of International Business and Economics
Rutgers University, NJ, USA*

and

John R. Dilyard

*Associate Professor
St Francis College, Brooklyn, USA*

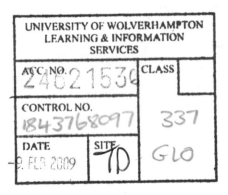
THE GLOBALIZATION OF THE WORLD ECONOMY

An Elgar Reference Collection
Cheltenham, UK • Northampton, MA, USA

Published by
Edward Elgar Publishing Limited
Glensanda House
Montpellier Parade
Cheltenham
Glos GL50 1UA
UK

Edward Elgar Publishing, Inc.
136 West Street
Suite 202
Northampton
Massachusetts 01060
USA

A catalogue record for this book is available from the British Library.

ISBN   1 84376 809 7

Printed and bound in Great Britain by MPG Books Ltd, Bodmin, Cornwall

Contents

Acknowledgements

The editors and publishers wish to thank the authors and the following publishers who have kindly given permission for the use of copyright material.

Blackwell Publishing Ltd for article: Joseph E. Stiglitz (1999), 'Reforming the Global Economic Architecture: Lessons from Recent Crises', *Journal of Finance*, **54** (4), August, 1508–21.

Claudia Buch for article: Claudia M. Buch, Ralph P. Heinrich, Lusine Lusinyan and Mechthild Schrooten (2000), 'Russia's Debt Crisis and the Unofficial Economy', *Kiel Working Paper*, **978**, April, 1–3, 1–38.

Cambridge University Press, the Centre for Economic Policy Research and Centre International D'Etudes for excerpt: Barry Eichengreen and Richard Portes (1987), 'The Anatomy of Financial Crises', in Richard Portes and Alexander K. Swoboda (eds), *Threats to International Financial Stability*, Chapter 1, 10–58.

Eastern Economic Association for articles: James Tobin (1978), 'A Proposal for International Monetary Reform', *Eastern Economic Journal*, **4**, July–October, 153–9; S. Stanley Katz (1999), 'The Asian Crisis, The IMF and the Critics', *Eastern Economic Journal*, **25** (4), Fall, 421–39; Peter B. Kenen (2002), 'Currencies, Crises, and Crashes', *Eastern Economic Journal*, **28** (1), Winter, 1–12; Paul A. Volcker (2002), 'Globalization and the World of Finance', *Eastern Economic Journal*, **28** (1), Winter, 13–20; Dominick Salvatore (2002), 'The Euro: Expectations and Performance', *Eastern Economic Journal*, **28** (1), Winter, 121–36; Ajit Singh (2003), 'Capital Account Liberalization, Free Long-term Capital Flows, Financial Crises, and Economic Development', *Eastern Economic Journal*, **29** (2), Spring, 191–216.

Economic Policy Institute (www.epinet.org) for article: Robert A. Blecker (1999), 'The Ticking Debt Bomb: Why the U.S. International Financial Position Is Not Sustainable', *Economic Policy Institute Briefing Paper*, **85**, 1–22.

Elsevier for article and excerpts: Carlos Diaz-Alejandro (1985), 'Good-bye Financial Repression, Hello Financial Crash', *Journal of Development Economics*, **19** (1/2), September–October, 1–24; H. Peter Gray (1999), 'Macro Financial Stability Policy: An Overview for a Globalized World', in H. Peter Gray (Series ed.) and Irene Finel-Honigman (ed.), *Research in International Banking and Finance: European Monetary Union Banking Issues: Historical and Contemporary Perspectives*, **14**, 3–18; Terutomo Ozawa (2001), 'Borrowed Growth: Current-account Deficit-based Development Finance', in Khosrow Fatemi (ed.), *International Public Policy and Regionalism at the Turn of the Century*, Chapter 7, 95–113.

Federal Reserve Bank of Chicago for article: George G. Kaufman (2000), 'Banking and Currency Crises and Systemic Risk: Lessons from Recent Events', *Economic Perspectives*, Third Quarter, 9–28.

Federal Reserve Bank of Kansas City for article: Andrew Crockett (1997), 'Why Is Financial Stability a Goal of Public Policy?', *Federal Reserve Bank of Kansas City Economic Review*, **82** (4), Fourth Quarter, 5–22.

Institute for International Economics for article: John Williamson (2000), 'What Should the World Bank Think about the Washington Consensus?', *World Bank Research Observer*, **15** (2), August, 251–64.

International Monetary Fund for article: Catherine L. Mann (2000), 'Is the U.S. Current Account Deficit Sustainable?', *Finance and Development*, March, 42–5.

Journal of European Financial Services, University of Insurance and Banking, Warsaw, Poland for article: C.V. Helliar, A.A. Lonie, D.M. Power and C.D. Sinclair (2000), 'The Risks of Investing in Emerging Markets: Fund Managers' Perspectives', *Journal of European Financial Services*, **4** (1), 7–29.

Kiel Institute for World Economics for articles: Claudia M. Buch (1999), 'Chilean-Type Capital Controls – A Building Block of the New International Financial Architecture?', *Kiel Discussion Paper*, **350**, June, 1–25; Stanley Fischer (2003), 'Financial Crises and Reform of the International Financial System', *Review of World Economics/Weltwirtschaftliches Archiv*, **139** (1), 1–37.

Levy Economics Institute for articles: James K. Galbraith (2002), 'The Brazilian Swindle and The Larger International Monetary Problem', *Levy Economics Institute Policy Note*, **2002/2**, 1–6; Wynne Godley and Alex Izurieta (2002), 'Strategic Prospects and Policies for the U.S. Economy', *Strategic Analysis*, 1–29.

Sandy Masur Dornbusch for article: Rudi Dornbusch (2001), 'Malaysia: Was It Different?', *National Bureau of Economic Research Working Paper*, **8325**, June, 1–16.

Oxford University Press for article: T.N. Srinivasan (2000), 'The Washington Consensus a Decade Later: Ideology and the Art and Science of Policy Advice', *World Bank Research Observer*, **15** (2), August, 265–70.

M.E. Sharpe, Inc. for article: David Felix (1997–98), 'On Drawing General Policy Lessons from Recent Latin American Currency Crises', *Journal of Post Keynesian Economics*, **20** (2), Winter, 191–221.

Taylor and Francis Ltd (http://www.tandf.co.uk/journals) for article: Christian E. Weller (2001), 'Financial Crises After Financial Liberalisation: Exceptional Circumstances or Structural Weakness?', *Journal of Development Studies*, **38** (1), October, 98–127.

United Nations Publications for excerpts: Kwang W. Jun and Thomas L. Brewer (1997), 'The Role of Foreign Private Capital Flows in Sustainable Development', in Juergen Holst, Peter Koudal and Jeffrey Vincent (eds), *Finance for Sustainable Development: The Road Ahead*, 109–37; John R. Dilyard and H. Peter Gray (2002), 'Increasing the Contribution of Foreign Investment to Sustainable Development: Domestic and International Policy Measures', in *Finance for Sustainable Development: Testing New Policy Approaches*, 135–57.

World Scientific Publishing Co. Pte. Ltd for article: Paul C.H. Chiu (2000), 'Taiwan's Experience in Dealing with the Asian Financial Crisis and Examination of the Role of Short-term Capital Flows in the Emerging Market Economy', *Review of Pacific Basin Financial Markets and Policies*, **3** (4), 557–64.

Zed Books Ltd for excerpt: Jan A. Kregel (1998), 'East Asia Is Not Mexico: The Difference Between Balance of Payments Crises and Debt Deflation', in K.S. Jomo (ed.), *Tigers in Trouble: Financial Governance, Liberalisation and Crises in East Asia*, Chapter 3, 44–62, references.

Every effort has been made to trace all the copyright holders but if any have been inadvertently overlooked the publishers will be pleased to make the necessary arrangement at the first opportunity.

In addition the publishers wish to thank the Marshall Library of Economics, Cambridge University, the Library of the University of Warwick and the Library of Indiana University at Bloomington, USA for their assistance in obtaining these articles.

Introduction

H. Peter Gray and John R. Dilyard

The focus of this volume is the greater instability of national economies that has arisen in the wake of the deeper international economic and financial integration, known more generally as globalization. The closer a country's economic/financial relations with foreign countries, the more sensitive is that country's economy to repercussions, benign or adverse, from events that take place abroad; and, if weaknesses exist, the more vulnerable is that economy to adverse foreign disturbances. International transactions involving trade or capital serve as conduits for the transmission of shocks from one country to another.

When a trading partner undergoes a spontaneous shock such as a decrease in national income, its demand for imports will be reduced. The more closely integrated the two countries (A and B), the larger will be the absolute value of the effect of, say, a given decrease in national income in B on the demand for A's exports and the greater the possibility A's economy can be thrown into a recession. As long as the shocks are small and both the 'real' and financial sectors of individual countries are resilient, the deeper integration is well worth the greater sensitivity if only because the gains from trade will outweigh the costs of more frequent bouts of minor instability.[1] The exposure of a national economy to the risk of these occasional shocks, then, is a necessary cost of globalization.

Globalization, however, is more than just trade. The deeper integration among nations it engenders is found in both the so-called 'real' sectors (trade) and financial sectors of an economy. Unfortunately, these sectors have tended to be analyzed separately in economics. International trade theory tends to ignore the financial sector. The assumption of balanced trade implies that the existing exchange rate between the two national currencies corresponds, given the levels of domestic prices, to the terms-of-trade compatible with balanced trade; the possibility that capital flows will affect the demand and supply of currency (and hence its value) is not considered. The pattern of trade in more modern economies, however, has influenced and been influenced by foreign direct investment and its resulting effect on capital flows among nations. The greater interdependence created between the real and financial sectors makes it necessary for any discussion of stability (or lack thereof) in a globalized world to address both of them.

One way to illustrate a relationship between a nation's balance on current account and its net international investment position is seen in Figure 1.[2] If a nation's currency is undervalued, it will run a surplus on trade in goods and services: either exports will be greater than the appropriate (balanced trade) value and/or imports will decrease and replacement domestic production will expand. The figure illustrates a condition of deficit on the balance on current account (dissaving *vis-à-vis* non-residents). The deficit is shown as being effected by a mixture of the sale of existing foreign assets and increases in liabilities to foreign residents ('borrowings'). As a result of the dissaving (current expenditures greater than current receipts), the international net worth (INW) of the country *vis-à-vis* foreign residents, has been eroded.[3]

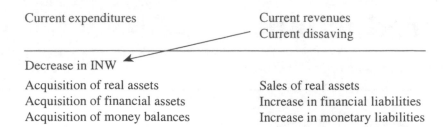

Figure 1　The relationship between the current balance and INW

Note　The entries above the line are current flows of incomes and expenditures and below the line are acquisitions of foreign assets and liabilities by residents. The above the line flows are equal and the surplus of expenditures over revenues is the current deficit or international dissaving. This imbalance is transferred to the asset position and represents the decrease in the INW. The six categories show how the change in INW was distributed among the different genera of assets and liabilities. The apparatus is formally known as 'flow-of-funds analysis' and identifies expenditures (on current purchases or asset acquisitions) as 'uses' and revenues (from the sale of current goods and services or of assets) as 'sources' of funds. This apparatus does *not* allow for changes in the values of pre-existing assets and liabilities in the currency of record.

In a world of flexible rates of exchange (determined by the net flow of funds), the initiative for imbalance can derive either from the capital or the current account. When inflows of capital into a country strengthen its currency's rate of exchange, the price competitiveness of the country's value-added is reduced. A deficit balance on goods and services is then induced (a use of funds) which will tend to match the net inflow of financial or real capital (a source of funds). Alternatively, underlying conditions such as home country tastes can change such that imports become more desirable; in order to re-establish balance on goods and services, the national currency needs to weaken. This process usually takes some time, however.

The greater degree of involvement in the 'real' sector is seen in the existing, much greater volume and value of the exchange of goods and services among nations as a result of broader and more efficient conduits for the production and exchange of goods. International trade has increased as a result of fewer and reduced impediments brought about by the elimination (or reduction) of tariffs and quotas on imports achieved through multilateral trade negotiations. These negotiations took place under the sponsorship of the (now defunct) General Agreement on Tariffs and Trade. The establishment of the World Trade Organization to ensure a level playing-field in the international exchange of goods and services has also introduced an apparatus for arbitrating disagreements over what are considered by one party to be unfair trade practices.[4] The growth of international trade between industrialized or rich countries and developing countries with large supplies of semi-skilled or even skilled labor, at costs which are substantially lower than in the industrialized world, has been the driving force for so-called 'export-led growth' and the elevation of many developing nations to the status of 'developed nation'.[5] Also very important are the huge reductions in the costs of maritime and air transportation which have been achieved mainly by the new technology of containerization and by the economies of scale larger carriers made possible. This deepening of integration has taken place and generated greater specialization within the bloc of industrial countries, as well as between the industrialized and the developing worlds.

Large-scale growth in direct investment by multinational corporations is another factor contributing to the huge increase in the value of international trade as it has improved the quality of the supply conduits between pairs of countries. This is particularly important because foreign affiliates from industrialized countries are often established in developing countries with the express purpose of producing under the parent's own quality standards goods which will enrich the marketing and distribution chain of the parent company in many industrialized countries. Foreign affiliates can also produce goods designed for incorporation in the final assembly process in an affiliate in an industrialized country. The role of multinational corporations hinges on the greater internal ability to transfer proprietary knowledge and management skills. In effect, then, globalization has improved the ease with which goods and services made in one country can be sold and used in a different country.

This process of the elimination of inefficiencies in the linkages or conduits has also been greatly enhanced by huge gains in information technology, which permit better information to be exchanged very quickly between an importer and an arm's-length supplier or among units of a multinational corporation. The development of international trade in the 60 years since the end of World War II would amaze any economist who studied international trade and linkages either between the two world wars or between 1945 and, say, 1958.[6] To this point, spontaneously generated instability in international trade in goods and services has not been a major source of widespread instability although individual goods and industries have experienced rapid changes.

The second area in which the efficiency of conduits has increased tremendously is financial. At the end of World War II, only residents of the United States were not restricted in making investments in foreign countries. The international financial system is now largely without controls over exports of capital by residents of *all* industrialized countries. This is a sea change from the traditional attitude towards international investment in which governments were the main actors and could be expected to moderate 'profit-seeking' activities in order to preclude violent instability in financial markets. It will become evident in the course of this volume that it is this financial integration which is likely to prove the more important source of instability, particularly between developed and developing countries.

Recent years have seen some major financial crises in countries as geographically and culturally disparate as Brazil, Chile, Russia, and Thailand. The elimination of barriers to the free international transfer of funds, often at the instigation of the International Monetary Fund, has grown more quickly than the capability of some nations to exert the appropriate controls over and to instill the necessary degree of sophistication in their own financial sectors. This does not mean that financial stress has not afflicted industrialized nations, but nations with more sophisticated financial institutions have proved better equipped to recognize and to take precautions against the sources of financial instability that exist when countries are allowing the free flow of capital among them – see Volcker (2002; this volume, Chapter 7). The inauguration of the elimination of controls over international capital movements in the industrialized world has been accompanied by a new system whereby exchange rates respond to the flows of funds among countries. Thus, a nation which is, for whatever reason, receiving a steady inflow of capital from abroad (foreign saving) will find its currency has strengthened and its current transactions will show a deficit.

Greater international mobility of capital contributes to major instability when there is a rush to invest in or to escape from the currency of a host country, and the disturbance generates stress within the host's domestic financial system and an imbalance on current transactions (showing either saving or dissaving *vis-à-vis* foreign countries). The trigger of instability does not, in principle, vary between industrialized and developing countries: the trigger is a sudden realization by owners of assets denominated in a (foreign) currency that that currency of denomination is likely to lose value in terms of the owner's own functional currency.[7] Thus, the expectation of the weakening of a national currency will trigger withdrawals of foreign-owned assets from that currency. Once some investors start to sell their assets, the process can become self-fulfilling. When an investor sells a substantial amount of an individual asset, the price of that asset in foreign currency will be reduced and, when the proceeds of the asset sales are sent home (or to a third currency which is expected to strengthen), the currency of denomination will weaken in the foreign exchange market. Provided that the volume of sales is big enough to make the price changes visible, the weakening of the currency will reinforce any thoughts other asset-owners may have of escaping from a vulnerable currency. The process can feed upon itself and could, when there is a sufficient volume of assets owned by non-residents, engender a flight from the currency which comes to be widely perceived as 'overvalued'.

This possibility requires that a currency can be 'overvalued' for a period of time (to set up the potential stress). Here it is necessary to understand the motivations for acquiring assets denominated in a foreign currency,[8] and for host countries to accept large inflows of portfolio investment. The former are normally attracted either by the expectation that the currency of denomination will strengthen within the foreseeable future; other purchases rely on the expectation of higher growth rates in local prices or higher yields than can be obtained in other markets. In both scenarios, a steady inflow can strengthen a currency and can be self-fulfilling in much the same way that a flight from a currency can be generated, though more gradually. The differences in the speed of reaction to a change in expectations suggest that a currency will appreciate slowly but steadily over a period of time but that any major decline will occur at a more rapid, unstable pace.

The argument for liberalizing international capital movements is essentially similar to the argument for free trade of goods and services: allowing capital to move internationally and to seek out the highest available expected rate of return on assets improves the global allocation of resources and the potential value of world output. More investment will take place in countries in which capital formation will have the highest payoff. Implicit in this argument is the assumption that the costs of instability are less than the gains. There is, in addition, a foreign exchange cost because there is a 'debt-carrying cost' to the host economy, so that the totality of the investments must generate enough foreign exchange earnings to allow for the asset-owners to repatriate their earnings/profits even if they do not liquidate the assets.[9] Adding to instability is the degree to which the foreign-owned assets are more easily encashable (or more liquid) than any underlying real assets created with the borrowed funds.[10] Thus, inward foreign direct investment (FDI) is likely to be a superior medium of international investment from both the host country's and the international financial system's points of view, simply because the assets owned by the multinational corporation are likely to be 'real' assets, which are not easily converted into financial assets that can be quickly encashed and repatriated. In this way, FDI does not add to the system's potential for instability.[11]

The threat of instability derives from a failure of the balance of payments on current transactions to allow the host currency to be seen as viable (i.e. there is a continuous stream of current deficits indicating the need to acquire liabilities to finance current expenditures). If the willingness of foreign asset-holders to continue to hold (or own) assets denominated in the host's currency weakens, the potential for a major instability grows. The existence of foreign-owned portfolio assets (bonds and stocks) indicates a potential danger if the performance of the host economy in terms of its current transactions is seen by foreign asset-holders as 'unsatisfactory'. The underlying problem is that for a host nation to reduce its current deficit, the country must both reduce its current expenditures (domestic and international) and weaken its currency, so that its export sector will become more price competitive in world markets.[12] The linkage here is self-evident: if a nation exceeds its perceived capacity to borrow, it will be disciplined by foreign asset-holders seeking to avoid losses. The timing of the corrective action will be forced on the host country when its currency weakens as assets leave and a smooth adjustment is ruled out. Instability in the financial sector will be quickly transferred to the real sector – see Crockett (1997; Chapter 2).

The total (domestic and foreign) current expenditures of a nation can be referred to as its *absorption* of resources. Some reasons for borrowing from abroad are warranted. An inflow of capital can be channeled into capital formation and, provided that the total capital formation generates extra net exports in excess of the costs of borrowing, the host economy will prosper. This is what Ozawa (2001; Chapter 4) refers to as 'borrowed growth'. However, borrowing from abroad (usually by the government) can also be used for consumption to raise the standard of living (to adapt Ozawa's terminology, 'borrowed consumption') and for 'social absorption' (expenditures on physical and social infrastructure).[13] Neither borrowed consumption nor borrowed social absorption can be expected to generate enough foreign exchange in the foreseeable short run to cover the costs of borrowing: it follows therefore that a nation should fund these expenditures domestically and not by incurring easily encashable liabilities with non-residents. Disregard of the costs of borrowing from abroad (running deficits on current account) is a prescription for serious financial instability. The greater the ratio of foreign-owned assets to international reserves, the less time is available for correcting the problem, and the more serious the dislocation is likely to be if there is a concerted withdrawal of assets from the currency.

A country-specific, though probably not unique, case of absorption financed by foreign borrowing is identified by Galbraith (2002; Chapter 15), who suggests that the Brazilian government deliberately maintained an overvalued currency in order to allow affluent Brazilians an opportunity to transfer assets out of their home currency. When the political system and the 'power élite' have identical interests in developing countries – particularly with respect to the freedom to export capital and to the desirability of a strong (read 'overvalued') currency – there is even more pressure on international reserves and an increased risk of instability.

The essential problem is a serious difference in the speed with which the real and financial sectors can adapt to a new set of external conditions. Net flows of financial capital can and will generate changes in the relative values of two (or more) currencies (the rate of exchange between them): these changes will impose changes in the pattern of international trade and require the reallocation of inputs among sectors. The changes that occur in financial markets are reflected in the prices of financial assets far more quickly than the real economy can adapt to the new conditions.[14] All of these changes will also require changes in the standard of living in the countries involved.

When the focus transfers from the costs of irregularities in flows of goods and services to international movements of financial assets, the cost–benefit ratio of globalization can increase substantially. Movements of international capital between nations with closely integrated capital markets create the possibility of larger fluctuations in exchange rates on two counts. First, the source of instability can, like trade, consist of fluctuations in the *flow* of ongoing capital movements, and the larger these flows, the greater the scope for fluctuations. Second, the more closely two national capital markets are integrated, the greater is the volume of accumulated *stocks* of foreign-owned capital in a market likely to be and the greater the potential for accumulated assets to be withdrawn. In this context, and given that integration and deregulation of financial transactions have resulted in a greater level of foreign-owned holdings of financial assets in nearly every country in the world, instability can impose greater costs on individuals and national economies under modern conditions. Financial instability in foreign exchange markets is an important potential 'downside' of globalization and governments (and economists) must anticipate the dangers before markets and data signal developments to the managers of mutual funds and unit trusts.

The linkage between the degree of integration of capital markets among countries ('financial globalization') and the damage that can be brought about by the repercussion from the suddenly perceived insupportability of prevailing exchange rates is important in any examination of recent international economic instability. These phenomena are not restricted to but manifest themselves most frequently in so-called developing, newly industrializing economies, that is in countries which are in the process of evolving from the stage of less developed to modern economies.

There exist three reasons for the greater instability potential in national financial sectors. First, a disequilibrium and potentially unsustainable rate of exchange can be maintained for a period of time until the magnitude of the imbalance between a 'justifiable' and the existing or market rate becomes apparent. A government can deliberately or out of simple unawareness disregard the overvaluation of its currency. Second, the development of large portfolio investments by individual families has grown as mutual funds and unit trusts have created funds denominated in different currencies and currency mixes. The managers of such funds read much the same data and will interpret these data using very similar analytic approaches. They are therefore likely to reach the same opinion about a single currency at much the same time: this is one source of the herd instinct in financial markets.[15] In this way, large sums of foreign-owned assets can be moved quite quickly and are very likely to trigger reinforcing action by other funds. Third, once an imbalance triggers a reactionary flight from the overvalued currency, the process can reinforce itself and the rate of exchange can go past its (new) equilibrium value and instigate even more painful adjustments in the real sector.

Financial markets are, within a national economy, inevitably closely interwoven. There is a danger, then, in focusing on examples of instability which are unique to a single source. The present collection of papers focuses predominantly on what are termed 'currency crises' having their origin in foreign exchange markets.[16] Kaufman (2000; Chapter 3) distinguishes between 'banking crises' and 'currency crises' and recognizes the potentially close interrelationship. Banking crises can be ignited by events in currency (foreign exchange) markets, but they can also occur spontaneously without a currency crisis. Currency crises, by definition, have their source in foreign exchange markets and their greater frequency under the current integration of national financial markets denotes their tie to globalization. If a currency crisis impairs the resilience of the banking sector, the consequences are, of course, more serious. The focus, then, is how the greater integration of national financial markets and the concomitant reduction in regulation of private international capital flows have contributed to the greater frequency of episodes of substantial instability.

This volume is arranged in five parts. Part I provides an overview of the general problem of international financial instability. Part II addresses the problems to which developing nations are particularly sensitive. These nations usually lack the sophistication in their economies, particularly in the financial sectors, to benefit fully from integration into the global financial system – see Dilyard and Gray (2002; Chapter 10) and Singh (2003; Chapter 13). Part III focuses on regional experiences of instability. Part IV addresses problems of instability in the industrialized world. Here the major problems are the unwillingness of the major governments to address the vulnerability of the US economy given its huge indebtedness (negative international net worth) and the ease of encashability of such a large volume of its liabilities as well as the domestic effects of the overvaluation of its currency.[17] Part V includes papers which review structural weaknesses in the international financial architecture.

Notes

1. This assumption, usually tacit, underlies the argument for free trade. It also implies that greater attention should be paid by national authorities to the resilience of their systems.
2. For a fuller description see Jean M. Gray and H. Peter Gray (1988–9), 'International Payments in a Flow-of-Funds Format', *Journal of Post Keynesian Economics*, **9** (2), 241–60.
3. Note that the net worth can also change if existing assets or liabilities change value in their currency of denomination.
4. The existing arrangements tacitly assume balanced trade and are effectively devoted to prevent countries from impeding imports or subsidizing exports in order to run current surpluses. Current surpluses are a means of 'exporting unemployment' or stimulating domestic growth (at the expense of another country's sluggishness).
5. Examples are Chile, Korea, Mexico, Taiwan and some of the more recent entrants into the European Union.
6. The formation of the European Economic Community in 1958 was a major step forward. The European Union now has 14 members and a common currency (adopted so far by 11 countries) and is, within the next few years, scheduled to permit entry by 10 East European countries, which are in transition from planned to market-driven economies.
7. An economic unit's functional currency is the currency in which the unit reports its profits and/or income, and in which it measures its performance.
8. Some large international loans, private and sovereign, are denominated in the lender's currency, but such loans have not been importantly affected by globalization. Some investments in real assets, land, and multinational affiliates can be taken as denominated in the currency of the host country. Portfolio assets, stocks and bonds, are denominated in the currency of the market in which they are traded, and it is this category of assets that has grown so importantly as a result of the liberalization of private capital movements.
9. The needed foreign exchange could be generated by other activities, at least in the short run.
10. If inflows of portfolio assets finance the acquisition of foreign portfolio assets by residents, then the international financial system has become less resilient. Portfolio assets can be quickly encashed if expectations change *and* the government with the threat of a run on its currency cannot require private entities, which own foreign portfolio assets, to sell them and repatriate the proceeds.
11. Multinational corporations do have large amounts of working capital whose composition is subject to perceptions about possible changes in rates of exchange.
12. This is the crux of the so-called absorption theory of balance-of-payments adjustment.
13. The concept of 'social infrastructure' is developed in H.P. Gray (2000), 'Globalization and Economic Development', *Global Economic Quarterly*, **1**, March, 71–95.

14. See Tobin (1978; Chapter 8, this volume).
15. International trade decisions are not affected in this way because of the much larger number of participants and products involved.
16. Kaufman (2000; Chapter 3) examines the linkages between banking and currency crises.
17. For an assessment of the implications of the vulnerability of the dollar, see H.P. Gray (2004), *The Exhaustion of the Dollar: Its Implications for Global Prosperity*. Basingstoke and New York: Palgrave-Macmillan.

Part I
Overview of Global Instability

[1]

The anatomy of financial crises

BARRY EICHENGREEN and
RICHARD PORTES*

Much as the study of disease is one of the most effective ways to learn about human biology, the study of financial crises provides one of the most revealing perspectives on the functioning of monetary economies. Indeed, epidemiological metaphors like fever and contagion feature prominently in the literature on financial crises. Financial crises, like contagious disease, threaten not only the host organism, namely the financial market, but the entire economic environment in which that host resides.

There exists a voluminous historical literature concerned with episodes labelled financial crises.[1] Yet the usefulness of much of this literature is limited by the absence of any definition of the phenomenon under consideration and hence of a minimal structure around which historical observation can be organized.[2] This criticism is not limited to the historical literature, since recent theoretical analyses of financial crises are uniformly deficient in this same regard. While no single definition may be appropriate to all purposes, any work on financial crises should proceed on the basis of an explicit statement of meaning. Since our purpose in this chapter is to provide a perspective on the present and prospective danger of a serious disruption to the global financial system, which we propose to explore by comparing the last full-fledged financial crisis – that of the 1930s – with conditions prevailing today, we adopt the following definition. A financial crisis is a disturbance to financial markets, associated typically with falling asset prices and insolvency among debtors and intermediaries, which ramifies through the financial system, disrupting the market's capacity to allocate capital within the economy. In an international financial crisis, disturbances spill over national borders, disrupting the market's capacity to allocate capital internationally.

This definition suggests an agenda for research, of which the following

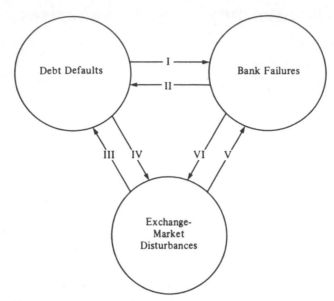

Figure 1.1   Asset-market linkages

questions form only a part. What are the distinguishing features of disturbances which give rise to financial crises? Rather than the nature of the disturbances, is it the financial system's response that differentiates crises from perturbations to financial markets? What is the mechanism through which a disturbance specific to a single market is generalized to the entire system? In particular, what are the roles of asset prices and solvency problems in the process of generalization and propagation? How are the market's allocative capacities disrupted, and what are the implications of this disruption for the course of the crisis itself?

Our definition implies a distinction between generalized financial crisis on the one hand and bank failures, debt defaults and foreign-exchange market disturbances on the other. This distinction is the presence of linkages, which are represented schematically in Figure 1.1. These linkages within the body economic give the essential anatomy of financial crisis.

Consider two examples which play a leading role in our historical analysis. Defaults on sovereign bonds, if sufficiently widespread and disruptive, impede the ability of the bond market to allocate capital across countries. But if these defaults are not accompanied by bank failures (if in Figure 1.1 the linkage labelled 'I' is interrupted), there may exist alternative channels, notably bank loans, through which the capital market's allocative functions may be carried out. Debt default need not give rise to financial crisis. But if, on the contrary, debt default heightens the commercial banks' susceptibility to failure, the danger of a generalized crisis is intensified. To take another example, an anticipated devaluation may threaten the banking system if depositors liquidate their accounts in an effort to avoid capital losses on their overseas assets (an example of the linkage labelled 'V'); but if they hold government securities instead, this linkage is broken and exchange-market difficulties need not be associated with financial collapse. Clearly, the extent and speed of transmission along these linkages depend on institutional arrangements in financial markets, including any institutionalized responses of policy-makers.

In this paper, we focus on the generalization and propagation of financial crises in an international setting. Ideally, these issues of generalization and propagation are studied historically: while all serious disturbances threaten the stability of financial institutions, it is only from the comparison of historical episodes during which different institutional arrangements prevailed that generalizations about the fragility or resilience of monetary economies can be derived. By analyzing the contrasting institutional arrangements of the 1930s and 1980s, we hope to identify configurations which render the international financial system particularly susceptible to collapse.

Our analysis of the generalization of financial disturbances underscores the critical role played by institutional arrangements in financial markets as a determinant of the system's vulnerability to destabilizing shocks. In both the 1930s and 1980s, the institutional environment was drastically altered by rapid change in foreign exchange markets, in international capital markets, and in the structure of domestic banking systems. But the implications of institutional changes have not all been similar. In the earlier period, they generally worked in the direction of heightening the system's vulnerability to shocks; recently, however, some have tended to work in the opposite direction. Our review of the course of crises suggests that the banking system and the linkages by which it is connected to the rest of the financial sector play a pivotal role in the propagation of crises. Our analyses highlight the importance of two sets of factors in the process of propagation: asset-market linkages running from debt defaults and exchange-market disturbances to the stability of the banking system (linkages I and V in Figure 1.1), and the role of economic policy in blocking these linkages and thereby insulating the banking system and the macroeconomy from threats to their stability.

I   The international financial crisis of the 1930s

A.   *The environment*

The 1920s were marked by three sets of developments which increased the international financial system's susceptibility to destabilizing shocks: flux in the foreign exchange market, rapid institutional change in the banking system, and dramatic shifts in the volume and direction of international lending. Each set of developments had its immediate origins in the dislocations associated with World War I.

Foreign exchange markets   The war and its aftermath marked the end of the classical gold standard. Most countries initially succeeded in maintaining their gold reserves and customary exchange rates by withdrawing gold coin from circulation and embargoing bullion shipments. But as hostilities dragged on and were financed through the issue of money and bonds, pressure mounted in foreign exchange markets. The German and Austrian exchanges collapsed by 1918. The British and French rates were propped up by American intervention but depreciated with the termination of support in 1919.[3] The postwar inflationary boom, the reparations tangle and deficit finance of reconstruction all wreaked havoc with national efforts to peg the domestic-currency price of gold.

Policymakers then confronted the question of the appropriate level at which to stabilize exchange rates. The history of subsequent efforts to reconstruct the system of fixed parities is familiar: Britain restored sterling's prewar parity in 1925 following a period of deflation; France opted against reversing half a decade of inflation, pegging the franc price of gold at five times the prewar level; Germany and other countries experiencing hyperinflation established new currency units; and Latin American countries reestablished gold standard parities in conjunction with budgetary reforms and newly independent central banks.[4]

The characteristics of the reconstructed gold standard added to the strains on the financial system. Paramount was the problem of misalignment, starting with the pound sterling, the traditional linchpin of the monetary mechanism. Due to high wages and to changes in the direction of trade, Britain's restoration of the prewar parity rendered the pound overvalued and difficult to defend with the Bank of England's slender reserves. Keynes (1925) estimated sterling's overvaluation at 10–15 per cent. In conventional accounts, an undervalued French franc figures also among the misaligned currencies.[5] Misalignment was related to the problem of maldistributed gold reserves, which came to be concentrated in the United States and France. This maldistribution gave rise elsewhere

14   **Barry Eichengreen and Richard Portes**

to complaints of a 'gold shortage', which induced countries to expand on prewar practice and supplement gold reserves with foreign deposits. The growth of foreign deposits rendered the reserve currencies increasingly vulnerable to destabilizing shocks.[6] Each of these difficulties reflected the failure of governments to coordinate their choice of exchange rates and to harmonize their monetary policies. Ultimately, the consequences of this failure would be far-reaching.[7]

International lending   The impact of the war on patterns of international lending and borrowing was equally profound.[8] The 1920s marked the rise of the United States and decline of Britain as external creditors. The transfer of business from London to New York, initiated by wartime closure of the London market to foreign borrowers and by the Liberty Loan campaign in the United States, was reinforced following the conclusion of hostilities by informal capital controls in the UK and abundant savings in the US. Before the war, Britain's foreign assets roughly matched the combined total of the remaining creditor countries, while the US was a creditor of negligible importance. In the 1920s (with the exception of 1923, when transfers to Europe were depressed by the Ruhr invasion), lending by the US, especially to countries outside the British Empire, consistently exceeded that by Britain.

The other side of this coin was rapidly mounting indebtedness in Central Europe and Latin America. Loans to Europe were used to finance the reconstruction of industry and infrastructure, the purchase of imported inputs and the provision of working capital. At the same time, the growth of lending can be understood as a response to the need to recycle German reparations in much the same way that OPEC investment in the US, in conjunction with US lending to LDCs, recycled oil revenues in the 1970s.[9] Loans to Latin America, in contrast, reflected favourable publicity and growing awareness of economic prospects in developing regions.[10] Table 1.1 summarizes the direction of US and British lending. American lending was widely distributed, going most heavily to Europe (where Germany was the leading debtor in absolute terms) and then to Latin America and Canada; British lending was directed predominantly towards the Empire, especially at the end of the decade.

Then, as recently, there was much discussion of the soundness of foreign loans, embellished by tales of loan pushing, excessive commissions, corrupt administration, and squandering of funds. Indeed, placing much of the business in relatively inexperienced American hands may have increased the market's tendency to fund risky projects.[11] It is important to note, therefore, that the macroeconomic performance of

Table 1.1. **US and British lending in the 1920s**

	US lending abroad by region (millions of dollars)			
	Europe	Canada	Latin America	Far East
1924	526.6	151.6	187.0	96.1
1925	629.5	137.1	158.8	141.7
1926	484.0	226.3	368.2	31.7
1927	557.3	236.4	339.7	151.2
1928	597.9	184.9	330.1	130.8
1929	142.0	289.7	175.0	51.5

	British investment in government and municipal securities (millions of pounds)	
	Foreign	Dominion and Colonial
1926	392.0	676.5
1927	406.7	703.3
1928	364.5	1036.0
1929	351.0	1061.6

Sources: For the US, Department of Commerce (1930); for Britain, Royal Institute of International Affairs (1937).

the debtors, and the consequent growth in their ability to service external debt, was more than respectable, and in the Latin American case rather impressive, during this period of large-scale foreign lending (1925–9). With the exception of Costa Rica and El Salvador, real GDP in those Latin American countries considered in Table 1.2 increased at then historically unprecedented rates in excess of five per cent per annum. Except for Brazil, Guatemala and (to a lesser extent) Costa Rica, the same is true of exports, despite a persistent decline in the prices of primary products. Initially, the ratio of debt service to exports (excluding reparations) remained manageable.[12]

Thus, in the 1920s as in the 1970s, foreign lending was associated with expanding trade and rosy prospects, at least in the short run, for economic growth in the borrowing regions. Whether the loans were sound in the sense that export receipts would prove adequate to service them is essentially the question whether it was realistic to assume that the growth rates and financial stability (e.g., absence of real interest rate

16   **Barry Eichengreen and Richard Portes**

Table 1.2. **Annual growth rates of real GDP, industrial production and exports 1925–9, and debt/export ratio, 1929**

(in percentage points)

	GDP	Industrial production	Exports in US dollars	1929 Central govt foreign debt as percent of exports
Germany	1.7	5.0	9.9	6.6
Austria	2.7	6.3	4.0	77.5
Hungary	7.1	−0.4[a]	5.9	123.2
Australia	−0.4	4.1	−3.8	112.5
Canada	6.3[a]	8.8	−1.1	46.2
Argentina	5.7	5.2	4.8	41.8
Brazil	7.2	4.6	−1.6	66.3
Costa Rica	0.2	1.6	3.1	95.4
Chile	10.8	0.0	5.8	101.7
Colombia	7.5	4.5	11.6	55.7
Honduras	5.6	6.8	20.2	43.3
El Salvador	1.7	5.9	12.4	105.4
Guatemala	5.5	3.0	−3.4	54.0

Note: European figures exclude reparations. [a] indicates 1926–9. For Australia, industrial production is proxied by manufacturing production at constant prices. *Sources:* Latin American figures computed from Thorp (1984), Appendix Table 4. European figures computed from Mitchell (1976). Canadian figures computed from Urquhart and Buckley (1965). Australian figures computed from Butlin (1984).

shocks) of the 1920s would persist. The answer is surely more obvious with hindsight than it was at the time.

Banking structure and regulation   These changes in the direction of foreign lending were accompanied by equally profound developments in the structure and regulation of commercial banking. Following the lead of the United States, which had created the Federal Reserve System in 1914, in the 1920s many countries either established central banks or gave them added independence, in Latin America in conjunction with visits by US economic experts, in Central Europe as a condition of League of Nations stabilization loans.[13] One function of these central banks was to act as lender of last resort, although as we shall see there was considerable variation in the effectiveness with which they carried out this role. In a number of countries monetary reform was accompanied by new banking regulations patterned on the US model. In Chile, for example, a law of September 1925 established a 'Superintendencia de Bancos' charged with inspecting the books of banks and publishing a statement of their position annually. Banks were prohibited from extending individual loans in excess of ten per cent of the sum of paid-up capital and reserves and were required to observe minimum capital requirements which differed by city size and liability composition. Since there was considerable variation in the appropriateness of the US model, these reforms varied in their efficacy and implications for the stability of national banking systems.

A number of countries including Germany and Poland established publicly owned or controlled agricultural credit and mortgage banks which engaged in all forms of deposit and industrial banking and expanded rapidly.[14] Their implications for the stability of the financial system are not clear: on the one hand, public banks for political reasons sometimes extended loans to risky undertakings which did not attract private banks; on the other, the central authorities were particularly disinclined to let public enterprises fail.

A further feature of the development of banking structure in the 1920s was a pervasive amalgamation movement. While the immediate incentive for amalgamation was often savings on administrative costs, another advantage was the greater facility with which risk could be diversified and stability ensured through the dispersion of loans over different regions and sectors of the economy. Although present earlier, the amalgamation movement in commercial banking accelerated after World War I, spreading from England and Wales to Latin America, Hungary, Poland and Greece. In Germany and Czechoslovakia, large banks increasingly acquired control of their smaller counterparts, while in the US, restrictions on branch banking were circumvented through such mechanisms as the securities affiliate.

Along with the spread of the securities affiliate, financial innovation in the 1920s took the form of the adoption of 'investment' or 'industrial' banking on a national scale in the Succession States of what had been the Austro-Hungarian Empire. In English-speaking, Scandinavian and Latin American countries, intermediaries specialized in deposit banking, soliciting money on deposit and extending short-term advances to commerce and industry. The alternative of investment banking, which entailed long-term loans to industry, had traditionally prevailed in Central Europe. When the Succession States created new banking systems in the wake of World War I, they naturally emulated Austrian and German practice. Given the specialization of industry and agriculture in the newly partitioned Central European states, the fate of the

18   **Barry Eichengreen and Richard Portes**

Table 1.3. **Business cycle indicators for advanced countries, 1929–38 and 1973–83**

	GDP	Import volume	Terms of trade	Net capital outflow at 1929 prices $ million	World price level (US export unit values)
1929	100.0	100.0	100.0	355	100.0
1930	94.6	94.8	106.1	−145	89.6
1931	89.3	89.5	111.8	−1,422	69.4
1932	83.0	76.5	113.7	−1,661	59.0
1933	84.0	78.4	114.8	1,006	61.9
1934	89.2	79.6	111.1	−1,254	72.4
1935	94.3	81.8	108.0	−406	74.6
1936	101.6	85.7	100.6	−176	76.1
1937	107.0	97.4	103.9	−1,677	80.6
1938	109.3	87.0	108.3	−1,413	74.6
1973	100.0	100.0	100.0	8,919	100.0
1974	100.4	101.1	88.4	7,020	127.6
1975	99.8	92.7	90.3	12,507	142.6
1976	105.1	105.5	89.8	12,416	147.5
1977	109.1	109.5	88.7	13,429	152.7
1978	113.5	115.4	91.1	17,241	163.3
1979	117.3	124.0	87.3	16,265	185.9
1980	118.8	121.8	81.3	14,215	211.0
1981	120.4	118.4	80.2	15,792	230.4
1982	119.9	117.6	81.9	14,340	232.9
1983	122.8	122.0	83.4	11,702	236.5

Notes: GDP, import volume and terms of trade are weighted averages for 16 countries. The capital flows are deflated by the US export unit value index. The US export unit value in 1973 was 251 per cent of its 1929 level.
Source: Maddison (1985, p. 13).

banks' loan portfolios was tied to the fortunes of narrow industrial or agricultural markets. When a particular crop or industry was hit by the Depression, the shock to the banking system would prove severe.

B.   The crisis and its management

Our analysis of the financial crisis of the 1930s highlights two factors: first, the singular importance of linkages running from debt defaults and exchange market disturbances to the instability of banking systems; second, the critical role of policy in interrupting these linkages, thereby insulating the banking system and the macroeconomy from threats to their stability.

Table 1.4. **Business cycle indicators for 11 developing countries, 1929–38 and 1973–83**

	Latin America				Asia			
	GDP	Export volume	Terms of trade	Import volume	GDP	Export volume	Terms to trade	Import volume
1929	100.0	100.0	100.0	100.0	100.0	100.0	100.0	100.0
1930	96.1	81.2	81.5	77.4	101.1	91.3	90.4	89.5
1931	90.0	90.0	67.9	51.9	101.4	86.6	83.5	82.3
1932	86.7	73.0	71.4	39.5	103.8	77.7	84.2	78.5
1933	93.2	75.7	68.8	45.5	104.5	80.0	82.1	71.2
1934	101.0	85.4	76.5	52.5	99.4	82.6	86.6	76.7
1935	106.3	91.9	75.2	56.4	104.2	84.7	92.3	82.6
1936	113.4	93.3	80.6	61.7	109.9	94.1	94.9	81.0
1937	120.8	101.8	89.1	76.8	110.0	n.a.	n.a.	n.a.
1938	121.4	(81.4)	(84.9)	(70.9)	106.9	n.a.	n.a.	n.a.
1973	100.0	100.0	100.0	100.0	100.0	100.0	100.0	100.0
1974	106.7	100.4	95.8	126.4	101.6	101.7	97.5	109.1
1975	109.7	100.1	88.5	119.5	110.0	107.8	91.9	110.9
1976	116.0	112.1	94.1	112.0	110.2	132.0	97.0	121.9
1977	122.3	123.2	94.7	110.9	119.3	142.9	102.0	132.9
1978	127.3	141.2	87.9	121.2	131.7	163.6	97.7	157.5
1979	136.1	152.6	87.5	141.8	136.8	171.8	94.5	165.3
1980	143.9	167.7	92.1	169.7	145.2	189.6	91.2	176.3
1981	143.9	190.3	85.6	175.1	153.0	209.6	86.4	183.0
1982	142.3	194.0	83.1	132.3	161.6	220.4	81.2	176.5
1983	139.3	214.7	80.2	103.7	174.1	245.7	75.9	193.3

Notes: The above indices are all weighted averages. Latin America includes Argentina, Brazil, Chile, Colombia, Cuba and Mexico. Asia includes China, India, Indonesia, Korea and Taiwan.
Source: Maddison (1985, p. 14).

Exchange market disturbances   The first indication of serious financial distress was exchange-rate depreciation by primary producers starting in 1929. While misalignments within the North Atlantic community may have played some role in early exchange-market difficulties, the most disruptive pressures originated on the real side, notably in markets for agricultural commodities and primary products. So long as US import demands and foreign lending were maintained, these pressures remained tolerable. But in 1928–9 the indebted countries of Central Europe, Latin America and Oceania were subjected to dual shocks. First, the Wall Street boom both reflected and induced portfolio shifts by US investors, choking off American capital exports: after peaking in the summer of 1928, they fell by 46 per cent within a year (see Table 1.1). Next,

20   **Barry Eichengreen and Richard Portes**

commodity exports declined precipitously following the US cyclical downturn commencing in the summer of 1929 (see Table 1.3). Primary-producing countries were seriously affected (as shown in Table 1.4), since the US accounted for more than 40 per cent of the primary-product consumption of the 15 leading industrial countries.

The exchange rate and the external debt were directly linked through the government's reserve constraint. Gold and foreign-exchange reserves could be allocated either to debt service or to merchants and currency dealers who, under gold standard statutes, could demand gold for export. In principle, borrowing countries could have chosen to default on their external debts while defending the gold standard, to let their exchange rates go while maintaining debt service, or to default and depreciate simultaneously. Initially, they chose to sacrifice the exchange rate and honour the debt. One might speculate that policymakers viewed debt as even more sacrosanct than the gold standard, although that is doubtful in view of the frequency of default in the nineteenth century (matched only by the frequency of suspensions of convertibility). In fact, their motives were pragmatic: while default automatically precluded additional foreign borrowing, depreciation had less impact on credit-worthiness. It was even suggested that, insofar as depreciation stimulated exports, it might facilitate foreign bond flotations. Nevertheless, policymakers themselves saw depreciation as a threat to the national credit, albeit one less serious than default.

The pre-sterling depreciations were a Latin American and Antipodean phenomenon, starting with Uruguay in April 1929 and followed in rapid succession by Argentina, Paraguay, Brazil, Australia, New Zealand, Venezuela, Bolivia and Mexico. Australia's experience is especially revealing, since both default and devaluation were resisted so strongly.[15] The Australian economy was adversely affected by both declining wool and wheat prices and increasingly stringent London credit conditions. As early as the first semester of 1929, the Commonwealth Bank had been alarmed by the decline in its sterling balances and by its inability to float new loans in London. But despite the rising opportunity cost of debt service, little consideration was given to the option of default, in the hope that faithful maintenance of service might permit floating new loans in London. Instead, to curb imports the banks rationed foreign exchange and increased their rates against sterling while attempting to stay within the gold points. These expedients were viewed as temporary, and their reversal was anticipated as soon as new loans could be floated. The authorities obtained additional breathing space through the passage of legislation (patterned after the British Gold Standard and Currency and Bank Notes Acts of 1925 and 1928) which concentrated Australian gold holdings in the authorities' hands. Citizens were required to exchange gold for notes, and specie exports were discouraged by specifying a minimum quantity of gold (400 ounces fine) which could be obtained on demand. Hence there was additional scope for depreciation without destroying the gold standard facade.

To strengthen the trade balance and stave off depreciation, Australia adopted no fewer than seven new tariff schedules between April and December 1930. Exports were promoted by a 'Grow More Wheat Campaign' and by bounties or bonuses for wine-making and gold mining. Ultimately, these efforts proved inadequate due to deteriorating world market conditions and to resistance within Labour circles to further deflationary policies. When in December 1930 a political impasse over the budget deficit threatened to unleash a wave of capital flight, those in banking circles who viewed devaluation as damaging to Australian credit acceded to the others who insisted that devaluation would be acknowledged instead as a beneficial step 'towards recognition of the true state of affairs'.[16] In January the currency was depreciated substantially, at which point it held until sterling's devaluation the following September. The authorities continued to hope that additional borrowing on the London market might prove possible; hence little serious consideration was given to the alternative of default except by Labour heretics such as Jack Lang in New South Wales.

Debt default   Even after suspending convertibility, many countries found it difficult or impossible to maintain service on their external debt.[17] The debt crisis that followed fell into three phases.[18] The first, spanning calendar year 1931, is dominated by Latin American defaults. During the second, from January 1932 through June 1933, default spread to Southern and Eastern Europe. The third, whose opening coincided with the Monetary and Economic Conference of 1933, was dominated by Germany's reduction of service on its foreign debt.

Macroeconomic events, rather than disturbances limited to financial markets, played a leading role in the onset of the debt crisis. The Great Depression affected the ability of governments to generate both the tax revenues needed to service debt and the foreign exchange required to transfer revenues abroad. Plummeting economic activity and rising unemployment increased budgetary expenditures at the same time as revenues fell. The decline in export values and volumes led to a rapid contraction of foreign exchange earnings (see Table 1.4). In much the same manner that an isolated bank failure can be infectious given depositors' incomplete information about the solvency of other banks, defaults by a few countries caused investors to revise their expectations

for continued debt service by others. International lending all but
evaporated following Bolivia's January 1931 default, and with the
collapse of lending, the incentive to keep debt service current was further
reduced.[19]

The Latin American defaults that dominated the first phase of the
crisis exhibited common features. Typically they resulted from the
interaction of declining primary-commodity prices with government
budget deficits (due both to expenditures on nonproductive projects and
to the macroeconomic slump).[20] Debt crisis and domestic political
instability interacted in a vicious circle: political instability hindered
attempts to achieve fiscal reform, while the crisis environment and the
draconian policies adopted to redress the debt and budget problems
threatened to undermine the most stable of governments. Although
Bolivia's default was in large part a function of a 40 per cent fall in the
dollar price of tin, a long history of budgetary mismanagement culminating in the government's overthrow also played a role, as the British
consul had recognised fully three months before default:

> The unlimited depredations on the State coffers by the late head of the
> country and his minions have left the country bled white, and there are
> no resources left on which to fall back. In fact there is every prospect
> that Bolivia will be obliged to default on her obligations in connection
> with foreign loans falling due in December.[21]

In Peru, as in Bolivia, the onset of the Depression exacerbated
political unrest which culminated in revolution. While Peru's new
government put a stop to what the British consul described as the
previous administration's 'reckless squandering' of funds, it was still
forced to halt debt service in March 1931 on the grounds that the
Treasury was bare of funds.[22] Chile, which also experienced revolution
and suffered greatly from the decline in nitrate and copper prices,
defaulted four months later. Brazil, hit by a disastrous fall in coffee prices
and similarly undergoing revolution, defaulted in October.

Default spread to Europe one year to the day after its appearance in
Latin America. Compared with the Latin American republics, most
Central and East European countries had suffered less from the collapse
of primary-commodity prices (due to greater export diversification) and
had pursued more austere budgetary policies. They were hesitant to
interrupt service on the grounds that much of their debt had been
arranged under League of Nations auspices. Nonetheless, Hungary's
default in January 1932 was followed in rapid succession by those of
Greece, Bulgaria and Yugoslavia.

The final phase of the crisis was ushered in by Germany's default. The
German authorities had previously limited the transfer of funds to

extinguish maturing loans but refrained from interfering with interest transfers. As in Latin America, default was associated with political upheaval. One of the first steps of the National Socialist Party upon taking power in 1933 was to convene a conference of bondholders' representatives with the intention of rescheduling the debt. Arrangements were made to transfer a share of accrued debt service into foreign currency, to issue scrip in place of the rest, and to convert maturing coupons into funding bonds. With few exceptions, the dollar obligations of German states, municipalities and corporations were brought under the control of the Reichsbank's Conversion Office.

Strikingly, debt default had limited repercussions in the foreign exchange market. The currencies of most defaulting Latin American countries had already depreciated, while the currencies of the major European debtors were under exchange control. Moreover, in contrast to the 1980s, the deterioration of long-term foreign assets posed no direct threat to the banking systems of the creditor countries. Links from debt default to bank failures were broken because foreign lending took place not through bank loans but through the issue of bonds, few of which were held by banks in the creditor countries. Banks might participate in the syndicate which organized the loan and serve as purchasers of last resort if the market failed to take up the entire issue. But even in such instances, banks could resell their share of the issue once bond-market conditions improved.

Commercial banks also purchased foreign bonds as investments, although information on the extent of this practice is sketchy and incomplete. For the United States, the Comptroller of the Currency provided only aggregated information on the foreign bond holdings of National Banks. According to these data, foreign bonds accounted for but a small share, on the order of 7.5 per cent, of the bond holdings of National Banks, and bonds for less than a third of total assets. The Comptroller provided no information which might be used to estimate what share of these foreign bonds were subject to default risk. But unlike the Comptroller, who listed foreign bonds only as a group, the Vermont Bank Commissioner in 1930 reported the book value of the individual foreign bonds held by each state-chartered bank and trust company.[23] Table 1.5 lists foreign government bonds held by mutual savings banks, trust companies and savings and loan associations in Vermont on 30 June 1930. *Ex post*, and perhaps also *ex ante* given the relatively small discounts from par, most of these bonds appear to have been subject to relatively little default risk. Of the 58 banks under the Commissioner's supervision, one closed its doors in 1930, but due to a bad domestic loan rather than foreign bonds, of which the bank in question in fact held

24   **Barry Eichengreen and Richard Portes**

Table 1.5. **Foreign government bonds held by Vermont mutual savings banks and trust companies, 30 June 1930**

	Book value $000
National Debt	
Dominion of Canada	453
Government of Argentina	277
Government of Newfoundland	296
Kingdom of Belgium	1,083
Kingdom of Denmark	1,209
Kingdom of Norway	896
Kingdom of Sweden	4
Republic of Chile	751
Republic of France	54
Republic of Uruguay	437
United Kingdom of Great Britain and Ireland	159
United Kingdom of Great Britain and Northern Ireland	23
Provincial Debt	
Province of Alberta	317
Province of British Columbia	195
Province of Manitoba	69
Province of New Brunswick	20
Province of Nova Scotia	14
Province of Ontario	913
Province of Quebec	48
Province of Saskatchewan	245
Miscellaneous Canadian bonds	927

Source: State of Vermont (1930).

none. While foreign bonds accounted for a larger share of the portfolios of the banks of certain other states, it is hard to see how foreign defaults alone could have posed a serious threat to the US banking system. It is likely that the same conclusion holds for the UK and other creditor countries.

A more serious threat was posed by the liquidation of foreign bank deposits. The exception to the debtor-country rule of giving priority to debt over convertibility concerned the treatment of short-term credits. These credits typically originated in connection with commercial transactions. As the Depression deepened, not only did credits to finance international transactions become redundant, but financial uncertainty induced foreigners to convert them into domestic currency. Commercial banks in the indebted regions consequently experienced sudden withdrawals of foreign balances. Their governments responded with exchange control and prohibitions on the repatriation of short-term capital. For example, when in October 1931 Argentina experienced accelerating depreciation, it imposed exchange control and froze short-term liabilities, which were owed predominantly to British creditors. After nineteen months an agreement was reached with Britain, under the provisions of which a long-term loan was floated to provide funds to transfer the frozen accounts. What is noteworthy is that Argentina, at the same time as it faithfully maintained service on its long-term debt, did not hesitate to restrict foreign access to short-term liabilities. The difference is attributable to the higher costs of leaving short-term debt unfettered, given its volatility in response to changes in anticipated returns, and the greater benefits of leaving service on long-term debt uninterrupted in the hope that additional long-term borrowing might again prove possible for the creditworthy.[24]

Short-term credits, bank failures and intervention

The preceding discussion has focused on links between exchange-rate convertibility and debt. A noteworthy aspect of Argentine experience is the absence of the next link in the chain, from debt and exchange rates to bank failures. While, as noted above, sovereign default was not a major source of instability of creditor-country banking systems, the same was not always true of debtor-country banks. Short-term debt was an important item on the liability side of many debtor-country-bank balance sheets, even if, due to their greater size, it represented a small item on the asset side of creditor-country-bank balance sheets.

In particular, foreign attempts to repatriate short-term credits in the summer of 1931 posed major threats to the solvency of the Austrian and German banking systems. Serious difficulties surfaced in Europe with the run on the Austrian Credit-Anstalt in May 1931. The problems of the Credit-Anstalt, while largely of domestic origin, were greatly compli-cated by its dependence on foreign credits. Austria had been the second European state (after Sweden) to stabilize its currency, and the early date of its stabilization in conjunction with League of Nations sponsor-ship promoted a sizeable inflow of foreign funds to the banking system. The Credit-Anstalt had participated fully in the amalgamation movement of the 1920s, absorbing the Bodenkreditanstalt and its portfolio of dubious industrial loans, and in 1929, when the market value of these loans declined precipitously, this amalgamation returned to haunt it.[25] Regulations forced the Credit-Anstalt to publish its 1930 balance sheet on 11 May 1931, revealing that it had lost more than half its capital, the criterion according to which it was officially declared insolvent. This announcement provoked large-scale withdrawals by domestic and

26 **Barry Eichengreen and Richard Portes**

Table 1.6. **Short-term indebtedness of selected European countries, 1930–3**

(millions of US dollars)

Country	Date	Central Government	Local authorities	Central bank	Other banks	Other debtors	Total	Gross Foreign Debt
Austria	IX 1932	14.1	0.3	121.9		19.4	156	583[a]
Hungary	XI 1931	42.8	21.8	25.3	106.7	124.0	320	695[a]
Bulgaria	XII 1931	4.2	3.4	1.1	10.3	23.4	42	n.a.
Poland	XII 1931	0.4	—		5.1	27.9	33	1,130[a]
Romania	1932			13.5	23.7	41.9	79	965
Denmark	XII 1932		—	25.0		36.2	61	361
Finland	XII 1932	7.5	1.4	4.7	24.4	17.5	55	296
Norway	I 1933		2.2			19.7	106.9	129	373
Germany	IX 1932	148.0		193.6	918.4	963.3	2,223	4,670

Note: [a] denotes 1930 value; n.a. denotes not available. Gross foreign indebtedness for Poland includes direct foreign investment.
Sources: League of Nations (1933, 1937, 1938) and Royal Institute of International Affairs (1937).

foreign creditors.[26] A $14 million credit obtained through the Bank for International Settlements was exhausted within five days, and a subsequent loan from the Bank of England lasted little longer. The government's next step was to freeze foreign balances, and on 16 June 1931 foreign creditors agreed to a two-year suspension of transfers provided that the Austrian Government guaranteed the debts. A second standstill between other Austrian banks and their creditors followed. Although this freeze of foreign transfers did not put a halt to domestic withdrawals, which continued through 1931, the Credit-Anstalt's doors remained open by virtue of large rediscounts with the National Bank. This aspect of Austrian experience suggests a lesson common to Europe and Latin America: shocks with the potential to destabilize the banking system did not lead to generalized collapse because central banks acted in lender-of-last-resort capacity and simply did not permit this to occur.[27]

The Austrian run alerted creditors to the precarious position of other countries dependent upon short-term credits from abroad, notably Germany and the Successor States of Eastern Europe. Table 1.6 indicates the extent of short-term foreign indebtedness of the German banking system. Even had German banks not shared many of the weaknesses of their Austrian counterparts, they would have suffered withdrawals given depositors' incomplete information about their position and the signal provided by the Credit-Anstalt crisis.[28] The Darmstadter Bank, which failed on 13 July 1931, had invested heavily in textiles in general and in the bankrupt Nordwolle firm in particular, as well as in the nearly insolvent municipalities of the Rhine–Ruhr region. Foreign deposits figured prominently on the liabilities side of its balance sheet. Between mid-1930 and July 1931, German statistics show withdrawals of 2.5 to 3 RM billion in short-term foreign credits, or roughly half of the gross short-term liabilities of the 28 most important German banks. In the six weeks ending 13 July 1931, the Darmstadter lost 30 per cent of its deposits, culminating in a run that forced the closure of all German financial institutions. As the price of state support, the Reich fused the Darmstadter with another bank and replaced its board of directors. To prevent capital flight, the Reichsbank was given a monopoly of trans-actions in foreign exchange. Under the provisions of an agreement coming into force in September, transfers of short-term debt were suspended for six months and then for a year starting February 1932. Nonperforming assets were written down and new capital was secured with the aid of the Treasury and, indirectly, the Reichsbank.

Next to Austria and Germany, Hungary was most seriously affected by the liquidation of short-term credits. In the Hungarian case, first the Credit-Anstalt disclosures led to a withdrawal of foreign credits, and then the German banking crisis precipitated a domestic run. The government declared a three-day bank holiday, limited withdrawals and instituted exchange control. Together with heavy rediscounts by the Central Bank, these measures prevented widespread failures. The experience of Romania, the next largest short-term external debtor, differed in that official exchange control was only introduced in May 1932, and in its absence rediscounts with the National Bank were provided even more liberally.

The role of the lender of last resort in containing bank failures is evident in Latin America as well. As noted above, Argentina escaped bank failures because of the substantial rediscount and other credits extended to commercial banks by the Banco de la Nacion: rediscounts rose from 80 million pesos at the end of 1928 to 160 million pesos in April 1931, while advances to banks against government bills rose from 190 to 250 million pesos. Where rediscounts were less liberally provided, instability was greater: in Peru, for example, the Banco del Peru y Londres suspended payments in October 1930, occasioning a banking moratorium lasting through the end of the year. The authorities

28   **Barry Eichengreen and Richard Portes**

Table 1.7. **Indices of prices of bank shares and industrial shares, 1930–3
(1929 = 100)**

		VI 1930	XII 1930	VI 1931	XII 1931	VI 1932	XII 1932	VI 1933	XII 1933
Belgium	Banks	66	55	47	36	30	35	35	35
	Industrial	72	55	52	35	29	36	35	29
Canada	Banks	85	80	72	69	45	50	54	47
	Industrial	62	45	34	28	18	22	39	40
Denmark	Banks	93	96	92	75	70	78	91	101
	Industrial	92	90	88	81	71	74	85	90
France	Banks	89	76	73	46	47	54	52	50
	Industrial	85	66	62	41	44	47	48	43
Germany	Banks	88	74	66	n.a.[a]	35	35	37	...
	Industrial	86	62	53	n.a.[a]	36	47	56	52
Netherlands	Banks	94	83	82	56	47	57	66	58
	Industrial	73	51	43	30	21	30	33	32
UK[b]	Banks[c]	92	97	89	68	82	96	96	104
	Industrial	75	64	56	49	45	57	63	70
USA	Banks[d]	67	43	38	21	14	23	21	15
	Industrial	77	55	47	29	18	24	42	43
Sweden	Banks	104	101	93	70	50	53	53	58
	Industrial	90	80	73	48	31	35	39	39
Switzerland	Banks	98	96	97	61	49	61	60	60
	Industrial	89	75	77	50	45	54	68	66

Notes: [a] No quotation.
   [b] 31.XII.1928 = 100.
   [c] Banks and discount companies.
   [d] New York bank shares.
Source: League of Nations (1934).

responded by encouraging amalgamations and, after 1931, by increasing rediscounts.

The United Kingdom and the United States are the two prominent exceptions to this pattern, the UK because the banking system was not threatened, the US because of the extent to which it was. The relationship between the prices of industrial and bank stocks shown in Table 1.7 can be taken to indicate the condition of national banking systems relative to the condition of national economies. The table confirms that the British banking system weathered the crisis exceptionally well while the American banking system suffered profoundly.

In the British case, external credits again play a role, but in a rather different fashion.[29] The extent of Britain's short-term liabilities, while known to experts, was heralded by the publication of the Macmillan Committee Report in the summer of 1931. Combined with uncertainty about the defensibility of the sterling parity due to a budgetary impasse and British creditors' inability to withdraw funds from Austria and Germany, it led to a run on the pound which forced Britain from the gold standard in September. But since the discount market and the Government, not only the banks, relied on foreign funds, and since the run took the form mainly of sales of foreign-owned Treasury bills and withdrawals of credits previously granted to the discount market, it posed little threat to the banking system. In the three months ending September 1931, total deposits of the ten London clearing banks fell by £70 million, not an insignificant amount but small in comparison with experiences on the Continent.

Even in the United States, where agricultural foreclosure and industrial insolvency are typically emphasized as explanations for bank failure, foreign credits played a role. Signs of widespread financial distress surfaced in June 1931, when foreigners reduced their holdings of dollar acceptances and transferred their deposits from commercial to reserve banks. With Britain's abandonment of the gold standard these movements accelerated. In part these withdrawals of foreign deposits reflected the imposition of exchange control abroad, which rendered the United States one of the few remaining sources of liquidity for foreigners scrambling for funds.

Foreign withdrawals were particularly damaging to the banking system because they reinforced domestic sources of weakness. In the course of the 1920s, US commercial banks had greatly augmented the security and real estate components of their portfolios.[30] Collapse of the security and mortgage markets therefore rendered their asset position especially vulnerable. Real estate loans, which tended to be geographically undiversified due to restrictions on branch banking, increased the vulnerability of thousands of small unit banks to sector-specific shocks. Their desperate attempts to restore liquidity induced them to call in open-market loans and sell securities. Similar responses occurred in other countries although, as Table 1.8 makes clear, the liquidity position of US banks had eroded particularly dramatically over preceding years.[31] In response, US banks restricted loans, giving rise to widespread complaints among manufacturing firms about a shortage of credit. The scramble for liquidity reinforced the collapse of the bond market. The prices of domestic bonds fell so dramatically that by June 1932, when the rate on 3-month acceptances had fallen below one per cent, domestic industrial bonds were quoted on an 11 per cent yield basis and second

30   **Barry Eichengreen and Richard Portes**

Table 1.8. **Bank cash resources as percentage of total deposits, 1929–32
(end of June)**

	1929	1930	1931	1932
France	7.4	9.7	13.9	33.6
Switzerland	n.a.	n.a.	11.3	22.9
United Kingdom	11.3	11.5	11.7	11.5
United States	7.3	7.4	7.6	8.2
Italy	6.9	6.6	6.2	5.9
Germany	3.1	2.7	3.6	3.4
Poland	8.5	8.8	10.7	9.0
Sweden	2.1	2.3	2.1	3.8
Czechoslovakia	6.7	7.3	7.2	7.4
South Africa	10.3	10.0	9.1	10.1
Argentina	17.9	14.2	13.4	17.5
Australia	15.6	13.4	19.2	17.8
Canada	13.3	12.1	10.9	12.2
Chile	14.4	12.6	9.5	26.4
Japan	9.1	9.0	10.1	9.8
New Zealand	12.3	13.0	13.7	11.5

Note: n.a. signifies not available.
Source: League of Nations (1934).

grade rails yielded 19 per cent. While some component of these yields indicates the magnitude of the risk premium, their high level may also reflect distress sales and therefore the generalized effects of the financial crisis, which severely disrupted the domestic bond market's ability efficiently to allocate funds among competing uses in much the same manner that the collapse of the market in foreign bonds reduced international investment to a trickle.[32]

Although the literature on the American Depression emphasizes the two waves of bank failures in the late autumn of 1930 and early spring of 1933, in fact failures continued throughout. In October 1931, for example, 522 banks with deposits amounting to $470 million were forced to suspend payments, and in the 12 months ending in June 1932, 2,429 US banks failed. Again, the pattern of failure mirrors the actions of the authorities. In the spring of 1932 the incidence of bank failures declined as the Federal Reserve expanded credit through rediscounts and open market operations, but this expansionary initiative was reversed soon thereafter, permitting a resurgence of commercial bank insolvencies.[33]

The US case provides a graphic illustration of linkages running from bank failures to other markets and to the macroeconomy. Although it is still disputed whether monetary stringency, much of which resulted from bank failures, was a factor in the onset of the Great Depression, it is widely agreed that these monetary factors were central to its singular depth and long duration. The inability of the Federal Reserve to prevent widespread bank failures, along with its inability to interrupt the linkages running back from bank failures to financial markets and to the macro-economy, is a central explanation for the severity of the crisis in the United States. Thus, one reason for the exceptional depth of the Great Depression in the US was that policy was used less effectively than in other countries to prevent the transformation of financial market disturbances into a generalized financial crisis.

II   Fifty years later

A.   *The periods compared*

A summary of the apparent similarities and differences between our two periods will be useful background for our analysis. In the 1930s as in the 1980s, illiquidity was not confined to any one country or region. In neither instance can the problems of debtor countries be attributed exclusively to domestic causes – external shocks from the world economy were transmitted through sharp rises in real interest rates and falls in commodity prices and the economic activity of industrial countries. The burden of reparations inhibited expansion just as the burden of debt service does in many countries today (McNeil, 1986).

There can be no exact dating of recent troubles in international financial markets, nor *a fortiori* a precise correspondence between 1929 and 1979. Nevertheless, to take 1979 as the beginning of the contemporary period of interest is not merely a convenient metaphor. Admittedly, one cannot identify at that point a classical panic, preceded by 'mania', then 'distress', and followed by sharp, generalized price falls (Kindleberger, 1978). But conditions in the world economy and financial system clearly did deteriorate from the second oil shock to the Mexican collapse of August 1982, which marks the onset of the 'debt crisis' in popular consciousness.

Any simple analogy with 1932, however, would be equally inappropriate. For just as the contemporary debt crisis began the American economy entered a period of strong expansion which compensated, until recently, for the drag on world economic activity caused by the overhang of LDC debt and restrictive macroeconomic adjustment policies adopted to deal with it.

We have seen many debt reschedulings but not widespread, extended interruptions of service and amortization on the scale of the 1930s; even the deterioration of relations between Peru and the IMF in August 1986 is not strictly comparable to the defaults which began in January 1931. There have been wide swings in nominal and real exchange rates but no significant currency collapses, nor any resort to inconvertibility or new exchange controls to protect any major currency. Real interest rates rose to historically exceptional heights, but there was no worldwide dramatic fall of investment. Large government budget deficits in industrialized countries have in most cases (with a major exception!) been brought under control, with many crisis budgets but no collapse of government finances. There have been large trade imbalances and repeated threats of a plunge into overt protectionism, but in practice we have seen only the gradual accretion of non-tariff barriers to trade. Failures of individual financial institutions have been isolated, without generalized runs or significant contractions in the credit base. One authority judges that the crisis was worst in 1982–4 and is now over (Kindleberger, 1986).

We are less sanguine, and we stress in particular the need for continued and improved international policy coordination in providing the regulatory and macroeconomic environments necessary to prevent financial crisis. But despite greater interdependence in the world economy – and partly in response to it – institutional change and economic policies have tended to break, block or attenuate the linkages of Figure 1.1. A further difference from the 1930s is more difficult to analyse: the growing assertiveness of the United States and the political consensus among the major industrialized countries in dealing with international debt problems (Diaz Alejandro, 1984; Portes, 1986). It has been more difficult for any single debtor country, particularly in Latin America, to break ranks, and the cohesion of the creditors' cartel contrasts sharply with feeble efforts at coordination among debtors.

As noted, in both the 1930s and 1980s, the preceding decade had been marked by major changes in the structure and management of the international political economy. Before World War I, the United Kingdom played the pivotal role in the world economy, using its investment income to run a trade deficit that allowed other countries to pursue export-led growth. When World War I and its aftermath cut that income, the United States assumed the financial role of the world's leading creditor without taking on the corresponding responsibility of running an import surplus with open markets, thus leaving a structural weakness in the system. Now the transition from the United States to Japan as dominant lender is similarly occurring without a shift by Japan into import surplus (though in this case, with little immediate weakening of American political dominance).

Yet differences between the periods preclude simple generalizations. In the 1970s, the banks did not act merely as intermediaries in placing LDC bond issues among many dispersed bondholders, but rather took on very large direct exposure, with corresponding risk to themselves and the financial system.[34] Although there was significant cross-border lending among banks in the earlier period, the density of international interbank relationships now is incomparably greater. For both reasons, creditors have been much better organized in the 1980s than in the 1930s, a change that has favoured rescheduling rather than default.[35] But banks appear to have paid no more attention to sovereign risk in the lending of the 1970s than in that of the 1920s. And they lent at considerably shorter maturities than those of the 1920s bond issues.

An institutional difference of considerable practical importance is the International Monetary Fund. To some extent, the IMF acts as international lender of last resort, while also serving the capital market in a signalling capacity, providing information on domestic adjustment programmes and helping to differentiate among borrowers. There are also stronger domestic lenders of last resort (new, in some countries), with more extensive supervisory and regulatory roles now than fifty years ago despite recent moves towards deregulation; and there is deposit insurance in many countries. The macroeconomic background differs as well, with much greater experience of stabilization policies, a system of floating exchange rates in existence for over a decade, and extended international discussion of domestic macroeconomic policies in economic summits, the OECD and the EEC. Finally, there is greater political stability in relations among the industrialized creditor countries, and perhaps greater internal political stability in the LDC debtors.

B.   The environment

Our description of the international financial environment begins with the breakdown of the Bretton Woods payments settlement and exchange rate systems in the early 1970s. A detailed history is not needed here. But the major events have brought deep structural change closely analogous to that of the 1920s, in the exchange rate system, in international lending, and in financial institutions.

The changes in the exchange rate system during 1971–73, while in the opposite direction to those of the mid-1920s, were equally profound and far-reaching.[36] Official convertibility of dollars into gold was abandoned in August 1971, and the adjustable-peg exchange-rate mechanism gave way to unrestricted floating in March 1973. The 'reform' negotiations of the C20 and its successors could not reconstruct or replace the constraints

34　Barry Eichengreen and Richard Portes

which Bretton Woods had imposed on the autonomy of national monetary authorities. The new freedoms and powers were *de jure* rather than
de facto, however, as policy-makers, academic analysts and the markets
soon discovered. The same capital mobility which made the old exchange
rate system untenable also made true autonomy infeasible.

Among the many complementary explanations for the breakdown of
the Bretton Woods exchange rate system, we stress capital mobility as
fundamental. So did the architects of the system and their predecessors.
Nurkse (1944) identified 'disequilibrating' capital flows as a major cause
of the disturbances of the interwar period. Keynes insisted that controls
over capital movements be an essential component of the postwar
monetary order, and the Bretton Woods Agreement made no provision
for convertibility for capital account transactions. But the progressive
relaxation in the early 1950s did extend to capital flows. Their volume
and speed grew dramatically as a function of technological innovation
and profit opportunities. Since the authorities were unwilling to make the
Bretton Woods exchange rate system their sole policy target, official
convertibility and the adjustable peg could not withstand the pressures
arising from the growing sophistication, scope and integration of international capital markets. This process has of course continued, and we
return to it below.

Currency convertibility and the international institutions established
at Bretton Woods survive. Moreover, the political relationship between
France and Germany in the context of the European Community gave
rise in 1979 to the European Monetary System, with its exchange rate
mechanism providing a 'zone of (relative) monetary stability' among
most of the EC currencies.[37] Even outside the exchange-market intervention in the EMS, the major currencies have not floated freely since
1973. Exchange rates have been regarded as important indicators or even
targets for monetary policy, leading to intervention, whether unsterilized
or sterilized.[38] This raises the question whether, by the end of the 1970s,
the resulting exchange rate system was well-suited to absorb major
macroeconomic and financial shocks, or whether the system propagated
or even magnified such disorders, which might then be transmitted to
capital markets and the financial system (linkages III and V in
Figure 1.1).

The explosive growth of international lending in the 1970s is also
familiar to contemporary observers.[39] Analysts still differ, however, in
the importance they assign to supply and demand factors affecting
international lending during the period. Econometric explanations of its
volume and price perform no better than econometric models of
exchange rate behaviour. It is clear that the 1970s saw a striking,

unexpected growth of liability financing of balance-of-payments deficits under little apparent constraint for most countries; and that aggregate liquidity in the world economy was correspondingly demand-determined.

The process of institutional change in the banking system during the 1970s was also driven by the powerful forces of internationalization and the technological change which stimulated and facilitated it. The pace of internationalization may have slowed somewhat in the past five years.[40] This has not eased the regulatory authorities' task in keeping abreast of these changes. The problems of the banking system in 1974–5, from spectacular bank failures like Franklin National and Herstatt to many lesser difficulties, were surmounted.[41] But the Basle concordat of 1975 was just the beginning of a much more active, continuous process of consultation among central banks, in good part through the continuing work of the Cooke Committee. This internationalized prudential supervision also forms an important part of the environment in which the events of the past several years have transpired.

C.   *Disturbances and their management*

The two major sources of recent instability are those of fifty years earlier: disturbances in the foreign exchange market and sovereign debt.

Major exchange rate swings and misalignments, as well as sharp deterioration in the debt-servicing capacity of individual countries, have undoubtedly threatened domestic financial institutions and the international financial system. There have been isolated, individual cases of bank failures, some quite spectacular, at least judging by the reaction of the media. Banco Ambrosiano, Johnson Matthey and Continental Illinois offered high-grade material to all from sensational journalists to sober academics. The scandals and political fallout were greater in Rome and London than in Chicago, but financially the most serious was Continental Illinois, then the twentieth largest US bank and a major participant in the international interbank market. Despite a classic run by foreign holders of its CDs, the bank was saved by the regulators (without bailing out its officers and shareholders), and there were no spread effects nor generalized financial crisis resembling the 1930s.

Stresses in foreign exchange markets, international lending and the banking system are striking, and they suggest analogies with the interwar period. These comparisons help to explain why there has so far been no collapse like that of the 1930s and shed light on the continuing vulnerability of the financial system. We shall therefore turn to data on the size of imbalances and shocks, on the capacity of the exchange-rate system to

cope with misalignments and volatility, and on how the debt crisis has
been managed. We then consider the linkages represented in Figure 1.1
and the roles of policy and institutional change in attenuating them.

Exchange rates   The exchange rate system operating since 1973 has
survived both unexpectedly high volatility and substantial misalignments
without exchange-market collapse or any overall drift towards controls.[42] Central bank intervention has doubtless helped; few would argue
that it has been destabilizing, though many would judge its influence to
be marginal. It has certainly not eliminated short-run volatility. Nor has
market learning reduced volatility as the floating-rate period has gone
on. Even the EMS has had only limited effects: among the major EMS
currencies, only the Deutschmark and lira experienced clear declines in
overall volatility (with respect to all currencies) from 1978 to 1984.[43] On
most assessments, however, the EMS has succeeded in reducing volatility among the currencies participating in its exchange-rate mechanism,
as one would expect.[44]

Yet more than a decade of learning among market participants and the
authorities has apparently not delivered the supposedly stabilizing
effects of speculative activity. The EMS may be interpreted as one
response to this disappointment, while the rapidly developing forward
and futures markets now provide ample opportunities to protect against
exchange-rate instability. Recent evidence suggests, however, that these
opportunities are not used fully to insulate trade, and that exchange-rate
volatility does in fact have empirically significant effects on the volume of
international trade.[45] And the new markets and instruments can be used
not only to hedge but also to gamble. We must therefore regard short-run
volatility still as evidence of instability which might itself spread through
the financial and real economies.

Even more dangerous, however, are the large exchange-rate swings
and misalignments of long duration which have characterized the period
since 1973. Williamson (1985, p. 17) cites maximum swings in real
effective exchange rates during 1973–82 of 22 per cent for the Deutschmark, 19 per cent for the French franc, 32 per cent for the US dollar, 35
per cent for the yen, and 60 per cent for the pound. His graph
(reproduced as our Figure 1.2) is striking testimony to the magnitude of
these gyrations and their extended duration. His calculations of misalignments give one measure, admittedly controversial, of the exchange-rate
imbalances creating strains on other elements of the financial system.
Table 1.9 gives these estimates of divergencies from 'fundamental equilibrium exchange rates' in 1984:Q4. One need not fully accept the
methodology or conclusions to judge that the misalignments are likely to

Table 1.9. **Estimates of exchange-rate misalignments, 1984:Q4**

	Effective exchange rate relative to estimated fundamental equilibrium	Fundamental equilibrium rate US dollar	Nominal appreciation needed against US dollar (percentage)
US dollar	137	n.a.	n.a.
Japanese yen	89	¥ 198	24
Deutschmark	87	DM 2.04	50
French franc	92	FF 6.51	44
Pound sterling	107	$ 1.52	25

Note: n.a.: not applicable.
Source: Williamson (1985, p. 79).

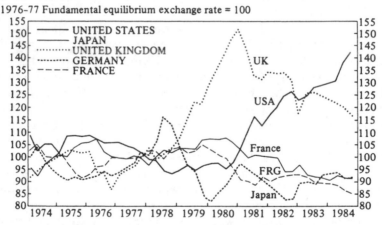

Figure 1.2 Composite measures of real effective exchange rates, five major countries, 1974–84.
Source: Williamson (1985, p. 103)

have been two to three times the magnitude of those estimated by Keynes for the 1920s.

Even in the absence of an agreed model of exchange-rate determination, there is consensus that changes in such fundamentals as the current account and purchasing power parities (or even 'safe haven' effects) cannot fully explain these shifts. Nor are they solely due to inappropriate monetary policies and exchange-rate targets (as represented by the pegs of the 1920s). An unbalanced *mix* of monetary and fiscal policies within the United States and among the major industrial

38   **Barry Eichengreen and Richard Portes**

countries is a more comprehensive explanation, especially insofar as it underlies the wide swings in nominal and real interest rates and international interest rate differentials. Yet it is increasingly agreed that speculative 'bubbles', with or without rational expectations, also played a role in accentuating recent exchange-rate swings.[46] If so, then the exchange rates are still highly uncertain for participants in trade and financial markets, however much they hedge.

This longer-run uncertainty may reduce trade volumes just as volatility appears to do, and direct investment may suffer as well. Large and sustained misalignments impede trade by encouraging protectionist policy responses. Since debt servicing capacity derives from trade flows, there is an indirect link from the exchange-market disturbances of the past decade to debt defaults (linkage III in Figure 1.1). Yet this differs from the link we identified for the earlier period, in which convertibility crises and the threat of exchange control induced withdrawals of short-term funds, which in turn could provoke default. Nor do exchange-rate misalignments appear to have threatened the banking systems in either creditor or debtor countries (linkage V). But exchange-rate uncertainty and volatility may have increased the importance of this link by offering banks new opportunities for speculation. Some have participated aggressively in these markets (often seeking to build up earnings depleted by bad loans), and some of these have not succeeded (Franklin National and Herstatt were early victims).

A more important example of linkage III can be found in the LDC debtor countries themselves. In several cases, exchange-rate over-valuation has led to massive capital flight by domestic residents, seriously exacerbating debt-servicing difficulties.[47] Insofar as overvaluation is a direct result of government policy, exchange-market intervention rather than post-1973 exchange-rate flexibility is the cause of the problem.

On balance, we are inclined to accept the judgment of Cooper (1983) that flexible exchange rates have served more as a shock absorber than as a source of destabilizing influences in the financial system or as a link in their transmission. The misalignments which this flexibility has permitted, by removing a constraint on monetary and fiscal policies, have not themselves provoked financial crisis or exacerbated financial instability, whatever their negative effects on trade and investment. Indeed, it is the process of correcting the misalignments without the appropriate coordination of macro policy mixes which might be highly destabilizing.[48]

Debt   As in the 1920s, the growth and export performance of major borrowing countries in the latter half of the 1970s gave some cause for optimism regarding the recycling process and the prospects for debt

Table 1.10. **Annual growth rates of real GDP and exports, 1975–9**

	GDP	Exports in US dollars
Argentina	1.1	27.2
Brazil	6.6	15.9
Chile	7.4	25.7[a]
Mexico	6.2	32.7[a]
Venezuela	4.7	13.1[a]
Peru	0.9	28.0[a]
Nigeria	1.2	22.5[a]
India	2.6	15.7
Indonesia	7.4	21.6
Korea	10.6	30.9
Malaysia	8.8	30.3
Philippines	6.6	18.6
Egypt	n.a.	6.9
Turkey	3.7	12.5
Yugoslavia	6.4	12.4

Note: [a] more than 50% increase in 1979 over previous year.
Source: International Financial Statistics 1983 Yearbook.

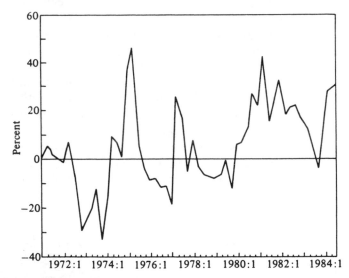

Figure 1.3   The real interest rate of nonoil LDCs, 1971:1–1984:3.
Note: The real rate is measured as the six-month lagged LIBOR adjusted with the three-month forward rate of inflation of export unit values of nonoil LDCs.
Source: Dornbusch (1985, p. 341)

service.[49] Table 1.10 gives data comparable with Table 1.2 for the earlier period. In both cases, however, the assumption that expansion would continue without major shocks proved to be false.

The problems which ensued were indeed similar. The major external shocks which hit the debtor countries were global, not country-specific. The second oil shock, the OECD recession and the industrialized countries' restrictive monetary policies created serious fiscal problems in the debtor countries (aggravated by domestic mismanagement) and cut the prices and volumes of commodity exports. Nominal interest rates finally rose to meet and exceed inflation, bringing a sharp switch from negative to positive real rates. Higher nominal rates also reduced debtor liquidity by shifting the burden of debt repayment towards the present (the tilt effect). Then as inflation subsided, nominal interest rates fell less quickly, and real rates rose further (see Figure 1.3).

Voluntary lending to LDCs by the commercial banks evaporated after the Mexican crisis of August 1982; the Polish debacle of early 1981 had already hit lending to Eastern Europe and put Hungary and Romania in deep trouble.[50] A wave of debt reschedulings followed: there were a total of 36 'multilateral debt renegotiations' in 1975–81 covering $19.6 billion of debt; then 10 in 1982 ($2.4 billion), 32 in 1983 alone ($51.7 billion), with some slackening in 1984, but a record number of 41 reschedulings signed in 1985 dealing with $92.8 billion of debt.[51] Lenders reacted to new information about global economic conditions and individual debtors with a generalized, discrete change of regime in credit markets. Rather than a continuous tightening of terms and constraints for borrowers, there was a shift to credit rationing.

This change of credit-market regime was a response to macroeconomic shocks exogenous to the credit markets whose effects conveyed new information to lenders.[52] Imperfect information about one or at most a few borrowers was generalized to others, and lenders' overall perceptions changed. The 'disaster myopia' emphasized by Guttentag and Herring (1984, 1985) was dispelled by such information; and when the disaster scenario suddenly took on a non-negligible subjective probability, lenders whose sole protection was to try to maintain short loan maturities could react only by pulling out of the market wherever possible.

The magnitude of the shocks which so dramatically affected lenders' behaviour can be seen in Tables 1.11–1.18 and Figures 1.3 and 1.4. The rise of 20 percentage points in real interest rates on floating-rate debt from 1980 to 1981 is extraordinary. The fall in the real commodity price (excluding oil) of 26 per cent from 1980:Q1 to 1983:Q1 is of a similar magnitude to fifty years previously. Although the terms of trade of

Table 1.11. **Average real percentage interest rate on LDC floating-rate debt, 1977–83**

1977	1978	1979	1980	1981	1982	1983
−11.8	−7.4	−9.7	−6.0	14.6	16.7	15.9

Source: Maddison (1985, p. 47).

Table 1.12. **Commodity price indices, 1979–85 (1980 = 100)**

	1979	1980	1981	1982	1983	1984	1985
Coffee (NY)	112.5	100.0	76.8	83.4	84.9	93.7	88.6
Copper (London)	90.3	100.0	79.8	67.8	72.9	63.0	64.9
Petroleum (Venezuela)	60.8	100.0	116.1	116.1	101.6	97.9	97.9[a]
Rubber (Singapore)	88.6	100.0	78.8	60.2	74.7	67.2	53.3
Sugar (EEC Import price)	87.4	100.0	83.7	82.0	79.5	72.6	72.4
Tin (London)	92.1	100.0	84.5	76.5	77.4	72.9	68.7

Note: [a] Quarter II.
Source: International Financial Statistics 1985 Yearbook.

Table 1.13. **External shocks, 1979–83**

	Percentage change in terms of trade from 1975–78	Real income effect as percentage of GDP	Sum of real interest rate and terms of trade effects on GDP (percentage)
Argentina	3	0.2	1.6
Brazil	−29	−2.3	−5.0
Chile	−27	−4.9	−6.2
Mexico	26	1.8	1.2
Peru	−22	−3.7	−4.2
Venezuela	64	15.9	16.2
Colombia	−18	−2.0	−2.8
Indonesia	36	6.1	6.2
Korea	−3	−0.9	−3.8
Malaysia	14	4.9	4.8
Thailand	−14	−2.9	−3.3
Philippines	−16	−3.2	−3.9

Source: Sachs (1985, pp. 527–28).

42   **Barry Eichengreen and Richard Portes**

Table 1.14. **Gross external liabilities and short-term component, 1978–83**

(billion US dollars, end-year)

		1978	1980	1981	1982	1983
Argentina	Total	13.3	27.3	33.7	43.6	46.0
	S	3.4	10.5	11.0	16.5	9.4
Brazil	Total	53.4	70.0	79.9	91.0	95.5
	S	7.1	13.5	15.3	17.4	14.2
Mexico	Total	35.7	57.1	77.9	85.5	93.7
	S	4.9	16.2	25.0	26.1	10.1
Peru	Total	9.7	10.0	10.3	12.2	12.4
	S	2.1	2.1	2.5	3.1	1.4
Venezuela	Total	16.8	29.6	31.9	31.8	32.2
	S	8.0	15.5	17.0	14.7	14.5
Nigeria	Total	5.5	9.0	11.9	14.2	19.7
	S	2.4	3.5	4.4	4.3	6.7
Korea	Total	17.3	29.3	34.2	38.3	40.4
	S	4.5	10.1	11.6	13.6	12.1
Indonesia	Total	18.0	29.9	22.7	26.5	30.2
	S	1.8	2.8	3.3	4.8	4.6
Philippines	Total	10.8	17.4	20.8	24.2	23.9
	S	3.9	7.6	9.4	11.3	9.4
Yugoslavia	Total	12.5	18.5	20.7	20.0	20.3
	S	1.2	2.1	2.5	1.8	1.9

Note: Short-term liabilities S are those of *original* maturity less than one year.
Source: World Bank, *World Debt Tables, 1985–86.*

Table 1.15. **Ratio of gross external liabilities to exports of goods and services, 1978–84 (percentage)**

	1978	1980	1981	1982	1983	1984
Argentina	169	244	285	449	471	464
Brazil	369	301	296	388	392	345
Mexico	313	232	256	310	327	301
Peru	401	206	243	292	323	331
Venezuela	154	133	130	158	186	182
Nigeria	45	33	61	110	179	160
Korea	101	130	125	135	133	128
Indonesia	159	94	91	125	151	147
Philippines	220	214	242	302	294	304
Yugoslavia	147	134	131	131	154	144

Source: World Bank, *World Debt Tables, 1985–86.*

Table 1.16. **Exposure of US banks to LDC debtors, 1982 and 1986**

| | Percentage of capital | | | | Billion $US |
| | June 1982 | | March 1986 | | March 1986 |
	9 money center banks	All US banks	9 money center banks	All US banks	All US banks
Mexico	50	38	38	22	24.2
Brazil	46	31	37	22	23.7
Korea	19	14	11	9	9.4
Venezuela	26	16	16	9	9.7
Argentina	21	13	14	8	8.5
Chile	12	9	9	6	6.3
Philippines	14	8	8	5	5.0
Colombia	8	5	4	2	2.3
Non-OPEC LDCs	227	154	141	88	96.4
OPEC	35	60	33	18	19.4

Note: Banks' capital defined as equity, subordinated debt and loan-loss reserves. 'All US Banks' are those completing Country Exposure Report. Their total capital base rose from $66.2 b in June 1982 to $109.7 b in March 1986.
Source: Federal Reserve Board.

Table 1.17. **Exposure of US and UK banks in Mexico, Brazil, Argentina and Venezuela as percentage of capital, 1982 and 1984**

	End 1982	End 1984
Bank of America	128	122
Chase Manhattan	139	142
Manufacturers Hanover	234	173
Chemical	155	134
Bankers Trust	131	114
First Chicago	123	103
Citicorp	n.a.	140
National Westminster	n.a.	73
Barclays	n.a.	62
Lloyds	n.a.	165
Midland	n.a.	205

Sources: Cline (1983, p. 34) for 1982 and Lever and Huhne (1985) for 1984.

44   **Barry Eichengreen and Richard Portes**

Table 1.18. **Bank share price/earnings ratio as percentage of overall market P/E for UK and US, 1970–86**

	NYSE	London
1970	n.a.	66.9
1975	n.a.	118.4
1980	62.0	52.5
1981	69.8	49.7
1982	48.8	39.7
1983	49.5	51.4
1984	45.5	47.5
1985	49.6	56.7
1986 (Jan–July)	56.8	46.1

At 15 August each year except 1986.

Source: Financial Times, Datastream.

non-oil LDCs (NLDCs) had peaked in 1977:Q1, the decline of 18 per cent from 1979:Q1 to 1983:Q1 was still substantial. The total effect in terms of real income is shown in Table 1.13; for the non-oil debtors (excluding Argentina), there were losses in GDP from three to six per cent. As a real income loss, this might be tolerable; as a required increase in transfer abroad, it was indeed onerous.[53]

Consequences for the debt burden are shown in Tables 1.14 and 1.15. Beginning in 1980, total indebtedness rose rapidly for the NLDCs, and by 1982 their debt-export ratios far exceeded the levels recorded in Table 1.2 for 1929 (which refer, however, only to central government debt, whereas the recent data cover all foreign liabilities). Most may still have been 'solvent' on a suitable long-run calculation,[54] but with uncertain expectations, the distinction between insolvency and illiquidity for a sovereign debtor is both theoretically imprecise and politically untenable. Certainly liquidity was impaired by the withdrawals of short-term funds in 1982–3 evident in Table 1.14; together with capital flight, they significantly increased the disaster probability. That reaction could have activated the linkages I, V and VI which proved so devastating in the 1930s. The 'debt strategy' was designed entirely to contain it.

The dangers are evident from the data on bank exposure in Tables 1.16 and 1.17 and on bank share prices in Table 1.18. The US banks did not begin to recover from the 1982 plunge in their relative price/earnings ratios until 1986, partly because of their subsequent problems with energy and real estate loans. The UK banks have fared somewhat better but show no sign of regaining the standing they enjoyed in the 1970s.

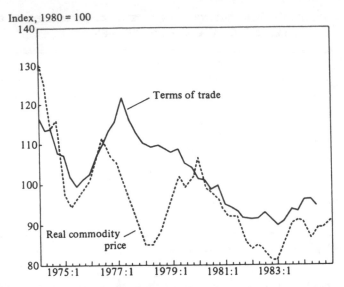

Figure 1.4   The nonoil LDCs' terms of trade and the real commodity price, 1974:1–1985:1.
Note: The real commodity price is the *Economist* index of commodities deflated by industrial countries' unit export values. Terms of trade are exports unit value index divided by imports unit value index. Terms-of-trade data extend through 1984:3.
Source: Dornbusch (1985, p. 324)

Many useful case studies treat the impact of the debt crisis on individual countries and regions and their responses.[55] Nevertheless, we require much more empirical evidence on the role of information about debt-servicing difficulties and their causes. How do the markets perceive such information, process it, and then react to individual borrowers and classes of borrowers? For example, we have two contradictory assessments of market evaluations of Mexican securities in the period leading up to August 1982, one finding a continuous deterioration from the previous winter, the other observing a discontinuous plunge shortly before the crisis became manifest.[56] How the market performs before a crisis is important in assessing whether shifting more sovereign debt into the market through securitization is likely to make the system more or less stable.

The response of policy-makers to the debt crisis assumed that it was essentially and almost everywhere a problem of liquidity rather than solvency, ignoring questions about the legitimacy of that distinction. This approach may have been adequate in the short run, when the key to avoiding financial crisis was maintaining confidence. On plausible

46   **Barry Eichengreen and Richard Portes**

assumptions about growth, interest rates, adjustment policies, industrial-country macro policies, and the provision of bridging loans, projections showed substantial improvement in the debt indicators during 1984–6 and a progressive dissipation of the crisis thereafter.[57]

The US government's optimism did not last; hence the Baker Plan in autumn 1985. For the objective of avoiding a financial crisis, however, the strategy has been almost completely successful so far in keeping both creditors and debtors on board. Neither the reasons nor the prospects for continued success are entirely obvious. There exist clear, level-headed, well-informed evaluations of the costs and benefits of default to debtors which imply that there are cases in which the benefits exceed the costs.[58] As long as rescheduling continues to eschew debt relief, this will remain the case; yet historical comparisons suggest the likelihood of some element of write-off, some ultimate sharing of the burden between creditors and debtors.[59] The question is whether there are circumstances in which debt relief or write-offs are possible without financial crisis.

The answer requires a judgment of the overall health of the international banking system and a scenario for how the authorities would react. Recently the banks have been building up their capital base while writing off some sovereign debt (see Table 1.16). There remain problems on the asset side. Keeping maturities short has little systemic advantage, since that just increases the competition, when trouble threatens, to exit first and leave the problem to other banks. It can be argued that some of the banks' off-balance-sheet activities that have grown so fast recently are relatively risky. On the other hand, securitization on the liability side of banks' balance sheets reduces their dependence on the highly volatile international interbank market.

Linkages   The discussion of recent disturbances and their management now permits a comparison between the two periods of the operation of the linkages we have stressed.

(i)   Whereas the events threatening debt default endangered the banks of some debtor countries in the 1930s, the creditor-country banks did not then hold enough sovereign debt to make it a problem for them. In the current period, there have been a few instances of the former linkage (Argentina had domestic financial difficulties at a critical juncture in its debt-servicing problems). The major effort today, with banks having assumed the credit risks formerly borne by purchasers of sovereign bonds, is to contain any menace this poses for the financial system. So far, direct policy intervention by national authorities and international institutions has succeeded almost entirely in protecting the banking system from major harm.

(ii)   There have been no bank failures so spectacular as themselves to provoke debt default.

(iii)   In the 1930s, withdrawals of short-term funds sometimes brought the authorities to restrict convertibility in order to avoid debt default. Recently, exchange-rate overvaluation without exchange controls has brought capital flight, which has played a greater role in the buildup to debt crisis than in the earlier period (although capital movements were important in the *propagation* of crises in both periods). Failure to block this linkage has been a key weakness in present-day arrangements relative to those of the 1930s. There is a further, indirect linkage from exchange-market disturbances to debt-servicing difficulties which is a major threat today: exchange-rate misalignments have caused pressures for protectionist trade policies, which impede the ability of debtor countries to earn the export surpluses they require.

(iv)   Whereas debt default did not generally force down the debtor's exchange rate in the 1930s, the burden of debt service has clearly had that effect even for non-defaulting debtors today. Pressures from the government budget and the need to run current account surpluses both work in this direction, insofar as depreciation relieves the financial burden of supporting an overvalued rate while raising net exports.

(v)   Instability in the foreign exchange markets was a major cause of generalized financial instability in the 1930s. In the recent period, it has endangered banks only insofar as some of them have sought too aggressively to profit from speculation in these markets.

(vi)   In the earlier period, bank failures caused pressures on the home country's currency by provoking capital flight, and occasionally on the currency of a major foreign creditor (recall how the pound weakened due to the problems of Austrian and German banks). Recently, tremors in the US banking system appear to have made the foreign exchange markets nervous, but this has not been a significant consideration.

Institutional change and public policy

Partly in reaction to the problems faced by the banks, international credit flows have in the past few years shifted from bank lending towards direct credit markets. Simultaneously, there has been an explosion of new financial markets and financial instruments, primarily because technological innovation has substantially reduced transactions costs.[60]

In principle, reduction in interbank linkages should reduce systemic vulnerability. The 'Cross Report' (Bank for International Settlements, 1986), however, points out some countervailing aspects of recent trends: the quality of banks' loan assets may decline; the narrower base of the system may make it less responsive to sudden liquidity needs; non-bank capital markets may have less information on borrowers, less opportunity to screen and to monitor performance, and less capacity to arrange refinancing packages for those in debt-servicing difficulties; and many of the new services banks are providing appear to be underpriced, so that they are not providing earnings commensurate with their risks.

These trade-offs are complicated, and the pace of change has been so rapid that there is little contemporary experience from which to generalize. On the basis of interwar experience, these developments appear to be mainly positive from the viewpoint of financial stability. Our study of linkages suggests that incomplete and imperfect information favours the generalization of adverse shocks into full-fledged crises; that macroeconomic instability is the prime source of those shocks; and that appropriate action by the regulatory and monetary authorities can block the most dangerous linkages. Such action in the 'debt strategy' has avoided defaults and widespread bank failures to date. But it was the system of bank lending to sovereign borrowers that permitted the accumulation of excessive debt burdens, and the rescheduling process which has so far prevented defaults is maintaining almost the full weight of those burdens on the debtors.

In the 1930s, as during the century of international lending before World War I, creditors too assumed a share of the losses created by adverse shocks. The problem then was that when the shocks were global, the contagious, infectious nature of default contributed to financial crisis, disrupting the allocative mechanisms of the international capital market. We now have much more sophisticated public health measures, both macroeconomic and regulatory. They can cope with the dangers of securitization while the financial system switches from relationship-towards transaction-based banking.

Securitization will get more information into the market place. This should reduce adverse selection; substitute more frequent, smaller, visible shocks for the major upheavals which arise when relationships go wrong; and remove from the banking system the heavy burden of having to act as a buffer when shocks do occur. It is not evident that underpricing of new financial services exceeds the inadequacy of spreads in allowing for the default risk on bank lending to sovereign borrowers in the 1970s ('disaster myopia'); while the *ex-post* rates of return on international lending of the 1920s appear to have been relatively favourable for the lenders.[61]

Calls for more formal international-lender-of-last-resort (ILLR) arrangements[62] should not obscure the substantial development of both domestic and international LLR facilities over the past fifty years, as well as a much more sophisticated regulatory system. In the 1930s, financial weakness affected mainly the large banks in Europe, while in the United States it characterized the entire spectrum of the banking system. Now small banks are protected on the liability side by deposit insurance which limits runs,[63] and large ones in difficulty are handled directly by domestic LLRs. Internationally, the 'Paris Club' arrangements have for over two decades effectively handled rescheduling of official or government-guaranteed lending to sovereign debtors. The International Monetary Fund acts in a signalling capacity, providing the capital market with information on debtors and so reducing the risk that the difficulties of one will be transmitted infectiously to others who are creditworthy. IMF conditionality helps to maintain the standing of the debtor and its obligations, thereby limiting the risk of contagious transmission of financial illness to its creditors. And in contrast with the 1930s, the IMF can act to promote a rescheduling before default, whereas then default was needed to provoke direct negotiations between a sovereign debtor and representatives of its creditors.[64] This *ex ante* bargaining should in principle benefit both creditors and debtors; in practice, who gains how much from rescheduling is highly controversial.

Coordination of prudential supervision has taken place primarily under the auspices of the Bank for International Settlements. The Basle concordat of 1975, as revised in 1983, explicitly disclaims any ILLR responsibilities. The authorities' key principle is to exercise supervision on a consolidated basis. They do have a clear understanding of how responsibilities are shared between home and host central banks, and the individual regulatory authorities are much more experienced than they were fifty years ago. It has been difficult for them, however, to keep abreast of internationalization and financial innovation.

The key problem facing any LLR is moral hazard.[65] The classic answer is that the LLR is responsible for the money supply – avoiding financial crisis by containing any threat to the credit base – rather than for the survival of any particular financial institution. The internationalization of the interbank market has made this distinction harder to maintain, however, and no authority or institution currently has responsibility for the world money supply. There is no true ILLR, although the functions which one might fulfil are much better understood now than they would have been in the 1930s (as can equally be said of domestic LLRs).

Nevertheless, success in blocking the transmission of destabilizing shocks in the 1980s owes much to the ILLR-style activities of certain participants . The US Federal Reserve Board and Treasury sometimes seem to forget that the United States is supposed to have lost its hegemonic role. Whether by itself, as when domestic monetary policy

50   **Barry Eichengreen and Richard Portes**

was eased in autumn 1982 in response to signs of financial distress,[66] or in collaboration with the IMF, notably in dealing with Mexico in both 1982 and 1986, or coordinating its major Western partners, as at the Plaza Hotel in 1985, the United States has shown itself capable of leadership. Neither the commitment to 'hands-off' economic policies nor the decline of internationalism in the United States has inhibited decisive action when American vital interests are at stake.

Sometimes others play this role, as did the Governor of the Bank of England in arranging a bridging loan for Hungary through the BIS in spring 1982. Yet unless and until more formal institutional arrangements are established, the United States will continue to be the key player – if it wishes – in forcing action on debt strategy, exchange rates and macro-economic policy coordination, and hence in preventing financial crisis.

III   The future

There are still plausible disaster scenarios. Marris (1985) on macro policy imbalances and their consequences (the 'hard landing') and Lever and Huhne (1985) on debt both permit the imagination to run to deep financial crisis. We believe, however, that greater understanding today of the linkages in financial crisis may have helped to reduce the danger of a serious crisis. Market participants and policy-makers may have learned from the experience of several smaller disturbances since the early 1970s that disaster probabilities are not negligible and appropriate precautions should be taken.

The main dangers lie not in disturbances originating in financial markets but in malfunctions of the real economy. Even though we have not experienced a crisis that seriously disrupted its allocative role, the international capital market still does not appear to be working properly, with the bulk of net flows now going from areas of high real marginal productivity to areas of lower productivity. Sustained high unemployment still fosters protectionism and threatens trade policy conflicts, with the 'inward-looking' consequences characteristic of the 1930s.[67] Although there has been more international macroeconomic policy cooperation recently, it is not fully institutionalized and may prove transient[68] – there is no international monetary constitution providing rules on exchange-market intervention and choice of reserve asset, constraints on fiscal and monetary policies, or responsibility for the ILLR function. Policy-makers still try to maintain their autonomy in an increasingly interdependent world. Paradoxically, even that objective, in the sense of expanding their opportunity set, might best be achieved through international economic policy coordination. Markets could not do the job, even if individual domestic policies were independently 'optimal'.

IV   Conclusions

In this paper, we have contrasted the international financial crisis of the 1930s with the recent performance of the global financial system. We have sought to provide a perspective on the prospects for continued stability in international capital markets. While exhibiting fundamental differences in the operation of these markets currently and during the 1930s, our analysis nonetheless yields conclusions regarding conditions conducive to both the maintenance of stability and the onset of crisis.

The most important of these conclusions concern the roles of regulatory and stabilization policies. Financial crises spread most quickly when information is least complete, and they result in major externalities for particular sectors and the macroeconomy. On both imperfect information and externality grounds, there is a rationale for government intervention. Financial crises pose a greater threat under some institutional configurations than others. Even when the benefits of financial deregulation are apparent, there is a role for regulatory policy in channeling financial innovation in directions that leave the world economy less vulnerable to financial collapse. Finally, we have seen that financial crises are as much the result of macroeconomic shocks as they are of perturbations originating in financial markets. Perhaps the most important policy to prevent financial crises is therefore to provide a stable – and, in an increasingly interdependent world, internationally coordinated – macroeconomic environment within which financial markets may function.

The main difference between now and fifty years ago is that we have been there before and do not want to return. Informed policies can help us to avoid epidemic and keep our anatomy lesson to the conference room rather than the mortuary.

NOTES

* We thank H.M. Stationery Office for permission to cite documents from the Public Record Office, Anita Santorum for research assistance, and Jane Maurice for cheerful secretarial help beyond the call of duty. Anthony Harris, Joan Pearce and our discussants offered very useful comments, as did the seminar group at the Institute for International Economic Studies (Stockholm), where an early version of the work was presented in April 1986.
1 The most comprehensive recent survey is by Kindleberger (1978).

52 Barry Eichengreen and Richard Portes

2 This same point is made by Goldsmith (1982), p. 42.

3 Other exchanges, including those of Italy, the Netherlands, Spain, Sweden, Japan, Argentina and Brazil, remained stable even at the end of the war.

4 See the introduction to Eichengreen (1985a) for details.

5 Documenting the franc's undervaluation is problematic, however; see Eichengreen and Wyplosz (1986). Conventional accounts typically suggest that the franc was some 10 to 15 per cent undervalued relative to the dollar.

6 The transition from the gold to gold-exchange standard is analysed in Eichengreen (1985b). We return below to the role of foreign deposits.

7 Two views of the policy coordination problem are Clarke (1967) and Eichengreen (1985b).

8 The information summarized here is taken from Eichengreen and Portes (1986).

9 The parallels between the two experiences are explored by Balogh and Graham (1979).

10 Many articles in the financial press could be cited. An example is the *Financial Times* (18 December 1929), which even at this late date calls Peru 'apparently a country with a bright future.'

11 See for example Winkler (1933) or Securities and Exchange Commission (1937). Mintz (1950, ch. 4) presents evidence that a few aggressive issue houses were responsible for a disproportionate share of the loans which ultimately went into default.

12 The Table 1.2 data on ratios of public debt to GNP must be interpreted with care, since the importance of state and municipal borrowing varied enormously across countries. The low ratio for Germany, for example, reflects the tendency for borrowing to originate with municipalities and not the Reich.

13 Latin American experience is described in Eichengreen (1986) and Central European reforms in Nurkse (1946).

14 League of Nations (1931), p. 14.

15 Details are to be found in Schedvin (1970).

16 Schedvin (1970), pp. 166–7.

17 Insofar as exchange-rate fluctuations due to devaluation disrupted trade, a linkage to which contemporaries attached much importance, export receipts and debt capacity were reduced still further. For example, Condliffe (1933, p. 221) writes that 'exchange instability resulting from the breakdown of the international gold standard was one of the principal causes of further economic deterioration in 1932 and figured prominently among the factors which limited and checked the revival of prices and productive capacity in the third quarter of that year'. For similar comments, see Nurkse (1944). We return below to evidence on the impact of exchange-rate volatility on trade.

18 This periodization follows Condliffe (1933), chapter ix.

19 The situation in 1931 differs from Sachs's (1982) description of pre-World-War-I lending and default. Before World War I, Sachs argues, default by one country did little to interrupt the flow of capital to other borrowers. The difference between the periods may be that default in 1931 was seen as a response to global rather than country-specific shocks.

20 Eichengreen and Portes (1986) report regressions in which both the extent of terms-of-trade deterioration and the growth of the central government budget deficit are significantly correlated with the incidence and extent of default.

21 British Public Record Office (PRO) FO371/14198, Dispatch to Foreign Office by R. C. Mitchell, 'Political Situation in Bolivia', 22 September 1930.

22 PRO FO 371/14253, Dispatch from Mr Gurney (Lima), 'Annual Report of the Peruvian President to Congress', 18 September 1930; Madden *et al.* (1937), p. 111.

23 Bank Commissioner of the State of Vermont (1930). Vermont appears to be the only state for which this information is available. See White (1984) for further discussion of these data.

24 See Leguizamon (1933) for additional analysis.

25 Kindleberger (1984). p. 372. It is popularly thought that origins of the run were both economic. caused by the bank's uncertain liquidity, and political, caused by French alarm over the recently proposed Austro-German customs union.

26 A recent account of this episode is James (1984).

27 It could be argued that the provision of deposit insurance and improvements in bank regulation have reduced the extent of these externalities. We return to this point below.

28 See League of Nations (1934) for another statement of this view.

29 Details are to be found in Cairncross and Eichengreen (1983) and the references cited there.

30 Between June 1922 and June 1929, the real estate loans of commercial banks had risen by 128 per cent and their security loans by 77 per cent, in comparison with all other loans and investments. which rose by only 30 per cent.

31 The ratio of cash reserves to total deposits was consistently lower only in countries which ultimately turned to exchange control (Germany, Austria, Czechoslovakia) and in the exceptional Swedish case.

32 This is similar to the argument advanced by Bernanke (1983).

33 This episode is the subject of Epstein and Ferguson (1984).

34 Beenstock (1984) argues that this difference has no significant systemic consequences; and the 1970s may turn out to have been a quite exceptional period in this regard. with the growth of securitization and off-balance-sheet operations in the past few years.

35 There were negotiations between debtor countries and the bondholders' organizations after the defaults of the 1930s, but they were difficult to organize. See Eichengreen and Portes (1986).

36 See Williamson (1977) for an account of this period.

37 See Padoa Schioppa (1985) for background on the operation of the EMS and the detailed discussions and assessments in the report (and background documents) of the Treasury and Civil Service Committee of the UK House of Commons (1985).

38 The studies which supposedly showed the inefficacy of sterilized intervention were ignored when the United States changed its policy stance in September 1985.

39 Recent accounts, from somewhat different viewpoints, include Cline (1984) and Lever and Huhne (1985).

40 OECD (1983) describes the picture at the beginning of the 1980s, and Bryant (1987) offers a more recent and more analytical assessment.

41 See Kindleberger (1978, 1986) and Spero (1980).

42 Generally. capital controls have been progressively liberalized or removed, notably in the UK. It can be argued that they have played an important role in

54 **Barry Eichengreen and Richard Portes**

keeping the EMS together – or that the demands of keeping the system together have required capital controls (Giavazzi and Giovannini, 1986). This view is likely to be tested soon, as France and Italy proceed to relax exchange controls.

43 See Kenen and Rodrik (1986).
44 See Rogoff (1985), Padoa Schioppa (1985), and House of Commons (1985).
45 See de Grauwe and de Bellefroid (1986) and Kenen and Rodrik (1986).
46 See Frankel and Froot (1986) and references cited there.
47 The estimates in *World Financial Markets* (March 1986) are particularly striking, though controversial (according to the *Financial Times*, 21 August 1986, the Bank of Mexico estimates capital flight under the current government at $2 billion, in contrast to the Morgan Guaranty estimate of $17 billion). A more academic but still debatable analysis stressing the role of capital flight in Latin American debt problems, and the root cause of exchange rate overvaluation, is given by Sachs (1985).
48 The views of Marris (1985) are discussed below.
49 Diaz Alejandro (1984) argues that an observer in 1980–81 could not reasonably have foreseen a crisis of the magnitude experienced in 1982–4. On the other hand, Portes (1977) predicted a debt-servicing crisis for several East European countries in the early 1980s, beginning with a rescheduling for Poland in 1980–1.
50 See Portes (1982).
51 World Bank (1986).
52 As suggested by theory; see, for example, Guttentag and Herring (1984). Their argument that an extended period without adverse shocks creates conditions in which a shock will then provoke discontinuous market behaviour is more specific and rigorous than the 'financial instability hypothesis' of Minsky (1982), who argues that the danger of financial crisis builds up over an extended period of prosperous times.
53 Cf. note 20 above.
54 See Cohen (1985).
55 Notable among these are Kraft (1984), who gives an 'inside', circumstantial narrative of the negotiations which dealt with the initial Mexican crisis, and Fraga (1986), who makes an interesting comparison of Brazil's recent experience with Germany and reparations fifty years before.
56 Compare Guttentag and Herring (1985) with Edwards (1986).
57 'With reasonable recovery in the global economy, the problem of international debt should prove manageable and the degree of its current risk to the international system should decline' (Cline, 1983, p. 121).
58 See Kaletsky (1985) and Lever and Huhne (1985).
59 See Eichengreen and Portes (1986) for calculations of the *ex-post* rates of return earned by creditors in such cases.
60 Cooper (1986) describes these changes and argues convincingly that they are explained better by technical change than as innovative risk-sharing arrangements or as responses to cross-border differences in taxation and regulation.
61 Eichengreen and Portes (1986).
62 For example, see Guttentag and Herring (1983).
63 The models of the US Federal Deposit Insurance Corporation and Federal Savings and Loan Insurance Corporation have been increasingly followed in Europe and elsewhere.

64 Eichengreen and Portes (1986).
65 Solow (1982) provides a recent discussion of the theory relevant to LLR
    functions, which are treated further in Kindleberger (1978) and Kindleberger
    and Laffargue (1982). It can be argued that financial deregulation has led to
    more risk-taking by financial intermediaries, hence to more LLR interven-
    tion, exacerbating moral hazard (and weakening monetary control). This
    goes beyond our scope here.
66 See Carron (1982).
67 See Cooper (1983).
68 See Portes (1986).

REFERENCES

Balogh, Thomas and Andrew Graham (1979). 'The Transfer Problem Revisited:
    Analogies Between the Reparations Payments of the 1920s and the Problem
    of the OPEC Surpluses', *Oxford Bulletin of Economics and Statistics* **41**,
    pp. 183–92.
Bank for International Settlements (1986). *Recent Innovations in International
    Banking*, Basle.
Beenstock, Michael (1984). *The World Economy in Transition*, London:
    Macmillan.
Bernanke, Ben S. (1983). 'Nonmonetary Effects of the Financial Crisis in the
    Propagation of the Great Depression'. *American Economic Review* **73**,
    pp. 257–76.
Bryant, Ralph (1987). *International Financial Intermediation: Issues for Analysis
    and Public Policy*, Washington: Brookings Institution.
Buiter, Willem and Richard Marston (eds) (1985). *International Economic
    Policy Coordination*, Cambridge: Cambridge University Press.
Butlin, N. G. (1984). 'Select Comparative Economic Statistics, 1900–1940',
    Source Paper No. 4, Department of Economic History, Australian National
    University.
Cairncross, Alec and Barry Eichengreen (1983). *Sterling in Decline*, Oxford:
    Blackwell.
Carron, Andrew (1982). 'Financial Crisis: Recent Experience in US and Inter-
    national Markets', *Brookings Papers on Economic Activity*, No. 2,
    pp. 395–422.
Clarke, S. V. O. (1967). *Central Bank Coordination, 1924–31*, New York:
    Federal Reserve Bank of New York.
Cline, William (1983). *International Debt and the Stability of the World
    Economy*, Washington, DC: Institute for International Economics.
    (1984). *International Debt: Systemic Risk and Policy Response*, Washington,
    DC: Institute for International Economics.
Cohen, Daniel (1985). 'How to Evaluate the Solvency of an Indebted Nation',
    Economic Policy **1**, pp. 139–67.
Condliffe, J. B. (1933). *World Economic Survey, 1932–33*, Geneva: League of
    Nations.
Cooper, Ian (1986). 'Financial Markets: New Financial Instruments', paper
    presented to CEPR Workshop, London.

56　**Barry Eichengreen and Richard Portes**

Cooper, Richard (1983). 'Managing Risks to the International Economic System', in Herring, Richard, ed., *Managing International Risk*, Cambridge: Cambridge University Press.

Diaz Alejandro, Carlos (1984). 'Latin American Debt: I Don't Think We Are in Kansas Anymore', *Brookings Papers on Economic Activity*, No. 2, pp. 335–89.

Dornbusch, Rudiger (1985). 'Policy and Performance Links between LDC Debtors and Industrial Nations', *Brookings Papers on Economic Activity*, No. 2, pp. 303–56.

Edwards, Sebastian (1986). 'The Pricing of Bonds and Bank Loans in International Markets', *European Economic Review*, **30**, pp. 565–90.

Eichengreen, Barry (1985a), ed, *The Gold Standard in Theory and History*, London: Methuen.

   (1985b). 'International Policy Coordination in Historical Perspective: A View from the Interwar Years', in Buiter and Marston (1985), pp. 139–78.

   (1986). 'House Calls of the Money Doctor: The Kemmerer Missions to Latin America, 1923–1931', in Ronald Findlay *et al.* (eds), *Debt, Stabilization and Development: Essays in Honor of Carlos F. Diaz Alejandro*, Oxford University Press, forthcoming.

Eichengreen, Barry and Richard Portes (1986). 'Debt and Default in the 1930s: Causes and Consequences,' *European Economic Review* **30**, pp. 559–640.

Eichengreen, Barry and Charles Wyplosz (1986). 'The Economic Consequences of the Franc Poincare', unpublished manuscript

Epstein, Gerald and Thomas Ferguson (1984). 'Monetary Policy, Loan Liquidation, and Industrial Conflict: The Federal Reserve and the Open Market Operations of 1932', *Journal of Economic History* **44**, pp. 957–86.

Frankel, Jeffrey and Kenneth Froot (1986). 'The Dollar as an Irrational Speculative Bubble', Marcus Wallenberg Papers on International Finance, **1**, No. 1.

Fraga, Arminio (1986). *German Reparations and Brazilian Debt*, Princeton Essays in International Finance No. 163, Princeton, NJ: International Financial Section, Princeton University.

Goldsmith, Raymond (1982). 'Comment on Minsky', in Kindleberger and Laffargue (1982), pp. 41–43.

Giavazzi, Francesco and Alberto Giovannini (1986). 'The EMS and the Dollar', *Economic Policy* 2, pp. 455–85.

de Grauwe, Paul and Bernard de Bellefroid (1986). 'Long-Run Exchange Rate Variability and International Trade', mimeo.

Guttentag, Jack and Richard Herring (1983). *The Lender-of-Last-Resort Function in an International Context*, Princeton Essays in International Finance No.151, Princeton, NJ: International Financial Section, Princeton University.

   (1984). 'Credit Rationing and Financial Disorder', *Journal of Finance* **39**, pp. 1359–82.

   (1985). *The Current Crisis in International Lending*, Washington, DC: Brookings Institution.

House of Commons, Treasury and Civil Service Select Committee (1985). *The Financial and Economic Consequences of UK Membership of the European Communities: The European Monetary System*, Vols. I, II, and Memoranda, London: HMSO.

James, Harold (1984). 'The Causes of the German Banking Crisis of 1931', *Economic History Review* **38**, pp. 68–87.

Kaletsky, Anatole (1985). *The Costs of Default*, New York: Twentieth Century Fund.

Kenen, Peter and Dani Rodrik (1986). 'Measuring and Analyzing the Effects of Short-Term Volatility in Real Exchange Rates', *Review of Economics and Statistics*, pp. 311–15.

Keynes, John Maynard (1925). 'Is Sterling Overvalued?' *The Nation and Athenaeum*, 4 April.

Kindleberger, Charles (1978). *Manias, Panics and Crashes*, New York: Basic Books.

  (1984). *A Financial History of Western Europe*, London: Allen & Unwin.

  (1986). 'Bank Failures: the 1930s and the 1980s', in *The Search for Financial Stability: The Past Fifty Years*, San Francisco, California: Federal Reserve Bank of San Francisco.

Kindleberger, Charles and Jean-Pierre Laffargue (eds) (1982). *Financial Crises: Theory, History and Policy*, London: Cambridge University Press.

Kraft, Joseph (1984). *The Mexican Rescue*, New York: Group of Thirty.

League of Nations (1931), *Commercial Banks, 1913–1929*, Geneva: League of Nations.

  (1934). *Commercial Banks, 1925–1933*, Geneva: League of Nations.

  (1937). *Balance of Payments 1936*, Geneva: League of Nations.

  (1938). *Balance of Payments 1937*, Geneva: League of Nations.

Leguizamon, Guillermo A. (1933). 'An Argentine View of the Problem of Exchange Restrictions', *International Affairs*, pp. 504–17.

Lever, Harold and Christopher Huhne (1985). *Debt and Danger: The World Financial Crisis*, London: Penguin.

Maddison, Angus (1985), *Two Crises: Latin America and Asia 1929–38 and 1973–83*, Paris: OECD.

McNeil, William C. (1986). *American Money and the Weimar Republic*, New York: Columbia University Press.

Marris, Stephen (1985). *Deficits and the Dollar: The World Economy at Risk*, Washington, DC: Institute of International Economics.

Minsky, Hyman (1982). 'The Financial Instability Hypothesis: Capitalist Processes and the Behaviour of the Economy', in Kindleberger and Laffargue (1982), pp. 13–38.

Mintz, Ilse (1950). *Deterioration in the Quality of Foreign Bonds Issued in the United States, 1920–1930*, New York: National Bureau of Economic Research.

Mitchell, B. R. (1976). *European Historical Statistics*, London: Macmillan.

Morgan Guaranty Trust Company of New York, *World Financial Markets*.

Nurkse, Ragnar (1944). *International Currency Experience*, Geneva: League of Nations.

  (1946). *The Course and Control of Inflation*, Geneva: League of Nations.

OECD (1983). *The Internationalization of Banking*, Paris.

Padoa Schioppa, Tommaso (1985). 'Policy Cooperation and the EMS Experience', in Buiter and Marston (1985), pp. 331–55.

Portes, Richard (1977). 'East Europe's Debt to the West', *Foreign Affairs* **55**, pp. 751–82.

  (1982). 'La crise polonaise et les relations économiques est-ouest', *Politique étrangère*, no. 1, pp. 75–90.

58   **Discussion by Robert F. Gemmill**

(1986). 'Finance, Trade and Development: Issues in Transatlantic Cooperation', CEPR Discussion Paper No. 100.

Rogoff, Kenneth (1985). 'Can Exchange Rate Predictability be Achieved without Monetary Convergence? Evidence from the EMS', *European Economic Review* **28**, pp. 93–116.

Royal Institute of International Affairs (1937). *The Problem of Foreign Investment*, London: Oxford University Press.

Sachs, Jeffrey (1982). 'LDC Debt in the 1980s: Risk and Reforms', in *Crises in the Economic and Financial Structure*, ed. Paul Wachtel, Lexington, Mass.: D.C. Heath.

(1985). 'External Debt and Macroeconomic Performance in Latin America and East Asia', *Brookings Papers on Economic Activity* No. 2, pp. 523–64.

Schedvin, C. Boris (1970). *Australia and the Great Depression.* Sydney, Sydney University Press.

Securities and Exchange Commission (1937). *Report on the Study and Investigation of the Work, Activities, Personnel and Functions of the Protective and Reorganization Committees*, Washington, DC, GPO.

Solow, Robert (1982). 'On the Lender of Last Resort', in Kindleberger and Laffargue (1982), pp. 237–47.

Spero, Joan (1980). *The Failure of the Franklin National Bank*, New York: Columbia University Press.

State of Vermont (1930). *Annual Report of the Bank Commissioner of the State of Vermont for the Year Ending June 30, 1930*, Rutland, Vermont: The Tuttle Company.

Thorp, Rosemary (1984), ed., *Latin America in the 1930s*, London: Macmillan.

Urquhart, M. C. and K. A. H. Buckley (1965). *Historical Statistics of Canada*, Cambridge: Cambridge University Press.

U.S. Department of Commerce (1930). *American Underwriting of Foreign Securities*, Washington, DC: GPO.

White, Eugene (1984). 'A Reinterpretation of the Banking Crisis of 1930', *Journal of Economic History* **44**, pp. 119–38.

Williamson, John (1977). *The Failure of World Monetary Reform*, London: Nelson.

(1985). *The Exchange Rate System*, Washington, DC: Institute for International Economics.

Winkler, Max (1933). *Foreign Bonds: An Autopsy*, Philadelphia: Roland Swain.

World Bank (1986). *World Debt Tables*, Washington, DC: IBRD.

[2]

Why Is Financial Stability a Goal of Public Policy?

By Andrew Crockett

A number of developments in recent years have combined to put the issue of financial stability at the top of the agenda, not just of supervisory authorities, but of public policymakers more generally. These developments include: the explosive growth in the volume of financial transactions, the increased complexity of new instruments, costly crises in national financial systems, and several high profile mishaps at individual institutions.

The growth in the volume of financial transactions and the increasing integration of capital markets have made institutions in the financial sector more interdependent and have brought to the fore the issue of systemic risk. International capital flows, though generally beneficial for the efficient allocation of savings and investment, now have the power in unstable conditions to undermine national economic policies and destabilize financial systems.

Andrew Crockett is General Manager at the Bank for International Settlements. He presented this paper at the Federal Reserve Bank of Kansas City's 1997 symposium, "Maintaining Financial Stability in a Global Economy," in Jackson Hole, Wyoming, August 28-30, 1997. The views expressed are those of the author and do not necessarily reflect those of the BIS or the Federal Reserve System. Helpful comments on an earlier draft of this paper were provided by Svein Andresen, Claudio Borio, Peter Dittus, Danile Nouy, Patrick Honohan and Bill White.

The increased complexity of new instruments makes it harder for senior management in financial firms, let alone supervisory authorities, to understand intuitively the risks to which the institutions concerned are exposed. There are fears that the models underlying the pricing of the new instruments may not be sufficiently robust, that the mathematics of the models may have become disconnected from the realities of the marketplace, or that the operational controls within financial institutions may be inadequate to control the resultant risks.

The crises in financial systems that have occurred have demonstrated the close linkages between financial stability and the health of the real economy. In Mexico, for example, what began as a currency crisis led to a serious recession and created huge strains in the banking system, further deepening the recession. The consequences of the Mexican crisis destabilized several other Latin American countries, notably Argentina, and threatened for a while to have even wider repercussions. In industrial countries, financial strains in Scandinavia and Japan, among others, had adverse consequences for the real economy.

Lastly, there have been a number of well-publicized losses at individual institutions, due to the breakdown of operational or other controls. Episodes such as Drexel Burnham, Procter &

Gamble, Orange County, Metallgesellschaft, Barings, Daiwa, and Sumitomo, though reasonably well contained, demonstrate how quickly losses can mount, and illustrate the systemic risks that would be inherent in a larger scale mishap.

The central case for making the health of the financial system a public policy concern rests on two propositions: firstly, that, left to itself, the financial system is prone to bouts of instability; and secondly, that instability can generate sizable negative spillover effects (externalities). It will be the purpose of this paper to examine these propositions more closely, and in the light of this examination, to consider what forms public policy intervention in the financial sector might take. More specifically, I will address the following questions: what do we mean by financial stability? Why should official intervention (as opposed to reliance on market forces) be required to promote stability? And what concrete approaches can be employed?

I. WHAT IS FINANCIAL STABILITY?

A distinction is commonly made nowadays between monetary stability and financial stability (interestingly, this distinction would not have been so easily recognized a generation ago, either by economists or public officials). Monetary stability refers to the stability of the general price level; financial stability to the stability of the key institutions and markets that go to make up the financial system. While these are conceptually separate objectives of policy, the linkages between the two are now increasingly recognized.[1]

The debate on monetary stability has progressed further and its definition has reached a greater degree of consensus than is the case with financial stability. Nobody disputes that the avoidance of excessive inflation is an appropriate objective. And nobody doubts that it is public policy (specifically, monetary policy) that ultimately determines the inflation rate. Remaining debates, as became evident last year at Jackson Hole, surround issues such as how to accurately measure inflation; what, within a relatively narrow range (usually 1-3 percent), should be considered an optimal inflation rate; whether the objective should be expressed in terms of the inflation rate or the price level, and how quickly one should return to price stability after having been forced away from it.[2]

No such general consensus applies in the case of the definition of financial stability. For the time being, at least, each writer can supply his own. In my case, I will take financial stability to apply to both institutions and markets. In other words, stability requires (i) that the key *institutions* in the financial system are stable, in that there is a high degree of confidence that they can continue to meet their contractual obligations without interruption or outside assistance; and (ii) that the key *markets* are stable, in that participants can confidently transact in them at prices that reflect fundamental forces and that do not vary substantially over short periods when there have been no changes in fundamentals.

This does not, however, provide a full definition. Which are the "key institutions" whose stability is important? And what is the degree of price stability in financial markets that is required?

Stability in financial institutions means the absence of stresses that have the potential to cause measurable economic harm beyond a strictly limited group of customers and counterparties. Occasional failures of smaller institutions, and occasional substantial losses at larger institutions, are part and parcel of the normal functioning of the financial system. Indeed, they serve a positive function by reminding market participants of their obligation to exercise discipline over the activities of the intermediaries with whom they do business.

Similarly, stability in financial markets means the absence of price movements that cause wider economic damage. Prices can and should move to reflect changes in economic fundamentals. And the prices of assets can often move quite abruptly when something happens to cause a reassessment of the future stream of income associated with the asset, or the price at which this income stream should be discounted. It is only when prices in financial markets move by amounts that are much greater than can be accounted for by fundamentals, and do so in a way that has damaging economic consequences, that one is justified in talking about "instability" or "crisis" in the financial system.

A practical issue that is worth addressing at this point is whether all financial institutions and all markets should be treated similarly. Are problems in the banking sector to be considered in the same light as problems at nonbank financial institutions? Is the failure of a big bank the same as that of a small bank? And should central banks be as concerned about excessive volatility in asset prices as they are about instability among financial institutions? These are issues that have been, and remain, controversial.

Consider first the question of which institutions are important for financial stability. This raises two further issues: are banks special? And are some institutions "too big to fail"? Two reasons are usually given for believing that banks warrant special treatment in the preservation of financial stability.[3] The first is that banks' liabilities are repayable at par on demand, while their assets are typically comparatively illiquid. This makes them more liable to runs that cause illiquidity and even insolvency. The second is that banks remain responsible for the operation of the payment system. This means that difficulties at one institution are transmitted, semi-auto-

matically, to the rest of the financial system, with the risk, at the extreme, that the payments system could seize up.

Both of these reasons continue to have force, though perhaps not to the same extent as previously. While illiquid loans remain a disproportionate share of banks' assets, holdings of marketable securities have tended to increase. And the "moneyness" of banks' liabilities may have become less of a distinguishing characteristic, as banks increase their reliance on marketable claims to meet funding requirements, and nonbank institutions issue liabilities that are repayable on demand. Banks continue to dominate the payments system, and the failure of one bank immediately generates losses to those banks exposed to it in the settlement system. Cascading losses through these arrangements have the potential to undermine the payments systems, which is the basis for monetary exchange in all economies. But interlocking claims and settlement exposures among other entities at the core of the financial system have grown sizably as nonbank financial intermediaries have come to greater prominence. These have increased the potential for knock-on effects among them.

The conclusion is that banks remain "special," in that instability in the banking system has a greater capacity to generate systemic contagion than difficulties elsewhere in the financial sector. But the distinctions are becoming more blurred, with problems at key nonbank institutions having growing potential for significant spillover consequences.

In many respects size has become more important than an institution's formal character in determining its systemic significance. Regulators frequently deny that there is a "too big to fail" doctrine. One can understand why they do, since to make it explicit would court moral hazard. Still, it is only realistic to recognize that certain institutions are so central to the financial system that their failure would constitute a systemic crisis. Their obligations to counterparties are so large that failure to discharge them would cause widespread contagion. This group of institutions includes both banks and nonbanks.

Next, what about price volatility in asset markets? How much price movement can take place before we should classify markets as being "unstable"? And which markets are of particular concern for the health of the financial system and the economy more generally?

There are obviously no hard-and-fast answers to these questions. Any price movements that exceed what can be justified on grounds of changing fundamentals have the potential to result in resource misallocation. Sustained price volatility that generates uncertainty, leading to an unwillingness to enter into long-term contracts, hampers economic performance through discouraging the mobilization and allocation of savings through the financial system. And sudden or sharp price movements that place the liquidity or solvency of prudently run financial institutions at risk have more immediate dangers.

As to which markets should be the focus of concern, once again the criterion should be the capacity to cause wider economic damage. Financial and other asset markets, because of their broad linkages to saving and investment decisions, obviously have a greater potential impact on other macroeconomic variables than do developments in markets for goods and services. This impact can occur through wealth effects, as the prices of financial assets change; through changing the expected returns on savings and investment; or through generalized effects on consumer and business confidence.

A further point concerns the capacity for contagion among financial markets. Just as difficul-

ties at one financial intermediary appear to have the effect of undermining confidence more generally, so experience suggests that sharp movements in one market can destabilize others. Examples of this phenomenon include the broadly similar movements in international equity prices in 1987, following the price break on Wall Street; the general upward movement in bond yields in 1994; and the spread of exchange rate difficulties in Europe in 1992-93 and in Southeast Asia in 1997.

In conclusion, there is still no clear-cut definition of what constitutes financial instability. What may distinguish the financial system from other areas of economic activity, however, is the potential for healthy flexibility to develop—in a short period of time—into more troublesome instability and eventually, in extreme circumstances, into crisis. This is because precautionary action taken by individuals in the face of asymmetric information can in certain circumstances have the effect of amplifying, rather than dampening, natural volatility. This potential brings us closer to an understanding of why the maintenance of stability is often considered to be a natural responsibility of public authorities.

Assessing the point at which movements in asset prices, or in the financial position of intermediaries, risk becoming self-perpetuating is obviously a matter of judgment. Because the costs of mistakes are so high, it is of key importance to understand the dynamics of the process. It is also important to come to an assessment of the ways in which the financial instability interacts with the real economy to intensify (or moderate) an initial shock. It is for this reason that, whatever the specific arrangements in place in any country to monitor or underwrite the health of individual institutions, there needs to be close cooperation between the authorities responsible for the supervision of individual institutions, those responsible for broader systemic stability, and those concerned with stability in prices and the real economy.

II. WHY IS OFFICIAL INTERVENTION REQUIRED TO PROMOTE STABILITY?

There can be little doubt that financial stability, properly defined, is a "good thing." It creates a more favorable environment for savers and investors to make intertemporal contracts, enhances the efficiency of financial intermediation and helps improve allocation of real resources. It provides a better environment for the implementation of macroeconomic policy. Instability, on the other hand, can have damaging consequences, from the fiscal costs of bailing out troubled institutions to the real GNP losses associated with banking and currency crises.

The only qualification to be made is that stability must not be confused with rigidity. Market prices must be allowed to move as supply and demand conditions change. And financial institutions should not be prevented from going out of existence when they are unable to make a profit. The trick is to permit the necessary flexibility in market prices and structures, without generating instability that has damaging consequences on confidence and real economic activity.

Financial stability is a public good in that its "consumers" (i.e., users of financial services) do not deprive others of the possibility of also benefiting from it. In this sense, public authorities have an interest in seeing that it is "supplied" in an appropriate quantity. This does not mean, however, that public authorities should necessarily intervene in financial markets so as to promote stability. There is no public agency directly concerned with stability in the market for foodstuffs or automobiles (although govern-

ments generally accept a responsibility for health and safety and for competition). Is finance any different?

It cannot be denied that all financial instability has costs for someone. The collapse of a financial firm imposes direct costs on shareholders, who lose their investment; on employees, who lose their jobs; and on depositors and unsecured creditors, whose claims may be forfeit. Instability in asset prices creates losses for those whose investments prove unsuccessful. In this (i.e., the direct or "private" costs of instability), financial firms and markets are not qualitatively different from other sectors of the economy. And while there are always pressures to compensate private losses, it is generally assumed that the public interest is served best by allowing market disciplines to work—unless there is evidence of market failure.

In what follows, I will examine the argument that the financial system is particularly subject to market failure, and that the consequences of such failure justify public policy intervention. It will be convenient to divide this discussion into two parts: that concerned with the potential for instability at financial *institutions*; and that concerned with excessive volatility in prices in financial *markets*.

Instability at financial institutions

The reasons why difficulties at a financial firm may give rise to public policy concerns may be grouped under several (overlapping) heads:

(a) Losses to depositors and other creditors may be exacerbated because of the unique vulnerability of financial institutions to "runs."

(b) The scope for losses to spread to other financial institutions through "contagion" or direct exposures is high.

Table 1

EQUITY PRICES IN 1987 AND BOND YIELDS IN 1994

	Equity price movements in 2 weeks of October 1987*	Bond yield rise end-January through end-July 1994 (basis points)†
United States	-20.2	142
Japan	-12.2	89
Germany	-14.2	142
France	-16.7	159
United Kingdom	-24.8	236
Italy	-11.3	235
Canada	-18.5	297
Netherlands	-18.9	124
Belgium	-10.7	156

* 9th to 23rd October 1987.
† Ten-year benchmark.
Sources: National sources.

(c) There may be budgetary costs from the perceived need to protect depositors or bailout troubled institutions.

(d) There may be more widespread macro-economic consequences from instability in the financial sector.

(e) A loss of confidence in financial interme-diation may lead to financial "repression" result-ing in suboptimal levels of savings and misallocation of investment.

The first two of these points concern the potential for an "instability bias" in the financial system; the last three to the external costs gen-erated by such instability. Let us now consider them in slightly more detail.

"Runs" and the protection of individual insti-tutions. There are two broad reasons why the authorities may wish to be involved with the stability of individual institutions (other than contagion risk, which is dealt with below). One rests on the vulnerability of banks to runs; the other on economies of scale in monitoring the behavior of complex firms.

A well-known feature of banks is that they issue liabilities that are redeemable on demand at par, while they hold longer term assets that are less readily marketable and have an uncertain value. Under normal circumstances, this does not pose a major problem, since deposit with-drawals are subject to the law of large numbers and well-managed loans that are held to maturity are mostly repaid at face value. A bank's holding of capital covers the risk of loan loss, and a cushion of liquid assets is sufficient to preserve confidence in its ability to meet withdrawals.

If, however, something happens to disturb confidence, the situation can be destabilized. Depositors perceive that those who withdraw

ECONOMIC REVIEW • FOURTH QUARTER 1997   *11*

their funds first will be able to do so without loss or penalty; those who delay may find that the bank's capital has been eroded by a "fire-sale" of less marketable assets. What this means is, firstly, the value of a bank (like other firms) is greater as a going concern than it is in a forced liquidation. Secondly, because of the leverage inherent in banks' operations, forced liquidation is more likely than in the case of nonfinancial firms. This argues in favor of an outside agent to preserve potentially solvent institutions as going concerns, or else to intervene to gradually wind down firms that have become insolvent.

A slightly different argument for intervention to protect depositors is that they have inadequate information to protect themselves. Monitoring financial institutions is costly, and pooled monitoring may be more efficient than individual monitoring. (Note that this argument may apply to all firms, not just those, like banks, whose liabilities are repayable at par on demand.) In this view, the public authorities are performing a service (like that of a rating agency) that it would be too difficult or too costly for individual depositors to perform for themselves. This argument can be given a political slant by recognizing that, to be realistic, certain depositors will always act foolishly when faced with the incentive of high returns. Since political pressure to provide compensation for losses is bound to ensue, it is better for the authorities to step in to avert losses, or rationalize the process by which compensation is provided.

"Contagion" effects at other financial institutions. Potentially more serious than the losses that accrue to individual depositors at a failed institution is the danger that difficulties may be propagated more widely. Such contagion can take place through two main channels: firstly, the pattern of interlocking claims among financial institutions; and secondly, the potential for difficulties at one institution to provoke a loss of

confidence in others thought to be similarly placed.

There can be little doubt that the exposure of financial firms to other financial intermediaries has grown dramatically in recent years. A major factor has been the increase in trading activities. Daily foreign exchange trading has increased threefold over the last decade and stood at $1.25 trillion in 1995. Well in excess of 80 percent of these trades are between dealing counterparties. Derivatives and securities trading has grown even faster and is also dominated by interdealer activity. The place where the resulting inter-intermediary exposures get concentrated is the interlocking network of payments and securities settlement systems. Although individual exposures are of short duration, at any point in time they are very large in size. In many cases, the unsecured exposure of financial institutions to a single counterparty exceeds capital. It is this fact that has led some observers to conclude that a disruption transmitted through the payment system is the largest single threat to the stability of the financial system.[4]

Contagion can also occur indirectly, when strains at one financial institution provoke a loss of deposits from, or an unwillingness to enter into transactions with, other firms that are also thought to be vulnerable. Following the Barings collapse, for example, a number of small to medium-sized investment banks in London and elsewhere were reported to have suffered deposit withdrawals, even though there was nothing to suggest that they had incurred losses similar to Barings'. In other words, contagion can be indirectly as well as directly induced.

Contagion is one of the basic reasons why public authorities are concerned with the health and survival of individual financial institutions. This relates to the "public good" aspect of financial stability. Confidence in the financial system

benefits individual participants without imposing costs on others. If the failure of one institution causes a contagious loss of confidence
elsewhere, the adverse consequences to the system as a whole may be much greater than those
resulting from the initial disruption.

Resolution costs. Turning now to the spillover
consequences of instability, the transfer costs of
resolving financial crises are the most readily
quantifiable, and in many ways the most striking. To public policy officials, the costs that fall
on the public budget surely provide the most
persuasive evidence of the need to do whatever
is necessary to strengthen financial systems.

The U.S. public is acutely aware of the savings
and loan debacle of the 1980s, the resolution costs
of which are estimated at anywhere between 2
percent and 4 percent of GDP. These costs,
however, pale in comparison with the fiscal
costs incurred in a number of other countries.[5]
In France, the losses incurred by a *single* bank,
Credit Lyonnais, are now put at some $30 billion,
or over 2 percent of GNP. Honohan estimates the
fiscal costs of resolving crises in developing
countries alone as being as much as $250 bil-
lion.[6] A World Bank Study estimates that 14
countries had to devote more than 10 percent of
GNP to the resolution of banking sector crises
(Table 2).[7] And a by now well-known IMF
study concludes that almost three-quarters of
IMF member countries encountered "significant" banking sector problems during the period 1980-96; of these as many as one-third
warrant the designation "crisis."[8] Part of the
resolution costs of these crises fall on the banking system and its clients. More frequently,
however, the government budget is left to pick
up the lion's share.

GNP costs of financial instability. The resolution costs of financial sector crises are, of
course, transfer costs. They cannot be taken as

an accurate guide to losses in economic welfare,
which could be either greater or smaller. They
could be smaller than the transfer costs if the
real assets financed by failed banks remained in
existence and continued to yield productive
services. On the other hand, the cumulative misallocation of financial resources represented by
bad loans suggests that the overall loss to society
from inefficient financial intermediation may
have been even larger than the losses that eventually fell on the budget or on the shareholders
and other claimants of banks. How can one go
about assessing the macroeconomic costs of
instability?

Even if instability does not lead to crisis, they
can make it harder for the authorities to gauge
the appropriateness of a given policy stance.
Financial fragility complicates the interpretation of the indicators used to guide monetary
policy decisions. Somewhat more seriously,
weaknesses at financial institutions can limit the
willingness to lend, thus creating "head winds"
for the expansion of demand. Overall economic
performance suffers as a result.

Where financial difficulties are more serious,
the impact on GNP can be larger and more
direct, whether or not the authorities decide to
support the financial system. In Mexico, for
example, the interaction of financial sector difficulties and a currency crisis led to a sharp
setback to GNP. By mid-1995 industrial output
in Mexico had fallen 12 percent from its level
two quarters earlier. Even in Argentina, which
successfully defended its exchange rate, GDP is
estimated to have temporarily fallen some 7
percent below trend as a result of the "tequila
effect." The banking crisis of the 1980s in Chile
saw output growth drop from 8 percent in the
five years preceding the crisis to only 1 percent
in the five years after it.

Among industrial countries, it is harder to

Table 2

Country (time period of crisis)	Estimate of total losses/costs (percentage of GDP)
Latin America	
Argentina (1980-82)	55
Chile (1981-83)	41[a]
Venezuela (1994-95)	18
Mexico (1995)	12-15[b]
Africa	
Benin (1988-90)	17
Cote d'Ivoire (1988-91)	25
Mauritania (1984-93)	15
Senegal (1988-91)	17
Tanzania (1987-95)	10[c]
Middle East	
Israel (1977-83)	30[d]
Transition countries	
Bulgaria (1990s)	14
Hungary (1995)	10
Industrial countries	
Spain (1977-85)	17
Japan (1990s)	10[e]

[a] 1982-85.
[b] Accumulated losses to date.
[c] In 1987.
[d] In 1983.
[e] Estimate of potential losses.
Source: Goldstein (1997) based on Caprio and Klingebiel (1996a).

detect cause-and-effect relationship between financial instability and GDP. In the United States, the savings and loan crisis had little measurable impact on growth, costly though it was to the budget. In Nordic countries and in Japan, the consequences are more readily apparent. Growth in Finland averaged 4.5 percent in the years preceding the outbreak of the banking crisis, and was *minus* 4.0 percent in the three succeeding years (though doubtless not all of the difference is attributable to financial difficul-

ties). In Sweden and Norway, there were economic downturns following the strains in the banking system, though again other factors were also at work. And in Japan, the "head winds" caused by financial sector weaknesses held growth in the mid-1990s below the underlying potential of the economy.

It bears repeating here that the relationship between financial instability and macroeconomic instability is two-way. Macroeconomic instability is usually a major factor in financial diffi-culties, often because an unsustainable expan-sion induces unwise lending. Credit-fueled "bubbles" in financial asset and property prices frequently play a contributory role, especially when a large share of lending is used to finance the acquisition of real estate or financial assets whose price is, for a time, rising rapidly.[9] A recession then reveals serious weakness in lend-ing portfolios. When the financial system en-counters difficulties, problems can quickly worsen macroeconomic performance. Weak-ened intermediaries cease to lend, losses in the financial sector create negative wealth or income effects, generalized uncertainty inhibits invest-ment, and the public sector is often forced to rein in real expenditure to help offset the budgetary cost of increased transfers.

Instability and the development of the finan-cial sector. Beyond the direct effects of financial instability on real economic activity, there can be indirect adverse consequences for longer run growth potential if financial intermediation is stunted. As Akerlof has shown, in any market where participants have asymmetric informa-tion, moral hazard and adverse selection reduce exchange below levels that could be beneficial if market participants had better information (the market for lemons). The market for intertem-poral exchange is characterized by extreme asymmetry of information between providers of funds and potential borrowers. The potential negative consequences are, however, offset by the existence of specialized intermediaries. Fi-nancial intermediaries perform the role of agents for lenders, screening out uncreditworthy borrowers, monitoring borrowers' performance after a loan is made, adding creditworthiness through the commitment of their own capital, and creating liquidity through providing for the ready marketability of claims.

All of this, however, depends upon the preser-

vation of confidence in the stability of the net-work of financial intermediaries: if lenders lose confidence in the continued stability of the insti-tutions to whom they have entrusted their funds, or in the integrity of the markets in which they have invested, they will seek to reduce their exposure and place their assets elsewhere. In the limit, they may choose consumption over sav-ing, or may place their savings in nonproductive but "safe" forms (such as precious metals). If this happens, the contribution of the financial sector in providing improved methods of risk pricing and management, and in adding liquidity and creditworthiness, will be much diminished. Mishkin indeed defines a financial crisis as "a disruption to financial markets in which adverse selection and moral hazard problems become much worse, so that financial markets are unable to channel funds efficiently to those who have the most productive investment opportunities."[10]

Instability in financial markets

While there is broad (though not universal) acceptance that the stability of financial institu-tions should be an objective of public policy, this is much less true with regard to financial asset prices or financial flows. The majority view is that free markets are the best guarantors of equi-librium in prices, and that official intervention should be limited to removing market imperfec-tions, e.g., by promoting the disclosure of rele-vant information and preventing the emergence of monopoly practices. Yet financial markets can, in principle, be subject to the same kind of "instability bias" and adverse spillovers that affect financial institutions.

Instability bias arises if a disturbance affecting prices generates forces creating further moves in the same direction. These are generally based on extrapolative expectations, which can result from asymmetric information, reinforced by herd instincts. Certain technical features of markets, such as margin requirements, can also play a role. In a rising market, those who invest on margin find their net worth rising, and are thereby enabled to make further leveraged purchases, pushing prices still higher. The opposite effects come into play in a falling market, with margin calls forcing liquidation of holdings and exacerbating price declines.

The importance of such instability biases are very hard to assess on a priori grounds. The sudden drop in equity prices in 1987 suggests that they can sometimes be significant, though the relative infrequency of such occurrences provides some reassurance. Swings in exchange rates could be taken as evidence that similar pressures work in currency markets; though full-blown currency crises are more apt to be result of attempts to defend a fixed rate at an unsustainable level.

Volatility in financial asset prices has the capacity to create "spillover" effects of various kinds. Firstly (and perhaps least troublesome), is the added difficulty it creates for the authorities in formulating macroeconomic policies. Movements in asset prices influence all of the channels by which monetary policy traditionally affects the real economy: the interest rate channel, the wealth channel, the exchange rate channel. Moreover, they can, if severe, have pervasive effects on confidence. There is at present a lively debate about whether and how monetary policy should respond to asset price movements. The fact that the debate is still unresolved is evidence of the uncertainties created for policymakers when financial markets are unstable.

Another type of spillover effect occurs when asset price movements undermine the stability of financial institutions. This can happen if intermediaries are heavily exposed to certain categories of assets (e.g., equities or real estate), or

if their lending is secured on such assets. It can also occur if financial institutions have mismatched foreign currency or interest rate books, or if higher volatility suddenly increases the costs of hedging options positions.

Lastly, asset price volatility can create real economic costs if the authorities are led to take extreme measures to restore stability. Perhaps the most prominent examples of such costs occur in currency crises. Instability in foreign exchange markets is almost invariably accompanied by sharply higher interest rates in the country whose currency is under downward pressure. And higher interest rates usually provoke a downturn in economic activity, whether accompanied and exacerbated by a financial sector crisis or not.

What are the specific markets that are particularly vulnerable to instability, and what is the nature of the spillover effects? Let us briefly consider four.

Firstly, the foreign exchange market. Two types of instability should be distinguished: the turmoil that surrounds speculation against a pegged exchange rate; and the volatility that seems to characterize floating rates. The defense of pegged rates, especially when it is ultimately unsuccessful, is most likely to be classified as a currency "crisis." In such a case, it can be argued that the problem is as much one of policy as of market instability. Should the authorities have selected a fixed rate regime? Should they have changed the peg (or the regime) earlier? Should they have pursued a different mix of policies? Some have argued, however, that attacks on a fixed peg can also be speculatively induced.[11] Where there are dual or multiple equilibria in exchange rate relationships, the movement from one to another may owe more to market dynamics than to fundamentals.

Where exchange rates are floating, volatility is harder to explain, especially when movements in fundamentals are modest. Swings in relative real values among the U.S. dollar, Deutsche Mark and Japanese Yen have approached 50 percent or more in the past decade and a half. Such swings complicate macroeconomic policies; generate the potential for resource misallocation and give rise to protectionist pressures. While it can be argued that exchange markets are responding to policy divergences (actual and expected), the link is often not at all clear.

Secondly, instability in equity markets can also have external consequences. Stock market volatility can undermine the stability of financial institutions who are directly or indirectly exposed to equity prices; exacerbate the investment cycle (via Tobin's "q"); and, if prices fall sharply, have adverse effects on confidence. However, although stock market crashes have a fascination for lay opinion, the impact of equity price instability has for most of the time been relatively mild. This may be because there are nonlinearities at work. Modest movements in equity values do little if any harm; but a larger movement has a disproportionately greater potential both to set up self-perpetuating forces and to do real economic damage.

Thirdly, much the same can be said of price fluctuations in bond markets. Despite the generalized run-up in bond yields in 1994, adverse spillovers were rather well contained. So long as the central bank is thought able to stabilize inflation, the scope for extreme movements in bond prices is limited.

Fourthly and finally, real estate, though not strictly speaking a financial asset, can be subject to "bubble" phenomena. A real estate bubble complicates the formulation of monetary policy while it is being created, and can leave a string of failures in its wake when it bursts. Some of the difficulties faced in mid-1997 by Southeast Asian economies can be traced, in part to real estate bubbles.

What should be concluded from the foregoing brief survey? If there are disequilibrium tendencies in financial and other asset markets, and if price volatility has had adverse spillover consequences, does this argue for making the stability of asset prices a focus of public policy concern in the same way as the stability of financial institutions?

Here the answer is, at best, not clear-cut. Few economists would be confident that governments could be better at determining equilibrium prices than markets. Even when prices move by an amount that is clearly greater than "fundamentals" justify, it can rarely be said that the price was more appropriate before the move than after it. And frequently, the blame for price volatility is due to unstable policies just as much as to unstable markets. So the broad consensus among economists (with which I agree) is that official policy to stabilize financial asset prices should be focused more on sustainable policies and removing market imperfections, than on direct actions to limit price movements.

One should recognize that there can, occasionally, be exceptions to this general rule. When currencies become substantially misaligned (as in 1985, say), governments may try to give a lead to markets (albeit through statements concerning policies). And if domestic asset prices were to fall to an extent that threatened financial stability, it would not be surprising to see a policy response aimed at stabilizing prices. In fact, central banks responded to the 1987 stock market crash by easing the provision of liquidity to financial markets. In general, however, official responses to extreme price movements tend to be ad hoc, rather than part of a cohesive "policy" on financial market stability.

III. APPROACHES TO ENSURING FINANCIAL STABILITY

The foregoing section has listed a number of reasons why financial instability has negative externalities. These are probably sufficient to make achieving and maintaining stability a public policy goal. It is of less help, however, in determining how public authorities should promote stability. This section reviews several broad approaches to promoting stability, implying varying degrees of intervention by the authorities. The principal focus is on policies to promote stability at financial institutions, since these have been the subject of more coherent analysis. At the end of the section, however, there are a few observations on preventing instability in key market prices.

Reliance on market forces

With the possible exception of New Zealand, where certain special circumstances apply, no countries have adopted the position that market forces can be relied on as the sole guarantor of stability at financial institutions. But while official support for the pure market solution is limited, there is a stronger academic tradition in this vein, going back to the free banking school, and finding recent expression in the writing of Dowd.[12] Other academics have questioned whether the contagion effect that lies behind official concern with systemic stability is in reality all that significant.[13]

The case for the market solution is, to simplify, as follows: when all actors, including depositors, counterparties, managers, and shareholders of financial institutions realize they are "on their own," they will exercise a much higher degree of care, and financial institutions will thereby be forced to operate in a sounder and more prudent fashion. The failure of an individual institution will become less likely, and the risk of systemic contagion will be almost nonexistent. The moral hazard implied by official intervention will be removed, with favorable consequences for the efficiency of resource allocation.

The case against can be put on several levels. Most fundamentally, it is argued that there are events that may occur very infrequently, that cannot be predicted, and that have the capacity to destabilize the financial system if not resisted. These could include political events such as the outbreak of war or the election of radical governments; economic events, such as the 1929 stock market crash; or natural disasters such as a major earthquake in a large metropolitan center. If governments were to stand aside from helping the financial system under such extraordinary circumstances, financial institutions would have to carry such a large cushion of capital as to greatly reduce their capacity to contribute to economic welfare in normal times.

More prosaically, it is pointed out by Goodhart and others that political pressures make it very hard for elected authorities to refuse assistance to institutions whose depositors have powerful electoral influence.[14] Since most market participants know this, any ex ante announcement by governments not to support the financial system lacks credibility. Moral hazard is not, therefore, avoided. Thus, despite the attraction of reliance on market forces, most observers accept that it is insufficient, by itself, to guarantee stability in all circumstances.

Safety nets

The most effective way of ensuring continued confidence in financial institutions is to provide their users with some sort of explicit safety net. The main types of safety net are deposit insurance schemes, and the presence of a lender of last resort. The primary drawback of safety nets is moral hazard, which appears in a particularly overt form with deposit insurance. Insured depositors have no incentive to monitor the institutions with whom they place their funds. Borrowing institutions are therefore able to pursue risky strategies and, at the limit, to "gamble for resurrection" when their capital has been eroded. The potential for imprudent behavior is exemplified by the savings and loan episode in the United States.

Various means have been suggested to address the moral hazard issue. These include limiting the coverage of deposit insurance, charging risk-based insurance premia, and limiting insurance coverage to a specific category of institutions (100 percent reserve banks). None is entirely satisfactory. Limiting the coverage of insurance schemes means that uninsured depositors can still precipitate a "run" when they fear for bank solvency. Risk-based insurance premia are difficult to calculate on a formulaic basis. And 100 percent reserve banking, despite impressive academic support from Henry Simons to Milton Friedman and James Tobin, has never gained much support.[15] Probably most observers conclude that 100 percent reserve banks would not be successful in winning a major share of the market during normal times, and therefore the issue of how to safeguard stability at other institutions would not go away.

Lender-of-last-resort support has been a recognized role of central banks since Bagehot. The object is to provide support to solvent but illiquid institutions to avoid the possibility that they would have to liquidate assets in a "fire sale" that would generate losses and lead to an avoidable insolvency. Aside from the practical difficulty of distinguishing between insolvency and illiquidity, the lender-of-last-resort role does not avoid the problem of moral hazard.[16] One answer to this is "constructive ambiguity"—a phrase made popular by Jerry Corrigan meaning that central banks reserve the right to intervene

to preserve stability but give no assurances, explicit or implicit, to individual institutions. Such an approach is intended to make institutions act more prudently by making them uncertain whether they would be rescued in a crisis. In some circumstances, however, "constructive ambiguity" may turn out to be a cloak for "too big to fail," if the lender of last resort is more willing to take the risk of allowing a small institution to go under than a large one.

Regulation

If there were no safety net, regulation would be justified by the need to protect the interests of depositors and other creditors. With a safety net, the justification shifts to one of protecting the deposit insurance fund (often taxpayers) and avoiding moral hazard. In practice the focus of regulation has shifted significantly over time, and may now be in the process of a further shift. Three different focuses for regulation can be distinguished.

Regulation to protect franchise values. Until about 20 years ago, regulation in most countries had the effect of limiting competition in the financial industry. Entry to the industry was controlled, there were restrictions on interest rate competition, and cartel-type practices were tolerated. In a number of countries, including the U.S. and Japan, there was strict segregation between commercial and investment banking activities. Since franchise values were high as a result, losses were less likely and, when they did occur, more often led to industry-sponsored takeover or rescue than to outright failure.

Several developments in the 1970s and 1980s undermined this form of regulation. The growing dominance of the free market philosophy made protective practices less acceptable. Liberalization and deregulation increased competition which in turn eroded banks' profitability and diminished franchise values. With relatively thin capital cushions, this made banks more vulnerable to adverse external shocks. As a result regulation to limit competition and bolster the profitability of financial institutions was no longer a practicable or acceptable means of ensuring systemic stability.

Risk-based capital adequacy. In recent years the dominant form of regulation to promote systemic stability has been risk-based capital adequacy. Instead of limiting banks' activities, regulators have sought to ensure that banks are adequately capitalized against the risks they run. This is the philosophy behind a series of documents issued by the Basle Committee on Banking Supervision. Supervisors have divided assets into a number of "risk classes" and specified the amount of capital to be held against each.

Such an approach has several advantages. The notion of relating capital to risk is in conformity with the reason financial institutions hold capital in the first place. And the increased capitalization of the banking system that has followed from the decisions of the Basle Committee has undoubtedly improved systemic resiliency. Nevertheless, certain aspects of the way the approach has been implemented have drawbacks, which are becoming increasingly recognized.

Firstly, and most importantly, there is the potential for a discrepancy between risk, as calculated by the financial institution itself, and risk as measured by regulatory criteria. To take two obvious examples: the Basle Committee risk weights make no distinction between high and low quality credits within the same risk weight category (e.g., between a AAA borrower and a junk bond issuer); nor do they take account of the possibility of risk reduction through diversification. Most financial firms now find that there is a significant discrepancy between the "economic capital" they consider appropriate to

cover the total risk of their portfolio and the "regulatory capital" they are required to hold under the Basle ratios.

This would not matter much from the viewpoint of stability if the only problem were an excess of prudence on the part of supervisors. Indeed, it could well have advantages, since the additional capital cushion required by supervisors could be considered the "price" to be paid for the safety net provided by the lender of last resort. As some writers have pointed out, however, this is not the only implication. Even adjusting for supervisory caution, a portfolio's riskiness may appear significantly different when internal risk models are used than when the Basle risk weights are applied. It is possible for banks with higher risk appetites to deliberately add risk to their portfolios (e.g., through the use of credit derivatives) without having an effect on the regulatory capital required to meet the Basle ratios.[17]

A second problem with the current approach is that it focuses only on certain categories of risk. One gap in the original Basle Accord has now been plugged with the extension of capital requirements to market risk as well as credit risk. But several of the most recent examples of serious losses in the financial sector have come from operational risk (Barings, Daiwa), legal risk (swaps with UK local authorities) and model risk (Metallgesellschaft). As a result of these perceived shortcomings, growing attention is now being given to using regulation to better harness market incentives in support of stability.

Regulation to support market forces. In any market, self-regulation is a powerful force. The strongest incentive to act with prudence and integrity comes from those with most to lose when they fail to do so. Recent thinking has therefore focused on ways of strengthening the incentives on individual institutions to manage their own affairs prudently and on their counterparties to exercise appropriate discipline: in the jargon, "incentive-compatible financial regulation."[18]

Consider the assessment of risk. The managers of a financial institution have a strong incentive to monitor accurately their risk exposure. It therefore seems likely that an internal assessment of risk will be a better measure than a simplified external formula. This philosophy has been accepted by the Basle Committee and incorporated in the market risk amendment to the Capital Accord. The market risk amendment allows firms to use their own models (subject to external validation) to measure the risk in their trading portfolio then prescribes a "multiplication" factor which translates value at risk into required capital holding.

It seems, therefore, as though the debate is moving towards a distinction between the *measurement* of risk, which is best done by those who are closest to the portfolio, and have the tools to do it; and the *capitalization* of risk, decisions on which raise public policy issues. Since the authorities, by underwriting the stability of the financial system are in essence providing financial institutions with catastrophic risk insurance, it is legitimate for them to limit the potential recourse to such insurance by requiring a minimum *level* of capital holding.

Conceivably, one could go even further and assign responsibility for decisions on capital holding to the private sector as well. This is the philosophy behind the so-called "pre-commitment" approach. An institution would itself choose how much capital it would assign to cover the value at risk in its portfolio. If losses exceeded the calculated probability, then the institution would be subject to some kind of penalty. This is an intriguing idea, though it would present a number of complex practical

issues. Moreover, it is not clear that it would lead to an appropriate pricing of the safety net.

The idea of harnessing self-disciplining forces is also behind the proposal of the Group of Thirty to develop industry-led standards for risk management, internal operating controls and public disclosure.[19] The proposal would call for major international institutions to commit to standards that they would undertake to meet themselves and to require of their counterparties. When endorsed by supervisors, these would then presumably spread, through market pressures, to all institutions. Being developed by practitioners, these standards, it is argued, are more likely to provide an appropriate balance between benefits and costs. In particular, by allowing the industry to propose more efficient ways of reducing risk, they would reduce the danger that firms would cut corners in an effort to avoid burdensome official regulation.

Before ending this section, a word should be added on policies to preserve stability in financial market prices. Theory provides much less help in addressing this issue than that of stability in financial institutions. Certain approaches to providing a more stable market environment would not be controversial. These include the encouragement of stable and sustainable macroeconomic policies; fuller disclosure and dissemination of relevant financial data; and the outlawing of anticompetitive practices in financial markets. Other measures have also attracted a measure of support, such as the use of "circuit-breakers" when prices move by more than a certain threshold amount.

What to do when a significant "bubble" is thought to be developing, or when a bubble bursts, is a matter on which there is little agreement. Public authorities can warn about "irrational exuberance," but central bankers are in general unwilling to adjust macroeconomic policy to stabilize financial asset prices. If prices were to fall, the reaction might be different, if only because experience suggests that price falls tend to be more rapid and disorderly than price rises.

IV. CONCLUDING COMMENTS

There is persuasive evidence that financial stability provides a favorable environment for efficient resource allocation and more rapid economic growth.[20] Instability has been associated with lower levels of saving and investment, fiscal costs, and setbacks to GNP. It is, therefore, unavoidable that securing stability should be a concern of public policy authorities.

What is less clear, however, is whether the maintenance of stability requires an activist approach on the part of the authorities, or alternatively whether it can best be achieved by reliance on market forces. Arguments against a pure laissez-faire approach include the following: that there are disequilibrium tendencies within the financial system that can, via contagion, turn instability into crisis; and that the costs of a financial crisis for economic welfare are so great that it is irresponsible to take chances. On the other hand, too great a level of support for the financial system, or support in inappropriate ways, can lead to inefficiency and moral hazard.

A consensus therefore seems to be developing among central bankers that regulation should, as far as possible, be directed at reinforcing the self-disciplining tendencies of the market. This probably means less detailed or prescriptive

regulation, and a greater reliance on the internal controls of market participants, supported by mechanisms that sharpen the incentive for prudent behavior.

It may be worth ending with a few observations on regulatory structure. A tendency has developed in recent years to draw a distinction between the function of institutional supervision; responsibility for systemic stability; and responsibility for price stability. These are indeed separate functions, and there may be cases in which the pursuit of any one of them is handicapped by the simultaneous pursuit of the others.

There are also powerful linkages, however. Systemic stability is linked to the health of the individual institutions that comprise the system; and instability in the financial system can both cause and be caused by instability in the real economy. What this means is that there must be close collaboration between those responsible for monetary and financial stability, respectively, and that both must be aware of the financial condition of the key institutions. Moreover, in order not to stifle innovation, all concerned need to have a healthy respect for market forces and recognize the need, in a market economy, for bankruptcy as an ultimate sanction. for unsuccessful enterprises.

This does not lead to any universally applicable conclusions concerning regulatory structure. It should, however, give pause to those who believe that separating functions is a straightforward and costless measure to tackle perceived shortcomings in present arrangements.

ENDNOTES

[1] *BIS Annual Report*, 1996-97.

[2] Federal Reserve Bank of Kansas City's 1996 symposium, "Achieving Price Stability," held in Jackson Hole, Wyoming, August 29-31.

[3] Goodhart, C.A.E., Philipp Hartmann, David T. Llewellyn, Liliana Rojas-Suares, and Steven R. Weisbrod. 1997. "Financial Regulation: Why, How and Where Now?" Monograph for the Central Bank Governors' Meeting at the Bank of England, June 6.

[4] Corrigan, E. Gerald. 1996. "Remarks at the Symposium on Risk Reduction in Payments Clearance and Settlement Systems," New York, Goldman Sachs and Co., January 25.

[5] Goldstein, Morris. 1997. "The Case for an International Banking Standard," Institute for International Economics, Washington, D.C., April.

[6] Honohan, Patrick. 1996. "Financial System Failures in Developing Countries: Diagnosis and Prescriptions," unpublished manuscript. Washington: International Monetary Fund.

[7] Caprio, Gerard, and Daniela Klingebiel. 1996. "Bank Insolvencies; Cross-Country Experience," unpublished manuscript. Washington: World Bank.

[8] Lindgren, Carl-Johan, Gillian Garcia, and Matthew Seal. 1995. "Bank Soundness and Macroeconomic Policy." Washington: International Monetary Fund.

[9] Borio, C.E.V., N. Kennedy, and S.D. Prowse. 1996. "Exploring Aggregate Asset Price Fluctuations Across Countries: Measurements, Determinants and Monetary Policy Implications." *BIS Economic Papers*, no. 40, April.

[10] Mishkin, Frederic S. 1991. "Anatomy of a Financial Crisis," National Bureau of Economic Research Working Paper no. 3934.

[11] Eichengreen, Barris, and Charles Wyplosz. 1993. "The Unstable EMS," Brookings Papers on Economic Activity, no. 1, pp. 51-143.

[12] Dowd, Kevin. 1988. "Private Money," Institute of Economic Affairs, Hobart Paper, no. 112.

[13] Kaufman, George. 1994. "Bank Contagion: A Review of the Theory and Evidence," *Journal of Financial Services Research*, no. 8, April, pp. 123-50.

[14] Goodhart, C.A.E., Philipp Hartmann, David T. Llewellyn, Liliana Rojas-Suares, and Steven R. Weisbrod. 1997. "Financial Regulation: Why, How and Where Now?" Monograph for the Central Bank Governors' Meeting at the Bank of England, June 6.

[15] Simons, Henry. 1948. *Economic Policy for a Free Society*. Chicago: University of Chicago Press. Also, Friedman, Milton. 1959. *A Program for Monetary Stability*. New York: Fordham University Press. Also, Tobin, James. 1985. "Financial Innovation and Deregulation in Perspective," *Bank of Japan Monetary and Economic Studies*, no. 3, September, pp. 19-29.

[16] Of course, it is usually accepted that the management of a failed institution should forfeit their positions and the shareholders should lose their money: the debate surrounds the extent to which uninsured depositors should be protected.

[17] Yellen, Janet L. 1996. "The 'New' Science of Credit Risk Management at U.S. Financial Institutions," presented at the Conference on Recent Developments in the Financial System, Bard College, April 11, and reproduced in BIS Review.

[18] Greenspan, Alan. 1996. "Remarks to 32nd Annual Conference on Bank Structure and Competition," Federal Reserve Bank of Chicago, May, and reproduced in BIS Review, No. 58.

[19] Group of Thirty. 1997. "Global Institutions, National Supervision and System Risk," A Study Group Report, Washington.

[20] King, Robert G., and Ross Levine. 1993. "Finance and Growth: Schumpeter Might Be Right," *Quarterly Journal of Economics*, August, pp. 717-37.

[3]

Banking and currency crises and systemic risk: Lessons from recent events

George G. Kaufman

Introduction and summary

Many countries worldwide have experienced serious banking and/or currency (exchange rate or balance of payments) problems in recent years with high costs in terms of reduced income and increased unemployment to their own countries as well as others. A study by the International Monetary Fund (IMF) reported that more than 130 of the IMF's 180-plus member countries had experienced serious banking problems between 1980 and 1995, and this was even before the recent banking crises in East Asia—Korea, Thailand, Malaysia, and Indonesia—as well as in Russia (Lindgren, Garcia, and Saal, 1996).

A map of countries experiencing banking crises is shown in figure 1. Lindgren et al. define serious problems to include banking crises that involve bank runs, collapses of financial firms, or massive government intervention, as well as less damaging but extensive unsoundness of institutions. With the primary exception of the U.K., the Benelux countries,[1] and Switzerland, most of the countries that avoided bank problems had no or nearly no modern banking systems. Currency crises were even more frequent than banking crises. They are typically defined as historically large depreciations in exchange rates and/or large declines in foreign reserves. Another IMF study of 53 industrial and developing countries identified 158 currency crises and only 54 banking crises in approximately the same time period (IMF, 1998a). Many countries suffered more than one such crisis during this period. A third study by Kaminsky and Reinhart (1996 and 1999) of 20 countries from 1970 to 1995 identified 71 currency crises and 25 banking crises.

This article examines these twin banking and currency crises to attempt to identify their causes, particularly any similarities and interconnections, and their implications both for the country in which they occur and for other countries through possible contagion. Lastly, the article evaluates the effectiveness of alternative public policy initiatives introduced to mitigate if not prevent these crises and their accompanying potentially severe damage to the economy.

Not only have banking and currency crises been frequent in number worldwide, but they have often been extremely costly in terms of both declines in real output and increases in transfer payments (wealth transfers) from taxpayers to bank depositors and other financial claimants whose funds were explicitly or implicitly insured or guaranteed at par value by the government. Thus, these crises are a major public policy concern. The IMF estimated that cumulative losses in gross domestic product (GDP) from potential (trend) growth in the 158 recent currency crises in 53 countries averaged 4.3 percent of the trend GDP values in each country and 7.1 percent in the 96 crises in which any output losses were suffered (IMF, 1998a). This is shown in table 1. The average time to return to trend value was about one and a half years. The output loss was greater in emerging economies than in developed economies, although the crises lasted somewhat longer in industrial than emerging economies. The estimated cumulative output loss from potential output in the 54 banking crises was significantly greater than in the currency crises, averaging 11.6 percent in all crises and 14.2 percent in the 44 crises

George G. Kaufman is the John F. Smith Professor of Finance and Banking at Loyola University Chicago and a consultant to the Federal Reserve Bank of Chicago. An earlier, longer version of this article was published in Financial Markets, Institutions, and Instruments, May 2000, Vol. 9, No. 2. The author is indebted to Bill Bergman, Douglas Evanoff, and James Moser of the Federal Reserve Bank of Chicago; George Benston of Emory University; and participants at conferences at the Pacific Basin Finance and Economics Conference, Taipei, Taiwan; the Federal Reserve Bank of New York; and the Bank of the Netherlands, Amsterdam, for helpful comments in the development of this article.

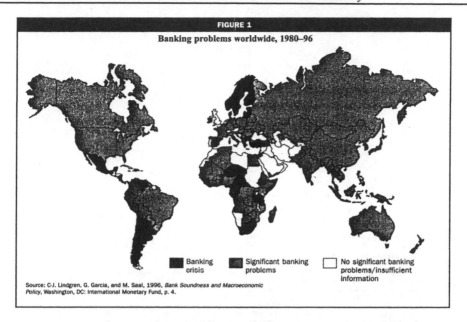

FIGURE 1

Banking problems worldwide, 1980–96

■ Banking crisis ▨ Significant banking problems □ No significant banking problems/insufficient information

Source: C-J. Lindgren, G. Garcia, and M. Saal, 1996, *Bank Soundness and Macroeconomic Policy*, Washington, DC: International Monetary Fund, p. 4.

that experienced an output loss. The loss was again greater for emerging than industrial economies. Moreover, banking crises last 3.1 years on average, twice as long as currency crises. In countries that experienced both a banking and a currency crisis simultaneously, the estimated output loss was greater than when each crisis was experienced separately. The average cumulative output loss was 14.4 percent in the 32 such crises observed and this time was greater for industrial than emerging economies.[2] The average time for recovery averaged about the same as for a banking crisis alone, but increased sharply for industrial countries to nearly six years.

The estimated transfer payments in support of deposit guarantees in banking crises topped 10 percent of GDP in a number of countries and exceeded 40 percent in Argentina, Thailand, Korea, Indonesia, and Malaysia (table 2).[3] The magnitude of comparable transfer payments in currency crises from taxpayers to protected domestic or foreign creditors, including repayment of any loans from official international institutions, has not been estimated, but appears to have been sizable in a number of recent crises. Both the income loss and transfer payment estimates exclude the costs to other countries that may either have been adversely affected by the above problems or provided assistance to the countries experiencing the problems.

The large magnitude of these numbers and the fact that many of the crises occur concurrently across countries and give rise to widespread fear of contagion or systemic risk clearly indicate why banking and currency crises attract the attention of bankers, policymakers, and the general public worldwide. But the causes, characteristics, dangers, and other features of these crises are not often clearly delineated and analyses of these problems frequently suffer from vagueness. For example, while liquidity and solvency problems at banks may be readily visualized and differentiated, the idea of an illiquid or insolvent country is more difficult to convey. However, a sharp depreciation in exchange rates may trigger defaults by private borrowers, including banks, and by sovereign governments on their foreign-currency-denominated debt and even on their domestic currency debt, if the costs of their foreign currency debt increase sufficiently. Until recently, the explanation and analysis of banking and currency crises were largely undertaken by different researchers, many of whom were largely unaware of or uninterested in each others' contributions. This occurred in part because, until recently, currency crises were more balance of payments current (trade) account than capital (financial) account crises and the focus more of macroeconomists, while banking

					Cumulative loss of output
TABLE 1					
Costs of crises in lost output relative to trend (1975–97)					
	Number of crises	Average recovery time[a]	Cumulative loss of output per crisis[b]	Crisis with output losses[c]	Cumulative loss of output per crisis with output loss[d]
		(years)	(% points)	(percent)	(% points)
Currency crises	158	1.6	4.3	61	7.1
Industrial	42	1.9	3.1	55	5.6
Emerging market	116	1.5	4.8	64	7.6
Currency crashes[e]	55	2.0	7.1	71	10.1
Industrial	13	2.1	5.0	62	8.0
Emerging market	42	1.9	7.9	74	10.7
Banking crises	54	3.1	11.6	82	14.2
Industrial	12	4.1	10.2	67	15.0
Emerging market	42	2.8	12.1	86	14.0
Currency & banking crises[f]	32	3.2	14.4	78	18.5
Industrial	6	5.8	17.6	100	17.6
Emerging market	26	2.6	13.6	73	18.8

[a]Average amount of time until GDP growth returned to trend. Because GDP growth data are available for all
countries only on an annual basis, by construction the minimum recovery time was one year.
[b]Calculated by summing the differences between trend growth and output growth after the crisis began until
the time when annual output growth returned to its trend and by averaging over all crises.
[c]Percent of crises in which output was lower than trend after the crisis began.
[d]Calculated by summing the differences between trend growth and output growth after the crisis began until
the time when annual output growth returned to its trend and by averaging over all crises that had output losses.
[e]Currency "crashes" are identified by crises where the currency component of the exchange market pressure
index accounts for 75 percent or more of the index when the index signals a crisis.
[f]Identified when a banking crisis occurred within a year of a currency crisis.
Source: International Monetary Fund, 1999, *World Economic Outlook: May 1998*, p. 79.

problems were primarily the domain of microeconomists. (Analyses of both types of crises include Glick, 1999; Kaminsky and Reinhart, 1996 and 1999; McKinnon and Pill, 1998; and Rogoff, 1999.)

Banking and currency breakdowns also tend to be feared more than breakdowns in most other sectors of the economy, because the public does not appear to understand the operations of these sectors very well. Both sectors deal in finance and intangibles, which make them more difficult for the public to comprehend than sectors that deal in tangibles, such as steel, automobiles, and even communications. As a result, for many, these sectors are shrouded in mystery and lend themselves readily to fictitious accounts of their operations, particularly of the implications of problems and breakdowns. Thus, for example, most of us are more familiar and comfortable with the way firms produce automobiles and what can go wrong than with the way banks produce deposits and loans and what can go wrong there. After all, one can always kick the tires on an automobile, but it is harder to kick the interest rate on a deposit or loan. To the extent that

the adverse implications of breakdowns are exaggerated, the resulting tales of horror are widely reported in the press as facts and become the stuff that popular novels and movies are made of, which further fan the flames of fear. Thus, failures in the financial sector lead to greater and stronger calls for government intervention and remedies.

Triggering event

Crises have triggering events or shocks. A banking crisis is generally ignited either by the economic (or legal) insolvency of one or more large banks or similar financial institutions or by widespread depositor runs on large banks or similar financial institutions perceived to be insolvent and unable to repay their deposits or other debt claims on time and at par value. A currency crisis is generally started either by a sharp, substantial, and disorderly decline in the exchange rate in one country, frequently, although not always, from levels set by a fixed (pegged) or crawling peg exchange rate standard, or by a speculative run (attack) on a country's currency that exerts downward pressure on

TABLE 2

Estimated transfer cost of selected banking crises

Country	Period	Estimated cost/ GDP (percent)
United States	1980s	2.5
Japan	1990s	20.0p
Norway	1987–89	4.0
Spain	1977–85	16.8
Sweden	1991	6.4
Bulgaria	1990s	14.0
Hungary	1991–95	10.0
Israel	1977–83	30.0
Mexico	1990s	20.0p
Argentina	1980–82	55.3
Argentina	1989–90	13.0
Brazil	1994–95	5–10.0
Chile	1981–83	41.2
Uruguay	1981–84	24.2
Venezuela	1994–95	18.0
Turkey	1982–85	2.5
Finland	1991–94	8.4
Korea	1997–	60.0p
Indonesia	1997–	80.0p
Thailand	1997–	45.0p
Malaysia	1997–	45.0p

p = Preliminary

Note: Includes all depository institutions; costs are to governments and depositors.

Sources: Caprio and Klingebiel, 1999, Lindgren, Garcia, and Saal, 1996, Rojas-Suarez and Weisbrod, 1996, *Wall Street Journal*, October 22, 1998, and July 27, 1999, and Standard and Poor's, various years.

the exchange rate (Eichengreen, Rose, and Wyplosz, 1996).[4] Thus, banking and currency crises both involve an actual or potential depreciation in the value of financial claims. This reflects a failure by banks or countries on a fixed or semi-fixed exchange rate to keep their promise to redeem or exchange, respectively, claims at a given rate (price). For banks and other privately owned financial institutions, this results in insolvency and either reorganization or liquidation. For countries, although they survive, they are likely to experience losses from higher foreign debt burdens and from economic, political, and/or social turmoil and subsequent defaults and restructuring. (A broad spectrum of views on the causes and triggering events of recent banking and currency crises appears in Bisignano et al., 2000, Hunter et al., 1999, and Summers, 2000.) Kaminsky and Reinhart (1996) develop a broad set of stylized facts (regularities) describing recent banking and currency crises.

Potential impact on the economy

The health of the banking and international sectors is viewed to be important not only because these sectors are perceived to be particularly vulnerable or fragile, but because they are both economically important and closely intertwined with other sectors in the economy and, therefore, perceived to be likely to infect other sectors with their problems (Davis, 1995). A relatively small individual problem may be turned into a much larger and broader crisis. Bank liabilities comprise the major form of money in developed economies and nearly everyone in such economies touches and is touched by money and credit in their everyday life. The insolvency or near insolvency of one or more important banks is believed to reduce credit, particularly loans, to the market or markets served, ignite depositor runs either to other "safe" banks or to riskless Treasury securities and currency, reduce deposits and the money supply, disrupt the operation of the payment system, increase uncertainty, disturb financial markets, and cause, at a minimum, fire-sale losses that will drop security prices below their otherwise equilibrium levels. Such effects endanger the solvency of other economically solvent banks and could ignite further runs (Council of Economic Advisers, 1999). These adverse effects are magnified if the insolvent banks are physically closed or deposits frozen for a significant length of time, so that some or all depositors do not have immediate access to some or all of their funds. Dermine (1996, p. 680) has noted that

> The issue is not so much the fear of a domino effect whereby the failure of a large bank would create the failure of many smaller ones; strict analysis of counterparty exposures has reduced substantially the risk of a domino effect. The fear is rather that the need to close a bank for several months to value its illiquid assets would freeze a large part of deposits and savings, causing a significant negative effect on national consumption.

This does not happen in the U.S. today. With rare exceptions, insured depositors at failed banks have access to the full value of their funds the next business day and uninsured depositors to the estimated recovery value of their claim the next business day through an advance by the Federal Deposit Insurance Corporation (FDIC) serving as receiver (Benston and Kaufman, 1998, and Kaufman and Seelig, 2000). However, this is not true in many other countries, where uninsured depositors may have to wait long periods of time until the appointed receiver actually recovers the funds through the liquidation of the bank's assets, and even insured depositors at failed institutions may have to wait some time to regain access to the full value of their deposits. In either case, if depositors or other stakeholders suffer losses, the adverse effects of problems at a single bank or small group of banks could be transmitted quickly throughout the banking sector, beyond to the entire financial sector, and possibly even beyond to the macroeconomy, causing sharp and abrupt declines or aggravating already extant declines in aggregate output (Federal Reserve Bank of Minneapolis, 1999). At the same time, asset prices, particularly in real estate and stock markets, are likely to decline sharply. Not infrequently these prices had previously been bid up sharply with financing provided in large measure by rapid bank credit expansion permitted if not fostered by the central bank.

It is the suddenness of the transmission of shocks as well as the breadth of the potential impact that appears to differentiate the financial sector from most other sectors as a cause of crises. As former president of the Federal Reserve Bank of New York, Gerald Corrigan (1991, p. 3), has noted: "More than anything else, it is the systemic risk phenomenon with banking and financial institutions that makes them different from gas stations and furniture stores." Indeed, there appears to be little fear of contagion and systemic risk in most other, nonfinancial sectors of more or less equal importance, such as automobiles, computers, transportation, and even agriculture (food).

Banking problems may also ignite currency problems, particularly in smaller, open economies on fixed or semi-fixed exchange rate standards. If the banking and any accompanying macroeconomic and asset price bubble problems are sufficiently severe, domestic and foreign depositors at insolvent or near-insolvent banks are likely to shift their deposits to perceived safer banks, including foreign-owned domestically or nondomestically domiciled banks, possibly in foreign-currency-denominated deposits. This is particularly likely if, as the problem increases in magnitude, doubts arise about the government's ability or commitment to maintain full deposit guarantees. At the same time, other domestic and foreign investors are likely to shift their funds abroad, again partially or totally in foreign currency. Such capital outflows (runs) exert downward pressure on the country's exchange rate. If the country attempts to protect its exchange rate by selling its foreign reserves, aggregate bank reserves are reduced by a like amount. Unless offset by increases through other central bank operations, those sales intensify the banking and macroeconomic problems by forcing further bank asset sales and monetary contraction and

encouraging further capital outflows. This makes it more difficult for the country to avoid a currency depreciation.

Currency crises characterized by a sharp depreciation in exchange rates are likely to increase both the burden of debt denominated in foreign currency to domestic borrowers and the probability of default on such debt. The former will reduce the profitability of domestic debtor firms and even threaten their solvency. The latter is likely to reduce capital inflows, particularly in the short run. Both effects will exert downward pressure on aggregate income. Likewise, a sharp depreciation in the currency of one country relative to its trading partners will increase the price of its imports and thereby also, at least in the short run, its rate of inflation. The volume of imports is likely to decline. In time, the lower exchange rate will stimulate increased exports. These effects are likely to reduce the exports both of the country's trading partners and of its export competitors to third countries and may set off one or more rounds of competitive depreciation (beggar-thy-neighbor responses), possibly accompanied by increased trade and capital barriers. If so, aggregate incomes in all affected countries will be reduced.

Just as banking problems can ignite currency problems, currency problems can ignite banking problems. If a country experiencing a speculative run on its currency attempts to protect its exchange rate from depreciation by selling foreign currency, the resulting reduction in its international reserves will reduce bank reserves and, unless offset (sterilized) by the central bank, ignite a multiple contraction in money and credit that could threaten the solvency of banks. Concurrently, to avoid, or at least delay, a depreciation from a speculative run, countries frequently increase their rates of interest to discourage additional capital outflows and attract capital inflows. But the higher rates may dampen domestic economic activity, increase loan defaults, and threaten bank solvency. Speculative runs on a currency also are likely to include runs from domestic currency deposits to foreign currency deposits, possibly even at the same banks. This is a run on domestic currency, not on banks, but in time may invite a run on banks. If a country does not prevent a depreciation and if accompanying declines in aggregate income are sufficiently large, loan defaults are likely to increase and could drive some banks into or near to insolvency. Loan defaults are likely to be more frequent and larger if banks and/or bank customers had borrowed in foreign currencies on an unhedged basis and were forced by the depreciation to make larger domestic currency payments than expected. Thus, even banks that fully hedge their foreign currency borrowing by foreign currency loans to domestic borrowers are likely to suffer defaults when the domestic currency depreciates significantly. The borrowers' exchange rate risk becomes the bank's credit risk.

Thus, currency and banking crises are mutually reinforcing, particularly under fixed or semi-fixed exchange rates. However, Kaminsky and Reinhart (1996) report that, while banking crises statistically predicted balance of payments crises in the countries they studied, balance of payments crises did not predict banking crises. That is, they find that, although often happening concurrently, banking crises have been an important cause of currency crises far more often than the other way around.

Systemic risk

What makes banking and currency crises different from most other crises and particularly frightening to many people are the accompanying cries of contagion or systemic risk. Systemic risk refers to the risk or probability of breakdowns (losses) in an entire system as opposed to breakdowns in individual parts or components and is evidenced by comovements (correlation) among most or all the parts. Thus, systemic risk in banking is evidenced by a high correlation and clustering of bank failures in a country, a number of countries, or globally; and in currencies, by a clustering of deprecations in exchange rates in a number of countries. Systemic risk may also occur in other parts of the financial sector, for example, in securities markets as evidenced by simultaneous declines in the prices of a large number of securities in one or more markets in a country or across countries. Systemic risk may be either or both domestic and/or transnational.

Although systemic risk is frequently proclaimed during banking and currency crises, its meaning is ambiguous. It means different things to different people, particularly with respect to causation. One popular definition refers to a "big" shock that produces near simultaneous adverse effects for most or all of the domestic economy or system. That is, systemic "refers to an event having effects on the entire banking, financial, or economic system, rather than just one or a few institutions" (Bartholomew and Whalen, 1995, p. 4). Likewise, Mishkin (1995, p. 32) defines systemic risk as "the likelihood of a sudden, usually unexpected, event that disrupts information in financial markets, making them unable to effectively channel funds to those parties with the most productive investment opportunities." How the transmission occurs is unclear.

Other definitions focus on potential spillover to others. For example, the Bank for International Settlements (BIS) defines systemic risk as "the risk that the failure of a participant to meet its contractual obligations may in turn cause other participants to default with a chain reaction leading to broader financial difficulties" (BIS, 1994, p. 177). This definition emphasizes causation as well as correlation (correlation with causation) and requires strong direct interconnections or linkages among the institutions, markets, sectors, or countries involved, so that when the first domino falls, it falls on others, causing them to fall and, in turn, to knock down others in a chain or "knock-on" reaction. For banks, this may occur if, for whatever reason, bank A defaults on a loan, deposit, or other payment to bank B that produces a loss greater than B's capital and forces it to default on a payment to bank C with losses that are larger than C's capital, and so on down the chain (Crockett, 1997). The smaller a bank's capital–asset ratio, the more leveraged it is and the more it is likely to be driven into insolvency by insolvencies of banks located earlier on the transmission chain and to transmit losses to banks located later on the chain.

For countries, this may occur through direct trade linkages so that if country A experiences problems or a depreciation in its exchange rate that reduce its imports from country B, it causes B's aggregate income to decline, reducing its imports from country C, and so on down the chain. What makes direct causation (chain reaction) systemic risk in financial sectors particularly frightening to many is both the lightning speed with which it is believed to occur and the perception that it can infect "innocent" as well as "guilty" parties, so that there is little or no protection against its damaging effects.

A third definition of systemic risk also focuses on spillover, but does not involve direct causation and requires weaker interconnections. Rather, it emphasizes similarities in third-party risk exposures among the units involved. When one unit experiences an adverse shock that generates severe losses, uncertainty is created about the values of other units potentially subject to the same shock. To minimize additional losses, market participants will examine other units (for example, banks or countries) in which they have economic interests to see whether they are at risk. The more similar the risk exposure profile with that of the initial unit economically (in terms of macroeconomic behavior, markets, or institutions), politically, or otherwise, the greater is the probability of loss and the more likely are the participants to withdraw funds as soon as possible and possibly induce liquidity and even more fundamental problems. This is referred to as a "common shock" effect and represents correlation without direct causation (indirect causation).

Because information on either the causes or magnitude of the initial shock or on the risk exposures of the other units potentially at risk is not generally available immediately, accurately, or free, and analysis of the information is not immediate or free, participants require time and resources to sort out the identities of the other units at risk and the magnitudes of any potential losses. As credit markets deteriorate, the quality of private and public information also deteriorates and uncertainty increases further. Moreover, because many of the participants are risk averse, they will transfer funds, at least temporarily during the period of confusion and sorting out, as quickly as possible to well-recognized safe or at least safer units without waiting for the final analysis. In periods of great uncertainty and stress, market participants increasingly tend to make their portfolio adjustments in quantities (runs) rather than in prices (interest rates). That is, at least temporarily, they will not lend at any rate, Thus, there is likely to be an immediate flight or run to quality away from units that appear potentially at risk, regardless of whether further analysis would identify them ex post as having similar exposures that actually put them at risk (guilty) or not (innocent). At this stage, common shock contagion appears random, potentially affecting more or less the entire universe and reflecting a general loss of confidence in all units. Moreover, because these runs are concurrent and widespread, such behavior by investors is often referred to as "herding" behavior.

The runs are likely to exert strong downward pressure on the prices (upward pressures on interest rates) of the securities of affected institutions and countries. At the same time, many of the affected countries are likely to force their interest rates up even further to reduce additional capital outflows and encourage inflows. Thus, liquidity problems are likely to temporarily spill over to units not directly affected by the initial external shock. At some later date, after the sorting out process is complete, some or all of these flows affecting innocent banks or countries may be reversed. During the sorting out period, the fire-sale driven changes in both financial quantities (flows) and prices (interest rates) are likely to overshoot their ultimate equilibrium levels and intensify the liquidity problems, particularly for more vulnerable units (Kaminsky and Schmukler, 1999).

A distinction is often made between rational or information-based systemic risk and irrational, non-information-based, random, or "pure" contagious systemic risk (Kaufman, 1994, and Kaminsky and Reinhart, 1998). Rational or informed contagion assumes that investors (depositors) can differentiate among parties on the basis of their fundamentals.

Random contagion, based on actions by uninformed agents, is viewed as more frightening and dangerous as it does not differentiate among parties, impacting innocent as well as guilty parties, and is therefore likely to be both broader and more difficult to contain. It is likely that innocent parties may be impacted immediately during the sorting out period under common shock contagious systemic risk, but in time will be sorted out by investors and depositors from guilty parties. Thus, the empirical borderline between rational and irrational contagion is fuzzy and in part depends on the time horizon applied. Likewise, definitions of "innocent" and "guilty" are not always clear and precise. Innocent parties may be defined as units that are widely perceived to be economically well behaved. That is, banks that are perceived to be solvent and not overly leveraged and countries that are perceived to have high foreign reserves relative to their foreign liabilities and to be following sound monetary and fiscal macroeconomic policies. Guilty parties then are insolvent, near-insolvent, or excessively leveraged banks and countries with low reserves or poor financial management.

The importance of the distinction between innocent and guilty parties for evaluating contagious systemic risk underlies the recent argument by the U.S. Council of Economic Advisers that international assistance should be offered to "those cases where problems stem more from contagion than from poor policies, ... [that is,] countries with sound economic policies may be subject to attack because of contagion" (Council of Economic Advisers, 1999, p. 285). It is largely the perceived randomness of the contagion that appears to make it more frightening in banking and exchange rates than elsewhere and justifies special protective public policy actions.

Recent changes in environment

It may be argued that contagious systemic risk has become both more likely and more important in recent years as a result of both 1) economic development that increases the importance and interdependence of banking and the global interdependence of countries, and 2) advances in computer and telecommunications technology that permit funds to be transferred more easily, quickly, and cheaply across large distances and national boundaries and connect both banks and countries more closely. At the same time, financial liberalization and deregulation of both bank activities and international capital controls have permitted vastly increased national and transnational capital flows to occur and participants to increase their risk exposures. Gross international capital flows through both banks and security markets have increased almost twentyfold since the 1970s from about $50 billion annually to nearly $1,000 billion (Eichengreen et al., 1998). Nevertheless, net international capital flows, as measured by the negative of the net current account, relative to GDP are still below the levels reached under the gold standard and those of the 1920s. For example, Bordo, Eichengreen, and Kim (1998) report that this ratio peaked at 6 percent for 12 major countries in the late 1910s, declined to 1 percent in the 1960s, and recovered only to 2 percent by 1990. (See also Folkerts-Landau et al., 1997, and Goodhart and Delargy, 1998.)

Through time, as income and wealth have increased, many more economic units have been brought into contact with banks and other financial institutions and markets. Thus, disturbances in the banking and financial sectors are likely to impact a larger proportion of the population than in earlier periods. One could ask how many individuals were affected directly or even indirectly by the Tulip Bulb Bubble in Holland in the 1630s or the South Sea Bubble in England in 1720. It is unlikely to have been very many, either in absolute numbers or as a percentage of the population, particularly relative to the numbers affected by more recent financial crises.[5]

Advances in technology have made bank and currency runs both easier and faster. Large depositors and other banks can withdraw funds almost instantaneously. Even small depositors no longer need to line up physically at banks to withdraw their funds. They can transfer their funds to other banks by telephone

and computer and obtain, at least temporarily, currency at ATMs (automated teller machines). "Silent" electronic runs now dominate "noisy" paper runs. Not only can funds be withdrawn faster and more cheaply, but runs can start faster upon receipt of any adverse news about the financial health of institutions and countries.

Trading activity for financial assets, including both futures and options as well as cash securities and trading by the banks for their own accounts, has increased sharply and has vastly increased the volume of interbank clearings. The notional value of derivative contracts has increased nearly ninefold from $8 trillion in 1991 to near $70 trillion in 1999. Spot and forward currency transactions increased from $600 billion per day in 1989 to $1,500 billion per day in 1998 (Bank for International Settlements, 1998b). To the extent that interbank claims are not settled immediately on a gross basis with good funds (payment versus payment or delivery), risk exposures have increased both domestically and internationally. In addition, the volatility of capital flows from the ability of participants to change the directions and reverse their investments almost immediately has increased. Thus, for example, external bank and securities lending to the largely "sick" East Asian countries dropped abruptly from $23 billion in the second quarter of 1997 to an outflow of about the same magnitude in the fourth quarter and $35 billion in the first quarter of 1998 (figure 2). The reversal in private capital flows was even greater, as part of the decline in 1997

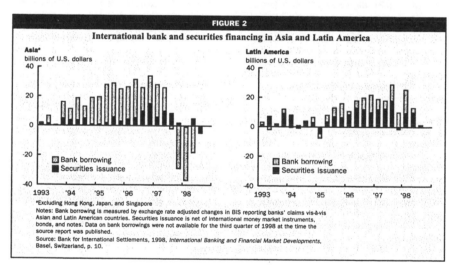

FIGURE 2

International bank and securities financing in Asia and Latin America

Notes: Bank borrowing is measured by exchange rate adjusted changes in BIS reporting banks' claims vis-à-vis Asian and Latin American countries. Securities issuance is net of international money market instruments, bonds, and notes. Data on bank borrowings were not available for the third quarter of 1998 at the time the source report was published.

Source: Bank for International Settlements, 1998, *International Banking and Financial Market Developments*, Basel, Switzerland, p. 10.

and 1998 was offset by increased official flows from international institutions and individual countries (Haldane, 1999). Net private inflows into these countries totaled $103 billion in 1996 and dropped to near zero in 1997 and to an outflow of $28 billion in 1998 (Council of Economic Advisers, 1999). The reversals in net private capital flows may also be large relative to a country's GDP. For example, recent reversals in flows were equal to 18 percent of Mexico's GDP in 1981–83 and 12 percent in 1993–95, 15 percent of Thailand's GDP in 1996–97, 11 percent of Venezuela's GDP in 1987–90, and 9 percent of Korea's GDP in 1996–97 (Lopez-Mejia, 1999).

It is sometimes argued that financial liberalization and deregulation effectively were responsible for the increases in both the frequency and seriousness of banking and currency crises in recent years. On the surface, there appears to be some truth to this. Capital flows to developing countries increased sharply following the liberalization of capital controls by these countries (Folkerts-Landau et al., 1997, and Little and Olivei, 1999). In addition, a number of studies have reported that most recent banking and currency crises occurred after financial deregulation or liberalization. For example, Kaminsky and Reinhart (1996) report that some 70 percent of banking crises were preceded by deregulation and that financial liberalization was statistically significant in explaining banking crises, although not currency crises. By permitting increased competition and reducing protection for existing institutions, financial deregulation may be expected to increase the number of bank failures. Liberalization of capital controls sharply increased capital inflows in many countries that could reverse just as sharply and ignite pressures for depreciation. But, more importantly, the liberalization and deregulation were poorly implemented and sequenced in most countries that experienced crises, rather than being inappropriate and unnecessary. (Surveys of recent cross-country financial liberalization experiences appear in Williamson and Mahar, 1998, and Eichengreen et al., 1998. Also see Gruben, Koo, and Moore, 1999.)

Particularly for banking, the deregulation was generally introduced to correct serious extant problems in the industry that had resulted in widespread and massive silent insolvencies and severe misallocations of resources from excessive government regulation and credit controls. When deregulation was finally implemented, it was often only after the problems had already been accumulating in size for some time, but the losses were unbooked and not yet widely recognized by the public. Thus, when the losses could no

longer be concealed and exploded into public awareness, they were often incorrectly but understandably associated in the public's eye with the concurrent visible deregulation rather than with the earlier and less visible fundamental causes. But, as is argued later, by increasing risk, the government guarantees and credit controls that accompany most forms of government regulation frequently increased the probability of insolvency. Moreover, once insolvent, the banks were likely to be permitted to continue to operate and generate additional losses rather than being resolved. As a result, the magnitude, although possibly not the frequency, of banking insolvencies is likely to be greater than before the introduction of these guarantees. The deposits financing the negative net worth of the insolvent banks are effectively off-balance-sheet government debt and liabilities of the taxpayer. At some point, the combined cost of the increased burden on taxpayers and the lost efficiency and output from the misallocation of resources increases sufficiently to cause government regulation to lose support and be increasingly replaced by market regulation. Likewise for liberalization of capital flows; the cost of misallocation of resources from capital controls that directed foreign credit and the loss of potential increases in income from greater capital flows generate pressures for change.

But market discipline does not work in a vacuum. To be effective and superior to government regulation, market regulation requires a number of institutional preconditions. For banking, market regulation requires a system of laws and property rights, particularly regarding contract enforcement, bankruptcy and repossession, incentives that reward success and punish failure, well-trained and knowledgeable bankers and bank supervisors, and relatively stable macroeconomic conditions. These conditions are particularly important because, with only rare if any exceptions, governments appear unable to avoid providing at least some explicit or implicit guarantees and downside protection for bank depositors, other creditors, and occasionally even shareholders. Some parties, at minimum shareholders, must be at risk and permitted to share in any government losses to encourage the correct risk incentives and to avoid privatizing only bank profits and socializing the losses. Market discipline must be permitted to increase to offset the decline in regulatory discipline. For transnational capital flows, basically the same preconditions are required.

In many if not most instances in recent years, deregulation and liberalization were introduced before the preconditions were in place (McKinnon, 1993). In the resulting absence of either government or market discipline, the outcome is often increased risk taking with resulting large losses and disruptions that are widely considered, incorrectly, the result of the deregulation and liberalization per se. Indeed, the transition from government regulation to market regulation is often a dangerous road that is full of potholes and steep drop-offs that, if not navigated carefully, can damage the process if not derail it altogether. If the appropriate prerequisites are not in place at every step of the deregulation process, the result may be worse than the starting point. That is, deregulation wrongly done may be more damaging to the economy than the government regulation that it was intended to replace. If, as is usual, deregulation and liberalization are introduced after many years of government control and repression, they are likely to expose the extant economic insolvency of banks and the overvaluation of the country's currency. As a result, until the adjustment is complete, banking failures could increase further and capital inflows could increase to unsustainable levels that magnify the likelihood of abrupt and disruptive reversals (McKinnon and Pill, 1996). As is often the case in economics, many of the problems lie in the transition from one equilibrium to another.

A study of 53 countries from 1980 to 1995 by Demirgüç-Kunt and Detragiache (1998) finds that financial liberalization increases the likelihood of banking crises, but that the probability decreases the stronger in place are the institutional preconditions for liberalization and market discipline in terms of contract enforcement, lack of corruption and bureaucratic interference, and respect for the rule of law. Moreover, the more repressed is the financial sector at the time liberalization is introduced, the more do gains from liberalization outweigh the costs of any banking crises.

Corrective policies (solutions) and associated problems

What lessons may be derived from our analysis of the large number of banking and currency crises worldwide in recent years? Unfortunately, the major lesson appears to be that there are no silver bullets or easy answers to either preventing such crises or solving them quickly at no or low cost after they have developed. Although countries experiencing either or both crises have many similarities and the guilty parties can generally be identified after the event, nearly all crises differ in significant ways and the guilty parties are often difficult if not impossible to finger ahead of time. Nevertheless, some conclusions with respect to potentially corrective public policies appear warranted.

Because systemic risk in banking and finance is widely perceived to be destructive to the aggregate economy, governments have almost throughout history introduced a wide array of public policies intended to reduce the frequency and magnitude of its impact. Indeed, Corrigan (1991, p. 3) has argued that it is systemic risk "more than any other factor—that constitutes the fundamental rationale for the safety net arrangements that have evolved in this (U.S.) and other countries." Because the seriousness of systemic risk is often judged by whether it is information based and impacts only guilty parties or is irrational and nets innocent parties as well, different policy strategies may be appropriate to each type of systemic risk.

If contagious systemic risk is assumed to be information based and affects only guilty parties, then solutions should focus both on strengthening each party's abilities to absorb adverse external shocks, that is, reducing their vulnerability, and on reducing the magnitude and frequency of any such shocks through appropriate macroeconomic policies. In the absence of government intervention, the market place will determine the optimal vulnerability of each party. If deposit or currency values depreciate, losses would be suffered by shareholders, depositors, and other creditors in the case of bank failures and possibly by a broader range of participants in the case of exchange rate depreciations. But it is precisely the fear of such losses that encourages participants to protect themselves by reducing their vulnerability. The long-term economic benefits of governments repeatedly compensating guilty parties ex post for actual losses or ex ante guaranteeing (insuring) them against potential losses from bank insolvencies or currency depreciations appears, at best, highly questionable. However, this does not rule out government actions to prevent or offset temporary overshooting of price and quantity adjustments, which frequently occur during the information gathering and processing segments of the sorting out period, through lender of last resort type activities. But the new, post-shock price equilibrium and the extent of overshooting are both difficult to define, and governments at times may unwisely attempt to restore the old pre-shock equilibrium price structure with unfortunate consequences.

If, however, the systemic risk affects both guilty and innocent parties, then a stronger although not airtight case can be made for providing, at least, temporary liquidity assistance to harmed but perceived economically solvent parties to tide them over until the market has recognized their innocence and both prices and flows have adjusted accordingly. But, an analysis of the historical record suggests both that the market can generally differentiate innnocent from guilty parties and that there is little evidence of severe and lasting damage to innocent parties in either common shock or causation contagious systemic risk, even in the period before government intervention.[6] Moreover, it often appears difficult for governments to differentiate between guilty and innocent parties and, at least, recent history suggests that governments have frequently tended to define innocence rather broadly and often provided assistance to insolvent parties. This tends to delay the adjustment process and increase aggregate costs to the economy. For U.S. banks, particularly in the period before the Federal Reserve System, monitoring of their interbank exposures appears to have been practiced seriously. If a bank experienced a significant run, the other banks in the market area, generally operating in concert through the local clearinghouse, would examine the bank's financial condition to determine whether it was suffering from a liquidity or a solvency problem. If it was only a liquidity problem and the bank was economically solvent, the other banks would effectively recycle the lost deposits back to the bank through loans and interbank deposits. If it was a solvency problem, the other banks would generally not recycle the deposits and permit the bank to fail.

After the Federal Reserve was established, bank monitoring began to change from a private to a public responsibility. The Fed's initial lender of last resort activity through the discount window was supplemented in 1933 by the insurance of at least some bank deposits by the FDIC. As the ultimate guarantor of the safety net, the government now had a direct financial stake in the security of the protected institutions and needed regulation to control its potential losses. As Federal Reserve Chairman Alan Greenspan (1999, p. 10) has noted, "the safety net requires that the government replace with law, regulation, and supervision much of the disciplinary role that the market plays for other businesses." The introduction of the safety net effectively also transferred the timing of the resolution of insolvent banks from the market place, which had little if any discretion, to the regulators, who had considerable discretion.

Because large units suffering adverse shocks are perceived to be a greater threat to ignite more damaging systemic risk and threaten the stability of the financial system, governments have been particularly concerned with protecting such units and their stakeholders from serious harm. Such policies are popularly referred to as "too-big-to-fail," even though in some countries, such as the U.S., the firms are generally permitted to fail. Rather, more accurately, such institutions are "too-big-to-liquidate" or "too-big to-impose-losses on important stakeholders" (Kaufman,

1990). Thus, in the U.S., the government may at times extend the safety net below depositors and other creditors at very large banks beyond the de jure non-FDIC insured $100,000 per account coverage and protect them against loss. More recently, however, Chairman Greenspan (2000) has stated that he views no institution as too big to either fail or liquidate (unwind) in an orderly fashion. What the authorities wish to avoid is a quick (disorderly) reaction. But stockholders would not be protected and appropriate discounts or "haircuts" would be imposed on nonguaranteed deposits.

Bernard and Bisignano (1999) make a convincing case that much of the large flows on the international interbank market in more recent years at interest rates that hardly discriminate among borrowers were fueled by the belief that central banks would intervene to prevent losses. There is also a perception that the U.S. government might intervene in the threatened insolvency of some large nondepository non-FDIC insured financial institutions, such as insurance companies, pension funds, finance companies, and hedge funds, for example, as it was recently perceived to do in Long-Term Capital Management. This is particularly likely if banks are among the major creditors and if the rapid unwinding of large and complex derivatives positions may be feared to produce uncertainty and large fire-sale losses. The safety net is not likely to be stretched under smaller institutions of the same type. In such interventions, the government's concern is likely to be as much on limiting adverse spillover to financial markets as to other institutions.

Ironically, regulators and governments frequently encourage and even force banks to engage in risky portfolio activities to further their economic, social, or political goals in the form of credit allocation. In the U.S., for example, until the thrift and banking debacle of the 1980s, the government encouraged and even forced federally chartered thrift institutions to channel short-term deposits into long-term fixed-rate residential mortgages. Such policies were possible only because of the simultaneous government guarantees. Absent these guarantees, depositors would have fled from institutions with such large risk exposures and the institutions would have either failed or changed their operating strategy. Indeed, before deposit insurance in 1934, savings and loan associations made primarily only three- to five-year rollover mortgages. Thus, they assumed relatively little interest rate risk. Use of banks by governments to pursue goals other than safety and efficiency increased the vulnerability of the institutions and prolonged the length and increased the cost of the recent banking crises in the U.S., Mexico, Japan, and many more countries (Kaufman, 1997a).

Because governments typically underprice the guarantees and insurance that they provide, the insurance and guarantees have encouraged depositors and banks to engage in greater moral hazard behavior than would be permitted by private insurers, whose primary objective is minimizing losses to their shareholders. The increased risk taking by banks in the form of greater credit, interest rate, and foreign exchange rate risk as well as lower capital ratios both increased the likelihood of banking crises and the costs to solvent banks and taxpayers. In addition, the agency problems tend to be greater for government provided insurance than for privately provided insurance. Evidence developed by Calomiris (1999) suggests that the magnitude of both banking and currency crises has been greater on average in the post-safety net era than before. As a result, the costs of government policies to restrict systemic risk frequently have exceeded the benefits, although all the costs may not become widely visible until long after any benefits—reduced runs and supported asset values—are enjoyed. Such guarantees appear to be a classic example of the time inconsistency problem in economics. The benefits of the guarantees are observed today and the costs only tomorrow. Given that the public and policymakers generally apply high discount rates to evaluating the present value of future outcomes of policy actions, Kindleberger (1996, p. 149) appears often to be correct when he argues that "today wins over tomorrow."

More recently, public policy strategies to limit systemic risk in banking have focused more on restricting the safety net and attempting to have regulatory discipline resemble market discipline more closely. These strategies would limit, if not eliminate, losses from bank insolvency through more timely resolution of economically floundering banks before their economic or market value capital turns negative. Contagious systemic risk can only transmit insolvencies if the losses at each and every party on the transmission chain exceed their capital. If banks are resolved before their market value capital turns negative, systemic risk transmitting losses is eliminated. These corrective structures include measures such as "prompt corrective action" and "least cost resolution." In the U.S., they were enacted in varying and yet unknown degrees of effectiveness in the Federal Deposit Insurance Corporation Improvement Act (FDICIA) of 1991 (Benston and Kaufman, 1988, 1994, 1995, and 1998, and Kaufman, 1997a and b).

Policies similar to those applied to banks have been used to deal with currency crises. But, because domestic governments cannot print the currencies of other countries, large scale purchases of domestic

currency with foreign currency to maintain exchange rates and the provision of guarantees of foreign currencies effectively require the assistance of one or more other countries or of multinational international organizations (Fischer, 1999). Through time, as with banks, such support was first provided by private parties, generally bankers, and then by foreign governments (Bordo and Schwartz, 1998). Most recently, it has been provided by official international institutions, such as the IMF, World Bank, and regional development banks. For example, in Mexico in 1994, the IMF effectively guaranteed dollar-denominated Mexican government securities and in 1997, all deposits, including dollar-denominated deposits, at Indonesian, Korean, and Thai banks (Lindgren et al., 1999). These policies have been subjected to the same criticisms as have been leveled at the similar bank policies (Meltzer, 1999). They increase moral hazard behavior by countries and private investors that in turn increases the vulnerability of the international sector to future shocks. In addition, the benefits of such support are likely to accrue as much, if not more, to foreign creditors than to domestic citizens, who have to repay the loans. For example, Kho and Stulz (2000) find that the announcement of the IMF guarantee program in Korea resulted in large and statistically significant excess returns to shareholders of large U.S., French, and German banks that tended to have Korean exposures, as well as shareholders of Korean banks. However, smaller and insignificant excess returns were generally found in response to the announcements of IMF support programs in the other East Asian countries. The largest gains at U.S. banks were to those with the greatest exposure to Korea. Lastly, international institutions are just as likely to be unable to differentiate among guilty and innocent parties and too often support guilty parties.

Corrective policies, appropriate or inappropriate, are more difficult for currency crises than banking crises for at least two reasons. One, countries are sovereign and it is difficult for other countries or international organizations to impose enforceable conditions on them without their cooperation and agreement. This is evidenced by the frequent disregard of the IMF's conditionality requirements by assisted countries or the "dumbing down" of the conditionality features as the assisted countries protest their perceived harshness. Two, as noted, international organizations are not central banks that can print unlimited quantities of the currency of any country. They can only borrow other countries' currencies in limited quantities. Thus, the assistance packages often include the worst of all worlds. They may be too small to prevent a devaluation or mitigate most of its effects, but too large to avoid moral hazard responses, increasing the likelihood and costs of future crises.

Many of the more recent capital inflows into developing countries appear to have been undertaken on the perception of government or international institution guarantees and would likely have been significantly lower had such perceptions not existed. But, even smaller capital flows from one or more larger countries can swamp the economies of smaller countries and cause substantial pressures on their exchange rates in rapidly changing directions that could damage even well-managed countries (Little and Olivei, 1999). Short-term international capital flows to emerging economies are considerably more volatile than long-term flows. This is evident from figure 2, which shows bank loans, which are primarily short term, and securities issuances, which are primarily longer term, and from figure 3 for investments other than long-term direct and portfolio. Indeed, direct international investment has been relatively stable in recent years. A large part of the decline in bank loans was in the form of particularly short-term international interbank loans (Bernard and Bisignano, 1999). As a result, some propose restricting only "bad" short-term capital inflows and not "good" long-term (portfolio and direct) capital inflows (Council on Foreign Relations, 1999, and Wyplosz, 1999). However, as argued earlier, this may increase risk taking by private and government debtors by reducing the ex ante threat of foreign investors disciplining them on a timely basis by withdrawing their funds. (Some critics go even further and question the benefit of permitting any

international capital flows on an unregulated basis; for example, Bhagwati, 1998. Edwards, 1999, provides a counter argument.)

In summary, a number of difficulties plague the use of government policies to prevent or mitigate perceived systemic risk in either banking or balance of payments without introducing counterproductive and harmful longer-term effects. These include problems in:

■ Differentiating innocent (economically sound) parties or sectors that require only temporary liquidity assistance from guilty (economically unsound) parties or sectors that require longer-term support that if provided could often fail to lead to recovery and could delay adjustment, result in substantial misallocations of resources, and increase losses in the longer run. While governments and bank regulators may have more timely and superior information about troubled banks in emerging economies, this is less likely in industrial countries. Thus, at least in industrial countries with well-developed money and capital markets, it is likely to be more efficient to provide liquidity assistance indirectly through open market operations and let the market allocate the funds to perceived solvent parties than to attempt to do so directly to the government-perceived solvent banks through the central bank's discount window or otherwise (Kaufman, 1991, and Capie, 1998). This would also ease the pricing problem noted below.

■ Determining the correct amount of any assistance to be provided. Too little would not solve the problem and be wasted and too much would misallocate resources and create the potential for moral hazard problems that could exacerbate the problem.

■ Determining the correct price of the assistance to discourage excessive moral hazard behavior on the part of the recipients.

■ Avoiding political considerations and interference (forbearing), so that the assistance is provided where needed on the basis of economic considerations only.

■ Implementing necessary actions that could harm powerful political groups or government allies, such as requiring banks to officially declare loans in default as nonperforming. These actions would cause the borrowers to be declared legally bankrupt, reducing the market prices of their shares and possibly ousting their management.

■ Discouraging the adoption of simple and intuitively appealing but ineffective policies, such as restoration of banking or currency controls, that, although

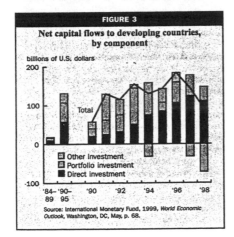

FIGURE 3

Net capital flows to developing countries, by component

billions of U.S. dollars

Total

☒ Other investment
☒ Portfolio investment
■ Direct investment

'84–   '90–   '90   '92   '94   '96   '98
89   95

Source: International Monetary Fund, 1999, *World Economic Outlook*, Washington, DC, May, p. 68.

they were inefficient and ultimately motivated the deregulation, concealed the problem for some time (time inconsistent solutions).

- Introducing fundamental structural legal reforms that are necessary for market discipline to be effective, such as enforceable contracts, property rights, bankruptcy laws, and a credible court system. (For a description of the importance of the legal system in finance, see Laporta et al., 1998.)

Long-term solutions

The most feasible long-run solutions to systemic risk in both banking and exchange rates lie with increased reliance on market forces and market discipline. (A wide rage of potential solutions is discussed in Bisignano et al., 2000.) But this does not imply either that there will not be failures—indeed these are likely to be relatively frequent but small crises—or that there is no role for government policies. Government policies may be required to improve the effectiveness of market discipline, particularly if other government policies have weakened the incentives for such discipline.

The evidence from recent currency crises clearly highlights the key role of government protected economically insolvent banks in fostering the underlying economic conditions that precipitated the speculative runs and eventual depreciation of the currencies by financing unsustainable increases in real estate and stock market prices (Adams et al., 1998, BIS, 1997 and 1998, and IMF, 1998a and b). For example, although varying widely among countries, bank credit extended to the private sector expanded greatly in the four major East Asian countries—Indonesia, Korea, Malaysia, and Thailand—in the years leading up to the crises. In Malaysia, the ratio of private sector bank credit to GDP doubled from 71 percent to 142 percent between 1990 and 1996, the year before the crisis, and in Thailand, the ratio increased by 67 percent between 1990 and 1995 (World Bank, 1998). Much of this credit went to real estate, which is traditionally viewed as risky. Each of the four countries had such loans in excess of 20 percent of total bank loans, a level considered vulnerable by the IMF (Lindgren et al., 1999). These loans helped push up real estate prices sharply and, when these prices dropped abruptly, went into default and contributed significantly to the severity of the crises.

The banks were able to grow their risky loans this rapidly in part because they were not fully exposed to market discipline until the domestic government's explicit or implicit guarantees lost their credibility. By that time, it was too late. In addition, state-owned and -controlled banks are rarely subject to market

discipline and, as effectively arms of government policy in allocating credit to targeted sectors or allies, are notorious for badly misallocating credit (Kaufman, 1999). The banking problems in transitional economies are attributable largely to loans to insolvent state-owned or -controlled and, recently, to poorly privatized enterprises and, at least in Russia, also to finance securities and foreign exchange speculation. To properly understand the operation and implications of these banks, their balance sheets should be combined with those of their government, rather than viewed separately.

To enhance the role of market discipline for larger banks in an environment of partial government guarantees, they should be required to issue a minimum percentage of term debt of a relatively short maximum maturity that is subordinated to the government's claim. Similar to the bank insurance agencies, these claimants have only limited upside potential relative to their downside risk and, because they cannot run, may reasonably be expected to monitor their banks carefully. This would supplement monitoring and discipline by both shareholders and regulators (Benston and Kaufman, 1998, Board of Governors of the Federal Reserve System, 1999, Evanoff and Wall, 2000, and U.S. Shadow Financial Regulatory Committee, 2000). The interest rate the market demands on such explicitly uninsured debt sends a highly visible signal to the market of the issuing bank's perceived financial condition and makes it harder for the regulators to delay imposing sanctions required under prompt corrective action.

In addition, most governments can greatly upgrade the quality, prestige, and independence of their bank supervisors (Caprio, 1998, and Bisignano et al., 2000). Supervisors must be able to understand the nature and consequences of bank activities and have the respect and authority of the bankers in order for their reports and recommendations to have credibility and be evaluated seriously. This also requires that they be adequately compensated relative to the bankers that they supervise.

Moreover, in some countries, the government guarantees are perceived to extend beyond banks and other financial institutions to other major firms. Thus, corporate leverage ratios in general are at levels vastly inconsistent with the degree of macro instability in the economy. In Korea and Thailand, for example, the debt to equity ratios are four to five times the levels in the U.S. and much of Western Europe (figure 4) and are possible only because of the perceived guarantees. It does not take much of an adverse shock, at times only a slowdown in growth rates or small

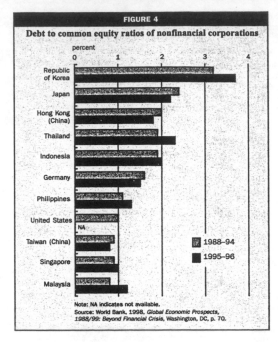

FIGURE 4

Debt to common equity ratios of nonfinancial corporations

percent

Note: NA indicates not available.
Source: World Bank, 1998, *Global Economic Prospects,
1988/99: Beyond Financial Crisis,* Washington, DC, p. 70.

protected by capital and its exchange rate to be protected by foreign reserves or be prepared to permit the rate to float.

The above structural and political reforms are often not easy to introduce. Important and powerful sectors and parties, for example, risky real estate and corporate borrowers and their allies, benefited from the existing arrangements, even if the economy as a whole may not have, and are understandably reluctant to surrender this advantage. Otherwise, the reforms would already have been introduced. Evidence from past banking and currency crises suggests that major reforms (for good or bad) are generally easier to introduce the more severe the crisis and the more discredited the old policies and the more visible their costs. Thus, mild crises rarely lead to fundamental and lasting reforms. It took the severe banking and thrift crisis in the U.S. in the 1980s to enact the reform FDICIA legislation that reduced the discretionary power of the regulators and the severe currency crises in Korea and Thailand in the late 1990s to begin to reduce heavy government intervention in large domestic financial and nonfinancial firms.

Conclusion

Costly banking and currency crises have plagued most countries in recent years, significantly reducing their GDP and causing sizable transfer payments among domestic sectors. Thus, these crises are of concern to both monetary and bank regulatory policymakers. Considerable time and efforts are being devoted to identifying the causes of these twin crises and developing solutions to reduce both the probability of their occurrence in the future and their severity if and when they do occur. Banking and currency crises have a number of common characteristics and are frequently interconnected, so that one may ignite the other.

Because the banking and currency sectors are widely perceived to be fragile, government guarantees are often introduced that protect at least some claim holders from loss. But the guarantees or safety-nets were often poorly designed. As a result, they frequently increased rather than decreased the relative fragility of these sectors, so that subsequent breakdowns were frequently more serious and costly. At least part of the cost was shifted from the claim holders directly affected to the insurance agency or government, so that the cost was less visible. In addition,

increases in interest rates, to drive these firms into insolvency. If the government protects shareholders as well as debtholders, little if any market discipline will exist. These countries require the introduction or intensification of an equity culture, in which losses as well as profits are privatized, rather than profits privatized and losses socialized. Market discipline implies a system of rewards (carrots) and punishment (sticks). Without sticks, market discipline is ineffective. Many countries need to put the discipline meaningfully into market discipline. It is of interest to note that the sharpest rebound in gross capital inflows to emerging Asian economies in 1999 occurred in equity financing. The inflow exceeded even precrisis levels and suggests that, for the moment anyway, foreign investors prefer less leverage (IMF, 2000).

Lastly and perhaps most importantly, governments can reduce the likelihood of systemic risk and crises in both banking and exchange rates by pursuing stabilizing macroeconomic policies that reduce the frequency and magnitude of adverse shocks. This is easiest for larger diversified industrial countries and most difficult for smaller, open, undiversified, developing countries. The less able a government is to stabilize its economy, the more it must require its banks to be many countries in recent years introduced programs of financial deregulation and liberalization to both increase the influence of market forces and encourage greater efficiency and economic development. Unfortunately, these changes were often introduced before the underpinnings that permit market forces to operate efficiently and successfully were fully in place. In the absence of either effective market or effective regulatory discipline, breakdowns increased in frequency and magnitude.

This article argues that lasting solutions to these crises need both to avoid the difficulties from poor implementation and to be incentive compatible, so that policymakers "do the right thing." With respect to banks, adverse moral hazard and principal–agent problems associated with government guarantees may be reduced by limiting the guarantees so as to introduce at least partial market discipline and by designing a structure of regulatory discipline that both mimics market discipline and offsets any declines in market discipline that the regulation itself may introduce.

Ironically, however, limiting government-provided guarantees to increase emphasis on market discipline requires that governments significantly upgrade the quality, prestige, and independence of their bank supervisors both to monitor the condition of the banking system and to implement appropriate sanctions on troubled institutions on a timely and effective basis to turn the institutions around before they reach insolvency. A system of regulatory prompt corrective action with sanctions that become progressively harsher and more mandatory as a bank's financial position deteriorates and least cost resolution based on the provisions included in FDICIA in the U.S. could serve as an anchor. To improve market discipline, it is also necessary in some countries to establish or strengthen an equity culture in which losses as well as profits are privatized. This requires putting in place the legal, cultural, social, and political structures that permit markets and market discipline to operate effectively.

Similarly for currency or exchange rate problems, guarantees by either the domestic government or official international organizations that eliminate entirely or even significantly reduce potential losses to creditors if the domestic currency is depreciated have eventually contributed to deprecations and their associated problems as often as they have prevented them. To reduce the likelihood of exchange rate breakdowns, increased emphasis must both be transferred to market forces to discipline wrongdoers and be placed on stabilizing macroeconomic policies to reduce the need for guarantees that delay and disguise the adverse implications of poor policies.

Lastly, systemic risk for both banking and exchange rates appears to be more serious in perception than in reality. The historical evidence suggests that direct causation (chain reaction) contagion rarely if ever occurs. Common shock contagion occurs more frequently, but primarily on a rational, information-based basis. Banks and countries with similar risk exposure to those of the bank or country experiencing the initial adverse shock will also be adversely affected. But to the extent that neither information nor processing of information is free or immediate, innocent banks or countries may be adversely impacted temporarily during the sorting out period. However, the effect is rarely sufficiently strong to drive innocent banks into insolvency or depreciate innocent counties' currencies permanently. Rather than providing full guarantees and safety nets, the public interest would be better served if public policy were directed at reducing both the time required for market participants to sort out the innocent from the guilty parties and the costs of doing so. This may be achieved by improving the timely and accurate disclosure of relevant information, including that provided by the governments themselves.

NOTES

[1]The Benelux countries consist of Belgium, the Netherlands, and Luxembourg.

[2]More recent estimates by the IMF place the cumulative four-year total output loss (the sum of losses from both currency and banking crises) of the Tequila crisis in the mid-1990s at 30 percent for Mexico and 15 percent for Argentina and of the East Asia crisis of the late 1990s at 82 percent for Indonesia, 57 percent for Thailand, 39 percent for Malaysia, and 27 percent for Korea (IMF, 1999b). In addition, recent estimates place the decline in real GDP from peak to trough in the crises countries in these years at 10 percent for Mexico, 19 percent for Indonesia, 14 percent for Thailand, 8 percent for Korea, and 4 percent for Russia (Summers, 2000).

[3]Estimates of the transfer payments generally have a wide range of error and, until all insolvent institutions in the country are completely resolved, can vary greatly from observation date to observation date. The estimates are more or less equal to the aggregate negative net worth of the protected economically insolvent institutions. Because this amount is partially determined by the actual proceeds from the sale of the institutions' assets since insolvency and the projected proceeds from future sales and recoveries, it is highly sensitive to the state of the economy and the level of interest (discount) rates on the observation date. The poorer the state of the economy on this date, the smaller will be the projected proceeds from asset sales and the larger the necessary transfer payments. Conversely, the better the state of the economy,

the smaller the necessary transfer payments. The total will be known with certainty only after all the assets are sold and any embedded put options or other buyback agreements have expired.

[4]For example, nominal exchange rates declined (depreciated) in the 1990s crises countries from their peaks shortly before the beginning of the crisis in each country to their troughs by 54 percent in Mexico, 527 percent in Indonesia, 57 percent in Korea, 58 percent in Thailand, and 76 percent in Russia (Summers, 2000).

[5]A recent article noted that Amsterdam merchants lost little if anything in the Tulip debacle and that, while shares in the South Sea Company lost 90 percent of their value, commercial bankruptcies in England rose only slightly (Chancellor, 1999).

[6]See Kaufman (2000) and Fernándes-Arias and Rigobon (2000).

REFERENCES

Adams, Charles, Donald J. Mathieson, Garry Schinasi, and Bankim Chadha, 1998, *International Capital Markets*, Washington, DC: International Monetary Fund, September.

Bank for International Settlements, 1998a, *68th Annual Report, 1998*, Basel, Switzerland, June.

_____, 1998b, "International banking and financial market developments," *BIS Quarterly Review*, November.

_____, 1997, *67th Annual Report, 1997*, Basel, Switzerland, June.

_____, 1994, *64th Annual Report, 1994*, Basel, Switzerland, June.

Bartholomew, Philip F., and Gary W. Whalen, 1995, "Fundamentals of systemic risk," in *Research in Financial Services: Banking, Financial Markets, and Systemic Risk*, Vol. 7, George G. Kaufman (ed.), Greenwich, CT: JAI Press, pp. 3–18.

Benston, George J., and George G. Kaufman, 1998, "Deposit insurance reform in the FDIC Improvement Act: The experience to date." *Economic Perspectives*, Federal Reserve Bank of Chicago, Second Quarter, pp. 2–20.

_____, 1995, "Is the banking and payments system fragile?," *Journal of Financial Services Research*, December, pp. 209–240.

_____, 1994, "The intellectual history of the Federal Deposit Insurance Improvement Act of 1991," in *Reforming Financial Institutions and Markets in the United States*, George G. Kaufman (ed.), Boston: Kluwer Academic Publishing, pp. 1–17.

_____, 1988, *Risk and Solvency Regulation of Depository Institutions: Past Policies and Current Options*, New York: New York University, Salomon Brothers Center, monograph, No. 1988-1.

Bernard, Henri, and Joseph Bisignano, 1999, "Information, liquidity and risk on the international interbank market: Implicit guarantees and private credit market failure," Bank for International Settlements, working paper, September.

Bhagwati, Jadish, 1998, "The capital myth," *Foreign Affairs*, May/June, pp. 7–12.

Bisignano, Joseph R., William C. Hunter, and George G. Kaufman (eds.), 2000, *Global Financial Crises: Lessons From Recent Events*, Boston: Kluwer Academic Publishing.

Board of Governors of the Federal Reserve System, Study Group on Subordinated Notes and Debentures, 1999, "Using subordinated debt as an instrument of market discipline," staff study, No. 172, December.

Bordo, Michael D., Barry Eichengreen, and Jong-woo Kim, 1998, "Was there really an earlier period of international financial integration comparable to today?," National Bureau of Economic Research, working paper, No. 6738, September.

Bordo, Michael D., and Anna J. Schwartz, 1998, "Under what circumstances, past and present, have international rescues of countries in financial distress been successful?," Rutgers University, working paper, October.

Calomiris, Charles W., 1999, "Victorian perspectives on financial fragility in the 1980s and 1990s," Columbia University, working paper.

Capie, Forrest, 1998. "Can there be an international lender-of-last-resort?," *International Finance*, December, pp. 311–325.

Caprio, Jr., Gerard, 1998, "Banking on crises: Expensive lessons," in *Research in Financial Services*, Vol. 10, George G. Kaufman (ed.), Stamford, CT: JAI Press, pp. 3–20.

Caprio Jr., Gerard, and Daniela Klingebiel, 1999, "Bank insolvency: Bad luck, bad policy, and bad banking," in *Modernizing Financial Systems,* Dimitri Papadimitriou (ed.), New York: St. Martin's Press, pp. 267–301.

Chancellor, Edward, 1999, "When the bubble bursts ...," *Wall Street Journal,* August 18, p. A18.

Corrigan, E. Gerald, 1991, "The banking-commercial controversy revisited," *Quarterly Review,* Federal Reserve Bank of New York, Spring, pp. 1–13.

Council of Economic Advisers, 1999, *Annual Report, 1998,* Washington, DC: U.S. Government Printing Office, February.

Council on Foreign Relations, 1999, *Safeguarding Prosperity in a Global Financial System: The Future International Financial Architecture,* Washington DC: Institute for International Economics.

Crockett, Andrew, 1997, "Why is financial stability a goal of public policy?," in *Maintaining Financial Stability in a Global Economy,* Federal Reserve Bank of Kansas City, August, pp. 7–36.

Davis, Philip E., 1995, *Debt, Financial Fragility, and Systemic Risk,* Oxford: Oxford University Press.

Demirgüç-Kunt, Asli, and Enrica Detragiache, 1998, "Financial liberalization and financial fragility," World Bank, working paper, No, 1917, May.

Dermine, Jean, 1996, "Comment," *Swiss Journal of Economics and Statistics,* December, pp. 679–682.

Edwards, Sebastian, 1999, "How effective are capital controls?," *Journal of Economic Perspectives,* Fall, pp. 65–84.

Eichengreen, Barry, Andrew Rose, and Charles Wyplosz, 1996, "Contagious currency crises: First tests," *Scandinavian Journal of Economics,* December, pp. 463–484.

Eichengreen, Barry, Michael Mussa, Giovanni Dell'Ariccia, Enrica Detragiache, Gian Maria Milesi-Ferrett, and Andrew Tweedie, 1998, *Capital Account Liberalization: Theoretical and Practical Aspects,* Washington, DC: International Monetary Fund, occasional paper, No. 172,

Evanoff, Douglas D., and Larry D. Wall, 2000, "Subordinated debt as bank capital: A proposal for regulatory reform," *Economic Perspectives,* Federal Reserve Bank of Chicago, Second Quarter, pp. 40–53.

Federal Reserve Bank of Minneapolis, 1999, "Asking the right questions about the IMF," *1998 Annual Report.*

Fernández-Arias, Eduardo, and Roberto Rigobon, 2000, "Financial contagion in emerging markets," in *Wanted: World Financial Stability,* Eduardo Fernández-Arias and Ricardo Hausmann (eds.), Washington, DC: Inter-American Development Bank, pp. 33–47.

Fischer, Stanley, 1999, "On the need for an international lender of last resort," *Journal of Economic Perspectives,* Fall, pp. 85–104.

Folkerts-Landau, David, Donald Mathieson, and Garry J. Schinasi, 1997, *International Capital Markets,* Washington, DC: International Monetary Fund, November.

Glick, Reuven, 1999, "Thoughts on the origins of the Asian crisis," in *The Asian Financial Crisis: Origins, Implications, and Solutions,* William C. Hunter, George G. Kaufman, and Thomas Krueger (eds.), Boston: Kluwer Academic Publishing, pp. 33–63.

Goodhart, Charles, and P. J. R. Delargy, 1998, "Financial crises: Plus ça change, plus c'est la même chose," *International Finance,* December, pp. 261–287.

Greenspan, Alan, 2000, "Banking evolution in contemporary context," *Proceedings of the 36th Annual Conference on Bank Structure and Competition—The Changing Financial Industry Structure and Regulation: Bridging States, Countries, and Industries,* Federal Reserve Bank of Chicago, forthcoming.

_____, 1999, "Statement before the Committee on Banking and Financial Services, U.S. House of Representatives," Washington, DC, February 11.

Gruben, William C., Jahyeong Koo, and Robert R. Moore, 1999, "When does financial liberation make banks risky?: An empirical examination of Argentina, Canada, and Mexico," Federal Reserve Bank of Dallas, working paper, No. 99-05.

Haldane, Andy, 1999, "Private sector involvement in financial crises," *Financial Stability Review,* Bank of England, November, pp. 184–202.

Hunter, William C., George G. Kaufman, and Thomas H. Krueger, eds., 1999, *The Asian Financial Crisis: Origins, Implications, and Solutions*, Boston: Kluwer Academic Publishing.

International Monetary Fund, 2000, *World Economic Outlook*, Washington, DC: International Monetary Fund, April.

_____, 1999a, *World Economic Outlook*, Washington, DC: International Monetary Fund, May.

_____, 1999b, *World Economic Outlook*, Washington, DC: International Monetary Fund, October.

_____, 1998a, *World Economic Outlook*, Washington, DC: International Monetary Fund.

_____, 1998b, *International Capital Markets*, Washington, DC: International Monetary Fund, September.

Kaminsky, Graciela L., and Carmen M. Reinhart, 1999, "The twin crises: The causes of banking and balance-of-payments problems," *American Economic Review*, June, pp. 423–500.

_____, 1998, "On crises, contagion, and confusion," George Washington University, Washington, DC, working paper, December.

_____, 1996, "The twin crises: The causes of banking and balance-of-payments problems," Board of Governors of the Federal Reserve System, international finance discussion papers, No. 554, March.

Kaminsky, Graciela L., and Sergio Schmukler, 1999, "What triggers market jitters: A chronicle of the Asian crisis," Board of Governors of the Federal Reserve System, international discussion paper, No. 634, April.

Kaufman, George G., 2000, "Banking and currency crises and systemic risk: A taxonomy and review," *Financial Markets, Institutions, and Instruments*, Vol. 9, No. 2, May.

_____, 1999, "Helping to prevent banking crises: Taking the 'state' out of state banks," *Review of Pacific Basin Financial Markets and Policies*, March, pp. 83–99.

_____, 1997a, "Preventing banking crises in the future: Lessons from past mistakes," *Independent Review*, Summer, pp. 55–77.

_____, ed., 1997b, *Research in Financial Services: FDICIA—Bank Reform Five Years Later and Five Years Ahead*, Greenwich, CT.: JAI Press.

_____, 1994, "Bank contagion: A review of the theory and evidence," *Journal of Financial Services Research*, April, pp. 123–150.

_____, 1991, "Lender of last resort: A contemporary perspective," *Journal of Financial Services Research*, October, pp. 95–110.

_____, 1990, "Are some banks too large to fail? Myth and reality," *Contemporary Policy Issues*, October, pp. 1–14.

Kaufman, George G., and Steven A. Seelig, 2000, "Treatment of depositors at failed banks and the severity of bank crises," Loyola University Chicago, working paper.

Kho, Bong-Chan, and René M. Stultz, 2000, "Banks, the IMF, and the Asian Crisis," *Pacific Basin Financial Journal*, May, pp. 177–216.

Kindleberger, Charles P., 1996, *Manias, Panics, and Crashes,* third edition, New York: Wiley.

Laporta, Rafael, Florencio Lopez-de-Silanes, Andrei Shleifer, and Robert W. Vishny, 1998, "Law and finance," *Journal of Political Economy*, December, pp. 113–155.

Lindgren, Carl-Johan, Tomás J. T. Baliño, Charles Enoch, Anne-Marie Gulde, Marc Quinton, and Leslie Teo, 1999, *Financial Sector Crisis and Restructuring Lessons from Asia*, Washington, DC: International Monetary Fund, occasional paper, No. 188,.

Lindgren, Carl-Johan, Gillian Garcia, and Matthew I. Saal, 1996, *Bank Soundness and Macroeconomic Policy*, Washington, DC: International Monetary Fund.

Little, Jane Sneddon, and Giovanni P. Olivei, 1999, "Why the interest in reforming the international monetary system?," *New England Economic Review*, September/October, pp. 53–84.

Lopez-Mejia, Alejandro, 1999, "Large capital flows: Causes, consequences, and policy responses," *Finance and Development,* September, pp. 28–31.

McKinnon, Ronald I., 1993, *The Order of Economic Liberalization,* Baltimore, MD: Johns Hopkins Press.

McKinnon, Ronald I., and Huw Pill, 1998, "International overborrowing: A decomposition of currency and credit risks," *World Development,* July, pp. 1267–1282.

_____, 1996, "Credible liberalization and international capital flows: The overborrowing syndrome," in *Financial Deregulation and Integration in East Asia,* T. Ito and T. Krueger (eds.), Chicago: University of Chicago Press, pp. 7–42.

Meltzer, Allan H., 1999, "What's wrong with the IMF? What would be better?," in *The Asian Financial Crises: Origins, Implications, and Solutions,* William C. Hunter, George G. Kaufman, and Thomas Krueger (eds.), Boston: Kluwer Academic Publishing, pp. 241–260.

Mishkin, Frederic S., 1995, "Comment on systemic risk," in *Research in Financial Services: Banking, Financial Markets, and Systemic Risk,* Vol. 7, George G. Kaufman (ed.), Greenwich, CT: JAI Press, pp. 31–45.

Rogoff, Kenneth, 1999, "International institutions for reducing global financial instability," *Journal of Economic Perspectives,* Fall, pp. 21–42.

Rojas-Suarez, Liliana, and Steven R. Weisbrod, 1996, "Banking crises in Latin America: Experiences and issues," in *Banking Crises in Latin America,* Ricardo Hausmann and Liliana Rojas-Suarez (eds.), Washington, DC: Inter-American Development Bank, pp. 3–21.

Summers, Lawrence H., 2000, "International financial crises: Causes, prevention, and cures," *American Economic Review,* May, pp. 1–16.

U.S. Shadow Financial Regulatory Committee, 2000, *Reforming Bank Capital Regulation,* Washington, DC: American Enterprise Institute, March.

Williamson, John, and Molly Mahar, 1998, "A survey of financial liberalization," *Essays in International Finance,* No. 211, Princeton, NJ: Princeton University Press, November.

World Bank, 1998, *Global Economic Prospects 1998/99: Beyond Financial Crisis,* Washington, DC: World Bank.

Wyplosz, Charles, 1999, "Speculative attacks and capital mobility," in *Central Banking, Monetary Policies, and the Implications for Transition Economies,* Mario Blejer and Marko Skreb (eds.), Boston: Kluwer Academic Publishing, pp. 273–295.

[4]
Borrowed Growth: Current-account Deficit-based Development Finance

TERUTOMO OZAWA

I.   INTRODUCTION

A rapidly growing economy tends to encounter a situation in which internal saving is exceeded by domestic investment. How to cope with this deficiency of savings is a critical issue in formulating an effective strategy of economic growth. Any open-economy that invests more than it saves at home will end up with a familiar Keynesian disequilibrium in which the current account (CA) becomes negative (i.e., $CA = S - I$, assuming $G = T$). And this CA deficit needs to be financed by capital inflows (external borrowing), since CA necessarily equals capital account. In other words, rapid growth is financed by a surplus on capital account or a net capital (foreign savings) inflow. This type of CA deficit-based development finance may be called "*borrowed growth*".

Borrowed growth is a double-edged sword for developing countries in particular. Helped by capital inflows, "input-driven" industrialization *à la* Krugman (1994) is made possible and, indeed, accelerated—and results in a miraculous economic growth. At the same time, however, once foreign investors sense some danger of weakness in the developing country's performance, a herd mentality takes over, causing an abrupt and exaggerated reversal in capital flows. All this leads to the familiar pattern of "manias, panics and crashes" *à la* Charles Kindleberger (1996). The upshot is a currency crisis and a resultant financial debacle. The "East Asian miracle" (World Bank, 1993) and what may be called the "East Asian debacle", which have both recently occurred in tandem, are *nothing but the results of excessive debts created through the liberalized financial markets by way of CA deficits*. This exaggerated swing from miracle to debacle represents the perils of borrowed growth. Indeed, a string of the recent currency and financial crises in Mexico, East Asia, Russia, and Brazil have occurred because of the mismanagement (or "non-management") of borrowed growth—and were aggravated by inappropriate policy responses. In addition, some advanced and mature economies also experience the similar phenomenon of borrowed growth, as will be explained below.

The purpose of this chapter is first to conceptually explore the "business-cycle-magnification" effect of the CA-deficit-based finance of economic growth—that is, the danger of "externally originated (via capital account) BOP imbalance", and then to examine the implications of this phenomenon for the recent Asian experience of "boom and bust—and quick rebound" and America's longest boom with its record high CA deficit. The paradox of "CA deficit but strong currency" for the U.S. economy is noted and explained by a role reversal between the CA and the capital account with respect to their autonomous versus accommodating characteristics.

II. STAGES OF ECONOMIC GROWTH AND CA DEFICITS

Borrowed growth, which occurs in developing and advanced countries alike, can best be understood in terms of the stages theory of balance of payments. For developing countries, borrowed growth is predicated as an ineluctable feature of their *outer-dependent* development strategy in the "stages theory of the balance of payments (BOP)" (Kindleberger, 1963). Rapidly growing developing countries are likely to experience CA deficits, whereas those countries which have succeeded in building a strong industrial base start to run CA surpluses. On the other hand, once a country becomes fully developed and mature, it is prone to have CA deficits. Since one country's CA deficit is necessarily some other country's (or countries') CA surplus, a group of deficit countries is necessarily matched by a group of surplus countries in balancing out each other's CA in the world as a whole.[1]

As a country develops over time, it usually goes through the six sequential stages of external financial relations: (1) "immature debtor-borrower", (2) "mature debtor-borrower", (3) "debtor-lender and debtor-repayer", (4) "immature creditor-lender", and (5) "mature creditor-lender", and finally, (6) "creditor-drawer and borrower" (Halevi, 1971). Along these stages, the CA initially deepens in deficit but gradually improves, eventually resulting in a surplus; it thereby traces out a J-shaped (stretched-out) curve during the course of economic development.

In other words, when at the start of economic development, an economy opens up for international trade and investment, its CA registers a growing deficit, especially if left to free market forces without restrictions on cross-border transactions. This is rather an inevitable consequence of a successful take-off to sustained growth. Advanced capital goods, technologies, services, and hitherto-unavailable consumer goods are necessarily all imported from the advanced world to modernize the country's industrial base and market demand conditions. Whatever it can produce (normally natural resources/primary goods) is exported but this is not sufficient to cover the value of imports. Hence, the resultant CA deficit needs to be financed by borrowings from abroad. As the economy succeeds in industrialization, however, this deficit is eventually reversed and usually turned into a surplus.

Stated in terms of the stages theory of BOP, the above-described situation matches the first two stages of "debtor-borrower" (the bottom initial segment of the J-shaped curve). These early stages represent the most critical (danger-laden) period for a rapidly catching-up economy, since its rising CA deficits require more and more foreign borrowings unless otherwise controlled—and plunging deeper and deeper into debts with rapidly ballooning investment income payments. This tendency is all the more pronounced if exchange rates are fixed, since domestic borrowers are falsely assured that their debts specified in foreign currency are the same as home-currency debts. Yet a devaluation of home currency, which may be triggered by sudden capital withdrawals by foreign investors, would wreak havoc to the debtors. This period can, therefore, be identified as the *"perilous CA deficit phase"*.

On the other hand, the subsequent two stages of "creditor-lender" are accompanied by CA surpluses, the phase that can be identified as the *"robust CA surplus phase"*. Those countries that reach this phase have successfully entered, or are at the height of, their industrialization drive in which the "secondary" sector (manufacturing and construction) *à la* Colin Clark (1935) plays the dominant role as an engine of growth—and the "primary" and the "tertiary" (service) sectors the supporting roles. They are specialized in "making things" and their rising national incomes derive mostly from manufacturing goods and exporting them. Their technological progress is focused on product development and production processes. Export and domestic output in manufacturing are mutually reinforcing, making the logic of cumulative causation (or "virtuous cycle") work (Kaldor, 1985; Eatwell, 1982; Cantwell, 1987).

Finally, the last stage of "creditor-drawer and borrower" may be labeled as the *"mature CA deficit phase"*. There are basically two types of advanced countries which are in this phase: one is those mature economies which are living off their past investments abroad and/ or are capable of borrowing because they have high credit-rating and offer good attractions as hosts for multinational corporations' operations and as financial markets for foreign investors. The other type is those advanced countries which enjoy the privilege of having their currencies used as international reserves by other countries; hence they are able to reap seigniorage. In other words, they can keep running CA deficits by exporting their own currencies so long as the rest of the world is willing to hold their currencies as assets. These two types are not meant to be exclusive of each other; their characteristics combine to create a situation in which an advanced country experiences a prolonged period of borrowed growth.

In what follows, the perilous CA deficit phase will first be examined. How a rapidly catching-up economy manages this particular phase is a critical issue in this age of liberalized capital movements. Policymakers in those afflicted economies have failed to control the composition of capital inflows (foreign direct investment, bank loans, portfolio investment, and speculative investment) during the borrowed-growth period. Conventional IMF-sanctioned macroeconomic stabilization measures are designed to solve internally caused CA imbalances. They are not equipped for specifically dealing with flows of hot global money.

III.   THE FINANCIAL AND THE INDUSTRIAL SECTORS: INTERACTION

CA and capital account represent the two external sectors of an open economy, the former the "industrial/real" sector and the latter the "financial/money" sector. They interact closely in economic development and growth. Industrial-sector transactions require money-sector transactions for finance and settlement of trade accounts, but the financial sector often becomes autonomous (no longer accommodating) in this age of hot capital flows, compelling CA to accommodate.

In this connection, the so-called intertemporal theory of production and trade *à la* Fisher (Fisher, 1930; Krugman and Obstfeld, 1997), which has been developed within the framework of conventional neoclassical trade theory (typically presented in terms of a production transformation curve and indifference curves), provides a good starting point in analyzing the interface between the industrial and the financial sectors. This intertemporal theory predicts that any rapidly developing country is likely to import "present spending or purchasing power" (investment goods for domestic capital formation) by exporting "future spending or purchasing power". This means a low relative price of future spending (namely a high relative price of present spending), which indicates a high rate of interest, since highly productive investment opportunities exist. Thus, such a developing country has an intertemporal comparative advantage in present spending; it borrows from overseas to finance productive investment opportunities. In other words, cross-border finance satisfies the needs of its industrial sector. Consequently, domestic capital formation takes place through a CA deficit. This model of intertemporal comparative advantage describes an *ideal* growth situation with BOP equilibrium *over time*—ideal, especially if all imports are only investment goods. The financial side of trade equilibrium is satisfied by capital inflows which foreign investors are willing to provide. And what is borrowed today will be paid back out of what it can produce in the future. There is no BOP problem in the long run.

The reality, however, is more complicated, of course. What is borrowed (today's debt) may not be used to build up a country's productive capacity. If it is squandered for consumption alone (instead of investment), the country will not be able to pay off debt out of future output. A currency and financial crisis will then ensure. This illustrates how important it is to manage capital-account transactions judiciously and to use borrowed capital for productive domestic investments. The financial sector (via the capital account) inevitably interacts with the industrial sector in economic development and growth.

In short, an open economy (S = I + CA) thus has a higher degree of freedom in development finance than a closed economy (S = I), because the former can avail itself of its external balance (CA). For a closed economy, domestic savings are the only source of finance, and if domestic savings are not sufficient, it is constrained from growth. But for an open economy, if domestic savings are not sufficient to finance the desired capital formation, it can borrow foreign savings via a CA deficit. In this situation, CA transactions are autonomous—or *masters,* so to speak—while capital-account transactions are accommodating—or *servants*. But CA-deficit-based finance is accompanied by high risks of excessive capital inflows. For example, it may so happen that unfettered capital inflows are so large that a recipient developing country subsequently ends up with an even larger CA deficit. A sudden surge in capital inflows may not be properly channeled into productive capital formation, spilling into unproductive, purely speculative types of investment and into a greater CA deficit. The domestic need for capital formation thus may be overwhelmed by unnecessary huge capital inflows. In other words, a *role reversal* occurs: capital-account transactions become masters, whereas CA transactions become servants.

Moreover, in the context of an *open* economy with unfettered capital flows across borders, the rapid growth stage exposes a developing country to the forces of "cumulative causation" (both upward and downward) which are generated in both the industrial and the financial sectors simultaneously. These forces cause both "super-growth" and "super-crisis" (or a magnified boom-and-bust cycle) in the following scenario:

(a) High domestic investment (accompanied by high saving) → (b) high growth → (c) capital inflows → (d) growth acceleration or super-growth → (e) more capital inflows (which mean a growing CA deficit) → (f) a danger of inflation (due to a rise in money supply caused by capital inflows) and diminished investment opportunities in the industrial/real sector → (g) speculative and excessive investment in the "financial/money-and-quasi-money sector" (i.e., securities, and real estate) → (h) signs of a collapse (busting) of a boom (bubble) → (i) defaults on domestic debts → (j) a quick exit of hot global money → (k) depletion of official reserves → (l) currency crisis (home currency meltdown) → (m) defaults on foreign debts → (n) financial/banking crisis → super-crisis.

The boom (super-growth) period is thus covered by the first-half sequence of (a) through (g), while the bust (super-crisis) is represented by the second-half sequence of (h) through (n). The whole sequence involves interactions (initially complementary/augmenting but later deleterious/subversive) between the industrial and the financial sectors.

IV. CAPITAL ACCOUNT: TYPES OF CAPITAL FLOWS

Foreign (private) capital inflows comprise three major types: (1) foreign direct investment (FDI) by multinational corporations, (2) portfolio investment by securities firms and investment funds, and

(3) bank loans. FDI is the most stable type, and not so easily reversible. It involves not only financial capital but also—and more importantly—human capital (industrial knowledge) and physical capital (machinery, equipment, and intermediate inputs). Portfolio investment is speculative by nature, consequently footloose and susceptible to herd mentality. It is a source of instability, since it is easily "cashable" and instantly reversible (Gray, 1999). In fact, it is portfolio investments (including currency speculations) that trigger a crisis when they are suddenly withdrawn from the host financial markets. But they are also the ones that come back quickly, as soon as the host countries show some promising signs of economic recovery, thereby assisting a rebound in the local financial markets. Thus, they are ironically *both* crisis-triggering and rebound-assisting. In contrast, although short-term in nature, bank loans are relatively stable. However, they tend to be overextended in good times, especially under the moral hazard of bailout by both the debtor nation's central bank and the IMF. They are also slow in returning to (overwithdrawn from) the once-afflicted emerging markets even when the latter show signs of recovery.[2]

It is now widely recognized that FDI is the type of capital inflow that is desirable for developing host countries, since FDI brings advanced technology, long-term capital, managerial/organizational knowledge, and access to export markets. It is generally posited that an appropriate sequence of capital inflows into a developing country is to liberalize long-term capital inflows (particularly FDI) ahead of short-capital inflows (Eichengreen *et al.*, 1999). And there is an increasing opinion that short-capital inflows, especially hot speculative money in the foreign exchange markets, need to be controlled.

V.   TWO GENRES OF BOP IMBALANCES: CONVENTIONAL VS. NEW

As mentioned, there has recently been a role reversal between CA transactions and capital-account transactions. The former used to be masters, and the latter servants. When the Bretton Woods system of pegged exchange rates operated with discretionary controls on short-term capital flows and foreign exchange over the 1950–71 period, CA transactions used to be the *primary/autonomous* part of international economic activities, whereas their capital-account counterparts played the *secondary/accommodating* role by financing CA activities (Meade, 1951). In those days, CA deficits, when they appeared, were the result of the internal disequilibrium caused by

excessive domestic demand over real domestic output, as best stipulated in the Keynesian "absorption" theory of BOP (Alexander,
1953). Hence, to correct a serious CA deficit, which is regarded as
the result of a country "living beyond its means" (since $CA = Y - [C + I + G]$), tight macroeconomic policies (monetary and fiscal) are
called for and applied to reduce domestic expenditure. The only
way for an economy to grow was then to raise domestic savings to
finance investment. Under the Bretton Woods system, the BOP
served as a guidepost for macroeconomic stabilization.

Those countries that could not manage had to seek a bailout
from the IMF. The IMF, however, imposed its conditionalities or
austerity program on the borrowing governments to solve internal
disequilibrium (excessive spending). The governments then had to
implement IMF-imposed deflationary policies (to force the country
to live "within its means"). If such an austerity program was judged
unworkable, the IMF allowed a devaluation of currency in the name
of "fundamental disequilibrium". These IMF prescriptions—the
austerity program and devaluation—were appropriate and effective
to deal with *internally originated (via CA)* BOP crises, since capital
flows (capital-account transactions) were controlled.

With liberalization of cross-border capital movements and rising
liquidity in the global economy, however, the whole situation began
to change. Capital-account transactions have grown larger in
volume, as a more autonomous type of capital flows (especially, hot
money) rose in importance, overwhelming CA transactions.[3] In this
type of situation, short-term capital flows (portfolio investments and
bank loans) become autonomous in nature—and no longer accommodating in the traditional sense. When a country is flooded with
capital inflows (hence with a huge surplus on its capital account),
the country is compelled either to let its currency appreciate or to
inflate its economy (if exchange rates are fixed). This expansionary
pressure created by imported liquidity in turn causes CA deficits for
the very purpose of relieving such pressure via imports. In other
words, even if the country runs a rising external deficit, it is still
possible that its currency keeps appreciating. This phenomenon
may be called the "CA deficit but strong currency" paradox.[4] This
type of CA deficit is *externally originated (via capital account) BOP
imbalance* where the capital account becomes a master (and the CA
a servant), an imbalance which is diametrically opposite to the *internally originated (via CA) BOP imbalance* where the CA is a master
(and the capital account remains a servant). In fact, therein lies the
very danger of CA-deficit-based finance (Ozawa, 1998).

The IMF has recently been criticized for its continued imposition of the outdated austerity programs on the bailed-out Asian governments. Those beleaguered Asian countries had been maintaining fundamentally sound macroeconomic conditions: relatively well-balanced budgets, stable money supply, and price stability. In the case of the Asian crisis, those debtors who misused borrowed money (denominated in foreign exchange) were mostly the private banks, which in turn lent to domestic firms in local currency. Hence, when conventional IMF prescriptions were applied, things were made worse. The bailed-out economies were driven into a severe recession, with super-high interest rates and tight fiscal conditions. Consequently, businesses collapsed, causing even more bad loans— thus aggravating the banking crisis. Banks contracted loans and precipitated a serious credit crunch. In short, the conventional IMF remedies that were once developed to cope with internally originated BOP imbalances proved to be not a medicine but rather a poison for those countries with externally originated BOP imbalances.[5]

VI. THE ASIAN EXPERIENCE

How effectively have the East Asian countries managed the perils of borrowed growth? First of all, Japan was lucky, since its catch-up growth occurred during the period of the original IMF regime of fixed exchange rates with officially sanctioned foreign exchange controls. In order to maintain an official exchange rate (Y360 to the U.S. dollar), the Japanese government pursued a BOP-guided monetary policy for growth. Exports were initially encouraged so as to earn as much foreign exchange as possible and build up official reserves. Economic development was promoted so long as its deficit-creating effect on the BOP remained manageable. But, once the BOP started to show a deficit which could no longer be financed by foreign reserves, tight monetary policy was immediately applied to slow down the pace of economic growth (to reduce imports) and promote exports. As soon as the BOP conditions improved, however, Japan quickly returned to expansionary monetary policy and resumed high growth.[6] This "stop and go" cycle was then repeated many times until Japan escaped from the perilous CA-deficit phase and moved into the robust CA-surplus phase.

Since in those days capital-account transactions were closely controlled, the BOP imbalances Japan faced were only of the *internally originated* type. Japan was protected by the legitimate capital controls under the IMF system. Its financial sector, particularly the banking industry, was strategically used as a vital instrument of high catch-up growth. Japan adopted what may be called "bank-loan capitalism" in which "central-bank-based finance of development" was actively used for the purpose of avoiding external dependence—that is, instead of CA-deficit-based finance (Ozawa, 1999a). In other words, Japan's catch-up industrial strategy was institutionally protected; in effect, it enjoyed an "infant BOP protection", so to speak—thanks to the original IMF system which gave immunity to Japan's capital and foreign exchange controls.[7] Japan escaped from the dangers of externally originated BOP imbalances.

Not only did Japan minimize external borrowing but it discouraged inward FDI. Japan, however, eagerly purchased technology via licensing agreements from the West, thereby acquiring the technological assets of advanced Western multinationals in an unbundled fashion (Ozawa, 1974). Licensing served as an effective substitute for inward FDI, since Japan had a well-developed absorptive capacity for foreign technology. (Actually this was another form of "borrowed growth" in the industrial/real sector.) When Japan finally began to liberalize capital-account transactions in the early 1980s, it was already structurally developed enough to withstand any major currency fluctuations under managed float. Short-term capital flows were then liberalized without disrupting the real sector.

Although the Japanese experience is peculiar to the postwar economic environment and perhaps not comparable with the present-day situation, one fundamental fact still holds. *Japan's conservative approach to CA management* is perhaps something developing countries should pay attention to. In this respect, China's gingerly approach to CA management and capital-account liberalization is in line with, and comes closest to, the Japanese model. Even a neo-liberal mainstream economist, Paul Krugman (1998) approvingly notes:

> "Why hasn't China been nearly so badly hit as its neighbors? Because it has been able to cut, not raise, interest rates in this crisis, despite maintaining a fixed exchange rate; and the reason it is able to do that is that it has an inconvertible currency, a.k.a. exchange controls. Those controls are often evaded, and they are the source of lots of corruption, but they still give China a degree of policy leeway that the rest of Asia desperately wishes it had."

Moreover, China has been steadily accumulating CA surpluses since the start of the 1990s (except for 1993 when it temporarily registered a deficit of $11.9 billion). Its official reserves stood at $150 billion at the end of 1998 (Economic Planning Agency, 1999).

Taiwan's fiscal conservatism is likewise an approach akin to the Japanese strategy. Taiwan is managing the stability of its New Taiwan dollar effectively at both economy and company levels. Its CA has long been in the black. When exports dropped, it introduced temporary exchange controls such as a ban on Taiwanese firms' non-delivery forward contracts and a reporting requirement of foreign-exchange remittances in excess of US$1 million and certain forward trades of US$5 million or more to the central bank, all designed to discourage speculation. Taiwanese business owners are traditionally conservative in corporate finance, in that many are owned by families, and external borrowing is normally kept to a minimum. Their leading firms have had very low debt-to-equity ratios in the neighborhood of 30%. More importantly, Taiwan has been running solid CA surpluses ever since the start of the 1980s (in 1996, for example, its CA surplus amounted to US$110.3 billion or 4.0% of GDP).

Singapore has been similar in its CA management. It has been running CA surpluses throughout the 1990s, with $14.6 billion both in1966 and 1997. The Hong Kong government, too, has been maintaining its currency-board-fixed exchange rate of HK$7.8 to the U.S. dollar; in August 1998, it even supported local stock prices by investing $15.2 billion in Hong Kong's 33 biggest companies to fend off currency speculators (Mungan, 1998).

In contrast, all those troubled economies in Asia exhibit two characteristics which are the opposite of the approaches taken by Japan, China, Taiwan, Singapore, and Hong Kong. They all have become hooked to footloose global money because they allowed borrowed growth to take its own course by (1) permitting unfavorable CA conditions to develop and (2) prematurely liberalizing capital-account transactions. Thailand, where the Asian crisis originated, had continually been running CA deficits since the mid-1960s (except in 1986 when it recorded a small 247 million surplus). Its CA deficit hovered around 8% of GDP prior to the crisis. In 1987, Thailand began a series of deregulation on interest rates and banking transactions and opened Bangkok International Banking Facilities (BIBF), which served as a duct for capital inflows when rising local interest rates widened the rate differential *vis-à-vis* the outside world. Borrowed money from overseas was then poured by poorly supervised and inexperienced local bankers into speculative real estate and stock markets, eventually culminating in a boom-and-bust cycle.

Indonesia and Malaysia were likewise caught in the trap of the perilous CA-deficit phase (Indonesia from a $1.9 billion deficit in 1985 to a $7.8 billion deficit in 1996; Malaysia from a $613 million deficit in 1985 to a $4.9 billion deficit in 1996). Both instituted swift capital liberalization, which made them dependent on ("addicted to") foreign capital. Indonesia's financial liberalization measures introduced in 1983 and 1988 had resulted in large interest differentials (5–10%), causing rapid capital inflows.

Korea had closely followed the footsteps of Japan's self-reliant financial approach to industrialization until the late 1980s when it experienced a ballooning CA deficit. In fact, it once used central-bank-based development finance via "policy loans" in a more top-down and micro-managed fashion (Ozawa, 1999b). To finance the deficits, the Korean government then began to take advantage of the favorable climate in international credit markets instead of drawing down foreign reserves. Capital-account liberalization was implemented in the latter half of the 1980s to prepare for the opening of capital markets in the early 1990s (Park, 1994). Until the recent currency crisis in November 1997, Korea had been able to maintain a stable market exchange rate tied to the U.S. dollar, although its real exchange rate remained appreciated (i.e., over-valued) for political reasons (Lee, 1998). *Chaebols* competed with each other in expanding industrial capacities through borrowing of foreign short-term capital. Overcapacity, an export-market slump (hence, a high CA deficit), and the rising short-term debt-foreign reserves ratio, and recession-caused business bankruptcies in the late 1990s all coalesced into an inevitable condition for a currency and financial crisis which occurred in November 1997.

It is clear that those Asian countries that fell victim to the financial crisis were all trapped in the snare of "externally originated BOP-imbalance", as they prematurely liberalized their financial markets— prematurely since they were not ready to deal with massive inflows of short-term capital. These excessive short-term capital inflows contributed to the business cycle magnification, creating a fragile boom destined for its eventual bust; hence they were not really needed for a healthy economic expansion. In fact, some argue that high saving rates at home alone were sufficient to finance respectable rates of economic growth *without* borrowing foreign savings through CA deficits. For example, a study made by the Nomura Research Institute (Kan, 1999) demonstrates that during the period 1991–96, even without external borrowings, Thailand could have grown at an annual rate of 6.7% (instead of 8.2%), Malaysia at 7.5% (instead of 9.0%), Indonesia at 7.5% (instead of 7.8%), the Philippines at 2.4% (instead of 2.8%), South Korea at 7.1% (instead of 7.4%), and China at 11.7% (instead of 11.5%) (see Table 7.1).

TABLE 7.1 *Growth Rates Without Capital Inflows (Foreign Savings)*

1991–96	S: Saving[1] (domestic)	F: Capital inflow[1]	I: Investment[1] = S+F	G: Growth rate[1]	ICOR[2] = I/G	S-based growth rate = S/ICOR
ASEAN						
Thailand	34.9	7.7	42.6	8.2	5.2	6.7
Malaysia	35.0	6.5	41.5	9.0	4.6	7.5
Indonesia	32.1	2.6	34.7	7.8	4.4	7.2
Philippines	19.0	3.2	22.2	2.8	8.1	2.4
South Korea	35.4	1.5	36.9	7.4	5.0	7.1
China	40.1	–1.0	39.2	11.5	3.4	11.7

[1] As percentage of GDP
[2] ICOR: Incremental capital-output ratio.
Source: A study made by the Nomura Research Institute cited by Kan (1999), p. 17.

This hypothetical case, however, assumes that *all* domestic savings—and they alone—are channeled into domestic capital formation without any CA deficit (or surplus), namely a balanced CA. The assumption of a balanced CA means, however, that a developing country is restricted from importing all the necessary capital goods (including modern technology) for fast catch-up growth and therefore, it may not be able to grow at such a brisk rate—that is to say, incremental capital–output ratio (ICOR) will increase under import restrictions. Nevertheless, the study does point to rather small net contributions of capital inflows to total growth in those high-saving countries when the risks of externally caused BOP imbalances are taken into account.

VII. AMERICA'S BORROWED GROWTH

The unprecedented 9-year expansion of the U.S. economy is increasingly linked with a bull market in stocks. An economic expansion means continuous upward pressures on national income, which equals to output, Q, times price, P, in a macroeconomic framework. So far (as of this writing), inflationary pressures have luckily been contained, although the labor market is considerably strained with an ever- rising shortage of skilled workers, and oil prices have shot up considerably. Expansionary forces are more and more generated by what Alan Greenspan calls "the wealth-induced excess of demand"[8] (i.e., demand created by rising stock prices, which make people feel richer and hence spend). And this "excess" demand is spilling into a record CA deficit, which is estimated at around $300 billion in 1999.

Thus, America is clearly in a mode of borrowed growth, in the sense that it enjoys CA-deficit-financed growth. But, the U.S. has many unique features as a deficit country. First of all, it is not so much U.S. borrowers but foreign investors that bring money to its capital markets. The U.S. is not really borrowing in order to finance its deficit—that is, a situation of internally originated (via CA) BOP imbalance, but rather it is freely accepting capital inflows that fuel its boom, thereby resulting in a CA deficit—that is, a situation of externally originated (via capital account) BOP imbalance. Moreover, the U.S. dollar is currently the world's dominant (most eagerly accepted) currency, allowing a high level of tolerance for a CA deficit without weakening its value. Hence the paradox of "CA deficit but strong currency" applies to the U.S. economy.

In addition to its external debt, already amounting to $1.5 trillion, the private sector of the U.S. economy borrows heavily *internally* as well. At the end of the third quarter of 1999, for example, the debts of corporations and households stood at $4.2 trillion (46% of GDP) and $6.3 trillion (69% of GDP), respectively (totaling 115% of GDP).[9] Especially worrisome is the buildup of household debt in the form of margin debt, which at New York Stock Exchange member firms alone shot up 25% to $229 billion in the last two months of 1999.[10] In addition to using borrowed money to make investments in such new areas as Internet-related, e-commerce-related fields, corporations thus also borrow to buy more stocks, further driving up stock prices. The U.S. economic expansion is thus sitting on two time bombs—external and internal debts.

This debt-driven boom, notably since late 1997, can be summarized in the following way: Capital inflows (after the Asian crisis) → continuation of a bull stock market → more internal borrowings → further rises in stock prices → wealth-driven consumption → more investment (especially combined with the Internet Revolution) → upward pressures on national income → greater CA deficits → price-pressure moderation due to rising imports → interest rate pressure moderation → a greater stock market boom → continuous capital inflows → a strong dollar (especially against the Euro) → the "CA deficit but strong currency" paradox.

In the fourth quarter of 1999, the U.S. CA deficit reportedly reached a record 4% of GDP as a result of its strong growth rate of 5.8%. This high-strung borrowed growth may no longer be classified merely as "mature" CA-deficit-based finance; it is perhaps becoming more of the "perilous" type. The global financial markets may begin to question the capacity of the U.S. to finance its rising external debt and the wisdom of its soaring internal debt, particularly margin debt—now that the Asian crisis is over, offering increasingly attractive returns on investment relative to those already overvalued ones in the United States. Any sudden withdrawal of investments from the U.S. will lead to a rough landing of the stock market boom. Indeed, the next debt crisis may occur in the U.S., as some warn.[11]

VIII. CONCLUSIONS

An open economy (with a macroeconomic constraint: $S = I + CA$) certainly has a higher degree of freedom in financing its economic growth than a closed (autarkic) economy ($S = I$). The former can make use of foreign savings in addition to domestic savings through a CA deficit, whereas a closed economy's source of funds is restricted to its own savings. Thus, the availability of foreign savings (i.e., investible capital) through a CA deficit makes an open economy grow much faster without creating upward pressures on prices, since imports of goods and services in excess of exports provide a net increase in aggregate supply at home. Particularly when imports are centered on capital goods, they directly add to domestic capital formation—that is, a buildup in the country's productive capacity.

No country can keep running CA deficits forever, however, since the deficits need to be financed by external borrowings. So far as a rapidly catching-up country is concerned, however, the Kindleberger-Halevi stages theory of BOP predicts that its deficit condition will be automatically managed over time and turned into a surplus once the country succeeds in industrialization and structural upgrading by exploiting dynamic comparative advantages. What is envisaged is a success case of borrowed growth—and this is consistent with the long-term equilibrium model of intertemporal trade. The developing country initially imports current spending (i.e., borrowing to build up its productive capacity) in exchange for future spending (repaying in terms of exporting at a later date). Initial deficits are thus canceled out (paid off) by eventual surpluses over time.

It should be noted, however, that in this age of financial globalization, hot money flows are rampant across borders. This increases the risks of over-expansion (super-growth) and over-contraction (super-crisis). The perilous CA-deficit phase is rendered all the more treacherous, as the phenomenon of an internally originated

110   *Terutomo Ozawa*

CA deficit changes to that of an externally originated CA deficit. This was indeed the case of the recent Asian crisis. The well macro-managed economies (stable prices, small government deficits, and high growth rates) of Thailand, Indonesia, Malaysia, the Philippines, and South Korea all fell into the trap of an externally originated CA deficit. Initially, inflows of hot money (a surplus on capital account) stimulated speculative investments and created a boom, but it soon aggravated CA deficits and cast doubt on the sustainability of pegged exchange rates, eventually inducing foreign speculators to bet on devaluation of the Asian currencies and foreign investors to pull out money. All this culminated in a sudden currency crisis and the resultant financial (banking) and economic collapse.

Similarly, America may be entrapping itself into a hazardous mode of CA-deficit-based finance by running an ever-widening external deficit. One may argue that the U.S. situation is distinct and less perilous, since its external debt is denominated in its own currency, the U.S. dollar, unlike the crisis-hit Asian countries which borrowed in foreign currencies; besides the dollar reins supreme as the most widely accepted international currency. But U.S. external debt ($1.5 trillion) is compounded by an even larger internal debt (at least $11 trillion). Both debts are basically supported by lenders' expectations about U.S. stock prices. Indeed, America's borrowed growth (or better still "borrowed prosperity") may be in a "perilous" phase of expansion.

REFERENCES

Alexander, S. (1953) 'Effects of a Devaluation on a Trade Balance,' *IMF Staff Papers*, II(April): 263–278.

Cantwell, J.A. (1987) 'The Reorganization of European Industries After Integration: Selected Evidence on the Role of Transnational Enterprise Activities,' *Journal of Common Market Studies*, 26:127–152.

Clark, C. (1935) *The Conditions of Economic Progress.* London: Macmillan.

Eatwell, J. (1982) *Whatever Happened to Britain? The Economics of Decline,* London: Duckworth.

Economic Planning Agency (Japan) (1999) *Azia Keizai 1999* [Asian Economy 1999], Tokyo: Finance Ministry Printing Office.

Economist (2000) 'A Tale of Two Debtors,' January 22, 2000.

Economist (2000) 'Debt in Japan and America: Into the Whirlwind,' January 22, 2000.

Eichengreen, B., *et al.* (1999) *Liberalizing Capital Movements: Some Analytical Issues*, Washington, DC: IMF.

Fisher, I. (1930) *The Theory of Interest,* New York: Macmillan.

Gray, H.P. (1999) *Global Economic Involvement,* Copenhagen: Copenhagen Business School Press.

Halevi, N. (1971) 'An Empirical Test of the 'Balance of Payments Stages' Hypothesis,' *Journal of International Economics,* 1:103–117.

Kaldor, N. (1985) *Economics without Equilibrium,* Armonk, New York: M.E Sharpe.

Kan, S. (1999) 'Azia Tsuka Kiki to Nihon Keizai eno Eikyo [The Asian Currency Crisis and its Impact on the Japanese Economy],' in Urata, S. and Kinoshita, T. (eds.), *Niju Isseiki no Azia.*

Kasa, K. (1999) 'Time for a Tobin Tax?,' *FRBSF Economic Letter,* 99–12:April 9. *Keizai* [Twentieth-Century Asian Economy], Tokyo: Toyo Keizai Shimposha: 1–22.

Kindleberger, C.P. (1963) *International Economics,* New York: Irwin.

Kindleberger, C.P. (1996) *Manias, Panics and Crashes: A History of Financial Crises,* third edition, New York: John Wiley.

Krugman, P. (1994) 'The Myth of Asia's Miracle,' *Foreign Affairs,* 73(6), November:62–93.

Krugman, P. (1998) 'Saving Asia: It's Time to Get Radical,' *Fortune,* Sept:75–80.

Krugman, P. and Obstfeld, M. (1997) *International Economics,* Reading, MA: Addison-Wesley.

Lee, Y-S. (1998) 'A Political Economy Analysis of the Korean Economic Crisis,' *Journal of Asian Economics,* 9(4):627–636.

Meade, J.E. (1951) 'The Theory of International Economic Policy,' Vol. 1. *The Balance of Payments,* London: Oxford University Press.

Mungan, C. (1998) 'Hong Kong Spent Some $15.2 Billion to Buy Up Stocks,' *Wall Street Journal,* October 21:A15.

Ozawa, T. (1974) *Japan's Technological Challenge to the West: Motivation and Accomplishment, 1951–1974,* Cambridge, MA: MIT Press.

Ozawa, T. (1998) 'Tandem Growth and Crisis: Did East Asia Emulate Japanese Model of Finance?' Paper presented at the Third South China International Business Symposium, November 23–26, 1998: printed in Antonio, N.S. and Chan, T-S. (eds.), *Proceedings,* Vol. 1:25–38.

Ozawa, T. (1999a) 'The Rise and Fall of Bank-Loan Capitalism: Institutionally Driven Growth and Crisis in Japan,' *Journal of Economic Issues,* 33(2), June.

Ozawa, T. (1999b) 'Bank-Loan Capitalism and Financial Crisis,' in Rugman, A. and Boyd, G. (eds.), *Deepening Integration in the Pacific Economies,* Cheltenham: Edward Elgar.

Park, Y.C. (1994) 'Korea: Development and Structural Change of the Financial System,' in Patrick, H. and Park, Y.C. (eds.), *The Financial Development of Japan, Korea, and Taiwan: Growth, Repression, and Liberalization,* New York: Oxford University Press, 325–372.

UNCTAD (1998) *World Investment Report 1998,* New York: UN Publications.

Wall Street Journal (1999), 'U.S. Boom: Living on Borrowed Dime?' December 31, 1999: C1.

Wall Street Journal (2000a) 'Stock-Purchase Borrowing Worries Greenspan,' January 27, 2000: A2.

Wall Street Journal (2000b) 'Greenspan Warns on Stock-Market Gains,' January 14, 2000: A2.

112   *Terutomo Ozawa*

Wallich, H.C. and Wallich, M.I. (1976) 'Banking and Finance," in Patrick, H. and Rosovsky, H. (eds.), *Asia's New Giant: How the Japanese Economy Works*, Washington, DC: Brookings Institution, 249–315.

World Bank (1993) *The East Asian Miracle: Economic Growth and Public Policy*, New York: Oxford University Press.

Yoshitomi, M. (1998) *Nihon Keizai No Shinjitsu* [The Truth about the Japanese Economy], Tokyo: Toyo Keizai Shinposha.

NOTES

1. This author was reminded of the logic of general equilibrium analysis by H. Peter Gray in private correspondence.

2. These different characteristics are reflected in the coefficient of variation. In general, it is much higher for portfolio investment than for FDI. According to UNCTAD (1998, pp. 14–15), interestingly, bank loans exhibited a much larger volatility coefficient than both FDI and portfolio investment in selected (12) developing countries over the period 1992–97.

3. Most capital flows go through the foreign exchange markets. As Kasa (1999) put it colorfully, "On a typical day in the foreign exchange market roughly $1.5 billion change hands. This means that in less than a week foreign exchange transactions have exceeded the annual value of world trade." When other types of capital flows which are not transacted through the foreign exchange markets (e.g., physical flows of the hard currencies such as the U.S. dollar to be used as a store of value in non-U.S. territories) are included, the volume of capital flows easily exceeds more than seven times the value of trade.

4. During the super-dollar days of the Reagan administration in the early 1980s, Ron Stanfield, a colleague in my economic department asked me a question: "How come the dollar is so strong, though we run a huge trade deficit?" My answer was that capital inflows (capital-account transactions) were over-whelming trade-account transactions, because foreign investors wanted to keep their money in the politically stable and strong U.S. economy. In fact, the Reagan administration said that a strong dollar was a sign of U.S. economic strength. I owe him the above conceptualization of the "CA deficit-strong currency" paradox. This paradox can be best explained in terms of "externally originated BOP imbalances"; massive inflows of foreign capital (and a strong demand for the U.S. dollar abroad) keeps the dollar strong despite America's large CA deficit.

5. A similar view is expressed in Yoshitomi (1998), although this chapter's analyses are different in origin and details.

6. This BOP-guided monetary policy Japan once pursued is well known. For an excellent analysis of it, see Wallich and Wallich (1976).

7. The immunity was certainly meant to be temporary. The IMF kept pressure on Japan to liberalize its financial markets. But Japan had been able to buy time until it entered the robust CA-surplus phase of BOP.

8. As quoted in "Greenspan Warns on Stock-Market Gains," *Wall Street Journal*, January 14, 2000, A2.

9. As cited in "U.S. Boom: Living on Borrowed Dime?" *Wall Street Journal*, December 31, 1999: C1.

10. This makes the Federal Reserve Board Chairman, Alan Greenspan, worried to such an extent that the Fed may initiate curbs on stock borrowing by raising the 50% margin requirements which has not been changed since 1974. "Stock-Purchase Borrowing Worries Greenspan," *Wall Street Journal*, January 27, 2000: A2.

11. See, for example, "A tale of two debtors," and "Debt in Japan and America: Into the whirlwind," *Economist*, January 22, 2000.

[5]

MACRO FINANCIAL STABILITY POLICY
AN OVERVIEW FOR A GLOBALIZED WORLD

H. Peter Gray

ABSTRACT

The integration of national financial systems as a result of the introduction of a unified currency or by the reduction in barriers to movements of portfolio capital is likely to reduce the ability of some firms to withstand adverse shock without confronting insolvency. This micro financial instability can contribute to an increased probability of macro financial instability (or crisis). The increased danger of instability is a direct result of the economic gains brought about as a result of financial integration.

The new conditions could require that heavier capital requirements be imposed on banks (with similar measures being imposed on other firms selling financial services). Such requirements must be agreed upon internationally and supplemented by more and equally effective regulation and supervision of banks and financial firms. This may require some supranational regulatory system to the despair of those who attach importance to the preservation of national economic independence.

Research in International Banking and Finance, Volume 14, pages 3-18.
Copyright © 1999 by JAI Press Inc.
All rights of reproduction in any form reserved.
ISBN: 0-7623-0597-5

3

4   H. PETER GRAY

INTRODUCTION

The philosopher's stone of economic and financial analysis is successfully to build a macroeconomic system on the bases of microeconomic foundations. Because of the huge complexity of inherently dynamic, globally integrated economic-financial systems subject to endogenous disturbances and exogenous shocks, the likelihood of success is about that of turning base metals into gold. This paper addresses the question of financial instability in terms of the distinction and connection between micro financial instability and macro financial instability. The micro foundations of macro instability will be seen to follow the general rule of being difficult, if not impossible to disentangle. While the argument is couched in terms of commercial banks (in keeping with the focus of the volume), major bouts of instability can occur simultaneously in equity markets and foreign-exchange markets as well as in deposit intermediaries. It is probably legitimate to argue that, in the existing globalized international system, crises in foreign exchange markets may be the most important kind of adverse shock— particularly for industrializing/developing countries. Instability can and is likely to infect other components of the financial sector (interactivity contagion) so that the modern integrated system of financial markets carries with it the risk of instability in deposit intermediaries being caused by a wider range of disturbances.[1]

Micro financial instability occurs when one financial institution fails (possibly bringing a few more vulnerable firms down with it), but neither the general price level of financial assets nor the wealth of households and corporations is noticeably affected. Macro financial instability involves the failure of one or more major institution as well as a number of minor institutions and a consequent large reduction in the total value of financial assets in the economy affected (Herring and Litan 1994).

Macro financial instability can affect a nation, a region, or the world.[2] When a national or a regional system is subjected to macro financial instability, the damage to its financial institutions (deposit intermediaries) causes it to sink into serious recession either as a result of the reduction in wealth[3] or because of the macroeconomic stringency imposed on the economy as a remedy for the causes or the direct consequences of the macro financial instability. In an international economy there are export markets to provide aggregate demand and support and assistance from supranational institutions to help to reestablish solvency and confidence in the damaged financial system. When the world financial system suffers a crisis (mega-financial crisis), there is no external source of aggregate demand to aid in the recovery and the consequent reduction in output and demand is more likely to be dominated by the loss of wealth.[4]

At the end of the twentieth century there are several portents of potential macro financial instability: (1) the recent, unresolved crises in financial markets in East Asia and, particularly so if the Japanese system loses the confidence of holders of its liabilities; (2) the vulnerability of Latin American financial systems to crisis

(the Latin American countries are following the earlier pattern of the Asian industrializing nations of accepting inflows of easily encashable portfolio liabilities
from abroad but without the high rates of economic growth); (3) the underlying
potential vulnerability of the hegemonic currency with its implications of mega-
financial instability (Gray 1996); (4) the unknown implications for macro financial instability of global integration of financial markets with the power of derivatives to impose serious strain on a national system; and (5) the integration of
many major European currencies into the euro with all of the stresses and strains
of economic adjustment that this event is likely to impose.[5] What matters for
mega-financial instability is whether there is a domino effect from one market or
sector to another: if so, the whole question of global financial stability relies upon
the existence of firewalls or barriers to contagion (within or between sectors).
Given the trauma that financial crisis imposes, it is not clear that after-the-fact,
lender-of-last-resort actions can simply reinflate a depressed economy.

Central bankers and chancellors of the exchequer or finance ministers have not
revealed that they have fully appreciated the implications of events or of the global integration of financial markets for macro financial instability or that they
have taken adequate steps to guard against contagion.[6] Certainly Chapters 3 and
4 of this volume suggest that micro financial instability has not been banished by
what has been, by and large, a very successful period of macroeconomic performance. Indeed, one could take the view that the recent Keynesian successes of the
world economy have, to a degree, been purchased by the willing acceptance of a
reduction in financial resilience or stability efficiency (Gray and Gray 1981, pp.
55-61; Gray 1996).[7]

This paper is not so presumptuous as to lay claim to solving the problem set out
above: that would require a new *Principia*.[8] The purpose is, rather, to examine the
way in which inadequate resilience (ability to withstand an adverse shock without
becoming insolvent) on the part of deposit intermediaries and other financial
firms can contribute to *macro financial* instability. Some policy considerations
are put forward. The paper does not address the problem of identifying and anticipating possible shocks of a magnitude capable of inducing macro-financial instability when financial firms are being operated prudently and within the limits set
by the authorities.[9] Some early warning systems (Salvatore 1998) would seem to
be a good guide for national systems plus recognition that, in the globalized banking system, it is important that supervision in all countries be effective. Such a
requirement could impair national independence ("nationhood") but it may be a
necessary cost of global financial integration.

The paper first addresses the underlying conditions of instability. It then considers how inadequate resilience at the bank or financial firm level could contribute
to macro financial instability and how weak institutions can enhance the danger of
instability in the event of an exogenous shock. The final section addresses the
important questions of prudential management on a global scale and its incorpo-

ration of equally disciplined and effective supervision of financial systems in a globalized and interdependent world.

INSTABILITY IN ASSET MARKETS[10]

Market instability is a recognized phenomenon but little analytic effort has been devoted to it. Hicks's (1946, p. 65) famous diagram refers to instability in a market for goods: an unstable but market-clearing flow equilibrium is bounded by stable situations on either side of the instability. The range of instability is, it must be assumed, so small that there is no need for concern with induced consequences (at least, Hicks saw no need to address the possibility). Figure 1 provides a diagram of a potentially unstable market for financial *assets*: it has an obvious genetic dependence on Hicks's original figure.

The excess demand curve for assets shows a market clearing at P_1. As drawn, the market is stable for values greater than P_1 (an increase in price will reduce demand) and unstable for prices below P_0. A shock which shifts the excess demand curve to the left by an amount equal to a, will precipitate a decline in asset prices to P_3. The ability of the system to withstand an adverse shock (its resilience) is indicated by a and the potential damage done by the underlying instability by b.

The resilience of a financial firm derives from the level of reserves, from the degree of portfolio diversification, and the quality of its assets. The range of instability, b, derives from any actions of asset holders which reinforce the effects of the original shock (this is contagion among financial institutions as an insolvency in one "bank" destroys the assets of another "bank" and brings that bank down in a vicious cycle).[11] The greater b, the greater are: the reinforcement of the original shock by induced actions; the greater is the decline in the prices of financial assets brought about by instability; and the greater the reduction in the total value of financial and real assets and of net worth on the part of households and corporations. The loss of wealth will reduce aggregate demand and create excess capacity. It is also to be expected that a decline in the value of financial assets will sap entrepreneurs' confidence and make financial institutions more wary of approving extensions of credit. All of these effects reinforce each other and can help to explain why mega-financial instability of sufficient magnitude can engender depression.[12]

A consideration of macro prudential policy requires understanding the two magnitudes, what can cause a to be eroded or buttressed and what contributes to the magnitude of b. The two concepts do not lend themselves to precise measurement but what is needed is some identification of phenomena which are likely to decrease a and to increase b as well as any tendency for the two effects to be interdependent.[13]

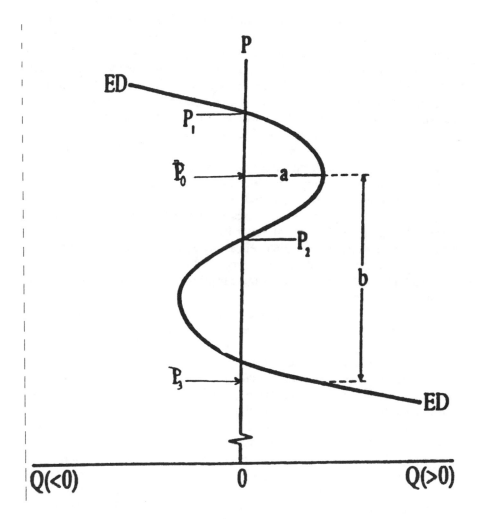

Figure 1.

Guttentag and Herring (1986, p. 2) identify two kinds of shocks for deposit intermediaries in a closed system: *credit shocks* are large-scale defaults by borrowers and *funding shocks* are large-scale withdrawals by depositors.[14] A credit shock that impinges directly on a large number of financial institutions must imply some exogenous shock but, at the firm level, a default by one or two major borrowers can exceed the reserves of an individual financial firm.[15] There is a danger that banks and other sources of credit may suppress potential losses from overextended borrowers unless their reporting is carefully and effectively overseen. This may be particularly relevant to credit card debt when individuals become overextended and banks have little firsthand knowledge of their debtors. When the "day of reckoning comes," several banks may declare insolvency in a short space of time as funding shocks are induced.[16] The existence of important banks and financial firms following prudent policies will increase the system's a and suggests that an endogenous shock is unlikely to bring about macro financial instability: micro financial instability will be more frequent but there is a reduced risk of contagion and a will be reduced for the system.[17]

When the resilience (a) of a national system is considered, it is, in some sense, the average a of all of the institutions (weighted by the liability base of the institutions). Higher capital reserves will increase a as will careful supervision, good risk diversification, or conservative lending policies. Following Eichengreen and Portes (1987, p. 28), it is necessary to understand that the relationship between micro and macro instability depends crucially upon the type of shock experienced by the system as well as upon the inherent ability of banks to remain solvent in the event of an adverse shock. An adverse shock that impinged heavily on carefully managed banks will be less likely to trigger instability than a smaller shock which impinges on weak banks.

The problem with (heavy-handed, ultra-conservative) ex ante prudential policy is that it tends to hamper initiative in the financial sector through regulations of activities because the potential of new initiatives to cause instability are not understood. Such regulations could dampen useful innovation and encourage counterproductive innovation by financial firms (Maehara 1994, p. 154). In more general terms, there exists an inevitable tradeoff between the severity of ex ante requirements (enhancing a)[18] and the allocative efficiency of the economy in that regulation in pursuit of greater micro financial stability may sap the ability of the financial sector to promote allocative efficiency and growth (Smith and Walter 1997, pp. 154-157):[19] in other words, overly careful regulation will inhibit the financial sector from fulfilling the task of enhancing dynamic economic performance. If, as Herring and Litan (1994, p. 11) suggest, the market mechanism provides a better way to monitor the insolvency risk of overexposed (low-resilience) banks than ex ante regulation (especially when innovations in financial instruments exceed the ability of regulators to keep pace), the probability of insolvency by some institutions (micro financial instability) would be increased. This is one way to restrict the damage done to allocative efficiency in the real sector and innovation in the financial sector: such a policy will allow the market to eliminate those institutions with little resilience. In the absence of a suitable policy (of deposit insurance), asset holders would need to be more aware of the conduct of the institutions to which they entrust their assets. An approach based on careful regulation of capital adequacy and on careful oversight of potential loan losses will mainly reduce the danger of endogenous macro financial instability though it will also have positive benefits when there is an adverse exogneous shock (see below).

A policy of "too big to fail" could preserve some insolvent deposit intermediaries ex post. This could be seen as an incentive for excessive risk-taking by a large bank with destabilizing potential. This would be mistaken provided that the regulators enforce any loss on shareholders and discharge the senior executives and members of boards of directors judged responsible for the insolvency. It is an interesting question as to the need to license bankers (and directors) at large banks so that those guilty of excessive risk-taking could have their licenses revoked after an insolvency. Unfortunately, regulators are not always willing to take or are capable of such action and are not necessarily able to locate good bankers.[20]

The range of instability, *b*, depends very much on the degree to which reactions to the shock reinforce the original shock. This can, as noted, take place within a sector (deposit intermediaries) or between sectors (banks and the equities market).[21] The more widespread the shock, that is, the larger proportion of banks suffering from an adverse shock, the more likely are all banks to be weakened and the greater the probable mutual reinforcement. Banks that have adequate net worth (and loan loss reserves) to withstand the first shock may not be able to withstand aftershocks and in this way will contribute to the increase in *b*. Similarly, the greater the fall in the value of real assets (especially those financed by mortgage liens), the greater the reduction in bank resilience.

It is not possible to consider this phenomenon without confronting the question of the degree of confidence of households and executives.[22] There would seem to be a tendency for there to be an inverse relationship between *a* and *b*: the larger is *a*, the smaller is *b* likely to be and, inevitably, an adverse shock which exceeds *a* will destroy confidence and increase *b* even though the resilience of individual banks has not changed.[23]

DIFFERENT EFFECTS OF DIFFERENT SHOCKS

This section examines the probable impact of three different kinds of shocks on a system in which the individual values of *a* have substantial variance around the mean.[24] The posited wide variance in the individual values of *a* could be taken as indicating lax or ineffective supervision of individual intermediaries by the monetary authorities as well as different attitudes toward risk exposure (and the risk-return tradeoff) in banks.

1. *An endogenous shock* will almost inevitably originate in banks with small resilience (*a*) if only because these are the most extended and the most vulnerable to credit or funding shocks. The failure of one bank can lead to the failure of other financial institutions usually through a credit shock (but an induced funding shock could cause failure).[25] The danger that such a shock will be large enough (> *a*) to trigger a general decline in asset values through contagion either within a sector or between sectors, depends upon the ex ante measures enforced by the monetary authorities and the size of the credit shock.[26] Capital reserves required ex ante

coupled with careful supervision of excessive risk and/or risk concentration could eliminate or restrict contagion to a small number of similar institutions and deposit insurance could preclude any general loss of confidence in institutions not directly affected by the shock. Under such conditions, the downward spiral indicated by *b* would not be triggered. The instability would be micro financial.

2. The damage inflicted by an *exogneous shock* with a concentrated impact will depend directly on the magnitude of the shock and the degree of resilience of those institutions which bear the brunt of the shock. There is, therefore, a potentially random element in such a shock. However, the likelihood of macro financial instability depends directly upon the resilience of the institutions affected directly and indirectly on the shock and its repercussions.

3. The damage inflicted by an *exogenous* shock with a broad even effect will resemble an endogenous shock in that it is likely to bring about the failure of some weaker institutions and to weaken other banks. Given the resilience of the banking system (*a*) it is the magnitude of the shock which will determine the likelihood of macro financial instability. The more likely a country is to be affected by an exogenous shock, the higher should ex ante standards or resilience be and the greater the cost in terms of the contribution of the financial sector to national economic performance.[27]

THE ENHANCED DANGERS OF A GLOBAL SYSTEM

In an internationally integrated system of financial markets, two additional sources of instability are identified by Guttentag and Herring (1986): *transfer shock* is really a special kind of credit shock applying to foreign loans and results from a marked reduction in the ability or willingness of foreign debtors to acquire the [hard] currency in which their obligations are denominated,[28] and *foreign-exchange shocks* which involve the loss of capital value and income that follow from a change in exchange rates. These sources of instability were defined in terms of a financial system in an industrialized country with assets denominated in both home and foreign currency and took cognizance of the possibility that the consequences of a foreign-exchange shock could limit the soundness of some assets (i.e., the ability of debtors to meet their obligations). In an industrializing/developing country subjected to a sudden and substantial weakening of its currency, a *transfer shock* will adversely affect some debtors as the cost of imported goods rises but may beneficially affect some other debtors for whom the price competitiveness of their products in foreign markets in industrialized countries will have increased as a result of currency depreciation. Any loans denominated in foreign currency will enhance the profits of a bank in a country which has just experienced a depreciation of its currency. In an industrialized country these two sources of instability are likely to be mutually reinforcing and represent an additional source of *adverse* disturbance for banks which engage in international lending.

Banks and (other financial firms) operating in an internationally integrated system have a higher degree of exposure to shocks whether they be uninational banks making foreign loans or multinational banks with a network of affiliates in other countries.[29] The potential reduction in resilience which follows from international activity depends upon the degree to which banks are able to hedge their exposures and to avoid any greater risk element in foreign lending because of less familiarity with the borrower's commercial culture and because lenders may not fully appreciate differences between the reporting standards of their home country and those in the borrowing country.

Globalization involves deepening integration between the already-integrated financial systems of the industrialized countries and those of developing and newly industrializing countries. The inability of several developing countries to service their foreign debt in 1982 brought the world financial system closest to mega-financial instability since World War II.[30] Industrializing/developing (i/d) countries are more prone to adverse financial and real shocks, in part because they are likely to be less effective in the design and enforcement of prudential financial regulation. The consequent greater risk and uncertainty and the danger of adverse shock are deemed to derive from nine major characteristics of financial markets in the developing world.

1. Financial markets in the developing world are more prone to adverse real and financial shocks which reduce the values of financial assets because of the relatively greater reliance on a small number of export products. When manufacturing affiliates are the marginal supplying unit in the global network of a multinational corporation, a global recession can focus a shock on what are probably the most vulnerable financial systems.

2. The level of foreign-exchange reserves needed by industrializing/developing countries has traditionally been measured as a fraction of necessary imports: now, in an era in which convertible foreign currencies are invested in equity markets, it is necessary to have much larger reserves.

3. Governments in developing countries, particularly in fast-growing countries, have less reliable sources of information (data) and are less skilled in the use of policy to assure the stability of financial firms. In the same way, their authority to inflict short-run costs on the home economy and on "crony" banks is inadequate.

4. Given the influx of portfolio investent into emerging stock markets, there is a danger of a loss of confidence and an abrupt exodus of funds from financial markets, the economy, and the currency, so that the task of the authorities is substantially more difficult.[31]

5. The dangers of a foreign-exchange crisis are greater in developing countries as short-run foreign-exchange problems can be more easily sup-

pressed in fast-growth economies in a globalized world either by continuous net inflows of portfolio capital seeking high returns or by ever greater (official) borrowing from abroad. The new technologies have both facilitated the transfer of funds to capital markets in i/d countries, but they have also geared up the speed with which funds can be transferred as a result of a herd instinct response to a shock.

6. Financial linkages are the mechanism whereby instability in real and financial markets in an unstable developing country is transmitted to the industrialized world. The vehicle is likely to be stress on or the failure of affiliates of financial firms based in industrialized countries, who suffer from their exposure to events in the developing world and the decrease in capital adequacy of the parent bank.

7. Accounting and disclosure standards in some developing and newly industrializing countries are neither as well developed nor as well understood by foreign investors (outsiders) and are not easily regulated by bank executives or regulators. The true condition of borrowers was difficult to ascertain in Thailand because borrowed funds were frequently used within a firm for purposes other than those for which they were intended (Waldman and Scherer 1997; McDermott and Wessel 1997).[32]

8. Where national economies are closely integrated in regional blocs (official or informal), a financial crisis in one country almost inevitably spreads to other members of the bloc (unless the bloc's financial hegemon has great strength and is prepared to use it).

9. Limits on the degree of individual action by employees may be less effectively administered in affiliates in foreign countries: a grotesque example is that of the Singapore affiliate of Barings Merchant Bank (Leeson and Whitley 1997).

In industrializing/developing economies, a diminution of either allocative or stability efficiency can have high perceived social costs. These countries would also suffer from heavier micro-prudential constraints in industrialized countries which would impede the transfer of the flow of saving from the industrialized world (always provided that the funds were not easily encashable and were directed to sound projects). This is the conundrum faced by those people and institutions concerned with effective prudential regulation.

Herring and Litan (1994, pp. 4-9) found the problems of macro-prudential (systemic) regulation to be more complex when financial markets are integrated within the bloc of industrialized countries than in a world of largely independent national markets. This difficulty will grow as more countries at different levels and rates of development are integrated into the world financial system. Regulation of an integrated system will need ever greater international cooperation to avoid the costs to allocative efficiency of micro-prudential regulation of individual financial firms.

The ability of a bank to generate profits and to enhance capital out of retained earnings is made easier if banks are not burdened by heavy capital adequacy requirements (provided always that the loans are good enough and the global economy tranquil enough to avoid a credit shock). This aspect has serious implications for a level playing field among banks which compete in a globalized financial system. There is a danger that the burden of ex ante restrictions will provide an incentive for national regulatory authorities to compete in terms of the laxity of the effectiveness of supervision. Such laxity, whether in industrialized countries or in industrializing/developing countries and whether instigated by the desire to help indigenous banks gain market share or by too close relationships between government and banks, will decrease the global value of a. Bryant (1987, p. 139) identifies a similar phenomenon: a competition in laxity among developing countries attempting to establish themselves as offshore banking centers.

The danger that national systems of supervision/regulation will vary in reliability or effectiveness could, if attention to the problem of potential instability increases and if the differences are known to exist, make international cooperation still more difficult to achieve. It seems unlikely, particularly under existing political conditions, that these concerns would lead to an attempt to create a supranational system of regulation. The European Union has not yet been able to create such a body despite its ability to create a single currency. The institution of such a supranational body may not have been negotiable at Bretton Woods: still less now when the International Monetary Fund is advocating complete freedom of capital movements without any announced concern with the effects of such a policy on the probability of macro- or mega-financial instability (Fischer 1997).

CONCLUSION

The danger that micro financial instability (the insolvency of financial firms) will contribute to a major bout of instability lies outside the analytic range of Herring and Litan and Maehara (1994). Their recommendation of allowing the market system to enforce resilience by causing overextended banks to fail and tacitly assumes that the other banks are well capitalized. The analysis assumes a tranquil world: this assumption may need reconsideration. The danger of weak financial firms is that their insolvency will be precipitated by *and will strengthen* an adverse shock that is capable of triggering the downward cycle of instability. Since macro financial instability is likely to be caused by an event outside the system (in another country or another sector), the assumption of a tranquil, globalized world could neglect a crucial aspect of financial instability.

The difficulties of establishing adequate resilience are enhanced by the fact that globalization and prudential regulation enforce a loss of nationhood by limiting the discretion of national governments to implement policies which reflect their society's objective functions (policy targets) (Gray 1999, chap. 10). The political and economic aspects of globalization may conflict. If globalization and integration are to be politically acceptable, the gains in economic efficiency must exceed the psychic cost of the impairment of nationhood. This issue confronts all forms of integration and can present difficulties in the absence of a strong consensus because, too often, the economic gains are long term and the psychic and economic costs are immediate.

The integration of financial markets both within the European Union where the euro will replace many national currencies, and within the world where capital markets have become more and more integrated by the reduction of barriers and transaction costs and by the large gross flows of portfolio capital, weakens nationhood. It is a danger signal that the European Union has decided to launch the euro before it has addressed the issue of bank supervision. If the launching of the euro brings macroeconomic strains in its wake, then banks are likely to be overextended and the danger of crisis enhanced.

Financial markets enforce the consensus degree of financial tightness and policy, particularly the generosity of the domestic social contract, is likely to be determined by the "low bidder" (Gray 1999, chap. 10). It is difficult to conceive of a country not losing its ability to maintain self-recognition without its own currency or an independent monetary system (although competing for the World Cup every other year may be an adequate substitute).

This paper has addressed the problems inherent in the globalization of capital markets at an abstract level. It has argued that, without serious attention being paid to the need for prudential regulation of weak banks (and the whole range of financial firms) in the form of resilience-creating measures, the dangers of macro financial instability, and possibly even mega-financial instability, are likely to increase as a result of the greater probability of micro financial instability. The potential decrease in the resilience of national systems, brought about by the greater exposure to adverse shock that follows from globalization, could require that heavier capital requirements be imposed than are currently required (by the Basel Concordat). Because the effectiveness of regulation is also important in controlling any reduction in resilience, it is not only that capital adequacy standards must be harmonized but also that the effectiveness of regulation be equalized. Equalization implies supranational control of the regulation of firms producing financial services: this would eliminate yet another strand of national identity.

FitzGerald (1996) points out that any involvement of the International Monetary Fund in restoring financial stability in the event of crises at the national or world levels will require authorization of IMF borrowing and/or the innate authority to create special drawing rights. Some conservative countries could oppose this, leaving the provision of the international public good to the combination of Europe, Japan, and the United States. This has been identified as a "committee hegemon" in Gray (1996) and presents the obvious problem of the time required for generating political agreement in the face of events which require quick action. Given the existing weakness of the Japanese financial system and the potential for rivalry between the euro and the U.S. dollar, there may be legitimate reasons to question the feasibility of an inherently stable integrated capital markets throughout the world (even when those countries which do not currently have access to the major markets, are not included).[33]

ACKNOWLEDGMENT

The author is obliged to John Dilyard for in-depth discussions of several aspects covered in this paper.

NOTES

1. Two examples may be of help here: when positions in equities are financed by mortgages on real property, banks can be damaged by a sharp loss of value in equities that transmits itself to real property; when a country's currency experiences inflows of portfolio capital and becomes overvalued, a flight from the currency can devastate the value of its stock market (Gray 1999b).

2. Because its much greater implications for invoking the paradigm shift that is depression, we have coined the term "mega-financial instability" for world instability.

3. There exists an in-between kind of instability when a substantial component of a country's deposit institutions fails but the collapse is limited to a particular kind or genus of institution. The classic example of this kind of collapse is the U.S. savings and loan industry in the mid-1990s. At considerable expense, the U.S. government managed to prevent these failures from affecting other institutions and other markets. This experience resembles micro financial instability because its effect was limited and did not pervade the macroeconomy of the country.

4. It is probable that the value of real assets will decline with that of financial assets as the demand for them shifts sharply to the left: this enhances the perceived loss of wealth. Indeed, the two are likely to be mutually reinforcing.

5. Reliance on export markets as a source of aggregate demand requires the willingness of the unaffected regions to run deficits on current account in their balances of payments and/or a hegemon which will undertake that role. Depression involves a paradigm shift. Keynes realized that when one nation was prepared to conduct expansionary fiscal policy, it was important that the expansionary force not be lost in a global morass of depression. This accounts for Keynes's (1933) reservations about the desirability of free trade in a depression. Failure to recognize the paradigm shift explains Robbins's inability to comprehend Keynes on this issue (O'Brien 1988).

6. For an analysis of the effects of international financial integration on national markets and economies, see Oxelheim (1996).

7. It is possible that the creation of the euro will aggravate the weaknesses of the dollar by siphoning off balances or by explicit competition for the role of dominant currency although this should not occur, if at all, before the EU has adjusted to its common currency (I am obliged to Ilhan Meric for making this last point).

8. Central bankers and people who share their responsibilities are, by nature and with cause, secretive. It may well be that arrangements have been made to counter any serious instability that may arise in the industrialized world but unless they are understood, they cannot deter speculative attempts to induce a run on a national currency.

9. FitzGerald (1996) suggests that the extension of credits through the IMF to countries which have undergone bouts of macro financial instability (for example, Mexico in 1994) has used up polit-

ical capital in that there was substantial dissatisfaction in Europe with what was effectively a bail-out of U.S. investors.

10.   The reference is à propos: Newton spent a lot of intellectual capital pursuing the alchemist's dream (Keynes 1973).

11.   In 1997 Chairman Alan Greenspan of the U.S. Federal Reserve System coined an expression which sums up endogenous instability (in the U.S. equity markets): a market for financial assets can be severely overvalued because of "irrational exuberance" in which the future is discounted too optimistically. Such an endogenous shock derives from a universal over-optimism not from the excess risks incurred by one or a few individual firms nor from the characteristics of the exogneous shock (Eichengreen and Portes 1987, p. 28). The solution of this problem falls within a liberal interpretation of the purview of monetary policy. On the issue of "speculative bubbles," see Canterbery (1998).

12.   This section derives from Gray (1992).

13.   The same effect will exist in equities as the sale of assets by one individual may sap the willingness of others to hold either the same or other equities.

14.   Depression brings about a paradigm shift as economic units now see their main objectives as restoring some crudely conceived historic measures of adequate (real) net worth and liquidity (Gray 1990). In Keynesian terms the marginal and average propensity to save increases sharply for those with income, the risk premium on real and financial investments increases, and economic behavior is defensive rather than expansionist.

15.   The emphasis is on ex ante measures (i.e., prudential supervision of deposit intermediaries and other financial firms). The loss of net worth following a major crisis cannot be fully offset by the availability of credit with its connotation of debt for the private sector.

16.   This paper uses the term "shock" to mean an event which affects the prices of financial assets (or, for assets which are not traded, their net present values). Because the paper separately identifies the size of the shock and the possibility that it will trigger self-reinforcing adjustments by actors in financial markets, the term does *not* carry the implication of "very large potential effects" used in Guttentag and Herring (1982, p. 2).

17.   The Darmstädter und National Bank suffered a killing shock as a result of the bankruptcy of a single German textile firm in 1931 (in part because of the nervousness of depositors after the near failure of Credit Anstalt in Vienna).

18.   This is the major point of Herring and Litan (1994) and Maehara (1994) that insiders will be better able than regulators to identify suspect institutions and can act accordingly. The point loses its validity when banks lend money to highly leveraged financial firms: the bail-out of a hedge fund, Long-Term Capital Management, by the Federal Reserve System and a consortium of major U.S. financial firms in October 1998, suggests that banks do not possess the perceptivity that Herring and Litan and Maehara suggest. Major losses by commercial banks in Russia do little to bolster confidence in the inherent macro financial stability of the system.

19.   This is implicit in the conclusion of Herring and Litan (1994) and Maehara (1994).

20.   To identify a tradeoff can be misleading if it instills into the mind of the reader that the tradeoff is constant through time. At a time of general fragility, the social cost of macro financial instability will greatly exceed the cost of sluggish movement toward an efficient allocation of resources (and vice versa).

21.   The danger also exists that regulatory, deposit-insurance agencies will assess the problem in terms of minimizing the loss of insurance reserves. This would be equivalent to a bank lending officer never making a bad loan.

22.   This is a problem that is more relevant in Europe, Japan, and Canada than in the United States but is steadily becoming more relevant in the latter.

23.   Here the case of Long-Term Capital Management is a huge and an interesting example of interdependence.

24.   For a study of this, see Tversky and Kahneman (1982).

25.   The recommendation of Herring and Litan (1994) and Maehara (1994) that the industry be allowed to identify weak institutions and that, inferentially, these be "encouraged" to fail by their competitors, would have the effect of increasing the aggregate *a* and, in this way reducing the vulnerability to exogenous adverse shock.

26.   The system is considered to be closed: an international system is considered in the following section.

27.   When instability occurs in an equity market, it is necessarily a result of a funding shock, that is, of a net withdrawal of funds of major proportions.

28.   The distinction between ex ante and ex post prudential policies is is developed in Maehara (1994, pp. 154-156).

29.   This point recalls the recent contagion among the Asian industrializing countries that were subjected to withdrawals of portfolio capital when the economy of a neighbor (Thailand) underwent an exogenous shock resulting in the depreciation of the baht. For an account of the Thai experience, see Maehara (1998).

30.   Even sovereign debt does not escape this risk.

31.   Note the potential for contagion when the value of foreign equities is sharply reduced: while the asset-holder may not be a bank the bank may find itself the indirect loser as the asset-holder may not be able to meet commitments to the bank.

32.   The most obvious evidence in support of this hypothesis is the ostensibly negative capital of eight U.S. money market banks at the time of the 1982 Latin American financial crisis. Bennett (1983) indicates that three banks had exposure to Argentina, Brazil, Chile, Mexico, and Yugoslavia in excess of 200 percent of equity.

33.   Singh (1992) argues that the existence of stock exchanges in developing countries is a second-best solution but he does not address the macro-instability implications. For a study of the potentially adverse effects of portfolio inflows, see Salehizadeh (1998).

34.   Singh (1992) calls this phenomenon "crony capitalism."

35.   See Boote and Thugge (1997) for an examination of countries that do not have access to private capital markets and which are restricted to financing through supranational institutions and government-to-government concessionary lending.

REFERENCES

Bennett, R. A. 1983. "Top Banks' Third World Loans Detailed." *New York Times*, March 18, p. D3.

Boote, A. R., and K. Thugge. 1997. "Debt Relief for Low-Income Countries: The HIPC Initiative." *International Monetary Fund Pamphlet Series No. 51*. Washington, DC.

Bryant, R. C. 1987. *International Financial Intermediation*. Washington, DC: The Brookings Institution.

Canterbery, E. R. 1998. "Irrational Exuberance and Rational Speculative Bubbles." Presidential Address given at the Annual Meetings of the International Trade and Finance Association, Atlantic City, NJ, May 29.

Eichengreen, B., and R. Portes. 1987. "The Anatomy of Financial Crisises." Pp. 10-58, in *Threats to International Financial Stability*, edited by R. Portes and A.K. Swoboda. London: Cambridge University Press.

Fischer, S. 1997. "Capital Account Liberalization and the Role of the IMF." Presented at "Asia and the IMF," Hong Kong, September.

FitzGerald, E. V. K. 1996. "Intervention versus Regulation: The Role of the IMF in Crisis Prevention and Management." *UNCTAD Discussion Paper* No. 115, May.

Gray, H. P. 1990. "A Model of Depression." *Banca Nazionale del Lavoro Quarterly Review* (September): 269-288.

Gray, H. P. 1992. "Hicksian Instability in Asset Markets and Financial Fragility." *Eastern Economic Journal* 18 (Summer): 249-258.

Gray, H. P. 1996. "The Ongoing Weakening of the Hegemonic System." *Banca Nazionale del Lavoro Quarterly Review.*

Gray, H.P. 1999. *International Economic Involvement in the New Global Economy: A Paradigm of Modern International Economics.* Copenhagen: Copenhagen Business School Press.

Gray, J. M., and H. P. Gray. 1981. "The Multinational Bank: A Financial MNC?" *Journal of Banking and Finance* 5 (March): 33-63.

Guttentag, J. M., and R. J. Herring. 1982. "The Insolvency of Financial Institutions: Assessment and Regulatory Disposition." In *Crisis in the Economic and Financial Structure*, edited by P. Wachtel. Lexington, MA: Heath Books.

Guttentag, J. M., and R. J. Herring. 1986. "Disaster Myopia in International Banking." *Princeton Essays in International Finance* (September).

Herring, R. J., and R. E. Litan. 1994. *Financial Regulation in the Global Economy.* Washington, DC: The Brookings Institutions.

Hicks, J.R. 1946. *Value and Capital.* Oxford: Oxford University Press.

Keynes, J. M. 1933. "National Self-Sufficiency." *The Yale Review* XXII (June): 755-769.

Keynes, J. M. 1973. "Newton, the Man." Pp. 363-374 in *Essays in Biography: The Collected Writings of John Maynard Keynes*, Vol. X, edited by D. Moggridge. London: Macmillan.

Leeson, N., and E. Whitley. 1997. *Rogue Trader: How I Brought Down Barings Bank and Shook the Financial World.* Boston: Little Brown and Company.

Maehara, Y. 1994. "Comment." Pp. 153-162 in *Financial Regulation in the Global Economy*, edited by R.J. Herring and R.E. Litan. Washington, DC: The Brookings Institution.

Maehara, Y. 1998. "Financial Stability in Southeast Asia." *Journal of Asian Economics* 9 (Summer): 227-236.

McDermott, D., and D. Wessel. 1997. "*Caveat* Lender: Asian Banks Contribute to a Bust in the Economic Boon." *Wall Street Journal*, October 6, p. 1.

O'Brien, D. P. 1988. "Lionel Charles Robbins, 1898-1984." *The Economic Journal* 98 (March): 104-125.

Oxelheim, L. 1996. *Financial Markets in Transition: Globalization, Investment and Economic Growth.* London: Routledge.

Salehizadeh, M. 1998. "Financial Flows to Mexico: Implications for Foreign Investors." *The International Trade Journal* XII (Spring): 23-48.

Salvatore, D. 1998. "Capital Flows, Current Account Deficits, and Financial Crises in Emerging Market Economies." *The International Trade Journal* XII (Spring): 5-22.

Singh, A. 1992. "The Stock Market and Economic Development: Should Developing Countries Encourage Stock Markets? *UNCTAD Discussion Papers*, No. 49, Geneva.

Smith, R. C., and I. Walter. 1997. *Global Banking.* New York: Oxford University Press.

Tversky, A., and D. Kahneman. 1982. "Judgement under Uncertainty: Heuristics and Biases." Pp. 3-22 in *Judgement under Uncertainty: Heuristics and Biases*, edited by D. Kahneman, P. Slovic and A. Tversky. New York: Cambridge University Press.

Waldman, P., and P. M. Scherer. 1997. "Hi-Tech Trauma: A Company's Travails show why the Economy in Thailand is Shot." *Wall Street Journal*, September, 8, p. 1.

[6]

CURRENCIES, CRISES, AND CRASHES

Peter B. Kenen
Princeton University

INTRODUCTION

Last year, I agreed to write a monograph reviewing recent efforts to reform the international financial system—the so-called architecture exercise. To prepare for that task, I spent some months reading the descriptive and analytic literature on recent currency crises, especially the Mexican crisis of 1994-95 and the Asian crisis of 1997-98. Tonight, I want to share with you some of what I learned about those crises and the best responses to them. Before doing that, however, I want to share with you some of my concerns about the way in which many of our colleagues have gone about modeling those crises and other complex events.

Rigorous theoretical work must always begin with a stylized representation of the events we seek to explain. We must suppress or simplify a welter of detail in order to focus on a manageable number of institutional arrangements and behavioral relationships. The usefulness of our subsequent work, however, will depend crucially on the quality of the stylized representation that emerges from that process. If we abstract from key features of the situation or episode we want to explain, we cannot expect to shed much light on it.

Unfortunately, many of our colleagues devote too little effort to that vital task. Some seem quite content to adopt someone else's stylized representation, because they are eager to pursue their main objective—showing that they can devise a more rigorous or parsimonious explanation for that same stylized representation. Others devise their own stylized representations but appear to base them on a quick reading of the handiest materials instead of immersing themselves thoroughly in the most authoritative sources.

You should perhaps bear in mind that I am not the best judge of the current literature. Some of it, indeed, lies beyond my grasp. Unlike many of my colleagues, I did not major in mathematics. When I was a graduate student at Harvard, we were allowed to substitute proficiency in mathematics for a second foreign language, and the requisite level of mathematical proficiency was ludicrously low by present-day standards. As I was reluctant to take the time to learn a second foreign language, I decided to try the mathematics exam. When the results were posted, I was heard to exclaim, "Wow. I passed." But Bob Dorfman, who set the exam, overheard me and corrected me. "You didn't pass," he said. "We passed you." Nevertheless, I am still usually able to cull from a fairly abstruse algebraic exercise the stylized facts on which it was based. And I am distressed by what I have found. Without naming names, let me cite three examples.

Peter Kenen: Department of Economics, Fisher Hall, Princeton University, Princeton, NJ 08544. E-mail: pbkenen@princeton.edu. This article is based upon the Presidential Address given by Peter Kenen on February 23, 2001 at the 27th Annual Eastern Economic Association Conference in New York, NY.

Eastern Economic Journal, Vol. 28, No. 1, Winter 2002

One key characteristic of the Asian crisis was the extent to which Asian banks and firms had built up huge foreign-currency debts in the years before the crisis but had not hedged their foreign-currency exposure. When creditors began to demand repayment, debtors had either to buy foreign currency or default on their debts. There was therefore a large, inelastic demand for foreign currency at the start of the crisis, which explains why the Asian currencies depreciated hugely when they were set free to float. Yet one leading paper on the Asian crisis assumes that private-sector debt was denominated mainly in domestic currency.

Another recent paper got that fact right, but the author could not explain why Asian banks and firms did not hedge their foreign-currency exposure. One must conclude, he said, that there were no forward foreign-exchange markets for the Asian currencies. Had he read the descriptive literature on the Asian crisis, he would have known that the Thai central bank intervened massively on the forward foreign-exchange market in the run-up to the crisis. In fact, it encumbered almost all of its reserves by selling dollars forward. Hence, there must have been a market.

A third well-known paper asserts quite rightly that a central bank cannot serve as a lender of last resort to its country's banks without printing money and thus risking inflation and currency depreciation. And the same problem arises, it says, when a government seeks to recapitalize its country's banks, because it risks running a big budget deficit and having to print money in order to finance it. The paper goes on to assert, however, that the International Monetary Fund (IMF) can perform those tasks without raising the money supply of the country involved. Therefore, it says, the IMF should provide large-scale financing to countries that experience banking crises, as that is the only way to resolve those crises without risking inflation and currency depreciation. Last year, I quoted this assertion on the final exam in an undergraduate course on international monetary economics and asked the students to refute it. To give them a hint, I told them to follow an IMF loan from the Fund itself to a country's banking system, using simple T-accounts, and most of them did that correctly. They showed that the loan must go through the books of the central banks on its way to the stricken commercial banks and will therefore raise the money supply.

All of us know that graduate students have to impress potential employers with their analytic skills. But I wish we had some way to insist that they acquire command of the facts before choosing the stylized facts they want to explain. To do that, of course, they must read the relevant descriptive literature, which means that we must assign it, even if we have to read some of that dull stuff ourselves. And let us then judge the quality of their analytic work—and that of the job-market candidates who pass through our institutions—by asking how well they have posed the questions they seek to answer. We should not be content to ask whether they have used the best technique or definition of equilibrium to derive their answers.

So much for my state of mind. I turn now to the state of the world and, in particular, the state of the international financial system in the wake of the recent crises. I will deal with three questions: What was different about the recent crises, compared to earlier crises? What was different about the official response to those crises? What should be done differently to cope with future crises?

KEY CHARACTERISTICS OF THE RECENT CRISES

The title of this paper is borrowed from the title of a book by Paul Krugman—*Currencies and Crises*. I have added "crashes" not merely to avoid outright plagiarism but because the recent crises did indeed lead to crashes. There were, in fact, three sorts of crashes.

First, currencies crashed when they were set free to float. The Mexican peso, Thai baht, Malaysian ringgit, and Korean won lost half their dollar values in a matter of weeks. The Indonesian rupiah fell even farther when that country's currency crisis was compounded by a political crisis. But political uncertainties also played a significant role in the Mexican, Thai, and Korean crises. Stephen Haggard [2000] provides a fascinating account of the interactions between economics and politics in the Asian crisis. Second, domestic credit flows imploded when the currency crises triggered banking crises. Finally, capital formation contracted sharply when credit flows imploded, and that caused output to fall steeply.

I have already mentioned the most important reason for the currency crashes. They cannot be blamed on hedge funds or other greedy predators—the villains conjured up by Mahathir Mohamed to explain Malaysia's plight. They were due to the large, inelastic demand for foreign currency coming from domestic banks and firms having large foreign-currency debts. If greed played a role in the Asian crisis, it was the greed of Asian banks and firms that took on those huge debts in order to finance their participation in the building boom and property bubble that led up to the Asian crisis. Once the crisis struck, it was not greed but fear that caused the currency crashes.

In the Thai case, foreign creditors fled because the creditworthiness of the Thai banks had been impaired by the collapse of the boom and bubble, and when the foreign creditors fled, those to whom they had lent so freely had to buy dollars to pay off their debts. As soon as the baht collapsed, moreover, the creditors of other Asian countries began to run down their claims, because those countries' banks and firms were seen to be equally vulnerable. The Thai currency crisis was the result of an incipient banking crisis. Elsewhere, however, especially in Indonesia, the banking crises were the result of the currency crises. And the currency crises were due in turn to a self-fulfilling creditor panic, as rational defensive behavior by individual creditors led to the very catastrophe that each of those creditors feared.

In the Mexican case, by contrast, the foreign-currency debt of the private sector played a secondary role in producing the currency crisis, although it helped to produce the subsequent credit crunch and the resulting fall in output. It was, instead, the foreign-currency debt of the Mexican government—the large stock of so-called *tesobonos*—that played the main role in the critical phase of the Mexican crisis. There was a self-fulfilling creditor panic, but it reflected the creditors' fear that the Mexican government would default on the *tesobonos*. And Mexico was perilously to default on the eve of the rescue mounted by the U.S. Treasury and the IMF.

The IMF is often blamed for the subsequent implosion of domestic credit in the Asian countries—the cause of the crash in investment and output. The Fund's critics charge that it forced the Asian countries to pursue orthodox policies under conditions that really called for unorthodox policies—reflation rather than deflation. Alan Blinder [1999], Paul Krugman [1998], Jeff Sachs [1997], and Joe Stiglitz [1999] took this line at one time or another. The implosion of domestic credit, they said, was due to the tightening of monetary policy favored by the Fund, and the sharp drop in output was due to the tightening of fiscal policy, as well as the implosion of domestic credit. There is some truth to these charges, but three points must be made.

First, the tightening of monetary policies was initiated by the Asian countries themselves, not at the behest of the IMF, in an effort to stabilize their countries' currencies. Furthermore, the tightening was not severe. The Fund did insist that Indonesia's central bank adopt a much tighter monetary policy, but that was after the Bank Indonesia had injected huge amounts of liquidity into the banking system to rescue several banks that were tottering at the brink of insolvency, and prices were rising rapidly as the rupiah plummeted [Lane et al., 1999].

Second, the tightening of fiscal policy was aimed at releasing real resources to exploit the expenditure-switching effects of the currency depreciations. It derived from the belief that the endogenous effects of the crisis would not have large output-reducing effects. In one case, indeed, it derived from the insistence of the country's own government that output would rise, not fall; on that optimistic supposition, a significant contraction of domestic expenditure would have been needed to exploit the export opportunities afforded by the depreciation of the country's currency. The Fund revised its fiscal targets for the crisis-stricken countries as soon as it became apparent that output was falling rapidly in those countries, that tax revenues were thus falling too, and that the countries could not meet the Fund's initial fiscal targets without raising taxes or slashing government spending. As output continued to fall, moreover, the Fund urged the Asian countries to shift sharply toward fiscal expansion, and it criticized one Asian country for failing to follow the Fund's advice that it should raise government spending.

Third, the critics of IMF orthodoxy pay too little attention to the principal cause of the sharp fall in output during the Asian crisis. The tightening of Asian monetary policies was partly responsible for the collapse of domestic lending that led to the fall in investment and output, but it was not the main villain. The credit crunch was due mainly to the depreciations of the Asian currencies. These had the effect of raising hugely the domestic-currency values of Asia's large foreign-currency debts and the domestic-currency cost of servicing those debts. They had disastrous balance-sheet effects on Asian banks and firms. Insolvent lenders faced insolvent borrowers, and credit flows imploded. It is easy to show, moreover, that the resulting fall in investment was the main cause of the fall in output.

IMPLICIT GUARANTEES, CRONY CAPITALISM, AND ALL THAT

Many accounts of the Asian crisis have blamed it on the implicit guarantees that the Asian governments gave their banks and firms and to the contingent liabilities arising from those guarantees. Michael Dooley [2000], for example, says that the Asian crisis had to occur as soon as the governments' contingent liabilities came to exceed the governments' assets. Craig Burnside, Martin Eichenbaum, and Sergio Rebello

[1998] say that the crisis had to occur as soon as it became apparent that the Asian governments could not honor their contingent liabilities without running large budget deficits and would then have to monetize those deficits, causing domestic inflation and currency depreciation.

These are elegant models, in that they appear to explain both the cause and the timing of the Asian crisis. But they are much too neat. They are based on factoids, not stylized facts. Both models imply that the foreign creditors of Asian banks and firms should have seen the crisis coming. But the pre-crisis behavior of capital inflows, equity prices, and other variables suggest that the crisis was unanticipated. True, the problems of Thailand built up steadily in 1996-97, and the baht began to weaken several months before the onset of the crisis in mid-1997. But the other countries' problems erupted abruptly, when foreign investors and others realized suddenly that those countries looked like Thailand in several distressing respects.

Furthermore, both models imply that foreign investors and others were able to add up the implicit guarantees given by the governments of the Asian countries and could therefore calculate the governments' contingent liabilities. But that was impossible, because of the heterogeneity of the guarantees. Some of the implicit guarantees had obvious cash values, but others did not. What baht or dollar value would one attach to the implicit promise that troubled banks would not be closed when they were truly insolvent? What baht or dollar value would one attach to an implicit promise of more "directed lending" to a troubled company?

It makes more sense to treat these and other guarantees, and "crony capitalism" generally, as having contributed importantly to the vulnerability of the Asian countries and to the intensity of the Asian crisis once it was quite clear that the guarantees would not be honored fully. And blame for the crisis itself should be pinned on the creditor panic triggered by the incipient financial-sector crisis in Thailand and propagated thereafter by the unusually heavy dependence of Asian banks and firms on foreign-currency debt. As for the buildup of that debt, it must be blamed on the serious mistake made by many emerging-market countries in the 1990s—the rush to liberalize and open up the financial sector without paying sufficient attention to the corresponding need for strong prudential supervision.

THE POLICY RESPONSE

I have already discussed the orthodox aspects of the IMF response to the Asian crisis. Let me turn now to the unorthodox aspects—the large number and heterogeneity of the policy conditions attached to the use of IMF credit, and the size of the financial packages assembled by the IMF.

All of the crisis-stricken Asian countries were obliged to adopt far-reaching financial-sector reforms, not just those required immediately to repair the damage done to their banking systems by the crisis itself. Furthermore, they had to commit themselves to many other reforms that had no obvious bearing on their prospects for recovery. Indonesia was made to eliminate food subsidies and raise the prices of several food products, cut its import tariffs, discontinue the various privileges granted to the National Car, lift restrictions on foreign investment in several sectors, and abolish domestic monopolies, such as those dealing in garlic and cloves. Korea was made to rescind prohibitions on the foreign ownership of financial institutions, halt directed lending by Korean banks, and liberalize trade with Japan. In fact, the number of so-called structural conditions contained in these two programs exceeded the number contained in the typical IMF program for a transition economy—one that was seeking to switch all the way from plan to market.

After the Mexican crisis, emerging-market countries and their foreign creditors were warned that they should not expect the official community to provide large-scale financing of the sort that Mexico received in 1995. A report endorsed by the governments of the major industrial countries put the point bluntly:

> ... neither debtor countries nor their creditors should expect to be insulated from adverse financial consequences by the provision of large scale official financing in the event of a crisis. Markets are equipped, or should be equipped, to assess the risks involved in lending to sovereign borrowers and to set the prices and other terms of the instruments accordingly. There should be no presumption that any type of debt will be exempt from payments suspensions or restructurings in the event of a future sovereign liquidity crisis [Group of 10, 1996].

In 1997, however, the IMF assembled $17 billion in official financing for Thailand, $36 billion for Indonesia, and $58 billion for Korea. The contributors included the IMF itself, the World Bank and Asian Development Bank, and various national governments. It must be noted, however, that the amounts of financing made available up front were far smaller than these numbers.

There were two reasons for this difference. The first was the ordinary practice of the IMF, which doles out its financing in quarterly installments, in order to monitor and guarantee compliance with the various policy conditions attached to that financing. The second was the novel practice of combining IMF funding with bilateral funding. In the Thai case, the bilateral funding was disbursed in tandem with IMF funding. In the Korean case, however, it was set aside as a "second line" of defense. Hence, Korea could not use it, even in December 1998, when Korea ran out reserves and had used up all of the money that was currently available from the IMF. At the end of March 1999, Thailand had drawn down $13 billion of its $17 billion package, but Korea had drawn down only $28 billion of its $58 billion package. In short, the official community relied primarily on adjustment and only secondarily on financing in its attempt to cope with the Asian crisis.

What was the rationale for this strategy? There was, of course, the usual concern about moral hazard—that large-scale official financing would encourage both creditors and debtors to behave imprudently. But that was not the main concern that shaped the official response to the Asian crisis. The IMF did not interpret the Asian crisis as a pure creditor panic. If creditors fled, they had good reason—the deep-seated structural defects of the Asian economies. Therefore, the Fund concluded, foreign investors would not return and capital inflows would not resume until the Asian countries had displayed their willingness to correct those defects, especially flaws in the financial sector.

Nevertheless, the IMF believed that they could do that quickly, so that exchange rates and output would stabilize quickly, even though capital inflows might not resume immediately. In other words, the Fund expected a rapid revival of confidence, thanks to its own intervention—the policy commitments it extracted from the Asian governments and the financing they would obtain if they fulfilled those commitments. In addition, the Fund—and most of the rest of us—expected the depreciations of the Asian currencies to do what the textbooks predict: raise exports, reduce imports, and thus raise total output, as well as improve the trade balance. By running trade surpluses, moreover, the Asian countries would be protected from any delay in the revival of capital inflows, and that would minimize their need for large-scale official financing. There was indeed a remarkable shift in the trade balances of the Asian countries; they ran large trade surpluses in 1998. But not for the predicted reason. There was no significant increase in exports, but there was a very large decrease in imports, due to the fall in Asian output caused by the balance-sheet effects of the currency depreciations. I have described this elsewhere as "dysfunctional" adjustment [Kenen, 2000].

Taken as a whole, the strategy adopted by the IMF seems to have been built on precarious premises. It assumed that orthodox policy changes and far-reaching structural reforms could be implemented promptly and would restore confidence quickly, so that capital outflows would cease. Hence, modest amounts of up-front financing would be sufficient to achieve and sustain exchange-rate stability. This strategy could have worked if these suppositions had been satisfied, but it was apt to fail if anything went wrong—and something was bound to go wrong. That's Murphy's Law. If governments procrastinated, and they did, the restoration of confidence would be delayed, and it was. If confidence was not restored quickly, capital outflows would continue, and the amount of financing provided would then be too small to keep the Asian currencies from depreciating further.

The Fund's insistence on far-reaching structural reform during the crisis itself may have made matters worse by convincing panicky creditors that the Asian crisis was due to deep-seated structural flaws that had to be corrected promptly. Because they were not corrected promptly, confidence was not restored. The Fund was quite right to insist that some things be done quickly. Insolvent banks had to be closed or recapitalized, and plans to deal with corporate debts had to be devised, even if they could not be implemented speedily. By calling for other reforms, however, such as trade liberalization, removing restrictions on the foreign ownership of domestic banks, and abolishing domestic monopolies, the Fund may have undermined its own strategy by implying that all of these tasks were essential to resolve the Asian crisis.

By insisting on those reforms, moreover, the Fund created uncertainty about the amounts of official financing that would be available to the crisis-stricken countries. There is a strong case for doling out IMF credit in tranches. If all of it were made available immediately, the Fund would have no way to penalize a government that reneged on its commitments. To put the point differently, the tranching of IMF credit enhances the credibility of a government's policy commitments and, to that extent, may actually contribute to the restoration of confidence. But the availability of IMF credit is itself important for restoring confidence. It is not meant merely to buy time for policy changes to take hold and capital inflows to resume. It has a key role to play in arresting a capital outflow due to a loss of confidence.

There is, admittedly, an inherent conflict between two sensible objectives. The need to ensure compliance with policy commitments calls for the gradual, conditional disbursement of IMF credit, but the need for exchange-rate stabilization and the restoration of creditor confidence call for reliable up-front financing. At the margin, however, the conflict should be resolved in favor of up-front financing. In "modern" crises, involving large capital outflows, rather than "old-fashioned" crises, involving large current-account deficits, it is hard to estimate the so-called financing gap and thus ascertain the amount of financing required to buy time for resolving a crisis. The size of the financing gap will depend on the size of the subsequent capital outflow, which will in turn depend on the amount of financing provided. But the larger the amount of up-front financing, the smaller the risk of a continuing capital outflow. Therefore, front-loading can actually reduce the total amount of financing required. Fortunately, the Fund has moved in this direction. It adopted a more openhanded stance in the Brazilian crisis of 1998-99 than in the Asian crisis of 1997-98, and it has gone on doing that.

WHAT SHOULD BE DONE IN THE FUTURE

The Fund has drawn several lessons from the Asian crisis. In addition to providing more up-front financing, it has concluded that the scope of conditionality should indeed be limited. The Fund should not insist opportunistically on far-reaching structural reforms. It should limit itself to the policy changes and structural reforms that are deemed essential to cope with a crisis [IMF, 2001]. There is no consensus, however, not in the official community nor among academic economists, concerning the appropriate scale of IMF financing, and there is still a striking disjuncture between official rhetoric and official practice.

Every official communiqué says that large-scale financing should be provided only in truly exceptional circumstances. Nevertheless, "systemically important" countries appear to receive it routinely, including, most recently, Argentina and Turkey. Smaller countries, by contrast, have been denied large-scale financing and have therefore been forced to restructure their external debts. Ukraine, Pakistan, and Ecuador provide recent examples.

Some of the Fund's critics, moreover, want it to adopt a wholly different strategy. Last year, an advisory commission appointed by the U.S. Congress and chaired by Allen Meltzer issued a report that called for a radical transformation of the Fund's mandate [International Financial Institution Advisory Commission, 2000]. As a national central bank cannot create foreign currency, it cannot serve as a lender of last resort to its banking system when foreign creditors panic and run down their foreign-currency claims on the banking system. Therefore, the IMF should serve as the lender of last resort to countries that have sound banking systems but are nevertheless beset by creditor panics. But now comes the really radical part. The Fund should do nothing else. It should not provide financing to countries afflicted by sovereign debt problems, adverse shifts in their terms of trade, or any other sort of balance-of-payments problem. Had this been its mandate in the 1990s, the Fund could not have come to the aid of Mexico, which could not roll over the *tesobonos*; it could not have come to the aid of Thailand, Indonesia, or Korea, which did not have sound banking systems. Thereafter, moreover, it would have been barred from assisting Brazil or Argentina, which had debt-related problems rather than banking-sector problems.

Others, including Stanley Fischer [2000], former first deputy managing director of the IMF, believe that the Fund can function as a lender of last resort, but not in the very restrictive sense proposed by the Meltzer report. They acknowledge the flaws in the analogy between the IMF and an international central bank. The Fund cannot create money; it cannot close down a country in the same way that a central bank can close down a commercial bank; and it cannot engage in anything like prudential supervision of its members' policies. Nevertheless, they favor large-scale official financing for countries that suffer reversals in capital flows like those that hit the Asian countries in 1997-98.

There is, however, another approach—which is the approach I favor. The IMF should always provide "bridge financing" to countries with balance-of-payments problems, regardless of the reasons for them, and it should be prepared to provide larger amounts of financing to countries with open capital markets. But it should not attempt to function as a lender of last resort—to furnish financing sufficiently large to offset a creditor panic fully. It must not relieve private creditors of the need to assess risks soberly. It must not relieve member governments of the obligation to strengthen their banking systems, undertake adequate prudential supervision, and follow appropriate policies— especially debt and exchange-rate policies. When creditor panics occur, moreover, the governments of the debtor countries must be prepared to suspend their debt payments, including those of the private sector, and then to engage their creditors in the restructuring of their debt payments.

There has been much talk about the need to involve the private sector in the resolution of emerging-market crises. That will not happen, however, until the official community has shown that it is prepared to withhold large-scale official financing from "systemically important" countries. Furthermore, the official community must cease to insist that countries resolve their debt problems in a market-friendly manner. In early 1998, foreign banks agreed to roll over their short-term claims on Korean banks and agreed thereafter to convert those claims into long-term claims. But that debt settlement was far from voluntary. The governments and central banks of the major industrial countries applied enormous pressure to their own countries' banks. In other cases, moreover, where no such pressure was applied, debtor countries had to "bribe" their creditors by offering very attractive terms to those who agreed to roll over their claims. They bought immediate relief but will have to pay for it later. Argentina affords the most recent example.

I have set out elsewhere [Kenen, 2001] the case for a more "coercive" approach to the resolution of debt problems—those arising from creditor panics and those that occur when a country has managed to run up an unsustainable debt burden. I have also sought to answer those who oppose that approach. Let me deal briefly here with two of their objections.

Some critics say that the threat of a mandatory standstill will serve merely to accelerate the creditors' rush for the exit [Fischer, 1999; Lipton, 2000]. An IMF paper on the subject goes so far as to say that this is the test by which all such proposals must be judged [IMF, 2000]. Experience to date, however, suggests that a "voluntary" rollover of debt cannot be achieved until reluctant creditors have already left or have run down their claims to levels at which they are willing to roll them over. That was true even in the Korean case. There is thus no way to know *a priori* which will provoke the more drastic reduction in foreign creditors' claims—the threat of a mandatory standstill or the run-down that must often occur before foreign creditors will be content to engage in a voluntary rollover.

Some critics say a mandatory standstill will lead to litigation—that there is no feasible way of protecting debtor countries from lawsuits by their creditors when the debtors suspend their debt payments. This is a serious objection, but there is an answer—adding a standstill clause to all debt contracts, or to the subset of contracts involving foreign-currency debt. This approach was suggested by Canada's finance minister, Paul Martin [1998], and was also mentioned in the report of a working group set up under the auspices of the U.S. Treasury:

> It is also worth considering the addition of options to sovereign bonds and interbank credit lines that would allow a debtor government or debtor banks to extend the maturity of a bond or credit line for a specified period of time at a predetermined spread. Such options could be exercised to ease pressure on the government and the banking system in the event of a liquidity crisis. Such provisions could have an effect opposite to the effect of the put options that have been exercised in certain recent crises. These put options have reduced the maturity of various credits and thus exacerbated market pressures [Group of 22, 1998].

A similar suggestion was made by Willem Buiter and Anne Sibert [1999], and I have proposed a variant of the Buiter-Sibert scheme [Kenen, 2001]. Under all of these proposals, creditors entering into a debt contract having a rollover option or buying a bond with a rollover option could not sue a debtor who exercised the option; they would have consented implicitly to the resulting suspension of debt-service payments when they agreed to the terms of the contract or bought the bond having the rollover option.

The governments of emerging-market countries would, I am sure, be reluctant to include rollover options in their own securities or require their inclusion in private-sector contracts. Furthermore, it would take time to build those options into the whole stock of emerging-market debt. Therefore, it may be necessary for the IMF to warn that it will cease to provide large amounts of official financing to governments that have not adopted these options by some deadline date. In fact, the Fund should eventually set out a comprehensive set of preconditions that governments must meet in order to qualify for anything more than modest amounts of bridge financing. Although I have not discussed all of them here, let me list them briefly:

- It should have subscribed to the IMF's Special Data Dissemination Standard (SDDS) and be meeting its main requirements, especially those pertaining to the reporting of reserves, reserve-related liabilities, and the external position of the country's private sector.

- It should have invited the IMF and World Bank to conduct an assessment of its domestic financial sector and, if advised to do so, have entered into a long-term contract with those institutions, committing itself to specific reforms aimed at reducing its vulnerability to future financial crises.

- It should have introduced so-called collective action clauses into its government's foreign-currency bonds, so as to facilitate negotiations with its private-sector creditors in the event of a future debt-related crisis.

- It should have adopted legislation requiring the inclusion of 90-day rollover options in all foreign-currency obligations, public and private, and adopted the procedures required to trigger the exercise of those options.

Countries that fail to meet these preconditions might nevertheless receive large-scale official financing, but only if the Fund's Executive Board decides by a large super-majority that a refusal to provide large-scale financing would put other countries at serious risk or impair the functioning of international financial markets.

Regular reliance on large-scale financing—trying to make the Fund into a lender of last resort—would be counterproductive. It would perpetuate imprudent behavior by private-sector lenders and discourage the governments of emerging-market countries from adopting appropriate policies and the long-run reforms required for them to take proper advantage of the opportunities afforded by active participation in international capital markets. Crisis financing cannot buy far-reaching structural reforms, but those reforms are urgently needed in many emerging-market countries.

REFERENCES

Blinder, A. S. Eight Steps to a New Financial Order. *Foreign Affairs*, September/October 1999, 50-63.

Buiter, W., and Sibert, A. C. UDROP: A Contribution to the New International Financial Architecture. *International Finance*, July 1999, 227-47.

Burnside, C., Eichenbaum, M., and Rebello, S. Prospective Deficits and the Asian Currency Crisis. Working Paper 6758. Cambridge: National Bureau of Economic Research, 1998.

Dooley, M. P. A Model of Crises in Emerging Markets. *Economic Journal*, January 2000, 256-72.

Fischer, S. Reforming the International Financial System. *Economic Journal*, November 1999, F557-76.

_____. *On the Need for an International Lender of Last Resort.* Essays in International Economics 220. Princeton: International Economics Section, Princeton University, 2000.

Group of 10. *The Resolution of Sovereign Liquidity Crises: A Report to the Ministers and Governors.* Washington: International Monetary Fund, 1996.

Group of 22. *Report of the Working Group on International Financial Crises.* Washington: Group of 22, 1998.

Haggard, S. *The Political Economy of the Asian Financial Crisis.* Washington: Institute for International Economics, 2000.

International Financial Institution Advisory Commission. *Report.* Washington: U.S. Congress, 2000.

International Monetary Fund. *Involving the Private Sector in the Resolution of Financial Crises—Standstills—Preliminary Considerations.* Washington: International Monetary Fund, 2000.

_____. Streamlining Structural Conditionality in Fund-Supported Programs: Interim Guidance Note. Washington: International Monetary Fund, 2001.

Kenen, P. B. On Dysfunctional Adjustment and Financing, in *Reforming the International Monetary and Financial System*, edited by P. B. Kenen and A. K. Swoboda. Washington: International Monetary Fund, 2000.

_____. *The International Financial Architecture: What's New? What's Missing?* Washington: Institute for International Economics, 2001.

Krugman, P. The Confidence Game. *The New Republic*, October 1998.

Lane, T. , Ghosh, A., Hamann, J., Phillips, S., Schultze-Ghattas, M., and Tsikata, T. *IMF-Supported Programs in Indonesia, Korea, and Thailand: A Preliminary Assessment.* Occasional Paper No. 178. Washington: International Monetary Fund, 1999.

Lipton, D. A Refocusing of the Role of the International Monetary Fund, in *Reforming the International Monetary and Financial System*, edited by P. B. Kenen and A. K. Swoboda. Washington: International Monetary Fund, 2000.

Martin, P. *Remarks to the Commonwealth Business Forum.* Ottawa: Finance Canada, September 29, 1998.

Sachs, J. The Wrong Medicine for Asia. *The New York Times*, November 3, 1997.

Stiglitz, J. Must Financial Crises Be This Frequent and This Painful? in *The Asian Financial Crisis: Causes, Contagion and Consequences,* edited by P.R. Agénor, M. Miller, D. Vines, and A. Weber. Cambridge: Cambridge University Press, 1999.

[7]

GLOBALIZATION AND THE WORLD OF FINANCE

Paul A. Volcker

It is a special honor and challenge to speak before you in the presence of the man who inspired this annual Hutchinson Lecture, a man I know is much revered on this campus.

I confess it is quite a while since I have read a textbook on money and banking, but I could not resist seeing how Professor Hutchinson might have graded my performance as Federal Reserve Chairman. I discovered what tens of thousands of students must already know: he wrote with great clarity and conciseness about the theory and practice of monetary policy. But I have to tell you he wasn't big on personalities. I did find my name in two rather obscure footnotes dealing with abstruse matters of banking supervision—nothing to justify this Lecture, much less an honorary degree.

One other thing, more relevant to my comments this morning, struck me when looking through the book (at least the fifth, mid-1980s edition). Typical of most textbooks of that time, and of most monetary policy-making to this day, the concentration was heavily on domestic matters. My theme today is that day is passing. I will put the point as simply and as provocatively as I can: Full participation in the world of global finance simply isn't consistent with independent monetary policies by independent nations.

Globalization is a rather ugly five-syllable word that has reached into our daily vocabulary. Ugly or not, it describes a phenomenon that isn't going to go away. That's fundamentally a matter of technology. When it is possible to communicate and to transact business around the world so conveniently, so economically, and so rapidly, the urge to do business is irresistible. Governments can try to slow it down. But that's increasingly difficult to do without a network of controls so intrusive as to imply insulation from the benefits of participation in the global economy. The fact of the matter, of course, is that with the demise of the Soviet Union and the triumph of the ideology of global capitalism, there are very few countries that have any desire to opt for economic isolation.

The benefits of free international trade have long been evident in practice as well as theory. It is not possible, for instance, to think that the "Asian Tigers" of Korea, Taiwan, Hong Kong or Singapore could have reached such high levels of income so rapidly except through trade. Most of the other countries of Southeast Asia and China itself, have gained enormously from access to the markets of the developed world, as we have benefitted from the competition and cheap imports.

The freeing of financial markets in the emerging world, and even in some of the advanced countries of Europe, is more recent, in large part a phenomenon of the

Paul A. Volcker: 610 5th Avenue, Suite 420, New York, NY 10020.

Eastern Economic Journal, Vol. 28, No. 1, Winter 2002

1990s. It is a development that has been strongly urged and welcomed by most economists, political leaders, and certainly Western financial institutions. The theoretical
logic has seemed compelling. Perhaps more to the point, the perception is that there
is money to be made. The analysis is straightforward. Capital would flow to the areas
of the highest potential return. Emerging economies with abundant and disciplined
labor, often with large natural resources, and a growing base of skills and education
would be prime beneficiaries in terms of economic growth. The gains would be shared
with the investors, and by all of us who benefit from reduced costs and competition.

For a little while, it seemed to work that way. Here in the Western Hemisphere in
the early 1990s, Mexico and Argentina were big gainers, and East Asia attracted
increasing amounts of capital, helping to finance an investment boom. Private flows
to those areas widely exceeded official aid and finance to the point that some began to
question the relevance of the World Bank and other official lenders.

But then, quite suddenly, something funny happened on the way to success. First
in Mexico, and a couple of years later in East Asia, we learned again a lesson as old as
capitalism itself. For all their enormous and really irreplaceable benefits, financial
markets are volatile. It's not a phenomenon limited to weak emerging economies.
We've had a little taste of it in the bubble and subsequent humbling of NASDAQ
recently—and more importantly in our own banking and savings and loan crises a
decade ago. You will recall much more recently the concerns expressed about the
potential fragility of American financial markets in 1998, in the backwash of the Asian
and Russian crises.

But what we found so clearly in the latter half of the 1990s is that those countries
that presumably would be the prime beneficiaries of global finance were in fact in the
greatest jeopardy. Countries like Thailand, Indonesia, Malaysia and others that had
for decades experienced extremely high annual rates of economic growth of as much
as 7 or 8 or 9 percent compounded, countries that were praised for stabilizing prices
and ending budget deficits, were suddenly plunged into deep recession. Recovery has
been uneven. Even now, none have returned to the trend line of growth established in
the 1980s and early 1990s.

The obvious difficulty has been the shocks associated with enormous exchange
rate instability and related gyrations in interest rates. The result in emerging country after country was the virtual destruction of domestic banking systems. In some
cases, there was a strong inflationary impulse and strong budgetary pressures. Those
financial strains and disturbances have been inconsistent with sustained economic
growth.

The common reaction among officials and financial market participants alike has
been to view this all as temporary, a sort of learning process, a transitional stage to
the brighter future promised by orthodox analysis. In particular, the instinct has
been to point to institutional weaknesses in the emerging nations themselves.

- Banking systems have lacked adequate capital, effective supervision, and experience in risk management.
- Accounting systems are primitive and auditing weak, with lack of transparency.
- Business practices are poorly developed, and corruption is rife.

GLOBALIZATION AND THE WORLD OF FINANCE   15

As time has passed, there has been a certain amount of introspection as well. How is it that large and sophisticated financial institutions in the developed world—with state of the art regulation, model systems of risk management and the rule of law— permitted themselves to get so exposed to structurally weak emerging economies that their own stability was jeopardized? Much effort is underway to review capital standards, to develop and enforce more uniform accounting practices, and to search for better risk management techniques.

Now, I don't want to question the relevance of all that. After all, I spent most of my life concerned with questions of financial regulation and supervision. I am a believer. It is also true that my professional life extends back over half a century. And as Yogi Berra once said, "you can observe quite a lot just by watching." It is precisely that experience that has made me skeptical—skeptical to the point of disbelief—that the intellectual and official analysis of the recent financial crises has been at all adequate.

It may be comfortable for us in the developed world to think that weaknesses peculiar to Asian or Latin American institutions, or lapses in the supervision of our own institutions, were the essence of the crises we have seen in the last half of the 1990s. But if that was true, how do we explain that most of those Asian economies had sustained such high growth rates long before their financial markets were opened?

I referred earlier to the fact that we had banking and savings and loan crises in the United States itself in the 1980s and early 1990s. Not so many years ago, the Scandinavian countries experienced the virtual bankruptcy of their banking system, and we read almost every day about the seemingly endless travails of the Japanese banks. It is an interesting and, I think, significant fact that those financial crises in the developed world have not had the devastating effects on economic stability and growth that have been characteristic of the emerging world.

How do we explain the difference? What strikes me about the emerging nations as much as their institutional weaknesses is a fact so obvious that we overlook the implications. Their financial institutions and markets are small—tiny on a world scale. Typically, their *entire* financial system is composed of institutions that in the aggregate amount to only a fraction of the size of a *single one* of the large financial institutions in the developed world, for some countries only a small fraction. A single regional bank in the United States is apt to have more assets or deposits than all the banks in most of the countries of South America or Southeast Asia. And I would point out those regional institutions in the United States or Europe are rapidly consolidating, for fear that they are too small to compete effectively in turbulent world markets.

The clear implication is that the emerging markets and their institutions are particularly vulnerable to the sometimes abrupt shifts of sentiment and funds characteristic of open markets. I liken it to sailing a small boat in the ocean: when the winds begin to blow, the Coast Guard properly sends out *small* craft warnings; only an extreme storm would concern the Queen Elizabeths of the world.

We've seen enough over the years to realize the pattern is repetitive. The strong potential of a high growth, reasonably managed emerging market attracts foreign funds. More lenders and investors enter with funds that may be marginal from their individual point of view. But cumulatively these same funds are large relative to the size of the emerging economy and its banking system. At first markets boom, interest rates are held down, the exchange rate is relatively strong, and growth is enhanced. But sooner or later, something happens—a growing sense of inflationary and balance of payments pressures, perhaps the perception of political instability. Sentiment changes and funds flow out even faster than they entered. Interest rates soar, and the exchange rate may drop by 20 or 30 or even 50 percent or more in a matter of weeks. Official rescue efforts may or may not mitigate the crisis. But typically the economic damage is severe.

The lesson I draw is not that we can or should draw back from global markets: the potential for enhancing growth is real and the technological forces driving the process are too strong to resist. But neither, in my judgment, can we sit back and assume that events, and the efforts of individual countries, will take care of themselves. What is at issue here is whether a world of global finance will in practice bear out the rhetoric about the glories of free markets. Obviously a lot is at stake, politically as well economically, in the answer to that question.

Well, what to do? Slowly, there is greater recognition that the question revolves around the exchange rate system itself. The favored official answer—and certainly the typical academic answer to the systemic question—seems to be floating currencies. And there isn't much doubt that, in the absence of other perceived alternatives, governments in crisis are driven to that approach. But that also seems to me a counsel of despair in terms of a satisfactory policy over time. Nothing in the practical record of the past quarter century lends support to the theorizing that floating exchange rates will also be relatively stable.

It is also obvious that the typical small emerging economy isn't comfortable with that answer. Their economies typically lack diversification, are open internationally, and are much more heavily dependent on imports and exports than the United States, the European Union or Japan. They are engaged in highly competitive markets, with their industries sensitive to the price changes imposed by large currency fluctuations. They do not have a strong track record of internal stability to anchor price expectations. And, as I argued earlier, their financial institutions are inherently small and vulnerable to big changes in interest and exchange rates. So it's no wonder they are not very happy about the fashionable advice of economists. They long for stability. And they will naturally seek ways of attaining it.

One striking reaction by a number of emerging nations to the recent crises has been a reversal of long-standing policies to insist on national ownership of banking institutions. In the face of turbulent markets, the instinct to seek stability by increasing the size and diversity of financial institutions is surely sound. For a small country, the surest way—maybe the only way—to achieve that size and diversity is, in effect, to import it, by permitting their bank to become foreign owned. How could it be otherwise? It is exactly that instinct that is driving so many of the mergers and consolidations in the developed world, where institutions are so much larger to begin with.

More directly in the exchange rate area, we are seeing another way to "import" stability—the extreme opposite of floating. A number of countries have decided to cling to a larger more stable currency by means of "dollarization" or "euroization" or by the old-fashioned but newly revived technique of a currency board. That's not a decision to be taken lightly. It involves political as well as economic costs, and it

GLOBALIZATION AND THE WORLD OF FINANCE   17

brings me back to the question of monetary policy. For a country to adopt the dollar, or another foreign currency, means to abandon an independent monetary policy. In effect, for those countries, at least 50 percent of Harry Hutchinson's textbook becomes irrelevant.

The loss of monetary independence has been equated with loss of control over a nation's economic destiny. But for some countries it's fair to ask whether the perceived loss of national autonomy is real or illusionary. Can in fact a small and open economy effectively have an independent monetary policy and control its financial destiny? Can Indonesia, or Thailand, or Mexico, or Argentina really have freedom of choice in a world of globalized finance? Or, does the market itself (or when the crisis arrives, the IMF) impose limits—limits that may be more arbitrary and seemingly capricious than use of a foreign currency? The point can be put more positively. Wouldn't the benefits of the currency stability and lower interest rates inherent in linking the dollar or the euro be more beneficial to growth and efficiency over time than the purported loss of monetary autonomy?

None of this is of much direct concern to the biggest economies of the world— certainly not to the United States or the European Union. They are diversified, relatively closed, continental size economies. By their nature, they already have the benefit of a common currency, a common currency extending over hundreds of millions of people and trillions of dollars of GDP, and over 50 states and 11 nations. Only the most extreme changes in their exchange rates with the rest of the world arouse strong political or economic concerns. They have, by their behavior, demonstrated their determination to "go it alone".

The trouble is they have become almost totally passive with respect to management of exchange rates. That leaves us with a systemic problem. Passivity in the face of even large exchange rate changes among the United States, Europe, and Japan poses intractable problems for many small emerging economies. Those problems directly undercut the potential benefits of global finance.

How can the small exposed countries rationally stabilize their exchange rates, or passively let them float, when their major trading partners themselves have currencies that swing in value by 25 or 30 or even 40 percent or more over the course of a year or two? The inevitable result is abrupt changes in the competitive position of their industries and in the costs of imports—changes over which they have no control or influence. Their industries, with committed capital investments, supply relationships, and sales patterns cannot easily adjust, certainly not in a year or two, only to see the exchange relationships reverse.

I must emphasize what is apparent to any observer. Changes of the magnitude we have seen in the dollar/yen or the dollar/euro exchange rates simply can't be explained by so-called fundamentals or unexpected shocks. They have continued at a time of general price stability. Growth patterns among the major economies have differed, but without changing suddenly. We have had a decade remarkably free of outright recession among the major nations. We have had, in fact, the most stable economic environment in decades.

So why don't we do something about it? There is the belief that the global markets are simply too big to manage, that the potential flows of funds are so massive that any attempt to fix exchange rates is bound to fail. Influencing exchange rates has implications for monetary policy, and no really large country will contemplate giving up independence in monetary policy.

But I observe that precisely that kind of commitment is in fact being made unilaterally by a number of smaller Latin American, Asian, and European countries that have opted to attach themselves to a strong currency. Countries with a history of inflation, instability, and weak governments sense an urgent need for both currency stability and the lower interest rates that stability would foster. That need seems more pressing than concerns about monetary autonomy—an autonomy they recognize that has become as much illusion as reality in a world of global finance.

What is equally clear is that the sustainability and value of a link to a major currency is related to two important conditions. The first, of course, is that the anchor currency is itself reliably stable in terms of purchasing power and widely usable, qualities associated with the U.S. dollar and potentially the euro. The second condition is that financial and trading relationships with the anchor currency are close and dominant. Otherwise, the exposure to big fluctuations among the major currencies will create difficulties. The present problems of Argentina are a case in point. The attachment of the peso to the dollar a decade ago was hugely successful in stabilizing prices, encouraging industrial reorganization and financial discipline, and promoting growth. But the persistent depreciation of the euro, compounded by the devaluation of the Brazilian real has gravely weakened its competitive position in the past few years, recreating a sense of crisis. Plainly, it is that second condition that limits the practicality of many countries finding refuge in dollarization, euroization, or a currency board.

But that doesn't mean that things aren't changing. The most striking change is not in the emerging world but within Europe itself. There, 11 members of the European Union have made a decisive break with the past, giving up national monetary autonomy in favor of a common currency, the euro. That is a recognition of the fact that a true economic union with completely open borders and free flows of finance is simply not consistent with extreme volatility in exchange rates. And the ultimate protection against that volatility within Europe is a common currency.

Among the nations of Southeast Asia, where trade with the rest of the world is so widely diversified, there is discussion about the possibility of emulating the European approach by forming a regional currency in an attempt to provide a measure of stability. Success in that effort would be, to put it mildly, surprising. Unlike Europe, intra-regional trade is limited. There is an absence of both a strong national currency and a well-developed financial center to anchor the system. East Asia would remain exposed to the wide fluctuations in exchange rates among its major suppliers and export markets.

What those events and yearnings do suggest, however, is the strong possibility that over time we will see regional economic areas built around zones of free trade and close currency relationships. That tendency will be encouraged by NAFTA and a wider Western hemisphere free trade zone. In larger Asia, in the decades ahead, it could be the Chinese yuan rather than Japanese yen that emerges as the regional anchor.

GLOBALIZATION AND THE WORLD OF FINANCE   19

Then a larger question is posed. Will those regions remain open to each other and third nations, and thus be stepping stones toward a truly global system? Or will they gravitate, with or without conscious purpose, toward inward-looking blocs in political as well as economic regional isolation? I have come to the conviction that the full implication of a truly global system of trade and finance will ultimately be a common currency encompassing most of the world. But I am realistic enough to know that is not a project for my lifetime.

What we can do, and should do to achieve the benefits of global finance, is work toward greater stability among the major currencies. We could begin modestly. We don't need to know precisely what the right exchange rate is. We can allow for the fact that a presumed equilibrium rate could change over time, guided in part by persistent market trends. We can recognize the value, given the inconsistencies and vicissitudes of economic and political life, for some meaningful flexibility in exchange rates. But at the same time, we should be able to resist the extreme swings in exchange rates among the dollar, the yen, and the euro—swings that are driven more by the herd behavior of markets, and by the recurrent swings in market mood from exuberance to fear, than by any reasonable evaluation of a sustainable equilibrium.

Suppose, to be specific, the G-7, or the Big Three, the United States, Japan and Euroland, took the position that fluctuations in their currencies beyond a band of, say, 20 or 25 percent should be resisted. That's a pretty wide margin for market flexibility, but much smaller than the swings we have seen. Larger changes would be resisted, if necessary, by direct intervention in the market. No doubt, to be successful and credible, that intervention would need to be supported by an understanding that monetary policies would, if and as necessary, also take account of the desirability of greater exchange rate stability. The main central banks would be encouraged to consider how they might coordinate policies to that end, a process that has been only isolated and sporadic in the past.

Therein lies the point of contention—that the domestic aims of policy would be subverted. I cannot deny the obvious, that points of perceived conflict could arise. But my own experience suggests something else. More often than not, strong movements in exchange rates suggest a need for rethinking and modifying monetary and fiscal policies in the interest of domestic as well as external stability.

In ordinary circumstances, the kind of rather wide exchange rate band I have in mind would leave a lot of room for cyclical differences in monetary policy. Central banks would not need to move continuously in lockstep. Indeed, a growing sense in the market that exchange rates would revert toward a "central tendency" or sustainable equilibrium would in some instances free the hands of the monetary authorities.

In one sense, the aim would be modest: to avoid the extreme fluctuations that, in fact, bear no relationship to differentials in interest rates or inflation rates or to more fundamental shifts in competitiveness. But the consequences, in making it possible for emerging countries to live more comfortably with freedom of international capital movements, would be substantial. In the technical terms of economic text books, what it comes down to is whether markets, by sensible international policies, can be dominated by stabilizing speculation—a tendency for market operators themselves to step in against extreme movements for the simple reason that profits can be made. Plainly, more often than not it is the opposite that has been happening. The perception is that, in the jargon of the market, "the trend is your friend"; the way to make money is to join, even lead, the herd.

What will count in the end is credibility—a recognition that there is national interest in greater stabilization and a willingness to act. That credibility will require time to attain. I would argue that it is attainable. We have attained it in an area at least as difficult, turning away the inflationary expectations that dominated and constrained monetary policies a couple of decades ago in my country and many others. The Europeans, recognizing the risk of currency instability tearing apart the common market, went a long way toward establishing the necessary credibility within their regional market even before taking the leap into the common currency. The Swiss, among others, have demonstrated that it is feasible even for a small economy.

The kind of approach that I have suggested is much less demanding than the European experience. But if successful, it can be an important way station toward the much more distant vision of a true world currency. In the meantime, I believe that it can be—in fact, it must be within our lifetimes—a critical ingredient in a truly effective global financial system, a system that works to the benefit of all the countries of the world, large and small.

NOTE

This is the speech given by Paul A. Volcker at the University of Delaware on Monday, 30 April 2001. Mr. Volcker was awarded an honorary degree and gave the annual Hutchinson Lecture, named in honor of Harry D. Hutchinson, who taught economics for 30 years at Delaware and was well-known for his concern for students and his money and banking textbook.

[8]

A Proposal for International Monetary Reform*

JAMES TOBIN
Yale University

Over the last twenty years economists' prescriptions for reform of the international monetary system have taken various shapes. Their common premise was dissatisfaction with the Bretton Woods regime as it evolved in the 1950s. Robert Triffin awakened the world to the contradictions and instabilities of a system of pegged parities that relied on the debts in reserve currencies, mostly dollars, to meet growing needs for official reserves. Triffin and his followers saw the remedy as the internationalization of reserves and reserve assets; their ultimate solution was a world central bank. Others diagnosed the problem less in terms of liquidity than in the inadequacies of balance of payments adjustment mechanisms in the modern world. The inadequacies were especially evident under the fixed-parity gold-exchange standard when, as in the 1960s, the reserve currency center was structurally in chronic deficit. These analysts sought better and more symmetrical "rules of the game" for adjustments by surplus and deficit countries, usually including more flexibility in the setting of exchange parities, crawling pegs, and the like. Many economists, of whom Milton Friedman was an eloquent and persuasive spokesman, had all along advocated floating exchange rates, determined in private markets without official interventions.

*This paper is Prof. Tobin's presidential address at the 1978 conference of the Eastern Economic Association, Wash. D.C.

By the early 1970s the third view was the dominant one in the economics profession, though not among central bankers and private financiers. And all of a sudden, thanks to Nixon and Connally, we got our wish. Or at least we got as much of it as anyone could reasonably have hoped, since it could never have been expected that governments would eschew all intervention in exchange markets.

Now after five to seven years—depending how one counts—of unclean floating there are many second thoughts. Some economists share the nostalgia of men of affairs for the gold standard or its equivalent, for a fixed anchor for the world's money, for stability of official parities. Some economists, those who emphasize the rationality of expectations and the flexibility of prices in all markets, doubt that it makes much difference whether exchange rates are fixed or flexible, provided only that government policies are predictable. Clearly, flexible rates have not been the panacea which their more extravagant advocates had hoped; international monetary problems have not disappeared from headlines or from the agenda of anxieties of central banks and governments.

I believe that the basic problem today is not the exchange rate regime, whether fixed or floating. Debate on the regime evades and obscures the essential problem. That is the excessive international—or better, inter-currency—mobility of private financial capital. The biggest thing that happened in the world monetary system since the 1950s was

153

the establishment of *de facto* complete convertibility among major currencies, and the development of intermediaries and markets, notably Eurocurrency institutions, to facilitate conversions. Under either exchange rate regime the currency exchanges transmit disturbances originating in international financial markets. National economies and national governments are not capable of adjusting to massive movements of funds across the foreign exchanges, without real hardship and without significant sacrifice of the objectives of national economic policy with respect to employment, output, and inflation. Specifically, the mobility of financial capital limits viable differences among national interest rates and thus severely restricts the ability of central banks and governments to pursue monetary and fiscal policies appropriate to their internal economies. Likewise speculation on exchange rates, whether its consequences are vast shifts of official assets and debts or large movements of exchange rates themselves, have serious and frequently painful real internal economic consequences. Domestic policies are relatively powerless to escape them or offset them.

The basic problems are these. Goods and labor move, in response to international price signals, much more sluggishly than fluid funds. Prices in goods and labor markets move much more sluggishly, in response to excess supply or demand, than the prices of financial assets, including exchange rates. These facts of life are essentially the same whether exchange rates are floating or fixed. The difficulties they create for national economies and policy-makers cannot be avoided by opting for one exchange rate regime or the other, or by providing more or different international liquidity, or by adopting new rules of the game of balance of payments adjustment. I do not say that those issues are unimportant or that reforms of those aspects of the international monetary system may not be useful.

For example, I still think that floating rates are an improvement on the Bretton Woods system. I do not contend that the major problems we are now experiencing will continue unless something else is done too.

There are two ways to go. One is toward a common currency, common monetary and fiscal policy, and economic integration. The other is toward greater financial segmentation between nations or currency areas, permitting their central banks and governments greater autonomy in policies tailored to their specific economic institutions and objectives. The first direction, however appealing, is clearly not a yiable option in the foreseeable future, i.e., the twentieth century. I therefore regretfully recommend the second, and my proposal is to throw some sand in the wheels of our excessively efficient international money markets.

But first let us pay our respects to the "one world" ideal. Within the United States, of course, capital is extremely mobile between regions, and has been for a long time. Its mobility has served, continues to serve, important economic functions: mobilizing funds from high-saving areas to finance investments that develop areas with high marginal productivities of capital; financing trade deficits which arise from regional shifts in population and comparative advantage or from transient economic or natural shocks. With nationwide product and labor markets, goods and labor also flow readily to areas of high demand, and this mobility is the essential solution to the problems of regional depression and obsolescence that inevitably occur. There is neither need for, nor possibility of, regional macroeconomic policies. It would not be possible to improve employment in West Virginia or reduce inflation in California, even temporarily, by changing the parity of a local dollar with dollars of other Federal Reserve Districts. With a common currency, national financial and capital markets, and a single national monetary policy, movements of funds to exploit interest arbitrage or to speculate on exchange rate fluctuations cannot be sources of disturbances and painful interregional adjustments.

To recite this familiar account is to remind us how difficult it would be to replicate its prerequisites on a worldwide basis. Even for the Common Market countries, the goal is still far, far distant. We do not have to resolve the chicken-egg argument. Perhaps it is true that establishing a common currency and a central macro-economic policy will automatically generate the institutions, markets, and mobilities which make the system viable and its regional economic consequences everywhere tolerable. The risk is one that few are prepared to take. Moreover, EEC experience to date suggests that it is very hard to contrive a scenario of gradual evolution towards such a radically different regime, even though it could well be the global optimum.

At present the world enjoys many benefits of the increased worldwide economic integration of the last thirty years. But the integration is partial and unbalanced; in particular private financial markets have become internationalized much more rapidly and completely than other economic and political institutions. That is why we are in trouble. So I turn to the second, and second best, way out, forcing some segmentation of inter-currency financial markets.

My specific proposal is actually not new. I offered it in 1972 in my Janeway Lectures at Princeton, published in 1974 as *The New Economics One Decade Older*, pp. 88–92. The idea fell like a stone in a deep well. If I cast it in the water again, it is because events since the first try have strengthened my belief that something of the sort needs to be done.

The proposal is an internationally uniform tax on all spot conversions of one currency into another, proportional to the size of the transaction. The tax would particularly deter

short-term financial round-trip excursions into another currency. A 1% tax, for example, could be overcome only by an 8 point differential in the annual yields of Treasury bills or Eurocurrency deposits denominated in dollars and Deutschmarks. The corresponding differential for one-year maturities would be 2 points. A permanent investment in another country or currency area, with regular repatriation of yield when earned, would need a 2% advantage in marginal efficiency over domestic investment. The impact of the tax would be less for permanent currency shifts, or for longer maturities. Because of exchange risks, capital value risks, and market imperfections, interest arbitrage and exchange speculation are less troublesome in long maturities. Moreover, it is desirable to obstruct as little as possible international movements of capital responsive to long-run portfolio preferences and profit opportunities.

Why do floating exchange rates not solve the problems? There are several reasons, all exemplified in recent experience.

First, as economists have long known, in a world of international capital mobility flexibility of exchange rates does not assure autonomy of national macroeconomic policy. The Mundell-Fleming models of the early 1960s showed how capital mobility inhibits domestic monetary policy under fixed parities and domestic fiscal policy under flexible rates. Moreover, the availability of the remaining instrument of macroeconomic policy in either regime is small consolation. Nations frequently face compelling domestic institutional, political, and economic constraints on one or the other instrument, or on the policy mix.

Second, it may seem that we should welcome an exchange rate regime that increases the potency of monetary policy relative to fiscal policy; after all, monetary policy is the more flexible and responsive instrument of domestic stabilization. But the liberation of domestic monetary policy under flexible rates is in large degree illusory. One reason is the attachment of central bankers to monetarist targets irrespective of exchange rate regimes and the openness of financial markets. More fundamentally, monetary policy becomes, under floating rates, exchange rate policy. The stimulus of expansionary monetary policy to domestic demand is limited by the competition of foreign interest rates for mobile funds. Thus much—in the limit, all—of the stimulus depends on exchange depreciation and its effects on the trade balance, namely on shifting foreign and domestic demand to home goods and services. The depreciation may occur all right, but its effects on the trade balance can be perverse for a disconcertingly long short run, during which further depreciation, perhaps reinforced by speculation, occurs. Meanwhile the effects of depreciation on domestic currency prices of internationally traded goods are inflationary, even for an economy with idle resources and no domestic sources of inflationary pressure.

Furthermore, there are international difficulties in reliance on monetary policy in a floating rate regime. I quote from my 1972 lecture: ". . . When the export-import balance becomes the strategic component of aggregate demand, one country's expansionary stimulus is another country's deflationary shock. We can hardly imagine that the Common Market will passively allow the U.S. To manipulate the dollar exchange rate in the interests of U.S. domestic stabilization. Nor can we imagine the reverse. International coordination of interest rate policies will be essential in a regime of floating exchange rates, no less than in a fixed parity regime." The bickering between Washington and Bonn about these issues in the last year is just what I had in mind.

Third, governments are not and cannot be indifferent to changes in the values of their currencies in exchange markets, any more than they did or could ignore changes in their international reserves under the fixed-parity regime. The reasons for their concern are not all macroeconomic; they include all the impacts on domestic industries, export and import-competing sectors, that arise from exchange rate fluctuations originating in financial and capital transactions. The uncoordinated interventions that make floating dirty are the governments' natural mechanisms of defense against shocks transmitted to their economies by foreign exchange markets.

Fourth, another optimistic hope belied by events was the belief that floating rates would insulate economies from shocks to export and import demand. The same Mundell-Fleming type model that told us the relative impotence of fiscal policies and non-monetary demand shocks under floating rates also implied that trade balance shocks would be absorbed completely in exchange rates without adjustment of domestic output or prices. This will, of course, not be the case if the trade balance moves the wrong way (anti-Marshall-Lerner), or if, for any of the other understandable reasons enumerated above, governments intervene to prevent full exchange rate adjustment. It will not be the case anyway if exchange rate movements have consequences for asset demands and supplies, as they will, either via the capital gains or losses they produce for agents with long or short positions in foreign currency or via the expectations of future exchange rate movements which they generate.

The recent decline of the dollar against the Deutschmark, yen, and Swiss franc illustrates many of the above points. The U.S., on the one hand, and Germany and Japan on the other, clearly have divergent domestic histories, prospects, and objectives in terms of output growth and inflation. The changes in currency exchange rates have not served, as some proponents of flexible rates might have hoped, to permit these countries to pursue their differing policies without mutual interference. The Germans and Japanese have been reluctant to accept the effects of currency appreciation on their export industries, and so they have intervened to limit the appreciation. The 'Americans, concerned about the effects of depreciation on price indexes, have tightened monetary policy and raised interest rates in an attempt to stem the anti-dollar tide in the foreign exchange markets.

This history also supports the assertion I made above, that goods "arbitrage" is very slow relative to inter-currency financial speculation and portfolio shift. The net result of exchange rate movements and domestic price movements over the past few years has been to improve dramatically the competitive position of the U.S. vis-à-vis Germany and Japan. This is true when wholesale prices indices, converted to a single currency at prevailing exchange rates, are compared. Our trade-weighted real exchange rate is about 5% below 1977 and March 1973, and more than 7% below 1976. Germany's is 7% above 1973, though still below 1976 and 1977. Japan's is 3% above 1973, 7% above 1976, and 2% above 1977. The change is even more spectacular when labor costs are similarly compared. In 1970 U.S. hourly labor costs, including fringe benefits, were the highest in the world, 67% above Germany, 300% above Japan. In 1977 five countries had higher costs at exchange rates prevailing in December. Our costs were 16% below Germany, and now only 55% above Japan.* The U.S. is now a low-wage country! Yet we are suffering from the worst trade deficits in history.

I do not wish to be misunderstood. I think the hysteria over the recent decline of the dollar is greatly overdone, and that the

*For these calculations, made at the Institut der Deutschen Wirtschaft, Köln, I am indebted to Professor Herbert Giersch.

panicky pressure on our government to defend the dollar—pressure from European governments, from financial circles here and abroad, from the media—has been most unjustified. Moreover, anyone who thinks that the pre-1971 system of pegged rates would have handled better the recent flight from the dollar into marks, yen, and Swiss francs has a very short memory. Things would have been lots worse, with greater impacts on U.S. domestic policies and greater disruptions to international markets. My message is not, I emphasize again, that floating is the inferior regime. It is that floating does not satisfactorily solve all the problems.

One big reason why it does not is that foreign exchange markets are necessarily adrift without anchors. What we have is an incredibly efficient set of financial markets in which various obligations, mostly short-term, expressed in various currencies are traded. I mean the word "efficient" only in a mechanical sense: transactions costs are low, communications are speedy, prices are instantaneously kept in line all over the world, credit enables participants to take large long or short positions at will or whim. Whether the market is "efficient" in the deeper economic-informational sense is very dubious. In these markets, as in other markets for financial instruments, speculation on future prices is the dominating preoccupation of the participants. In the ideal world of rational expectations, the anthropomorphic personified "market" would base its expectations on informed estimates of equilibrium exchange rates. Speculation would be the engine that moves actual rates to the equilibrium set. In fact no one has any good basis for estimating the equilibrium dollar-mark parity for 1980 or 1985, to which current rates might be related. That parity depends on a host of incalculables—not just the future paths of the two economies and of the rest of the world, but the future portfolio preferences of the world's

owners, including Arabs and Iranians
ll as Americans and Germans. Reason-
, economists and traders, not to mention
reasonable members of both species, can
nd do have diverse views. In the absence of
any consensus on fundamentals, the markets
are dominated—like those for gold, rare
paintings, and—yes, often equities—by traders in the game of guessing what other traders
are going to think.

As a technical matter, we know that a
rational expectations equilibrium in markets
of this kind is a saddle point. That is, there is
only a singular path that leads from disequilibrium to equilibrium. If the markets are not
on that path, or if they don't jump to it from
wherever they are, they can follow any of a
number of paths that lead away from equilibrium—paths along which, nonetheless, expectations are on average fulfilled. Such deviant
paths are innocuous in markets—as for rare
coins, precious metals, baseball cards, Swiss
francs—which are sideshows to the real
economic circus. But they are far from innocuous in foreign exchange markets whose
prices are of major economic consequence.

This suggests that governments might
contribute to exchange market efficiency by
themselves calculating and publicizing estimates of equilibrium exchange rates, rates
expected some years in future. The floating of
the Canadian dollar in the 1950s was probably an empirical episode of considerable intellectual importance in solidifying economists'
acceptance of the theoretical case for flexible
rates. Floating rates had acquired a bad reputation, rightly or wrongly, in the interwar
period. The Canadian experiment seemed to
show that market speculation was stabilizing;
certainly there were no gyrations greatly
disturbing to Canadian-U.S. economic relations or to the two economies. One reason,
among others, appears to have been a general
belief in a long-run equilibrium not far from
dollar-dollar parity, an equilibrium that

accorded both with the interconnected structures of the two economies and with the policy
intentions of the Canadian government.
Those who extrapolated from the model to the
world-wide floating of the 1970s have been
disappointed. It is scarcely conceivable that
the various OECD countries could individually project, much less agree on, much less
convince skeptical markets of, a system of
equilibrium or target exchange rates for 1980
or 1985. So I must remain skeptical that the
price signals these unanchored markets give
are signals that will guide economies to their
true comparative advantage, capital to its
efficient international allocation, and governments to correct macroeconomic policies.

That is why I think we need to throw some
sand in the well-greased wheels. Perhaps one
might have hoped that the volatility of floating rates would do that automatically; given
the limitations of futures markets, uncovered
risks might permit wedges between national
interest rates and currency diversification
might limit intercurrency movements of
funds. In my 1972 excursion into this subject
I was skeptical on this point, and events since
have vindicated my skepticism. I said, "Increasing exchange risk will help, but I do not
think we should expect too much from it.
Many participants in short term money
markets can afford to take a relaxed view of
exchange risk. They can aim for the best
interest rate available, taking account of their
mean estimate of gain or loss from currency
exchange. Multinational corporations, for
example, can diversify over time. They will be
in exchange markets again and again: there
are no currencies they cannot use."

Let me return to my proposed tax, and
provide just a few more details. It would be an
internationally agreed uniform tax, administered by each government over its own jurisdiction. Britain, for example, would be
responsible for taxing all inter-currency
transactions in Eurocurrency banks and

brokers located in London, even when sterling was not involved. The tax proceeds could appropriately be paid into the IME or World Bank. The tax would apply to all purchases of financial instruments denominated in another currency—from currency and coin to equity securities. It would have to apply, I think, to all payments in one currency for goods, services, and real assets sold by a resident of another currency area. I don't intend to add even a small barrier to trade. But I see offhand no other way to prevent financial transactions disguised as trade.

Countries could, possibly subject to IMF consent, form currency areas within which the tax would not apply. Presumably the smaller EEC members and those ldc's which wished to tie their currency to a key currency would wish to do this. The purpose is to moderate swings in major exchange rates, not to break links between closely related economies.

Doubtless there would be difficulties of administration and enforcement. Doubtless there would be ingenious patterns of evasion. But since these will not be costless either, the main purpose of the plan will not be lost. At least the bank facilities which are so responsible for the current troublesome perfection of these markets would be taxed, as would the multinational corporations.

I am aware of the distortions and allocational costs that can be attributed to tariffs, including tariffs on imports of foreign-currency assets. I don't deny their existence. I say only that they are small compared to the world macroeconomic costs of the present system. To those costs, I believe, will be added the burdens of much more damaging protectionist and autarkic measures designed to protect economies, at least their politically favored sectors, from the consequences of international financial shocks.

I do not want to claim too much for my modest proposal. It will, I think, restore to national economies and governments some fraction of the short-run autonomy they enjoyed before currency convertibility became so easy. It will not, should not, permit governments to make domestic policies without reference to external consequences. Consequently, it will not release major governments from the imperative necessity to coordinate policies more effectively. Together the major governments and central banks are making fiscal and monetary policy for the world, whether or not they explicitly recognize the fact. Recently, it is quite clear from the differences and misunderstandings among the so-called three locomotives, they have not been concerting their policies very successfully. I would hope that, relieved of the need to stay in lockstep in order to avoid large exchange rate fluctuations, these governments might approach the task of policy coordination with a longer-range and more global view of their responsibilities.

The Risks of Investing in Emerging Markets:
Fund Managers' Perspectives

C.V. Helliar, A.A. Lonie, D.M. Power, C.D. Sinclair
Department of Accountancy & Business Finance,
University of Dundee, Scotland, UK,
Corresponding Author: Christine Helliar,
University of Dundee; phone 01382-344198; fax 01382-224419

The authors gratefully acknowledge the financial assistance provided by The Carnegie Trust for Scotland. They would also like to thank Professor G.A. Stout, members of the Department of Accountancy & Business Finance and participants at the Scottish Accounting Group Conference and the British Accounting Association Conference for their helpful comments and suggestions.

Abstract
This paper attempts to characterise the portfolio priorities of leading UK investment institutions with respect to emerging stock markets (ESMs) and to define the constraints under which these institutions normally operate when including equities from these emerging markets in their portfolios. The results suggest that important differences exist between the views expressed by the representatives of different groups of institutions visited in the course of the study both in terms of (i) their approaches to investment in ESMs and (ii) the importance they attach to different barriers to investment in these markets. Pioneering investors appeared to focus on a new, more embryonic group of emerging markets. Consequently, they faced a number of barriers to investing in these markets which were often different in kind from those faced by other institutions who arrived in emerging markets at a later stage.

The Risks of Investing in Emerging Markets...

Introduction

This paper attempts to establish the character of the portfolio priorities of leading UK investment institutions with respect to emerging security markets (ESMs) and to identify the constraints under which these institutions normally operate when including securities from these emerging markets in their portfolios. The general argument that investors should engage in international portfolio diversification (IPD) has become well-established in finance articles and textbooks (Solnik, 1974; Eiteman, Stonehill and Moffett, 1992). The case for investing in ESMs is simply an extension of the argument for IPD to include new or underdeveloped security markets. First, certain ESM countries have enjoyed some of the world's fastest rates of economic growth over the past 10 years[1] and IPD provides access to the securities of the companies which are the major contributors to this growth (Greenwood, 1993). Second, a number of industries which appear to have outstanding economic potential are represented only in ESM economies. Third, Markowitz principles of portfolio diversification provide investors with a particularly strong justification for choosing emerging market securities. The correlations between financial markets in ESMs and mature security markets are normally much lower than those between the various market indices of large, developed financial centres; according to Markowitz principles, including emerging market securities in a portfolio may reduce risks and increase returns. In so far as these low correlations are the outcome of differences in the rates of industrial and economic growth, different phases of the trade cycle, differences in the industrial composition of each economy or from opportunities resulting from changes in Government macroeconomic or regulatory policies, the gains are likely to persist over time.

The often excellent returns offered by securities in these markets have been well documented both in academic articles and in the financial press[2], especially after the Crash of 1987 when the correlations between the US stock market and the rest of the world's developed stock markets increased substantially (Roll, 1988; Le, 1991; Speidell and Sappenfield,

---

[1] For example, the compound annual growth rate of Malaysian Gross Domestic Product at constant prices between 1990 and 1993 was 12.7 per cent, that of China was 21.1 per cent and that of Chile 24.3 per cent. *Annual Abstract of Statistics*, various issues.

[2] For example, in 1993, the Polish market rose by 720 per cent, the Turkish market by 214 per cent and the Philippines market by 133 per cent. *Emerging Market Factbook* (1993).

1992). Moreover, the degree of international co-movements amongst these developed market indices (with the exception of Japan's Nikkei Index) has increased substantially from the pre-crash to the post-crash period (Arshanapalli and Doukas, 1993). For example, Divecha, Drach and Stefek (1992) report that over the 5-year period 1987-91 a US fund manager who put 20 per cent of his/her investment in emerging markets would have reduced annual portfolio risk from 18.3 per cent to 17.5 per cent while increasing the fund's annual return from 12.6 per cent to 14.7 per cent. Adopting a UK perspective, Sinclair, Lonie, Power and Helliar (1995) find that combining a domestic-based share portfolio with various proportions of equities from 18 emerging markets over a 5-year period increased the ratio of mean return per unit of risk from 0.002 to 0.217[1].

While risk measured by the variance of portfolio returns will normally be reduced by international portfolio investment, other types of risk are likely to be greater and the barriers to investment perceived by portfolio managers more formidable when emerging market securities are included in the portfolio. A principal objective of this research was to investigate whether the hazards of investing in such markets, which are often cited in academic texts, were considered to be important by practitioners and whether some of these barriers were regarded as sufficiently formidable to prevent investment altogether. A further objective was to highlight some of the problems experienced by investing institutions which have added the securities of emerging markets to their portfolios. Our interviews with leading professionals were designed to supply useful insights into how UK practitioners viewed potential barriers to investment in ESMs. Earlier studies have, in general, drawn inferences about barriers to IPD on the strength of information from market indices and other quantitative data. The interviews in this study provided an opportunity to assess the *relative* importance of different barriers when an array of possible barriers was considered.

Barriers to Investment in ESMs Identified in the Literature

The arguments in favour of adopting caution when investing in ESMs are well-documented in the literature. Emerging markets are believed to be prone to political risk involving military takeovers and it is often assumed that international investors are likely to suffer from unwarranted restrictions on the inflows and outflows of capital by these Governments

---

[1] However, as *The Economist* (January 6th, 1996, pp. 67-68) has noted, ESMs in general proved a poor investment in 1994 and 1995; 10 of the 15 markets analysed recorded a fall in market value in these years; Poland, China and Mexico declined by more than 40 per cent in dollar terms.

The Risks of Investing in Emerging Markets...

(Hartmann and Khambata, 1993). Emerging market countries are often susceptible to currency risk where there are rarely any forward foreign exchange markets and any large gains which may be earned on ESM equities may be eliminated by adverse movements in the exchange rate (Glen and Jorion, 1993; Hauser, Matityahu and Yaari, 1994). ESM markets are thought to suffer from a greater incidence of thin trading than their developed market counterparts (Gill and Tropper, 1988).

Another disadvantage which is highlighted in the literature is the heavy concentration of market capitalization in a relatively small number of securities (Mullin, 1993; Glen and Pinto, 1994) and the related problem of the low liquidity of these markets (Gill and Tropper, 1988). A further perceived barrier to investment in ESMs by large international investors is the argument that insider trading is endemic in these markets. Keane (1993) suggests that the absence of adequate monitoring rules and proper disclosure requirements in ESMs can contribute to the prevalence of insider trading. He makes the additional point that transaction costs in ESMs are high relative to those in developed markets and may discourage the potential investor from investing there. However, by far the most dramatic disadvantage of ESM investment according to the substantive literature on the barriers to emerging market investment is the allegedly high volatility of the returns on equities traded in these markets and the potential for dramatic downturns in ESMs where international investors may be left holding equities that no one wants to buy (Keppler, 1991; Wilcox, 1992). For example, Wilcox (1992) argues that the enormous volatility of emerging markets suggests that many international investors are "predominantly momentum players [attempting] to ride a wave of new information coming into the market [rather than] value-orientated investors" (p. 16). Other possible barriers (which were highlighted in a prior discussion with a retired fund manager) such as the absence of an active bond market, the lack of derivative instruments and the poor quality of financial information in emerging markets were also considered in the analysis. The importance of all of these barriers was investigated in the interviews undertaken as part of this study.

Method

To examine the barriers to investing in emerging markets, semi-structured interviews were conducted with eighteen representatives of different financial institutions: analysts, brokers, economists, traders, custody and settlements staff and fund managers. A wide cross-section of interested parties from several institutions was therefore questioned, between December 1994 and June 1995. The financial institutions visited were located in Dundee, Perth, Edinburgh and London. Table 1 summarises

10

Journal of European Financial Services

information about the responsibilities of the individuals who were interviewed by the team[1].

Table 1
Interviewees' Areas of Responsibility

No.	Institution	Location	Responsibility
1	Investment Bank	London	Custody & settlement of trades
2	Investment Bank	London	Economist providing information on emerging market economies
3	Investment Bank	London	Research Analyst investigating Eastern Europe
4	Investment Bank	London	Bond Trader
5	Investment Bank	London	Debt Origination
6	Fund Manager	Scotland	Fund Manager
7	Insurance	Scotland	Fund Manager
8	Fund Manager	London	Fund Manager - Eastern Europe
9	Broker	London	Research Economist deciding when it was right to target a market and providing indices
10	Broker	London	Global Research. Heading teams investigating potential new markets
11	Broker	London	New emerging markets/ Pioneering
12	Broker	London	Research Analyst investigating all emerging markets

We employed three main criteria in determining which institutions to visit. First, we required access to key personnel in relevant institutions - achieved in practice through departmental contacts with these institutions. Second, to increase the range of views about the importance of barriers in our sample, we sought a rough balance (a) between fund managers, brokers and investment bankers and (b) between individuals who were responsible for global portfolios and those who performed specialist functions such as custody and settlement. Third, the extent of our study was subject to the usual constraints of time and cost.

---

[1] With the exception of the two interviewees involved in custody and settlement, all of the above are directly involved in searching for new markets and securities in which to invest, either to invest directly themselves or in advising others where to place their investments.

The Risks of Investing in Emerging Markets...

Two members of the research team attended each interview; one team member participated in all 18 visits to supply a common perspective. Each interview lasted approximately 45 minutes; all were recorded, although a team member generally made detailed notes about the responses. A semi-structured questionnaire (which was pre-tested[1]) was used in all cases, although the relevance of different questions varied according to the role of the interviewee. The notes from the interviews were analysed and extracts taken from the tapes as soon as possible after the completion of each visit. Attempts were made to distil impressions and to group, or alternatively to differentiate, answers from the various institutional responses. These impressions, together with factual information supplied by respondents, form the basis of the remainder of this paper, which is set out as follows: section 4 summarises the three categories of participants in this study; section 5 explores the investment strategies of pioneering institutions and their perceptions about the importance of different barriers to IPD; section 6 examines the perceptions of fast-follower institutions about these barriers; section 7 considers the special problems faced by individuals in charge of custody and settlement procedures in UK institutions which invest regularly in India and Russia.

Sample

It was decided that, if possible, the individuals interviewed should represent two different stages of the investment process: those who undertook an advisory role in the selection of emerging market securities and those who made the actual investment decisions. We also wished to visit different types of institutions that were involved in analysing opportunities and taking investment decisions in these markets. The selection of interviewees was therefore made on the basis of talking with individuals in different types of organisation to try and discover whether similarities or differences existed between them in their approach to investing in emerging markets - for instance, whether the perceptions of insurance fund managers, pension fund managers and investment trust managers differed radically from those of the representatives of banks and brokers. Our preliminary hypothesis was that the position and function of interviewees in their various organisations - as well as the culture of the organisation itself - was likely to

---

[1] Most importantly, a retired fund manager went over each question with care and offered detailed suggestions. Departmental colleagues also provided constructive criticism.

Journal of European Financial Services

affect the interviewees' attitudes to ESM investment[1]. However, it became clear that we could not classify the interviewees by their type of institution or according to whether they were advisors or actual investors. Instead, we were able to separate the interviewees into three main classes.

The first group contained brokers, investment bankers and fund managers, all of whom were significant players in emerging markets in their own right, but whose primary importance was that they had assumed a *pioneering* role among UK institutions. They decided whether emerging markets had reached the stage when investment by other UK institutions appeared to be justified and subsequently acted as agents for many of these institutions in the countries in question. The brokers and bankers in this category provided vital evaluations of the companies, the markets and the regulatory frameworks in these countries. They had established databases of accounting information that enabled the fund managers to appraise potential investment opportunities at a company level. The second group were fund managers who invested in ESMs as part of their institution's portfolio strategy of global diversification, but only invested once the pioneers had paved the way. This second group were termed *fast-followers*[2]. The third category included individuals who initiated structured deals and undertook custody and settlement operations in ESM countries, termed *specialists*.

During the interviews the notion of what constitutes an "emerging market" often varied according to the role of the individual interviewed. In general, the pioneers and specialists employed the term with particular reference to newly established markets in countries such as China, Russia or the Ivory Coast, while the fast-followers considered that more developed markets such as Hong Kong and Singapore, which have now been promoted out of this category by the International Finance Corporation (IFC), were still "emerging". The IFC definition, which includes all markets not covered by the Financial Times World indices, is therefore not always regarded as appropriate by practitioners.

At the institutions visited, the structures of the investment desks which follow ESMs varied enormously. Some institutions had assembled

---

[1] Research in the area of risk and decision making has shown that attitudes to risk are often influenced by seniority within the firm and the desire for promotion. (Tversky and Kahneman, 1984; MacCrimmon and Wehrung, 1986).

[2] The terms "pioneer" and "fast follower" are derived from the literature on technological and commercial innovation. Lonie, Nixon and Grinyer (1988) refer to the appearance in this literature of the "offensive innovator" or pioneer, who is the first to market, and of the "defensive innovator" or fast follower who seeks to avoid the risk of launching a product which is technologically and commercially unproved.

teams dedicated to the analysis of emerging markets in which individuals accepted responsibility for different regional ESM areas, while in other institutions ESM portfolio selection was shared among those responsible for investment in specific geographical areas such as North and South America. The degree of specialisation therefore varied from one institution to another, usually according to the nature and the size of the investment being undertaken in the ESM. The heterogeneity of emerging security markets is so great that most investing institutions not only separate them on a geographical basis but frequently divide them further according to country-performance criteria.

Investing in ESMs: the Role of Pioneers

A group of brokers, fund managers and investment bankers, as shown in Table 2, (S, T, U, V, W, X, Y and Z) were categorised as "pioneers" and had attitudes to emerging markets which differed in a number of important respects from those of the representatives of other institutions visited. These latter institutions can be characterised as "fast followers" who normally pursue attractive ESM returns in the slipstream of pioneering institutions. These interviewees had different job descriptions and considered different markets from their fast-follower counterparts and their main aim was to find new investments for their funds or for their clients' funds. Thus they sought out new markets and decided whether the securities in these markets were suitable for actual investment. These pioneers were always in the forefront of investment in ESMs, and the fast-followers were only prepared to invest in these markets once the pioneers had established a foothold.

Table 2
Characteristics of the Pioneers Visited

Interviewee	Role of Interviewee	Markets Considered
S	Fund manager	Eastern European equities
T	Economist	Global emerging markets
U	Head of emerging market team	Global equities
V	Chairman and fund manager of investment trust investing in emerging markets	Global emerging markets
W	Research analyst for emerging markets	Eastern European markets
X	In charge of emerging market indices	Global emerging markets
Y	Responsibility for new markets	Eastern Europe; Middle East and Africa
Z	In charge of research	Global equities

The pioneers had a number of common characteristics which helped us to identify them as a coherent grouping. First, they were viewed by themselves, by the fast-followers interviewed and by the research team as more audacious and pioneering than the average fund manager. Thus there was common agreement that these were indeed pioneers. As Z put it:
"[T]he fund managers want stability and are more cautious [when investing] because they think emerging markets are too unstable. We are much more cavalier."

This boldness in initiating investment in markets which other institutions deemed to be too risky was apparent from the list of countries and the list of markets that the interviewees were monitoring as potential candidates for their portfolios. For example, U's emerging markets team viewed the Ivory Coast as "being on the leading edge of emerging markets" and reported that one of his team had just returned from a trip to investigate the possibility of investing in Kazakhstan. Interviewee U added that the only countries that his institution did not have a presence in were "those places that were ... either politically difficult or physically dangerous or were so small that there was no chance of any [profitable] investment opportunity from investing in these locations". In another interview, S (the manager of a London-based fund) pointed out that she only recommended investment in Eastern European countries such as Russia, Poland, Hungary, Estonia and the Czech Republic and would willingly have invested even more in Russia if her institution's rules had permitted it.

Second, the pioneering institutions where interviews took place maintained teams of specialists whose activities were devoted to the analysis of emerging markets. These teams were generally much larger in size and more closely focused on ESMs than those of the fast followers. The specialist teams were often supported by active research units responsible for the gathering of information, the analysis of data and, where necessary, the construction of indices for individual ESMs; for example, X and Z worked in research units of this character.

Third, some of the members of these emerging market teams - notably those under the supervision of interviewees at V and Z - had been recruited from emerging market countries and trained at the head office of the institution. Their expertise contributed to the process of emerging market security selection. As the emerging market team leader at U explained, "[I]t is worth having someone [a broker] on site".

Fourth, the pioneers moved very rapidly from country to sector to company level once they had decided to act, and did so several months (or even years) ahead of the fast followers who moved in a staged process towards the purchase of shares in individual companies in ESMs. As the interviewee, U, stated: "We look for a combination of factors which ... suggest that changes are under way. First, we look at the law. Then we examine the degree of commitment politically for implementation of reforms and, third, there is the availability and size of something to buy."

Once the pioneers have identified the target market and country, the fund manager S stated that: "[We] go out on a series of macro and micro trips ... The macro would focus on [meetings with] Central Bank officials and Finance Ministry officials ... and we would ask them what they think inflation [for example] will be. The micro would focus on visits to companies."

This willingness to travel seemed to be much more prevalent among the pioneering institutions; they usually sought to visit the factory, meet the company management and generally assess the company's earnings prospects. As S put it: "We come up with a total forecast return for the company which is based on three factors: real earnings growth, P/E expansion or contraction and currency appreciation or depreciation over the next three, six and twelve months."

Fifth, the pioneering approach of the London-based institutions visited resulted in a quite different appreciation of relevant risks by their representatives from that of the fast followers, essentially because in 1995 the former were concentrating on a group of emerging markets that the latter regarded as still too dangerous for portfolio investment. A striking example of this difference related to the quality of accounting information provided by companies in emerging markets. The head of an emerging markets team, U, argued that: "Accounts are generally produced but we don't usually believe them. The other thing about accounts ... is that not only is there an expectation that they lie but that they exaggerate the rosiness of the picture and the opposite tends to be the case. We find that they usually keep the profits down to minimise tax for family-run businesses."

And subsequently the same individual noted that: "The most difficult financial statements to look at are in countries which have accounting systems that are generous like Turkey; in terms of inflation-accounting rules, Turkey is more than generous."

Interviewee G pointed out that in Russia most foreign investors make their decisions on an asset valuation basis rather than on any other criteria because Russian forecasts of earnings based on company accounts are notoriously unreliable.

Another example of this difference in emphasis related to tax. For a number of the pioneering institutions, which are exempt from tax in the UK, the tax implications of investing in ESMs were regarded as highly significant although they are rarely discussed as a barrier to investing in emerging countries in the literature. A number of interviewees in this group remarked that the governments of some emerging market countries did not appear to take account of the effects of their domestic taxation on overseas investors who have tax-exempt privileges in their own countries; such investors may be unable to recoup taxes paid in emerging market countries even where double taxation treaties already exist - providing a powerful disincentive to investing in the emerging markets in question. Interviewee V, whose fund has tax-exempt status in the UK, indicated that he was forced to engage in a costly and complex operation which involved investing via a third country such as Mauritius to avoid a potential tax liability.

Sixth, the pioneers have visited some of these countries and introduced emerging market companies to the concept of Investor Relations and pointed out that international investors expected to receive accurate, detailed information on a timely basis about the companies in which they invest. Russia was highlighted by a number of interviewees as an example of a country where communication between the company and investors was poor. Pioneers, such as interviewee G, discussed the difficulties that they have encountered when they began to visit some of the Russian companies in which they had an interest as a shareholder or as a potential investor. On these visits they often have to explain to the Russian managers the nature of fund management and portfolio selection, how the capital markets work and the reasons for their visit. They indicated that most information in emerging countries such as Russia, whether official data or corporate disclosures, was scant, often unreliable and invariably out of date.

These pioneers recognised the benefits of international portfolio diversification (Solnik, 1974; Eiteman, Stonehill and Moffet, 1992) and would consider any country provided there was something large enough to invest in. None of the conventional barriers suggested in the literature seemed to deter them from seeking an investment in an emerging market. The major deterrents preventing them from making an investment were physical danger, the absolute size of an investment and taxation. Thus the pioneers' perceptions of the risks of investing globally did not seem to support the arguments discussed in the substantive literature on this topic.

The Fast Followers' Approach to an ESM Portfolio

Individuals (A, B, C, D, E and F in Table 3) at six fast-following institutions were interviewed by the team. These institutions proved to have a number of features in common and, taken as a whole, the fund managers exhibited a culture and an investment philosophy which were distinctive and contrasted with the culture and attitudes that seemed to prevail in the London-based fund. All of these institutions invested a substantial part - in two cases the greater part -

of their portfolio in overseas assets. None of the six engaged in pioneering investment in emerging markets; all waited prudently until assurances about liquidity, quality of information and overall risk had been forthcoming from lead institutions, usually Barings and Flemings. All adopted a phased approach to investing in ESMs which normally commenced with a holding in a unit or an investment trust dedicated to investment in a broad spectrum of companies in an emerging market which had met the Barings (or Flemings) conditions for portfolio eligibility. As the fund manager D put it, "We are not pro-active in emerging markets. We prefer to wait for others to fact-find for us." Or, as B argued, "We wait for other institutions to go into emerging market countries - we wait for their literature." Manager A spelled out the different stages involved in his institution's progress towards the targeting of the shares of individual companies in emerging markets: "We buy units in ESM unit trusts and learn how to manage the portfolio. ... Then, in 9-12 months time, if we have enough information, we do it ourselves once we have developed our own expertise. If it's an emerging market we haven't been in before, then we use an index"

D's approach was very similar: "We are cautious and sub-contract to start with, looking over the [sub-contractor's] shoulder. We then bring it in-house and probably start with an indexed position and then move to an aggressive strategy based on economic fundamentals and stock market data".

Journal of European Financial Services

Table 3
Characteristics of the Fast-Followers

Interviewee	Size of Portfolio	% Invested Overseas	Investment Horizon	% Invested in Emerging Market	Emerging Market Desk	Minimum Investment Size
A	£ 3.4bn	27%	6-12 month review period but longer-term horizon	Far East 6% and Small European Markets 1%	No	£ 100,000 or 1% of portfolio
B	£ 0.8bn	53%	2-3 years	Far East 6.5%	No	£ 2,000,000
C	£ 1.0bn	30-35%	Target horizon for each market	N/A	Two EM specialists	£ 5,000,000
D	£ 4.0bn	5-15%	6-month review but generally hold shares for several years	N/A	Far East three-person team	£ 5,000,000 in about 20 ESM companies
E	£ 5.0bn	55%	12-18 months	N/A	Yes - two person team	£ 500,000 or 1% of fund
F	£ 1.5bn	46%	5 years	Far East 7%	Far East three-person team	£ 500,000

The risk aversion which characterised the phased approach of the fast follower institutions to newly established emerging markets was strongly in evidence in their response to questions about possible investment in Russia. In contrast with the views of the pioneering fund manager all of the fast followers regarded such investment as too risky to be worthy of serious investigation in 1995. The response of E was typical of the fast followers' views on investment in Russia and, more generally, in Eastern Europe: "We have virtually nothing invested in Eastern Europe. We monitor the area, but don't currently invest there ... We don't like Eastern Europe because its not sufficiently mature. It's too risky and they don't have the structure in place ... The Morgan Stanleys of this world will invest in Russia and so forth because ... they have teams looking at these countries."

By contrast, S, the manager of a pioneering institution, pointed out that she recommended investment *only* in Eastern European countries such as Russia, Poland, Hungary, Estonia and the Czech Republic.

The Risks of Investing in Emerging Markets...

In general, the desire for high returns exhibited by the fast followers in the sample was tempered by a lower tolerance of risk than that of their pioneer counterparts. Nevertheless, many forms of risk associated with ESMs which, in the 1980s and early 1990s, were frequently portrayed as representing formidable barriers to investment in emerging markets were viewed without concern by all of the fund managers in 1995. Academic research suggests that currency volatility is a very significant factor in the overall volatility of funds (e.g. Eun and Resnick, 1988). According to our interviewees, however, currency risk, although sometimes significant in emerging market countries, was simply factored into the calculation of the costs and benefits of entry[1]. Similarly, share price volatility was not considered to be a significant barrier despite the literature which suggests that it is probably the major barrier to investment in emerging markets (e.g. Wilcox, 1992). The heavy concentration of market capitalization in a relatively narrow range of shares, the prevalence of insider trading in ESMs and the lack of complementary markets in bonds and derivatives were also not considered to be barriers to participation in emerging markets by the fund managers interviewed. For example, both of the managers A and F used virtually identical language about insider trading, arguing that it "makes the market work".

Political risk - notably in Russia and certain other Eastern European countries - was on occasion decisive for the fast followers A and D, but generally induced caution rather than dismissal from consideration[2]. Market

---

[1] Recent government actions in India and Brazil demonstrate that even popular emerging markets, which were formerly thought to be relatively immune from government interference, are susceptible to official intervention. In August 1995 the Brazilian authorities reimposed capital controls in a bid to stem heavy foreign exchange lows. In the Spring of 1995 the Indian government withdrew support for a large investment funded by foreign investors. Obviously, foreign exchange risk exists for investments in any foreign market unless the investment takes place through a specialised country fund. Forward markets in foreign exchange do not exist for currencies of emerging market countries, and any cover, it was argued, would be prohibitively expensive. Most of the investors questioned on this point make no attempt to hedge their currency exposure, even though they acknowledged that the very high returns characteristically offered by ESMs can be lost through a dramatic movement in a currency.

[2] The interviewees made the familiar point that political risk is always prevalent as governments in emerging markets are often unstable and a new regime with a fundamentally different philosophy from the old regime may gain power overnight. The new authorities may re-nationalise privatised industries, expropriate assets and introduce new laws restricting foreign investment. Less dramatically, the state plays a number of important roles in risk management which may not be assumed

Journal of European Financial Services

illiquidity presented more of a problem - the "biggest barrier" according to the fund manager E. This description is surprising, since illiquidity is not normally accorded the same weight as other barriers to investment in ESMs in the recent literature. Fast followers A and D also perceived that illiquidity was an obstacle to investment in certain emerging markets, although fund manager C believed that his institution's characteristically long-term investment in such markets greatly diminished the problem. Fund manager B concentrated on the purchase of "blue chips" in the larger ESMs to overcome this problem. Government restrictions on outflows of capital were an important determinant for D's pension fund and the manager A cited Russia and Taiwan as unattractive markets in this respect[1]. Lack of in-house expertise in specific emerging markets was not necessarily seen as a problem. Although D emphasised that his institution's in-depth targeting of shares was built on expert knowledge which took time to develop, fund manager A argued that, as an interim measure, they would not hesitate to sub-contract and hire an expert manager to look after a portfolio of ESM securities which represented particularly attractive prospects. Most of the fund managers were prepared to accept high transaction costs as long as returns were substantially higher. As manager C argued: "If the Indonesian market goes up by 80 per cent and you pay a little more on dealing costs, you can accept them."

    The fast follower E took entry and transaction costs rather more seriously when he said: "Take South Korea. There ... is a foreign premium of maybe 80-100 per cent [on the purchase of equities by non-nationals]. Once you have paid that premium and you revalue your purchases the next day you suffer an immediate loss. If you sell again you would get back that

---

immediately - or at all - by a new regime (see Lessard, 1995). Most of the literature on political risk is of little help to a fund manager who is contemplating investing in an ESM prone to such risk. However, Cosset and Suret (1995) employed modern empirical techniques to gauge the effects of political risk constraints on the performance of a portfolio of international stocks and concluded not only that diversification among politically risky countries improves the risk-return profile of optimal portfolios but actually produces a reduction in overall portfolio risk.

[1] Details of changes in the investment restrictions of a number of emerging market countries including Korea, Mexico and Taiwan over the 1980s are documented in Bosner-Neal, Brauer, Neal and Wheatley (1990). Also, the Emerging Stock Market Factbook (1991) reported that by 1990 some markets such as Argentina and Brazil had "no significant restrictions" while others such as Chile, Greece and Mexico were "relatively free" and noted that only a small minority of emerging markets still restricted the entry of foreign investors into their markets.

The Risks of Investing in Emerging Markets...

premium. But it's a big risk and the client needs to understand and be willing to take that risk and to live with it."

The overriding reason why the managers of the fast follower institutions were prepared to discount most of the risks associated with ESM investment was, not surprisingly, that large returns were often possible in such markets; pressures exerted by performance league tables were a powerful motivating force. However, some had longer-term purposes such as "trying to buy into GDP growth ... once we target a company we hold the shares for a number of years" (Fund manager D). Others, such as manager E, were driven by clients' stated preference for investing in emerging markets.

Some similarities in the attitudes of the fast follower fund managers and their pioneering counterparts were also notable. The actions of all fourteen pioneers and fast-followers interviewed were driven by the prospect of high returns. As the manager S stated: "If I can't expect to make 30 per cent, then it's not very interesting. As a minimum, 30 per cent is what emerging markets should be giving investors."

All managers planned to minimise transaction costs, if possible, by holding shares in ESMs for 3-5 years on average - although fund manager S stressed that shares in some countries such as Turkey were traded much more aggressively than in other markets because of the extraordinary volatility of the Turkish equity market. All aspired to a contrarian strategy in which they detected undervalued and out-of-favour shares possessing high potential or observed the signs of impending market collapse and left the ESM at a time when other investors were still arriving, attracted by soaring and unsustainable share prices[1]. All of the interviewees, as a rule, contemplated currency risk with equanimity.

There was more support for academic views about risks of investment in emerging markets among the fast-followers than there was among the pioneers; at least one of the fast-followers mentioned political risk (Hartmann and Khambata, 1993) and illiquidity (Gill and Tropper, 1988) as potential barriers to investment. However, there was not very strong support amongst the fast-follows for some of the other impediments to global investing such as currency risk (Glen and Jorion, 1993; Hauser, Matityahu and Taari, 1994), insider trading (Keane, 1993) or concentration of market capitalization (Mullin, 1993; Glen and Pinto, 1994).

---

[1] According to one interviewee, when deciding to sell investments in an ESM warning trends and key indicators such as fast diminishing international reserves, excessive short-term borrowing at high yields to fund equity purchases and a record ratio of trade (or budget) deficit to GDP were examined closely.

Journal of European Financial Services

The Role of Specialists in ESM Investment

A number of specialists were interviewed who had special responsibilities for trading bonds of emerging countries or for custody of securities and settlement of transactions involving ESM equities. Although we obtained some interesting insights into the selection of emerging market bond portfolios, it is on the latter role of custody and settlement that we wish to concentrate, as this seemed to be more important. Custody and settlement problems are rarely described in the literature on IPD as significant barriers to investing in emerging markets. However, it emerged from the interviews that for certain countries custody and settlement difficulties are arguably more important than any other consideration. The settlement rates for a number of Emerging Market Countries are shown in Table 4 and a visual inspection of the table indicates that delays in settling transactions in India are particularly acute[1] with only 16 per cent of trades being settled on time.

Table 4
Settlement Rates for Emerging Market Countries

COUNTRY	VOLUME (% of Total Trades)	SETTLEMENT (% Settling on Settlement Date)
Argentina	4.24	70.07
Brazil	9.30	92.37
Chile	0.10	95.52
Greece	2.49	63.61
India	1.70	15.68
Indonesia	10.32	59.63
Korea	3.04	79.47
Malaysia	29.12	71.04
Mexico	11.59	83.36
Portugal	3.14	96.50
Thailand	20.42	64.72
Turkey	4.55	85.33

---

[1] Settlement rates in Russia were not provided, and anecdotal evidence from those interviewed suggested that the problem was even more acute in Russia than in India.

The Risks of Investing in Emerging Markets...

There were four main concerns with the custody and settlement of securities. According to our interviews the first major problem for international investors with some of the emerging markets was the characteristic size of each holding. India was a good example of this. In India the denominations of share certificates were commonly very small, to cater for the domestic individual investor base rather than the requirements of large institutional shareholders. One London-based custodian interviewed stated that the share certificates from US$1m worth of Indian equities would fill a small room and that a trade of US$100,000 would consist of about 2,000 pieces of paper which would all need to be stored in a safe location. This requirement was viewed as a major disadvantage in a city such as Bombay which has one of the most expensive real estate prices in the world. The custody costs of Indian equity investments were therefore seen as prohibitive. One of the fund managers in the sample suggested that this cost was a reason for the popularity of Government Depository Receipts (GDR) in the period 1993-94[1], which enabled investors to hold claims to equities without incurring the normal custody costs.

Second, the specialists perceived that the share settlement system was another barrier to investing in some emerging markets, it was seen to be labour-intensive and resulted in literally millions of pieces of paper circulating at any one time. Again, the system in India was a good example of this problem; there were no standard share denominations; clerks could not use computerised systems to settle the trades and were thus compelled to process share certificates individually; they sat at their desks with sackfuls of paper surrounding them. A custodian in a London-based financial institution said of the Bombay stock exchange: "Basically, [the settlement process] is very labour intensive ... I would reckon that one of my settlement staff would process 10 Indian trades a day compared with 120 to 150 trades a day in a developed market".

In a manual system of this character there is obviously a high risk that share certificates and other documents go missing. International investors in this market also face the risk of fraud. In addition, the process of registering shares is inevitably lengthy; for example, in India registrars routinely take 10-12 weeks to transfer shares and official estimates suggested that about 15 per cent of share transactions were "objected to" at the registrars because the paperwork was not in order[2], which further delayed

---

[1] For example, it is estimated that US$2.5bn was invested through GDR issues in 1994 (GSCG Benchmarks, 1994).

[2] When a trade is completed, the broker reviews the paperwork to ensure that it is all in order. The broker then passes on the paperwork to the clearing house which

Journal of European Financial Services

the processing of a trade. In many of the emerging markets there was no central depository to store share certificates and international investors needed to rely on the local knowledge of their contacts on the ground to secure some location for storing the certificates.

Third, the absence of a legal framework which regulates dealing in securities was a barrier to investing in emerging market securities. Russia was a country cited as posing special problems in this area. A London-based custodian pointed out that in Russia most share dealing took place over-the-counter and local brokers were usually used by international investors both to identify the shares of high-potential companies and to execute any purchase or sale orders. She argued that most of these brokers were under-capitalised, posing a credit risk to international investors[1], and that the majority had offices which were not linked to electronic settlement systems, resulting in transactions being done by fax rather than on Swift. Her institution, like many others, were contemplating shifting their international business from individual broker firms to the larger banks[2] to try and avoid these difficulties, but at the time of the interviews, brokerage services were not yet offered by the banks.

The difficulties caused by the absence of a legal framework for security transactions were demonstrated by the process of settling a trade. When a trade had been executed, a sale and purchase agreement was completed which is the equivalent of a "confirmation" and a "contract" in developed equity markets. A power of attorney was often required to give the broker permission to deliver certificates to the registrar. Most registrars'

---

transfers the payments and certificates on a net basis to the custodian. The custodian re-registers the stock in the new owner's name at the registrar's office. It is often at the registrar that problems arise and the transfer is "objected to". For instance, transfer deed signatures may not match those on the share register. If they do not, the documents are passed all the way down the chain again, from the registrar to the custodian to the broker and so on. By this stage the broker has already been paid his fee and so has little interest in establishing who is the legal owner of the equities, unless the threat of withdrawal of business in the future can be used to galvanise him into action.

[1] When possible, investors try to arrange a delivery-*before*-payment method of settlement, rather than the usual delivery-*versus*-payment method to avoid fraud or delay in the settlement process.

[2] Around the time of the team's visits to UK institutions in mid-1995 well-known local Russian brokers were being poached by the Russian banks to set up brokerage sections in these banks.

offices were located in Moscow but each registrar was liable to require different documentation from other fellow registrars, including the purchase-and-sale document, authorised signatures and certificates of incorporation. There was no standardisation of the documentation required for share transfers and various combinations of up to 20 different items could be requested by registrars.

Fourth, the lack of share certificates and the difficulty of establishing proof of legal ownership appeared to inhibit some investors from investing in these markets. In countries such as India the interviewees argued that many local investors neglected to re-register their shares when they bought them, so that when an international investor purchased these equities and attempted to re-register them, it was often found that the seller was not, in fact, the registered owner of the stock. In other countries share certificates which would identify the owner of any shares did not exist at all. For example, in Russia an entry in the share register was the only proof of ownership and investors faced the risk that some individual might erase their name from the share register and replace it with another. Most international investors overcame this problem by taking a photocopy of the register once their name was entered and then arranging for the custodian to confirm that their name remained on the record by inspecting the register every month. As a result of this additional work, custody fees were very expensive - up to ten times the fees charged in developed markets. Brokers' commissions were also believed to be quite large, but the actual size of the commission could not be accurately quantified; brokers charged a negotiated percentage, but the formally recorded commission was irrelevant since there was no transparency in the price at which they purchased the shares (in local currency) on the local market for their international clients (who paid in dollars). Transaction costs were also relatively high in Russia, because, to receive dividends in roubles a special account normally had to be set up, which needed the approval of the exchange control authorities in Moscow. Repatriation of dividends or capital gains earned on equities sold in Russia was also difficult to arrange and required the permission of the state.

These custody and settlement problems associated with emerging markets highlight barriers which appear to be overlooked in the academic literature on investment in emerging markets, but represent serious impediments to investment in these countries. Only the pioneers were willing to invest in these countries and the fast-followers were not yet confident enough of the custody and settlement arrangements. The fast-follower practitioners viewed the custody and settlement problems as so severe that they would not risk their funds in these countries. The pioneers, on the other hand, saw these markets as offering great opportunities, where a

Journal of European Financial Services

lot of money could be made, until the fast-followers arrived, when such heady gains were unlikely to be available again.

Conclusion

ESMs have changed in character over the past decade and the interest generated by their exceptional returns has ensured that they are regularly considered by fund managers who are deciding on the allocation of the assets in their portfolios. Although barriers to investment remain formidable in a number of ESMs, in many cases the prospective returns to investment in these markets are so remarkable that fund managers, whose performances are ranked on a quarterly or a monthly basis, are increasingly finding it difficult not to become involved.

This study has examined the investment processes of investment in emerging markets and has considered the risks that need to be considered in the investment decision process. Our evidence shows that many of the institutions which have invested in emerging markets in recent years have been heavily dependent upon the efforts of pioneering financial institutions. The pioneers establish bridgeheads in these countries, evaluate the accessibility of security markets to outside investors and supply the financial databases (as well as the necessary assurances) that the fast followers require before initiating operations in these markets. There is therefore an important complementarity between the pioneering and fast follower institutions: the former accept high risks in pursuit of exceptional returns, while the latter, pursuing a more risk-averse strategy, help to consolidate and develop international investment in new financial centres.

The finance literature suggests that a number of risks are incurred in investing in emerging markets; foreign exchange risk (Glen and Jorion, 1993; Hauser, Maitityahu and Yaari, 1994), political risk (Hartmann and Khambata, 1993), illiquid markets and thin trading (Gill and Tropper, 1988) and insider trading (Keane, 1993). The visits to eighteen practitioners investing in emerging markets in our study seems to suggest that there is little evidence to support the view that these are the major barriers to investment in emerging markets. Of more importance to global investors were factors rarely cited in the literature, such as taxation, and especially custody and settlement. The custody and settlement barriers were the only ones that appeared to prevent the fast-followers from investing. Our results are based on interviews with eighteen practitioners, and clearly more work is required in this area to establish how generalisable these findings are across the investment community.

The Risks of Investing in Emerging Markets...

REFERENCES

ARSHANAPALLI, B. and DOUKAS, J. (1993): "International Stock Market Linkages- Evidence From the Pre-October and Post-October 1987 Period", Journal of Banking and Finance, 17, 193-208.

BOSNER-NEAL, C., BRAUER, G., NEAL, R. and WHEATLEY, S. (1990): "International Investment Restrictions and Closed-End Country Fund Prices", Journal of Finance, 45, 523-548.

COSSET, J.C. and SURET, G.M. (1995): "Political Risk and the Benefits of International Portfolio Diversification", Journal of International Business Studies, 26, 301-318.

DIVECHA, A.B., DRACH, J. and STEFEK, D. (1992): "Emerging Markets: A Quantitative Perspective", Journal of Portfolio Management, 18, 41-50.

ECONOMIST, (1996): "Shake, Slither and Schuss", Economist, January, 67-68.

EITEMAN, D.K., STONEHILL, A.I. and MOFFET, M.H (1992): Multinational Business Finance Wokingham: Addison-Wesley, .

EMERGING STOCK MARKET FACTBOOK (1991): New York: International Finance Corporation.

EMERGING MARKET FACTBOOK (1993): New York: International Finance Corporation.

EUN, C.S. and RESNICK, B.G. (1988): "Exchange Rate Uncertainty, Forward Contracts, and International Portfolio Selection", Journal of Finance, 23, 761-767.

GILL, D. and TROPPER, D. (1988): "Emerging Stock Markets in Developing Countries", Finance & Development, 25, 28-31.

GLEN, J.D. and JORION, P. (1993): "Currency Hedging for International Portfolios", Journal of Finance, 47, 1865-1886.

GLEN, J.D. and PINTO, B. (1994): "Emerging Capital Markets and Corporate Finance", Columbia Journal of World Business, Summer, 31-43.

GREENWOOD, J.G. (1993): "Portfolio Investment in Asian and Pacific Economies: Trends and Prospects", Asian Development Review, 11, 120-150.

HARTMANN, M.A. and KHAMBATA, D. (1993): "Emerging Stock Markets: Investment Strategies of the Future", Columbia Journal of World Business, Summer, 83-104.

HAUSER, S., MATITYAHU, M. and YAARI, U. (1994): "Investing in Emerging Markets: Is it Worthwhile Hedging Foreign Exchange Risk?", Journal of Portfolio Management, Spring, 76-81.

KEANE, S. (1993): "Emerging Markets - The Relevance of Efficient Markets Theory", ACCA Occasional Research Paper, 15, 1-23.

KEPPLER, A.M. (1991): "Further Evidence on the Predictability of International Equity Returns", Journal of Portfolio Management, Fall, 48-53.

LE, S.V. (1991): "International Investment Diversification Before and After the October 19, 1987 Stock Market Crisis", Journal of Business Research, 22, 305-310.

LESSARD, D.R. (1995): "Financial Risk Management for Developing Countries: A Policy Overview", Journal of Applied Corporate Finance, 8, No. 3, 4-28.

LONIE, A.A., NIXON. W.A. and GRINYER, J.R. (1988): "The Dependence of Innovation Upon Group Support - A Case Study", Business and Economics Review, 4, 27-34.

LONIE, A.A, POWER, D.M. and SINCLAIR, C.D. (1993): "The Putative Benefits of International Portfolio Diversification: A review of the Literature", British Review of Economic Issues, 15, 1-43.

MACCRIMMON, K.R. and WEHRUNG, D.A. (1986): "Taking Risks: The Management of Uncertainty" New York: Free Press.

MULLIN, J. (1993): "Emerging Equity Markets in the Global Economy". Federal Reserve Bank of New York Quarterly Review, Summer, 54-83.

ROLL, R. (1988): "The International Crash of October 1987". in ed. KAMPHUIS, R.W., KORMENDI, R.C. and WATSON, J.W.H., "Black Monday and the Future of Financial Markets Chicago", MAI Publications .

SINCLAIR, C.D., POWER, D.M. and LONIE, A.A. (1995): "An Investigation of the Argument for Increased Investment in Emerging Markets" in Global Structure of Emerging Financial Markets. D.K. Ghosh and E. Ortiz (Eds.)

SINCLAIR, C.D., LONIE, A.A., POWER, D.M. and HELLIAR, C.V. (1995): "An Investigation of the Stability of Returns in Western European Markets, 1989-1994", paper presented at the European Financial Management Conference, London, June 28-30.

SOLNIK, B. (1974): "Why not Diversify Internationally?". Financial Analysts Journal, 30, 48-54.

SPEIDELL, L.S. and SAPPENFIELD, R. (1992): "Global Diversification in a Shrinking World", Journal of Portfolio Management, 18, 57-67.

TVERSKY, A. and KAHNEMAN, D (1984): "Rational Choice and the Framing of Decisions", Journal of Business. 59, S251-S278.

WILCOX, J.W. (1992): "Global Investing in Emerging Markets". Financial Analysts Journal, 48, 15-19.

Part II
Instability in Developing Nations

[10]

INCREASING THE CONTRIBUTION OF FOREIGN INVESTMENT TO SUSTAINABLE DEVELOPMENT: DOMESTIC AND INTERNATIONAL POLICY MEASURES

John R. Dilyard
*H. Peter Gray**

EXECUTIVE SUMMARY

The developing world consists of two relatively clearly defined groups of countries: those which are growing at a sustainable rate, albeit with interruptions caused by short-term dislocations (industrializing/developing) and those whose performance is close to stagnation (poor countries). This distinction reinforces the observation of the Commission on Sustainable Development (CSD) that "poverty elimination" had become the "poor step-child" of the annual CSD sessions. The paper addresses an important aspect of the problem: can the inadequacy of official development assistance to nations in need of external finance be remedied by private portfolio and direct investment and, if so, what are the necessary policy measures for both the investing and recipient nations?

The policies will hinge on the adequacy of the institutions needed by both the more developed countries and poorer countries if they are both to attract and retain inward flows of private portfolio equity investment and to avoid financial crises.

The need for external finance derives from the low level of domestic savings and, possibly, the inability to generate export revenues to meet the developmental need for hard currency. Private investments, direct and portfolio, are possible sources of the needed finance. Neither direct nor portfolio investment is likely to be available to the developing countries in the amount needed because of inadequate resource bases and/or an inadequate "institutional infrastructure" and because of inadequate supplies of savings being generated in the consumer-driven economies of the industrialized world. Further, part of the supply of finance potentially available to the developing countries has been siphoned off by the needs of countries with economies in transition.

There is good reason to consider under-emphasis on poverty as a serious omission if, as seems reasonable, very poor countries will almost inevitably tend to devote any increase in available resources to consumption and to investment which generates consumption goods rather than to the other goals of Sustainable Development ("environmental protection and the creation of biodiversity" and "social programmes"). Failure of the participants in the Rio Summit to officially acknowledge and to repair the inadequacy of financing available to the very poor countries is a major concern.

In a globalized economic system with a liberalized international economic involvement, developmental strategy requires that nations seeking sustainable development take advantage of the benefits of international trade and investment by following a policy of outward industrialization allowing inflows and outflows of direct investment and utilizing portfolio finance where this is expected to be long-term. This paper addresses two sources of private foreign financing, direct investment and portfolio investment. The paper can be seen as validating Jun and Brewer (1997) in the greater contribution of direct investment to sustainable development, but it also shows the inadequacy of heavy reliance on the corporate sector because these channels of funding together will fail to eliminate the inadequacy of external funding, particularly for poor countries. The paper also examines why this should be so, and what steps must be taken if either direct and/or private portfolio investment are to be relied upon to eliminate the funding "gap" between the available flow and the amount which could be used efficiently.

It is necessary to recognize the need for developing countries to have sophisticated institutional infrastructure if they are to rely on private funds for financing sustainable development. In poor countries, such sophistication is probably not feasible because the ability to create the "institutional financial infrastructure" needed to

* H. Peter Gray is Professor Emeritus of Economics and Management, Rutgers University, United States; John Dilyard is Professor of Management, St. Francis College, United States.

attract private portfolio investment is acquired only as part and parcel of the process of the institutional evolution that is endemic in sustainable development. Middle-income or industrializing/development countries can benefit greatly from inflows of direct investment and, if they have developed or can develop the appropriate financial infrastructure, from inflows of modern portfolio investment.

T HE United Nations Commission on Sustainable Development recognizes the sovereignty of individual developing nations as well as the three goals of eliminating poverty;[1] the development of social programs; and the importance of limiting environmental degradation while recognizing the dangers of reductions in biodiversity. Developing nations have, therefore, the acknowledged right to allocate such economic gains as they may achieve according to their own set of priorities. The priorities among the goals will vary according to the level and rate of growth of income of individual countries and their cultures. It may also be reasonably assumed that the lower the level of per-capita gross domestic product, the greater will be the share of any incremental product that will be devoted to consumption (the elimination of poverty) and the smaller the share for the other goals identified by the Rio Summit.

Modern conditions divide the developing world into two relatively clearly defined groups of countries: those which are growing at a sustainable rate, albeit with interruptions caused by short-term dislocations (industrializing-developing or I-D countries) and those whose performance is close to stagnation (poor countries). The 1996 Human Development Report (UNDP, 1996, 3) identifies 101 countries (not including China or India but with 25 per cent of the world's population) as suffering from "failed growth," defined as having per-capita income lower in 1993 than before 1990. Boote and Thugge (1997, table 2) identify 41 heavily-indebted poor countries which stand in drastic need of debt relief.

The existence of such a large share of the world's population in countries with failed growth is both an important moral problem for the civilized world in the light of the goals agreed upon at the Rio Summit and offers the possibility of substantial damage to the global commons as poor countries are likely to commit large amounts of environmental damage in their

search for greater product.[2] Given this scenario, the distribution of income gains and sustainable development among the population of developing countries has significant importance for the global benefits to be derived from the reduction of pollution spillovers. It is, therefore, important that the Commission on Sustainable Development address the foreign financing of economic development in the non-industrialized world as well as the conditions in the recipient countries necessary for such financing.

Investment in I-D and poor countries works its effect mainly by augmenting the rate of economic growth and by contributing to any evolution in the host economy that accompanies economic growth. Portfolio investment, unless it incorporates foreign expertise and training related to a specific project, will serve to supplement domestic savings so that the rate of capital formation can be increased and, possibly, to ease any shortage of foreign exchange needed for the acquisition of foreign-made capital goods. Foreign direct investment (FDI) is likely to include technology transfer, foreign expertise and training of indigenous personnel, as well as a supplement to domestic savings. Access to foreign markets may also be generated when the affiliate is incorporated into a global network of production and distribution. The emphasis on economic growth leaves, as noted above, the partition of the economic gains among the three goals of the Rio Summit to the individual nation. This does not preclude some spillover gains to limiting environmental degradation and to the creation of social programs. The degree to which such spillover effects are generated will depend to a large degree on the concern of the multinational corporation with the aspirations of the host country there will be wide variability among multinationals.

Jun and Brewer (1997) noted that the top twelve recipient nations (including China, which we would contend is unique) receive about 80 per cent of FDI flows as well as a substantial part of private portfolio flows. These data reinforce the suggestion that the

---

[1] The Commission on Sustainable Development cited, as a criticism of progress reports, that "poverty elimination" had become the "poor stepchild" of the annual CSD sessions (*CSD Update*, vol. 3, November, 1996).

[2] Damage to the environment committed by very poor nations has different characteristics than the damage perpetrated by the industrialized nations and the richer developing nations. The decimation of the rainforests of the Amazon basin and the generation of carbon monoxide from petroleum consumption are obvious examples of the two kinds.

developing countries have been effectively divided into two blocs and that the more affluent developing countries enjoy a virtuous cycle of self-reinforcing development while the poor countries suffer a vicious cycle of self-reinforcing stagnation.

The purpose of this paper is to examine the way in which private capital flows are attracted to developing countries so that savings can be transferred from the developed countries in the form of direct and private portfolio investment flows to I-D and poor countries. Given that the Rio Summit relied upon the corporate sector to be the key actor in the "battle to save the planet" (Ismail, 1996), the role of private financial transfers and their distribution between the two groups of developing countries must constitute a primary area of focus. The paper identifies the adequacy or inadequacy of "institutional infrastructure" as an important factor affecting the ability of a developing nation to attract (and to retain) inward investment. Institutional infrastructure comprises the institutional setting, the rules and regulations and the efficiency of their enforcement that prevail in a country.[3] Inward private portfolio investment, particularly portfolio equity investment (modern foreign portfolio investment or MFPI) is extremely sensitive to the adequacy of "financial institutional infrastructure".

THE ROLE OF PRIVATE CAPITAL IN SUSTAINABLE DEVELOPMENT

All developing countries need to attract a flow of net inward foreign investment in some form and for an extended period as a supplement to domestic savings during the process of development.[4] Thus, a nation must be able to generate inflows of foreign funds in the form of direct investment, traditional private and official portfolio investment, modern portfolio investment (denominated in host-country currency — see below) or official development assistance (ODA) to supplement its sustainable development initiatives.

The financing of sustainable development must confront three problems: first, the adequacy of the total flow of available funds (the actual or potential flow relative to the amount which can be effectively and efficiently used);[5] second, the distribution of these funds among the two groups in the developing world; and third, the ability of the developing countries to avoid financial or environmental crises in which the direction of the flow of funds reverses and net capital flows return to the industrialized world.

In the absence of a substantial increase in ODA and other subsidized flows, the flow of private capital from the industrialized to the developing world is likely to be less than the perceived need of the developing countries. Since private capital seeks high risk-adjusted rates of return, global excess demand for savings can lead to competition among developing countries to attract inflows of investment and to turn the terms of trade against developing countries and in favour of multinational corporations and industrialized nations with surplus savings.[6] Even if the total foreign savings available for transfer to developing countries were, in some sense, adequate, it is probable that its distribution would be biased towards the I-D countries. It is therefore possible to perceive of a quasi-optimistic scenario in which the I-D countries do receive (almost) as much private investment as they can effectively utilize — largely in the form of FDI and portfolio capital — while poor countries continue to be underfunded.

The major problems facing poor countries are the lack of a policy framework that favours inward FDI, institutional infrastructure that allows FDI to be used effectively, the resources needed to attract inward FDI (Dunning and Narula, 1996) and the lack of financial infrastructure or the sophistication necessary to attract private portfolio capital even if the greater benefit allows a risk premium to be paid. I-D countries, however, may have local resources of sufficient quality to attract inward FDI and they may have financial infrastructure which is adequate to attract inward private portfolio investment under tranquil conditions but not adequate to retain inward portfolio investment in turbulent times.

Not all components of the gross inflow are equally valuable per unit of inflow. What matters is that they accumulate to the amount which the country can use effectively; there is, therefore, substantial substitutability among the different components.

---

[3] The concept is developed below. Institutional infrastructure must be clearly distinguished from "physical" infrastructure whose role in development is well recognized. The two types of infrastructure have features in common and some aspects, such as the existence of good communications networks, might be classified in either category.

[4] This is an assumption which could be disproved by reference to the remarkable success of Taiwan, Province of China, which has run current account surpluses and has a substantial positive balance of foreign assets owned over liabilities to foreigners. This example is more honoured in the breach than in the observance.

[5] The volume of funds which can be efficiently used depends, importantly, on the efficiency of the recipient government. Doubts about this efficiency are probably responsible for the current emphasis on private capital flows.

[6] This fact is best established and is most sophisticated in the competition to attract inward FDI (Guisinger and others., 1985).

Table 1. Net long-term resource flows to developing
countries, 1990–1997($ billion)

	1990	1991	1992	1993	1994	1995	1996	1997	1998*
Net long-term resource flows	100.8	123.1	152.3	220.2	223.6	254.9	308.1	338.1	275.0
Official flows	56.9	62.6	54.0	53.3	45.5	53.4	32.2	39.1	47.9
Private flows	43.9	60.5	98.3	167.0	178.1	201.5	275.4	299.0	227.1
From international capital markets	19.4	26.2	52.2	100.0	89.6	96.1	149.5	135.5	72.1
Private debt flows	15.7	18.6	38.1	49.0	54.4	60.0	100.3	105.3	58.0
Commercial banks	3.2	4.8	16.1	3.3	13.9	32.4	43.7	60.1	25.1
Bonds	1.2	10.8	11.1	37.0	36.7	26.6	53.5	42.6	30.2
Others	11.4	3.0	10.7	8.6	3.7	1.0	3.0	2.6	2.7
Portfolio equity flows	3.7	7.6	14.1	51.0	35.2	36.1	49.2	30.2	14.1
Foreign direct investment	24.5	34.4	46.1	67.0	88.5	105.4	126.4	163.4	155.0

Source: Calculated from World Bank, *Global Development Finance*, 1999.
* 1998 levels are estimated.

Table 2. The distribution of foreign direct investment
flows to developing countries, 1990–1997 ($ billion)

	1990	1991	1992	1993	1994	1995	1996	1997
Foreign direct investment to all developing countries	24.5	34.4	46.1	67.0	88.5	105.4	126.4	163.4
Direct investment in the top 12 developing countries	17.3	23.2	33.5	49.8	68.5	76.1	94.3	114.0
Direct investment in all other developing countries	7.2	11.2	12.6	17.2	20.0	29.3	32.1	49.4
Sub-Saharan Africa	0.8	1.6	1.6	1.9	3.3	3.5	4.3	5.2

Source: Calculated from World Bank, *World Development Indicators 1999*.

ODA is probably the most valuable because it carries no corresponding liability, but the shortfall of ODA for countries seeking sustainable development is well recognized and the authors see little evidence in the United States, at least, of any quick turnaround in attitude. Direct investment, with its concomitant transfers of proprietary technology, environmental management techniques, human capital and possible access to foreign markets for value added in the host country, is very valuable (Fry, 1996). The per unit value of inward portfolio investment depends upon the degree to which the foreign savings is locked into the recipient nation and upon the efficiency with which it is allocated to projects with a high expected rate of return.

Data on recent flows of all categories of capital (foreign savings) to developing countries are given in table 1. This paper focuses on three kinds of private capital flows: direct investment, traditional portfolio debt flows and portfolio equity flows. Two categories, direct and portfolio equity, are central to this paper because they are effectively denominated in the currency of the recipient country and have different characteristics from debt flows, which are usually defined in hard currency. What is of significance here is the division of flows (of each kind) between the top twelve recipients and the rest of the developing world. Details of the division in all three kinds are given in tables 2, 3 and 4.

Private portfolio flows have surged, particularly in

Table 3. The distribution of private debt flows to
developing countries 1990–1997 ($ billion)

	1990	1991	1992	1993	1994	1995	1996	1997
Private debt - all	15.7	18.6	38.1	49.0	54.4	60.0	100.3	105.3
Private debt in the top 12 countries	9.6	16.3	23.6	31.5	49.9	49.4	86.7	75.6
Private debt - all others	6.1	2.3	14.5	17.5	4.5	10.6	13.6	29.7

Source: Calculated from World Bank (1999). *World Development Indicators 1999*.

Table 4. The distribution of modern foreign portfolio investment
flows to developing countries, 1990-1997 ($ billion)

	1990	1991	1992	1993	1994	1995	1996	1997
MFPI, all countries	3.7	7.5	14.1	51.0	35.2	36.1	49.2	30.2
MFPI, top 12 countries	2.5	6.7	12.9	47.7	25.3	24.8	29.4	18.7
MFPI, all others	1.2	0.8	1.2	3.3	9.9	11.3	19.8	11.5

Source: Calculated from World Bank (1999). *World Development Indicators 1999*.

countries located in regions where sustained development seemed and seems feasible. The success of countries in East Asia, prior to 1997, and Latin America is identified in tables 5 and 6. Some East Asian developing countries are beginning to attract more inward investment as they have successfully begun to overcome the disruption caused by the 1997 crisis. However, the contribution of foreign investment to sustainable development depends upon the growth of the stock of the inward investment: hence the importance of the ability to retain inflows from past years. Direct and modern portfolio investments have very different degrees of reliability (sensitivity to a lack of confidence in the host economy) and, therefore, provide different levels of benefit per dollar of investment: this is largely due to the different characteristics of the assets.[7]

The benefits (and the potential costs) of inward FDI are well known and are discussed in detail in Jun and Brewer (1997). Here we are concerned with the lack of volatility and the steady growth of the stock of inward FDI. While the physical assets acquired as a result of FDI are defined in the currency of the recipient country, the real assets will not be vulnerable to a depreciation or devaluation of the

host country currency brought on by an excessive rate of inflation (a traditional macroeconomic problem) and financial assets of affiliates can be protected against weakness in the host currency by borrowing locally. When there is an overvaluation of the host currency brought about by excessive inflation, the terms of trade facing host-country enterprises improve without fundamental reason. Thus, a depreciation merely restores the original terms of trade or there will be, at most, a relatively minor weakening of the currency's real rate of exchange (the nominal rate adjusted for different degrees of inflation). The capitalized value of the affiliate's physical assets in the parent company's home currency and the price-competitiveness of exports from the affiliate will not be seriously affected in the long run (Gray and Miranti, 1990).[8]

While a host country's policy framework may explicitly attract or deter inflows of FDI in a macroeconomic sense, the detrimental effects of inadequate institutional infrastructure can be offset through the

---

[7] Data on FDI flows include changes in the outstanding portfolio of assets and liabilities of established MNC affiliates.

[8] This does not mean that the local affiliates benefit from the excessive inflation: indeed, they may temporarily lose their price competitiveness and find the host-country market depressed as the authorities seek to fight the inflation without depreciation. Further, a change in the real rate of exchange (terms of trade) that will engender a given current balance will, self-evidently, affect the value of the FDI asset in the home-country currency.

Table 6. Equity funds in emerging equity markets[a]

Country	Total Assets ($ million)	Number of Funds	GDP($ billion)
Argentina	230	6	297.5
Brazil	1,497	53	759.2
Chile	1,200	7	67.1
China	6,680	108	835.7
Colombia	40	2	73.1
India	3,450	60	311.4
Indonesia	597	27	233.5
Korea	5,150	94	461.8
Malaysia	875	20	
Mexico	1,348	12	330.0
Philippines	654	13	82.9
Taiwan, Province of China	3,953	29	272.0
Thailand	2,855	31	183.2
Regions Asia	40,125[b]	375	–
Latin America	9,750[b]	155	–

Sources: UNCTAD (1997, Table A.19)
Note: The number of funds includes funds from the more developed countries as well as from the industrialized countries.
[a] asset values and the number of funds are taken as of September 30, 1996.
[b] assets do not include the asset values of the country funds.

creation of special enclaves which contain adequate (or, at least, less inadequate) institutional infrastructure, such as export zones, by the host country. These measures may not be needed by the more affluent developing nations in their attempts to attract inward FDI but they offer a means for poorer nations to buffer any inward FDI from domestic malfunction.[9]

When branches or affiliates of foreign banks are present in the enclave, they can shelter multinationals' foreign affiliates from any adverse effects of inadequate financial infrastructure. He (1999) shows the importance of the presence of foreign banks. When foreign banks were allowed to establish themselves in the Shanghai region of China, their presence brought about spectacular increases in inward (non-financial) FDI and in gross regional product. Inadequate institutional infrastructure can affect the benefit to be derived by a foreign affiliate in a developing country because of differences in the ability of affiliates in developing economies to engage in activi-

ties which rely on sophisticated practices. One such possibility is the difficulty which obtains in assessing the likelihood that certain transferred technologies could precipitate a disaster because of inadequate supervision by the host government.[10] Per contra, Lundan (1996) shows that inward FDI in pollution-intensive industries can improve the pollution standards of the host country because the multinational corporation is limited in its pollution capability by the demands of its customers or because the firm finds the world-wide standardization of equipment to be beneficial.

Inward FDI may be expected to grow steadily as reinvested profits expand existing affiliates and as growth in the host economy increases the capability

[9] Enclaves are often made still more attractive by the offer of various investment incentives (Guisinger and others, 1985). Of course, the creation of enclaves only makes inward FDI more attractive and the local resources must be attractive enough to foreign multinational corporations to warrant inward FDI. This requires, at a minimum, a reliable well-trained workforce which, in turn, requires good educational infrastructure.

[10] There exist modern technologies which are disaster-capable, meaning that a malfunction can cause great harm outside the confines of the property of the producer ("disasters" are distinguished from "accidents" which take place within the confines of the producer's property). When the operation is deprived of adequate supervision by the parent multinational corporation and of adequate regulation by the host country, the result could be a disaster. The disaster in the Union Carbide (India) Ltd., pesticide plant in Bhopal causing over 1,750 people to be killed by poison gas is perhaps the best example (Gladwin and Walter, 1985). On the subject of sales of baby formula in developing countries with unsanitary water supply, see Beauchamp (1983).

Table 6. Private capital flows and private equity flows into I-D countries ($ billion)

Country	1986	1990	1991	1992	1993	1994	1995	1996	1997
Argentina									
NPCF	0.9	-0.2	2.9	5.6	13.6	10.1	9.7	16.1	19.8
PI(eq)	nil	0.0	0.4	0.4	5.5	1.2	0.2	0.9	2.2
Brazil									
NPCF	-0.1	0.5	3.6	9.7	16.2	12.3	20.0	29.7	43.4
PI(eq)	nil	nil	0.8	1.7	5.5	5.1	4.4	4.0	3.8
Chile									
NPCF	-.5	2.1	1.5	1.8	2.4	5.1	5.5	7.4	9.6
PI(eq)	nil	0.3	0.0	0.3	0.4	0.9	0.3	0.1	0.5
Colombia									
NPCF	1.6	0.3	0.2	0.7	2.1	4.3	4.7	7.7	10.2
PI(eq)	nil	nil	nil	nil	0.2	0.3	0.1	0.3	0.1
Indonesia									
NPCF	0.8	3.2	3.4	4.6	1.1	7.7	11.5	16.2	10.9
PI(eq)	nil	0.3	0.0	0.1	2.5	3.7	4.9	3.1	0.3
Malaysia									
NPCF	0.8	1.8	4.2	6.1	11.3	8.5	10.1	12.8	9.3
PI(eq)	nil	0.3	0.0	0.4	3.7	1.3	2.3	4.4	-0.5
Mexico									
NPCF	0.6	8.3	12.0	9.2	21.2	20.7	16.0	25.2	20.5
PI(eq)	nil	0.6	4.4	5.4	14.3	4.5	0.5	3.9	2.1
Philippines									
NPCF	0.4	0.6	0.4	-0.7	3.3	3.9	4.3	5.0	4.2
PI(eq)	nil	nil	nil	0.3	1.4	1.4	2.0	1.3	0.1
Thailand									
NPCF	-0.2	4.4	5.0	4.3	7.5	4.4	10.0	13.6	3.4
PI(eq)	0.0	0.4	0.0	0.0	3.1	-0.5	2.2	1.6	-0.3

Notes: NPCF = net private capital flows; PI(eq) = portfolio investment in equity markets (annual flow).
Source: World Bank (1999c). *World Development Indicators* (Washington, D.C.: World Bank)
The data set did not provide data for either Korea or Singapore.

of accommodating higher levels of technology thereby inducing the creation of new affiliates. The realized benefits of FDI also should provide confirmation that a policy framework supportive of FDI consistent with the goals of sustainable development complements well the return-seeking motives of FDI. Still, the type of FDI flowing into a country is not always under the control of the country; it simply may not possess assets and/or resources that can be exploited in an economical way without some sort of incentive housed within the policy framework. It is therefore crucial for sustainable development that incentives geared to attract FDI are consistent with the environmental concerns and objectives of the Rio Summit.

Inward debt investments constitute "traditional portfolio investment" and are ordinarily denominated in hard currency (that is, not the borrower's currency).[11] Such loans made to governments and or private entities in a developing country usually have long maturities and are endangered only by serious economic problems in the debtor country. A serious recession or a crisis can affect the ability of the debtor to service the debt or even result in default.[12] The long (original) maturities of these loans means that they can be traded in secondary markets in periods of

[11] However, see the account of the Thai crisis below.

[12] The existence and transparency of bankruptcy law is a component of the institutional infrastructure.

stress but that they cannot bring about a capital flight unless local firms (including the debtor) buy them back and, improbably, use hard currency to effect the purchase. Of course, reliance on debt investment is vulnerable to the drying up of supply in the event of bad performance by the debtor's economy and/or an increase in the risk premium when lending ultimately resumes.

Modern foreign portfolio investments (MFPI) usually comprise acquisitions of equities in (emerging) stock markets in developing countries: there are also some investments in debt instruments denominated in local currency and traded locally. The assets are, therefore, denominated in the currency of the host country and, unless closely tied to exports, are sensitive to economic conditions in the host country. The existence of an equity market of adequate efficiency in a developing country usually indicates that the country perceives itself to have achieved sustainable growth. Thus, poor countries are unlikely to be able to attract noteworthy inflows of MFPI.

In recent years investments in equity markets in I-D countries by asset-holders based in industrialized countries have increased substantially (tables 5 and 6). The most important way in which this flow of funds occurs is through the creation of mutual funds (unit trusts) in industrialized countries which specialize either in equities in one country or in a region. These funds are able to reduce transaction costs for investors, provide country-specific knowledge and proselytize investors on the virtues of international portfolio diversification as a sales promotion technique (notwithstanding caveats in the prospectus). Mutual funds can also give ultimate beneficiary owners of equities the impression, not always warranted, that by having a country specialist provide local day-to-day control over their assets their capital will be reasonably secure against sudden financial crises.[13]

As of September 1996 there existed 375 equity mutual funds specializing in Asian markets with asset values in excess of $40 billion (table 5). There also existed 31 funds which specialized in Thai securities with assets of $2.8 billion. While this was small in relation to international claims by foreign banks of about $70 billion, it was important because of its ease of encashment and lack of any fixed maturity (table 6). Equity investments are inevitably denominated in the capital importer's currency. Equities have no predetermined maturity and are traditionally regarded as long-term liabilities. However, in a liberalized system of markets and from a narrow international flow-of-funds aspect, the foreign-owned

equities are easily-encashable assets (though not, in a technical sense, liquid). They can be sold at the going market price in an established market quite quickly and promptly converted to the creditor's home currency in the foreign exchange market (subject to any dislocations which exist in a crisis situation and subject to the existence of capital controls). To the extent that the capital importing countries use these inflows to finance investment in long-term projects, the capital-importing country is financing long-term investments with easily encashable liabilities and is contravening good financial practice of matching the maturities of asset and liability. Only if the financial system is robust enough so that equity flows are not volatile or the central bank has sufficient reserves of foreign exchange or lines of hard-currency credit to negate any lack of confidence, could financing investment with easily encashable funds be an appropriate policy.

The existence of foreign-owned equities in an internationally-liberalized system drastically increases the host country's optimum volume of foreign-exchange reserves. This quantum has traditionally been defined in terms of necessary imports (a flow) but should now allow for the inclusion of encashable liabilities to foreigners (a stock). This represents a fundamental change in concept and sharply reduces the benefits of the MFPI. Note too that the benefits derived from the inflow of foreign saving into a local equity or stock market depends upon the efficiency of that market as an allocative device (Singh, 1992) as well as upon the additional volume of new issues of equity by locally-owned firms attributable to the reduced cost of equity capital.

Competition among mutual funds in the industrialized world has forced some firms to seek out new areas for investment. Helliar and others (1998) report on the criteria by which emerging equity markets are opened up for investment by British mutual funds. Clearly, foreign fund managers will seek to escape from the effects of a local crisis as best they can. The result of the infusion of foreign funds into local equity markets is a substantial overhang of potentially volatile foreign exchange. A crisis, whether originating in the domestic economy or in the foreign exchange market, is likely to generate a sudden outflow of funds and to expand a domestic political or economic crisis into a foreign-exchange crisis.[14] In principle, a country with a sophisticated macro-financial policy could instruct its monetary authority to hedge the value of foreign-owned equities, but this

---

[13] Certainly, an individual could never hope to manage effectively a portfolio of assets in a series of apparently unrelated volatile markets.

[14] Note that traditional portfolio investment has the lender's asset specified in the lender's (hard) currency so that it is the possibility of inability to service the debt — not the foreign exchange rate — that is crucial in traditional portfolio investment.

seems to call for almost as much financial sophistication as liberalization and will substantially raise the
cost of the funds.

According to Singh (1992), the purpose of the
original plan for emerging nations to develop stock
markets was to attract portfolio investment which
would replace debt as a source of hard currencies
given that commercial banks in industrialized countries were likely to be unwilling to make loans or buy
bonds in emerging markets. This original plan (put
forward by the World Institute of Development Economics Research in 1990) argued for the abandonment of control over international capital movements[15] and seems to show a sublime faith in the
idea that equity investments in countries which cannot sell debt to foreign banks are long-term and not
subject to sudden withdrawals.

PORTFOLIO EQUITY INVESTMENT

Classical economic theory sees net international
capital inflows as a source of saving which can be
used for capital formation and, at the same time, constitute assets that can be used by investors as a
means of achieving a diversified portfolio with a high
risk-adjusted rate of return. This interpretation and
the argument that the freedom of international capital movements will increase global allocative efficiency both rely on the assumption that economic systems are inherently stable with no important exogenous (or endogenous) shocks to engender a financial
crisis. The emerging equity markets must be assumed to have significant depth, breadth and resiliency. Indeed, in the absence of some assurance of
the possibility of repatriation of funds in a time of
stress, the volume of private portfolio equity investment in developing countries would remain quite
small.

A financial system consists of a series of inter-
linked financial markets which function under known
sets of regulations and procedures (including the existence or non-existence of a lender of last resort and
of insurance against the failure of deposit intermediaries). The greater the number of financial products
traded and the greater the inter-temporal and geo-
graphic range of those products, the more sophisticated is the system and the greater is its ability to
promote allocative efficiency under tranquil conditions. A well-functioning financial system will be
regulated by the financial authorities (in a national

system, the central bank) and the set of policies in
force and effectively administered (macro-financial
policy). Given the existing set of statutes, macro-
financial policy is designed to generate a combination
of products, practices and regulations which will promote an effective mix of allocative and stability efficiencies.[16]

Such policies are enhanced by central bank cooperation (lines of credit) and by the creation of supranational bodies (for example, the IMF), which are
designed to provide temporary assistance. Policymakers must recognize the need for transparency of regulations and practices and for the availability of reliable information so that people who are engaged in
any part of the system may have a full appreciation
of the way in which the system is designed to work
and works (or have reliable access to someone who
has such knowledge).[17] People for whom an understanding of the system is necessary include executives of both financial and non-financial corporations – especially executives engaged in international
financial transactions – and people employed in the
regulation and administration of the system. All of
these people need to be aware of the potential for the
foreign sector to generate adverse shocks.

The industrialized countries of the world have developed their financial sectors over the last century
and a half (and more) and possess a series of highly
specialized firms and operatives who are both well-
trained and well-equipped to cope with slow change:
these specialist firms create linkages among major
financial markets across space and time and provide
information. Within the industrialized countries, a
relatively fast rate of innovation resulting from the
liberalization of capital markets, the adoption of new
and different exchange-rate systems, the introduction
of computers and the ability to quickly transact financial operations throughout the integrated sector
has been accomplished with relatively little stress
(although the crises of the pound sterling and the
Italian lire in 1992 could be attributed in part to a
failure of national central banks and/or treasuries to
understand the degree to which new financial instruments, such as derivatives, could be profitably used
by private firms to punish badly overextended, vul-

---

[15] This required the elimination of section 3 of Article VI of the
International Monetary Fund's Articles of Agreement. The question of the absence of capital controls is considered in Section IV
below.

[16] Macro-financial policy can be seen as the financial equivalent of macro-organizational policy (Dunning, 1992) which is designed to make the country attractive to internationally-mobile
productive activities. This paper does not address "monetary policy" designed to reduce the variability of GDP around its trend.

[17] People who are active in only one aspect of the system, for
example, depositors in a financial intermediary, need have a
knowledge only of the institutions which they use and any related
institutions.

nerable national currencies).[18] Even given that advanced capitalist economies are likely to have efficient financial infrastructures does not mean that mistakes cannot happen and that crisis is impossible. In addition to the foreign-exchange crises of sterling and the lire, the near failure of Long-Term Capital Management in the United States in 1998 was only resolved by astute and massive rescue operations.[19] That these experiences did not result in major instability offers proof of a good measure of stability efficiency in the financial system of the industrialized countries.

Generally, the financial sectors of the industrialized countries have avoided severe crises despite the development of domestic and international strains as new regulatory frameworks, new technologies (including new financial instruments) forced new awareness of different dimensions of risk and as portfolio managers and other actors push their analytic models to the limit. Advanced capitalist economies can then be expected to have efficient financial infrastructures, provided that the rate of technological change does not exceed the capacity of actors to keep up-to-date with the intricacies of innovations and provided that prolonged tranquillity does not introduce underestimation of the probability of adverse shocks in the mindset of operators in the market.[20] One consequence of the generally adequate financial infrastructure in industrialized countries is that models of the financial sector in, and transactions among, these countries had substantial resistance to shocks and models of international transactions did not need to specify explicitly the components of financial infrastructure. Unfortunately, most pre-1997 analyses neglected to consider the question of the adequacy of financial infrastructure in developing countries.[21]

An efficient financial infrastructure implies the existence of a financial policy framework that provides for adequate prudential regulation. The latter is a static concept and, as Herring and Litan (1994)

and Maehara (1994) suggest, the goal of having prudential regulation keep up with technological innovations in times of rapid change may not, even in sophisticated systems, be feasible. This point overlaps with the idea that as technology advances, problems of enforcement grow and regulation will distort capital markets without an adequate increase in stability-efficiency. This is a strong argument for greater reliance on market forces (i.e. for liberalization) as a means of disciplining firms exposed to excessive risk.[22]

Good financial infrastructure requires: good macro-financial policy and the power to introduce the needed constraints and support systems vested in the central bank; the acceptance by the financial community of the authority of the central bank; good data so that the central bank and operators in financial markets are able to make rational decisions on a reliable basis; and ongoing research into the operations of the system. The greater the number of specialist institutions linking together markets for different kinds of assets and liabilities, the quicker the speed of reaction of these institutions to new information, the more reliable the information, the higher the levels of operator experience and skill in acting in the existing system of financial markets and the greater the mass of financial resources at the disposal of stabilizing institutions, the greater is the adequacy of financial infrastructure of the country. However, there is an internal problem here: the ability to generate good financial infrastructure depends upon the existence of good financial infrastructure. Macro-financial policy must be able to rely on the existence of good data and responsive financial firms if it is to be able to generate good macro-financial policy. Currently, the Chairman of the Board of Governors of the Federal Reserve System is regarded by the financial sector of the United States as a central banker par excellence. He would not be as successful were he to be the cen-

---

[18] For a discussion of the contribution of computer links to the growth of international financial flows, see Minsky (1986). For an assessment of central bank policy in Italy in 1992, see Salvatore (1998).

[19] The bail-out of Long-Term Capital Management in August, 1998, in New York required an infusion of $3.5 billion.

[20] The latter is the essence of Minsky's (1986) theorem, which can be seen as a variant version of "adaptive expectations". The theorem identifies a subtle but potentially serious reduction in the quality of the financial infrastructure as operators are lulled into a sense of false security by a prolonged absence of adverse shocks or by the creation of unidentified speculative bubbles, possibly caused by general or sectoral "irrational exuberance" (Canterbery, 1999).

[21] The crisis in East Asia in 1997 served as a catalyst for analysis of "why things went wrong". In general, analysts have

focused on what may generally be termed "inadequacies of capital markets" rather than on the broader range of characteristics of I-D and poor countries contained within the rubric of "institutional infrastructure" as the idea is developed here. Eichengreen and others (1998) have conducted the most broad-based assessment of which the authors are aware.

[22] Herring and Litan (1994) and Maehara (1994) both advocate allowing individual firms/banks to fail in the expectation that this will not generate a crisis and should cause others firms/banks to reduce their vulnerability and to enhance the stability efficiency of the system. In a system with good stability-efficiency, this is very likely to be so, but the stakes are high and, in many cases, the odds are not knowable. The proposal can be seen as compatible with ensuring that Minsky's (1986) fears of operatives being lulled into a sense of false and overoptimistic security will not occur, but it neglects the possibility that one failure can, in a taut system, start a chain reaction.

tral banker in a country in which good financial infrastructure did not exist.

The lack of an adequate financial infrastructure implies three things.[23] First, the transaction costs of using the system of financial markets will be higher, the greater the degree of inadequacy of the infrastructure. Second, the allocative efficiency of the system will be reduced as individual investors make suboptimal decisions as a result of their lack of understanding of the fine points of the system, from the inferior quality of information available, or from misguided attempts to steer funds to "cronies". Third, the probability of a major crisis is greater than would exist with adequate infrastructure because economic units will not correctly assess uncertainty and the danger of a vicious cycle. The last possibility is significantly enhanced in an open economy allowing transactions on both goods-and-services and capital accounts: it is this possibility of substantial instability that tends to be neglected in traditional analysis.

A system of markets, linkages and skilled operators (good financial infrastructure) is not created overnight and is likely to be very sensitive to culture, tradition, established practices as well as to the set of "formal institutions" inherited from the past. An I-D country may very well have a financial sector which operates with more-or-less satisfactory effectiveness in allocating capital in a closed economy and/or in an environment which is evolving only slowly and the country may have financial infrastructure which enables it to withstand some domestic shocks without creating a financial crisis.[24] Unsatisfactory financial infrastructure is likely to build up stresses over time so that the adequacy of a country's financial infrastructure is likely to deteriorate in the absence of a pause in economic growth and/or advances in financial technologies.[25] Given that institutions and expertise (infrastructure) require time to develop, a system that has been inherited from the past can toler-

ate only some (unknowable) rate of innovation of financial markets and practices without potentially drastic loss of effectiveness. The critical rate of innovation may easily be exceeded in a developing economy either when the economy has experienced rapid growth over a period of years — and expectations have adapted to assume the inevitable continuation of that growth (Tversky and Kahneman, 1982) — and/or has, in the process, become deeply exposed to the substantially more sophisticated global financial system developed by the industrialized economies with all of the possibility of exogenous shock which "membership" in the global system creates. All of the indigenous participants in a national financial system cannot be expected to have a full appreciation of the benefits and the potential costs of the new internationally-open system. Under these circumstances, there will be a gap between the quality of financial infrastructure in existence and the quality required if stability efficiency is to be adequate in the new more open and sophisticated financial system. It is this gap between the existing and the required quality of financial infrastructure which can be held largely responsible for the crises in Thailand and, through contagion, in other East Asian economies.[26] From a policy framework perspective, then, it is important that adequate regulations and procedures are created to support the function of a solid financial infrastructure: this is an example of (financial) institution building.[27]

In Thailand, financial infrastructure fell short of what was required in virtually every dimension: exchange-rate policy; the sophistication of private financial institutions, recognition of the need to hedge foreign-exchange exposures; culture; the accuracy of firms' financial statements; the effectiveness of prudential regulation; and the vulnerability to a panic withdrawal of non-residents investments in equities.[28] No single dimension was crucial in bringing about the ultimate flight from the baht and the abandonment of the dollar peg on July 2, 1997: all contrib-

---

[23] Qualifications to the efficiency of the market system usually emphasize the first aspect of greater transaction costs but neglect the second which derives from imperfect, and possibly asymmetric, information. Asymmetric information receives great stress in Eichengreen and others (1998) and the possibility of (deliberately) bad data relatively little analysis. In financial systems in developing countries, the second issue is of major importance because it contributes to the potential for instability (Rahman, 1998).

[24] One of the major benefits from the establishment of branches and affiliates of major global banks in an industrializing country is the introduction of better banking techniques which multinational banks bring with them. These techniques may spill over to indigenous banks if competition between the two groups is allowed.

[25] There is a similarity here to Minsky's theorem: small shocks will allow the financial infrastructure to be improved at some cost of short-run and localized dislocation (cf. Maehara, 1994).

[26] The problem of contagion is not addressed in this paper. Contagion has clearly been a problem in the East Asian crisis but it operates largely through the mindsets of foreign asset holders who, having misread the effectiveness of financial infrastructure in the country in crisis, take steps to reduce their positions in countries with similarly inadequate financial infrastructure and which are suddenly perceived to be potentially subject to similar adverse shocks. For analyses of the East Asian financial crises, see Letiche (1998) and Rahman (1998).

[27] For a definition of "institutions" see World Bank (1999, 22-23).

[28] What happened in Thailand was an exemplar for Indonesia, Korea, Malaysia and the Philippines except that these countries (with the exception of Korea) were shocked by contagion rather than by the original loss of confidence in a national currency.

uted, directly or indirectly, to the crisis. The individual strands of inadequacy can be examined sequentially.

In any crisis which finds its roots in the international sector, foreign-exchange policy needs to be examined first. In an attempt to attract foreign capital and to limit domestic inflation, the Thai government had, with the encouragement of the International Monetary Fund, tied the baht to the United States dollar so that its rate of exchange was fixed. Note that this policy optimistically assumed that the Thai economy had the stability efficiency to withstand any adverse shock that the U.S. economy could withstand. In practice, this proved to be untrue. At a time when the dollar strengthened against other major currencies in 1997, some relative inflation in Thailand caused the baht to strengthen in real terms against the currencies of its competitors on two counts. The net result was that the price-competitiveness of Thai exports was eroded.

In consequence, the central bank needed, if the pegged rate was to be sustained, to raise the yield on loans denominated in baht to finance the reductions in the rate of growth of exports. Banks and non-financial firms which had access to dollar or yen loans were able to borrow in these currencies at substantially lower rates and, in this way, to reduce apparent borrowing costs. Clearly, more sophisticated bankers and executives of non-financial firms would have recognized an interest rate premium to be a sign of potential weakness and would have borrowed in hard currency only if they could have saved a sum large enough to allow for an exchange rate-hedge and would have hedged their positions. It seems that both non-financial firms and banks which borrowed in hard currency to finance activities which yielded baht were naively relying on the continuation of the dollar/baht rate of exchange.[29] Once the peg to the dollar was seen to be in danger of collapse, the baht was subjected to serious withdrawals of foreign capital.

In Thailand, as elsewhere in East Asia, culture made transparent disclosure of financial conditions much more difficult to achieve with the net result that balance-sheet data hid the very highly-leveraged positions of many large firms (as well as the foreign exchange exposure of banks and some large non-financial firms). One way in which the vulnerability was hidden, in addition to lax accounting standards, was through substantial reliance on related-party

transactions and through off-balance sheet financing of debt. These conditions made it possible for bankers and executives of non-financial firms to take undue risks without these risks being fully appreciated by foreign lenders and investors.[30] One study (Rahman, 1998) emphasizes the inadequacy of the auditing process in Southeast Asia – particularly by international firms. The study reports "horror stories" of firms given a clean bill of health by an international accounting firm only to fail weeks later. Of course, the local managers of country or regional unit trusts/mutual funds should have been aware of the inadequacies of the auditing process in a region in which they were, ostensibly at least, specialists.

The level of prudential regulation of the financial sector was simply inadequate (as the lax accounting reporting suggests). In part, this was due to a traditional antipathy for disclosure on the part of the Thai banks.[31] Both the general disregard for accurate data and the suspicion of authority made the task of imposing adequate standards of prudential regulation more difficult as did the lack of apparent need for concern with malfunction.[32]

One major weakness of central bank policy was the fact that it used up by far the greater part of its foreign exchange reserves in trying to maintain the peg (in accordance with the IMF policy). When renunciation of the dollar peg proved inevitable, there were no reserves left to support the baht against the swings of speculation which occurred.[33] In consequence, the damage inflicted on Thai firms burdened with debt denominated in foreign exchange was unnecessarily great. The social cost of the crisis was

---

[29] This was not as naive as it may appear *ex post facto*. Rahman (1998) notes that rating agencies in New York did not reduce their ratings on sovereign debt of the five East Asian countries until well after the start of the crisis.

[30] This lack of familiarity of East Asian practice indicates a substantial weakness in the financial infrastructure of industrialized countries: financial firms were prepared to lend money and to acquire equities without a thorough understanding of the lack of reliability of their data. Clearly, the investment was not sufficient to precipitate a system-wide crisis in the larger and more robust global system.

[31] The Thai banking system contains a large number of banks owned by overseas Chinese who have a very strong antipathy for disclosure and which tend to operate within a network of overseas Chinese firms in the region (Australian Department of Foreign Affairs and Trade, 1995).

[32] Eichengreen and others (1998, 21-22) puts great emphasis on the contribution of the inadequacy of prudential regulation to crisis (to the point that the expression, "inadequacy of prudential regulation" is used six times in one paragraph). The study correctly points out that liberalization magnifies any inadequacy in the network of prudential regulation. Of course, opening the financial system up to a more sophisticated system will magnify the shortcomings substantially more.

[33] This point was made by Peter B. Kenen at the twenty-fifth Annual Conference of the Eastern Economic Association, March 12, 1999, at Boston, Mass.

Table 7. Variables Used in Studies of Determinants of Direct or Portfolio Investment

Grosse	*Singh and Jun*	*UNCTAD*
Market Growth	Market Size	Market Size
Exports/Imports	Market Growth	Change in Market Size
Interest Rates	Exports	Exchange Rates
Credit	Wage Rates	Exchange Rate Variance
Inflation	Taxes	
Fiscal Balance	Work Days Lost	
Foreign Exchange Reserves	Political Risk	
GDP per Capita	Operating Risk	
Price of Oil	Debt Management	
	Home Country Factors	

Mody and Srinivasan	*Taylor and Sarno*	*Dilyard*
Market Size	Credit Rating	Market Size
Cost of Investment	Exchange Rates	Debt Burden
Taxes	US T-Bill Rates	Interest Rate Differences
Labor Costs	US T-Bond Rates	Credit Rating
Propensity for Trade	Real US Industrial Production	Stock of direct investment
Stock of direct investment		Profitability of direct investment
Country Risk		Size of Stock Market
Infrastructure		

substantial in the region.[34] The crisis was reinforced when domestic banks became insolvent when the prices of real assets fell drastically and firms declared bankruptcy.

THE DIVISION OF PRIVATE FLOWS BETWEEN INDUSTRIALIZING/DEVELOPING AND POOR COUNTRIES

It is useful to summarize the argument to this point: both I-D and poor countries need inflows of private foreign investment to achieve sustained development.

Inward FDI requires a certain degree of institutional infrastructure (both financial and legal) which is likely to be available in the higher-income I-D countries but which must be steadily improved through time as MNCs develop higher levels of expectation about the needed level of sophistication in the institutional infrastructure.[35] Poor countries can only hope to achieve inward FDI if they have specific assets which attract MNCs in industries which rely heavily on available assets (Dunning and Narula, 1996).[36] For this they will require a high level of institutional infrastructure which is likely to be most effectively supplied in an enclave. Poor countries are also likely to need to have the capability of negotiating with MNCs and of formulating an inward-investment policy framework (with a full knowledge of the potential costs of such a plan). While the resources needed to attract inward FDI probably have high opportunity cost, the direct benefits and positive externalities should also be high.

---

[34] In addition to the usual indicators of cost, there is a real possibility that the Thai economy suffered as Thai-owned firms were so weakened by the crisis as to be acquired relatively cheaply by foreign MNCs. As yet there are no data on this phenomenon and it presents scope for a very interesting inquiry.

[35] The Commission of Sustainable Development highlights the important role of government in institution building for financial sector development.

[36] Dunning and Narula (1996, 1-3) identify the deficiency in "location-bound created assets" as a cause of the low rate of inward FDI in poor countries. This concept comes close to the idea of institutional infrastructure since the assets have to be created by the local (host) economy and cannot be supplied by the MNC except in a defined enclave in which event the foreign affiliate is effectively cordoned off from the host economy.

Table 8. Concentration of foreign direct investment in a select
group of countries, 1990-1997 (per cent)

	1990	1991	1992	1993	1994	1995	1996	1997
Share held by top 12	70.5	67.3	72.6	74.3	77.4	72.2	74.6	69.8
Share held by top 8	62.9	61.0	68.6	69.1	69.3	65.0	66.4	62.4
Share of top 12 held by top 8	89.2	90.6	94.6	93.1	89.6	90.1	89.0	89.4

Source: Calculated from World Bank, World Development Indicators, 1999.

Table 9. Concentration of private debt flows in a select
grouping of countries 1990-1997 (percent)

	1990	1991	1992	1993	1994	1995	1996	1997
Share held by top 12	61.1	87.6	62.1	64.3	91.7	82.4	86.4	71.8
Share held by top 8	62.8	68.6	56.0	56.4	58.6	67.4	65.6	56.3
Share of top 12 held by top 8	102.9	78.4	90.3	87.7	64.0	81.8	75.9	78.5

Source: Calculated from World Bank, World Development Indicators, 1999.

Inward traditional portfolio investment also requires a discernible degree of institutional infrastructure but will be judged mainly on the ability of the economy to avoid financial crises. Failure to exhibit a satisfactory level of institutional infrastructure will probably result in a higher cost of borrowing for some countries rather than a complete lack of availability. While financial infrastructure is important, the other dimensions cannot be neglected.

Inward modern foreign portfolio investment must be sustained in the event of recession or financial stress lest its exodus aggravate adverse conditions and instigate a financial crisis. Poor countries will not be able to attract MFPI because of the absolute lack of financial infrastructure. Industrializing/ developing countries must recognize the vital importance of good financial infrastructure and must take conscious steps to generate it.

Attracting inflows of private portfolio investment to a developing economy can be valuable as a supplement to other types of investment inflow. However, if the inflows are not retained and are dissipated by outflows, a policy of attempting to attract easily-encashable foreign capital may not be a good one (irrespective of the efficiency of the local equity market). The damage inflicted by a crisis is simply too great. The key to the retention of MFPI is strong financial infrastructure. Since one purpose of strong financial infrastructure is to deter the existence of financial stress and to preclude panic repatriation of funds in times of financial stress, there is a question as to whether completely unimpeded capital mobility

is appropriate for developing countries.[37]

The major argument for complete liberalization of capital movements (that is, the complete absence of controls on international funds transfers) is the enhancement of global allocative efficiency. There is nothing wrong with this goal[38] provided that the countries have adequate financial infrastructure and most analyses now address the ability of a country to effectively create various aspects of financial infrastructure (for example, prudential regulation and good macroeconomic policies). Indeed, financial capital movements are extremely difficult to control and have become more difficult in the light of recent technological innovations. Any regime of controls runs the danger of seriously distorting capital flows so that the cure may be worse than the disease.

Such a policy must address the level of sophistication of financial infrastructure in all of its dimensions. It is perfect freedom of capital movements which allows the easy encashability of assets and the

[37] The current policy of the IMF is, on the instructions of its policy-setting committee (which comprises finance ministers and central bankers), to amend the Fund's Articles of Agreement so that the Fund can promote the orderly liberalization of capital movements (Eichengreen and Mussa, 1998, 16). Analyses of the process are now subject to more caveats than in 1997 (Fischer, 1997, 1998).

[38] Particularly with respect to direct and traditional portfolio investment.

Table 10. Concentration of portfolio equity flows in a
select grouping of countries, 1990-1997 (per cent)

	1990	*1991*	*1992*	*1993*	*1994*	*1995*	*1996*	*1997*
Share held by top 12	66.7	87.7	91.4	93.5	71.8	68.7	59.8	61.9
Share held by top 8	52.7	83.2	67.5	76.1	56.9	48.6	43.4	54.9
Share of top 12 held by top 8	79.0	94.8	73.8	81.4	79.3	70.7	72.6	88.6

Source: Calculated from World Bank, World Development Indicators 1999.

Table 11. Portfolio equity and direct investment in a
select group of countries, 1993–1997 ($ billion)

	1993	*1994*	*1995*	*1996*	*1997*
Direct investment in:					
Argentina	*3.3*	*3.1*	*4.8*	*5.1*	6.6
Chile	*1.0*	*2.6*	*3.0*	*4.7*	5.4
South Korea	*0.6*	*0.8*	*1.8*	*2.3*	2.8
Malaysia	*5.0*	*4.3*	*4.1*	*5.1*	5.1
Mexico	*4.4*	*11.0*	*9.5*	*9.2*	12.5
Thailand	*1.8*	*1.4*	*2.1*	*2.3*	3.7
Equity investment in :					
Argentina	*5.5*	*1.2*	*0.2*	*0.9*	2.2
Chile	*0.4*	*0.9*	*0.3*	*0.1*	0.5
South Korea	*6.0*	*2.5*	*3.6*	*3.7*	1.3
Malaysia	*3.7*	*1.3*	*2.3*	*4.4*	(0.5)
Mexico	*14.3*	*4.5*	*0.5*	*3.9*	2.1
Thailand	*3.1*	*(0.5)*	*2.2*	*1.6*	(0.3)

Source: Calculated from World Bank (1999). *World Development Indicators* (Washington, D.C., World Bank).

concomitant conversion of local funds into hard currency.

A financial system in which data are not reliable and operators are ignorant of the implications of membership in a global system is in danger of having inadequate stability efficiency.[39] The benefits foreseen by advocates of complete mobility of international capital would, if adequate stability efficiency is to be maintained, require a highly sophisticated financial sector in each and every country.

Rahman (1998, 36) calls for international accounting firms to take the necessary steps so that the quality of audit services provided by their national practices all over the world does not fall short of practices

[39] The real cost of a crisis in an I-D country depends very much on the degree to which the other countries in the world are able to maintain an open market for the crisis country's exports. This requires an importer of last resort and is a role to be filled by the world's financial hegemony. The cost to the crisis country exceeds the bankruptcies of existing firms: it includes the very weakened condition of surviving firms and the high probability that the better of these firms will be acquired by foreign multinational corporations at the expense of national net worth.

in North America and Europe. This recommendation is based on the failure of firms that had received a "clean bill of health" only a few months earlier but it conjures up severe problems of extraterritoriality. Clearly Rahman is correct in the sense that common accepted standards of accounting would preclude the possibility of bad investments by lenders and mutual fund managers in the industrialized world but, like the Panglossian vision of a world with completely liberalized movements of portfolio capital, the approach neglects the adequacy of financial infrastructure (the state of preparedness of the financial sector to conform to the conditions required). Eichengreen and others (1998) offer a sensible review of the problems that must be confronted before freedom of financial capital can be as widespread as liberalized international trade now is. But the study fails to consider the cost of the inordinately larger reserves of foreign exchange which are required as well as the (opportunity) costs of the expenditure of resources in developing the necessary financial infrastructure (with its heavy demands on human capital) as a cost to be offset against the marginal benefits of freedom of international capital movements.

THE SIMILARITIES OF THE DETERMINANTS OF THE TWO INFLOWS: AN EMPIRICAL STUDY

As important as ODA is to promote economic development, it is not sufficient to sustain development. Ultimately, other sources of capital will be needed, and I-D countries are turning increasingly to the private sector to foster economic growth. The private sectors of I-D countries are, however, not sufficiently strong to generate all the private capital needed for continuing economic development. What cannot be raised internally therefore must come from external sources. External private capital flows into a developing country in two forms, direct and portfolio, with portfolio consisting of modern portfolio investment (equity) and debt.

Generally speaking, those entities that engage in direct and portfolio equity investment do so for different sets of strategic reasons. Direct investment in real assets implies the desire to control assets, while portfolio investment uses the ownership of assets to earn a definable return or gain.[40] As the ability of firms, institutions and individuals to invest in the private sectors of other countries becomes more complex in a globalized financial marketplace, however,

the distinction between what functions as direct or portfolio investment can become less clear (Dunning and Dilyard, 1999). For example, it is conceivable that a firm can engage in a portfolio of several (relatively small) direct investments in several countries with the idea that those investments that do not meet previously established criteria will be divested. On the other hand, a consortia of investing entities, each making what essentially is a portfolio investment, could pool their resources to exert functional control over the firm in which the investment has been made.

Historically, studies addressing the determinants of private investment in I-D countries have treated direct and portfolio investment as distinct entities, concentrating primarily on internal country-specific (pull) factors to explain direct investment and external (push) factors to explain portfolio investment. Country-specific factors include domestic market size and/or growth, the history of exchange rate variability, and those such as interest rates, inflation, political risk and the existing stock of direct investment that address the general environment for direct investment. External factors, on the other hand, refer mostly to the interest returns available in alternative locations (developed countries) for portfolio investment; the expectation of higher rates of return on equity and bond investment in I-D countries pushes investment to those countries. Recent studies by Grosse (1997), Mody and Srinivasan (1998), Singh and Jun (1995), UNCTAD (1993), and Taylor and Sarno (1997), however, have expanded the list of explanatory variables for both types of investment to include internal and external variables. Recognizing that the functional purposes of direct and portfolio investment can be similar, Dilyard (1999) developed a common set of explanatory variables applicable to both. Table 7 presents a summary of the variables identified in all of these studies.

In his empirical study of the net flows of direct and private portfolio[41] investment to three East Asian and three Latin American countries[42] from 1980 to 1995, Dilyard used the following set of variables to explain each type of flow:

- Gross domestic product (market size);
- The ratio of total annual interest paid on all debt (domestic and foreign) to gross national product (debt burden);

[40] The operational distinction between direct and portfolio equity investment actually revolves around control, with 10 per cent ownership of a company deemed (by the UN, World Bank and others) to be sufficient to exercise managerial control.

[41] Private portfolio investment was defined as equity and all non-guaranteed debt, including bonds and bank loans.

[42] The East Asian countries were Indonesia, Malaysia and Thailand, while the Latin American countries were Argentina, Brazil and Chile.

- The ratio of short-term debt to total private debt (debt burden);
- The difference between the average annual rate on US Treasury Bonds and the average interest rate on all new private debt added during the year (interest rate differences);
- The difference between the average annual US prime lending rate and the average interest rate on all new private debt added during the year (interest rate differences);
- A comparison of the country's credit rating as determined by Institutional Investor magazine and the average credit rating for all rated countries (credit rating);
- The stock of all inward direct investment from all sources (stock of existing direct investment);
- The combined gross domestic product of developed (OECD) countries (market size);
- The stock of all outward-bound direct investment from OECD countries to I-D countries (a push factor)
- The profitability of US direct investment in an I-D host country (investment environment);
- The year-end capitalization level of the I-D country's stock market (a pull factor);
- The year-end capitalization of developed country stock markets (a pull factor).

Dilyard modelled the combined net flows of direct and portfolio investment against these variables using time series analysis techniques. Adjusting for the incidence of high degrees of correlation among variables common to this type of analysis, he found that either or both direct and portfolio investment in each of the two regions was strongly influenced by GDP, credit rating, the profitability of direct investment, and the size of the country's stock market.

These variables are pertinent to the role of private investment in sustainable development because they point to the environment in which investment can flourish. A large domestic market (GDP), a growing private sector (size of stock market), signs that the economy can support private investment (profitability), and evidence of fiscal and/or monetary infrastructure (credit rating) are all viewed positively by potential private investors. Thus, continuing inflows of private investment, in all its forms, is evidence that foreign investors view favourably the prospects of ongoing or sustained development in a country.

Applying this analysis to the concentration of direct and portfolio investment shown in tables 2, 3 and 4 suggests that only a small number of countries are expected to have sustained development. In fact, the concentration of investment flows can be shown to be even more severe by focusing on the six countries used in Dilyard's study plus China and Mexico. Dur-

ing the 1990s, these eight countries have been the destination of the vast majority of direct and portfolio investment.

The concentration of direct investment in these eight countries is demonstrated in table 8. On average, 90 per cent of the direct investment going to the twelve countries in tables 2, 3 and 4 and roughly two-thirds of the direct investment flowing to all I-D countries have gone to these eight countries from 1990 to 1997. This trend is mirrored in private debt. As table 9 shows, the eight countries were recipients of, on average, a little over 60 per cent of net private debt flows to all I-D countries. Debt flows, however, experienced more volatility than direct investment. Some of this volatility is due to the inclusion in debt flows of debt from private creditors that actually is guaranteed by a third party. Economically stronger countries tend to receive proportionally smaller amounts of this kind of debt than private, non-guaranteed debt. Thus, the large ($40 billion) increase in private debt going to I-D countries from 1995 to 1996 is likely made up of a significant portion of private, but guaranteed, debt.

If the distribution of direct investment and private debt suggests a strong relationship between a country's economic health and its receipt of private capital, what does the pattern of equity investment say? As is seen in table 10, the eight countries attracted anywhere from two-thirds to four-fifths of all equity investment in I-D countries from 1991 to 1993, but a lower amount from 1994 through 1997. Given the relative stability of direct and portfolio debt investment flows, one might expect the behaviour of portfolio equity investment to also be relatively stable.

Equity investment can be notoriously volatile and reacts quickly to any news that is expected to affect economic growth either positively or negatively.[43] Thus, even countries that appear to be an attractive location for direct investment may have undercurrents that frighten away portfolio equity investment. As evidence, examine the pattern of portfolio equity and direct investment in Argentina, Chile, South Korea, Malaysia, Mexico and Thailand from 1993 to 1997 (table 11). Each of these countries had at some point in that period either an economic crisis of its own or were adversely affected by the contagion of crises occurring in the region.

The response to these economic concerns in portfolio equity investment was rather immediate and dramatic capital flight. The problem was exacerbated as

---

[43] As evidence of this statement, one only need examine the recent turmoil in the United States stock market being caused by a combination of inflation fears, disappointing corporate earnings reports, and expectations on Federal Reserve Bank policy pronouncements.

well by its suddenness; these countries had the outward appearance of internal economic strength. Once weakness was revealed, the assumption of stability disappeared. The duration over which this capital flight occurred was (and is) a combination of the severity of the problem, investor expectations about the future and the existence of buying opportunities.[44]

Direct investment, on the other hand, did not experience the same kind of volatility as did portfolio equity investment. Indeed, in many cases direct investment actually increased. One reason this may have been occurring is that the flight of equity investment had created bargain basement buying opportunities for direct investment.[45]

It is difficult, of course, to use aggregate data to get inside the heads of those who engage in portfolio equity or direct investment, particularly with regard to their reactions to internal economic conditions. The empirical data presented here suggests that it is in portfolio equity where the most susceptibility to uncertainty occurs and where the lessons of East Asia (and more recently Eastern Europe) are most acute. As noted earlier, one of the problems that surfaced in Thailand in 1997 was the revelation of an amorphous financial infrastructure that brought about a crisis that not only severely damaged Thailand's economy but infected other country's as well. It also is instructive to note that the underlying causes of Thailand's weak financial infrastructure were largely irrelevant to the consequent capital flight; all that mattered was that which was believed to be true was proven false.

It is impossible to know how less severe capital flight would have been from these countries had the underlying economic fundamentals been shown to be more robust. Likewise, it is impossible to know how less violent the more recent reactions to similar uncertainties about the financial infrastructure of Russia would have been had the events in Thailand not occurred. The badly negative responses to unfavourable news about I-D countries' financial sectors, however, reinforce our premise that a sound financial infrastructure is a necessary component of sustainable development.

Arguably, a different set of policies, particularly

those relating to financial infrastructure and prudent supervision, could have kept the crisis in East Asia from occurring. While a greater degree of disclosure of financial conditions (both at the national and firm level), rules, regulations and practices might have made those entities investing in East Asia more aware of the full nature of the financial environment in which they were participating, it may also have depressed the level of investment in the first place. This relationship between financial infrastructure and policy frameworks and the level of FDI and portfolio investment, which is revealed through empirical studies that address the determinants of those kinds of investment, thus becomes increasingly important when formulating and implementing policy.

POLICIES FOR INSTITUTION BUILDING

Both domestic and foreign private investment are responsive to the quality of institutions in a developing country. This fact requires that policymakers give active attention to the need for building institutions and that they recognize the difficulties of the task. Better institutions (World Bank, 1999b, 22-3) facilitate economic growth in much the same way that improved physical infrastructure contributes to economic growth. However, where the need for upgrading physical infrastructure in both quantity and quality is made clearly apparent (to both taxpayers and policymakers) by bottlenecks and increases in transaction costs, the need for upgrading institutional infrastructure is less obvious. Moreover, improvements in institutional infrastructure may encounter resistance because they require reversing precedent, confronting cultural values, or even worse, threaten the narrow economic interests of the members of the élite.

The need for good institutional infrastructure is not limited to the financial sector, though there is a strong case to be made that the need for good institutions in that sector is paramount.[46] Foremost among these in a world in which the superior efficiency of a system relying on free markets and private sector development are the existence of property rights (legal)

---

[44] Whenever a large amount of investment flows out of or into a stock market over a relatively short period of time, the possibility that investors are responding to a herd instinct in addition to (or in place of) more quantifiable factors is present. While this behaviour is not based on financial reasoning, its impact on the affected market can be profound.

[45] For example, East Asian cement manufacturers, which are faced with high over-capacity and flagging demand, have been the target of much acquisition activity.

[46] Gray (2000) identifies eight areas in which the quality of institutions ("socio-economic infrastructure") is important: legal; educational; technological; financial; communications; cultural; government administration; and the political system. "Socio-economic infrastructure" is a slightly broader concept than "institutional infrastructure": the former includes the ability and the willingness of the population to work within an existing set of institutions, as well as the set of institutions itself. That this distinction can be important in the financial sector is shown by some features of the Thai financial crisis in 1997. With reference to FDI, this distinction may be taken to include the attitudes and work ethic as well as the skills of the labour force.

and the probity and constructive commitment of those in political power (government administration).

Foreign direct investment is, by definition, private. Nations seeking to attain sustainable development must compete among themselves for a share of the flow of FDI from richer to poorer countries. To attract FDI to generate offshore production of goods and services destined for markets in OECD countries, with all of the current account benefits that this genus of MNC affiliates promotes (Fry, 1996), an efficient set of institutions that both accommodates and nurtures private sector development is essential. While the benefits of good institutional infrastructure apply to both foreign-owned and domestic firms, foreign-owned capacity is, because of its international mobility, much more locationally sensitive to the quality of institutional infrastructure.

Fortunately, inward FDI does not require that the availability of good institutional infrastructure be nation-wide. Countries in the early stages of achieving sustainable development can create enclaves (restricted geographical regions) in which both good institutional and physical infrastructure are provided.[47] Successful development in enclaves can create spillover effects and lead to wider improvements in infrastructure and, in the process, provide growth impetus to the rest of the national economy.

Traditional foreign portfolio investment also requires good institutional infrastructure. Evidence of an example of this need is the decision of the Japanese Government in November 1999 to shift the focus of its aid to Indonesia from financial ODA to the loan of financial experts.[48] The cited reasons for the change in policy are the "lack of legal know-how and the country's shattered banking system". The legal structure and the collapse of the banking system interact in that the non-existence of an operational bankruptcy law and the huge volume of bad debts in the banking system combine to render the banks incapable of transmitting financial transfers to firms in the export sector.

Modern foreign portfolio investment is probably the source of external funds (saving) that is most sensitive to the quality of institutional infrastructure. Only very high quality institutions can both attract and retain MFPI which can be so subject to herd reactions by foreign portfolio managers.

Policy formulation depends upon awareness on the part of policymakers and elected legislators of the need for high quality institutional infrastructure. The first step in promoting institution building is the provision of evidence of the importance of institutions so that policymakers recognize the building of institutions as an integral part of the search for sustainable development.[49] From recognition in general it is a short step to identification of what constitutes qualitative improvements in the various sectors. Identification of those institutions which can most usefully be improved does not mean that the process is simple: conservatism, vested interests, fear of foreign domination and cultural values and tradition can all impede institution building. The process is, then, a long one and it must be conducted with standing commitment and a long-term outlook (thus differing from physical infrastructure which usually can be identified with individual, possibly major projects). The upgrading of institutional infrastructure will require broad-based educational programs if new institutions are to be accepted by those affected.

Governments must recognize, in addition, the importance of both legislation and new, refined regulatory systems. The legal and regulatory dimensions must precede the upgrading of institutional infrastructure because there is an inevitable lag between facilitating more sophisticated practices and the ability of people working in the affected sector(s) to learn to adapt to the new system.

Finally, as the analysis of the recent financial crisis has shown, the rate of institution building required is positively related to the rate of change imposed by circumstance. In context, circumstances can be beyond the control of policymakers, as when new technologies force different procedures upon the national economy. However, a rapid rate of change can also be imposed by opening up the economy (or a sector) to a more sophisticated international system and this constraint must be recognized by policymakers in both countries and in supranational bodies. If institution building has some maximum rate of accomplishment built into the process as the ability of ordinary people to accommodate (institutional) change approaches its limit, then the recognition of that constraint must be explicitly identified in the decision-making process.

INWARD FDI AND THE ENVIRONMENT[50]

The thrust of this paper has been that for both I-D countries and, where possible, for stagnating countries inward direct investment is the preferable for-

[47] This is most clearly seen when the inward FDI is seeking to exploit (depletable) primary resources. Here it is essential that the host government have the inherent skills to negotiate an agreement with the foreign corporation that retains for the host country the Ricardian rent which belongs to the primary resources.

[48] "Japanese Aid to Jakarta to shift to Technical Expertise", *The Straits Times*, 13, November, 1999.

[49] The emphasis on the financial sector in this paper should not be seen as refuting the generality of the argument.

[50] This section draws heavily on OECD (1999), particularly the articles by Gentry and Zarsky.

eign conduit for financing sustainable development.[51] This raises the question of how direct investment can be expected to affect the two objectives of sustainable development other than growth in per-capita income: the preservation or improvement of the environment — reducing the *rate* of environmental depredation — and the development of desirable social programs. It is important to recognize, at this juncture, that any analysis of the effect of FDI on environmental depredation requires that a distinction be drawn between the direct and the indirect effects. The operations resulting from inward FDI generate the direct effect (for example, emissions from factories of affiliates of multinational enterprises (MNEs) or the side-effects of mining a primary resource) and the environmental repercussions of any induced economic growth constitute the indirect effects. A part of any consumption pollution brought about by economic growth may be offset by the reduction of some pollution generated by sheer pressure on resources. Clearly, the indirect effects are likely to include the generation of desirable social programs as well as increased pollution generated by additional consumption.[52] Since the indirect effects are unlikely to be very sensitive to the cause of economic growth (domestically-generated growth or FDI-induced growth) and since economic growth is seen as inherently desirable, this section does not explore the potential indirect effects.[53]

There exist both favourable and unfavourable direct effects. Simple logic suggests that countries seeking to attract inward FDI will regard sacrificing environmental quality as one of many possible incentives which can be offered to internationally-mobile investments. This possibility suggests that these developing countries will become pollution havens and that their environmental quality will be sacrificed for

the sake of FDI-generated economic growth.[54] The reverse of this possibility is that established affiliates will transfer to the host nation production processes from the parent corporation and affiliates in more environmentally-sensitive economies and, in the process, reduce the total rate of environmental depredation in the host.

Examples of both kinds of FDI can be found, of course, but it is difficult to substantiate the predominance of either, in part because the generation of reliable data is extremely difficult.[55] There is also a wide range of possible ways in which pollution can be measured and different measures are likely to provide conflicting results. The problems are enhanced when MNEs based in environmentally-sensitive countries attempt to preserve the image of being environmentally friendly by subcontracting out the "dirty" production processes to other, possibly host-country firms. This is referred to as "cascading pollution". Zarsky (OECD 1999) finds evidence that supports both hypotheses. In an attempt to clarify the puzzle, Zarsky (OECD 1999, 52-57) develops a conceptual framework of linkages of which the macro linkages are the most important. The most pessimistic of these is the inability of national or supranational governments to control the behaviour of firms whose activities are internationally-mobile in a world in which poor countries cry out for sources of greater output and the regulation of pollution generation has been consigned to the level of individual states. In some countries, voters have relatively short time horizons so that longer-term problems, such as environmental depredation, are not given the attention they deserve. This concern echoes Kindleberger's (1986) concern with the lack of international public goods in the modern global economy. While recognizing the problems of both analysis and policy, it is worth noting that MNEs are, as a major global phenomenon, less than fifty years old: the society of nations has not yet addressed, with any degree of commitment, the problem of how to regulate the environmental implications of MNEs at the global level. Concern over the environment is necessarily urgent but there is need for commitment rather than despair. The beginnings of such a commitment are to be seen in the growth in the political strength of the environmentally concerned in the more affluent countries.

---

[51] ODA possibly excepted for the stagnating countries unable to attract adequate amounts of inward FDI.

[52] OECD (1999, 15) seems unduly concerned with the indirect effects: "This approach recognizes that although an investment might be judged 'environmentally-friendly' at the plant level, its operations may contribute to a larger-scale of economic activity at the macro level, which may in turn lead to additional environmental harms". If the source of net environmental damage is generated by the induced economic growth (an indirect effect), this implies that growth is harmful *per se* — unless the role of cascading pollution is important (see below). The argument reverts back to the point made in the first footnote to the effect that poverty elimination had become the "poor stepchild" of the annual CSD sessions.

[53] It is certainly possible, and even probable, that the establishment of foreign affiliate enterprises will give impetus to the improvement of the quality of socio-economic infrastructure – partly by spillovers from the affiliates' activities and partly by increasing the need for higher quality infrastructure.

[54] Given the fungibility among the various investment incentives and performance requirements, environmental quality may be sacrificed not only in terms of the affiliate's operations but also in terms of the mix of incentives offered (Gray and Walter, 1983).

[55] One way to improve the quality of empirical studies is to generate a series of interview-based studies at the industry level such as Lundan's (1996) study of the pulp and paper industry.

There is general agreement that MNEs from environmentally-sensitive countries are more likely to create "environmentally-friendly" affiliates because of the need to maintain a good environmental image in their home country and in other markets in which they compete. Concern for an MNE's general reputation can be an important lever for governments and non-government organizations (NGOs) which seek to ensure that FDI in developing countries is not motivated by the search for pollution havens. Perhaps more important in efforts to ensure that FDI is environmentally-friendly is that any lack (or waiver) of environmental regulation in a country which attracts an exporting affiliate be seen as an implicit subsidy of "dirty production". In this way, the goods produced by the affiliate would be subject to countervailing duties on importation into an environmentally-friendly country (Lundan, 1996, Chap. 2).

Other factors which limit the potential of the polluter haven hypothesis is that cost savings from dirty production are more likely to be realized in countries which are badly in need of inward FDI. Often, industries that would manage to effect substantial cost savings from lax enforcement of environmental controls tend to be heavily capital-intensive so that the exposure to political risk and similar socio-economic weaknesses in potential host countries is substantial.

While Gentry (1999, 37-42) analyses the various options open to governments and NGOs in industrialized countries to exert some control over the degree of environmental depredation which can be exercised by affiliate enterprises, the OECD volume refers only tangentially to the level of socio-economic infrastructure available in host countries. In addition to a lack of voter concern in some countries, the world operates seemingly as a series of independent states so that there is no major collective political understanding and commitments.

To regulate an industry or to put together a winning incentive package calls for a sophisticated set of institutions. These institutions are most likely to be found in I-D countries in which the willingness to cater to pollution-unfriendly processes is likely to be small (or, at least, significantly smaller than in stagnating countries). Since "dirty production" can be seen as an implicit subsidy, affiliates in a pollution haven will be limited to countries in which the affiliate is market-seeking. Countries with sufficiently large domestic markets are I-D countries and will not be sufficiently desperate for inward FDI that they will subsidize polluting industries.

CONCLUSIONS

Reliance on the (private) corporate sector to be the key actor in achieving the goals of the Commission on Sustainable Development will not be adequate. The dichotomy of developing countries into those making steady progress and those in stagnation identifies a group of poor countries that have not yet reached the level of sophistication in institutional infrastructure needed to attract substantial inward FDI or private portfolio investment. This conclusion does not mean that the corporate sector cannot play the major role in the further development of countries which have achieved (even low levels of) sustainable development and these are the countries which we have assumed to be most likely to divert a substantial part of incremental income to social programmes and environmental protection.

Models of economic development have not sufficiently emphasized the need for adequate institutional infrastructure, particularly financial infrastructure. This may be due, in part, to the predilection of economists for analyses which fail to recognize instability in financial markets and interruptions in the development process because of malfunctions of any kind.

It is recognized that many of the countries that are currently stagnating may not have institutional infrastructure which allows them to utilize adequately inflows of ODA. While governments and super-national global institutions may be responsible for the distribution of ODA, it would be valuable for the Commission on Sustainable Development to confront the question not only of how the volume of ODA can be increased but also to develop some criteria which might serve to guide the distribution of ODA among the stagnating economies.■

References

Altomonte, Carlo, Richard J. Bolwijn and H. Peter Gray (1999). "Open Industrialization as a Developmental Strategy: The Example of East Asia" in Khosrow Fatemi, ed., *The New World Order: Internationalism and Multinational Corporations* (London: Elsevier Science Ltd.).

Amsden, Alice H., Jacek Kochanowicz and Lance Taylor (1994). *The Market meets its Match* (Cambridge, Mass.: Harvard University Press).

Australian Department of Foreign Affairs and Trade (1995). *Overseas Chinese Business Networks in Asia* (Canberra: Australian Department of Foreign Affairs and Trade, East Asian Analytical Unit).

Beauchamp, T. (1993), "Marketing Infant Formula" in Theodore H. Moran (ed.),*Governments and Transnational Corporations*, (London: Routledge for the United Nations Library on Transnational Corporations).

Boote, Anthony R. Boote and Kamau Thugge (1997), *Debt relief for low-income countries: The HIPC Initiative*, Washington: International Monetary Fund, Pamphlet Series, No. 51.

Canterbery, E. Ray (1999), "Irrational exuberance and rational speculative bubbles", *International trade journal*

XIII, (Spring, 1999), pp. 1-34.

Dilyard, John R. (1999). "The Determinants of Private Foreign Investment in Developing Countries", Ph. D. dissertation, Rutgers University, Newark, NJ.

Dunning, John H. (1992). "The Global Economy, Domestic Governance, Strategies and Transnational Corporations: Interactions and Policy Implications ," *Transnational Corporations*, No. 1, December, pp. 7-45.

Dunning, John H. and Rajneesh Narula (1996), "The investment development path revisited: some emerging issues" in Dunning and Narula (eds.), *Foreign Direct Investment and Governments: Catalysts for Economic Restructuring*, (London: Routledge), pp. 1-41.

Dunning, John H. and John Dilyard (1999). "Towards a General Paradigm of Foreign Direct and Foreign Portfolio Investment," *Transnational Corporations*, No. 8, April, forthcoming.

Eichengreen, Barry and Richard Portes (1997). "The Anatomy of Financial Crises" in R. Portes and A.K. Swoboda, eds., *Threats to International Financial Stability* (London: Cambridge University Press), pp. 10-58.

Eichengreen, Barry and Michael Mussa (1998). "Capital Account Liberalization and the IMF," *Finance and Development*, No. 35, December.

Eichengreen, Barry, Michael Mussa, Giovanni Dell'Ariccia, Enrica Detragiache, Gian Maria Milesi-Ferretti, Andrew Tweedie (1998). "Capital Account Liberalization: Theoretical and Practical Aspects," IMF Occasional Paper 172 (Washington D.C.: International Monetary Fund).

_____ (1999). "Liberalizing Capital Movements: Some Analytic Issues," *Economic Issues*, vol. 17 (Washington, D.C.: International Monetary Fund).

Fischer, Stanley (1997). "Capital Account Liberalization and the Role of the IMF," paper presented at the Seminar "Asia and the IMF," Hong Kong, China, September.

_____ (1998). "The Asian Crisis and the Changing Role of the IMF," *Finance and Development*, No. 35, June, 2-5.

Fry, J. Maxwell (1996), "How Foreign Direct Investment in Pacific Asia improves the Current Account", *Journal of Asian Economics* 7, Fall, pp. 459-486.

Gladwin, Thomas and Ingo Walter (1985), "Bhopal and the Multinational", Wall Street Journal, January 16.

Gray, H. Peter (1992). "Hicksian Instability in Asset Markets and Financial Fragility," *Eastern Economic Journal*, No. 18, Summer, pp. 249-258.

_____ (1996). "Culture and Economic Performance: Policy as an Intervening Variable," *Journal of Comparative Economics*, No. 20, December, pp. 278-291.

_____ (2000). "Globalization and Economic Development," *Global Economic Quarterly*, vol. I, March (forthcoming).

Gray, H. Peter and Jean M. Gray (1994). "Minskian Fragility in the International Financial System" in Gary Dymski and Robert Pollin, eds., *New Perspectives in Monetary Macroeconomics: Explorations in the Tradition of Hyman P. Minsky* (Ann Arbor: University of Michigan Press), pp. 143-168.

Gray, Jean M. and H. Peter Gray (1981). "The Multina-

tional Bank: A Financial MNC?" *Journal of Banking and Finance* vol. 5, March, pp. 33-63.

Gray, H. Peter and Paul J. Miranti (1990). "International Financial Statement Translation: The Problem of Real and Monetary Disturbances," *International Journal of Accounting*, vol. 23, No. 2, pp. 19-31.

Gray, H. Peter and Ingo Walter (1983). "Investment-Related Trade Distortions in Petrochemicals," *Journal of World Trade Law*, vol. 17, July/August, pp. 283-307.

Grosse, Robert (1997), "Foreign Direct Investment in Latin America", *in Generating Savings for Latin America Development*, Chapter 6, Robert Grosse (ed.). (Coral Gables: North-South Centre Press).

Guisinger, Stephen E. and Associates (1985), *Investment Incentives and Performance Requirements*, (New York: Praeger Publishers)

He, Qiang (1999). "The Financial Sector and Economic Development," Faculty of Management, Rutgers University, (mimeo).

Helliar, C.V., A.A. Lonie, D.M. Power and C.D. Sinclair (1998). "The Risk of Investing in Emerging Markets: An Investor's Perspective," Department of Accountancy and Finance, University of Dundee, Scotland. (mimeo)

Herring, Richard J. and Robert E. Litan (1994). *Financial Regulation in the Global Economy* (Washington: The Broodings Institutions).

Hudgins, Sylvia C. (1999). "Capital Flows Provided by Modern Portfolio Investment: An Empirical Examination of Country-Specific Equity Funds of Indonesia, Malaysia, Philippines and Thailand," paper presented at the Annual Meetings of the International Trade and Finance Association, Casablanca, May.

Ismail, Ambassador Razali (1996), "What has been accomplished at Rio: Agenda 21 and the UN Commission on sustainable development", speech delivered at the Symposium on Global Accords for Sustainable Development: Enabling Technologies and Links to Finance and Legal Institutions, Cambridge, Mass., 5-6 September.

Jun, Kwang J. and Thomas L. Brewer (1997), "The role of foreign private capital flows in sustainable development" in Juergen Holst, Peter Koudal and Jeffrey Vincent (eds.), *Finance for Sustainable Development: The Road Ahead*, (New York: United Nations)

Kindleberger, Charles P. (1986). "International Public Goods without International Government," *American Economic Review*, vol. 76, March, pp. 1-13.

Kregel, J. A. (1998). "Yes, It" Did Happen Again -- A Minsky Crisis Happened in Asia," The Jerome Levy Economics Institute Working Papers, No. 234, April.

_____ (1998). "East Asia is not Mexico: The Difference between Balance of Payments Crises and Debt Deflations," The Jerome Levy Economics Institute Working Papers, No. 235, May.

Letiche, John M. (1998). "Symposium on Money and Financial Markets in Asia: A Challenge to Asian Industrialization," *Journal of Asian Economics*, vol. 9, Summer, pp. 179-236.

Lundan, Sarianna M (1996). *Internationalization and Environmental Strategy in the Pulp and Paper Industry* (Ann Arbor, Michigan: UMI).

Maehara, Yasuhiro (1994). "Comment" in Herring and Litan, eds., *Financial Regulations in the Global Economy* (Washington: The Broodings Institutions), pp. 153-162.

Minsky, Hyman P. (1986). *Stabilizing an Unstable Economy* (New Haven: Yale University Press).

Mody, A. and K. Srinivasan (1998), "Japanese and U.S. firms as foreign investors: Do they march to the same tune?", Canadian Journal of Economics, 31(4), pp. 778-799.

OECD (1999). *Foreign Direct Investment and the Environment* (Paris: OECD).

Rahman (1998). "The Role of Accounting Disclosure in the East Asian Financial Crisis: Lessons Learned?" Division on Investment, Technology and Enterprise Development, Enterprise Development Strategies, Finance and Accounting Section, Geneva (mimeo).

Salvatore, Dominick (1998). "Capital Flows, Current Account Deficits and Financial Crises in Emerging Market Economies," *International Trade Journal*, vol. XII, No. 1, Spring.

Singh, Ajit (1992). "The Stock-Market and Economic Development: Should Developing Countries encourage Stock-Markets," UNCTAD Discussion Paper No. 49, Geneva.

Singh, Harinder and Kwang. W. Jun (1995), "Some New Evidence on Determinants of Foreign Direct Investment in Developing Countries", *World Bank Policy Research Working Paper #1531*, (Washington, D.C.: World Bank).

Taylor, M. P. and L. Sarno (1997), 'Capital Flows to Developing Countries: Long-and Short-Term Determinants", *The World Bank Economic Review*, 11(3), pp. 451-470.

The Straits Times (1999). "Japanese Aid to Jakarta to shift to Technical Expertise," 13 November.

Tversky, Amos and Daniel Kahneman (1999). "Judgement under Uncertainty: Heuristics and Biases," in Daniel Kahneman, Paul Slovic and Amos Tversky, eds., *Judgement under Uncertainty: Heuristics and Biases* (New York: Cambridge University Press), pp. 3-22.

UNCTAD (1993), *Explaining and Forecasting Regional Flows of Foreign Direct Investment*, (New York: United Nations)

UNCTAD (1997). *World Investment Report, 1997: Transnational Corporations, Market Structure and Competition Policy* (Geneva: United Nations).

World Bank (1999a). *Global Development Finance* (Washington, D.C.: World Bank).

———— (1999b). *World Development Report 1999/2000* (New York: Oxford University Press).

———— (1999c). *World Development Indicators* (Washington, D.C.: World Bank), CD-ROM.

[11]

THE ASIAN CRISIS, THE IMF AND THE CRITICS

S. Stanley Katz, Ph.D.
East West Center, Honolulu

INTRODUCTION

For Thailand, Indonesia, South Korea and Malaysia, the much-celebrated "Asian Economic Miracle" came to an abrupt end in 1997. After three decades of virtually uninterrupted expansion, these countries saw their financial systems collapse, their economies falter and millions of their citizens returned to poverty, all within a few months. The financial crisis spread quickly to the Philippines and Hong Kong, and then to Brazil and Russia. That it did not spread further was due as much to good luck as to good planning.

Every country's financial angst has its own origins and remedies. Earlier crises had often originated in the fiscal exuberance of developing country leaders. The International Monetary Fund (IMF) would then be called in and would "consult" with the errant officials. On the basis of assurances that they would rein in the government's budget, restore confidence in the banking sector and maintain reasonable price stability, the country would be offered financial assistance from one or another of the Fund's special facilities. While there is some debate over the general effectiveness of IMF policies, particularly their long-run impact, the Asian crisis presented a very different set of conditions to the Fund. It was triggered not by financial excesses of governments but by those of the private sector. It reflected, moreover, a set of new and more complex factors stemming from the globalizing of financial markets that made the crisis both more opaque and contagious. The Asian situation thus required remedies different from those that had been tried in the past.

This paper discusses the major causes of the Asian crisis and comments on the scope and timing of the IMF's response. It then considers, in light of the IMF's Asian experience and given the fact that globally-integrated financial markets daily move amounts greater than most countries' annual GDPs, alternative proposals for ensuring that local financial pressures do not escalate into major crises.

PERSPECTIVE

It is useful to start by recalling the origins of today's international financial system. In June 1944, even before WWII had ended, the United States and Great Britain convened a group of economists and financial experts from forty-four nations at Bretton Woods, New Hampshire to design the financial/economic architecture for the post-War world. Their goal was to put the pieces of the international financial system back together in a way that would underwrite continued growth and stability and pro-

S. Stanley Katz: 3344 Hadfield Greene, Sarasota, FL 34235. E-mail: stanley_katz@msn.com.

Eastern Economic Journal, Vol. 25, No. 4, Fall 1999

scribe any return to the destructive trade and financial practices of the 1930s [Acheson, 1969, 81–84].

The Bretton Woods conferees had as their starting point a lucid and comprehensive memorandum prepared by a team of experts that included, among others, John Maynard Keynes, Harry Dexter White and Dean Acheson. Based in part on that document, within three weeks the conferees were able to agree on the main policies and institutions that they believed would create a sound, long-lasting post-War economic and financial system. The main pillars were the International Bank for Reconstruction and Development (the "World Bank"), the International Monetary Fund (IMF), and (after some political maneuvering) the General Agreement on Tariffs and Trade (GATT) [ibid.].

The shadow of the Depression of the 1930s loomed large over the Conference. It was obvious that European and American follies—inward-looking exchange rate policies, competitive currency devaluations, beggar-thy-neighbor trade practices, liquidity hoarding and the like—had intensified and deepened the Depression. The new IMF was to serve as both a firewall against any recrudescence of such practices and a stabilizer of the international monetary system. To carry out these roles, the Fund was granted unprecedented oversight and interventionist authority. Reconstructing Europe's infrastructure and industry was the charge of the new World Bank. Unwinding the legacy of trade restrictions and moving the industrialized nations to an open, global trade régime was the role of the GATT.

Although the Bretton Woods architecture proved both prescient and durable, it was far from perfect, and its fault-lines soon began to appear. The conferees, for example, had not envisaged the emergence of a new variety of financial crises, one that affected not the industrialized nations but the newly independent developing ones. While this turn had not been anticipated, the conferees had in fact provided enabling language in the IMF's *Articles of Agreement* [IMF, 1974, 2] that permitted the Fund to craft responses to the Third World's financial problems. For the most part they took the form of what would now be called "patches"—ways of working around unforeseen problems by adding new lines of program instructions. The Fund's patches did help to calm, if not cure, the financial problems of stress-prone developing countries.[1] Authority for these new programs is implicit in the first *Article* of the Fund's *Articles of Agreement*.

IMF ROLE AND RESPONSIBILITIES

The first *Article* provides the Fund with considerable, but not unlimited, latitude in discharging its primary stabilizing responsibilities. It states that the Fund is:

> To facilitate the expansion and balanced growth of international trade, and to contribute thereby to the promotion and maintenance of high levels of employment and real income, and to the development of the productive resources of all members;
>
> To promote exchange stability, to maintain orderly exchange arrangements among members, and to avoid competitive exchange depreciation; and

To assist in the establishment of a multilateral system of payments in
respect of current transactions between members and in the elimination of foreign exchange restrictions which hamper the growth of world
trade [Gwin, et al., 1989, 4–5].

To check on compliance, the IMF was to monitor member countries' progress
toward agreed-upon payments arrangements and provide short-term financing to
enable them to deal with transitory difficulties without resorting to measures that
might threaten their own or international prosperity.

The IMF's structure as laid down at Bretton Woods has remained relatively
unchanged over the years. Few *Amendments* have been added since 1945 when the
Fund's *Articles* were adopted. On the other hand, a large number of patches in the
form of special-purpose financing facilities and programs have been added, most
during the past two decades.

THE IMF RECORD

Well into the 1960s, the IMF did a credible job of helping the countries of Western
Europe stabilize their exchange rates, deal with transitory current account imbalances and build an international monetary system based on convertible currencies
tied to the U.S. dollar. The Fund and most observers acknowledge, however, that
these successes were made possible by the vast amount of capital transferred to these
countries under the U.S. Marshall Plan and successor programs.

Following the liberalization of their capital accounts and the U.S. decision to remove the dollar as the anchor of the international currency system, the major industrialized countries moved toward floating exchange rates. This violated the Fund's
Articles, which were promptly amended to fit the new reality. The Fund was instructed,
as part of these new arrangements, to "exercise firm surveillance over the exchange
rate policies of members." In fact, this mandate had little real meaning. The industrialized countries were by then able to meet virtually all of their liquidity needs from
the private capital markets. Since they had no need for IMF resources, the Fund's
new "firm surveillance" responsibilities [Kenen, 1989, 69–81] were essentially null
and void.

Although the IMF continued its annual rounds of consultations with member-
country governments, its influence on the policies and programs of the industrialized countries was by now greatly diminished. The IMF's open membership policy
had, however, resulted in a three-fold increase in members classified as "developing
countries." This new group, the less-developed nations of Asia, Latin America and
Africa, had become increasingly dependent on the IMF for advice and assistance,
especially the latter. The shift in the Fund's client base brought a new set of needs
and challenges. These low-income client countries needed financial assistance that
was more concessional (longer grace periods, extended maturities and below-market
interest rates) than had been required by industrialized members. And, increasingly,
they required relief from foreign exchange debt service burdens that were hobbling
their efforts to develop.

Contacts and consultations between the Fund and it low-income member countries became closer, more frequent and more comprehensive. The Fund's conventional "Stand-by Arrangements" were now accompanied by full-scale country analyses and country-specific assistance programs. New patches were added to deal with low-income countries' needs for longer repayment periods and below-market interest rates. The Fund had established, in 1963, the *Compensatory Financing Facility (CFF)* to help these countries overcome temporary shortfalls in export earnings. The *CFF* was followed in the 1970s and 1980s by an alphabet-soup of new special financing arrangements intended to better meet developing countries' needs. These included the *Extended Fund Facility* (1974), the *Supplementary Financing Facility* (1979), the *Structural Adjustment Facility* (1986), the expanded *Compensatory and Contingency Financing Facility*, (1988) the *Enhanced Structural Adjustment Facility* (1988) and, most recently, the *Supplemental Reserve Facility* (1997), the latter created to accelerate disbursements to deal with the Asian financial crisis [IMF, 1999].

The purpose of these new program patches was to provide more and easier access to IMF credits by the low-income countries. To qualify for such help, the Fund required the country's authorities to formulate a "Letter of Intent" that spelled out how they proposed to correct the country's domestic and international financial imbalances. Since public sector extravagance was the cause of many of these countries' difficulties, IMF "conditionality," (spelled out in the Letter of Intent) typically called for reducing the central government's budget, raising interest rates, improving tax collection, devaluing the country's currency, and preparing a time-bound plan for meeting outstanding external debt obligations.

Fund policy at first required that, in order to gain access to the Fund's special financing facilities, prospective borrowers had to be current on payments due foreign commercial banks. The Fund thus seemed to rank debt service to foreign banks ahead of a country's development efforts, and it opened itself up to charges that it had become a bill collector for foreign bankers. The debt problems of developing countries, in many cases the legacy of imprudent earlier borrowing, had meanwhile worsened as bank credits dried up and net official assistance declined. Paradoxically, both the World Bank and the IMF had by the late 1980s become net importers of capital from their developing member countries.

The next major IMF patch was the "Brady Plan." The Plan was framed in 1989 by the staff of the then-U.S. Treasury Secretary to deal with a financial crisis brewing in Mexico. The Fund had by then moved away from requiring countries to be current in their external debt service payments as a pre-condition for drawing on its special facilities. The Brady Plan went a step further. It recognized that debt service burdens were crippling the economy of Mexico (and of other developing countries); and it proposed that the foreign banks responsible for Mexico's staggering debt problems should bear, by means of write-offs or discounting of debt instruments, some of the costs of providing relief. By most assessments, the Brady Plan did help to defuse the gathering Mexican financial crisis. However, it turned out to be a one-time, special-country case. The Plan depended on "voluntary" participation by foreign commercial banks. It has not proved very popular as a means of providing developing countries' debt service relief [Sachs, 1989].

While the Fund has continued to provide assistance and advice to its developing country members, it has become increasingly clear that their problems were broadly developmental, rather than narrowly financial. Most developing countries need medical personnel and delivery systems; improved nutrition and education; functioning legal, financial and commercial institutions; skills and technology; and long-term capital investments in infrastructure. Besides these constraints, there is a fundamental mismatch between the short- and medium-term loan assistance the Fund can provide and these countries' requirements for grants and for long-term, concessional loans for development.

Overall, the developing country financial conundrum has in no sense been solved, nor has it gone away. Rather, it was pushed aside by the financial and economic implosion of the Soviet Union in 1989/90. The Fund's industrialized members pressed the IMF to rush into the breach and to play a role for which it had not been intended and for which it was not well equipped: to macro-manage and bankroll the transformation of Russia and the former Soviet Union from centralized to market-based economies. Neither the IMF's loans and recommended banking sector reforms nor the ill-advised "shock therapy" (prescribed by misguided but influential "transition experts") has met with success. IMF loans to Russia now total some $20 billion. The second $640 million tranche of a recent $4.5 billion loan (most of which is earmarked for interest due on past IMF loans) is in abeyance as the Russian economy has become increasingly anarchic and dysfunctional. In the meantime, charges of money laundering by, among others, the Russian mafia and some senior government officials, possibly involving the proceeds of earlier IMF loans, are being investigated [Charlton, 1999].

THE ASIAN FINANCIAL CRISIS

In the past two years the Fund has faced yet another problem: the financial crisis that has swept through some of East Asia's former economic leading lights and has spread from Asia to Russia and Brazil. While the Asian crisis appears to be in remission, at least for the present, recovery has been uneven and uncertain, and many of the conditions that sparked and fueled the Asian crisis remain unaddressed.

It seems like only yesterday—in fact it was in 1993—that the World Bank published its upbeat *The East Asian Miracle—Economic Growth and Public Policy* [World Bank, 1993]. The Bank reported that for most of the three prior decades, the East Asian "tigers," with South Korea as the leader of the pack, and the "Newly Industrializing Economies"—Indonesia, Malaysia, and Thailand—had generated increases in gross domestic product at the unprecedented rate of 5 percent to 7 percent a year. Questions were raised about whether the "miracle" was genuine in terms of having achieved a shift in productivity or whether it was simply the result of pouring more resources into these economies. Yet the benefits were tangible. An estimated 350 million East Asians had been lifted out of poverty. It appeared that the countries had broken out of the poverty trap and had entered the ranks of dynamic and self-sustaining economies.

Now, less than six years later, that glowing scenario has turned to ashes. During 1997 and 1998,[2] South Korea, Thailand, Malaysia and Indonesia experienced various degrees of financial and economic collapse. Scores of banks and corporations have gone bankrupt, per capita income has plunged, billions in savings have evaporated, millions of workers have lost their jobs and some have taken to the streets. The specter of collapse spreading further through Asia and to other corners of the global economy remains very much alive.

Since the first signs of the impending crisis appeared in each of these countries' financial sectors, one wonders if the IMF understood from the outset what was happening, and whether its remedies were timely and appropriate; or, conversely, if the Fund's prescriptions made a bad situation worse. One of the underlying causes of earlier financial crises in Central and Latin America and in Africa had been excessive spending by governments. Chronic public sector budget deficits had generated price inflation and trade account imbalances that led to overvalued currencies and the flight of capital. The IMF's conventional prescription in such cases called for reducing central government expenditures and increasing revenues by improving tax collections, raising interest rates to dampen speculation and keep funds in the country, devaluing the country's currency to increase exports and contain imports, improving governance and reforming banking. Although serious doubts have been expressed about the Fund's overall, longer-term impact, these remedies appear to have helped restore a degree of fiscal and financial equilibrium in the short run in countries able to muster the political will and public support needed to implement them.[3]

The crises in East Asian countries, however, reflected few of the characteristics of earlier financial crises in Central and Latin America. Government budgets had been recording substantial surpluses, price inflation had been modest, real interest rates were positive, saving rates were high, and current account balances were positive. For most of their "miracle" period, in fact, these Asian countries had experienced, besides stunning rates of domestic growth, rapid expansion of exports and trade account surpluses and a build-up of their foreign exchange reserves [World Bank, 1998, *passim*].

To promote their exports, the East Asian countries had liberalized their current accounts, but not their capital accounts, and had made their national currencies freely convertible into foreign exchange for current account transactions. Most had also pegged their national currency to the U.S. dollar, thereby all but eliminating exchange risks and the cost of hedging for traders and investors. While it was acknowledged that a corresponding liberalization of capital account transactions would be beneficial in the longer term, these countries' central bankers recognized that large, sudden movements of capital could be risky without a banking system able to prevent such transactions from destabilizing the country's financial sector and economy [ibid., 6]. Nor was it overlooked that restrictions on capital transactions protected owners of domestic firms and industries—usually members of powerful extended families, government officials and, in the case of Korea, the *chaebols*—from equity dilution and unfriendly takeovers. In the so-called Asian model, enterprises were in any case highly leveraged, and borrowing rather than equity had long been their main source of fresh capital. The debt/equity ratio of South Korean corporations, for example, was over 317 percent in 1996, twice the U.S. level [ibid., 8].

At the urging of the IMF, the United States, Japan and other capital exporting countries, these East Asian countries reluctantly began in the mid-1990s to liberalize their capital accounts. The intended sequence was to open the short- and medium-term end of the capital spectrum to foreign bankers and traders first. Long-term foreign capital transactions remained subject to formal and informal constraints and were to be liberalized "in due course."

Since interest yields were higher in these East Asian countries than in the industrialized countries' capital markets, and since their currencies had been pegged to the U.S. dollar, Japanese, European and American banks and other intermediaries began to pile up what they considered to be risk-free, high-yielding loans. At the same time, domestic banks, start-up financial institutions, corporations and a variety of other private intermediaries in these Asian countries found that they could borrow capital more cheaply and more readily abroad than they could at home. In the mid-1990s, for example, a run-of-the-mill Asian investor could borrow Japanese yen at nearly zero interest, invest in a Bangkok skyscraper, and expect to earn a 20 percent annual return.

From the perspective of both borrowers and lenders, East Asia became the modern-day version of the California gold rush. While world trade grew on average by about 5 percent a year between 1990 and 1997, aggregate global private capital flows grew at nearly six times that rate. Between 1990 and 1997, private capital flows to developing countries rose five-fold, from $42 billion to $256 billion. Nearly two-thirds of that amount went to East Asia [ibid., 7].

In the absence of reporting and monitoring requirements and of virtually any other requirements for transaction transparency, the central banks of these Asian countries had no way of knowing how much their banks, business firms and individuals were borrowing overseas. Even if they had had this information, they lacked the experience, skills and legal system that would have permitted them to moderate or check excessive capital inflows. Nor did the central banks of Japan, the United States, or European countries take soundings of the large amounts of capital moving electronically to East Asia. By 1996, annual net private capital inflows to these four East Asian nations amounted to between 5 percent and 15 percent of their annual gross domestic product (GDP). The Bank for International Settlements reported that in 1996 European Union banks' loans outstanding in East Asia amounted to $318 billion. The corresponding figure for Japanese banks was $261 billion, and for U.S. banks it was $46 billion [ibid.].[4]

As the volume of capital transfers grew, confidence soared and real estate and other forms of collateral at greatly inflated prices were used in place of due diligence assessments of borrowers by lenders. At the same time, the quality of collateralized assets declined. With the expectation that outstanding loans would continue to be rolled over, short-term borrowing was used increasingly for long-term investments. Hotels, apartment houses and office buildings were built in Seoul, Kuala Lumpur, Bangkok and Jakarta funded largely by short-term foreign loans, often with only the slightest prospect of earning positive returns in the near future. In South Korea, the *chaebols*, flush with borrowed funds obtained from friendly, often captive merchant bankers, invested in firms and industries whose debt servicing costs were higher than their prospective net earnings.

428   EASTERN ECONOMIC JOURNAL

The combination of speculative domestic borrowers and abundant, but mostly short-term foreign capital overwhelmed these Asian countries' understaffed, inexperienced and immature financial institutions. By 1996, problems that had been obscured or ignored while the good times rolled began to show up. The pace of economic growth faltered, trade surpluses turned to deficits as imports rose and competitiveness eroded. The supply of fresh foreign credits slowed from a flood to a trickle; and when the inflated collateralized property bubble burst, non-performing assets on the books of borrowers and lenders multiplied.

Expectations and confidence quickly switched from positive to negative as foreign bankers and money managers began to question the ability of their borrowers to service their debts and of the countries to maintain the pegged value of their currencies. The most egregious sin in the bankers' craft is to be the last one out, and the herd instinct quickly took over. Foreign lenders refused to renew outstanding short-term loans, began to dump assets and headed for the nearest exits. Despite costly but futile efforts to prop them up, starting with the Thai baht, these countries' currencies began to tumble, property and equities prices crumbled, and liquidity dried up as bankers called in outstanding loans in an attempt to cover their mounting negative asset positions.[5]

What had started as a problem in Thailand's financial sector quickly spilled over into the real economy. As fear took over, there were runs on large and small otherwise solvent banks. Many were forced to close. Their otherwise viable customers, unable to obtain funds to meet ordinary operating needs, were forced to follow. Bankruptcies and downsizing multiplied, and millions of East Asians lost their jobs, their incomes and their savings. They and their families were plunged back into the poverty from which they had only just escaped.

From Thailand it was only a short hop to other nominally vulnerable Asian countries. Overseas bankers and intermediaries, sensing that South Korea, Indonesia and Malaysia were overextended—a condition they had helped to create—set in motion the same process of financial withdrawal and economic contraction. The result was a regional economic crisis that left neighboring countries wondering if they would be next.[6]

While the flight of foreign capital was a proximate cause of the crisis in East Asia, there were others. Pressure on these countries from the IMF, the United States, Japan and European Community countries to liberalize their capital markets were ill-advised and premature. It was widely recognized that these Asian countries' financial institutions and capital markets were shallow and fragile. It was obvious as well that they lacked the institutional framework—the laws, people, processes, administrative checks and balances, experience and information and regulatory mechanisms—required to deal with a large and potentially disruptive inflow of foreign capital.

These institutional deficiencies were all the more critical given the fact that the previous decade had seen a proliferation of new banking and quasi-banking institutions in East Asia with little equity capital and less experience, nearly all engaged directly or indirectly in intermediating foreign capital. This rapid growth in interbank lending played a major part in the rapid accumulation of short-term debt by new and inexperienced banks and quasi-banking institutions. Nor was any tally kept of the foreign loans that had been taken up in these countries' non-banking sector by private firms, non-banking financial entities, the *chaebols*, and well-connected private individuals.

When the East Asian governments liberalized their banking sectors and capital markets, they initially opened up the short maturity end of these markets. This segment is typically characterized by short-term financial instruments and short-term rent-seeking (quick profits). For these reasons, this segment of capital markets can be highly volatile, with violent swings occurring within hours. Long-term capital, which is more often invested in plant and equipment, infrastructure and equities and cannot be so easily liquified, was to be liberalized "later." While the reason for this sequence was political, the price paid was financial and economic. Because of the shortage of long-term capital during the prior period of economic boom, short-term credit was used to finance long-term investments. The resulting mismatch of borrowing and lending terms was one of the main ingredients of the Asian financial crisis.

In the industrialized countries, little official notice was paid to the explosive growth of short term and frequently speculative capital transfers to East Asian borrowers. Moreover, new and complex financial instruments (involving, for example, deep discounts, strips and swaps, and new financial intermediaries such as hedge funds and region- and country-specific mutual funds) introduced new agents of volatility into an already overburdened financial scene. When combined with the ability of foreign and domestic traders and money managers to move huge sums of capital from country to country with a few keyboard strokes, these new factors should have caused alarms to go off in the central banks of Japan, Europe and the United States. If they did, they were not heeded, and the danger that large, volatile and mis-matched capital movements posed for East Asian nations was ignored.

THE IMF AND THE ASIAN CRISIS

What was the IMF doing all this time? For most of its existence, the IMF has been one of Washington's best kept secrets. More recently, however, it has become a favorite target of pundits and critics of every persuasion. At one extreme are those who are convinced that the IMF doesn't put out fires but starts them, and who suggest that the IMF building in downtown Washington, D.C. should be turned into a parking lot. Others believe that the Fund can be only as effective as its member countries permit, and that while it has made mistakes, it plays a necessary role in the international financial system. Yet another view is that the world of international finance has moved far beyond the vision and capabilities of the existing Bretton Woods institutions, and what is needed is, in effect, a global central bank. Finally some, both inside and outside the Fund, think the organization is fine as it is and simply needs more money to do its job.

The East Asian financial crisis has added to the debate about the IMF's future. A look at the Fund's performance in Thailand, Indonesia and South Korea can help illuminate this discussion [IMF, 1999].

Thailand

By the time Thai authorities called in the IMF fire brigade, the baht had been under attack by investors and speculators for some five or six months. The government had depleted a large part of the country's foreign exchange reserves in a futile attempt to maintain the baht's value, and both economic activity and the exchange rate were in steep decline. In late August 1997, the Fund's Executive Board approved a financial package for Thailand of $4.0 billion, to be disbursed over 34 months. For its part, Thailand, in a Letter of Intent, undertook a set of financial sector reforms that included identifying and closing some 50 non-viable financial institutions and recapitalizing the banking system. To provide the necessary budget for the proposed recapitalization, the Thai government agreed to shift from a budget deficit to a surplus equal to about 1 percent of GDP, in part by raising the value-added tax. Interest rates were to be raised to stem the outflow of investment capital, and the baht was to become subject to a managed float. An initial Fund disbursement of $1.6 billion was approved, not a very substantial amount given the heavy pressures the baht was experiencing.

Three months later, in late November 1997, the IMF Executive Board's review of the Thai situation revealed that, the IMF package notwithstanding, the baht had continued to lose value and the economic slowdown was sharper and more pervasive than Fund staff had anticipated in August. The IMF program was modified, but mainly it reiterated the need for a budget surplus and for major financial sector reforms. In December, the Fund made its second disbursement—a modest $810 million.

As the Thai crises deepened and as financial distress began to spread to neighboring Asian countries, the Thai Letter of Intent was progressively modified—in February 1998, and again in May, August and December. Each modification reversed the Fund's initial contractionary prescriptions. Fiscal and monetary measures were turned from negative to positive in order to stimulate domestic economic activity, to stabilize the baht and to create a much-needed social safety net. Interest rates were reduced and the Fund's previously ordained budget surplus was transformed into a deficit target.

The contraction of the Thai economy continued. Real GDP declined by an estimated 8 percent in 1998. Weak domestic demand was reflected in a sharp drop in imports that produced a current account surplus. The domestic money supply was meanwhile expanded and financial sector restructuring continued. To their credit, Thai government officials resisted the temptation to impose capital and currency controls (as neighboring Malaysia had done, with unexpected short-term benefits for that country's recovery!), and sought instead to increase foreign direct investment. For its part, the Fund continued its release of financial tranches: $270 million in March of 1998, $135 million in June and in September and $140 million in December [ibid., 3-6].

Indonesia

The IMF's involvement in the Indonesian crisis began a few months after Thailand and followed an essentially similar pattern. The Fund's initial response followed traditional lines: reduce central government budget expenditures, increase interest rates and float the rupiah. As in the Thai case, this prescription failed to account for the fact that Indonesia's financial and economic stress had originated in excessive borrowing by the private sector rather than by the government. Unlike the Thai case, however, in Indonesia the borrowing spree had involved private individuals, families and corporations rather than banks. Again, the Fund underestimated the severity of the economic downturn and (notwithstanding years of visits and consultation) failed to grasp the breadth and depth of the country's cronyism. Fund staff assumed that the economy could be turned around with conventional remedies. Instead, the crisis deepened and spilled out into the streets in the form of angry rioting and looting.

Back in Washington, the IMF Executive Board approved an initial program of financial assistance for Indonesia early in November 1997. Financial support of some $10 billion was committed for a three-year period and $3 billion was released for immediate disbursement. The IMF program was one of fiscal restraint. It included a budget surplus target of 1 percent of GDP; restructuring the financial sector, including closing a large number of undercapitalized private banks and merging of state banks; and a plan for improving the institutional, legal and regulatory framework of the financial system. In addition, foreign trade and investment were to be liberalized, a flexible exchange rate policy introduced and interest rates raised.

During the following months it became clear that the Fund's reform prescriptions and financing were unable to restore confidence in either the economy or in the rupiah. The economy's slide deepened. Following another IMF review, a "Memorandum of Economic and Financial Policies" was issued early in January 1998. Its main new features were a reversal in fiscal policy from contractionary to expansionary, the cancellation of several capital expenditure projects of questionable origin and priority and, in response to public demonstrations, emergency measures to ensure more adequate food supplies at affordable prices.

The rupiah continued to fall and economic conditions continued to deteriorate. Three months later, in April 1998, yet another review was held, and another "Supplemental Memorandum of Economic and Financial Policies" was issued. It continued the structural reforms of the financial sector and began to address the need for restructuring foreign exchange indebtedness and the problems of bank closings and domestic liquidity shortages that were stifling Indonesia's banking and corporate sectors. The country's social safety net was also to be strengthened through added support for small and medium-sized firms and new public works programs.

A "Second Supplemental Memorandum of Economic and Financial Policies" followed in June 1998. It acknowledged that the economic situation had worsened and that confidence had been further eroded by social disturbances and a change in government leadership. The budget deficit target was then raised to 8 percent of GDP. New and revised Letters of Intent and "Memoranda of Economic and Financial Policy" followed in July, September, October and November of 1998. As poverty and social unrest spread, each successive Letters of Intent added more strands to the social safety net and reinforced on-going financial sector reform efforts. Following its normal performance-linked disbursement procedures, the Fund parceled out financial support in tranches: $1 billion in April 1998, $1 billion in July, supplemented by some

$6 billion of informal debt rescheduling by bilateral creditors; and approximately $950 million in September, in November and in December of 1998 [ibid., 7-12].

South Korea

For many of the same reasons, South Korea had also become vulnerable to the contagious financial crisis. Responding to pressures from the Uunited States and the IMF, the Korean Government had removed a number of restrictions on foreign participation in the manufacturing and banking sectors. The government had been an active participant in the banking sector, and links between the *chaebols* and the banks fed a rapid expansion of unsound investments, much of it funded by short-term merchant bank borrowing abroad. These weaknesses became increasingly visible both within and outside the country. Exports stagnated, the current account turned negative and price inflation accelerated. The Korean won came under increased pressure and foreign bankers and traders headed for the doors.

The Korean government approached the IMF for assistance in December 1997, and a program of assistance and reform was agreed upon. It included comprehensive financial sector restructuring that, among other things, called for closing or recapitalizing scores of under-capitalized merchant banks and severing the long-standing, close relationships among the government, the *chaebols* and the banks. In addition, it provided for further trade and capital account liberalization and for a target budget surplus equal to 2 percent of GDP to fund the recapitalization of the banking sector.

The Fund's staff had seriously underestimated the severity of the South Korean economic recession. Besides writing its conventional prescriptions, the Fund had set much too short a time frame within which reforms were to be implemented. The Korean economy continued to contract and scores of banks and businesses closed their doors. Meanwhile, a Letter of Intent was agreed upon in December 1997 that essentially reiterated the previous reform régime. As the Korean financial and economic crisis worsened, additional Letters of Intent were issued in January, February, May, July and November of 1998. These prescribed the by-now-familiar remedies but included a few new ones as well: a switch from a budget surplus to a deficit target of 5 percent of GDP, increased social safety net expenditures, financial sector restructuring, including recapitalizing and/or closing banks, debt workouts with foreign creditors, trade and investment account liberalization, an easing of interest rates and greater corporate transparency.

The Fund parceled out its financial assistance in tranches tied to Korea's implementation of its Letters of Intent. Some $5.6 billion was disbursed in early December 1997, followed later in the same month by $3.5 billion from the Fund's new *Supplemental Reserve Facility* and by an additional $2.0 billion at the end of that month. Fund disbursements of financial assistance to Korea in 1998 amounted to $2.0 billion in January, in February and in May; and $1.0 billion in August and in December [ibid., 13-17].

ASSESSMENT[7]

It is clear with the benefit of hindsight that the Fund missed or misunderstood many of the essential differences between East Asia's financial problems and those it had dealt with elsewhere in the past. Asian's financial stress had arisen not as a result of public sector profligacy but because of imprudent and excessive foreign borrowing by these countries' private sectors. Having missed, at least initially, this basic causal difference, and having assumed therefore that recovery would respond to its traditional remedies, the Fund proceeded to compound its error by underestimating both the severity and tenacity of the Asian crisis. The Fund's prescriptions for budget surpluses and higher interest rates reinforced the contractionary forces at work in these economies when they should have done the opposite. A first opportunity to stop the Asian crisis in Thailand before it became virulent and contagious was therefore missed [World Bank, 1998]. Since the problem initially involved liquidity and confidence, the Fund might have been able to nip the crisis in the bud had it abandoned its usual carrot-and-stick approach and had instead front-loaded the disbursements of its financial support. In that case, confidence in these countries' currencies and economies might well have been restored before too much damage was done.

From a broader perspective, Fund staff hubris may have gotten in the way of sound economic analysis. Asian countries have highly trained and sophisticated economists and financial experts who knew a great deal more than Fund staff about what was happening in their economies. The Fund might have sought their views and advice earlier in the review process, but apparently chose not to do so. Observers (in Asia and elsewhere) complain that the Fund has become smug and exclusionary and too convinced of the rectitude of its own analyses and prescriptions. This institutional culture, combined with its usual protracted bureaucratic processes involving, among other things, Letters of Intent, "Standby Agreements," scheduled formal Executive Board Reviews, fixed agendas, and loan disbursement tranches tied to performance—appears to have hurt the Fund's overall effectiveness.

It appears that Fund staff, faced with a rapidly emerging financial crisis, chose to emphasize the need for structural reform.[8] While reforms are important in the longer term, they may have diverted attention from the need for quick and decisive action to check intensifying financial crises. In the past, the Fund could address currency and liquidity problems and structural reforms in a single package, with disbursements of Fund assistance tied to progress in reforms. That dual-track approach was perhaps appropriate when financial crises developed more slowly, when aggregate capital transfers were smaller and slower, and when transfers involved mainly government borrowers. Now the amounts are huge, the speed is instantaneous, and the borrowers are predominantly from the private sector. The window of opportunity for effective IMF intervention in this changed environment is days if not hours. The Fund's traditional gentlemanly pace hardly meets these new circumstances.

The Fund's recent Asian experience suggests that its efforts to deal with incipient currency and liquidity problems should in the future take precedence over efforts to achieve structural and institutional reforms. While both may be necessary, they involve different time frames and different in-country institutions and officials. Heading off financial problems requires a focused and rapid response; structural reforms cut across many sectors and are longer-term.

It has been suggested that the Fund should leave structural and institutional reforms to the World Bank and the regional banks. This would strip the Fund of its most persuasive reform lever, with no assurance that another financial institution would fill the gap. Moreover, the implicit division of labor presupposes a degree of consensus, cooperation and coordination among the IMF, the development banks and, most importantly, the concerned countries that is highly unrealistic given their divergent interests, objectives and decision-making processes. A further consideration is that in most cases one or another of the Fund's member countries is likely to be pressing IMF management to go easy on reforms and get the check in the mail. In any event, the IMF's Asian experience, while less than brilliant, does not indicate the need to separate the organization's financial carrots from its structural reform sticks—only that they be applied with greater sensitivity to the country's circumstances, needs and priorities.

The proposal that the IMF rush in with financial assistance raises the issue of "moral hazard."[9] The usual analogy is that people will worry less about smoking in bed if they have fire insurance on their homes. In international finance, moral hazard arises if lenders and borrowers are assured in advance that the Fund (a government or another institution) will guarantee the repayment of their loans in the event of a financial crisis. In that case, borrowers and lenders might be less concerned with the quality of the underlying assets. Moral hazard may be more of an issue in theory than in fact. It places little value on the time, costs and difficulties involved in obtaining financial guarantees and in collecting on them. In any case, it is doubtful that lenders would extend loans or that borrowers would seek them for doubtful projects even if they might eventually be able to recover their principal in the event of a financial crisis. It should be possible to build enough uncertainty, time delays and ambiguity into guarantee arrangements to forestall unsound lending.

THE FUTURE

The Bretton Woods architecture is showing its age. The economic and financial world the conferees envisaged and, in particular, the kinds of problems they expected the IMF to deal with, are history. The question now is whether the Fund's mandate and patched-up programs are adequate to cope with—and impact—today's huge, seamless and fast-moving financial markets. This issue is being framed even more broadly in terms of whether to try to upgrade the IMF and the current international financial architecture, or whether to retire it and replace it with new, forward-looking institutions.

This question has brought little in the way of consensus. Upgrading proposals typically include variations of the following:

> ***Enhanced Transparency and Accountability***. Macro-economic
> data as well as transactional information should in the future be based
> on uniform definitions and standards and should become rapidly and

readily available to all public, private and international participants
in international financial markets.

***Stronger Financial Systems and Financial Market Restructur-
ing***. The intent is to recognize that the liberalization of capital markets is an essential component of a well-functioning market-based
economy, but that it should follow, not lead, the strengthening of
financial sector institutions and the establishment of systems to
record, monitor and, as appropriate, regulate capital transfers.

***Oversight of Foreign Direct Investment and Regulation of
Speculative Flows***. This proposal would involve the imposition of
reserve requirements on foreign borrowing or a negative interest rate
or excise-type tax on short-term withdrawals, as well as the prioritiz-
ing of long-term capital investments so that resources would be directed to high priority investments, not to speculative or lower priority ventures.

Avoiding the Mismatch of Borrowing and Investment. This proposal would seek to avoid the use of short-term loans to finance long-
term investments and to prevent short-term credits from being repeatedly rolled over as a substitute for long-term financing.

In addition to these upgrading proposals, a more fundamental proposal has been
made that would require major improvements in the coordination of financial and
monetary policies at the international level. In place of current periodic summits and
ministerial-level "Interim Committee" meetings, a permanent secretariat would monitor and promote policy consistency and coordination among the major financial-cen-
ter countries. The secretariat might simply represent an expansion of IMF or OECD
monitoring roles and might mainly involve more frequent and/or continuing high
level contact among these countries' central bankers. An extension of this proposal
would establish a mechanism to provide closer coordination among the major security regulatory agencies, including the U.S. Securities and Exchange Commission, in
order to ensure the orderly development and operation of international security markets.[10]
     Another proposal would make the future IMF a combined international lender of
last resort and a manager of potential financial crises, corresponding in essence to the
Federal Reserve System in the United States. The Fund, it is argued, is well posi-
tioned to perform both functions. As a crisis manager, the Fund would take the lead
in formulating and negotiating rescue and workout plans with member countries and
their public and private sector creditors in order to forestall financial problems. As a
crisis lender, the Fund would take the lead in mobilizing and disbursing country-
specific financial rescue packages. To function as a lender of last resort, the Fund
would have to be granted authority to create and issue Special Drawing Rights (SDRs)

on an as-and-when needed basis and to allocate them directly to countries in need rather than to countries based on their IMF quotas [Fischer, 1999].

There is a strongly held contrary view that patching up an antiquated system is not the answer. What is required instead is a new Bretton Woods Conference that will visualize and create policies and institutions to meet the future needs of a global financial/economic system. A core institution to be established under this formulation would be a global central bank with the authority to oversee the international financial activities of all member countries, much as the Federal Reserve does for the 50 American states [Soros, 1998]. A step in that direction was in fact taken with the inauguration of the European Central Bank in 1999. The Bank was established to coordinate the monetary and fiscal policies of its eleven member countries—to establish a single currency, the euro, and to prescribe exchange rate bands, budget deficit ceilings, and convergent interest rates for the European Community as a whole. Since high-visibility matters of national sovereignty are at stake at nearly every turn, it remains to be seen how the scope and responsibilities the European Central Bank develop [Reuters, 1998]. There is also a suggestion that we are already on the way to the *de facto* creation of three currency areas—a European euro area, an Asian yen area and a North American dollar area. Whatever its pros and cons, this type of trilateral arrangement would surely facilitate the coordination of international financial policy.

These micro-measures would no doubt help ensure greater international financial stability and, presumably, fewer contagious financial crises. But on the larger question of architecture for the future, reams of papers and hours of discussions have produced little in the way of over-arching concepts or consensus. What has been produced so far comes nowhere near the vision and intellectual content of the architecture that emerged from Bretton Woods a half-century ago. This suggests that the needs and designs for such future architecture are too opaque and complex to be captured by a series of *ad hoc* meetings, papers and piece-meal proposals. What is required is an approach that is consecutive, comprehensive, and systemic. In the view of many observers, that can happen only if and when the United States takes seriously its role as leader of the new global economy. A decisive step in that direction would be for the United States to convene a "Bretton Wood II" Conference and invite leading experts from all major nations to contribute to the design of the economic and financial architecture for the coming decades.

The lack of an overall economic-financial blueprint is not for want of expertise or analytical tools. Rather, it is because patching up the old Bretton Woods system has worked fairly well so far; and for Washington and other capitals, that is the safest and least contentious route. The problem is that this piece-meal approach will not meet the exigencies of the new international economic-financial paradigm that has been created by the conjuncture of the "triumph" of market economics and the internationalization of information and technology. Individuals and firms from every corner of the globe can now buy, sell, and invest in what is a virtually seamless, timeless, and borderless global economy. All that they require is a computer, a modem, a telephone line—and financing.

With no visible signs of a multilateral initiative to meet this latter need, an *ad hoc* informal financial network has emerged pretty much spontaneously to fill the vacuum. Its main features are two: the *de facto* linking of financial markets around the world, and the nearly total absence of oversight, regulation or control. This stopgap arrangement has proven capable of financing transactions amounting to trillions of dollars, yen, marks and sterling a day. One of its less salutary features, however, has been the relative ease with which it can be manipulated by speculators and predators to bring down vulnerable, but otherwise viable, economies such as those in East Asia.

Presumably near the top of a Bretton Woods II agenda would be the question of how best to consolidate the newly created financial market linkages within an integrated financial system that will serve the larger objectives of maximizing benefits, minimizing costs and increasing stability across the entire international commercial and financial spectrum. Subsidiary issues, including transaction transparency, accountability, oversight arrangements, and the future roles of the IMF and the World Bank, which so far have been mainly discussed as discrete topics, would also be subsumed by broader considerations of the future economic-financial system as an integrated whole.

Another agenda item for Bretton Woods II would presumably be the unfinished (some would say unstarted) business of Third World development. This need was not foreseen by the conferees at Bretton Woods, and neither the World Bank nor the IMF was initially mandated or equipped to take on the task of development. Their responses have been a series of improvisations, some of which have yielded significant benefits. In other cases, however, their efforts have been less than successful—as in the recent Asian crisis. A fundamental flaw in both agencies' approach to development (a product of their original mandates and operating principles) has been the expectation that within a decade or two the developing countries would be able to repay their Bank and Fund borrowings and still have foreign exchange left over for development.

In summary, major changes in the global economy during the past decade have exposed the shortcomings of the patched-up Bretton Woods arrangements and the folly of continuing along that path. Needed now is new economic and financial architecture that, among other things, can deal with the new global economy and develop an effective approach to Third World development. Efforts to design such a forward-looking blueprint would be best undertaken in an international setting with participation by all important nations. It is suggested for this purpose that the United States convene a second Bretton Woods Conference. It is likely that most concerned countries would applaud such an initiative and would send their best and brightest financial and economic experts to participate. Like the conferees at the first Bretton Woods, these experts would be charged with conceiving and designing the next century's international economic and financial architecture. One would hope they would respond to this challenge no less brilliantly than did their esteemed predecessors.

438   EASTERN ECONOMIC JOURNAL

NOTES

This article is based on a lecture delivered on February 2, 1999, for the *Great Decisions 1999* series, University of North Carolina at Chapel Hill, NC.

1. An assessment of whether the IMF's prescriptions have helped or hindered the recovery of Latin American and African countries is presented by Stein, H. and Nissanke, M. elsewhere in this journal. The fact that discussions of an IMF-World Bank debt relief initiative for "Highly Indebted Poor Countries," first announced in September 1996, continued at the recently concluded annual meetings of these organizations adds weight to the view that the IMF has had only modest success in helping such countries deal with their external debt problems.
2. This paper is concerned primarily with the development of the Asian crisis during 1997-98.
3. See Note 1 above for an assessment of the IMF's successes and failures.
4. Later data were not available at the time of this writing. However, detailed, up-dated data on capital transfers are presented in UNCTAD's *1999 World Investment Report*.
5. The theoretical basis for the observed pattern of East Asia's financial sector stress, expansion and instability leading ultimately to crisis (the so-called *Minsky Financial Instability Hypothesis*) was formulated by Minsky [1992]. The "Minsky Hypothesis" has been expanded and elaborated to take account of contemporary conditions (such as partial market liberalization and the sequencing of liberalization) by Arestis and Glickman [1999]. For a discussion of the sequencing of financial market liberalization see Edwards [1989] and McKinnon [1993].
6. While the East Asian crisis appears to have moderated, its causes have still to be addressed. In this connection, U.S Treasury Secretary Robert Rubin, in a major policy address on April 21, 1999, indicated that the spring meeting of G-7 countries (concurrent with the meeting of Fund Governors) would take up a "powerful program of reform." The program is expected to include a new IMF "patch" in the form of a window that would permit the use of IMF financial resources to preempt an incipient crisis; greater private sector involvement in resolving future financial crises; and $70 billion of additional debt relief for heavily indebted developing nations.
7. An assessment of the IMF role in the Korean crisis that is relevant to other affected East Asian countries is presented in Nam [1998].
8. A standing joke in developing countries has it that the initials "IMF" stand for "It's Mainly Fiscal."
9. For a discussion of "Moral Hazard" see Fischer [1999].
10. The elements of a possible future international financial structure are presented in terms of "seven building blocks" by Camdessus [1998].

REFERENCES

Acheson, D. *Present at the Creation: My Years in the State Department*. New York: Doubleday, 1969, 81–84.

Arestis, P. and Glickman, M. *Financial Crisis in South East Asia: Dispelling Illusion the Minsky Way*. Manuscript, 1999.

Camdessus, M. *Toward a New Financial Architecture for a Globalized World*. Statement at the Royal Institute of International Affairs, London, U.K. 8 May 1998.

Charlton, A. IMF: Russian Aid Package Abandoned. *Associated Press*, 14 January 1999.

Edwards, S. On the Sequencing of Structural Reforms. *OECD Working Papers*, 70. Paris: OECD, Department of Economics and Statistics, 1989.

Fischer, S. *On the Need for an International Lender of Last Resort*. Washington, D.C.: IMF. Lecture delivered at Joint Meeting of the American Economic Association and the American Finance Association, New York, 3 January 1999. http://www.inf.org/external/np/speeches/1999/010399.MTM.

Gwin, C., Feinberg, R., et al. *The International Monetary Fund in a Multipolar World: Pulling Together*. Washington, D.C.: Overseas Development Council, 1989.

Kenen, P. The Use of IMF Credit, in *The International Monetary Fund in a Multipolar World: Pulling Together*, edited by C. Gwin et al. Washington D.C.: Overseas Development Council, 1989, 69–81.

International Monetary Fund. *Articles of Agreement*. Washington, D.C.: IMF, 1974, 2.

ASIAN CRISIS, IMF, AND CRITICS   439

_____. *IMF Evolves in Response to Over Half a Century of Challenge and Change.* January 1999. http://www.imf.org/external/pubs/ft/survey/sup0998/14.htm.

_____. *The IMF's Response to the Asian Crisis.* Washington, D.C: IMF, 17 January 1999. http://www.imf.org/External/np/exr/facts/asia.MTM.

McKinnon, R. *The Order of Economic Liberalization: Financial Control in the Transition to a Market Economy, 2nd Ed.* Baltimore: Johns Hopkins University Press, 1993.

Minsky H. A Theory of Systemic Fragility. in Altman, E. I. and. Sametz, A.W. (eds). *Financial Crises: Institutions and Markets in a Fragile Environment.* New York: John Wiley & Sons, 1992.

Nam, D. *Some Observations on the Reform Policies in Korea.* Monograph presented at World Bank Seminar on Banking Reform, 5 October 1998.

Reuters. ECB to Set Rates as Situation Requires—Duisenberg. 27 November 1998.

Sachs, J. Strengthening IMF Programs in Highly Indebted Countries, in *The International Monetary Fund in a Multipolar World: Pulling Together*, edited by C. Gwin et al. Washington D.C.: Overseas Development Council, 1989, 102.

Soros, G. *The Crisis of Global Capitalism.* New York: Perseus Books Group, 1998.

UNCTAD. *World Investment Report 1999: FDI and the Challenge of Development.* Geneva: UNCTAD, September 1999.

World Bank. *The East Asian Miracle—Economic Growth and Public Policy.* New York: Oxford University Press, 1993.

_____. East Asian Crisis: An Overview; and The Financial Sector: At the Center of the Crisis. *East Asia: The Road to Recovery.* New York: Oxford University Press, 1998, *passim.*

_____. *Global Economic Prospects 1998/99, Summary.* New York: Oxford University Press, 1998.

[12]

THE ROLE OF FOREIGN PRIVATE CAPITAL FLOWS IN SUSTAINABLE DEVELOPMENT

Kwang W. Jun and Thomas L. Brewer*

EXECUTIVE SUMMARY

This paper focuses on linkages between foreign capital flows to developing countries and sustainable development in the host economies. The purpose of the paper is to present an analytical framework for assessing the contribution of those flows to sustainable development and to present a set of policy guidelines for improving that contribution. Although the paper considers diverse types of foreign capital flows, it emphasizes foreign-direct-investment (FDI) flows in particular. This emphasis is appropriate, because of the distinctive potential contributions of FDI to sustainable development through various channels including technology transfer. Given the widespread changes in policies toward FDI in host countries in recent years and the emergence of FDI as the most significant and stable source of external finance, the potential effects of FDI on economic growth, poverty alleviation, and environmental quality have become increasingly important.

Private international capital flows to developing countries have increased dramatically during the 1990s, while official development finance has remained at relatively low levels. Private FDI flows in particular have increased steadily and significantly in the past decade, reaching approximately 100 billion dollars per year and becoming the single largest source of development finance. The large FDI flows to the developing world appear sustainable as firms continue to globalize their production processes and as governments pursue policies to liberalize their trade and investment regimes. However, FDI in developing countries remains highly concentrated. About 80 per cent of FDI flows are in only twelve countries, with China leading the list.

Issues concerning the assessment and improvement of the contributions of FDI to sustainable development are, therefore, increasingly important, particularly in those developing countries where inward FDI is concentrated. Because of the international environmental effects of FDI projects, such as air and water pollution, outside the countries where the projects are located, it is also important that other governments and international agencies recognize the stakes of the international community in environmental consequences of FDI. Further, the fact that parent firms located in home countries have a degree of control over the projects of their foreign affiliated firms in host countries inevitably adds an international dimension to issues of responsibility about the environmental consequences of FDI projects.

The paper presents an analytical framework for the assessment of the effects of FDI on sustainable development by way of the transfer of technology and management know-how, expansion of markets and employment opportunities, among other concomitant benefits. These benefits of FDI are considered within the broad context of a notion of sustainable development that

---

* Kwang Jun is Principal Financial Economist, International Economics Department, World Bank. Thomas Brewer is Professor, Georgetown University, United States.

includes a concern with environmental quality and human capital as well as the effects of FDI on economic growth. In addition, the paper specifically addresses issues concerning costs and risks associated with FDI. It thus considers a variety of plausible hypotheses about both beneficial and detrimental consequences of FDI for sustainable development.

Cross-country experience and empirical evidence are reviewed to ascertain the actual impact of FDI on sustainable development. In considering this evidence, it is important to recognize that the contributions of FDI to sustainable development occur through many other channels besides the provision of financial capital. In particular, transfers of environmental protection technology as part of the bundle of goods and services that accompany FDI projects can make significant contributions to sustainable development. Further, although the causal relationship between FDI and economic growth is often interactive, the two are positively correlated empirically. When assessing the effects of FDI on the environment, industry-specific patterns and trends also need to be taken into account -- the fact that there has been a shift away from FDI in extractive industries and toward FDI in services.

The effects of FDI on sustainable development depend on government policies as well as corporate practices. The trend of the liberalization of trade policies -- as well as investment policies -- in many developing countries should continue to lead to increases in FDI flows and also increase their potential contributions to sustainable development. The liberalization of trade policies is particularly important, because FDI projects that are based on protectionist import-substitution policies can be counterproductive in their economic growth effects. At the same time, any tendencies on the part of transnational corporations (TNCs) to circumvent environmental protection regulations by shifting the location of production internationally needs to be monitored. Strong competition policies also need to be in place to counter any monopolistic structural or behavioural tendencies by TNCs. In addition to such host country policies, the policies of home countries are important, for instance, in screening outward FDI projects for their environmental effects when they receive political risk insurance through national agencies.

At the multilateral level, the World Bank Group activities, including those of the International Finance Corporation (IFC) and Multilateral Investment Guarantee Agency (MIGA) as well as the lending operations of the IBRD and IDA, along with supporting research work and policy dialogues, have all begun to take into account much more consistently the environmental effects of projects. Among United Nations agencies, the analytical work on environmental practices, technology transfer policies, employment practices of TNCs by United Nations Conference on Trade and Development (UNCTAD) can increase understanding of the linkages between FDI and sustainable development. At the World Trade Organization (WTO), the increasing interest in expanding the agreements from the Uruguay Round to provide more comprehensive rules concerning investment -- in combination with greater sensitivity to the environmental issues associated with both investment and trade -- may also enhance the contributions of FDI to sustainable development.

I. INTRODUCTION

This paper assesses the contribution of foreign capital flows to sustainable development and presents policy guidelines for improving that contribution. The paper emphasizes FDI flows in particular, because of the distinctive contributions of FDI to sustainable development. Such an assessment is especially timely, because of the many changes in policies toward FDI in host countries in recent years and because FDI has become a significant and stable source of external finance.

The significant recent increases in the importance of FDI worldwide and in many individual developing countries are well known and easily documented -- whether measured in terms of the absolute amounts of flows or in relative terms as ratios to gross national product (GNP), capital formation or trade. However, it is not merely the increases in FDI flows, as recorded in balance of payments accounts, that makes FDI a potentially significant contributor to sustainable development. There is typically a diverse array of international transfers of goods, services, technology and people that accompany the FDI projects of TNCs[1]. It is precisely the nature and the diversity of these ancillary international flows that make FDI distinctive in terms of its potential contributions to economic growth and sustainable development. However, "...the channels that transmit growth-inducing factors can also transmit growth-inhibiting factors. For example, TNCs can act monopolistically within host economies, and production techniques introduced by TNCs can have negative environmental impacts".[2]

This paper, therefore, considers the potentially negative effects of FDI on sustainable development as well as the positive effects. It reviews evidence on this issue, and it presents a simple analytical framework for understanding the numerous and diverse linkages between FDI and the several elements of sustainable development. It also considers the effects of public policies and suggests ways that such policies can improve the contribution of FDI to sustainable development. Before turning to those concerns, however, the paper first briefly presents data on FDI flows and other types of financial flows to developing countries in order to document the basic trends and patterns in foreign capital flows that have become evident during the 1990s.

II. INTERNATIONAL CAPITAL FLOWS: TRENDS AND PROSPECTS

The early 1990s saw a dramatic surge in private capital flows to developing countries. Net long-term flows nearly quadrupled between 1990 and 1993, amounting to about 150 billion dollars

---

[1] It should further be noted that many of the economic activities associated with FDI projects are not revealed at all, indirectly or directly, in balance of payments data, because the transactions do not transcend national boundaries. Thus, for many purposes, it is data on the activities of foreign-owned firms (FOFs), rather than balance of payments (BOP) statistics, that are the most relevant. However, since separate aggregate data on FOFs do not exist for most economies, including developing economies in particular, this paper necessarily relies on BOP data.

[2] UNCTAD-DTCI (1996, p. 99).

in 1993. Although there was a sharp slowdown in the growth of private capital flows in 1994 and early 1995, following the rise in global interest rates and the Mexico crisis, private capital flows further increased to 182 billion dollars in 1995 (table 1). In 1996, the rapid growth of private capital flows appears to have resumed, thanks to the buoyant commercial bank lending and international bond issues, to exceed 200 billion dollars for the first time, and to account for more than 80 per cent of the aggregate resource flows to developing countries.

Table 1. Aggregate net long-term resource flows to developing countries, 1990-1996
(billion dollars)

	1990	1991	1992	1993	1994	1995	1996[*]
Aggregate net resources flows	100.4	122.9	148.4	211.8	205.0	238.7	278.2
Official development finance	56.5	65.8	55.7	54.5	52.2	56.8	43.8
Official grants	29.4	37.5	31.9	29.4	32.5	32.9	30.7
Official loans	27.1	28.3	23.7	25.1	19.8	23.8	13.0
Bilateral	11.6	13.3	11.3	10.3	9.3	12.6	-2.5
Multilateral	15.5	15.0	12.4	14.8	10.5	11.2	15.5
Total private flows	43.9	57.1	92.7	157.3	152.8	181.9	234.4
Private debt flows	16.5	16.1	35.8	44.7	40.7	58.0	95.5
Commercial banks	1.4	2.3	10.4	-1.6	8.6	33.8	42.5
Bonds	2.3	10.1	9.9	35.8	28.6	26.6	47.6
Others	12.8	3.7	15.5	10.5	3.5	-2.4	5.4
Foreign direct investment	24.2	33.8	45.9	67.7	79.4	91.8	93.2
Portfolio equity flows	3.2	7.2	11.0	44.9	32.7	32.1	45.7

Source: World Bank Debtor Reporting System
Note: [*] Estimated

To put this level of flows in comparative perspective, net private flows in 1981, which was the peak before the onset of the debt crisis, amounted to 66 billion dollars or about 30 per cent of current levels. The importance of private capital flows relative to the economies of the recipient countries has also increased significantly from 3.7 per cent of developing countries' fixed investment in 1990 to 14 per cent in 1995, more than double the rate attained before the debt crisis. In parallel with the surge, there has been a noticeable shift in the composition of private flows -- away from traditional bank lending to more FDI and portfolio flows.

The long-term prospects for sustained private flows to developing countries as a whole remain promising. Although short-term variations in emerging-market investment and cross-country differences will persist, the long-term structural factors that underpin upward trends in private capital flows to developing countries are expected to provide a continuous impetus for large investment flows in the private sector.

While cyclical factors have played an important role in triggering the recent surge, the structural forces driving the globalization of production and capital markets have been even more important. These factors include continuing diversification of institutional portfolios, financial innovation, technological advances, and falling transportation and communications costs. International investors are becoming more cautious and selective, but the rapid recovery of investment after the Mexico crisis in countries with strong fundamentals suggests that investor interest in emerging markets will continue as long as the markets provide higher risk-adjusted returns and portfolio-diversification opportunities. Moreover, with the improving prospects for fiscal consolidation in major industrial countries, real interest rates are likely to remain low. At the same time, the sustained growth in world trade will help drive continued large private flows -- especially FDI -- to developing countries.

On the recipient side, sound economic fundamentals in developing countries are set to pull investors in. The two main determinants drawing private capital flows -- improved creditworthiness and increased financial integration -- are expected to spread to more developing countries. Most private capital flows have gone to countries whose progress on macroeconomic stabilization and structural and financial sector reforms has been greatest -- and whose gains in creditworthiness and expected rate of return have therefore been greater. Privatization programmes, especially in transition economies, are likely to help attract larger foreign investment flows. Further improvement in business climates and growth prospects of developing countries will be conditional on sustained reforms. On the source side, institutional investors are leading the way in portfolio flows. In industrial countries, the reinforcing process of demographic changes, deregulation, and financial innovations results in an increasing proportion of household savings to be channelled through institutional investors. At the same time, the renewed commercial banking flows is facilitated by the improving financial situation at major international banks and the greater scope for project-financing activities (especially in infrastructure projects), often with the participation of export-credit agencies.

The globalization of production and an increasingly liberal trade regime foster FDI -- the single most significant and stable component of private flows. The favourable prospects for the growth and long-term sustainability of FDI flows to developing countries are supported by the continued globalization of corporate production, a major factor underpinning FDI flows. Technological advances and declining transportation and communications costs allow firms to divide production processes into discrete activities that can be transferred to locations that offer the greatest cost and efficiency gains. Trade integration will also lead to a continued growth in FDI -- from industrial countries to developing countries and increasingly among developing countries. Although capital repatriation from mature equity investments may limit the growth of net FDI, sustained economic growth and increasing export orientation in many developing countries are likely to boost FDI inflows. And the expanded scope for investment in recently opened industries and privatized services (for example, infrastructure) will further support the growth of FDI flows to developing countries.

Nevertheless, private capital flows to developing countries remain heavily concentrated in a handful of mostly middle-income countries. The top twelve recipients account for three quarters of total private flows, and about 80 per cent of FDI flows.[3] An uneven regional distribution of investment flows also persists: East Asia has emerged as the dominant region attracting 60 per cent of total private flows to the developing world, compared to only 10 per cent directed towards the Middle East/North Africa, Sub-Saharan Africa, and South Asia regions combined. Low-income countries (excluding China) also fare poorly in terms of FDI inflows as a percentage of their GNP, which is estimated at roughly half that of middle-income countries (table 2).

Table 2. Net foreign direct investment as a ratio of GNP, 1990-1996
(Per cent)

Region	1990	1991	1992	1993	1994	1995	1996[a]
All developing countries	0.6	0.8	1.0	1.4	1.6	1.7	1.4
Sub-Saharan Africa	0.3	0.7	0.5	0.6	1.1	0.7	0.8
East Asia and the Pacific	1.2	1.4	2.0	3.2	3.2	3.3	2.7
South Asia	0.1	0.1	0.2	0.2	0.3	0.5	0.8
Europe and Central Asia	0.1	0.3	0.5	0.7	0.8	1.2	0.6
Latin America	0.7	1.2	1.2	1.2	1.4	1.3	1.5
North Africa and the Middle East	0.6	0.4	0.4	0.8	0.7	0.4	0.4
By income group:							
Low-income countries	0.6	0.7	1.4	3.2	3.5	3.2	2.5
Middle-income Countries	0.5	0.8	0.9	1.0	1.0	1.2	1.1
Memorandum:							
Low-Income countries (excluding China)	0.3	0.3	0.4	0.5	0.7	0.8	0.6

Source: World Bank Debtor Reporting System data.
Note: [a] Estimated.

---

[3] For 1990-1996, the top twelve developing country recipients of FDI flows were China, Mexico, Malaysia, Argentina, Brazil, Indonesia, Thailand, Hungary, Poland, Chile, Greece and Colombia.

The growth of FDI flows to developing economies in the past decade brought with it a substantial accumulation of FDI stock (table 3). And the potential benefits of FDI, compared with other forms of capital flows. as perceived by host countries have also increased further in the aftermath of Mexico crisis. which was at least in part triggered by the volatile short-term portfolio flows (World Bank, *World Debt Tables*. 1996, pp. 17-19). The increases in FDI in developing countries during the 1990s have occurred in the context of total worldwide increases in FDI, and a significant amount of the FDI has. of course. gone to one developing country. China. Yet, the steady increases to all other developing countries are also evident in that table.

Table 3. Inward foreign-direct-investment flows and stocks in host countries
(Billion dollars)

Region	Flows							Stocks
	1984-1989 (average)	1990	1991	1992	1993	1994	1995	1995
World	115	204	158	168	208	226	315	2,658
Developed countries	93	170	114	114	129	133	203	1,933
Developing countries*	22	34	41	50	73	87	100	693
China	1	3	4	11	28	34	38	129
All Others	20	30	37	39	46	53	62	564

Source: United Nations Conference on Trade and Development. Division on Transnational Corporations and Investment. *World Investment Report. 1966*. annex table 1. pp. 227-231 (for flows), and table 3, pp. 239-243 (for stocks).

Note: *The data for developing countries in this table exceed those in table 1. due mainly to a broader definition of developing economies used.

Overall, then, the absolute amounts of FDI inflows in developing countries have been increasing during the 1990s, and they have become more important relative to other types of capital flows as well. Although these data are useful as approximate indicators of patterns and trends in foreign capital flows to developing countries. they are not by themselves adequate for assessing their contributions to sustainable development. For that task, it is necessary to disaggregate the notion of sustainable development into its constituent parts and similarly to identify more precisely the types of international business transactions and other activities of transnational corporations (TNCs) that commonly accompany FDI projects. These and other considerations are included in the next section, which presents a simple analytic framework for assessing the contributions of FDI to sustainable development.

III. ASSESSING THE CONTRIBUTION OF FOREIGN DIRECT INVESTMENT TO SUSTAINABLE DEVELOPMENT: A FRAMEWORK FOR ANALYSIS AND EVIDENCE

Sustainable development

The framework for analysis presented here explicitly acknowledges the interactions between economic growth and environmental quality that are at the core of the notion of sustainable development. More generally, it incorporates a variety of ecological and social objectives as well as economic objectives encompassed by the widely-accepted notion of sustainable development. Thus, the following objectives are included in the notion of sustainable development underlying this paper (Serageldin, 1994, p. 2):

- Economic objectives: growth, efficiency.
- Ecological objectives: ecosystem integrity, carrying capacity, biodiversity.
- Social objectives: empowerment, participation, social mobility, social cohesion, cultural identity, institutional development.

Further, it is important to recognize that four types of capital can be distinguished and that all four are important to sustainable development (Serageldin and Steer, 1994): *human-made capital*, such as machines and buildings; *natural capital*, such as soil, air and water; *human capital*, such as investments in education and health; and *social capital*, such as good governance and a sense of civic community. Although traditional economic analysis, of course, focuses on human-made capital, analyses of sustainable development tend to focus on the other three because they have been neglected in the past in economic growth studies and policies.

Foreign direct investment and transnational corporations

This broad and inclusive notion of capital is particularly appropriate and useful in discussing the contributions of FDI to sustainable development, because FDI entails much more than financial capital flows that are reflected in the FDI flow data reported in host countries' balance of payments accounts. The essence of FDI, in fact, is that it involves the international transfer of a package or bundle of assets of diverse types that are particularly important for the development of human capital. This is precisely what is distinctive about FDI relative to other forms of foreign capital flows and a key reason why it is commonly considered to be potentially beneficial to sustainable development in the host economy. There are, nevertheless, many complex and contentious issues about the nature, extent and costs of the contribution of FDI to human capital in the host country -- issues that are addressed below -- in addition to issues about the effects of FDI on natural and social capital.

Foreign direct investment is but one of several strategic alternatives that TNCs can employ for international transactions -- along with trade, licensing and strategic alliances. Their choices among these alternatives are based on complex calculations about costs, revenues and risks associated with each one as they decide to undertake various kinds of international business initiatives. In many instances, however, these forms of international business transactions are not substitutes for one another, but rather complements. Thus, TNCs commonly choose a combination of FDI plus one or more of the other forms in order to accomplish their objectives for a given foreign country. Furthermore, it is important to recognize that their strategic objectives can vary across these alternatives as well as among FDI projects. Common objectives associated with FDI projects include, in particular, gaining access to foreign markets, gaining access to efficient production locations or gaining access to raw materials -- and, increasingly in some industries, gaining access to technology (including in developing countries in some instances). As a result of these diverse objectives and types of international business transactions that may be associated with any one FDI project, it is difficult to generalize about the effects of FDI. These factors that need to be taken into account in assessing the contributions of FDI to sustainable development are represented in the simple diagram of figure 1, which includes TNCs' strategic alternatives as well as types of international business flows and types of capital formation for sustainable development.

Figure 1. TNCs' strategies, international flows of resources and capital formation in host countries

TNCs' strategies	→	Flows to host country	→	Effects on capital
FDI/subsidiaries		Funds		Human-made
Joint ventures		Technology		Human
Strategic alliances		People		Natural
Trade		Goods		Social
Licensing		Services		

Economic impact of FDI: cross-country experience and empirical evidence

There are several methodological and conceptual issues inherent in attempts to assess empirically the economic impact of FDI in developing countries. The methodological issues concern the difficulties of specifying clear, direct causal linkages between FDI and economic growth through empirical statistical analysis, because they are interactive over time, and they exhibit variability over time and across countries in the periods of leads and lags. In any case, the scatter plot of FDI and

GDP for thirty developing countries in figure 2 reflects a positive relationship. Furthermore, there is ample evidence (based on academic research and country cases) that provides strong support for the positive role of FDI in promoting economic growth in host countries. For example, the ratio of inward FDI to total output was found to have a positive influence on growth (Blomström, Lipsey and Zejan, 1996). Moreover, the positive growth impact of FDI flows was more significant compared with other types of external flows (Husain and Jun, 1992) and compared with domestic investment (Borenzstein, De Gregorio and Lee, 1994). At the same time, cross-national and longitudinal empirical studies -- as well as simple economic reasoning about the basis of firms' investment decision-making in general -- strongly suggest that FDI flows respond positively to recent increases in GDP and presumably to expectations of future increases. In a review of the evidence of causal linkages between FDI and economic growth in Central and Eastern Europe, in particular, the *World Investment Report* concluded that "...in determining whether FDI leads or lags economic growth, individual economies, or groups of economies, have to be examined separately" (UNCTAD-DTCI, 1996, p.66).

Figure 2. Foreign direct investment and host-country economic growth

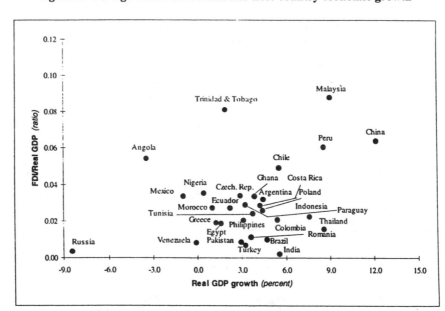

Source: World Bank, Debtor Reporting System and World Bank data.
    Note: Calculations are based on averages for 1993-1995 for the top thirty and recipients of FDI in 1995 of developing and economies in transition.

In order to understand the contribution of FDI to economic growth, however, it is also important to disaggregate FDI and its economic effects into more specific elements. Thus, for instance, on the basis of a recent and extensive review of the theoretical and empirical literature on the effects of TNCs' activities on economic development, particularly in developing economies, Caves (1996, pp. 235) observes: "[TNCs'] effects on the LDC's rate of economic growth might seem to provide the ultimate relationship to be investigated. Unfortunately, it seems a rather ineffective focus for research... No overall theoretical prediction connects the stock of foreign investment in the LDC to the rate at which its national income grows. Even if foreign investment should have spillover effects that raise the *level* of national income, these need not (necessarily) translate into an ongoing favourable effect on the *rate* [italics added] of growth." He thus prefers -- and reviews (pp. 233-234) -- research on the more specific ways in which TNCs' activities affect host economies, including capital flows and domestic savings. He suggests that because capital flows are relatively small, because they can reduce the rate of return for domestic savers (who then save less), and because they can preempt investment opportunities for domestic entrepreneurs, it is unlikely that foreign capital inflows add to investment in the local economy dollar for dollar, and there is some empirical evidence to suggest that in fact foreign capital inflows are partially offset by reductions in domestic investment. It might also be noted that the initial balance of payments impact of FDI could be negative in some instances where the foreign-invested projects induce large imports in early phases of the product cycle and require a long gestation period, and the likely rise in profit remittances may constrain the growth of net transfers from FDI during the mature phase.

Beyond its role as a source of risk capital for investment and its effects on international funds flows, however, FDI can provide an engine for growth in many other ways -- by transferring new technology and business practice, by stimulating innovation and investment, and by securing access to international goods and capital markets. In a number of countries, FDI has been a driving force in the expansion and diversification of manufactured exports. Foreign direct investment can also increase efficiency directly by producing at lower cost and indirectly by increasing competition in domestic goods and factor markets, contributing to the host country's international competitiveness over time.

Drawing from comparative cross-national data on the ratios of foreign capital flows to gross domestic capital formation in developing countries, as summarized in table 4,[4] several patterns and trends are evident. First, the ratios have been increasing for developing countries as a group during the 1990s. Second, the increase has been particularly pronounced for China, whose numbers tend to skew the means for the group of all developing countries. Third, since 1991 the ratios have been higher for developing countries than for developed countries.

---

[4] In as much as these data include mergers and acquisitions by foreign firms, they overstate to that extent the initial contribution of FDI to physical capital formation; on the other hand, in as much as many countries' FDI data exclude reinvested earnings, these data understate to that extent the contribution of FDI projects to physical capital formation over time.

Table 4. Ratio of inward FDI flows to gross fixed capital formation
(Per cent)

	1984-1989 (average)	1990	1991	1992	1993	1994
World	3.1	4.0	3.1	3.2	3.8	3.9
Developed Countries	3.9	4.9	3.3	3.1	3.5	3.3
Developing Countries	2.8	3.2	4.0	4.8	6.3	7.5
China*	1.8	2.6	3.3	7.8	20.0	24.5
All others	3.0	3.3	4.1	4.3	4.4	5.1

Source: UNCTAD-DTCI, *World Investment Report. 1996*, annex table 5, pp. 249-259.

Note: *The data for China may overstate actual inflows as they include outflows from China to Hong Kong, which are then returned to China.

Foreign direct investment, human capital, and technology flows

As noted above. however, it is not capital flows *per se* that are necessarily the most important contribution of FDI to sustainable development. In particular, the effects of FDI on human capital through employment-related activities and technology transfers are of special interest. Caves (1996, pp. 227-229) finds. for instance, that the preponderance of the evidence on TNCs' activities in developing countries is that they tend to pay higher than average wages, they "invest heavily" in training, and they increase the number of local nationals that are employed in managerial and engineering positions, as projects mature. In short, the contribution of TNCs through FDI projects to human capital can be substantial.

Data on the effects of FDI and associated flows of technology, people, goods and services on natural capital and social capital are less abundant, in part because they are inherently more difficult to generate and measure. This is a methodological problem that is of course, not limited to analyzing the linkages between foreign capital flows, on the one hand, and natural capital (or social capital) on the other; it is a more encompassing problem that extends to practically any analysis concerning the relationships among human-made capital formation and natural and social capital.

Foreign direct investment and the environment

There are two quite different sets of issues about linkages between FDI and the environment. One concerns the well-known issues about the relationships between economic growth in general and the environment. and the other concerns issues that are uniquely about the relationships between FDI and the environment. It would of course be impossible in this short and specialized paper to make an original contribution to the former issue. However, we can note that we share the perspective presented in the *World Development Report, 1992: Development and the Environment,* that:

> "... the adverse impact of economic growth on environmental degradation can be greatly reduced. Poor management of natural resources is already constraining development in some areas, and the growing scale of economic activity will pose serious challenges for environmental management. But rising incomes combined with sound environmental policies and institutions can form the basis for tackling both environmental and development problems. The key to growing sustainably is not to produce less but to produce differently. ... [However,] failure to address environmental challenges will reduce the capacity for long-term development" (World Bank, 1992, p. 36).

Beyond agreement with these general statements about the relationship between economic growth and the environment, we also note that there is evidence that many countries have simultaneously achieved improvements in both the quality of the environment and economic growth. Indeed, for many specific forms of environmental quality such as adequate urban sanitation systems, there is a direct link with income levels. Further, there is evidence for the economically advanced countries that many forms of air pollution, for instance, declined over the two-decade period from the early 1970s to the late 1980s even as their economies grew by about 80 per cent; over that period, particulate emissions declined by 60 per cent, sulfur-oxide emissions by 38 per cent, lead emissions by as much as 85 per cent in North America, and at the same time the amount of forested lands has increased (World Bank, 1992, p. 40). Yet, at the same time, there have also clearly been many ways in which environmental degradation has worsened as a result of economic growth and lax environmental-protection policies.

The most relevant issues for the present paper, therefore, are whether and how FDI entails unique environmental effects. Are there environmental protection issues that are specific to FDI? Are there ways in which FDI is especially detrimental to the environment? Can FDI make any distinctive contributions to environmental protection and sustainable development? These are difficult questions, for which there is limited empirical evidence. There is, of course, anecdotal evidence based on specific cases of environmental degradation by FDI projects. However, there is no *a priori* reason to suppose that TNCs are consistently more inclined toward environmentally irresponsible behaviour than domestic firms – or for that matter that they are consistently less inclined. An extensive UN study of the environmental effects of TNCs, for instance, observed that the involvement of TNCs in ten of the most serious environmental issues "varies from minor to major, from direct to indirect, from contributor to potential problem solver of the problem. ... [Thus], one can identify major and direct involvement of transnational corporations in the issue of managing hazardous chemical, processes and wastes but only very minor or very indirect involvement by them in issues such as desertification or species loss" (United Nations Centre on Transnational Corporations, 1985, p. 14).

There are two specific and inherently internationalized issues about the environmental consequences of TNCs' activities that are of particular interest. One is that TNCs' decisions about the international location of production can be influenced by differences in countries' environmental protection policies. The other is that decisions about the activities of a TNC's foreign affiliates are made by a parent corporation located in a different country and that, therefore, the parent firm may be less sensitive about the environmental consequences of its decisions concerning the affiliate than would be a locally-owned firm in the foreign country.[5]

International location of production

Transnational corporations that engage in FDI are in a unique position to choose -- and even to change -- the location of their operations, and they therefore have the potential to decide where any environmental degradation from their production process occurs. Because TNCs can establish productive facilities in different countries through FDI, they can in effect choose in which countries to pollute. They are thus free, at least in the abstract, to select countries for the locations of their production facilities on the basis of the laxity of the environmental protection polices of prospective host countries. Yet, one study concluded that "There is as yet very little evidence of any serious shifts in the international pattern of investment due to variations in national environmental policies" (United Nations Centre on Transnational Corporations, 1985, p. 47). The attractiveness of the local market, macro-economic conditions and cost considerations other than environmental protection costs typically dominate the FDI decisions of TNCs. For instance, the fact that the United States is the principal recipient country of FDI, including in particular FDI in pollution-intensive industries such as chemicals and metals, suggests that relatively strict environmental-protection policies are not deterrents to FDI.

On the other hand, there has been a salient and continuing issue about the possible deterrent effects of environmental liability on FDI in Central and Eastern Europe. As a result, the World Bank and the OECD conducted a joint study (Klavens and Zamparutti, 1995) to assess the importance of environmental issues to TNCs considering FDI projects in manufacturing, mining and construction in that region. On the basis of survey responses from 255 TNCs (from a list of the 1001 largest firms in those sectors worldwide), the study reached the following conclusions:

- Environmental issues do not generally discourage foreign investors from *considering* investments in Central and Eastern Europe.
- Environmental issues are secondary, but critical factors once companies begin to consider investing *in particular plants*. Environmental factors tend to influence the choices of specific sites, but not the decision of whether to invest at all. Although about one sixth of the firms reported that environmental problems were "very important" in decisions to reject

---

[5] For further discussion of these and other issues concerning the environmental practices of TNCs, see for instance Gladwin (1977), Gladwin and Walter (1976) and Pearson (1987).

specific sites for projects, most of those firms also continued to search for other investment opportunities.
- The firms' principal concern was the cost of liability for the cleanup of any contamination from the past.

Practices of TNCs and local firms

Another important issue is whether foreign-owned firms or locally-owned firms tend to have more environmentally sensitive practices. The fact that the parent corporation of a TNC is not located in the same country as a foreign affiliate causes concern about whether the executives of a TNC have a relatively strong sense of responsibility for the environmental consequences of their decisions.

This is an issue on which there is some evidence. In particular, a review of the linkages between private capital flows and environmental performance in four Latin American countries has been undertaken by Gentry (forthcoming) and collaborators in Argentina, Brazil, Costa Rica and Mexico. A key conclusion is that, for the most part, the foreign firms are ahead of the domestic firms in their integration of environmental considerations and improvements into their operations -- though there are examples of significant negative environmental impacts arising from the actions of foreign as well as domestic firms.

Beyond this evidence, there are a variety of plausible hypotheses about differences between TNCs and local firms in their environmental practices and consequences. As the following list (United Nations Centre on Transnational Corporations, 1985, pp. 7-9) suggests, there are some reasons to suppose that TNCs are more likely to follow environmentally benign policies than are local firms:

- TNCs are often under greater scrutiny by the public, the press and government regulators in host countries.
- TNCs are subject to pressures from their home governments and public opinion to be environmentally responsible in their foreign as well as domestic activities.
- TNCs can more easily transfer environmentally sound technology internationally through their own internal channels.
- TNCs' affiliates tend to be larger and more profitable than local firms and can thus more easily afford the costs of environmental management activities.

However, there are also reasons to suppose that TNCs are less likely to follow environmentally benign policies than are local firms:

- TNCs' products and production processes tend to be less appropriate to local conditions with regard to climate, diet and culture and thus more likely to have adverse environmental consequences.
- TNCs tend to have a less intimate understanding of complex local ecological systems than

do local firms.

There can therefore, obviously, be considerable variability across FDI projects in their environmental consequences and the environmental practices of the firms, as the following two cases illustrate.

Two contrasting cases

The following example in box 1 is illustrative of an infrastructure project in Central Europe that was not only profitable to the investor, but made a significant improvement in the level of pollution control for a power generation facility. The case in box 2, by contrast, not only illustrates the use of FDI to escape one country's environmental policies, but also the difficulties that national governments sometimes have in regulating TNCs' environmental practices.

Box 1. Example of the transfer of environmentally sound technology:
Asea Brown Boveri in Poland

Asea Brown Boveri (ABB), an electro-technical equipment, energy and transportation TNC headquartered in Zilrich, Switzerland, is a major supplier of combustion technologies for energy generation and of environmental-control technologies. It initiated a joint venture in Poland in 1989 which converted a former state-owned operation into a privately-owned company, ABB Zamech.

In a large turnaround programme, restructuring projects retrofitted new combustion and power generation technologies and know-how, providing simultaneous productivity gains and pollution abatement.   The total quality management practices of ABB were transferred, together with environmental management practices and extensive functioning training of staff. The venture has been very successful so far. Results for the first operating year gave a return on sales of 5.2 per cent and a return on equity of 43.7 per cent.

Source: United Nations-Transnational Corporations and Management Division , *World Investment Report,* 1992 (New York: United Nations, 1992), box IX.3, p. 238; as adapted from Business Council for Sustainable Development (BCSD), "Report on Technology Cooperation," (Geneva: BCSD, 1992), pp. 8 and 31.

Box 2. Example of difficulties in international control of TNCs' environmental practices

In July 1976, there was an explosion at the chemical plant, Icmesa, near Seveso, north of Milan; Icmesa was owned by Givaudan, a Swiss subsidiary of the Swiss pharmaceutical manufacturer Hoffmann-La Roche. The explosion released a cloud of chemicals, and tens of thousands of nearby residents were exposed to highly toxic dioxin. The firm delayed notifying local government authorities for 27 hours and then did not explain the toxic nature of the chemicals. Only nine days later did they confirm that there was dioxin on the ground, five days after tests had found evidence of such pollution -- thereby prolonging exposure and making cleanup more difficult.

The subsequent arrangements for waste disposal involved an Italian subsidiary of a German firm, which subcontracted the removal to a Swiss-based firm, whose only employee was an executive of a firm that was a subsidiary of Hoffmann-La Roche. The disposal was ultimately undertaken by a French firm. None of these firms, including Hoffmann-LaRoche, would disclose the disposal site, which was eventually determined to be in northern France.

This case demonstrates some special difficulties that countries encounter in protecting the environment because of the very nature of TNCs. First, the international nature of the production location decision was motivated by cross-national differences in environmental protection policies. The facility was established in Italy, because it would have been illegal to manufacture its products in Switzerland -- though they were actually exported to Switzerland (and to the United States). Second, the complex international arrangements for waste disposal were inherently difficult to monitor because they involved firms from four different countries. Third, there were serious problems in assessing liability and imposing penalties because of legal limitations on the responsibilities of firms that are related but located in different countries.

Source: Adapted from United Nations Centre on Transnational Corporations, *Environmental Aspects of the Activities of Transnational Corporations: A Survey* (New York: United Nations, 1985), pp. 93-94.

Sectoral patterns

There are two shifts occurring in the sectoral composition of FDI flows that are relevant to the issue of the environmental effects of FDI. One is the increases in infrastructure in developing countries, especially in Asia. Significant increases in FDI in large-scale infrastructure projects make it especially important that TNCs become sensitive to the effects of such projects on sustainable development, because of their potentially problematic and large-scale environmental effects -- for instance, from the construction and operation of an electricity generating plant and distribution system. These increases in infrastructure FDI are evident in terms of both the absolute amounts of flows as well as their proportions in the total flows to developing countries (UNCTAD-DTCI, 1996, pp. 18-29, and 285-295). Thus, by the end of 1994, the levels of FDI stocks in infrastructure were approximately 3.1 billion dollars in Central and Eastern Europe and 10.5 billion dollars in South, Southeast and East Asia (excluding China). However, the stocks were barely more than 1 billion dollars in Africa or in Latin America and the Caribbean; and the amounts of inward FDI in infrastructure in developing countries in flow and stock measures were still far below the levels in developed countries. In any case. it should be noted that any data on FDI flows and stocks significantly underestimate the contributions of TNCs to infrastructure projects because their non-equity contributions in the form of technical know-how, in-kind contributions in equipment, R&D cost-sharing, lease financing. and trade credits are typically quite large. though not easily measured and aggregated in national economic statistics.

The second shift in the composition of FDI is that the percentage of FDI in the services sector has been increasing while the proportion in the extractive sector has been declining over the past decade. Of course, such a shift is only indirectly and approximately indicative of a decline in the environmental degradation potential of FDI -- and only in relative terms in any case. They do, however, at least belie a common popular image of TNCs as being concentrated in pollution-intensive extractive and manufacturing industries. In fact, they are increasingly in light manufacturing, high-tech and service industries -- in developing economies as well as in developed economies. One implication of the decreased FDI in extractive industries, though, is that "...the responsibility for environmental protection has been shifting, at the margin, from transnational enterprises to local" firms in that sector (United Nations Centre on Transnational Corporations, 1985, p. 47).

Foreign direct investment and social capital

As for the effects of FDI on social capital, in the absence of data, we can again only offer a few generalized comments. There is one opportunity that is uniquely available to TNCs to circumvent government policy -- namely through the manipulation of transfer prices -- and thus contribute to the corruption of business and political relationships. Because the prices of the goods and services that are traded internationally among entities of TNCs are administered prices, they are determined within firms -- and not market-based prices resulting from arms-length negotiations between unrelated entities. They are therefore subject to considerable manipulation as firms seek to minimize tariffs and/or corporate tax liabilities in a world with highly variable rates across countries. Because the topic of transfer pricing is in itself complex and far beyond the scope of this paper to explore in detail, we can only acknowledge that the issue of the propriety of TNCs' transfer-pricing practices is a legitimate concern of governments and that it is inherently difficult to monitor.

A second area in which TNCs are sometimes subject to criticism about their effects on the social capital component of sustainable development, as defined above, is that they are intrusive in the local culture. To the extent that social capital is defined to encompass notions of community and cultural integrity. then TNCs may sometimes be detrimental to social capital. However, they may also represent and foster an open, and inclusive cultural cosmopolitanism that is beneficial to the host society and thereby make important positive contributions to social capital. The entire topic of social capital formation -- and its relationship to foreign investment -- is of course one that needs much more systematic research in the future than it has received.

In any case. the environmental and other effects on the host economy of FDI projects depend on the policies of the host government as well as the practices of private investors. The contributions of foreign capital flows are a consequence of the combination of public-sector policies and private-sector practices. In particular. the domestic regulatory policies as well as the international-trade policies, investment policies. and intellectual-property-protection policies, among other host-government policies, are all crucial to improving the contributions of foreign investment to sustainable development. We thus turn to issues concerning government policies and how they can increase the contributions of foreign capital flows to sustainable development.

IV. IMPROVING THE CONTRIBUTION OF FOREIGN CAPITAL FLOWS TO SUSTAINABLE DEVELOPMENT: POLICY IMPLICATIONS

The issue of how best to improve the contributions of foreign capital to sustainable development can be divided into three parts: (1) how to attract more of it (on the assumption that it is on balance beneficial to sustainable development); (2) how to increase its beneficial consequences; and (3) how to reduce its detrimental consequences. These questions are addressed below in regard to the policies of host governments. home governments. multilateral and regional organizations, and transnational corporations.

Attracting foreign capital

Investors are particularly interested in the totality of the investment climate in any individual developing country as they assess its prospects for a project. This is true whether the project is for market-access or production-efficiency reasons or some other strategic objectives. The specific elements of the macroeconomic environment of interest thus include real-income growth and price stability, as affected by overall macro-policy regime. In addition, they are interested in the degree of openness, transparency and stability in a broad range of international economic policies, including policies toward foreign investors. trade and intellectual property.

Host country policies are therefore a principal determinant of the amount and character of private capital flows that it receives. In this respect, consistent and stable macroeconomic policies are fundamental for establishing creditworthiness and fostering a private sector conducive to investment and attracting foreign capital in the form of both debt and equity. Particularly important are ensuring sustained growth of domestic savings, a low rate of inflation, a stable and realistic exchange rate, and the avoidance of relative-price distortions. Appropriate macroeconomic policies and an open foreign-exchange regime alone, however, may not be sufficient for developing countries to sustain large private capital inflows. Equity flows in particular, whether portfolio or FDI, also depend on a healthy private sector which demands an adequate legal framework, transparent tax codes, and modern and cost-effective transportation and telecommunications. In some cases, regional integration conforming with multilateral standards can help to promote private-sector development through creation of larger domestic markets and the coordination of infrastructure initiatives.

Weak institutions and obtrusive regulations discourage flows. Institutional problems are found in areas such as over-stringent bureaucracy and the involvement of too many institutions. In a number of countries (such as Czech Republic. Mexico. and Thailand), the streamlining of inter-agency procedures and the creation of a single investment enabling agency have facilitated increased FDI, and similar arrangements could be considered elsewhere. In addition, inefficient regulatory structures for FDI often create distortions in the economy. Foreign interest can also be discouraged by high-cost public sector monopolies that raise the price of basic services, by limits on entry into certain sectors of the host economy. and by excessive restrictions on the freedom to employ expatriates. It is important for developing countries to sustain efforts to establish a transparent regulatory framework that is internationally competitive and does not discriminate between domestic and foreign investors.

These issues on the stability of macroeconomic policy and political environment are typically more important to investors than incentive packages that may be developed for particular projects. Although foreign direct investors do. of course. often seek and obtain a variety of subsidies for their projects from host governments. the value of these incentives for enticing investors and their cost-effectiveness for host governments remain controversial. There is much research (for example, Guisinger and Associates. 1985) on such incentives -- and associated performance requirements -- and they have recently begun to attract renewed in interest in international policy-making circles (Brewer and Young. 1997). Further. the agreements from the Uruguay Round of trade negotiations on Subsidies and Countervailing Measures and on Trade-Related Investment Measures (TRIMs) have put investment subsidies and performance requirements on the agenda of the World Trade Organization. As a consequence. the use of investment incentives may become subject to more restraint in the future.

Increasingly. therefore. only those subsidies that can be justified on the grounds of externalities that create a wedge between the private and social benefits of investments are likely to be offered by host governments and found acceptable by multilateral rules and institutions. Of course, externalities concerning environmental protection and human capital formation are particularly deserving of attention within the context of the goals of sustainable development. Thus, one important way in which host governments can improve the contribution of FDI to sustainable development is to focus their subsidies specifically on those projects that offer social benefits in terms of their contributions to natural capital and/or human capital that cannot be fully captured by the terms of private transactions. At the same time, host governments should make the complementary commitment not to offer subsidies that cannot be justified on such grounds and that instead merely transfer wealth from local taxpayers to foreign shareholders.

FDI may also be facilitated by appropriate tax and regulatory policies in source countries.[6] Bilateral investment treaties between host and source countries can help to ensure that tax policies do not distort investor decisions to unduly discourage FDI. A number of industrial countries provide incentives for outward FDI. While this has encouraged direct investment from these countries, it

---

[6] A detailed review of policy measures to facilitate foreign direct investment flows to developing countries was provided to the World Bank Development Committee in Spring 1991. See Section III of World Bank (1991).

may also discriminate against host country investors and other foreign investors, who do not have access to subsides. Industrial countries have worked to develop general rules against subsidizing foreign investment as well as guidelines for foreign investment aimed at increasing the responsiveness of FDI to host country development objectives (OECD, 1991).

Maximizing the beneficial effects

There are two key ways by which host governments can maximize the beneficial contributions of FDI to sustainable development. One is to adopt strong competition policies internally, and the other is to adopt liberalized trade and investment policies internationally. The two, furthermore, are consistent and complementary.

Strong domestic competition policies are important in order to maximize the beneficial, efficiency-increasing effects of having more competitive domestic industries and in order to minimize any monopolistic tendencies of TNCs. In the past, in the context of import-substitution economic growth policies, many host governments in developing countries offered foreign investors protected positions in the domestic market. Such an approach not only stifled import competition, it also often stifled domestic competition as well when investors were assured favoured treatment, for instance in government purchasing of goods and services. Such policies constrain some of the potentially most beneficial effects of foreign investment through increases in the efficiencies of firms that must adapt to a more competitive industry structure created by new, foreign-based entrants. In contrast, strong competition policies that constrain firms' restrictive business practices and that foster competitive industry structure will maximize the efficiency-enhancing effects of the entrance of foreign investors into local markets.

At the same time, it is important that TNCs be allowed to link their local operations to international networks of suppliers and customers including their own affiliates and parent firms in other countries in order to maintain internationally competitive operations. This means liberalized international economic policies concerning trade and technology transfer as well as investment. These policy directions have already been well established in recent years through many unilateral actions by developing countries and by the array of multilateral liberalization agreements being implemented by the World Trade Organization.

Cross-country experience suggests host-country policies leading to greater benefits of capital inflows. Aside from the need for non-distortionary policies conducive to sustained growth and stable business environment, an open economic regime to promote closer linkages with global markets is important (Jun and Singh, 1996). In addition, the adequate development of physical infrastructure as well as human resources are essential to enhance the productivity of foreign investment (Stiglitz, 1993).

Minimizing the detrimental effects

Host governments can develop more effective environmental-protection regimes -- and other policies that are conducive to sustainable development. Not only host governments, but also home governments. multilateral and regional institutions and the TNCs themselves all have opportunities and responsibilities to limit some of the detrimental effects of FDI. including environmental degradation in particular.

Regional and inter-regional organizations can be instrumental in reducing the potentially negative consequences of FDI for natural capital, for instance, through the binding rules concerning environmental protection contained in the North American Free Trade Agreement (NAFTA)[7] or the non-binding statement of principles concerning investment of the Asia Pacific Economic Cooperation forum (APEC).[8] Whether the new Multilateral Agreement on Investment (MAI) being negotiated at the Organization for Economic Cooperation and Development (OECD) will have any provisions concerning environmental protection remains to be seen.[9]

At the multilateral level. the project finance operations of the International Finance Corporation (IFC). the political-risk-insurance operations of the Multilateral Investment Guarantee Agency (MIGA). the lending operations of the International Bank for Reconstruction and Development (IBRD) and International Development Association (IDA). along with the supporting research work and policy dialogues in many parts of the World Bank Group, have begun to integrate environmental concerns into their activities. At the United Nations, the analytical work on environmental practices. technology transfer policies. employment practices of transnational corporations by UNCTAD can increase understanding of the linkages between FDI and sustainable development. The increasing interest in the nexus between environmental and trade issues at the World Trade Organization (WTO) may also enhance the contributions of FDI to sustainable development -- particularly since at least some investment issues are also now being addressed within that organization.[10]

The home governments of TNCs can also play an important role in protecting against the detrimental effects of FDI. For example. they can screen projects for their environmental effects before granting them "political-risk-guarantees." Since environmental effects, of course, often transcend international boundaries -- through air or water pollution. for instance -- and thus occur even in the home countries of the TNCs. the governments of those countries have an incentive and responsibility to take into account the environmental impact of projects that they subsidize through their guarantee and other incentive programmes for FDI projects in developing countries.

Finally, TNCs themselves have incentives and responsibilities to minimize the detrimental consequences of FDI projects. including their environmental degradation effects in particular. Toward this end. guidelines have. in fact. been developed by both private-sector and public-sector organizations. Thus. "The Business Charter for Sustainable Development" developed by the

---

[7] NAFTA allows the signatories. for instance. to maintain or add environmental regulations that are not discriminatory and that have a reasonable scientific basis. even though they may limit trade.

[8] The APEC "Non-binding Investment Principles" include a provision that "Member economies will not relax health, safety. and environmental regulations as an incentive to encourage foreign investment."

[9] For preliminary discussions of the provisions of the MAI, see OECD (1996).

[10] For an analysis of international environmental institutional arrangements and rules, see Preston and Windsor (1992, pp. 211-234.)

International Chamber of Commerce is appended as an annex. Such guidelines must be adapted to the circumstances of particular projects; however, they provide useful starting points, from which corporations can develop more tangible. operational programmes that prevent environmental degradation.

V. SUMMARY AND CONCLUSIONS

In sum, although FDI flow data provide approximate indicators of changes in the absolute and relative magnitudes of FDI over time and differences across countries. they are not fully indicative of the overall significance of FDI to physical capital formation -- let alone the other three types of capital (human, natural and social) identified above in the notion of sustainable development. Indeed. data on FDI as a financial flow do not fully reflect the technology transfers that accompany FDI, nor do they fully reflect the contributions of FDI to human capital. And it is precisely the technology spillovers and their contributions to human capital that offer much potential for the contributions of FDI to sustainable development. Yet, the precise contributions of foreign capital flows, especially in the form of FDI, to the development of natural capital and social capital in host countries are inherently difficult to assess through rigorous empirical analysis (and perhaps even impossible in many instances).

The contributions of FDI to sustainable development, in any case, depend very much on combinations of project features and host-government policies. Thus, for example, both theoretical and empirical analysis indicate that import-substitution projects that are protected by high tariffs (or non-tariff barriers) can have negative social rates of return.

A variety of public-sector institutions, as well as TNCs themselves, can develop policies that will increase the contributions of foreign capital flows to sustainable development. These include host government policies that create sound macroeconomic environments for business -- and in some instances carefully targeted incentives that do not transfer wealth from local economies to foreign investors.

Improving the contributions of foreign capital to sustainable development, however, requires much more than simply increasing the amounts of foreign investment in developing counties. It also requires host-government policies that foster competition (and control restrictive business practices) within the economy and that allow the diverse types of international transactions that are essential to the successful operation of typical FDI projects. Such policies will maximize the potentially beneficial contributions of FDI projects to sustainable development.

Host governments -- as well as home governments and international institutions -- must also be mindful of the potentially harmful effects of FDI projects. Because of the common interests and responsibilities inherent in many environmental issues, all of these public-sector agencies need to monitor FDI projects for their environmental consequences. And, finally, of course, TNCs themselves also have similar responsibilities.

Annex. The Business Charter for Sustainable Development:
Principles for Environmental Management

[Editor's note: The Business Charter for Sustainable Development: Principles for Environmental
Management was adopted at the 64th Session of the International Chamber of Commerce Executive
Board on 27 November 1990, and first published in April 1991. It was prepared for the ICC
Commission on Environment.]

Introduction

Sustainable development involves meeting the needs of the present without compromising
the ability of future generations to meet their own needs.

Economic growth provides the conditions in which protection of the environment can best
be achieved, and environmental protection, in balance with other human goals, is necessary to
achieve growth that is sustainable.

In, turn versatile, dynamic, responsive and profitable businesses are required as the driving
force for sustainable economic development and for providing managerial, technical and financial
resources to contribute to the resolution of environmental challenges. Market economies,
characterized by entrepreneurial initiatives, are achieving this.

Business thus shares the view that there should be a common goal, not a conflict, between
economic development and environmental protection, both now and for future generations.

Making market forces work in this way to protect and improve the quality of the environment
-- with the help of performance-based standards and judicious use of economic instruments in a
harmonious regulatory framework -- is one of the greatest challenges that the world faces in the next
decade.

The 1987 report of the World Commission on Environment and Development, "Our
Common Future," expresses the same challenge and calls on the cooperation of business in tackling
it. To this end, business leaders have launched actions in their individual enterprises as well as
through sectoral and cross sectoral associations.

In order that more businesses joint this effort and that their environmental performance
continues to improve, the International Chamber of Commerce hereby calls upon enterprises and
their associations to use the following principles as a basis for pursuing such improvement and to
express publicly their support for them. Individual programmes developed to implement these
Principles will reflect the wide diversity among enterprises in size and function.

The objective is that the widest range of enterprises commit themselves to improving their
environmental performance in accordance with these Principles, to have in place management
practices to effect such improvement, to measuring their progress, and to reporting this progress as
appropriate internally and externally.

Note: The term environment as used in this document also refers to environmentally related
aspects of health, safety and product stewardship.

Principles

1.   *Corporate priority.* To recognize environmental management as among the highest corporate priorities and as a key determinant to sustainable development; to establish policies, programmes and practices for conducting operations in an environmentally sound manner.

2. *Integrated management.* To integrate these policies, programmes and practices fully into each business as an essential element of management in all its functions.

3.   *Process of improvement.* To continue to improve corporate policies, programmes and environmental performance, taking into account technical developments, scientific understanding, consumer needs and community expectations, with legal regulations as a starting point; and to apply the same environmental criteria internationally.

4.   *Employee education.* To educate, train and motivate employees to conduct their activities in an environmentally responsible manner.

5.   *Prior assessment.* To assess environmental impacts before starting a new activity or project and before decommissioning a facility or leaving a site.

6.   *Products and services.* To develop and provide products or services that have no undue environmental impact and are safe in their intended use, that are efficient in their consumption of energy and natural resources, and that can be recycled, reused, or disposed of safely.

7.   *Customer advice.* To advise, and where relevant educate, customers, distributors and the public in the safe use, transportation, storage and disposal of products provided; and to apply similar considerations to the provision of services.

8.   *Facilities and operations.* To develop, design and operate facilities and conduct activities taking into consideration the efficient use of energy and materials, the sustainable use of renewable resources, the minimization of adverse environmental impact and waste generation, and the safe and responsible disposal of residual wastes.

9.   *Research.* To conduct or support research on the environmental impacts of raw materials, products, processes, emissions and wastes associated with the enterprise and on the means of minimizing such adverse impacts.

10.   *Precautionary approach.* To modify the manufacture, marketing or use of products or services or the conduct of activities, consistent with scientific and technical understanding, to prevent serious or irreversible environmental degradation.

11.   *Contractors and suppliers.* To promote the adoption of these principles by contractors acting on behalf of the enterprise, encouraging and, where appropriate, requiring improvements in their practices to make them consistent with those of the enterprise, and to encourage the wider adoption of these principles by suppliers.

12.   *Emergency preparedness.* To develop and maintain, where significant hazards exist, emergency preparedness plans in conjunction with the emergency services, relevant authorities and the local community, recognizing potential transboundary impacts.

13.   *Transfer of technology.* To contribute to the transfer of environmentally sound technology and management methods throughout the industrial and public sectors.

14.   *Contributing to the common effort.* To contribute to the development of public policy and

to business, governmental and intergovernmental programmes and educational initiatives that will enhance environmental awareness and protection.

15.   *Openness to concerns.* To foster openness and dialogue with employee and the public, anticipating and responding to their concerns about the potential hazards and impact of operations, products, wastes of services, including those of transboundary or global significance.

16.   *Compliance and reporting.* To measure environmental performance; to conduct regular environmental audits and assessments of compliance with company requirements, legal requirements and these principles; and periodically to provide appropriate information to the Board of Directors, shareholders, employees, the authorities and the public.

Source: International Chamber of Commerce, *The Business Charter for Sustainable Development: Principles for Environmental Management.* ICC Publication No. 210/356 A, Paris, 1991; reprinted, with introductory note added by the editor, in UNCTAD-DTCI (1996), *International Investment Instruments: A Compendium, Volume III: Regional Integration, Bilateral and Non-governmental Instruments* (Geneva: United Nations), pp. 361-364.

References[11]

Ahmad, Yusuf, Salah El Serafy and Ernst Lutz. (1989). *Environmental Accounting for Sustainable Development* (Washington, D.C.: World Bank).

Blomström, Magnus, Robert E. Lipsey and Morio Zejan (1996), "Is fixed investment the key to economic growth?," *Quarterly Journal of Economics,* vol. CXI, no.1 (February), pp. 269-276.

Borenszstein, Eduardo, Jose De Gregorio, and Jong-wha Lee (1994), *"How Does Foreign Direct Investment Affect Economic Growth,"* International Monetary Fund Working Paper, International Monetary Fund, Washington, D.C.

Brewer, Thomas L., and Stephen Young (1996), "Investment policies in multilateral and regional agreements: a comparative analysis," *Transnational Corporations,* vol. 5, no. 1, pp. 9-36.

Brewer, Thomas L., and Stephen Young (1997), "Investment incentives and the new international agenda," *World Economy,* forthcoming.

Caves, Richard E. (1996). *Multinational Enterprise and Economic Analysis* (Cambridge: Cambridge University Press), second edition.

---

[11] The authors are indebted to Irene Ring for help in the development of the bibliography for the paper and also for her comments on a draft.

Daly, Herman E. (1996). *Beyond Growth: The Economics of Sustainable Development* (Boston: Beacon Press).

Daly, Herman E., and John B. Cobb, Jr. (1994). *For the Common Good* (Boston: Beacon Press).

Dixon, John A., and Sergio Margulis (1994). "Integrating the environment into development policymaking," in Ismail Serageldin and Andrew Steer, eds., *Making Development Sustainable: From Concepts to Action* (Washington, D.C.: World Bank), pp. 21-24.

Flaherty, Margaret, and Ann Rappaport (1981). *Multinational Corporations and the Environment: A Survey of Global Practices* (Boston: Center for Environmental Management, Tufts University).

Gentry, Brad (forthcoming). *Private Capital Flows and the Environment: Lessons from Latin America.*

Gladwin, Thomas N., and Ingo Walter (1976). "Multinational enterprise, social responsiveness and pollution control," *Journal of International Business Studies*, vol. 7, no. 2 (Fall-Winter), pp. 57-74.

Gladwin, Thomas N. (1977). *Environment, Planning and the Multinational Corporation* (Greenwich, Connecticut: JAI Press).

Guisinger, Stephen E., and Associates (1985). *Investment Incentives and Performance Requirements* (New York: Praeger).

Husain, Ishrat, and Kwang W. Jun (1992). "Capital Flows to South Asian and ASEAN Countries: Trends, Determinants, and Policy Implications," Policy Research Working Paper No. 842, World Bank, Washington, D.C.

International Chamber of Commerce (ICC) (1991). *The Business Charter for Sustainable Development: Principles for Environmental Management* (Paris: ICC).

Jun, Kwang W., and Harinder Singh (1996). "The determinants of foreign direct investment: new empirical evidence," *Transnational Corporations*, vol. 5, no. 2, pp.67-106.

Klavens, Jonathan, and Anthony Zamparutti (1995). *Foreign Direct Investment and Environment in Central and Eastern Europe: A Survey* (Washington, D.C.: World Bank).

Krishnan, Rajaram, Jonathan M. Harris and Neva R. Goodwin, eds. (1995). *A Survey of Ecological Economics* (Washington, D.C.: Island Press).

Krishnan, Rajaram (1995). "International economic relations, development, and the environment:

overview essay," in Krishnan, Rajaram, Jonathan M. Harris, and Neva R. Goodwin, eds. *A Survey of Ecological Economics* (Washington, D.C.: Island Press), pp. 285-294.

Munasinghe, Mohan (1994). "The economist's approach to sustainable development," in Ismail Serageldin and Andrew Steer, eds., *Making Development Sustainable: From Concepts to Action* (Washington, D.C.: The World Bank), pp. 13-16.

Organisation for Economic Co-operation and Development (OECD). (1991). *Declaration on International Investment and Multilateral Enterprises* (Paris: OECD).

Organisation for Economic Co-operation and Development (OECD). 1995. *Toward a Multilateral Agreement on Investment* (Paris: OECD).

Pearson, Charles S., ed. (1987). *Multinational Corporations, Environment and the Third World* (Durham, North Carolina: Duke University Press).

Preston, Lee E., and Duane Windsor (1992). *The Rules of the Game in the World Economy* (Dordrecht, Netherlands: Kluwer).

Serageldin, Ismail, and Andrew Steer (1994). "Epilogue: expanding the capital stock," in Ismail Serageldin and Andrew Steer, eds., *Making Development Sustainable: From Concepts to Action* (Washington, D.C.: World Bank).

Steer, Andrew (1996). "Annual overview: the year in perspective," *Environment Matters*, Annual Review (Fall), pp. 4-7.

Steer, Andrew, and Ernst Lutz (1994). "Measuring environmentally sustainable development," in Ismail Serageldin and Andrew Steer, eds., *Making Development Sustainable: From Concepts to Action* (Washington, D.C.: World Bank), pp. 17-20.

Stiglitz, Joseph E. (1993), "Measures for Enhancing the Flow of Private Capital to the Less Developed Countries," presented to the 46th Meeting of the Development Committee of the World Bank and the IMF.

United Nations Conference on Trade and Development-Division on Transnational Corporations and Investment (UNCTAD-DTCI) (1996). *World Investment Report 1996: Investment, Trade and International Policy Arrangements* (New York and Geneva: United Nations).

United Nations Conference on Trade and Development-Transnational Corporations and Management Division (UNCTAD-TCMD). (1992). *World Investment Report 1992: Transnational Corporations as Engines of Growth* (New York: United Nations).

United Nations Centre on Transnational Corporations (UNCTC). (1985). *Environmental Aspects of the Activities of Transnational Corporations: A Survey* (New York: United Nations).

World Bank (1996). *World Debt Tables, vol. 1: External Finance for Developing Countries* (Washington, D.C.: World Bank).

World Bank (1992). *World Development Report 1992: Development and the Environment* (Washington, D.C.: World Bank).

World Bank, Development Committee (1991). "The Role of Foreign Direct Investment in Development," (DC/91-5), Washington, D.C., World Bank.

[13]

CAPITAL ACCOUNT LIBERALIZATION, FREE LONG-TERM CAPITAL FLOWS, FINANCIAL CRISES AND ECONOMIC DEVELOPMENT

Ajit Singh
Queens' College, University of Cambridge

MAIN ISSUES AND THE INTERNATIONAL POLICY CONTEXT

The main objective of this paper is to review the theoretical issues and available empirical evidence on capital account liberalization. In addition to being of interest in its own right, capital account liberalizations is important to the debate on the New International Financial Architecture (NIFA) and to the post-Doha agenda at the World Trade Organization (WTO) in relation to foreign direct investment (FDI) flows. This paper focuses on developing countries and it considers policy from the perspective of (a) economic development and (b) the global rules of the game rather than the economic policy within individual countries. The paper essentially examines the question: what kind of global economic order in relation to capital flows can best serve the interests of developing countries?

Capital account liberalization is an area where economic theory is the most disconnected from real-world events. In analyzing liberalization of capital flows, it is customary to distinguish between short-term (for example, portfolio flows and short-term bank loans) and long-term flows (for example, FDI). Neoclassical theory suggests that free flows of external capital (including short-term capital) should be equilibrating and help smooth a country's consumption or production paths. However, in the real world, exactly the opposite appears to happen. Liberalization of the short-term capital account has invariably been associated with serious economic and financial crises in Asia and Latin America in the 1990s. The proponents of neoclassical theory argue that the case for free capital flows is no different from that for free trade; the former could simply be regarded as a form of inter-temporal trade. The first part of the paper addresses this central controversy in relation to developing countries and specifically asks the following questions:

- To what extent, if any, are trade liberalization and free capital flows analogous in their effects on social welfare? What are the conditions necessary to maximize their potential net benefits?
- What is the nature of the relationship between capital account liberalization and economic crises?
- Why do such crises occur far more in developing than in advanced countries?

Ajit Singh: Queens' College, University of Cambridge, Cambridge, CB3 9ET, United Kingdom. E-mail: as14@econ.cam.ac.uk

Eastern Economic Journal, Vol. 29, No. 2, Spring 2003

- Do free capital flows lead to faster long-term economic growth, which may compensate for the crisis and the economic instability associated with capital account liberalization?
- What kind of multilateral framework, if any, would be most appropriate for regulating international capital flows that would best serve the interests of developing countries?

In the light of the recent deep economic and financial crises in Asia, Latin America and Russia, many (but by no means all) economists today accept that because short-term capital flows are often volatile and subject to surges and sudden withdrawals, these flows could have seriously adverse consequences for developing countries. However, long-term capital flows, particularly FDI, are regarded as being much more stable, and for this and other reasons, are thought to have a positive influence on long-term economic development. It is therefore suggested that when liberalizing their capital account, developing countries may wish to liberalize only long-term capital flows such as FDI in the short- to medium-term, while still partially or wholly controlling short-term flows.

Even Joseph Stiglitz, who has been a fierce critic of precipitate capital account liberalization in developing countries, appears to favor free FDI flows. Thus Stiglitz finds striking "the zeal with which the International Monetary Fund (IMF) had requested an extension of its mandate to include capital market liberalization a short two years earlier at the Annual Meetings in Hong Kong. It should have been clear then, and it is certainly clear now, that the position was maintained either as a matter of ideology or of special interests, and not on the basis of careful analysis of theory, historical experience or a wealth of econometric studies. Indeed, it has become increasingly clear that there is not only no case for capital market liberalization, but that there is a fairly compelling case against full liberalization" [2000, 1076]. Stiglitz, however, emphasizes that his general strictures against capital account liberalization are primarily directed against short-term speculative flows. He writes, "The argument for foreign direct investment, for instance, is compelling. Such investment brings with it not only resources, but also technology, access to markets, and (hopefully) valuable training, an improvement in human capital. Foreign direct investment is also not as volatile—and therefore as disruptive—as the short-term flows that can rush into a country and, just as precipitously, rush out" [ibid., 1076].

This paper takes major issue, with the orthodox *laissez-faire* position [Summers, 2000; Fischer, 2001], of the desirability of speedy capital account liberalization in developing countries. It does, however, also part company with Stiglitz in important respects. I argue that although Stiglitz is right in suggesting that free-trade in capital is not the same as free trade in goods, he implicitly assigns too much virtue to the latter. I make this argument more in global economic terms rather than in those of the traditional concepts, such as infant industry protection. I further suggest that not only do developing countries need controls against short-term capital flows for many of the reasons Stiglitz puts forward, but they also require discretion to regulate FDI flows if it is thought to be desirable. This paper also argues that free movements of even FDI may contribute to financial fragility in developing economies and also may not serve the cause of economic development in a number of other ways.

These issues of capital account liberalization are, of course, not only of academic interest, but clearly of serious policy concern for developing countries. Note that the present paper concentrates exclusively on the international dimension of the policy debate on the subject. Orderly and fast progress toward capital account liberalization for all countries has been at the heart of the proposals by G7 countries for the New International Financial Architecture (NIFA). Similarly, the European Union and Japan have raised the question of the free movements of FDI as an important subject for study and eventual negotiations at the WTO. Unlike the aborted OECD Multilateral Agreement on Investment, these new proposals wholly exclude short-term capital flows and focus entirely on FDI. To date, these proposals have received little academic or public attention. Now, following the Doha WTO Ministerial Declaration, these issues are on the international agenda and merit urgent scrutiny. There is already a large literature on the NIFA.[1] However, the advanced countries' proposal for the free movement of FDI has not been studied much. The second half of the paper redresses this imbalance by focusing on FDI flows, specifically on the proposed new multilateral agreement on such flows.

To sum up, the main contribution of this paper lies firstly in bringing together the relevant theory and empirical evidence from diverse areas (theory of international trade, of international factor movements, of industrial organization, of finance, and of economic development) to bear on important international economic policy issues with respect to both short-term and long-term capital flows to developing countries. Secondly, the paper examines these multilateral arrangements entirely from a developing country perspective. Thirdly, it provides analysis and evidence to suggest that even unfettered FDI, a capital inflow favored by most economists, may not serve the developmental needs of many countries. Fourthly, the paper provides a critical analysis of the proposed new multilateral agreement (PMAI) being put forward at the WTO by some advanced countries. As mentioned above, very little work has been done on this specific topic before.

FREE TRADE VERSUS FREE CAPITAL MOVEMENTS: ARE THEY ANALOGOUS?[2]

Free Trade and Economic Openness: Analytical Considerations

The traditional case for free trade can best be put in terms of the two fundamental theorems of welfare economics. According to the first welfare theorem, a competitive equilibrium in the absence of externalities and non-satiation constitutes a Pareto optimum. The second theorem, which is more relevant for present purposes, states that any Pareto optimum can be realized as a competitive equilibrium in the presence of all-around convexity, provided suitable lump-sum transfers can be arranged among the participants. Most of these assumptions are erroneous or are not easily met in the real world. Nevertheless, neoclassical economists suggest that such considerations do not destroy the case for free trade; they only change the nature of the argument. Thus, Krugman concludes his classic defense of free trade in terms of modern theory as follows: "this is not the argument that free trade is optimal because markets are efficient. Instead it is a sadder but wiser argument for free trade as a rule of thumb in a world whose politics are as imperfect as its markets" [1987, 143].

However, as Chakravarty and Singh [1988] suggest, the politics of a world of increasing returns to scale are more likely to gravitate towards managed rather than free trade. Instead of either free trade or autarchy, this would be a world in between—a world of trade restrictions, government assistance to favored industries, and a plethora of special arrangements between countries, in other words, the messy real world. In place of all-around convexity, this real world is characterized by learning by doing [Arrow, 1962], dynamic economies and cumulative causation [Young, 1928; Kaldor 1978]. This is, therefore, the world of second best and of multiple equilibria. The purpose of policy is to move from a bad to a good equilibrium. The gains from such policy intervention, however, have to be balanced against the losses from government failure. Appropriate policy can therefore be prescribed only on a case-by-case basis [Occampo and Taylor, 2000; Gomery and Baumol, 2000]. Provided a mechanism exists to ensure full employment of each nation's resources, and if we abstract, for the moment, from the possibility of government failure, a policy of selective economic openness would be a source of great advantage for an economy for any one of the following reasons:[3]

(a) it may enable a country to concentrate its relatively specialized resources in areas of production where the world demand is highly income and price elastic;
(b) it may lead to diffusion of knowledge of a nature which can lead to considerable upgrading of the *quality* of local factors of production;
(c) it may lead to sufficient competitive pressure to eliminate X-inefficiency;
(d) trade may lead to changes in the distribution of income which can lead to a greater share of accumulation in national income;
(e) trade may facilitate what Schumpeter stressed so much: an accelerated process of creative destruction.

In general, trade openness works positively if the phenomenon of "learning" from contacts with the rest of the world is institutionalized through suitable adaptations on the policy side involving appropriate government interventions which make the domestic economy more responsive to change. This is a main lesson that emerges from the outstanding industrial success of East Asian economies during the second half of the 20th century.[4] Countries such as Japan and Korea established comprehensive technology and industrial policies to institutionalize such learning. It is important to appreciate that although Japan and Korea were "trade open" in the sense of being export or outward oriented, they were not so open on the side of imports. Both countries maintained, formally or informally, selective import controls for long periods during the course of their industrialization. The strategic interests of the U.S. hegemony permitted such selective openness without threatening retaliation.[5] To pursue these policies of selective economic openness, it is necessary for developing countries to have not only appropriate institutions to minimize the incidence of government failure, but also a world conjuncture that permits them to pursue commercial and industrial policies on a non-reciprocal basis that best suits their developmental requirements. Chakravarty and Singh [1988] point out that in such a world, selective economic openness may be a superior strategy than either free trade or autarchy. They also suggest that at a theoretical level, *learning over time* is a more relevant paradigm for developmental gains from trade than the neoclassical story that emphasizes the exploitation of arbitrage opportunities.[6]

To sum up, while the classical and neoclassical arguments for free trade suffer from serious conceptual and operational difficulties, selective trade or economic openness have substantive benefits that are more robust than the traditional neoclassical theory suggests. Such benefits can be realized, however, only in a world conjuncture in which full employment and other structural conditions outlined above are met, coupled with an appropriate set of domestic policies that go considerably beyond the limits of commercial policy as traditionally defined.

The Case for Capital Account Liberalization

The case for capital account liberalization was authoritatively put forward by Stanley Fischer, the former Deputy Managing Director of the International Monetary Fund, in the following terms:

- that the benefits of liberalizing the capital account outweigh the potential costs;
- that countries need to prepare well for capital account liberalization: economic policies and institutions, particularly the financial system, need to be adapted to operate in a world of liberalized capital markets; and
- that an amendment of the IMF's Articles of Agreement is the best way of ensuring that capital account liberalization is carried out in an orderly, non-disruptive way, that minimizes the risks that premature liberalization could pose for an economy and its policymakers. [1997]

Fischer suggests that, at a theoretical level, capital account liberalization would lead to global economic efficiency, allocation of world savings to those who are able to use them most productively, and would thereby increase social welfare. Citizens of countries with free capital movements would be able to diversify their portfolios and thereby increase their risk-adjusted rates of return. It would enable corporations in these countries to raise capital in international markets at a lower cost. It is suggested, moreover, that such liberalization leads to further development of a country's financial system, which in turn is thought to enhance productivity in the real economy by facilitating transactions and by better allocating resources. Some argue that free capital movements will help increase world welfare through another channel, namely transferring resources from aging populations and lower rates of return in advanced countries to younger populations and higher rates of return in newly industrializing economies. Such resource transfers will be Pareto optimal as both rich and poor countries would gain.

Summers succinctly sums up the core point of the orthodox perspective as follows: "... the abstract argument for a competitive financial system parallels the argument for competitive markets in general ... Just as trade in goods across jurisdictions has benefits, so too will intertemporal trade and trade that shares risks across jurisdictions have benefits" [2000, 2].

Orthodox economists recognize that capital account liberalization has risks. Markets sometimes overreact or react late or react too fast. However, Fischer argues that "...capital movements are mostly appropriate: currency crises do not blow up out of a clear blue sky, but rather start as rational reactions to policy mistakes or external shocks. The problem is that once started, they may sometimes go too far" [1997, 4-5]. In general, Fisher believes that capital markets serve as an important discipline for government macroeconomic policy "which improves overall economic performance by rewarding good policies and penalizing bad." [ibid., 4]

Two initial observations may be made with respect to this orthodox case for capital account liberalization. The first is that not all orthodox economists favor such liberalization. Bhagwati [1998] for example, a leading theorist and advocate of free trade in goods and services, regards capital account liberalization as inappropriate for developing countries. Secondly, as with the case of the neoclassical argument for free trade, the maintenance of full employment and macroeconomic stability constitute an important prerequisite for reaping the benefits of a globalized capital market. Specifically, as Rakshit [2001] suggests, the theoretical model of the beneficial effects of free capital movements makes the following assumptions:

(a) resources are fully employed everywhere;
(b) capital flows themselves do not stand in the way of attaining full employment or macroeconomic stability; and
(c) the transfer of capital from one country to another is governed by long-term returns on investment in different countries.

The validity of these assumptions under the current global economic regime is examined below.

The Analytical Case Against Free Capital Flows

The theoretical case against the view that unfettered capital movements are essential for maximizing the gains from trade and world economic welfare has been made by a number of economists from different schools of thought. First within the neoclassical tradition itself, Stiglitz [2000] argues that the concept of free movements of capital is fundamentally different from that of free trade in goods. Capital flows are subject to asymmetric information, agency problems, adverse selection, and moral hazard. Although such problems may occur also in trade in goods and services, they are intrinsic to financial flows and are far more significant.

Importantly, there are also diverging views about the price formation process in asset markets such as the stock market and the currency markets. Orthodox economists subscribe to the theory of efficient markets. In this view, prices are a collective outcome of actions of a multitude of individual economic agents whose behavior is assumed to be based on utility maximization and rational expectations. This price formation process is thought to lead to efficient prices in these markets. A powerful counter-view is that put forward by Keynes [1936] in Chapter 12 of the *General Theory* and encapsulated in his well-known "beauty contest" analogy, which highlights the role of speculation in determining prices.

Thus, in Keynesian analysis, which has been formalized in recent theoretical contributions, price formation in asset markets may often be dominated by speculators or, in modern parlance, noise traders. Moreover, theoretical work on Darwinian selection mechanisms indicate that the Friedman [1953] assertion that rational investors will always wipe out speculators is far from being valid in all situations.[7]

Further the critical school emphasizes that financial markets are particularly prone to coordination failures and often generate multiple equilibria, some of which are good and some of which are bad. In the absence of appropriate coordination by the government or international authorities, an economy may languish in a low-level equilibrium, producing suboptimal output and employment levels.

The post-Keynesian economists [see for example, Davidson, 2001], take a more radical stance. They put forward analyses and evidence in favor of Keynes' thesis "that flexible exchange rates and free international capital mobility are incompatible with global full employment and rapid economic growth in an era of multilateral free trade" [ibid., 12]. These economists also challenge the orthodox presumption that transparency and availability of more information would make the financial markets less prone to crisis. They point out that the crises are fundamentally due to the fact that the future is uncertain and people have different perceptions about it.

Keynes was very skeptical about the ability of the world economy under free trade and free capital movements to maintain balance of payments equilibrium between countries at full employment levels of output. In a famous passage he observed, "... the problem of maintaining equilibrium in the balance of payments between countries has never been solved ... the failure to solve the problem has been a major cause of impoverishment and social discontent and even of wars and revolutions ... to suppose that there exists some smoothly functioning automatic mechanism of adjustment which preserves equilibrium only if we trust to matters of laissez faire is a doctrinaire delusion which disregards the lessons of historical experience without having behind it the support of sound theory" [Moggridge, 1980, 21-2]. Consequently the Keynesian design for the postwar international financial system did not envisage free capital movements.

In summary, the orthodox theory that financial liberalization leads to global economic efficiency based on the analogy with free trade is flawed on several counts, including some within the neoclassical tradition itself.

EMPIRICAL RESEARCH ON FINANCIAL LIBERALIZATION AND ECONOMIC CRISIS

Banking and Currency Crises and the Real Economy

The theoretical expectation that free capital movements lead to smoother income and consumption trajectories for individuals and countries following economic shocks than would otherwise be the case, has been confounded by the experience of developing countries. Substantial empirical evidence suggests a close link between the liberalization of the financial system and economic and financial crises particularly in developing countries. Developed countries, including the United States, the UK and Scandinavian countries, have also been subject to such crises, but compared with developing countries, the incidence has been relatively low and the social costs correspondingly smaller. However, developing countries have suffered not only more but also deeper crises and virtual financial meltdowns.

Compared to this impressionistic evidence, the results of detailed econometric studies are more mixed. The empirical literature on this subject is vast and still growing at a fast rate. At least four kinds of studies are relevant. First, contributions to the financial literature support the orthodox case that financial liberalization in emerging markets reduces the cost of equity capital and has a positive impact on domestic investments. [Bekaert, Harvey and Lundblad, 2001; Henry 2000; Chari and Henry, 2002]. Secondly, studies on financial liberalization, banking, and currency crisis find that there is a close causal relationship between these variables, thus providing support for the anti-liberalization camp. Some of these studies will be reviewed below. A third strand of this literature concerns financial crashes and suggest that financial liberalization is much more risky in this respect for developing than for advanced countries. Leading contributions in this area are Martin and Rey [2002]. Wyplosz [2001], Mendoza [2001], McKinnon and Pill [1999]. The fourth part of this literature considers the relationship between capital account liberalization and long-term economic growth.

It is not our purpose here to systematically review this whole body of literature but rather to draw relevant conclusions for a multilateral global framework for short- and long-term capital flows from a developing country perspective. However, in order to indicate the nature and the kind of evidence produced by these studies, a few of them will be briefly examined below.

Kaminsky and Reinhart's [1999] paper explored the links between banking crises, exchange rate crises, and financial liberalization. The sample covered 1970 to 1995 and consisted of twenty countries, fourteen of which were developing. The authors found that both types of crises increased sharply since 1980. The average number of banking crises in their sample rose from 0.3 per year from 1970 to 1979 to 1.4 per year from 1980 to 1995. The two authors found that the banking crises and the currency crises are closely related and that the banking crises are often preceded by financial liberalization.

In their influential study Demigüc-Kunt and Detragiache [1998] examined banking crises from 1980 to 1984 for a sample of 53 developed and developing countries. They found that a banking crisis is more likely to occur where the financial system has been liberalized. They also found a two-way interaction between banking and currency crises. Where the banking systems are not sufficiently developed, with capital account liberalization, banks become vulnerable to external economic shocks. The authors' findings suggest that vulnerability is reduced with institutional development and strengthening of the banking system through prudential regulation. They also found that financial liberalization leads to an intensification of competition among banks and hence to greater moral hazard and risk-taking than before.[8]

The recent Asian crisis provides almost a laboratory experiment for examining the role of capital account liberalization in causing or exacerbating that region's severe economic downturn. Williamson and Drabek [1998] provide evidence to suggest that countries that did or did not have economic crises were differentiated only by whether or not they had liberalized their capital accounts. Most economists would now agree that even if premature financial liberalization without adequate prudential regulation was not the root cause of the crises in countries such as Thailand, Korea, and Indonesia, it greatly contributed to the occurrence and depth of the crises. Indeed, the economic fundamentals prior to the crises of the affected countries were better than those of India, but the latter country was spared the crisis because of its control over the capital account. Similarly, China managed to avoid a crisis and continued to have fast economic growth. China also had not liberalized its capital account.[9]

It is argued by some that even with the acute economic crisis of 1998-1999, over the long run Korea, with its economic openness, was a much more successful economy than India. This argument has some plausibility but overlooks the crucial fact that Korea's outstanding industrialization record over the previous three decades was not accomplished by a liberalized financial system but rather by a highly controlled one. However, when the system was liberalized in the 1990s it was followed by an unprecedented crisis [Demetriades and Luintel, 2001].

Social and Economic Costs of the Crisis

The Asian crisis was extremely important in terms of its economic and social impact on the populations of the affected countries. The World Bank notes that "In terms of lost output and the implications for poverty and unemployment, the Asian crisis represents one of the most acute periods of financial instability in this century" [2001, 73]. The crisis greatly increased poverty, reduced employment and real wages, and caused enormous social distress. Indeed the economic downturn was so enormous that in a country like Indonesia the social fabric of the country virtually disintegrated. This is why the Asian crisis is aptly termed, not just an ordinary slowing of GDP growth due to an economic shock or a normal cyclical recession, but an enormous meltdown. It is important to appreciate, however, that even if no meltdown occurs, economic slowdowns or recessions have bigger social costs in developing than developed countries because of their lack of publicly provided social security. There is evidence that in both country groups the effects of a downturn fall disproportionately on the poor and on women [Singh and Zammit, 2000; Stiglitz, 1999; World Bank, 1998/99].

Turning to an investigation of purely economic costs, there are good analytical reasons to believe that economic crises would negatively affect both investment and long-term growth [Pindyck, 1991; World Bank [2001]; Easterly et al., 2000]. In addition, recessions and meltdowns also have fiscal and redistributive implications that may affect the economy for a long period of time. Caprio and Klingebiel [1996] estimates indicate that the costs of a banking crisis are typically quite large, ranging from 3.2 percent of GDP in the 1984-91 U.S. savings and loans crisis to 55.3 percent

TABLE 1
Fiscal Costs of Banking Crisis in Selected Countries
(percentage of GDP)

Country	Date	Cost as a percentage of GDP
Argentina	1980-82	55.3
Chile	1981-3	41.2
Uruguay	1981-4	31.2
Israel	1977-83	30.0
Cote d'Ivoire	1988-91	25.0
Senegal	1988-91	17.0
Spain	1977-85	16.8
Bulgaria	1990s	14.0
Mexico	1995	13.5
Hungary	1991-95	10.0
Finland	1991-93	8.0
Sweden	1991	6.4
Sri Lanka	1989-93	5.0
Malaysia	1985-8	4.7
Norway	1987-89	4.0
United States	1984-91	3.2

Source: Caprio and Klingebiel 1996. Quoted in Chang, (2001)

for the 1980-82 Argentinian banking crisis (Table 1). On the basis of more recent evidence, Aizenman [2002] estimates the average cost of a currency crisis to be 8 percent of the pre-crisis GDP and the average cost of a simultaneous banking and currency crisis is 18 percent of pre-crisis GDP. He also reports that "the twin crises are mainly concentrated in financially liberalized emerging market economies" [ibid., 5].

In a pioneering study Easterly et al. [2000] investigated economic instability for a large cross-section of developed and developing countries from 1960 to 1990. As Table 2 indicates, developing countries typically suffer greater instability than developed countries with respect to output, employment, real wages, capital flows and terms of trade changes.[10] In neoclassical analysis it is customary to attribute instability to the lack of flexibility in labor markets, particularly to wage rigidity. However, Easterly et al. find that despite greater labor market flexibility (measured by changes in real wages) in developing countries, wages are also more volatile than developed countries (Table 2). The authors' results suggest that the characteristics of the financial system rather than the labor market are the more important causes of economic instability.[11] Their econometric analysis shows that financial variables are statistically significant in explaining both volatility of GDP growth and the likelihood of a downturn. They find that openness and policy volatility also have a significant influence on growth volatility. In general, the findings of Easterly et al. suggest that countries with weak financial systems display greater instability in GDP growth in part because these institutional shortcomings amplify the effects of the volatility of capital flows.

TABLE 2
Economic Instability and Related Variables:
Differences between Developing and High-Income OECD Countries

Variable	Developing Countries		High-income OECD Countries			
	Mean	Number of observations	Mean	Number of observations	t-Statistic for difference in means	P-value
Growth	0.007	163	0.027	23	-5.659	0.000
Standard deviation of growth	0.061	163	0.026	23	9.779	0.000
Median standard deviation of growth	0.052		0.022			
Standard deviation of employment	0.098	83	0.035	21	6.652	0.000
Standard deviation of real wage index	2.119	90	1.883	21	0.833	0.410
Standard deviation of real wage changes	1.197	85	0.321	21	8.116	0.000
Private capital flows / GDP	1.722	146	0.372	22	2.743	0.009
Standard deviation of private capital flows / GDP	2.662	138	2.311	22	0.808	0.420
Standard deviation of terms of trade changes	0.123	117	0.041	23	9.688	0.000
Standard deviation of money growth	0.219	148	0.077	20	6.757	0.000

Source: Easterly, W, Islam, R. and Stiglitz, J.E. [2000].

Capital Account Liberalization and Proximate Causes of Instability

The fundamental theoretical reasons why capital account liberalization may lead to economic instability were analyzed earlier. The present subsection briefly reviews some of the proximate reasons for this instability in developing countries, namely:

(a) Self-fulfilling expectations;
(b) volatility in capital flows;
(c) Increased competition among banks following liberalization as mentioned above;
(d) The changes in the global financial system and the short-termism of the leading players.

Self-fulfilling expectations. A large literature based on the self-fulfilling expectations suggests that capital account liberalization is much more likely to lead to financial crisis in emerging markets than in developed countries. This literature points to the role of factors such us moral hazard, credit constraints and overborrowing syndrome as factors to explain these different outcomes. Martin and Rey [2002), an important contribution to these studies, provide empirical evidence that after liberalization the probability of a financial crisis is negatively related to per capita income, whereas before liberalization these variables are only weakly related. The authors report that the results are robust to alternative definitions of financial crash. Their model of self-fulfilling expectations does not require any appeal to special factors mentioned above to explain these empirical facts. Rather, in their model, for intermediate levels of international financial transactions costs, pessimistic expectations can be self-fulfilling leading to a financial crash. The crash is accompanied by capital flight, a drop in income below the financial autarchy level, and market incompleteness.

Volatility. The volatility and the procyclical nature of private capital flows to developing countries is a well-attested feature of international capital movements during the last two decades [Williamson, 2002; Occampo, 2001; Singh and Zammit, 2000; Stiglitz, 2000]. Such inflows come in surges, often bearing no relationship to the economic fundamentals of the country, and leave the country when they are most needed; that is in a downturn. As Williamson and Drabek [1998] note, even in a country such as Chile which was deeply integrated with the world financial markets, private foreign capital suddenly withdrew in the event of a fall in copper prices. There is, however, an important debate on the comparative volatility of the different components of capital flows, which will be reviewed in the following sections.

Ramey and Ramey [1995] found that the effects of the volatility of capital flows was positively related to volatility of GDP growth, a result confirmed by Easterly et al. [2000]. The former two authors also reported a negative relationship between long-run economic growth and the volatility of GDP growth, a result again confirmed by Easterly et al. [2000], and also by World Bank [2001], among others. Table 3, from the latter publication, presents regression results of the effects of capital flows and their volatility on growth per capita, for a large sample of developing countries over successive decades, covering the 1970-1998 period. The table also contains the normal control variables used in such cross-section analyses (for example, initial GDP per capita, initial schooling, population growth rate, investment rates, and a measure of policy). Volatility of capital flows is measured by the standard deviation of the flows. The dependent variable is the rate of growth of GDP per capita. The table suggests an economically important and statistically significant negative relationship between capital flow volatility and GDP growth per capita for the 1970-1998 period as a whole.[12] It is interesting, however, that the negative relationship becomes weaker over time, with the value of the relevant coefficient rising from a statistically significant minus .322 during 1970-79 to minus .124 in 1990-98 when the coefficient was also statistically insignificant. Other results from Table 3 will be commented on in the following section.

The next issue is why the capital flows to developing countries are so volatile. Analysis and evidence suggests that both internal (for example, weak domestic financial systems, and frequent economic shocks) and external factors, particularly the animal spirits of foreign investors, are involved in making these flows volatile.

Kindleberger [1984] has observed that financial markets are subject to frequent crises, which he ascribes to periodic and alternating bouts of irrational exuberance

TABLE 3
Effects of Capital Flows and Their Volatility on
Growth per Capita by Decade.

Independent variable	Dependent Variable: Rate of GDP Growth per Capita			
	1970-98	1970-80	1980-89	1990-98
Capital flows	0.287[b]	−0.149	0.133	0.275[b]
Capital flows volatility	−0.344[b]	−0.322[b]	−0.188	−0.124
Initial GDP per capital	−0.508[b]	−0.345	−0.940[b]	0.159
Initial schooling	1.429	−1.749	3.640[a]	−0.446
Population growth rate	−0.513[b]	−0.438	−0.573[b]	0.869[b]
Investment	0.182[b]	0.309[b]	0.164[b]	0.094[b]
Policy	0.008[b]	0.007[b]	0.011[b]	0.013[b]
Inflation rate	−0.002[b]	−0.008	-0.001[b]	−0.004[b]
Openness of the economy	0.001	0.006	0.001	-0.024[b]
Adjusted R^2	0.75	0.59	0.57	0.38
No. of Countries.	72	56	74	100

a. Significant at the 10 percent level
b. Significant at the 5 percent level.
Source: World Bank [2001].

and pessimism of investors largely unrelated to fundamentals. Importantly, Kindleberger's historical analysis is implicitly endorsed by Alan Greenspan, the Chairman of the U.S. Federal Reserve himself, who recently commented on the 1987 U.S. stock market crash and the Asian financial meltdown of the 1990s:

> At one point the economic system appears stable, the next it behaves as though a dam has reached a breaking point, and water (read, confidence) evacuates its reservoir. The United States experienced such a sudden change with the decline in stock prices of more than 20 percent on October 19, 1987. There is no credible scenario that can readily explain so abrupt a change in the fundamentals of long-term valuation on that one day. ... But why do these events seem to erupt without some readily evident precursors? Certainly, the more extended the risk-taking, or more generally, the lower the discount factors applied to future outcomes, the more vulnerable are markets to a shock that abruptly triggers a revision in expectations and sets off a vicious cycle of contraction. ... Episodes of vicious cycles cannot easily be forecast, as our recent experience with Asia has demonstrated. [1998, 4-5]

This mirrors the Keynesian view of investor behavior and the significance of mass psychology in price formation in the financial markets, as discussed earlier. Keynes' insights on this subject have been formalized in current theoretical literature, which is able to provide a "rational" explanation for the herdlike behavior, contagion and other irrational manifestations of economic agents in financial markets [Shiller, 2000; Singh and Weisse, 1999; Singh, 1999].

It is also important to emphasize another major factor in causing the volatility of external capital flows to developing countries. Kaufman [2000] and Williamson [2002] have stressed the significance of changes in the nature and character of the financial markets in enhancing capital flow volatility. The intense competition in the world fund management industry together with the nature of rewards offered to fund managers have helped to make fund managers focus on the short run when making their investment decisions.[13] As Kauffman notes:

> In the new global financial system, most prominent banks, securities firms, and even a few insurance companies possess departments that emulate the trading and investment approach of the hedge funds. Even the corporate treasuries of a number of non-financial corporations are engaged in this activity. Once arcane and exotic, the hedge fund approach to investment has been mainstreamed. [2000, 61]

Finally, analysis and evidence for increased competition among banks following liberalization is provided by Furman and Stiglitz [1999] and Stiglitz [2000] among others.

EVIDENCE ON CAPITAL ACCOUNT LIBERALIZATION AND LONG-TERM ECONOMIC GROWTH

In principle it is possible for the instability caused by capital account liberalization to be more than compensated for by faster long-term economic growth arising from the greater availability of capital inflows. This is the promise held by the proponents of this policy regime [Fischer, 1997; Summers, 2000]. It will therefore be useful to review the available empirical evidence on this issue.

A good starting point is the broad brush approach adopted by Singh [1997a] in analyzing this issue. He considers the case of advanced countries whose experience, he suggests, is relevant for developing economies. This is because the former have operated under a regime of relatively free trade and capital movements for nearly two decades—a period long enough to make at least a preliminary assessment of the effects of this economic regime on performance. Evidence suggests that the record has been less than impressive despite the fact that the world economy during this period has not been subject to any abnormal negative shocks like the oil price increases of 1973 and 1979. Indeed, the economic performance of industrial countries during this later period has been much worse than in the earlier period of the 1950s and 1960s when they functioned under a myriad of capital controls.

- GDP growth in the 1980s and 1990s under a liberal regime regarding private capital flows was much lower than that achieved in the "illiberal" and regulated "golden age" of the 1950s and 1960s;
- Productivity growth in the last fifteen years has been half of what it was in the "golden age";
- The critical failure is, however, with respect to employment: 8 million people were unemployed in the OECD countries in 1970, but by the mid 1990s 35 million were unemployed, that is, 10 percent of the labor force.

Singh's analysis also shows that the poor performance of industrialized countries during the 1980s and 1990s cannot alternatively be ascribed to exogenous factors such as the exhaustion of technological opportunities, or to labor market imperfections. Industrial economies have more flexible markets today than they did in the golden age. In addition they have the benefit of a new technological paradigm of information and communication technology which many economic historians regard as on a par with the most important technological revolutions of the last two centuries. In view of all these factors—a new technological paradigm, more flexible markets, absence of economic shocks such as the oil shocks of 1973 and 1975—orthodox analyses would suggest that OECD economies should be growing today at a much faster rate than in the golden age. But as we see the opposite has been true.

Eatwell's [1996] and Singh's [1997a] analyses indicate that the poor performance of industrial countries in the recent period is closely linked to intrinsic features of the liberal financial regime. Coordination failures have led to suboptimal levels of the OECD and world aggregate demand, output and employment. When capital flows were regulated in the 1950s and 1960s, and there was successful coordination under the hegemony of the United States, balance of payments between countries was achieved at much higher levels of output and employment than has subsequently been the case under financial liberalization.

In contrast with the above broad brush approach, there exist numerous econometric studies of the effects of capital account liberalization on economic growth with definitely mixed results. Loungani recently reviewed the IMF contributions on the subject and reached the following conclusion:

> .....What impact do capital flows have on growth? The evidence is decidedly mixed and appears to depend, somewhat, on the particular flow studied (or the measure of capital market openness used), the sample period, the set of countries, and whether cross-section or panel data is used. Recent IMF work provides an illustration of mixed findings. In a much-cited study, Borensztein, De Gregorio, and Lee [1998] find that FDI increases economic growth when the level of education in the host country-a measure of its absorptive capacity- is high. Mody and Murshid [2002] find that capital inflows boost domestic investment almost one-to-one, but the strength of this relationship appears to be weakening over time. In contrast, Edison, Levine, Ricci, and Slok [2002], using the new measures of openness, do not find evidence of a robust link between international financial integration and economic growth. [2002, 6]

Two main conclusions emerge from the above review of empirical evidence on capital account liberalization, financial crisis, and GDP growth. First, there is strong evidence of a close relationship between liberalization and economic and financial crises in developing countries. This relationship is robust, and in the circumstances of these countries there are also strong analytical arguments for both its existence and robustness. Secondly, available evidence for the view that free capital flows promote faster long-term economic growth in developing countries is much weaker.

Aizenman reaches a broadly similar conclusion: ".....there is solid evidence that financial opening increases the chance of financial crisis. There is more tenuous evidence that financial opening contributes positively to long-run growth" [2002, 2] However, from the perspective of economic policy an important consideration is how to proceed from the short to the long term. The economic crises, and the instability that capital account liberalization is seen to generate in the short term, may compromise a country's future economic development by inducing capital flight and lowering domestic investment and long-term economic growth. In summary, in view of these facts and analyses, Stiglitz [2000] is fully justified in castigating the IMF for promoting universal capital account liberalization when most developing countries were not ready for such policies. Fortunately, in the wake of the Asian crisis the IMF has in the most recent period moderated its stance in this respect.

CAPITAL ACCOUNT LIBERALIZATION AND FDI [14]

As explained in the introduction, while Stiglitz finds a "compelling" case against any general liberalization of the capital account, he also suggests that there is a "compelling" case in favor of FDI. In view of the fickleness of the short-term capital flows and the gyrations of the markets, he comprehensively rejects the argument that capital account liberalization is desirable because it imposes discipline on countries by forcing them to follow good economic policy. However, he states that "far more relevant for the long run success of the economy is the foreign direct investment and the desire to acquire and sustain FDI provide strong discipline on the economy and the political process " [ibid., 1080]. Although he does not specifically address this issue, Stiglitz comes close to accepting the principles of the new proposal that is being put forward by the EU and Japan at the WTO for a multilateral agreement on investment (hereafter PMAI), covering only FDI. The background to this proposal is as follows. Three years ago the OECD countries failed to negotiate a Multilateral Agreement on Investment (MAI) among themselves, which was intended to be acceded to later by developing countries. PMAI is similar to MAI with the critical difference that, unlike the latter, the former will only be confined to FDI. This clearly represents a significant concession to developing countries. The advanced countries' preference would seem to be to establish a binding treaty at the WTO that would create a regime for FDI similar to that of (free) trade in goods. Since this agreement would be based on WTO's basic concepts, previous history suggests that it is likely to include the following kinds of elements:

* the right of establishment for foreign investors (the concept of market access);
* the principle of most-favored nation treatment;
* the principle of national treatment;
* investment protection, including matters relating to expropriation and the transfer of capital;
* additional disciplines relating to, among other matters, entry, stay, and work of key personnel;
* prohibition of performance requirements on foreign investors;

- rules on investment incentives;
- binding rules for settling disputes through the WTO dispute settlements mechanism.[15]

In favoring FDI Stiglitz seems to be a part of a general consensus among economists that suggests that compared with debt and portfolio investment, FDI, apart from its other merits, is the safest source of funds for developing countries. It neither adds to a country's debt, nor (being bricks and mortar) can it be quickly withdrawn from the country. Further, in view of the other virtues of FDI in bringing new technology, organizational methods, and, importantly, spillovers to domestic industry, its proponents claim that the case for PMAI becomes overwhelming.

Those propositions will be contested below and it will be argued that unfettered FDI is not in the best interests of many developing countries. As with short-term flows, FDI also requires appropriate regulation by these countries to enhance social welfare. Because such measures would be denied by PMAI, poor countries should resist the proposed agreement.

I begin this analysis by noting that developing countries' perspective on, and attitude towards, FDI has changed. In the 1950s and 1960s, developing countries were often hostile towards multinational investment and sought to control multinational companies' activities through domestic and international regulations. During the last two decades, however, emerging countries have been falling over themselves to attract as much multinational investment as possible.

This enormous shift in developing countries' stance toward multinational investment is associated with major changes that have occurred in the pattern of international capital flows to developing counties. The former may be regarded as both a cause and a consequence of the latter. The most important change in capital flows for the purpose of this paper is the emergence of FDI as a predominant source of external finance for developing countries during the 1990s. Between 1996 and 1998 FDI inflows to developing countries constituted about 10 percent of their gross capital formation. [Singh, 2001; UNCTAD, 2001]. It is also important to note that alongside these changes in the pattern of external finance, analysis and evidence suggest that developing countries' need for external finance has greatly increased. This is in part due to the liberalization of trade and capital flows in the international economy. UNCTAD [2000] suggests that because of these structural factors, developing countries have become more balance-of-payments constrained than before: the constraint begins to bite at a much slower growth rate than was the case previously in the 1970s and 1980s.

In these circumstances it is not surprising that developing countries have radically changed their attitude towards FDI. These counties, therefore, have competed intensely to attract FDI. This competition has resulted in a shift in the balance of power towards multinationals. An important objection to PMAI is that if approved, it would worsen this imbalance because the Agreement would essentially give the multinationals a license to (or not to) invest wherever or whenever they like regardless of the circumstance and needs of developing countries.

FDI AND FINANCIAL FRAGILITY

Leaving aside other characteristics of FDI (to be discussed later), we will consider it first simply as a source of finance, and examine its implications for balance of payments and macroeconomic management of the economy. In contrast to portfolio investments, FDI, because it involves normally a stake of 10 percent or more in a host country enterprise together with managerial control, is by definition supposed to reflect a long-term commitment.[18] The presumption is that the inflow of foreign capital in this form will be more stable than portfolio investments, which investors can easily liquidate following an internal or external shock.

There are, however, important arguments to suggest that the presumption of stability in net FDI inflows may not be correct. First, the distinction between FDI and portfolio investment has become much weaker with the growth of derivatives and hedge funds. As Claessens et al., [1995] observe, even at an elementary level it is easy to see how a long-term "bricks and mortar" investment can be converted into a readily liquid asset. They note that a direct investor can use his/her immovable assets to borrow in order to export capital and thereby generate rapid capital outflows.

Another reason why FDI may be volatile is because a large part of a country's measured FDI according to the IMF balance of payments conventions usually consists of retained profits. Profits are affected by the business cycle, and therefore display considerable volatility. This also prevents FDI from being countercyclical and stabilizing unless the host and home country economic cycles are out of phase with each other. That may or may not happen.

Further, there is evidence that, like other sources of finance, FDI flows can also surge at times. Apart from their contribution to volatility, these FDI surges, just like portfolio investment, can lead to equally undesirable consequences such as exchange rate appreciation and reduced competitiveness of a country's tradable sector.

Claessens et al. [1995] concluded that time series properties of the different forms of capital flows including FDI did not statistically differ and that long-term flows were often as volatile as short- term flows. Williamson [2002] has suggested that this study may have failed to find differences between flows because it measured volatility in terms of the second moments of the time series instead of the ones of a higher order. The latter are relevant with respect to occasional meltdowns, which occurred for example in the Asian crisis. UNCTAD's 1998 study of the stability of capital flows between 1992 and 1997 found that FDI was relatively more stable than portfolio flows, with important exceptions including Brazil, South Korea, and Taiwan.[17] Lipsey [2001] also concluded that the FDI flows were relatively more stable overall.

In favor of the FDI-stability thesis, it has been argued that during the Asian crisis and its aftermath, while bank lending and portfolio flows were sharply reversed, FDI continued much as before. However the motivation for this could have been what Krugman called the "fire-sale" of devalued assets as a result of the crisis. Evidence, however, seems to suggest that it is more likely that the relative stability of FDI is due in part to the fact that the governments abolished regulations preventing or limiting FDI in domestic enterprises (albeit under IMF conditionality in the affected countries). Multinationals have used this opportunity to increase their holdings in local firms at cheap prices [World Bank, 2001].

Even if FDI is somewhat less volatile than other flows other important implications of FDI for a host country's balance of payments need to be considered. These derive from the fact that an FDI investment creates foreign exchange liabilities not only now but also into the future. This characteristic leads to the danger that unfettered FDI may create a time profile of foreign exchange outflows (in the form of dividend payments or profits repatriation) and inflows (for example, fresh FDI) which may be time inconsistent. Experience shows that such incompatibility, even in the short run may easily produce a liquidity crisis. The evidence from the Asian liquidity crisis suggests that it could degenerate into a solvency crisis with serious adverse consequences for economic development [Kregel, 1996; Singh, 2001].

These considerations suggest that to avoid financial fragility the government would need to monitor and regulate the amount and timing of FDI. Since the nature of large FDI projects (whether or not for example these would produce exportable products, or how large their imports would be) can also significantly affect the time profile of aggregate foreign exchange inflows and outflows, both in the short and long term, the government may also need to regulate such investments. To the extent that the PMAI would not permit this kind of regulation of FDI, it would subject developing economies to much greater financial fragility.

It could in principle be argued that even if the financial fragility point is conceded, a PMAI may still benefit developing countries by generating greater overall FDI, which could compensate for the increased financial fragility. The validity of this proposition, however, is doubtful. We saw earlier that FDI has risen significantly in the 1990s. This occurred without any MAI and was clearly a product of a number of other factors.[18] Similarly, regulatory constraints on FDI and the total amount of FDI that a country is able to attract do not appear to be related. Malaysia [U.S., 1996] and China, [Braunstein and Epstein, 1999], for example, are large recipients of FDI despite having significant control and regulation over FDI projects.

FDI AND REAL ECONOMY, TECHNOLOGY TRANSFER, SPILLOVERS, INVESTMENT AND SAVINGS

Apart from FDI as a source of finance, two of the most important ways in which a developing country may benefit from such investments is (a) through transfer of technology and (b) from spillovers. The latter refer to the effects of FDI on raising productivity in local firms. These firms may be helped by foreign investment in a variety of ways, including the demonstration effect of the new technology and the enhancement of the quality of inputs which such investment may promote. On the other hand there may be few positive or even negative spillovers, if FDI forces local firms out of the market because of greater competition.

Both issues of technology transfer and spillovers have been widely studied, resulting in a large and controversial literature. The main lesson it provides in relation to the question of technology transfer is that a country is more likely to benefit from multinational investment if FDI is integrated into its national development and technological plans [Dunning, 1994; Freeman, 1989; Milberg, 1999; South Centre, 2000].

TABLE 4
Marginal Impact of Various Types of Capital Flows on Investment and Saving

	Dependent Variables											
	Investment	Saving	Investment	Saving	Investment	Saving	Investment	Saving	Investment	Saving	Investment	Saving
Independent Variable	(1A)	(1B)	(2A)	(2B)	(3A)	(3B)	(4A)	(4B)	(5A)	(5B)	(6A)	(6B)
Aggregate capital flows	0.72b	0.03										
Long-term capital			0.88b	0.10								
Bank lending					1.45b	-0.17						
FDI							0.84b	-0.03				
Portfolio investment									0.50	0.84a		
Short-term debt											0.23b	0.05
All other flows			0.22	-0.16	0.53b	-0.03	0.58b	-0.23	0.52b	-0.27	0.62	0.06
Growth rate, lagged	0.33b	0.33b	0.31b	0.36b	0.33b	0.46b	0.36b	0.45b	0.49b	0.48b	0.32b	0.39b
Change in terms of trade	0.01	0.04b	0.01	0.04b	0.01	0.05b	0.02b	0.05b	-0.00	0.04b	0.01b	0.05b
Inflation, lagged	-0.00	-0.00b	-0.00	-0.00b	0.00	-0.00b	-0.00	-0.00b	-0.00	-0.00a	-0.00	-0.00
Adjusted R²	0.70	0.70	0.70	0.70	0.71	0.72	0.72	0.71	0.72	0.73	0.73	0.73

a. Significant at the 10 percent level.
b. Significant at the 5 percent level.
Fixed-effects regressions of investment (or saving) ratios against capital flows based on an unbalanced sample, consisting of a maximum of 118 countries, spanning the period 1972-98. The method of estimation was two-stage least squares, when a good instrument could be found; otherwise simple ordinary least squares results are reported. Source: World Bank [2001].

This is why, other than Hong Kong, most successful Asian countries (including China and Malaysia as seen above) have extensively regulated FDI.

On the issue of spillovers, early studies were quite optimistic about the positive externalities from FDI on domestic industries. However, these studies suffered from severe methodological difficulties particularly in relation to the question of causation. More recent research using more up-to-date methodology as well as large microeconomic data sets arrives at much more pessimistic conclusions. In an influential study, Aitken and Harrison [1999] found that in Venezuela multinational investment had a negative effect on productivity of domestic plants in the industry. Such results are quite common from micro-level data [Hanson, 2001]. Similarly, the World Bank reaches the following conclusion from its comprehensive survey of the empirical studies of the effects of FDI on productivity growth in developing countries:

> The productivity benefits of capital flows—through the transfer of technology and management techniques and the stimulation of financial sector development—are significant in countries where a developed physical infrastructure, a strong business environment, and open trade regimes have facilitated the absorption of those flows, *but not otherwise*. (Italics added). [2001, 59]

A critical issue in evaluating the effects of FDI on the real economy is its impact on domestic savings and investments. Economic theory does not yield any unambiguous predictions about how domestic investment may be affected by foreign capital inflows. In general, this depends on the level of development of the economy, its degree of integration with international economy and its absorptive capacity. Table 4 shows the results of World Bank's analysis of the impact of various types of capital flows on investments and savings for a large cross-section of developing countries from 1972 to 1998. The results show that although FDI is positively associated with the investment, there is little relationship with savings. The long-term bank lending has a more important influence on investment than does FDI. Portfolio investment is, on the other hand, associated more with savings than with investments.

A more interesting analysis of this issue is reported in the recent study by Agosin and Mayer [2000]. This study examines the regional variations in the effects of FDI on the crowding in and out of domestic investment. The two authors' research covered 1970 to 1996 and included host countries from all three developing regions—Africa, Asia and Latin America. The results of the econometric exercise suggest that over this long period there was strong crowding in in Asia, crowding out in Latin America and more or less neutral effects in Africa. Agosin and Mayer conclude:

> ...the most far-reaching liberalizations of FDI regimes in the 1990s took place in Latin America, and that FDI regimes in Asia have remained the least liberal in the developing world... Nonetheless, it is in these countries that there is strongest evidence of CI (crowding in). In Latin America, on the other hand,...liberalization does not appear to have led to CI. [ibid., 14]

Turning finally, but for reasons of space, extremely briefly, to the relationship between FDI and long-term economic growth, Lipsey's comprehensive survey succinctly sums up the evidence on this issue as follows:

> ... As with the studies of wage and productivity spillovers, those of the effects of FDI inflows on economic growth are inconclusive. Almost all find positive effects in some periods, or among some group of countries, in some specifications, but one cannot say from these studies that there are universal effects. There are periods, industries, and countries where FDI seems to have little relation to growth, especially when other factors, mostly related to FDI also are included as explanations. [2001, 56-57]

What can be concluded for PMAI from the above analysis of various aspects of FDI? The main implication would appear to be that a global regime of unfettered FDI would not be Pareto-optimal for all developing nations. Countries have different (a) levels of economic development, (b) previous history, (c) endowments, (d) path trajectories, and (e) public and private sector capabilities of making effective use of FDI. Some may benefit from unrestricted FDI inflows and may have the absorptive capacity to cope with FDI surges and famines. Others may benefit more from its purposive regulation to avoid coordination or other market failures arising from unfettered FDI, as outlined above. A regime of unrestricted capital flows as envisaged in PMAI would deprive countries of policy autonomy in this sphere. In some cases, for example countries with ineffective or weak governments, this may not matter. However, in other countries regulation of FDI would bring net benefit because the correction of market failures would easily outweigh government failures. The so-called "developmental states" in Asia have been obvious examples of this. The PMAI would not serve the developmental needs of these countries. The main message of this paper is, therefore, that in the real world of second best, a case by case approach and selectivity is called for rather than a one-size-fits-all universal rules of the kind contained in PMAI.

CONCLUSION

The first part of the paper examined the theoretical and empirical case for short-term capital account liberalization in developing countries and found it wanting. Indeed, as Stiglitz suggests, there is arguably a compelling case against it. The second part considered the question of long-term capital account liberalization, specifically, that of FDI. Most economists, including Stiglitz, favor such capital flows into developing countries. On closer analysis, however, it is argued here than even FDI, if unregulated, may do more harm than good to many countries. It is therefore suggested that developing countries should resist the new multilateral agreement on investment, which Japan and the EU are proposing at the WTO, even though it will cover only FDI.

CAPITAL ACCOUNT LIBERALIZATION   213

NOTES

I am grateful for helpful comments from Philip Arestis as well as from session participants at the EEA meeting in Boston in March 2002. Since I could not attend the meeting, Philip kindly presented an earlier version of this paper on my behalf. That I am also indebted to Joseph Stiglitz's writings on the subject, despite important disagreements, will be clear from the paper. It is also a pleasure to record my gratitude to the editor and the four referees of this *Journal*, whose sometimes fierce comments greatly helped to improve the paper. This work was carried out at the Centre for Business Research at Cambridge University. The Centre's contributions are gratefully acknowledged. The usual caveat applies.

1. For a comprehensive survey and a recent contribution, see for example Feldstein [2002].
2. This section of the paper draws on Chakravarty and Singh [1988].
3. Such a mechanism, for example, existed in the "Golden Age" of the post-WWII era (1950-1973) when, under the aegis of a single hegemonic economic power, namely the U.S., European economies were able to maintain high levels of aggregate demand to ensure full employment [Glyn et al., 1990; Singh, 1995a].
4. See further Freeman [1989]; Singh [1995b]; Amsden [2001].
5. The US was willing to open its own markets to East Asian manufacturers without insisting on reciprocal opening of East Asian market. See further, Glyn et al., [1990].
6. See Passinetti [1981] for a fuller discussion of the learning approach to this issue.
7. On this set of issues, see for example, Stiglitz [1994]; Allen and Gale [2000]; Glen, Lee and Singh [2000].
8. A referee has objected that since Kaminsky and Reinhart [1999] and Demigüc-Kunt and Detragiache [1998] include both developing countries and advanced countries, it is not legitimate to draw conclusions about developing countries alone from this evidence. However, as argued in the text below, developing countries are more prone to financial crises following liberalization than Acs. Considering the two group of countries together will underestimate the strength of the relationship between financial liberalization, banking and currency crisis and underdevelopment rather than to overstate it.
9. For fuller discussion of these issues see Singh [2002a]; Jomo [2001]; Singh and Weisse [1999] and Rodrik [2000].
10. IMF [2002, Box 3.4, 126], broadly supports these conclusions.
11. A referee has pointed out that there is a greater difference in volatility between advanced countries and developing countries in terms of trade compared with capital flows. However, changes in terms of trade may be caused either by capital flows or current account balance, or both, as well as other factors. This important issue will not be pursued here.
12. Similar results are reported in IMF [2002].
13. For a fuller discussion of the issues involved in this argument see Cosh, Hughes and Singh [1990] and Singh [2000].
14. This and the following sections are based on Singh [2001].
15. See Singh and Zammit [1998] for a further discussion.
16. This is the empirical definition of FDI adopted by many countries to distinguish it from portfolio flows.
17. A referee has pointed out that the problems of FDI volatility create difficulties not just for developing countries but also for the U.S. where there has been a substantial drop in FDI recently.
18. See Singh [1997a; 1997b]; Singh and Weisse [1998] for a further discussion.

REFERENCES

Agosin, M. R. and **Mayer, R.** Foreign Investment in Developing Countries: Does it Crowd in Domestic Investment? United Nations Conference on Trade and Development, *Discussion Paper*, No. 146. February 2000.

Aitken, B. J., and **Harrison, A. E.** Do Domestic Firms Benefit from Direct Foreign Investment? Evidence from Venezuela. *American Economic Review*, June 1999, 605-18.

Aizenman, J. Financial Opening: Evidence and Policy Options, *NBER Working Paper* 8900, 2002.

Allen, F., and Gale, D. *Comparing Financial Systems.* Cambridge, MA: MIT Press, 2000.

Amsden, A. H. *The Rise of "The Rest": Challenges to the West from Late-Industriising Economies.* New York: Oxford University Press, 2001.

Arrow, K. The Economic Implications of Learning by Doing, *Review of Economic Studies*, 1962, 155-73.

Bekaert, G., Harvey, C., and Lundblad, C. Does Financial Liberalization Spur Growth? NBER Working Paper No. 8 245. Cambridge: MA: National Bureau of Economic Research, 2001.

Bhagwati, J. The Capital Myth: The Difference Between Trade in Widgets and Trade in Dollars, *Foreign Affairs*, 1998, 7-12.

Borensztein, E., Giorgio, J. De. and Lee, J-W. How does Foreign Investment Affect Growth? *Journal of International Economics*, June 1998, 115-35.

Braunstein, E. and Epstein, G. Towards a New MAI. In Jonathan Michie & John Grieve Smith (Eds.) *Global Instability and World Economic Governance.* NY: Routledge, 1999.

Caprio, G., and Klingebiel, D. Bank Insolvencies: Cross-Country Experience. *World Bank Policy Research Working Paper* 1620. Washington, DC: 1996.

Chakravarty, S. and Singh, A. *The Desirable Forms of Economic Openness in the South.* Helsinki: World Institute for Development Economics Research, 1988.

Chang, H.-J., ed. *Joseph Stiglitz and the World Bank: The Rebel Within.* London. UK: Anthem Press, Wimbledon Publishing Company, 2001.

Chari, A. and Henry, P. Capital Account Liberalization: Allocative Efficiency or Animal Spirits?, *NBER Working Paper* 8908, 2002.

Claessens, S., Dooloy, M. and Warner, A. Portfolio Capital Flows: Hot or Cool?, *World Bank Economic Review*, 1995, 153-174.

Cosh, A. D., Hughes, A. and Singh, A. Takeovers and Short Termism: Analytical and Policy Issues in the UK Economy. In *Takeovers and Short Termism in the UK, Industrial Policy Paper No, 3*, Institute for Public Policy Research, London, 1990.

Davidson, P. If Markets are Efficient, Why Have There Been So Many International Financial Market Crises Since the 1970s? in *What Global Economic Crisis?* edited by P. Arestis, M. Baddeley and J. McCombie. NY and UK: Palgrave, Hampshire, 2001.

Demetriades, P. O. and Luintel, K. B. Financial Restraints in the South Korean Miracle, *Journal of Development Economics*, April 2001, 459-79.

Demigüc-Kunt, A., and Detragiache, E. Financial Liberalization and Financial Fragility. In *Proceedings of Annual Bank Conference on Development Economics*, Washington, DC, April 1998, 20-21.

Dunning, J. Re-evaluating the Benefits of Foreign Direct Investment. *Transnational Corporations*, February 1994, 23-52.

Easterly, W., Islam, R., and Stiglitz, J. E. Shaken and Stirred: Explaining Growth Volatility, in *Annual World Bank Conference on Development Economics, The International Bank for Reconstruction and Development*, edited by B. Pleskovic and N. Stern. The World Bank, 2000, 191-211.

Eatwell, J. International Financial Liberalization: The Impact on World Development, *ODS Discussion Paper Series*, No. 12. New York: UNDP, 1996.

Edison, H., Levine, R., Ricci, L., and Slok, T. Capital Account Liberalization and Economic Performance: Survey and Synthesis, *IMF Working Paper*, 02/120, 2002.

Feldstein, M. Economic and Financial Crises in Emerging Market Economies: Overview of Prevention and Management. *NBER Working Paper Series*, Working Paper 8837, Cambridge, MA.: 2002.

Fischer, S. Capital Account Liberalization and the Role of the IMF. Paper presented at the seminar Asia and the IMF, held in Hong Kong, China: IMF, 19 September 1997.

_____. On the Need for an International Lender of Last Resort. *Journal of Economic Perspectives*, Fall 1999, 85-104.

Freeman, C. New Technology and Catching Up. *European Journal of Development Research*, 1/1, 1989.

Friedman, M. *Essays in Positive Economics.* Chicago: University of Chicago Press, 1953.

Furman, J., and Stiglitz, J. E. Economic Crises: Evidence and Insights from East Asia. *Brookings Papers on Economic Activity*, 2, Brookings Institution, Washington, DC, 1999a.

Glen, J., Lee, K., and Singh, A. Competition, Corporate Governance and Financing of Corporate Growth in Emerging Markets. *Cambridge Discussion Papers in Accounting and Finance*, AF46. Department of Applied Economics, University of Cambridge. Cambridge, 2000.

Glyn, A., Hughes, A., Lipietz, A., and Singh, A. The Rise and Fall of the Golden Age, in *The Golden Age of Capitalism*, edited by S. A. Marglin and J. B. Schor. Oxford: Oxford University Press, 1990.

Greenspan, A. Risk Mangement in the Global Financial System. Speech delivered to the Annual Financial Markets Conference of the Federal Reserve Bank of Atlanta, Miami Beach, Florida, 27 February 1998.

Gomery, R. E. and Baumol, W. J. *Global Trade and Conflicting National Interest*. Cambridge, Massachusetts: MIT Press, 2000.

Hanson, G. H. Should Countries Promote Foreign Direct Investment?, *G-24 Discussion Paper Series*, No. 9, New York: UNCTAD, February 2001.

Henry, P. B. Do Stock Market Liberalizations Cause Investment Booms? *Journal of Financial Economics*, 2000, 301-334.

Jomo, K. S. Growth After the Asian Crisis: What Remains of the East Asian Model? *G-24 Discussion Paper Series*, No. 10, United Nation Conference on Trade and Development. Centre for International Development Harvard University. United Nations, New York and Geneva, March 2001.

Kaldor, N. *Further Essays on Economic Theory*. London: Duckworth, 1978.

Kaminsky, G. L. and Reinhart, C. L. The Twin Crises: The Causes of Banking and Balance-of-Payments Problems. *American Economic Review*, 1999, 473-500.

Kaufman, H. *On Money and Markets: A Wall Street Memoir*. New York: McGraw Hill, 2000.

Keynes, J. M. *The General Theory of Employment Interest and Money*. New York, Harcourt, Brace and Company, 1936.

Kindleberger, C. P. *A Financial History of Western Europe*. London: George Allen and Unwin, 1984.

Kregel, J. A. Some Risks and Implications of Financial Globalisation for National Policy Autonomy. *UNCTAD Review*, United Nations, Geneva, 1996.

Krugman, P. R. Is Free Trade Passé?, *Journal of Economics Perspectives*, 1987, 131-43.

Lipsey, R. E. Foreign Direct Investors in Three Financial Crises. *NBER Working Paper*, No. 8084, 2001.

Loungani, P. Capital Flows. *IMF Research Bulletin*, September 2002, 1-3.

Martin, P. and Rey, H. Financial Globalization and Emerging Markets: With or Without Crash? *NBER Working Paper* 9288, 2002.

McKinnon, R. and Pill, H. Exchange-Rate Regimes for Emerging Markets: Moral Hazard and International Over-borrowing. *Oxford Review of Economic Policy*, 1999.

Mendoza, E. Credit, Prices and Crashes: Business Cycles with a Sudden Stop, *NBER Working Paper* 8338, 2001.

Milberg, W. Foreign Direct Investment and Development: Balancing Costs and Benefits. International Monetary and Financial Issues for the 1990s, *United Nations Conference on Trade and Development*, 1999, 99-115.

Mody, A. and Murshid, A. P. Growing Up with Capital Flows. *IMF Working Paper* No. 02/75, 2002.

Moggridge, D. *The Collected Writings of John Maynard Keynes, Vol. XXV*. Cambridge: Cambridge University Press, 1980.

Occampo, J. A. Rethinking the Development Agenda. Economic Commission for Latin America and the Caribbean. United Nations, 2001.

Occampo J. A. and Taylor, L. Trade Liberalization in Developing Economies: Modest Benefits But Problems with Productivity Growth, Macro Prices, and Income Distribution, in *Controversies in Macroeconomics Growth, Trade and Policy*, edited by H.D. Dixon. Massachusetts: Blackwell, 2000.

Pasinetti, L. L. *Structural Change and Economic Growth*. Cambridge: Cambridge University Press, Chapter 11.

Pindyck, R. S. Irreversibility, Uncertainty and Cyclical Investment. *Journal of Economic Literature*, 1991, 1110-48.

Rakshit, M. K. Globalization of Capital Markets: Some Analytical and Policy Issues, in *Globalisation and Economic Development, Essays in Honor of Waardenburg*, edited by S. Storm. Naastepad, UK, MA, U.S.A.: Edward Elgar, 2001.

Ramey, G., and Ramey, V. Volatility and Growth. *American Economic Review*, 1995, 559-86.

Rodrik, D. Development Strategies for the 21st Century, in *Annual World Bank Conference on Development Economics 2000*. International Bank for Recontruction and Development, The World Bank, 2000, 85-124.

Shiller, R. J. *Irrational Exuberance*. Princeton, NJ: Princeton University Press, 2000.

Singh, A. The Causes of Fast Economic Growth in East Asia. *UNCTAD Review*, Geneva, 1995a, 91-127.

_____. Institutional Requirements for Full Employment in Advanced Economies. *International Labour Review*, 1995b.

_____. Liberalization and Globalization: An Unhealthy Euphoria, in *Employment and Economic Performance: Jobs, Inflation and Growth*, edited by J. Michie and J. G. Smith. New York: Oxford University Press, 1997a, 11-35.

_____. Financial Liberalisation, Stockmarkets and Economic Development. *The Economic Journal*, Oxford, UK and Boston, U.S.A.: Blackwell Publishers, May 1997b, 771-82.

_____. Should Africa Promote Stock Market Capitalism? *Journal of International Development.* 1999, 343-65.

_____. The Anglo-Saxon Market for Corporate Control: The Financial System and International Competitiveness, in *Competitiveness Matters: Industry and Economic Performance in the U.S.*, edited by C. Howes and A. Singh. Ann Arbor, MI: The University of Michigan Press, 2000.

_____. Foreign Direct Investment and International Agreements a South Perspective. *Occasional Paper, Trade-Related Agenda, Development and Equity*. South Centre, October 2001.

_____. Asian Capitalism and the Financial Crisis, in *International Capital Markets: Systems in Transition*, edited by J. Eatwell and L. Taylor. Oxford University Press, Inc. 2002, 339-67.

Singh, A. and Weisse, B. A. The Asian Model: A Crisis Foretold. *International Social Science Journal*; 1999, 203-215.

Singh, A. and Zammit, A. Foreign Direct Investment: Towards Cooperative Institutional Arrangements between the North and the South, in *Globalisation, Growth and Governance*, edited by J. Michie and J. Grieve-Smith. Oxford: Oxford University Press, 1998.

_____. International Capital Flows: Identifying the Gender Dimension. *World Development.* 2000, 1249-68.

South Centre. *Foreign Direct Investment, Development and the New Global Economic Order: A Policy Brief for the South.* Geneva: South Centre. 2000.

Stiglitz, J. E. Reforming the Global Economic Architecture: Lessons from Recent Crises. *The Journal of Finance,* 1999, 1508-21.

_____. Capital Market Liberalization, Economic Growth, and Instability. *World Development*, 2000, 1075-86.

Summers, L. International Financial Crises: Causes, Prevention and Cures. *American Economics Review Papers and Proceedings*, May 2000, 1-16.

United Nations. *Trade and Development Report.* Geneva, Switzerland: UNCTAD 1998, 2000, 2001

Williamson, J. and Drabek, Z. Whether and When to Liberalize Capital Account and Financial Services. *Staff Working Paper* ERAD-99-03. World Trade Organization. Economic Research and Analysis Division. 1998.

Williamson, J. Proposals for Curbing the Boom-Bust Cycle in the Supply of Capital to Emerging Markets. *Discussion Paper* No. 2002/3. Helsinki: United Nations University, World Insitite for International Development Economics Research (WIDER), 2002.

World Bank. *Global Development Finance: Building Coalitions for Effective Development Finance.* Washington, DC: The World Bank, 2001.

_____. *World Development Report: Knowledge for Development* (1998/99). Washington, D.C. The World Bank, 1999.

Wyplosz, C. How Risky is Financial Liberalization in the Developing Countries? *CEPR* DP 2724. 2001.

Young, A. A. Increasing Returns and Economic Progress. *Economic Journal,* 1928, 527-42.

[14]

Financial Crises After Financial Liberalisation: Exceptional Circumstances or Structural Weakness?

CHRISTIAN E. WELLER

In this article, I argue that emerging economies are systematically becoming more susceptible to both currency and banking crises after financial liberalisation (FL). Using data for 27 emerging economies from 1973 to 1998, univariate and multivariate analyses indicate that the likelihood of currency crises and banking crises increase after FL. In particular, liberalisation allows more liquidity to enter an emerging economy, which finds its way into productive and speculative projects. What is common to both types of crises is a significant increase in speculative financing, thereby increasing the chance for borrower default. Thus, the outflow of international capital becomes more likely. The chance of a crisis occurring in response to changes in short-term loans is greater after FL than before. Similarly, the chance of a currency crisis occurring following a currency overvaluation is larger after FL than before. In comparison, the likelihood of a banking crisis occurring in response to an overvalued currency remains the same. Finally, the results show that the chance of a currency crisis declines over time, while the chance of a banking crisis increases after FL.

I. INTRODUCTION

Financial turmoil in emerging economies seems to occur more frequently in the past years. Most recently, the Asian crisis hit shortly after the shock waves from the Mexican peso crisis had subsided. In a survey of banking sector problems, the IMF found that two-thirds of its member countries have experienced banking sector problems between 1980 and 1996

Christian E. Weller, Economic Policy Institute, Washington, DC and Center for European Integration Studies, University of Bonn, Germany. The author is very grateful to Beth Almeida, Bernd Hayo, and Robert MacCulloch for their insightful comments on earlier versions of this article. He would also like to thank the referees of the journal for their productive comments.

The Journal of Development Studies, Vol.38, No.1, October 2001, pp.98–127
PUBLISHED BY FRANK CASS, LONDON

FINANCIAL CRISES AFTER FINANCIAL LIBERALISATION 99

[*Lindgren, Garcia and Saal, 1996*]. In almost all cases, we have witnessed not only the destabilization of the local banking system, but also the failure of the currency regime.

Since financial systems play a central economic role, financial crises result in serious repercussions. Stable currencies facilitate cross-border movements of trade and capital, while stable banking systems help to channel savings to investors. Crises, then, adversely affect international trade and capital flows, domestic credit, and, ultimately, output. The effects of financial crises are not isolated to the crises economies. Financial problems have often resulted in severe output contractions, which can lead to worsened trade balances of major trading partners and doubts over the repayment of international loans.

The literature reflects the significance of understanding financial instabilities. Often, however, the causes of a crisis are perceived as exogenous changes. Instead, the notion that financial liberalisation (FL) *in itself* could be a cause for greater fragility is only lately receiving some attention. In a discussion of the FL hypothesis and its adjustments over time, Arestis and Demetriades [*1999*] conclude that its theoretical foundations are weak, and that even where necessary preconditions, such as effective supervision or macroeconomic stability, exist, 'financial liberalisation could still become the main source of financial crises' [*ibid: 454*].

Empirical studies have also increasingly focused on the possibility that FL could lead to higher chances of financial crises, particularly on the combination of FL and weak institutional environments. Demirgüç-Kunt and Detragiache [*1999*] find, based on a study of 53 countries covering the period 1980–1995 that the chance of a banking crisis increases after FL. Strong institutions appear to mitigate this effect, but do not completely eliminate it. Also, Alba *et al.* [*1999*] conclude that the crisis in Thailand can be traced back to FL that was introduced in a weak institutional environment. Similarly, Demetriades and Fattouh [*1999*] find that the South Korean crisis had been caused by premature FL, before existing weaknesses in the financial system could have been addressed.

Notwithstanding the importance of strong institutions, FL can result in growing financial weaknesses, even if strong institutions exist [*Arestis and Demetriades, 1999*]. Building on the insights of Hyman Minsky [*1982, 1986*] and following the expansions by Grabel [*1993, 1995b*], I argue that emerging economies become more vulnerable to both currency and banking crises after FL. In this view, greater internal and external deregulation result in more instabilities as greater liquidity is used increasingly for unsustainable, speculative expansions. For instance, Chang *et al.* [*1998*] argue that the cause of the Korean crisis had been FL which allowed for large short-term capital inflows and for excessive investments. This is not to say that institutional or macroeconomic weaknesses may not raise the likelihood of crises, but that they are unlikely to disappear due to deregulation. Already existing structural weaknesses are likely to become even more severe in a more deregulated environment.

Employing a Minskyian-type framework to explore currency and banking crises offers considerable advantages over other approaches to the twin crises. While alternative approaches ascribe the occurrence of twin crises often to common macro causes, they fail to explore both the connection between financial market operations and deteriorating macroeconomic fundamentals, and the link between weaknesses in the foreign exchange markets and the banking sector. By providing not only an argument that links macroeconomic fundamentals and financial market operations, but also supporting empirical evidence for the growing vulnerability to currency and banking crises after FL, I hope to further our understanding of the mechanics of financial crises.

The rest of the article is organised as follows. In section II, I present an argument which connects FL to a greater likelihood of currency and banking crises. The theoretical argument serves then as the basis for univariate and regression analysis in section III. Finally, some concluding remarks follow in section IV.

II. FINANCIAL LIBERALISATION AND FINANCIAL CRISES

To avoid unnecessary confusion, I use the term currency and banking crises as commonly defined in the literature. Currency crisis are characterised by diminishing foreign exchange reserves and rising short-term interest rates either by themselves or in combination with a devaluation [*Eichengreen, Rose and Wyplosz, 1995; Sachs, Tornell and Velasco, 1996; Goldfaijn and Valdés, 1997; Kaminsky, Lizondo and Reinhart, 1997*]. Currency crises are distinct from speculative attacks, where devaluation can be avoided. Bank crises are characterised by deposit or credit contractions in the wake of a bank run. An indication of a looming bank crisis may be a deterioration of bank balance sheets. However, declining quality of bank balance sheets does not necessarily lead to bank runs. Increasing bad loan ratios are indicators for growing bank sector instabilities, while bank failures are considered crises [*Lindgren, Garcia and Saal, 1996*].

How do currency and banking crises become more likely after FL? FL is generally understood as the elimination of financial regulations in the domestic financial markets, such as credit ceilings, lending requirements, or entry restrictions to reduce excess demand for credit [*McKinnon, 1973; Shaw, 1973*]. The rationale for full deregulation of financial markets is that 'financially repressed' economies suffer from sub-optimal financial

FINANCIAL CRISES AFTER FINANCIAL LIBERALISATION   101

intermediation and from an inefficient allocation of financial capital. By eliminating interest rate ceilings and entry restrictions, financial intermediaries will collect more funds and provide more loanable funds. By eliminating lending requirements, financial intermediaries can allocate funds to their best uses, thereby raising the average productivity of capital, and ultimately the economic performance of an economy.

Additionally, FL often comprises external liberalisation through full or partial capital account opening, which raises the potential of more short-term capital mobility and more foreign direct investment flows. Through the elimination of internal and external government regulations, financial markets supposedly become more efficient. And the amount of loanable funds for investments increases. Also, banks should be able to attract more deposits after the elimination of interest rate ceilings. Similarly, deposit constraints on banks should decline with easier access to international capital markets. Finally, banks should be more willing to issue loans as interest rate restrictions are eliminated, and as domestic financial market competition increases. Consequently, financial stability should increase with FL as financial intermediaries become more efficient and more profitable.

Based on Minsky's [*1982; 1986*] 'financial instability hypothesis', a critique of FL has been developed that argues that FL helps to generate a more fragile financial environment [*Grabel, 1993; 1995b*]. The initial economic improvements often observed after the introduction of FL are both fuelling and driven by overly optimistic expectations, which are in turn determined by real short-term gains, especially in the financial market realm. Due to unrealistic assessments of future earnings streams, the additional liquidity that results from more deposits and from overseas capital inflows provides more capital for speculative investments. Thereby short-term gains are realised, while the conditions for financial instabilities are laid.

Financial deregulation can result in short-term economic gains, and may fuel overly optimistic expectations, which raise financial fragility. After domestic deregulation, previously credit constrained sectors may receive additional financing because interest rate constraints are reduced and additional capital is available.[1] More capital might increase business investment, thereby helping to expand both the real and the financial sector. Higher real interest rates, and expanding real and financial sectors will lead to more capital inflows from overseas. Larger capital inflows lead to a real currency appreciation, thereby attracting even more capital if investors speculate that the currency appreciation will continue.

Currency overvaluations are problematic in pegged exchange rate regimes if euphoric investors assess the associated risks inappropriately. If

FL leads to overly optimistic expectations, capital inflows allow monetary authorities to make credible statements that, in a pegged currency regime, the peg is stable. However, given that the stability of the currency peg is based on capital inflows, which are based on investor euphoria, market participants tend to underestimate the exchange rate risks and inadequately hedge against a devaluation [*Demetriades, 1999*].

Not only with respect to the exchange rate is it fair to say that, rather than a stable equilibrium, changes in economic fundamentals may merely produce periods of tranquility.

A continued appreciation helps to attract overseas capital because it fuels investors' euphoria. At the same time, deregulated financial markets may promise rising short-term gains through higher real interest rates and improving equity markets. Higher real interest rates in effect provide the incentive for firms to issue more equity. Thanks to internal and external deregulation, equity markets become more liquid as both domestic and international investors are channeling funds there [*Arestis and Demetriades, 1999*]. Greater stock market growth and liquidity attract more speculative investments to the equity market. As speculators' overly optimistic expectations cannot be met, greater stock market volatility follows [*Grabel, 1995a*].

At the same time as stock markets expand in emerging economies after FL, banks are increasing their lending in a more deregulated environment. Higher interest rates as well as increasing asset prices provide financial intermediaries with the incentives to expand their lending [*Grabel, 1993, 1995b*]. In particular, higher interest rates raise the profitability of bank lending (assuming that interest rates are still too low to create adverse incentive effects), and increased asset prices provide banks with higher collateral. Due to greater liquidity, investments both in productive and speculative investments should grow. Further, additional liquid capital that is invested in short-term speculative assets diverts funds from business investment finance, which is quite likely given that capital markets early during FL may promise high growth rates. Thus, bank credit can fuel an asset boom cycle [*Demetriades, 1999*].

A main tenet in the literature is that the internal and external deregulation fosters financial fragility by providing incentives for more speculative financing [*Grabel, 1993, 1995a; Arestis and Demetriades, 1999; Demetriades, 1999*]. Deregulation appears to foster investor euphoria, especially through increased asset prices, that inflate the collateral of borrowers, raise the expectations of lenders and increase domestic demand. Greater investor euphoria, however, lets investors, by definition, underestimate the risks involved in their portfolio allocations. Due to competitive pressures, financial institutions that do not engage in short-term

FINANCIAL CRISES AFTER FINANCIAL LIBERALISATION 103

speculative activities are punished through higher costs of capital. Thus, greater financial market competition may in fact create a 'too big to fail problem' due to herd behaviour. In other words, financial market speculation becomes, at least in the short run, self-fulfilling since more investors are engaging in speculative activities, thereby temporarily perpetuating a speculative boom.

In terms of a country's external relations, an overvalued exchange rate translates into a deterioration of the terms of trade, hence fuelling a weakening of the current account balance.

As a result, the financial sector grows due to real exchange rate and asset market gains, while the real sector slows down due to deteriorating terms of trade and a lack of access to investment finance. Consequently, output declines as exports become more expensive, and as demand for investment goods declines. Such a growing disparity between the financial and the real sector reflects the increasing speculative nature of finance in liberalised economies that is often observed following FL [*Grabel, 1998; Kaminsky and Reinhart, 1999; Lindgren, Garcia and Saal, 1996; Sheng, 1996; Benink and Llewellyn, 1994b; Bulino and Sundararajan, 1991*].

More speculative financing, though, raises the likelihood of borrower default risk. Also, maturity risk increases as short-term overseas investors become more likely to withdraw their funds if the higher default risk materialises. Alongside greater maturity risk, the exchange rate risk grows with the prospect of rapidly withdrawn short-term overseas capital [*Arestis and Demetriades, 1999*]. Withdrawal of foreign capital leads to an asset bust, and due to declining collateral to a wave of bad loans and to a credit crunch [*Alba et al., 1999; Demetriades; 1999*].

Stabilising measures for the exchange rate either fuel investors' expectations of an economic slowdown, such as higher interest rates, or they are limited in scope, such as the selling of reserves. Ultimately, the economy is marked by higher interest rates, a credit crunch, higher import prices, and depressed domestic demand.

Default risk increases. First, it may rise simply because the financial sectors expands faster than the real sector. This is particularly problematic if credit is expanded to an already weakening real sector. Both inadequate investment financing and deteriorating terms of trade should lead to a slowdown in the real sector. Second, FL provides incentives for more speculative financing thanks to overly optimistic investor expectations, fuelled by asset price bubbles and increased financial market competition. Third, default risk may rise due to increased foreign currency borrowing. An appreciating currency provides an incentive to borrowers to take out foreign currency denominated loans. However, borrowers may underestimate the risks associated with currency overvaluations, and thus inadequately hedge against the possibility of a currency depreciation [*Demetriades, 1999*]. Finally, monetary authorities may tighten interest rates to stabilise the exchange rate, thereby inducing a real economic slow down.

Higher default rates, though, lead domestic and international investors to reassess their overly optimistic expectations. Investor euphoria turns sour, and funds are withdrawn. A credit crunch ensues, and investments decline. The effects are more severe, the more important the role of short-term overseas capital is since it can be more quickly withdrawn and since it not only raises the maturity risk in financial markets, but also the exchange rate risk.

It has also been recognised that an overvaluation that helps to attract capital inflows through higher expectations about an economy's future performance may also foster an economic slowdown [*Kaminsky and Reinhart, 1999; Eichengreen, Rose and Wyplosz, 1995; Krugman, 1995b*]. Ironically, capital inflows may have helped to generate an overvaluation, fuelled overly optimistic expectations and a speculative financing boom, which may now make a devaluation, increasing borrower default, and therefore capital outflows more likely [*Grabel, 1995a*].

Finally, a lower interest rate differential due to rising interest rates abroad can lead to capital outflows.[2] Again, monetary authorities may try halt the outflow of capital through higher interest rates or the selling of reserves. In case of higher interest rates, the real sector may slow down, thus making capital outflows even more likely.

Adding to the greater chance of crises is the fact, that government finances are becoming strained. The need to support either domestic banks or domestic currencies comes in the wake of already deteriorating economic fundamentals, such as a slowing real sector. The demand on government budgets increases, while revenues are decreasing and expenditures are rising.

Obviously, FL does not have to lead inevitably to crises. It does, however, increase financial fragility, which can be diminished by government policies. One possibly stabilising aspect of FL may be greater international competition. Due to capital account liberalisation, barriers of entry for multinational banks (MNB) are lowered, which may reduce the risks banks incur in their portfolio. Banks may reduce their risk exposure once they have to compete with MNBs. If a domestic bank's net worth is above its safety threshold for prudent lending, more international competition may lead a bank to reduce its credit in order to lower its loan and risk exposure. The reduction in domestic bank credit is greater if MNBs engage in 'cherry picking' leaving only borrowers of lesser quality [*Weller, 2000a, 2000b*]. Obviously, the more a bank reduces its credit the less it is exposed to any of the above described risks, and the less likely it is to

FINANCIAL CRISES AFTER FINANCIAL LIBERALISATION   105

engage in speculative financing, thereby also lowering the chance of currency crises.

Other aspects of public policy should not be ignored here. In particular, strong regulation and supervision can help to stabilise financial systems in emerging economies. However, regulation and supervision alone are unlikely to reduce all risks associated with FL, particularly since euphoric investors are unlikely to assess the risks fairly. Demirgüç-Kunt and Detragiache [*1999*] find, based on a study of 53 countries covering the period 1980–95 that the chance of a banking crisis increases after FL. While strong institutions can mitigate the impact, banking crises remain more probable in a deregulated environment. Also, Alba *et al.* [*1999*] conclude that the Thai crisis can be traced back to FL, which was introduced in a weak institutional environment. Similarly, Demetriades and Fattouh [*1999*] find that premature FL had partially caused the South Korean crisis, before existing weaknesses in the financial system could have been addressed. Finally, in a critique of the FL framework, Arestis and Demetriades [*1999*] conclude that even where necessary preconditions, such as effective supervision or macro economic stability, exist, FL can still lay the foundation for financial fragility.

Because FL is by definition the elimination of financial market regulation, and because FL results in investor euphoria, there is a mismatch between the need for prudent regulation and the practice of regulation and supervision. While prudent supervision could set limits on credit expansion, effective regulation may not be achieved in a deregulatory environment. Also, in most cases, not all forms of speculative financing are subject to regulation and supervision. Further, causes of increased investor optimism that are a direct result of speculative financing, such as the wealth effect on consumer demand, cannot be regulated.[3] Put differently, where speculative financing is pervasive in a deregulated environment, even the most prudent regulation and supervision is unlikely to control financial fragility from growing. Finally, Arestis and Demetriades [*1999*] argue that at least some institutional weaknesses in financial supervision in emerging economies are a given, and that realistically speaking increased financial fragility after FL should be expected. Given also that effective financial supervision and regulation would have to address several issues at once – securities regulation, bank supervision, and foreign currency management to name a few – no supervisory system should be expected to fully address all issues. In particular, the introduction of FL means that domestic regulators in emerging markets are facing a new, deregulated environment, in which risks are most likely incorrectly assessed, at least until the first major market downturn occurs. Thus, deregulated markets are likely to run their course, thereby raising the chance of financial crises.

While proponents of financial deregulation would argue that internal and external liberalisation should increase the efficiency, and the stability of the local financial system, the argument laid out here leads to the opposite conclusion. Greater financial market openness should increase the likelihood of financial crises after FL since the deregulated environment allows for a dynamic environment, which fosters speculative finance built upon overly optimistic expectations. Initially improving economic fundamentals fuel investor optimism, even to a point where it could adequately be described by investor euphoria. Because institutions are often underdeveloped, because deregulated financial markets are supposed to rely on self-correcting mechanism, and because initially economic fundamentals are improving, there are no institutions sufficiently controlling this investor euphoria. Investors subsequently underestimate the risks associated with the resulting deregulation boom. Thus, financial crises after FL should be the rule rather than the exception [*Grabel, 1998*].

III. EMPIRICAL TESTS

In this section, I provide empirical evidence that emerging economies become more vulnerable to financial crises after FL. I first analyse banking crises followed by empirical evidence on currency crises.

Data

The variables for the empirical analysis are taken from a number of sources. Data on stock indexes are taken from *Datastream*; data on international debt positions are compiled both from the *Joint BIS-IMF-OECD-World Bank Statistics on External Debt*; data on loans extended by multinational banks are taken from the BIS' *Consolidated International Banking Statistics*; and all other data are provided in the IMF's *International Financial Statistics*.[4]

The data set used here comprised 26 emerging economies. The selection of countries used in this study was guided by three considerations. First, the study includes only emerging economies. Second, the sample of emerging economies was based on the samples used in earlier studies to allow for some comparability of results. Third, my sample of 26 countries includes several countries from each region.

The sample size is larger than most other studies on banking and currency crises, but smaller than the most comprehensive study on banking crises. My sample contains more emerging economies than several other studies on currency and banking crises [*Eichengreen et al., 1995; Frankel and Rose, 1996; Kaminksy and Reinhart, 1999*]. Notably, Kaminsky and Reinhart's [*1999*] seminal work on currency and banking crises uses a sample of 19 emerging and five industrialised countries [*Denmark, Finland,*

FINANCIAL CRISES AFTER FINANCIAL LIBERALISATION   107

Norway, Spain and Sweden]. However, my study includes fewer emerging countries than the most comprehensive study on banking crises [*Demirgüç-Kunt and Detragiache, 1999*], which included 34 emerging economies.

My selection of emerging economies does not fully overlap with the samples of earlier studies, largely because of data limitations. All 19 emerging economies included in Kaminsky and Reinhart [*1999*] are also part of my sample. However, I only include 23 of 34 emerging economies that were comprised in the sample used by Demirgüç-Kunt and Detragiache [*1999*], mainly because I use monthly data instead of annual data. Since changes in macroeconomic fundamentals leading to crises appear to occur rather rapidly, annual observations may be too infrequent to study the patterns during crisis and non-crisis times. But as I use monthly data, I exclude observations on GDP, and use industrial production as a measure of output instead. However, eight countries that were included by Demirgüç-Kunt and Detragiache [*1999*] are excluded. Three more countries were excluded because of incomplete data (India, Nigeria, and Syria).

The sample of countries used for the empirical analysis covers all regions of emerging economies. Ten countries are in South America (Argentina, Bolivia, Brazil, Chile, Colombia, Mexico, Paraguay, Peru, Uruguay, Venezuela), three countries are in Latin America (Guatemala, Honduras, El Salvador), five countries are in Asia (Indonesia, Korea, Malaysia, Philippines, Thailand), four countries are in the Middle East (Egypt, Israel, Jordan, Turkey), and four countries are in Africa (Guyana, Kenya, Tanzania, Zambia).

Analysis for Banking Crises

Hypotheses and variable definitions: Financial systems experience an increase in default, maturity, interest rate and exchange rate risks after liberalisation. Speculative financing becomes both more likely because of investor euphoria and more feasible because of financial market deregulation. Thus, default risk should rise, and consequently the exposure to other risks, too. Also, demands on the means of support that a government can offer should increase. Finally, the effectiveness of increased international financial competition in controlling speculative financing may be ambiguous in the face of growing investor optimism after deregulation.

First, default risk arises from overly optimistic credit expansions and from an asset market boom fuelled by investor euphoria. In the univariate analysis, I include both the level and the growth of real credit. It is possible that real credit levels are substantially higher prior to a crisis than at other times, but that lenders may have become worried about their credit exposure and may begin to reduce their lending. Thus, growth rates of real credit may be smaller prior to a crisis than at other times.[5] In fact, the summary statistics in Table 1 show that the level of credit is substantially higher before a crisis after FL than otherwise, and that real credit growth accelerates. Higher levels of real credit only indicate speculative financing, though, if they occur in an environment, where real production expands at a slower pace than financing. Thus, a widening gap between production and credit should signal increased speculative financing. In order to gain a sense of the dynamic of production prior to financial crises, I include again the level and growth rate of industrial production in the univariate analysis. As the summary statistics in Table 1 show both levels and growth rates of industrial production appear to be lower immediately before a banking crisis after FL. The gap between credit and production appears to widen after FL more than before FL (Table 1).

To control for the possibility of an asset market boom, I include stock market growth rates. Above average stock market growth rates suggest a growing asset market bubble. Given the rise in speculative financing often observed after FL, I expect stock market growth to be faster during the months immediately before a crisis than during non-crisis months.

Alongside higher default risk, maturity risk should also increase. Deteriorating economic fundamentals, such as increased borrower default, raise the chance the investors withdraw their funds. The exposure to maturity risk of any economy depends on its exposure to short-term external loans relative to official reserves, that could be used to defend a country's financial system against rapid outflows. In order to capture the dynamic development of maturity risk during the months leading up to a crisis, I include both the level and growth of short-term debt relative to official reserves. While it is ultimately the level of short-term loans that indicates a country's exposure to maturity risk, the growth rate relative to reserves can capture the attitude of international investors. A more rapid inflow of short-term capital relative to reserves immediately before a crisis suggests that investors misinterpreted the health of an economy especially during the months prior to a crisis. In the more deregulated environment after FL, both levels and growth rates of short-term capital flows should be greater after FL than before.

Next, the likelihood of maturity risk materialising depends to a large degree on what happens to economic fundamentals. Immediately before a crisis, I expect to observe an increase in the default risk, but also a growing sensitivity to interest rate differentials. In case economic fundamentals deteriorate relative to non-crisis periods it is likely that interest rate differentials widen if domestic rates are raised. The interest rate differential is captured by the difference between the respective economy's real interest rate, and the US' real interest rate. In order to correctly interpret any

TABLE I

SUMMARY STATISTICS FOR BANKING AND CURRENCY CRISES

Variable	Before FL					After FL				
	Overall	Banking Crisis		Currency Crisis		Overall	Banking Crisis		Currency Crisis	
		Tranquil Periods	Pre-Crisis Periods	Tranquil Periods	Pre-Crisis Periods		Tranquil Periods	Pre-Crisis Periods	Tranquil Periods	Pre-Crisis Periods
Industrial Production	83.510	83.653	87.769	86.148	83.017	109.473	109.353	108.369	108.727	116.585
Industrial Production Growth	3.849	4.015	2.027	4.346	5.246	5.646	6.373	5.346	6.760	2.635
Real Credit	93.876	95.015	84.542	81.910	106.585	123.75	115.454	152.002	119.595	164.440
Real Credit Growth	6.620	6.627	9.067	6.800	8.255	7.115	6.594	11.582	6.726	12.659
(Short-term Loans/Reserves)	7.442	7.615	5.302	4.512	15.784	1.867	1.931	1.846	1.495	3.031
Δ (Short-term Loans/Reserves)	15.509	16.126	100.080	109.710	-89.633	-21.012	-16.529	-49.515	-11.232	6.302
(Current Acct./Reserves)	-0.240	-0.240	-0.275	-0.209	-0.401	-0.077	-0.079	-0.100	-0.059	-0.163
Growth of Reserves	23.986	24.227	18.157	25.952	6.000	29.363	27.668	32.627	28.786	10.149
Real Interest Rate	-30.991	-36.302	-0.844	-30.048	-6.566	46558.35	62339.4	-0.096	66177.35	-0.664
Real Interest Rate Differential	-32.775	-37.971	-3.613	-31.549	-3.049	46556.06	62366.31	-2.058	66175.22	-3.193
Real M1	106.933	109.517	82.416	94.981	121.288	116.102	112.920	134.336	115.526	136.435
Real Deposits	67.622	67.712	70.560	N/A	N/A	143.968	140.573	151.141	N/A	N/A
Real M2	N/A	N/A	N/A	74.740	91.721	N/A	N/A	N/A	133.567	149.300
Real Exchange Rate	0.337	0.015	0.269	0.122	-4.968	-0.636	0.000	-5.921	0.053	1.786
(MNB Credit/Total Credit)	0.599	0.655	0.037	0.694	0.510	0.496	0.513	0.493	0.503	0.499
Δ (MNB Credit/Total Credit)	-0.018	-0.020	0.021	-0.004	-0.096	0.041	0.059	0.252	0.035	0.052

changes in the interest differential that may be observed I also include the emerging economies' real interest rate separately. Because of greater capital mobility, the interest rate differential should be greater after FL than before.

Fourth, rapid capital outflows and deteriorating economic fundamentals should weaken the external value of the currency. Thus, exchange rate risk increases, which is captured by the level of overvaluation of the currency. As has become common practice [*Eichengreen et al., 1995; Kaminsky and Reinhart, 1999*], the misalignment of a currency is measured by the real exchange rate's deviation from its mean during months that are classified as non-crisis months. A increase of the real exchange rate over its non-crisis average signals an undervaluation and a decrease an overvaluation. Because of the speculative nature of deregulated economies after FL, particularly because of external liberalisation, I would expect the overvaluation of a currency that should occur just before a crisis to be greater after FL than before.

A greater exchange rate risk has also direct feedback effects on the real economy. An overvalued currency leads to a deterioration in the terms of trade. Declining terms of trade, though, should lead to a worsening of the current account balance. Since official reserves can help to reduce a country's need for international capital in the face of declining current account balances, I include the current account balance relative to reserves in the analysis.

Fifth, among the potentially stabilising factors of FL is the influx of international capital into the domestic financial markets in the form of financial FDI. The level of MNB loans relative to total credit captures the size of multinational banks. Further, I also include the rate of change of MNB loans relative to total credit to see whether MNBs are more likely or less likely to fuel an expected credit boom prior to a crisis.

Finally, it is likely that the government is feeling already strains on the resources it could use to stabilise its financial system, such as official reserves. Thus, changes in official reserves are used as proxy for the changes of the ability of emerging economies' governments to stabilise their financial systems.[6] Official reserves may grow slower during the months immediately before a crisis than during non-crisis periods if the government needs to support its currency or its banking system in the wake of deteriorating economic fundamentals. To control for the demands a government may face from its financial system, I include real deposits and real M1 as proxies for the size of the financial system. Because of the speculative nature of economies after FL, the monetary base should be larger after FL than before, and it should be greater immediately prior to a crisis than during non-crisis periods. Thus, the possible demands on the government's resources should be largest during the months prior to a crisis after FL.

Univariate tests: In this section, I provide univariate evidence that shows that the economic environment is structurally different after FL from that before FL. Further, I demonstrate that the economic environment after FL leaves emerging economies more vulnerable to banking crises than before.

The data set is separated twice. Policies that comprise FL are often not introduced at once. Thus, the elimination of interest rate restrictions is chosen as the start of FL [*Fry, 1997; Demirgüç-Kunt and Detragiache, 1999*], and the data are divided into observations occurring prior to interest rate liberalisation and thereafter. Also, each observations falls either into a crisis month or a non-crisis month. For banking crises, crisis months are the 18 months prior to a banking crisis and the 18 months following a banking crisis. I classify as banking crises bad loan ratios of more than ten per cent, 'bank runs that lead to closure, merging or takeover by the public sector of one or more financial institutions, [or] ... if there are no runs, the closure, merging, takeover, or large-scale government assistance of an important financial institution (or group of institutions), that marks the start of a string of similar outcomes for other financial institutions' [*Kaminsky and Reinhart, 1999: 476*]. This definition has been widely used in the analysis of banking crises in emerging economies [*Balino and Sundararajan, 1991; Lindgren, Garcia and Saal, 1996; Sheng, 1996*]. In this analysis the month of when the banking sector problem is first discovered or reported is defined as the banking crisis months, and observations are classified according to whether they occur during the 36-month-window around a crisis (crisis) or not (non-crisis).

In order to control for country and time specific effects each variable is measured as the deviation from its average during non-crisis times.[7] Thanks to this manipulation, I am able to see systematic differences that are common to all economies. To show the robustness of the results, the deviations are recorded both for 18 and for 24 months prior to a crisis. The actual crisis month and the 18 (or 24) months after the crisis are excluded. To test the differences between crisis and non-crisis periods before and after FL, and the difference between crisis months before and after FL, I use a Wilcoxon rank sum test. A positive sign indicates that the mean prior to a crisis is larger than during tranquil periods, or that the mean after FL is smaller than before FL.

The univariate results for banking crises are reported in Table 2. Both before and after FL, crisis months appear to be significantly different from non-crisis months. Also, crisis months before FL appear to vary from crisis

TABLE 2

UNIVARIATE TESTS FOR BANKING CRISES

Variable	Equality of Tranquil and Crises Periods Before FL		Equality of Tranquil and Crises Periods After FL		Equality of Crises Periods Before and After FL	
	18-month	24-month	18-month	24-month	18-month	24-month
Pre-Crisis Period						
Industrial Production	-6.275***	-7.114***	3.197***	3.262***	5.034***	5.505***
Δ Industrial Production	1.022	-0.723	6.089***	5.215***	1.586	3.045***
Δ Stock Market	n.a.	n.a.	0.906	2.750***	n.a.	n.a.
Real Credit	-4.590***	-4.923***	-5.063***	-6.033***	-0.152	-0.742
Δ Real Credit	0.632	1.858*	-2.216**	-2.952***	-2.053**	-3.841***
Δ Short-term Loans/Reserves	-2.118**	-3.673***	-0.412	1.062	1.834*	3.947***
Real Interest Rate	0.754	1.009	-2.466***	-1.404	1.253	3.043***
Real Interest Rate Differential	2.112**	2.198***	-1.459	-0.374	0.812	2.737***
Real M1	2.485***	2.449**	-9.848***	-11.070***	-6.589***	-7.329***
Real Deposits	-5.754***	-6.867***	-3.845***	-4.403***	1.426	1.393
Real Exchange Rate (Deviation from Trend)	-0.623	-3.103***	11.056***	10.923***	4.579***	3.131***
Current Account/Reserves	3.667***	3.478***	8.502***	9.841***	0.468	1.781*
Short-term Loans/Reserves	-4.752***	-4.541***	-1.608	-1.325	4.105***	3.498***
Δ Official Reserves	0.112	0.515	0.243	0.239	-0.664	-1.221
MNB Loans/Total Credit	-4.800***	-4.347***	10.048***	12.350***	9.182***	9.936***
Δ MNB Loans/Total Credit	-1.711*	-3.103***	10.048***	7.212***	3.460***	5.864***

*= significance at the 5%-level, **= significance at the 2.5%-level; ***=significance at the 1%-level

FINANCIAL CRISES AFTER FINANCIAL LIBERALISATION   113

months after FL. Further, the univariate analysis supports the hypothesis that after FL banking crises are characterised by more optimistic credit expansions, and more speculative financing. Thus, maturity, interest rate, and exchange rate risk should also become more likely to materialise, especially as interest rate and exchange rate risks appear to be greater prior to crises. Only maturity risk, taken by itself appears to be lower after FL than before.

A financially more fragile environment after FL hinges on an increase in speculative financing, which signals rising default risk. The univariate results indicate an increase in speculative financing after FL that is not apparent before FL. The level of real credit is larger during the months directly before a crisis, before and after FL. In comparison, the growth rate of real credit is lower during crisis months before FL, and higher during crisis months after FL than during non-crisis months. Lenders slow down their credit expansion when credit is already high before FL, but increase the pace of credit expansion from an already higher than average level after FL. Moreover, rapidly expanding credit finances a slowing real sector after FL, whereas a slower credit expansion before FL finances an expanding real sector. Both the level and the growth rate of industrial production is below average during the crisis months after FL, while the level of industrial production is above average before FL with an average growth rate.

Further, there are signs that asset market bubbles may turn to asset market busts during the months prior to a crisis after FL. Similar to findings in earlier studies regarding banking crises [*Kaminsky and Reinhart, 1999*], stock market growth slows during the months before a crisis. This finding is consistent with a bursting asset bubble, which ultimately may take a toll on the financial system through a lagged increase in the default rates.

Maturity risk seems to stay the same prior to crisis after FL, whereas it appears to grow before FL. Both the level and change in short-term loans to reserves are greater during crisis months before FL, while both are the same after FL.[8]

Further, interest rate risk may grow in the pre-crisis months after FL. The real interest rate is higher prior to a crisis than during non-crisis months, whereas the real interest rate differential remains unchanged. Thus, changes in real interest rates appear to only avoid a narrowing of the interest rate differential between emerging economies and the US. The fact that real interest rates, though, have increased should further a deterioration in economic fundamentals, and thereby raise the default risk. In comparison, prior to FL the interest rate differential is narrowing during pre-crisis months.

The exchange rate risk appears to be also higher during the pre-crisis months after FL. After FL, the real exchange rate is overvalued immediately before a crisis as the real exchange rate falls below its non-crisis average. In comparison, there is some indication that the real exchange rate depreciates immediately before a crisis before FL.

In the wake of an overvalued currency, the current account balance worsens after FL. In fact, the current account balance relative to reserves becomes increasingly negative (Table 1), thereby possibly putting a strain on official reserves. A similar worsening of the current account balance before FL, though, may be related to increased imports due to expanding real production.

Even though risks increase, the vulnerability to banking crisis may still decline thanks to compensating factors, such as government support, or international competition. The monetary base expands during pre-crisis months after FL, thereby raising the potential demands on public resources when the crisis occurs. Prior to FL, though, real M1 shrinks during pre-crisis months, while deposits expand. While the strains on public resources grow before a crisis after FL, changes in official reserves are the same. Further, MNBs seem to lower their credit exposure faster than domestic banks, thus generally not fuelling a speculative financing boom after FL.

Multivariate analysis for banking crises: The univariate analysis ignores potential joint effects of the explanatory variables. Hence I expand the analysis by using a logistic regression, which has the advantages that it investigates the effects of several variables simultaneously, and that it controls for dynamic changes.

The dependent variable is a dichotomous variable which takes the value of one during the 18 months prior to a banking crisis and the value zero otherwise. The 18 months after a crisis and the actual crisis month are excluded.

In selecting explanatory variables, several considerations are of importance. First, where both levels and rates of change were included in the univariate analysis, levels rather than rates of change are chosen due to theoretical considerations. For instance, the level, not the rate of change, of short-term loans relative to reserves measures a growing maturity risk. Second, due to a high degree of collinearity I exclude the real interest rate, but keep the interest rate differential. The elimination of the real interest rate, which is meant to proxy for monetary policy is unproblematic since the components for M2, currency and broad money are included. Third, to avoid undue data limitations, I exclude MNB loans and stock market growth.

I estimate the coefficients for each sub-period separately using fixed effects logistic regressions. The results reported in regression (1) and (2) in Table 3 indicate that financial fragility is greater after FL than before. Lower

FINANCIAL CRISES AFTER FINANCIAL LIBERALISATION   115

industrial production during increases the chance of a banking crisis after FL, whereas it has no impact prior to FL. Also, more real credit prior to FL lowers the chance of a crisis, while it raises it after FL. Thus, above average credit expansion to a real sector with below average industrial production, as can be observed during pre-crisis months after FL, raises the default risk and increases the chance of a crisis unequivocally.

Not only do the empirical results show more speculative financing resulting in higher chances of banking crises after FL, but they also indicate a stronger response to a smaller maturity risk after FL. The level of short-term loans relative to official reserves during pre-crisis months is higher before FL than afterwards. But financial fragility rises significantly more in response to the same level of maturity risk, ceteris paribus, after FL than before (Table 3).

TABLE 3

MULTIVARIATE ANALYSIS FOR BANKING CRISES

Variable	Exp. Sign	Before FL (1)	After FL (2)	Parameter Comparison	Trend Variable (3)	Time Fixed Effects (4)
Industrial	–	0.0116	–0.0125***	1.198	–0.0161***	–0.0174***
Production		(0.0199)	(0.0029)		(0.0035)	(0.0042)
Real Credit	+	–0.0697***	0.0172***	–4.686***	0.0183***	0.0178***
		(0.0184)	(0.0023)		(0.0024)	(0.0030)
(Short-term	+	0.0851**	0.1611***	–1.441*	0.1856***	0.2280***
Loans/Reserves)		(0.0369)	(0.0377)		(0.0404)	(0.0465)
(Current Acct./	–	–3.155***	–2.2296***	–1.198	–2.3064***	–3.5355***
Reserves)		(0.7713)	(0.0377)		(0.6885)	(0.8907)
Δ Reserves	–	–0.0470***	0.0054	–4.999***	0.0059***	0.0062***
		(0.0104)	(0.0013)		(0.0013)	(0.0017)
Real Interest	–	0.00005	0.0004	–0.971	0.0004	0.0018
Rate Differential		(0.0002)	(0.0003)		(0.0003)	(0.0017)
Real M1	+	0.0040	0.0010	0.452	0.0020	0.0020
		(0.0063)	(0.0021)		(0.0022)	(0.0027)
Real Deposits	+	0.0698***	–0.0088***	4.688***	–0.0099***	–0.0123***
		(0.0167)	(0.0015)		(0.0016)	(0.0021)
Real Exchange	–	–0.0341***	–0.0254***	–1.046	–0.0261***	–0.0135***
Rate		(0.0074)	(0.0038)		(0.0039)	(0.0047)
Logged Trend	–	N/A	N/A	N/A	0.1886*	N/A
					(0.0975)	
Constant	+/–	–6.9145***	–1.5279***	–	–2.0369***	–3.4926***
		(1.6104)	(0.3002)		(0.4048)	(1.1860)
No. of Observations		1075	1074	–	1074	709
Time Fixed Effects		No	No	–	No	Yes
Log Likelihood		–56.9113	–496.6996	–	–494.766	–358.823
Chi-Square		145.72	150.23	–	154.09	172.94
Pseudo-R^2		0.5615	0.1314	–	0.1347	0.1942

* = significant at 10%; ** = significant at 5%; ***= significant at 1%.

With the same response to interest rate and exchange rate risks before and after FL, emerging economies appear to become more fragile after FL. There are no significant differences in the response to interest rate and exchange rate risks between the periods before FL and after FL. During both sub-periods a narrowing real interest rate differential has no impact on the chance of a crisis, and an overvaluation leads to an increase in the chance of a banking crisis. Since both interest rate and exchange rate risks are higher during the pre-crisis months after FL than before, financial fragility is greater after FL than before.

Also, the response to the current account balance remains stable before and after FL. Considering that there is no discernible difference in the deterioration of the current account balance during pre-crisis months, default risk should increase equally before and after FL.

Along with most risk categories, except maturity risks, increasing after FL, financial fragility also rises. Consequently, the same improvements in public resources, as proxied by changes in official reserves, have a significantly smaller dampening effect on emerging economies' chances of experiencing a banking crisis.

Further, more deposits reduce the chance of a crisis after FL, but raise it before FL. This indicates that greater liquidity improves a banking system's stability rather than destabilises it.

The effects of transitional turbulences that should subside over time may dominate the regression results. To control for time after FL, I introduce a logged time trend. I expect that policymakers become more familiar with the deregulated environment and can better respond to destabilising economic trends the longer an economy has been liberalised. Thus, the logged time trend represents something like a 'national learning curve'. The results of regression (3) in Table 3 show that the prior results are robust. Also, the results indicate that the likelihood of banking crises increases over time. Alternatively, the effects of time can be controlled by introducing fixed effects for each month since FL has been introduced as in regression (4) of Table 3. The results continue to be robust. After controlling for the time passed since the introduction of FL emerging economies are still more susceptible to banking crises than before FL.

Hypotheses and Variables for Currency Crises

Can we observe a similar rise in the vulnerability to currency crises after FL that emerging economies experience with respect to banking crises? I use the same univariate and multivariate analysis as employed for banking crises in the previous section.

Again, the likelihood of a currency crisis should increase with growing financial market speculation after FL. Overly optimistic credit expansions and asset market booms become once again indicators of a weakening macroeconomic environment. Similar to banking crises, investor euphoria is captured by a divergence in the level of industrial production and real credit prior to a crisis. After FL, real credit appears to grow to higher levels than real production. Also, Industrial production growth appears to slow, while real credit growth appears to accelerate (Table 1). Finally, above average stock market growth may indicate an asset market bubble.

Due to liberalised capital accounts, I would expect a more rapid outflow of short-term capital in the face of deteriorating economic fundamentals, thereby fostering a currency crisis. Thus, I expect the importance of short-term capital flows in determining an economy's vulnerability to crises to rise after FL. To account for the effects of capital mobility I include the level and growth of short-term debt to reserves, the interest rate differential between the respective economy and the US, and an indication of currency misalignments. There should be more short-term debt relative to reserves, a wider interest rate differential and an overvaluation immediately before a crisis.

Third, following currency overvaluations, the current account balance should deteriorate. I include the current account balance relative to reserves, which is expected to be lower during pre-crisis months.

Fourth, during pre-crisis months, public resources may be used to stabilise a currency. Thus, I expect a below average growth rate of official reserves, and an above average real interest rate, signaling a monetary tightening.

In comparison, the demand on public policy means may be greater if the monetary base is above average during the pre-crisis months. Due to financial deregulation, the monetary base may be greater after FL than before, therefore possibly leading to greater demands on public resources than before FL. Again, I use M1 and deposits as measures of monetary aggregates.

Finally, a greater presence of MNBs due to capital account liberalisation should lower the risk of currency crises as it induces banks to engage in less speculative financing.[9] The ratio of MNB loans relative to total credit and its change measure the impact of MNBs, which is expected to be lower during times of investor euphoria during pre-crisis months and after FL.[10]

Univariate analysis: Similar to the univariate analysis for banking crises, the data is subdivided first into observations that occur before and after FL and then into observations that occur during crisis and non-crisis months. To determine crisis months, I use a crisis index as a weighted average of changes in the nominal exchange rate (relative to the US dollar), and of changes in official reserves [*Eichengreen, Rose and Wyplosz, 1995;*

Kaminsky and Reinhart, 1999]. The weights of each component are chosen such that the conditional volatilities are the same.[11] A crisis is defined as a deviation of more than three standard deviations of the index from its mean. The 18 (or 24) months prior to a crisis are considered pre-crisis periods.

The univariate results in Table 4 suggest that the economic environment becomes more fragile in the one to two years prior to a crisis. Further, there appear to be significant and consistent differences before and after FL.

The results support some of the hypotheses. There is some evidence of more speculative financing after FL. Further, there is evidence of currency overvaluations and of deteriorating current account balances immediately before a crisis before and after FL. However, both the currency overvaluation and the decline in the current account balance appear to be greater after FL. In comparison, the evidence, suggests that short-term debt relative to reserves is greater before FL than after, but it tends to grow faster during pre-crisis months after FL than before. Also, in either case, the growth of official reserves slows down during pre-crisis months – more so after FL than before – which is consistent with the pattern observed for current account balances. Finally, interest rate differentials appear to be narrowing, rather than widening during pre-crisis months, with a stronger narrowing before FL.

There is some indication of more speculative financing after FL. Real credit rises above average during pre-crisis months and faster after FL than before. At the same time, the level and growth of industrial production fall below their long-term averages during pre-crisis months after FL. Thus, there is a noticeable divergence between credit and production during pre-crisis months after FL that does not exist before FL.

Further, there is not much support for asset bubbles before a crisis as stock market growth is higher during non-crisis times. Kaminsky and Reinhart [*1999*] found that stock market growth, appears to reach its peak about one year before a crisis. Thus, the end of an asset market bubble tends to precede a currency crisis. Considering that the decline in asset market growth is larger after FL, it is likely that the previous asset market bubble is also greater after FL, which is consistent with more speculation in a deregulated environment.

The results with respect to international capital mobility are mixed. Emerging economies experience real exchange rate overvaluations and subsequent current account balance declines leading up to a crisis, particularly before FL. However, the real interest rate differential narrows simultaneously, especially after FL. This may raise financial fragility, particularly if short-term debt relative to official reserves increases during pre-crisis months. Short-term loans relative to reserves are greater prior to

TABLE 4

UNIVARIATE TESTS FOR CURRENCY CRISES

Variable	Equality of Tranquil and Crises Periods Before FL		Equality of Tranquil and Crises Periods Before FL		Equality of Crises Periods Before and After FL	
	18-month	24-month	18-month	24-month	18-month	24-month
Pre-Crisis Period						
Industrial Production	3.061***	3.944***	2.572***	1.495	0.291	-1.572
Δ Industrial Production	0.659	1.929*	5.789***	5.798***	3.466***	2.686***
Real Credit	-10.113***	-11.261***	-8.487***	-7.572***	-2.249**	-1.702*
Δ Real Credit	2.168***	4.141***	-1.219	0.557	-2.132**	-1.962**
Δ Stock Market	3.314***	2.265**	3.780***	4.649***	-1.895*	-0.195
Short-Term Loans/Official Reserves	-12.744***	-13.866***	-10.088***	-4.765***	3.567***	5.093***
Δ Short-term Loans/Official Reserves	-4.689***	-4.331***	-7.252***	-8.819***	-1.263	-4.345***
Real Interest Rate	0.588	1.196	2.949***	3.456***	6.598***	7.329***
Real Interest Rate Differential	2.749***	2.992***	2.748***	3.347***	5.533***	6.469***
Current Account Balance/Reserves	14.468***	15.110***	11.426***	11.231***	-1.950*	-2.259**
Δ Foreign Exchange Reserves	8.767***	7.436***	11.326***	12.541***	0.350	2.957***
Real M1	-9.017***	-10.059***	-7.378***	-7.572***	-0.858	-1.597
Real M2	-6.850***	-8.378***	-3.327***	-7.639***	-0.742	-0.872
Real Exchange Rate (Deviation from Trend)	11.171***	11.696***	6.519***	8.220***	-2.014*	-1.099
MNB Credit/Total Credit	-2.723***	-5.835***	-2.813***	-4.623***	0.530	1.295
Δ MNB Credit/Total Credit	2.052**	-1.648*	-4.143***	-4.651***	-3.550***	-0.840

*= significance at the 5%-level, **= significance at the 2.5%-level; ***=significance at the 1%-level

crisis, especially before FL, leaving emerging economies more exposed to capital mobility. The rate of change of short-term loans relative to reserves is also above average during pre-crisis months. The results indicate a greater exposure to short-term capital mobility during the pre-crisis months, which appears to be more pronounced before FL.

Public resources are increasing below average prior to crises, while the potential demands on public resources, as measured by monetary aggregates are rising. The growth of official reserves is, especially after FL, below average. But real M1 and deposits increase to above average levels, aided by declining real interest rate after FL.

Greater international competition – a potentially stabilising policy – appears to grow prior to crises. Thus, in contrast to banking crises, MNBs expand their loans faster during pre-crisis months than domestic banks. Both levels and growth rates of MNB loans relative to total credit are above average during pre-crisis months after FL. Before FL, growth of MNB loans appears to slow, whereas the levels are still higher than during non-crisis periods. Since there is evidence of speculative financing after FL, it at least appears that MNBs are not reducing their credit exposure in response to observed speculative financing. Whether MNBs help to promote speculative financing is questionable since their average market share is below one per cent.

Multivariate Analysis for Currency Crisis

Analogous to my analysis of banking crises, I conduct a multivariate regression analysis to control for possible joint effects. The dependent variable takes the value of one during the 18 months prior to a currency crisis, and the value zero otherwise. Similar to the univariate analysis the 18 months after a crisis and the actual crisis month are excluded.

In the selection of the explanatory variables, I have considered the same factors as for banking crises. Hence, I include industrial production, real credit, and short-term debt relative to reserves, the interest rate differential, real M1, real deposits, current account balances relative to reserves, the growth of official reserves, and a measure of exchange rate misalignments.

Again, similar to banking crises, I estimate a fixed effects logistic models for both sub-sets. The results reported for regression (1), before FL, and regression (2), after FL, in Table 5 indicate that emerging economies have become more vulnerable to currency crises after FL.

More speculative financing increases the chance of currency crises. While the below average industrial production during the pre-crisis months does not have a significant impact on the chance of currency crises occurring, the above average level of real credit increases the likelihood of a crisis.

FINANCIAL CRISES AFTER FINANCIAL LIBERALISATION 121

TABLE 5

MULTIVARIATE ANALYSIS FOR CURRENCY CRISES

Variable	Exp. Sign	Before FL (1)	After FL (2)	Parameter Comparison	Trend Variable (3)	Time Fixed Effects (4)
Industrial	–	–0.0098*	0.0030	–2.195***	0.0080**	0.0097***
Production		(0.0050)	(0.0030)		(0.0033)	(0.0037)
Real Credit	+	0.0079***	0.0129***	–1.553*	0.0110***	0.0077***
		(0.0026)	(0.0019)		(0.0020)	(0.0022)
(Short-term	+	0.1048***	0.2177***	–1.800**	0.1681***	0.2317***
Loans/Reserves)		(0.0398)	(0.0485)		(0.0495)	(0.0592)
(Current Acct./	–	–3.2289***	–0.5823	–2.730***	–0.5425	–0.5403
Reserves)		(0.6501)	(0.7193)		(0.7297)	(0.8474)
Δ Reserves	–	–0.0187***	–0.0107***	–2.090**	–0.0107***	–0.0104***
		(0.0029)	(0.0025)		(0.0025)	(0.0027)
Real Interest	–	9.71e–07	0.0001	–0.443	0.0001	0.0002
Rate Differential		(0.0001)	(0.0002)		(0.0002)	(0.0003)
Real M1	–	0.0258	0.0053**	3.755***	0.0021	–0.0001
		(0.0048)	(0.0026)		(0.0027)	(0.0031)
Real M2	–	–0.0288***	–0.0101***	–2.550***	–0.0064**	0.0001
		(0.0069)	(0.0025)		(0.0027)	(0.0033)
Real Exchange	–	0.0032	–0.0165***	3.661***	0.0155***	–0.1064***
Rate		(0.0040)	(0.0036)		(0.0037)	(0.0042)
Logged Trend	–	N/A	N/A	–	–0.3521***	N/A
					(0.1041)	
Constant	+/–	–2.0046***	–3.0672***	–	–2.0286***	–3.0676***
		(0.3385)	(0.3306)		(0.4369)	(0.9298)
No. of Observations		899	1155	–	1155	832
Time Fixed Effects		No	No	–	No	Yes
Log Likelihood		–384.351	–472.983	–	–467.316	–386.018
Chi-Square		255.88	161.24	–	172.57	176.64
Pseudo-R^2		0.2497	0.1456	–	0.1559	0.1862

* = significant at 10%; ** = significant at 5%; ***= significant at 1%

Because speculative financing raises the chance of currency crises substantially, it is not surprising to find that emerging economies have also become more vulnerable to short-term capital outflows after FL. Even though the above average level of short-term ort-term loans is lower after FL than before, it raises the chance of a currency crisis more than before FL. Thus, the sensitivity to short-term capital flows has increased significantly thanks to FL.

Improvements in the current account balance have no stabilising effect after FL. The level of the current account balance is below average during pre-crisis months before and after FL, but it is higher after FL than before. While the lower level of the current account balance does not significantly raise the chance of banking crises, an improvement in the current account balance also does nothing to lower the chance of a banking crisis.

Similarly, faster reserve accumulations have a smaller stabilising effect after FL than before. However, overvalued exchange rates have a stronger destabilising effect after FL than before. Finally, the money variables appear to have opposite effects before and after FL. While an expansion of M1 is stabilising before FL, it seems to be destabilising after FL. An increase in M2, though, seems to destabilise a currency before FL, and stabilise it after FL.

Given the same set of economic fundamentals the chance of a currency crisis is higher after FL than before. Thus, the results not only show a structural difference after FL, they also suggest that this new structure in liberalised emerging economies is systematically more unstable than emerging economies before FL.

The possibility remains that the multivariate results capture some turbulences in the early stages of FL, rather than underlying structural weaknesses. To control for this timing effect, I again add a logarithmic time trend to the regression. The results of regression (3) in Table 5 show that the time trend is negative, indicating that the chance of a crisis declines the longer ago FL has been introduced, while the other results remain largely unchanged. Alternatively, I include time fixed effects to control for time specific changes after FL. The results are reported in regression (4) in Table 5. The inclusion of time effects in the regression changes only the effect of industrial production notably as the estimated parameter becomes positive. Put differently, increases in industrial production raise the chance of a currency crisis, which may reflect tendencies of over-production in the face of increasing liquidity.

IV. CONCLUDING REMARKS AND POLICY IMPLICATIONS

This article looks at the possibility that the vulnerability of emerging economies to currency and banking crises increases after financial liberalisation. Both univariate and multivariate tests suggest that the risk of encountering banking or currency crises rises after FL. Further, the results are sufficiently robust to suggest that the rise in currency and banking crises reflects an increases in structural weaknesses, rather than an increase in exceptional circumstances.

The empirical results indicate that the vulnerability of emerging economies to currency and banking crises increases after FL. External liberalisation allows more liquidity to enter an emerging economy, which, put somewhat simplistically, can then, thanks to internal liberalisation, find its way into productive and speculative projects. What is common to both types of crises is a significant increase in the divergence between real and financial trends, which is taken as an indication for growing trend of more speculative financing. Also, due to this divergence between the real and the financial sector, the chance of a crisis increases faster after FL than before.

FINANCIAL CRISES AFTER FINANCIAL LIBERALISATION 123

With a larger chance of borrower default in emerging economies, the outflow of international capital becomes more likely, and the chance of a financial crisis grows faster in response to changes in short-term loans after FL than before.

Similarly, a currency overvaluation raises the chance of a crisis in both cases. In the case of banking crises, currency overvaluations have the same negative impact before and after FL. A currency overvaluation, however, results in a significantly higher rise in the probability of a crisis after FL than before.

Since a deregulated environment may cause some turbulences initially, it is important to control for changes over time. After controlling for time, the chance of currency crisis declines over time after FL, even though the reactions to economic fundamentals remain similar, which suggests that other stabilising institutions, such as more transparency, may be improving. In contrast, the chance of a banking crisis seems to increase with time, which may indicate a growing optimism on the part of regulators. Earlier research [*Arestis and Demetriades, 1999*] has suggested that due to investor euphoria, market participants, which by extension would include regulators, underestimate the risks associated with a deregulated environment.

The main result of this research can best be summarised as evidence that shows that financing is not necessarily going where it is supposed to go in a less regulated environment, thus opening the possibility for crises. In particular, rising investor confidence and optimism result in increasingly speculative financing. This implies a few conclusions.

First, any economy that wants to liberalise its financial system should evaluate its need to liberalise very carefully. In particular, the rationale for FL is based on the assertion that a developing economy is mired in excess demand for credit. If such excess demand is not apparent, or if excess supply exists instead, other arguments in favour of FL have to be even more compelling. Demetriades and Fattouh [*1999*], for instance, show persistent excess credit in Korea during the 1980s and 1990s. Where excess credit can be observed, increased liquidity thanks to internal and external liberalisation is likely to be invested in speculative projects. In Korea, additional liquidity was used to fund speculative overseas investment, for example, loans to Russia.

Thus, other justifications for FL have to be considered in light of the rising chance of financial crises. In the Korean case, the consideration for liberalisation of local financial markets and the capital account were based on Korea's desire to join the OECD.

Second, if a decision is cast in favour of liberalisation the necessary institutions to stabilise the banks and currencies should be in place before opening one's borders. In other words, since greater vulnerability does not seem to be a string of exceptional cases, but rather a structural phenomenon, such institution building seems a necessary precondition rather than an acceptable afterthought to FL. A number of studies indicate that a weak institutional environment may have fostered the Asian financial crisis. For example, Alba *et al.* [*1999*] conclude that the crisis in Thailand can be traced back to FL that was introduced in a weak institutional environment. Similarly, Demetriades and Fattouh [*1999*] find that the South Korean crisis had been helped by the fact that FL was introduced before existing weaknesses in the financial system could have been addressed. Arestis and Demetriades [*1999*], though, argue that even the most efficient system of financial market supervision is unlikely to counter all emerging weaknesses following greater liberalisation as long as investors perennially underestimate the risks associated with deregulated financial markets. Thus, a cautious approach to FL seems warranted on the parts of all global financial market participants.

final revision accepted December 2000

NOTES

1. This assumes that interest rates will only rise to their credit rationing maximum [*Stiglitz and Weiss, 1981*].
2. In empirical studies of financial crises, rising interest rates abroad appear to have a significantly negative impact on the stability of an emerging financial system [*Kaminsky and Reinhart, 1999; Eichengreen, Rose and Wyplosz, 1995*].
3. Poterba [*2000*] provides a summary discussion of the wealth effect for the US, which show that the run-up in the stock market accounts for the majority of the increase in private consumption expenditures in the late 1990s.
4. See Table A6 in the Appendix for more details.
5. See the appendix for a complete list of variables, definitions and sources.
6. I assume that emerging market governments have made implicit or explicit commitments to stabilise their financial market systems, either through deposit insurance systems or through 'too big to fail' policies.
7. To avoid problems associated with different units, only percentages and indexes are used.
8. The fact that the ratio of short-term loans to reserves is smaller after FL is obviously not an indication that short-term borrowing is larger before FL as Table 1 shows. Financial fragility arises from the use of additional funds for speculative financing, which appears to be greater after FL.
9. Even though MNBs operate in more regulated economies, their operations are often restricted in such a way that they do not directly compete with domestic banks.
10. This assumes that MNBs do not engage in speculative financing as domestic banks do.
11. A formalisation of this index can be found in Kaminsky and Reinhart [*1999*].

REFERENCES

Alba, P., Hernandez, L. and D. Klingebiel, 1999, 'Financial Liberalization and the Capital Account: Thailand 1988–1997', *World Bank Policy Research Working Paper* No.2188 (Sept. 1999).
Arestis, P. and P. Demetriades, 1999, 'Financial Liberalization: The Experience of Developing Countries', *Eastern Economic Journal*, Vol.25, No.4, pp.441–57.
Balino, T. and V. Sundararajan, 1991, *Banking Crises: Cases and Issues*, Washington, DC: International Monetary Fund.

FINANCIAL CRISES AFTER FINANCIAL LIBERALISATION   125

Benink, H. and D. Llwellyn, 1994b, 'Fragile Banking in Norway, Sweden and Finland: An Empirical Analysis', *Journal of International Financial Markets, Institutions and Money*, Vol.4, No.3–4, pp.5–19.

Chang, H., Park, H. and C. Yoo, 1998, 'Interpreting the Korean Crisis: Financial Liberalization, Industrial Policy and Corporate Governance', *Cambridge Journal of Economics*, Vol 22, No.6, pp.735–46.

Demetriades, P., 1999, 'Financial Liberalization and Credit-Asset Booms and Busts in East Asia', paper prepared for World Bank Conference 'The Credit Crunch in East Asia: What Do We Know? What Do We Need To Know?' 30 Nov.–1 Dec. 1999.

Demetriades, P. and B.A. Fattouh, 1999, 'South Korea's Financial Liberalization: An Experiment in Faith', *International Affairs*, Vol.75, No.4, pp.779–92.

Demirgüç-Kunt, A. and E. Detragiache, 1999, 'Financial Liberalization and Financial Fragility', in B. Pleskovic and J. Stiglitz (eds.), *Annual World Bank Conference on Development Economics 1998*, Washington, DC: World Bank.

Eichengreen, B., Rose, A.K. and C. Wyplosz, 1995, 'Exchange Market Mayhem: The Antecedents and Aftermath of Speculative Attacks', *Economic Policy*, No.21, pp.251–312.

Frankel, J. and A. Rose, 1996, 'Currency Crashes in Emerging Markets: An Empirical Treatment', *Journal of International Economics*, Vol.41, Nos.3–4, pp.351–66.

Fry, Maxwell, 1997, 'In Favour of Financial Liberalization', *Economic Journal*, Vol.107, No.442, pp.754–70.

Goldfaijn, I. and Valdés Rodrigo, 1997, 'Are Currency Crises Predictable?' *IMF Working Paper* #97/159, Washington, DC: International Monetary Fund.

Grabel, I., 1993, 'Fast Money, "Noisy Growth": A Noise-Led Theory of Development', *Review of Radical Political Economics*, Vol.25, No.3, pp.1–8.

Grabel, I., 1995a, 'Assessing the Impact of Financial Liberalization on Stock Market Volatility in Selected Developing Countries', *The Journal of Development Studies*, Vol.31, No.6, pp.903–17.

Grabel, I., 1995b, 'Speculation-Led Economic Development: A Post-Keynesian Interpretation of Financial Liberalization Programmes in the Third World', *International Review of Applied Economics*, Vol.9, No.2, pp.127–49.

Grabel, I., 1998, 'Rejecting Exceptionalism: Reinterpreting the Asian Financial Crises', in J. Michie and J. Grieve Smith (eds.), *Global Instability and World Economic Governance*, Routledge

Kaminsky, G. and C. Reinhart, 1999, 'The Twin Crises: The Causes of Banking and Balance-of-Payments Problems', *American Economic Review*, Vol.89, No.3, pp.473–500.

Kaminsky, G., Lizondo, S. and C. Reinhart, 1997, 'Leading Indicators of Currency Crises', *IMF Working Paper* #97/79, Washington, DC: International Monetary Fund.

Krugman, P., 1995, 'Dutch Tulips and Emerging Markets', *Foreign Affairs*, Vol.74, No.4, pp.28–44.

Lindgren, C., Garcia, G. and M. Saal, 1996, 'Bank Soundness and Macroeconomic Policy', Washington, DC: International Monetary Fund.

McKinnon, R.I., 1973, 'Money and Capital in Economic Development', Washington, DC: Brookings Institution.

Minsky, H.P., 1986, 'Stabilizing an Unstable Economy', New Haven, CT: Yale University Press.

Minsky, H.P., 1982, *Can 'It' Happen Again?* Armonk, NY: M.E. Sharpe.

Poterba, J., 2000, 'Stock Market Wealth and Consumption', *Journal of Economic Perspectives*, Vol.14, No.2, pp.99–118.

Sachs, J., Tornell, A. and A. Velasco, 1996, 'Financial Crises in Emerging Markets: The Lessons from 1995', *NBER Working Paper*, No.5576,.

Shaw, E.S., 1973, 'Financial Deepening in Economic Development', New York: Oxford University Press.

Sheng, A., 1996, *Bank Restructuring: Lessons from the 1980s*, Washington, DC: World Bank

Stiglitz, J. and A. Weiss, 1981, 'Credit Rationing in Markets with Imperfect Information', *American Economic Review*, Vol.71, No.3, pp.393–410.

Weller, C., 2000a, 'Financial Liberalization, Multinational Banks and Declining Real Credit: The Case of Poland', *International Review of Applied Economics*, Vol.14, No.2.

Weller, C., 2000b, 'Multinational Banks in Developing and Transition Economies', *EPI Technical Paper* No.241, Washington, DC: Economic Policy Institute.

126   THE JOURNAL OF DEVELOPMENT STUDIES

APPENDIX

TABLE 6

VARIABLE DEFINITIONS AND SOURCES

Variable Name	Definition	Source
Industrial Production	Industrial production index (base=1990) (where not available, manufacturing production index, mining production index, crude petroleum production index, and gold output index are used.	IMF
Δ Industrial Production	12-month change in industrial production index (in per cent)	IMF
Δ Stock Market	12-month change in stock market index (in per cent)	Data-stream
Real Interest Rate	Real (CPI adjusted) interest rate (where not available, federal funds rate, treasury bill rate, long-term government bond rate are used) (in per cent)	IMF
Interest Rate Differential	Difference between real domestic interest rate and US rate (in percent)	IMF
Real M1	Index of CPI adjusted M1 with base=1990	IMF
Real M2	Index of CPI adjusted M2 with base=1990	IMF
Real Deposits	Index of CPI adjusted deposits with base=1990	IMF
Real Credit	Index of CPI adjusted credit with base=1990	IMF
Δ Real Credit	12-month change of CPI-inflation adjusted domestic credit (based on monetary survey) (in per cent)	IMF
Real Exchange Rate (Deviation from Trend)	Monthly difference of official exchange rate index (base=1990) adjusted for price level differences between emerging economies and the US and its average during non-crises periods. (in per cent)	IMF
Δ Official Reserves	12-month change of official foreign exchange reserves (in per cent)	IMF
Current Account/ Reserves	Current account balance relative to official reserves (in per cent)	IMF
Short-term Loans/ Reserves	Short-term outstanding debt relative to official reserves (in percent)	IMF; WB
Δ Short-term Loans/ Official Reserves	12-month change in total short-term outstanding debt relative to official reserves (in per cent)	IMF; WB
MNB Lending/ Total Credit	The ratio of loans by MNBs to total domestic credit (in per cent)	BIS; IMF
Δ MNB Lending/ Total Credit	12-month change in the ratio of loans by MNBs to total domestic credit (in per cent)	BIS; IMF

Notes: Balance of payments data and international debt positions are interpolated where appropriate. Sources are IMF, *International Financial Statistics*; World Bank, *World Debt Tables*; BIS, *International Banking and Financial Market Developments*; DataStream.

FINANCIAL CRISES AFTER FINANCIAL LIBERALISATION 127

TABLE 7

OVERVIEW OF COUNTRIES, FINANCIAL LIBERALISATION, AND
BANKING CRISES

Country	Financial Liberalization	Banking Crisis
Argentina	1977	03/1980; 05/1985; 1989; 12/1994
Bolivia	1985	10/1987
Brazil	1975	11/1985; 07/1994
Chile	1980	09/1981
Colombia	1980	07/1982
Mexico	1989	09/1982; 09/1992; 09/1994
Paraguay	1990	1995
Uruguay	1976	03/1981
Venezuela	1981 [1984–01/1989: Interest Rate Controls Reimposed] 1989	10/1993
Indonesia	1983	1992
Korea	1984–1988 [1988–1991: Interest Rate Controls Reimposed] 1991	11/1997
Malaysia	1980	07/1985
Phillippines	1981	01/1981
Thailand	1989	03/1979; 10/1983; 05/1997
Israel	1990	1985
Jordan	1988	08/1989
Kenya	1991	1993
Tanzania	1993	1988
Turkey	1980; [12/83–06/87: Interest Rate Controls Reimposed]; 1987	10/1983; 01/1991; 03/1994
Egypt	1991	
Zambia	1992	01/1995
Guatemala	1989	
Guyana	1991	1993
Honduras	1990	
El Salvador	1991	1989
Peru	1980 [interest rate control reimposed 1984–1990] 1990	04/1989

Sources: Demirgüç-Kunt and Detragiache [*1997, 1998*]; Kaminsky and Reinhart [*1996*]; Lindgren, Garcia and Saal [*1996*].

Part III
Regional Experience of Instability

[15]

The Levy Economics Institute of Bard College

Policy Note   2002/2

The Brazilian Swindle and The Larger International Monetary Problem

James K. Galbraith

The postwar liberal trading framework has become hopelessly distorted during the past two decades by the hegemony of the U.S. dollar, high interest rates, debt deflation, and capital flight; the asymmetries of a world so structured are proving intolerable. The economist John Maynard Keynes recognized this issue with characteristic clarity in the design of the Bretton Woods institutions--the World Bank and International Monetary Fund--in 1944. Keynes favored free markets and liberal trading arrangements insofar as they could be made to work, but he was also well aware that free markets are inherently unstable and prone to collapse. Keynes also understood that the characteristic structure of unregulated international finance placed bankers and creditors in the dominant position, and so would inevitably force adjustment by debtors. But what was locally rational in a financial transaction would prove disastrous for the system as a whole. As individual debtors contracted their economies in order to meet their interest payments, their demand for imports would diminish, and so would the exports of their suppliers. The entire economic system would contract, and in the end no one would be further forward in their ability to pay their debts.

THE INTERNATIONAL MONETARY FUND (IMF) has offered Brazil a $30 billion loan, most of it reserved for next year, on condition that the country continue to run a large primary surplus in the government budget. In this way the IMF maintains a strong arm over Brazil's next government, almost surely to be drawn from the left. Any significant move toward fiscal expansion would trigger revocation of the promised loan, followed by capital market chaos. Or so one is led to suppose.

Right now, Brazil is in the grip of recession. With declining demand for imports, the country has a surplus in its trade account (outflows less inflows of goods and services). It has, nevertheless, a substantial deficit in its current account (outflows less inflows of financial assets), most of which must be interest payments on external debts. These outflows are offset by capital inflows, which are not, however, mainly new investments--currently low, owing to the depressed state of internal demand--but operating loans to existing businesses and the sale of existing national assets to foreigners. In short, Brazil's external balance today is a matter of mortgaging or selling property to pay interest, meanwhile hoping that things will somehow get better.

The IMF's requirement that Brazil maintain a primary budget surplus amounts to a prohibition against fighting recession by increasing domestic demand, an action that would raise domestic investment and move the trade balance back into deficit (and the current account even more so), which in turn would require that foreign investors be found who are actually willing to bankroll new activity. Of course, such investors do not exist. If they did, the IMF would not be in the picture.

Conversely, the pressure to maintain a trade surplus is a device for balancing the existing willingness of foreigners to buy Brazilian assets against the existing burden of debt service. In part because of the political climate, that willingness is eroding more rapidly than Brazil can manage by shrinking real activity and curtailing imports. Panic therefore threatens from day to day. The short-run purpose of the loan is merely to shift the *timing* of panic so that it occurs under the new government instead of the old. A report in the *New York Times* on August 21, 2002, makes this clear:

> American and European banks have all been scaling back their lending to Brazilian exporters and manufacturers in the last six months. Most are refusing to comment on their willingness to jump back into that market on the heels of the fund's big loan deal.

Hence the loan represents no new money that would benefit Brazilians, except to the extent that wealthy Brazilian nationals also transfer their assets abroad, and that locals purchase durable imports while they can.

In the medium term, if the new government respects the conditions of the loan, the effect must be to finance a continuing reduction in private capital inflows, substituting debt to the IMF for exposure to private external investors while maintaining external debt payments to satisfy older creditors. It is probably not accidental that the net IMF loan for next year is roughly the same size as the present surplus on the capital account.

Nothing here holds out any hope that Brazil's high indebtedness and interest obligations can be reduced. There is no amortization plan. Therefore, unless something does turn up (for instance, massive price increases for orange juice and coffee, which are not very likely), the outlook is for another IMF loan, and another, and another, into the indefinite future, until the private foreign sector is safely divested of its Brazilian holdings.

There is also nothing in the loan that holds out the prospect for economic progress in Brazil itself. Neither increased public spending nor increased imports can be financed from it. Hence the loan represents no new money that would benefit Brazilians, except to the extent that wealthy Brazilian nationals also transfer their assets abroad, and that locals purchase durable imports while they can. It is a standstill, not a progressive package, whose purpose is to keep the wheels of finance spinning, aimlessly, on the Brazilian beach.

The IMF promises, in effect, to help maintain an illusion of business as usual, during which interval the new government can occupy its offices in Brasilia and enjoy the perquisites of power, but *only so long as* no actual changes of policy are made.

Who benefits? In the first place, private holders of Brazilian assets, who have an opportunity to escape before a severe devaluation. In the second place, foreign bankers, whose loans will receive interest longer than would otherwise be the case. And in the third place, domestic political forces inside Brazil that oppose growth in public services and social reform.

What is *not* clear is why a Brazilian government of the left, elected with a mandate to rule in the interest of the working population, should sacrifice its freedom of maneuver to these interests. It would be one thing if the loan held out a prospect of an early return to net new borrowing in support of state policy and private activity, but this is not the case. Instead, the loan is more properly thought of as a form of blackmail. The IMF promises, in effect, to help maintain an illusion of business as usual, during which interval the new government can occupy its offices in Brasilia and enjoy the perquisites of power, but *only so long* as no actual changes of policy are made. The threatened alternative, if the terms are broken, is financial chaos, no doubt accompanied by concerted efforts to destabilize the new regime.

In particular, has Luiz Inacio Lula da Silva worked for so many decades to build the Workers Party only to govern on such diminished terms? Or is he prepared seriously to consider an alternative strategy? If so, of what should it consist? And although disapproval by the U.S. government is a foregone conclusion, what should be the attitude of the people of the United States to such an alternative approach?

The Myth of "Sound" Financial Policies

Brazil is a large, resource-rich, industrialized developing country with a history of interventionist policies in several industrial areas, including aerospace, computers, and energy. It is the economic center of gravity in Latin America. The country's notorious flaw lies in income and wealth inequalities higher than virtually anywhere on earth, and a ruling elite very much aligned with the sectarian interests of the wealthy. A weak regulatory regime persists, particularly with respect to newly privatized sectors. Taxes have never been raised sufficiently to finance satisfactory mass urbanization, and the country's vast national resources have not been protected or developed in a sustainable fashion. Capital, moreover, has been free to take flight whenever policy threatened to move in these directions.

A case could once have been made for capital market openness in Brazil on the grounds that the country was short of capital resources and that these could only be acquired abroad. But that case was valid for the extremely short period between 1973, when the old Bretton Woods institutions were dismantled, and 1982, when the resulting explosion of private debt culminated in economic collapse. During the oil shocks, Brazil did manage to finance growth and its import bill from abroad, but of course it could not do so on a sustainable basis. Since then, Brazil and the rest of Latin America have labored under the dead hand of past debt, unpayable except by selling off existing capital assets. There is no serious case to be made that airlines, roads, power grids, and telecommunications networks actually function better under foreign ownership. At present the entire case for privatization is financial: it raises resources to permit the continued servicing of past debt.

There is no serious case that airlines, roads, power grids, and telecommunications networks actually function better under foreign ownership. At present the entire case for privatization is financial: it raises resources to permit the continued servicing of past debt.

For what purpose? The rationalizing argument behind current IMF programs is that countries that follow "sound" financial policies--balanced budgets, tight money, deregulation, and privatization of capital assets--will be rewarded with a stamp of creditworthiness. They should then benefit by being able to borrow from private capital markets on favorable terms, relative to their own histories and the record of countries who are less responsible. In principle this should mean they can run deficits on their trade accounts, loan-finance the purchase of capital goods imports to support development, and maintain high levels of economic growth and job creation. They should be able to do all of this and still attract inflows of direct foreign capital investment.

It has been clear for several decades, however, that this argument is a myth, that the promised land it envisions is a mirage. If it were not, would Brazil be able to complain? The country has a trade surplus and a primary surplus on the government budget. The only source of deficits in both accounts relates to the payment of interest on past debt. To run a surplus on the current account--reducing imports by another $20 billion or so--would require massive further deflation of the real Brazilian economy. This would destroy the tax base and greatly worsen the public budget. Thus, there is no way to improve Brazil's accounts from their current position, short of an export boom--which depends on external demand, over which Brazil has no control--or a write-down of past debt. But of course the very purpose of Wall Street's interest in Brazil is to be paid as much as possible for the past loans.

The Brazilian particulars illustrate a general point. The running of "sound" policies does not translate into favorable treatment on Wall Street. Instead, private investor judgments are driven largely by considerations over which national policies in developing countries have no influence at all. Most notably, these considerations include conditions in other developing countries and in the United States.

The rationalizing argument behind current IMF programs is that countries that follow "sound" financial policies-balanced budgets, tight money, deregulation, and privatization of capital assets-will be rewarded with a stamp of creditworthiness. It has been clear for several decades, however, that this argument is a myth, that the promised land it envisions is a mirage.

Conditions in other developing countries periodically affect Brazil through contagion in financial markets. Upheaval and financial crisis in Russia in 1998 directly affected the risk exposure of many emerging markets funds. Forced to account for the rising risk in Russia, they reacted by reducing exposure in other "risky" markets, such as Brazil, even though there was no connection between the Brazilian and Russian economies at that time. Similarly, contagion from Argentina--itself only recently a "model country" from the standpoint of the IMF--is affecting Brazil now. Brazil is being punished by the financial markets because of the failure of the IMF's sound-money prescriptions as they were applied in Argentina--even though Brazil did not follow the Argentine road of full acquiescence to the IMF's neoliberal schemes. The irony is, well, Latin American.

U.S. policies and internal conditions affect Brazil through their influence on relative rates of return facing investors. In the late 1990s, with a "flight to quality" compounded by the bubble mentality of the technology sectors, capital flowed into the United States and away from developing economies such as Brazil. Now that the bubble has collapsed, so has the appetite for emerging-country risk, and perhaps also the capacity to purchase Brazilian assets. This too is beyond Brazilian control.

It follows that the only route available to Brazilian policymakers *acting on their own* to restore growth and expand public goods and services in the short run must involve a reduction of debt payments. The easiest way to achieve this is straightforwardly to cut back on payments while imposing strict controls over capital flight. Alongside these measures, the real would be devalued, and interest rates reduced to accommodate both exporters and import substitution. This is the model followed by Russia in 1998, and the result was, in fact, a modest revival of domestic production after a terrible crash. Since that time, the crisis in Russia has eased, even though the vast damage done since the advent of shock therapy has not been overcome.

The case against a policy of debt reduction comes in two parts. One is specious, but the other must be taken more seriously. The specious argument holds that capital markets will punish Brazil for its defiance. The difficulty with this argument is straightforward: Brazil presently enjoys no benefit from its participation in world capital markets. Even the IMF package serves, from the standpoint of ordinary Brazilians, merely to keep up appearances. It is self-evident that to interrupt the recycling of IMF loans into debt service would change nothing in real terms, while the effective imposition of capital controls--if technically possible in Brazil's case--would slow the exit of private investors, and so the decline of domestic asset prices. It does no harm to a bankrupt entity to declare bankruptcy. The main effect is to halt the outflow of inside money. Although affected investors obviously do not welcome this sudden loss of freedom, there is no moral or ethical basis on which they can claim a greater "right to escape" than that of ordinary workers and other citizens to whom the market grants no such opportunities.

The more serious objection is that Brazil's internal political stability may be threatened by a policy undertaken in the national interest. This is the danger of subversion from the outside. The interests of international finance protect themselves by the means at their disposal. There is a long history of this in Latin America, including Brazil in 1964 and extending to present-day Venezuela, where the complicity of the U.S. State Department and doubtless other services in recent and continuing events is clear. In the Russian case, such risks are much smaller because the government rests on the bedrock of its security services, whose defects are well-known but whose loyalties do not seem to be in question. How well a new Brazilian government may be able to meet this danger is a matter of internal politics on which a distant observer cannot speak with any authority. But it is there--in the "crisis of confidence"--and not in the supposed power of a market that the true danger lies.

The running of "sound" policies does not translate into favorable treatment on Wall Street. Private investor judgments are driven largely by considerations over which national policies in developing countries have no influence at all.

Is There a Better Way?

Is there a better way, for Brazil and the world, than a complete rupture between countries in the North and South on financial matters? And are the national interests of the United States absolutely congruent with those of our leading financiers, so that policy with respect to international development can be safely left to their judgment and in their hands? Or is it possible that, to borrow a phrase, another world is possible after all?

Surely it has to be. The liberal economic vision--with multilateral clearing, relatively free and open trade, easy flow of technology, travel, migration, and human learning--has a core of virtues. It has helped to create a far more open and attractive world, in many important respects, than could ever have been achieved under the previous regimes of colonialism and empire. The world is today safer from global war than it was in the first half of the last century. Trade and peace do go hand in hand--most of the time. There are reasons why the enduring success of such a system remains an ideal for many intelligent and well-meaning people.

Particularly over the past two decades, the postwar trading framework has become hopelessly distorted by the hegemony of the U.S. dollar, unsustainably high interest rates, debt deflation, and capital flight. The asymmetries of a world so structured are intolerable.

At the same time, however, the world we inhabit fails to rise to the standard set by the liberal ideal. Particularly over the past two decades, the postwar trading framework has become hopelessly distorted by the hegemony of the U.S. dollar, unsustainably high interest rates, debt deflation, and capital flight. The asymmetries of a world so structured are intolerable, as they lead to unprecedented prosperity in the rich countries and deepening crisis for the poor. It is a minor miracle that they have not long since led to a full-scale revolt against U.S. global leadership. But the fact is, such a revolt may not be very far off. There already exists widespread rejection of American world leadership by the populations of developing countries worldwide, and the reputation once enjoyed by the United States as a pillar of multilateral order, having respect for differences and fair play, has long since been squandered. This cannot fail to translate into political terms sooner or later.

The British economist John Maynard Keynes had already recognized this issue with his characteristic clarity in the design of the Bretton Woods institutions--the World Bank and the IMF--in 1944. Keynes, as the third volume of Robert Skidelsky's biography makes especially clear, was an economic and a political liberal. He favored free markets and liberal trading arrangements insofar as they could be made to work. But he also had not forgotten the fact, which the Depression had driven home to all observers, that free markets are inherently unstable and prone to collapse.

Keynes understood that the characteristic structure of unregulated international finance placed bankers and creditors in the dominant position, and so worked to force adjustment by debtors. This was locally rational in financial transactions, but disastrous for the system as a whole. Individual debtors would be forced to contract their economies in order to meet their interest payments. Their demand for imports would diminish, and so would the exports of their suppliers. In the end, the entire economic system would contract, and no nation would be further forward in its ability to pay its debts.

The purpose of the Bretton Woods institutions, in Keynes's plan, was to evade this trap. The substantial mechanism was to be a multilateral clearing union, with authority to issue overdrafts to debtors--in effect, to print international money. Under Keynes's scheme, it would be creditors who would have to adjust by expanding their domestic economies, their employment, and their absorption of imports until their consumption of imports rose to match their sale of exports. Otherwise, creditors would face legitimate discrimination against their exports. In this way, the system would balance at high levels of employment (and the principal economic risk, of course, would be international inflation rather than global slump). No member country would, in Keynes's vision, be required to contract domestic economic activity and forgo full employment simply in order to meet international clearing obligations or pay debt service to foreigners.

Keynes did not get his way in the negotiations. The American side, led by Harry Dexter White, insisted on a system dominated by lender interests. As a result, the Bretton Woods institutions contributed almost nothing to postwar reconstruction until calamity threatened in 1948 and the Marshall Plan was put in place to avert it. After that, development largely proceeded under the impetus of cold and hot wars; one in Korea, which jump-started the recovery of Japan, and one in Vietnam, which provided a similar service for Korea and much of southern Asia.

The IMF began developing its modern regimens of debtor adjustment--devaluation plus deflation--for imposition in Europe in the late 1960s. There followed a brief moment, in the aftermath of the oil shock of 1973-74, when the IMF might have emerged as the principal conduit for the recycling of petrodollars to the oil-importing countries of the developing world, but the Nixon administration blocked this. Instead, the job of financing development was turned back to the major commercial banks, along with their European and Japanese colleagues. They made the necessary loans on commercial terms and at variable interest rates keyed to the London Interbank Offer Rate (LIBOR). Development from that point forward was to proceed on commercial terms and "free market" principles, at interest rates determined after the fact by the monetary authorities of the United States.

These arrangements were doomed from the beginning. They collapsed even sooner than they might have otherwise, when Paul A. Volcker and the Federal Reserve pushed American interest rates past 20 percent in their 1981 campaign against inflation. The result was a global crisis of debt, insolvency, and perpetual debtor adjustment that afflicts the entire developing world (except for India, China, and a handful of south Asian city-states) to this day.

The original authors of the IMF and World Bank generally supposed that the United States would remain in its immediate postwar position as a strong surplus country and creditor to the rest of the world. Thus dollars could be "scarce" and, if they were, international liquidity would have to be issued in some other medium. This rather soon proved to be a colossal misjudgment. Instead, the United States went into deficit and eventually became the world's largest debtor. The world became so awash in dollars that the proposed international unit of account--originally the bancor and in its etiolated modern form, the Special Drawing Right--faded into insignificance. Today, the dollar is the world's reserve currency, and the international position of the United States depends on this.

So long as the world is willing to take and hold U.S. assets, including liquid dollars, this system works--and shamefully to the interest of Americans. The resulting high value of the dollar means that we consume comfortably, and in exchange for very little effort, the products of hard labor by poor people. We live on the interest skimmed from the meager living available to factory workers in São Paulo, in exchange for providing otherwise unavailable liquidity to the world system. (Our situation is akin to that of, say, Australia in the late 19th century when gold fields were discovered, except that, in our case, no actual effort is required to extract the gold.) And meanwhile, we are not obliged to invest unduly in maintaining our own industrial base, which has substantially eroded since the 1970s. We could afford to splurge on new technologies and telecommunications systems whose benefits were, to a very great extent, figments of the imagination. And even when the bubble burst in those sectors, life went on, for most Americans, substantially undisturbed--at least for now.

> The original authors of the IMF and World Bank generally supposed that the United States would remain in its immediate postwar position as a strong surplus country and creditor to the rest of the world. This rather soon proved to be a colossal misjudgment.

But for how long will the system of dollar hegemony endure? There can be no definitive answer; the few economists who have worried about this issue are far from being in agreement. On one side, it is argued that the dominant currency holds a "lock-in advantage"; that is, there are economies associated with keeping all reserves in one basket. The United States in particular is in a strong position to oblige foreign central banks to absorb the dollars that private parties may not wish to hold, at least within elastic limits. Control of oil by U.S. allies and satellites will require other importers to buy dollars in order to buy oil, though it is not obvious that such control requires anyone to hold those dollars very long, except as a hedge against price increases or home-currency devaluations.

Against this, the question remains: Will foreigners be willing to add to their holdings of U.S. assets at a rate consistent with the U.S. current account deficit at full employment? The amount to be absorbed is in the range of half a trillion dollars per year. This was easily handled when asset prices were rising, but now that they are falling, dollar assets are not as safe as they once were. If foreigners are not willing to absorb them at the requisite rate, and if asset prices do not quickly fall to the point where stocks appear cheap, dollar dumping is, sooner or later, inevitable. Otherwise, the United States must slow the rate at which liquidity is issued by restricting its imports, which it can only do by holding down economic growth and keeping incomes well below the full-employment level. In that situation--which may already have arrived--the United States joins Brazil and other developing nations as a country effectively constrained by its debts. Indeed, the world prognosis from that point forward becomes grim, since high levels of American demand have been just about the only motor of growth and development (outside, perhaps, of China and India) in recent years.

The United States as a Debtor Nation

There are economists who advocate dollar devaluation, believing that the richer countries of the world would quickly rally to purchase increasing quantities of made-in-America exports, thus reversing the manufacturing decline of the past 20 years. But this is very unlikely. Exports to the rich regions may not be very price-sensitive.

This "elasticity pessimism" and the specter of financial vulnerability mean that for the United States, the combination of falling internal demand, falling asset prices, and a falling dollar represents a threat that can best be described as millennial.

And exports to the developing regions are very sensitive to income and credit conditions, which would get worse. At least in the short and medium term, there is no foolproof adjustment process to be had by these means. Where a high dollar provides U.S. consumers with cheap imports and capital inflows to finance domestic activity, a falling dollar would have opposite effects. A falling dollar would raise the price of imports into the United States, especially from the richer countries. Meanwhile, a declining dollar would hit at the value of developing countries' reserves, and so work, on that account, to diminish their demand for our exports. The most likely outcome from a dollar devaluation is therefore a general deepening of the world slump, combined with pressure on American financial institutions as global investors seek safer havens in Europe.

This "elasticity pessimism" (very much shared by Keynes in his day) and the specter of financial vulnerability mean that for the United States, the combination of falling internal demand, falling asset prices, and a falling dollar represents a threat that can best be described as millennial. (My colleague Randall Wray has called it the "perfect fiscal storm.") The consequences at home would include deepening unemployment. There would be little recovery of privately financed investment, amid a continued unraveling of plans--both corporate and personal--that had been based on the delirious stock market valuations of the late 1990s. The center of the world banking industry would move, presumably to continental Europe. Over time, the United States could lose both its position as the principal world beneficiary of the financial order and its margin of maneuver on the domestic scene. This would be not unlike what happened to the United Kingdom from 1914 to 1950.

It is not obvious that senior financial policymakers in the United States have yet grasped this threat, or that there is any serious planning under way to cope with it--apart from a simpleminded view among certain strategic thinkers about the financial advantages of the control of oil. Instead it appears that the responsible officials are confining themselves to a very narrow range of debt management proposals, whose premises minimize the gravity of the issue and whose purpose is to keep the existing bonds of debt peonage in place as long as possible.

A paper issued this year by the Derivatives Study Center, a Washington-based study group, outlines three major proposals for dealing with the problems of sovereign debt. One of these is the work of Anne Krueger of the IMF; the second, Treasury Undersecretary John B. Taylor; and a third, a group of private economists associated with the global debt relief campaign headed by Kunibert Raffer.

The IMF and Taylor proposals provide alternative ways of addressing a very narrow issue in debt negotiations, namely the incentive for renegade creditors to resist a write-down of their own assets and so to hold out for full payment. This is a classic free-rider issue, since the possibility of paying off any one creditor at face value rises as other creditors accept smaller payments. The IMF would deal with this problem via a new formal restructuring mechanism that would bind all creditors to terms acceptable to a majority. The Taylor proposal would accomplish much the same thing (though in a much more distant future) by providing that new debt contracts carry a collective action clause permitting the will of the majority of creditors to bind the entire group.

Neither the IMF nor the Taylor proposal addresses the systemic problem of excess and unpayable debt. Their thrust is merely to prolong the present prebankruptcy stage of financial relations for as long as possible--shaving and stretching out debt repayments so as to match the ability to pay to the willingness of foreign capital to acquire developing-country assets through liberalization and privatization. In this way, they implicitly assume what has already proven to be impossible, namely, that private capital markets will eventually produce "development" to which poor countries aspire. Nothing in either protocol would protect the populations or the public programs of any developing country.

The Raffer proposal makes an effort along these lines by proposing the creation of an international adjustment mechanism akin to the municipal bankruptcy proceedings available under Chapter 9 of the U.S. bankruptcy code. This proposal for "restructuring with a human face" would give citizens of debtor countries a legal right to be heard in debt negotiations, and so would permit countries to protect some of their social services and core infrastructure investments from disruption in the restructuring process. This proposal has an undoubted claim to enlightened sympathy, and would very materially ease the burdens of adjustment on poor countries in debt restructurings. But no more than the other proposals does it address the larger problem facing the world economy today, namely, the breakdown of a functional finance in support of the development process.

But *if,* as a result of a widespread diversification away from the dollar as a reserve asset, the United States runs a risk within, say, a decade or two, of joining those countries for whom the discipline of the international monetary order means continuous debtor adjustment, a new element will enter the picture. It would become part of the national interest of the United States, if not necessarily that of its financial industry, to collaborate in the reconstruction of a global order that serves the interests of debtors at least as well as creditors. It will become the American interest to switch sides in the debt wars and join forces with the developing countries whose interests lie in rebuilding a multilateral international monetary structure, thus providing a safe path to the orderly liquidation of the dollar overhang and the restoration of autonomy to growth-oriented national development policies.

What would this mean in practice? In broad terms, it would mean that the negotiations antecedent to Bretton Woods, so admirably recounted by Skidelsky, would have to be recreated. But this time, the United States would have to take the role that Britain, anxious to protect its national autonomy in difficult financial conditions, took in 1944. (In that environment, Britain spoke for all the habitually indebted nations of the world in favor of a global order that would force creditors to bear the burden of adjustment.) The role played by the United States would be taken by the world's emerging creditor power, the European Union.

There is every good reason to think that the outcome of such a revisited negotiation would be more favorable to the world's beleaguered debtors than was the case in 1944. The United States remains today a dominant diplomatic and military force, which the European Union is not. And the U.S. economy is far more globalized, with more natural links of trade and investment to the developing countries, than are the Europeans. Should the United States one day switch sides in the global financial struggles, remarkable things might happen in a fairly short time.

Such a change is difficult to imagine today. The political processes of the United States would first have to be thoroughly overhauled--the money changers once again would have to flee their positions in the temple. But circumstances have a way of dictating political position, sooner or later. It has only been a bit more than a century since the U.S. did in fact stand as the world's premier representative of debtor nations. It was only some 70 years ago that Franklin Roosevelt inaugurated the Good Neighbor Policy, acknowledging the sovereign right of Latin American countries to escape from the burden of unpayable debts. It may not take that long before we come full circle once again, if motivated by practical necessity in the pursuit of full employment. Perhaps the oncoming clash between Brazil's people and the global financial order will help motivate ordinary Americans to rethink on which side we should now stand.

References

Andrews, Edmund L. 2002. "Fears That Lending to Brazil May Dry Up." *New York Times,* August 21: C2.

Derivatives Study Center. 2002. *Sovereign Debt Restructuring.* Primer. Washington, D.C.: Derivatives Study Center, Economic Strategy Institute. www.econstrat.org/dsc%20sovdebt.htm

Krueger, Anne O. 2002. *A New Approach to Sovereign Debt Restructuring.* Washington, D.C.: International Monetary Fund. http://www.imf.org/external/pubs/ft/exrp/sdrm/eng/index.htm

Raffer, Kunibert. 1990. "Applying Chapter 9 Insolvency to International Debts: An Economically Efficient Solution with a Human Face." *World Development* 18:2: 301-311.

------. 2002. "Shopping for Jurisdictions--A Problem for International Chapter 9 Insolvency?" http://www.jubileeplus.org/analysis/articles/vultures_raffer.htm

Skidelsky, Robert. 2000. *John Maynard Keynes: Fighting for Britain* 1937-1946. Volume 3. London: Macmillan.

Taylor, John B. 2002. "Sovereign Debt Restructuring: A U.S. Perspective." Speech at the International Economics Conference on Sovereign Debt Workouts: Hopes and Hazards, Washington, D.C., April 2. http://www.ustreas.gov/press/releases/po2056.htm

Wray, L. Randall. 2002. "A Perfect Fiscal Storm." http://www.warrenmosler.com/docs/docs/perfect_fiscal_storm.htm

SENIOR SCHOLAR JAMES K. GALBRAITH is Lloyd M. Bentsen Jr. Professor of Government/Business Relations at the Lyndon B. Johnson School of Public Affairs, University of Texas at Austin. He extends his thanks to Dean Baker, Paul Davidson, Tom Ferguson, Steve Magee, and Wynne Godley for widely divergent but very helpful comments on an earlier draft.

[16]

On drawing general policy lessons from recent Latin American currency crises

The Bretton Woods Accords, reflecting the then ruling economic orthodoxy, were devised around the basic thesis that free international capital
mobility is incompatible with the preservation of reasonably free multilateral trade and full employment. Accordingly, capital controls were
enshrined in the Articles of Agreement of the IMF. The displacement
of the Bretton Woods adjustable peg exchange rates in the 1970s by
floating rates, however, has been paralleled by the displacement of the
old orthodoxy by a new one that holds that free capital mobility is
essential for the full realization of the welfare benefits from free multilateral trade and investment. Liberalized and globalized financial markets would reduce the cost of capital globally, deter mercantilistic power
plays by strong economies at the expense of weaker ones, and curb
domestic policies that distort relative factor prices or overheat the
economy.

This paper, however, argues that the Bretton Woods incompatibility
thesis remains valid. It builds its case by first showing that asymmetrical
power plays have continued under market liberalization, using the two
recent Latin American currency crises to make the point. It then dissects
the competing theoretical premises about financial market efficiency
that distinguish the two orthodoxies. This is followed by a presentation
of salient trends of the G–7 economies that suggest adverse interactions
between financial and real economy globalization. It concludes with
some policy inferences for both G–7 and developing economies. Given
the time constraints, all this is undertaken with "desperate brevity," to
use one of Schumpeter's favorite phrases.

The author is Emeritus Professor of Economics at Washington University in St.
Louis, Missouri. This paper was originally presented to the Twelfth Conference of
the Latin American Association of Faculties, Institutes and Schools of Economics
(AFEIEAL), October 14–16, 1996.

Journal of Post Keynesian Economics / Winter 1997–98, Vol. 20, No. 2   191
© 1998 M.E. Sharpe, Inc.
0160–3477 / 1998 $9.50 + 0.00.

**Mercantilistic crisis management by the G–7:
the Mexican and Cono Sur cases**

Ex-post assessments of Mexico's recent foreign exchange crisis by the
G–7, the Bretton Woods institutions, and other centers of economic
orthodoxy have been notably asymmetrical. Mexico has been fingered
as the chief culprit, its flawed economic performance finally causing
international financial markets to downgrade Mexico's creditworthiness. The prime victims were the portfolio investors; the Mexican
government had led them to overinvest by holding back data on the
fragile state of the economy until a belated accumulation of adverse data
tipped the balance toward downgrading and capital flight. A centerpiece
of the G–7 measures for avoiding future runs by international portfolio
investors has been, therefore, to authorize the IMF to establish a Special
Data Dissemination Standard,

> which offers countries having, or seeking, access to international capital
> markets, a voluntary means of providing regular, timely, and compre-
> hensive economic data. A key feature of the implementation . . . will be
> an electronic bulletin board maintained by the IMF at a World Wide Web
> site on the Internet. [*IMF Survey*, September 9, 1996, p. 290]

The orthodox *ex-post* assessments of the Cono Sur debt crisis of the
early 1980s were also asymmetrical (Devlin, 1989; Felix, 1994). They
singled out for criticism overvalued exchange rates and inadequate
prudential supervision of the Cono Sur banking system, but not loan
pushing by the international creditor banks that had encouraged overborrowing, or their back-to-back lending and tax avoiding instrumen-
talities that had facilitated the subsequent capital flight.

The asymmetry extends to post-crisis burden sharing. The effort of
Tesebono investors to liquidate their holdings and move into dollars,
which largely fueled the capital flight that led to Mexico's December
1994 crisis, had little to do with imminent default, since the Tesebonos,
although indexed to the dollar exchange rate, were merely peso-denominated. Mexico could therefore have limited access to the Banco
Central's foreign exchange window for capital flight while still fully
meeting its payment commitments to Tesebono holders. Indeed, Article
6 of the IMF Articles of Agreement authorizes it to do just that, as it also
authorizes the IMF to provide emergency credits only when not used to
facilitate capital flight.

The reverse, of course, happened. To dissuade Mexico from resorting to capital controls, Washington hastily cobbled together $51 billion of emergency credits, conditional on Mexico abjuring capital controls and committing itself to use only monetary and fiscal tightening to check the peso's fall. The arrangement converted Tesebonos into *de facto* dollar obligations of the government, enabling its holders to liquidate without loss. More important for Washington, the arrangement averted the threat that other developing countries under stress might follow Mexico's example, reversing the global trend toward free capital mobility and the integration of financial markets. Mexico's reward for playing the good soldier has been a sizeable increase of its foreign debt, a massive domestic banking crisis, and a deep depression from which, notwithstanding its recent reaccess to international financial markets, full recovery is likely to be years away.

A comparable asymmetry of burden sharing occurred during the 1980s Latin American debt crisis. The "concerted" lending packages of the creditor governments, lending banks, and Bretton Woods institutions to keep the debtor countries from defaulting were made contingent on the debtor governments guaranteeing *ex post* the foreign bank debts of their private firms. Ironically, the added monetary and fiscal burden of the *ex-post* guarantees fell heaviest on the Cono Sur economies. Having abolished most of their capital controls, they had wound up with predominantly unguaranteed private foreign debt when the debt crisis broke.

Although the lending banks had insisted on the *ex-post* guarantees as a precondition for contributing to the "concerted" loan packages, the creditor governments could have refused, telling the banks to take instead the customary recourse of doing workouts with their delinquent private debtors. But that was judged too risky for the international banking system. Some of the major U.S. and British lending banks had so overlent to Latin America that major writedowns of their private loans would have wiped out their equity capital and, via a panicky withdrawal of interbank deposits by other banks, might have elevated the debt crisis to a global banking crisis. The creditor governments could, of course, have assumed the monetary-fiscal burden of preventing that trajectory but found it politically easier to force it on the weakened debtor governments.

In each of the above cases there was also a major disconnect between the orthodox post-crisis and pre-crisis assessments of the same phenomena. In the Cono Sur case, the *tablita cambiaria* stratagem of disinflating by preannouncing a series of diminishing devaluations was assessed positively before the crisis, although it was producing real exchange rate appreciation in the Cono Sur countries. Only after the crisis was the strategem blamed for badly overvaluing the exchange rate. Prior to the crisis, the financing of rising current account deficits with rapidly increasing private foreign debt was not judged a cause for concern. As Walter Robichek, then Western Hemisphere Director of the IMF, reassured a 1980 Chilean seminar, "private firms can be expected to be careful in assessing the net return to be derived from borrowing funds as compared with the net cost, since their survival as an enterprise is at stake" (cited in Diaz-Alejandro, 1985). And the declining private saving rates accompanying the rising current account deficits were viewed as exemplifying welfare gains from market liberalization rather than an unviable consumption boom. It was only after the crises broke that these same trends were reappraised as crucial flaws.

Prior to its recent crisis, similar economic trends in Mexico were also viewed benignly. The Robichek Doctrine, refurbished as the Lawson Doctrine, helped rationalize an increasingly overvalued peso, rising current account deficit, declining private savings rate, and increasing private foreign indebtedness. As enunciated by Tony Lawson, Margaret Thatcher's Chancellor of the Exchequer, the doctrine held that countries that pursued free-market policies and balanced their fiscal budgets could always finance their current account deficits in the globalized financial markets. Thus, market-liberalizing Mexico, having eliminated its structural fiscal deficit, would remain a good credit risk unless its budgets slipped back into deficit.

The Lawson Doctrine held sway in Mexican and Wall Street financial circles right up to the cusp of the crisis. However, Washington financial circles defected earlier. By 1994, the U.S. Treasury, Federal Reserve, and, less firmly, the IMF and World Bank had become convinced that the Cono Sur–like trends in the Mexican economy needed checking, and began privately pressuring the Salinas government, albeit unsuccessfully, to do a corrective devaluation and tighten credit. Publicly, however, the Washington institutions continued to laud Mexico as a free-market success and exemplar to other developing countries. Asked after the crisis broke why they hadn't publicized their concerns, senior executives of the institutions responded that it would only have panicked the financial markets and precipitated the crisis earlier (U.S. General Accounting Office, 1996; Wessel, Carroll, and Vogel, 1995).

This puts a different spin on the the G–7's solution of the information problem. The Mexican trends that led the Washington institutions to defect from the Lawson Doctrine were quite visible to all, including foreign portfolio investors. But the investors suffered from cognitive dissonance, a disconnect between facts and preconceptions, which led them to draw false inferences from the facts. The Washington institutions had shared a similar disconnect right up to the crisis in the Cono Sur case. But this time they reacted to the adverse evidence by revising their preconceptions before the crisis broke. It was not the Mexican government, therefore, but the Washington institutions that had kept their reassessment hidden while engaging publicly in deceitful doublespeak, that bear the most guilt for misleading the financial markets. That they did so out of awareness that financial markets are prone to herd behavior and would have panicked casts doubt on the seriousness of the G–7's information solution for averting future crises. Is there much reason to think that providing timely pessimistic alerts over the World Wide Web will avert herd-like market reactions, or that they will even dare to circulate such pre-crisis alerts?

These asymmetries and doublespeak are manifestations of a basic dilemma now haunting G–7 macroeconomic policy making. Should globalization of financial markets be further encouraged by removing the remaining policy barriers to international capital mobility—the post–Bretton Woods orthodox position—or should it be restrained by strengthening the barriers, which harks back to the Bretton Woods incompatibility thesis?

On the theoretical issues

The economic case for maximizing free capital mobility relies on a strong macro version of the efficient market hypothesis. It holds that financial markets continually generate asset prices that—given currently available information about the fundamental determinants—are best estimates of the present values of the future income streams from capital assets. The incompleteness of information about the future introduces "white noise" errors in asset prices, which the markets, however, self-correct in accordance with excess demand market signals. The self-correction also squeezes out "noise traders" who, by speculating on asset price movements instead of evaluating assets on the basis of fundamentals, push prices away from equilibrium. This merely creates openings for rational traders who, knowing in which direction equilibrium lies, profit by taking countervailing positions at the expense of the noise traders.

Exogenous supply "shocks," primarily due to technological and structural change, and demand "shocks," primarily due to "policy surprises," alter fundamentals and therefore asset prices. But while supply shocks tend to be unavoidable, demand shocks can be minimized by policy approaches that focus on providing a stable legal framework for private markets and facilitating general access to information about fundamentals, but eschew "policy surprises," that is, efforts to block financial flows, alter fundamentals, or control asset prices.

This is the basic thesis embedded in the Robichek and Lawson Doctrines, and in the asymmetric allocation of blame after the currency crises. It also rationalized the asymmetric burden sharing as a "tough love" administering of short-term pain, for which the debtor economies would be amply compensated by long-run welfare gains from rescuing the financial globalization process. The *optimum optimorum* toward which the process was allegedly headed is a complete integration of national financial markets, with arbitraging financial flows unifying real interest rates and asset valuations across currencies, and worldwide competition between lenders minimizing the cost of capital, allowing global resource allocation to reach maximum efficiency.

Underpinning the incompatibility thesis of Bretton Woods is the darker Keynesian view of the behavior of financial markets, in which volatility is largely endogenously generated because the bandwagon overbidding and herd-like dumping of financial assets results from rational individual behavior under uncertainty. The fundamentals and their interactions in modern market economies are too complex and changeable over time for probability distributions of future profit trends to be derivable from statistical inference rather than subjective judgment.[1] The supply-side fundamentals that the efficient market hypothesis takes to be the long-term determinants of asset prices—trends in factor supplies and technological change—get deflected or reinforced by variations in the distribution of political and market power that affect the wage share, income distribution, effective demand, profit and risk assessments,

---

[1] This is Keynes as interpreted by Minsky and Post Keynesians (see Minsky, 1975, and the articles in Dymski and Pollin, 1994). The new Keynesians go only halfway. Noise trading generates overshooting, but prices still oscillate around equilibrium asset prices primarily determined by the evolution of factor supplies and technology. For Post Keynesians, that long-run path is merely a special case, attainable only if the aggregate demand and its composition and technological, financial, and wage trends happen to converge on a Golden Age outcome, but with market forces as likely to generate less desirable long run paths (Robinson, 1956).

financing conditions, and the level and composition of real investment. With asset pricing unavoidably shrouded in "Knightian" uncertainty, noise trading, which concentrates on estimating how market traders collectively will react to news about changes in fundamentals rather than how the changes might affect equilibrium asset prices per se, becomes an eminently rational trading strategy.

Moreover, the speculative surges increase the fragility of the banking system. This is because debt leveraging can augment the expected return from financial position taking, while wide swings of asset prices increase liquidity risk for long-term traders, which tends to increase the dominance of short-term market timing over the evaluating of fundamentals. Increased leveraging, market turnover and rising price volatility also weakens the ability of banks and other sources of credit to collateralize their credits effectively, while competition over market share restrains them from aggressively raising risk premia during bull markets. Conversely, pessimistic news hitting overextended financial markets can spark a selling wave and falling prices that may be accelerated by distress selling, settlement defaults, and a drying up of liquidity as banks raise risk premia and cut back credit lines. If the credit crunch extends to production loans, output cutbacks and shrinking aggregate demand will add to the defaulting and further weaken bank balance sheets. Systemic financial crises are thus a recurring threat from these financial dynamics, requiring precautionary constraints on financial trading as a necessary condition for stabilizing the real economy.

This Keynesian perspective applied to international capital markets shaped the Bretton Woods Accords, including the IMF's Articles of Agreement. It legitimized a range of "policy surprises," from counterspeculating forays by central banks, to lender of last resort credits from the IMF and central bank consortia, on up to direct capital controls, as useful policy instruments for keeping hot money flows from destabilizing exchange rates, multilateral trade, and full employment.

Neither view of how rational financial traders behave under uncertainty is, however, a logical corollary of a more basic theory about how market economies function. The efficient market hypothesis does not derive from general equilibrium proofs of the existence, stability, and optimality of laissez-faire economies, since the proofs merely relate to competitive market economies without modern financial markets. That is, they have been unable to incorporate money meaningfully as a store of value and standard for deferred payment. Similarly, Keynesian rationality does not derive from proofs that laissez-faire economies are unstable, but is a premise of such proofs. Each concept of rational behavior is thus an assertion about reality, whose validity depends entirely on how well it fits observable behavior.

In this regard, econometric tests and surveys of actual trading strategies have been destructive of the empirical validity of the efficient market hypothesis.[2] This has been especially so for foreign exchange trading. Professional Forex traders are found to systematically violate efficient market rationality while flourishing by trading strategies that conform to Keynesian rationality. Despite this, the issue is not completely settled. Too much ideological baggage is involved for hard-core believers in the optimality of free markets to yield, rather than to persist in trying to show, Ptolemaic fashion, that by ad-hoc respecification of the information set the negative evidence can be reconciled with the efficient market hypothesis.

That does not help much, however, since efficient markets are compatible with multiple exchange rate equilibria. By gang attacking a currency in equilibrium, rational speculators can make a killing if they can force the authorities to move to a new equilibrium exchange rate. The requisite is awareness by the rational traders that the government's ability to bear the political and economic costs of defending the exchange rate has critically weakened (Obstfeld, 1986). According to a prominent post-mortem analysis of the ERM crisis (Eichengreen and Wyplosz, 1993), the model fits well the cascade of devaluations that in 1992 collapsed the EC's exchange rate mechanism.

Real versus financial trends of the global economy

The incongruity between the phenomenally rapid expansion of international financial flows since the demise of Bretton Woods and the near global retardation of the growth of output, productivity, and the volume of trade provides further support for the incompatibility thesis.

Table 1 shows that global foreign exchange (Forex) turnover, excluding derivative trading, rose from $18.3 billion per day in 1977 to $1.23 trillion ($1.23 \times 10^{12}$) per day in 1995. Adding the market value of Forex options and related derivatives elevates the daily 1995 turnover to about $1.3 trillion. Most of the increase occurred after 1980, when the lifting of capital controls, pioneered by the United States and Canada, spread

---

[2] The test results are described in more detail in Felix (1996b) and in references cited therein.

Table 1
Global official reserves, forex trading, and exports, 1977–95

A. Reserves vs. forex trading volume[a]

	Global official forex reserves (U.S.$ bill.) (1)	Reserves + gold holdings[b] (U.S.$ bill.) (2)	Daily global forex turnover (U.S.$ bill.) (3)	Reserves/daily turnover (days) (1)/(3)	(2)/(3)
1995	1,202.0	1,330.0	1,230.0	1.0	1.1
1992	910.8	1,022.5	820.0	1.1	1.2
1989	722.3	826.8	590.0	1.2	1.4
1986	456.0	552.6	270.0	1.7	2.0
1983	339.7	496.6	119.0[c]	2.8	4.2
1980	386.6	468.9	82.5[c]	4.7	5.7
1977	265.8	296.6	18.3[d]	14.5	16.2

B. Exports vs. reserves and forex trading volume

	Annual world exports (U.S.$ trillions) (4)	Annual global forex volume[e] (U.S.$ trillions) (5)	Forex/exports (%) (5)/(4)	Reserves/exports (%) (1)/(4)	Reserves + gold/exports (%) (2)/(4)
1995	4.80	307.5	6406	25.0	27.9
1992	3.76	205.0	5452	24.2	27.2
1989	2.91	147.5	5068	24.8	28.4
1986	1.99	67.5	3392	20.5	27.8
1983	1.66	29.8	1795	20.5	29.9
1980	1.88	20.6	1096	20.6	24.9
1977	1.31	4.6	351	20.3	22.6

C. Memorandum items	1961–1965	1966–70
1. (Global forex reserves + gold)/exports	43.5%	32.3%
2. (Reserve position with IMF/)exports	3.1	2.8

[a] Net of double reporting of same transactions by intracountry and intercountry counterparties. Excludes trading in options and other derivatives.
[b] Official gold holdings valued at 35 SDRs per ounce.
[c] U.S. volume net only of double reporting of same transactions by domestic counterparties multiplied by 0.17, the average U.S. share of global forex turnover, 1989–1995.
[d] U.S. gross trading volume multiplied by 0.17.
[e] Daily global turnover of column (3) multiplied by 250 trading days.
Source : BIS, 1993, 1996; New York Federal Reserve Bank, 1992; IMF, *International Financial Statistics*, various issues.

to the other OECD countries, facilitating global trading in financial assets. The trading soon attenuated the link between international commodity trade and Forex turnover. Table 1 shows that global forex turnover rose from 3.5 times the value of global exports in 1977 to over 64 times the value of global exports in 1995. Concurrently, the ratio of global official reserves to daily Forex turnover plummeted from fifteen days in 1977 to one day in 1995.

One consequence has been a dramatic weakening of the power of central banks to counterspeculate collectively against unwanted exchange rate movements. A second has been a reversal of the initial decline in the ratio of official reserves to exports. Proponents of floating exchange rates had predicted that an important welfare benefit from floating would be the economizing on foreign exchange reserves, since they would no longer be needed to protect the rates. Table 1 shows, however, that, while the 1977 global reserve ratio was well below that of the 1960s, its subsequent rise has wiped out most of the decline. With the lifting of capital controls, the need to defend against the volatility of international capital flows evidently motivated the reversal. But the plummeting of the reserve/Forex turnover ratio indicates how inadequate the defenses are.

Tables 2 to 6, on the other hand, record a persistent worsening of key real growth indicators after the 1960s. Table 2 shows that the real GDP growth rates of both the G–7 and the remaining OECD countries dropped substantially and became more volatile after the 1960s, with no sustained reversal accompanying the burgeoning of capital flows in the 1980s. It also shows that the individual G–7 trends broadly conform to the group pattern, but with the Anglo-Saxon subgroup, which had grown less rapidly than the remaining G–7 in the 1960s, also declining less. Output trends among the developing countries have been more divergent. GDP growth in the 1970s, reflecting mainly diverging swings in the terms of trade, improved for almost half the developing countries while worsening for the rest. However, in the 1980s the growth rates of most developing countries dropped well below their 1960s pace, the only regional exception being South and Southeast Asia, where only half the countries had 1980s growth rates below those of the 1960s (Felix, 1996b, Table 5).

Table 3 shows that world, OECD, and G–7 exports of goods and services at constant prices also expanded more slowly after the 1960s. Among the G–7, the sole exception is the United States, whose export growth in the 1960s was, however, well below the G–7 average. The joint retardation of output and trade growth rather dims the glowing

Table 2
Annual real GDP growth and coefficients of variation of OECD countries, 1959–1994[a]

A. Individual G–7 countries

	Canada		France		Germany		Italy		Japan		U.K.		U.S.	
	Gr.	CV	Gr.	CV	Gr.	CV	Gr.	CV	Gr.	CV	Gr.	CV	Gr.	CV
1959–64	4.4	0.4	6.0	0.1	5.7	0.3	5.6	0.3	11.6	0.2	3.7	0.4	3.6	0.4
1965–70	5.1	0.3	5.3	0.2	4.7	0.6	5.5	0.2	10.5	0.3	2.4	0.2	3.6	0.6
1971–76	5.4	0.3	3.6	0.5	2.7	0.9	3.4	1.0	4.5	0.7	2.1	1.3	2.7	0.9
1977–82	2.4	1.1	2.5	0.3	1.7	1.0	3.0	0.7	4.3	0.2	1.1	1.9	1.8	1.4
1983–88	4.4	0.2	2.2	0.5	2.3	0.3	2.7	0.3	4.1	0.3	4.0	0.2	3.9	0.3
1989–94	1.3	1.6	1.7	1.1	3.0	0.7	1.3	1.0	2.5	0.8	1.0	1.9	2.1	0.7
1959–70	4.8	0.4	5.6	0.1	5.2	0.4	5.6	0.3	11.0	0.2	3.0	0.4	3.6	0.5
1971–82	3.9	0.7	3.1	0.5	2.2	1.0	3.2	0.8	4.4	0.5	1.6	1.6	2.3	1.1
1983–94	2.9	0.8	1.9	0.8	2.7	0.6	2.0	0.7	3.3	0.6	2.5	0.8	3.0	0.5

B. Country groups[b]

	G–7		OECD excluding G–7		All OECD	
	Gr.	CV	Gr.	CV	Gr.	CV
1959–64	5.0	0.1	5.3	0.1	5.0	0.1
1965–70	4.6	0.2	5.1	0.2	4.6	0.2
1971–76	3.3	0.7	4.1	0.5	3.4	0.7
1977–82	2.5	0.6	2.3	0.3	2.4	0.6
1983–88	3.6	0.2	2.7	0.3	3.4	0.2
1989–94	2.1	0.4	2.2	0.5	2.1	0.4
1959–70	4.8	0.2	5.2	0.1	4.8	0.2
1971–82	2.8	0.8	3.2	0.6	2.9	0.7
1983–94	2.8	0.4	2.5	0.4	2.8	0.4

[a] Growth rates are in percent; coefficients of variation are ratios.
[b] Group data are weighted averages, using comparative size of GDP as weights.
Source: OECD, *Economic Outlook*, appendix tables, various issues.

rhetoric about global economic integration, since the rising export/GDP ratios of the G–7 and the OECD shown in Table 4 merely reflect less retardation of trade than of output growth.

Table 5 shows that gross fixed investment of the G–7 and the OECD has also been expanding at substantially slower rates since the demise of Bretton Woods. This seems at odds with the doubling of the G–7 ratio of cross-border transactions in bonds and equities to GDP between the 1970s and the 1980s (Edey and Hviding, 1995, Table 4). It agrees,

202 JOURNAL OF POST KEYNESIAN ECONOMICS

Table 3
Annual growth of exports of goods and services at constant prices, 1959–94

I. Individual G–7 Countries[a]							
	Canada	France	Germany	Italy	Japan	U.K.	U.S.
	A. Six-year averages (%)						
1959–64	7.8	9.0	10.1	16.7	15.0	4.1	6.1
1965–70	9.9	10.7	10.8	13.4	17.2	6.0	5.5
1971–76	4.3	7.9	6.4	6.6	11.3	5.6	7.8
1977–82	5.4	4.2	4.6	4.0	7.4	2.1	4.0
1983–88	7.9	3.7	3.4	4.4	4.5	4.2	6.2
1989–94	6.4	5.0	6.0	6.9	4.6	4.1	7.7
	B. Twelve-year averages (%)						
1959–70	8.8	9.9	10.4	15.1	16.1	5.0	5.8
1971–82	4.8	6.1	5.5	5.3	9.4	3.8	5.9
1983–94	7.2	4.4	4.7	5.7	4.6	4.1	7.0

II. Country Groups[b]			
	G–7	OECD	World
	A. Six-year averages (%)		
1959–64	7.6	8.6	8.1
1965–70	8.3	8.8	7.9
1971–76	8.1	7.8	8.0
1977–82	4.6	5.0	4.5
1983–88	5.2	5.5	5.9
1989–94	6.5	6.4	5.7
	B. Twelve-year averages (%)		
1959–70	7.9	8.7	8.0
1971–82	6.4	6.4	6.2
1983–94	5.9	5.9	5.8

[a] 1959–70 data from IMF, *International Financial Statistics*, deflated by average of U.S. export and import price indices. 1971–94 deflated data from OECD, *Economic Outlook* annex tables.
[b] G–7 and OECD series are weighted averages using relative GDP as weights. World exports 1959–74 are deflated by the average of U.S. import and export price indices, 1975–94 are deflated by the IMF unit export price index.
Source: OECD *Economic Outlook*, annex tables; IMF *International Financial Statistics*, various issues.

however, with the finding of Martin Feldstein and associates that the high correlation between domestic saving and investment that had prevailed in the OECD countries during the 1960s has diminished very little since, despite the explosive expansion of international capital flows

Table 4
G–7 and OECD ratios of growth rates of export volume to GDP growth: 1959–94

	Can-ada	France	Ger-many	Italy	Japan	U.K.	U.S.	G–7	OECD
	I. Six-year averages (%)								
1959–64	1.8	1.5	1.8	3.0	1.3	1.1	1.7	1.5	1.7
1965–70	1.9	2.0	2.3	2.4	1.6	2.5	1.5	1.8	1.7
1971–76	0.8	2.2	2.4	1.9	2.5	2.7	2.9	2.4	2.3
1977–82	2.2	1.7	2.7	1.3	1.7	1.9	2.2	1.8	2.1
1983–88	1.8	1.7	1.5	1.6	1.1	1.1	1.6	1.4	1.6
1989–94	4.9	2.9	2.0	5.3	1.8	4.1	3.7	3.1	3.0
	II. Twelve-year averages (%)								
1959–70	1.8	1.7	2.0	2.7	1.4	1.8	1.6	1.7	1.7
1971–82	1.5	1.9	2.5	1.6	2.1	2.3	2.5	2.1	2.2
1983–94	2.3	2.3	1.7	3.4	1.4	2.7	2.6	2.3	2.3

Source: Tables 2 and 3.

(Feldstein, 1994). The flows have been transferring relatively few real resources on balance. Finally, Table 6 shows that the growth of labor, capital, and total factor productivity have all fallen precipitously since the 1960s in the OECD countries.

The global growth slowdown implies that some combination of lower accumulation of productive resources and their increased misallocation and underutilization set in after the 1960s. The search for general causes has produced a sizeable, but unconvincing, economic literature. It is unconvincing because, thus far, the literature has taken as axiomatic that the relation between financial liberalization and allocative efficiency is monotonically positive. The search has instead been for key market-distorting policies, factor supply rigidities, and exogenous technology and supply shocks that separately or in tandem must have more than offset the efficiency gains from liberalizing and globalizing the financial markets. But this is a perverse approach, given that product and labor markets have been liberalizing during the past two decades, and most governments since the 1970s have been privatizing and shrinking their range of economic activities. The literature has been trying to pin the blame for the global economic slowdown on factors that were strongest when the output, trade, and productivity trends were also strongest, and have been weakening as those trends weakened, while ruling out *a priori*

Table 5
Annual change of gross fixed investment at constant prices:
1959–94

I. Individual G–7 countries							
	Canada	France	Germany	Italy	Japan	U.K.	U.S.
A. Six-year averages (%)							
1959–64	5.0	8.7	8.4	5.7	8.4	5.9	4.7
1965–70	4.7	6.0	3.1	3.6	13.7	2.5	3.3
1971–76	6.5	3.3	–0.5	0.3	3.2	0.9	2.8
1977–82	4.1	0.5	1.4	1.4	3.6	–0.9	1.9
1983–88	6.9	1.9	2.6	3.0	6.6	6.9	6.6
1989–94	1.0	0.6	3.8	–0.5	2.8	–0.7	3.3
B. Twelve-year averages (%)							
1959–70	4.8	7.3	5.7	4.7	11.0	4.2	4.0
1971–82	5.3	1.9	0.5	0.9	3.4	0.0	2.3
1983–94	3.9	1.2	3.2	1.2	4.7	3.3	4.9

II. Country groups		
	G–7	OECD
A. Six-year averages (%)		
1959–64	6.9	6.9
1965–70	5.5	5.4
1971–76	2.5	2.5
1977–82	2.0	1.7
1983–88	5.6	5.4
1989–94	2.3	2.3
B. Twelve-year averages (%)		
1959–70	6.2	6.1
1971–82	2.2	2.1
1983–94	3.9	3.8

Source: OECD *Economic Outlook* annex tables, various issues.

the possibility that financial globalization, a major trend that *has* moved inversely to the real economy trends, might have contributed to the slowdowns. To redress the balance, let me cite direct evidence that the contribution may well have turned negative following the lifting of international capital controls.

Excessive absorption of resources in asset trading

Since 1955 the share of GDP generated by finance, insurance, and real estate (FIRE)—activities that service asset trading and the transfer of risk—has been rising almost monotonically in each of the G–7 countries. Until the early 1970s, the rising FIRE/GDP was accompanied by improving real growth rates of goods and nonfinancial services, supporting the orthodox view that financial deepening promotes real growth. But since then, real growth of the nonfinancial sectors has slackened even more than has overall GDP growth, implying that the increasing absorption of resources in FIRE activities had become socially counterproductive (Felix, 1996b, graphs 1–7).

Other data show a relative rise of resources devoted to finance proper. Finance's share of the OECD's labor force averaged 21 percent higher, and its share of total OECD investment averaged 104 percent higher in 1980–93 compared with 1970–79 (Edey and Hviding, 1995, Table 2). Since 1975, finance has been the fastest growing component of international service trade, rising at 13 percent per annum, while FDI in financial facilities led the growth of FDI in services during the 1980s (OECD, 1994, pp. 38–40).

Financial volatility and investment misallocation

Increasing exchange rate volatility and misalignments have accompanied the rapid expansion of international capital flows. The average monthly volatility of the dollar exchange rate with the franc, deutschemark, yen, and pound was 22 percent higher in 1980–84 and 35 percent higher in 1985–89 than in the already volatile 1970s (Blundell-Wignall and Browne, 1991, Table 7). And, while Latin America has been *numero uno* in exchange rate misaligning, the United States has not been far behind. During 1980–91, the ratio of the highest to the lowest annual *real* exchange rate[3] exceeded 3 to 1 in one-fifth of the Latin American countries, and averaged 2.3 to 1 for the region. But it was also 2 to 1 for the U.S. dollar, the world's dominant reserve currency, and 1.65 to 1 for the yen and 1.38 for the DM, the two lesser reserve currencies (Felix, 1996b, Table 12).

The distorting effect on investment strategies of the heightened volatility, which encompasses interest rates and other financial prices, helps explain why, despite the rapid spread of innovations in information and machine control technology, productivity growth has slackened since the end of Bretton Woods. Higher volatility increases liquidity and other risks of long-term investing, tilting private investors toward investments

[3] The rates are trade-weighted.

206   *JOURNAL OF POST KEYNESIAN ECONOMICS*

Table 6
Productivity in the business sector
(percentage changes at annual rates)

	Total factor productivity[a]			Labor productivity[b]			Capital productivity		
	1960–73[c]	1973–79	1979–95[d]	1960–73[c]	1973–79	1979–95[d]	1960–73[c]	1973–79	1979–95[d]
U.S.	2.5	0.2	0.5	2.6	0.4	0.9	2.3	–0.2	–0.2
Japan	5.4	1.1	1.1	8.4	2.8	2.2	–3.3	–3.7	–2.1
Germany[e]	2.6	1.8	0.4	4.5	3.1	0.9	–1.4	–1.0	–0.6
France	3.7	1.6	1.3	5.3	2.9	2.3	0.6	–1.0	–0.6
Italy	4.4	2.0	0.9	6.3	2.9	1.8	0.4	0.3	–0.9
U.K.	2.6	0.6	1.5	3.9	1.5	2.0	–0.3	–1.5	0.5
Canada	1.9	0.6	–0.1	2.9	1.5	1.1	0.2	–1.0	–2.4
Total of above countries[f]	3.3	0.8	0.8	4.5	1.6	1.4	0.3	–1.1	–0.7
Australia	2.2	1.1	0.8	3.3	2.4	1.4	0.1	–1.4	–0.2
Austria	3.1	1.0	0.9	5.5	3.0	2.1	–2.0	–3.1	–1.7
Belgium	3.8	1.3	1.2	5.2	2.6	2.1	0.6	–1.9	–1.0
Denmark	2.3	0.9	1.3	3.9	2.4	2.2	–1.4	–2.6	–0.9
Finland	4.0	1.9	2.5	5.0	3.2	3.5	1.4	–1.6	–0.4
Greece	2.5	0.7	–0.3	9.0	3.3	0.6	–8.8	–4.2	–2.0
Ireland	4.6	3.4	2.6	5.1	4.1	3.3	2.3	0.5	–0.2
Netherlands	3.4	1.7	1.1	4.8	2.7	1.6	0.8	–0.1	0.1
Norway[g]	2.0	1.7	–0.1	3.8	3.1	1.5	0.0	0.2	–1.8
Portugal	5.4	–0.2	1.6	7.4	0.5	2.4	–0.7	–2.5	–0.8
Spain	3.2	0.9	1.7	6.0	3.2	2.9	–3.6	–5.0	–1.5
Sweden	2.0	0.0	1.0	3.7	1.4	2.0	–2.2	–3.2	–1.3
Switzerland	2.1	–0.3	–0.2	3.2	0.8	0.3	–1.4	–3.5	–1.6

with faster payoffs.[4] It has led nonfinancial corporations to devote more of their investible funds to purchases of existing firms and buybacks of their stock shares and less to constructing new capacity. The propensity

---

[4] More formally, volatility raises the "hurdle rate," the minimum expected return that will induce investors to invest in projects involving front-end outlays—that is, fixed costs—and delayed net revenues. Since information about the future time shape of costs and revenues becomes more uncertain the longer the life of the project, delaying the project may reduce risk by allowing more information to be gathered. The hurdle rate of return therefore exceeds the cost of capital by also incorporating a premium from "waiting" in the investment decision. The waiting premium is a ratio of two present values: the present value today of the expected income stream were the project to be delayed, divided by the present value of the expected income stream from starting the project today (Dixit, 1992).

Table 6
Continued

Total of above smaller countries[f]	3.0	1.0	1.1	5.1	2.5	2.0	−1.5	−2.7	−1.0
Total of above North American countries[f]	2.5	0.2	0.4	2.6	0.5	0.9	2.1	−0.3	−0.4
Total of above European countries[f]	3.3	1.4	1.0	5.1	2.6	1.8	−0.7	−1.4	−0.6
Total of above OECD countries[f]	3.3	0.8	0.8	4.6	1.7	1.5	0.1	−1.3	−0.8

[a] TFP growth is equal to a weighted average of the growth in labor and capital productivity. The sample-period averages for capital and labor shares are used as weights.
[b] Output per employed person.
[c] Or earliest year available, i.e., 1961 for Australia, Greece, and Ireland; 1962 for Japan and the United Kingdom; 1964 for Spain; 1965 for France and Sweden; 1966 for Canada and Norway; 1970 for Belgium and the Netherlands; and 1972 for the United States.
[d] Or latest year available, i.e., 1991 for Norway; 1992 for Ireland and Portugal; 1993 for Germany, Austria, Belgium, Finland, Sweden, and Switzerland; and 1994 for Japan, France, the United Kingdom, Australia, Denmark, Greece, the Netherlands, and Spain.
[e] The two first averages concern western Germany. The percentage changes for the period 1979–95 are calculated as the weighted average of western Germany productivity growth between 1979 and 1991 and total Germany productivity growth between 1991 and the latest year available.
[f] Aggregates are calculated on the basis of 1992 GDP for the business sector expressed in 1992 purchasing power parities.
[g] Mainland business sector (i.e., excluding shipping as well as crude petroleum and gas extraction).
Source: OECD *Economic Outlook*, June 1996, annex table 59.

of large corporations in the Bretton Woods era to invest heavily in "greenfield" plants in order to exploit economies of scale in production and protect market share has been replaced by a propensity to invest primarily in improving the utilization rate of existing capacity by re-equipping the plants to handle variable production runs more economically, and to outsource cyclically sensitive and labor-intensive phases of production and distribution. Mergers, takeovers, and downsizing have displaced exploitation of scale economies in production as the preferred means of protecting market share.

The declining productivity growth of the United States thus reflects an increasing dualism between large and small firms. Large firms have pretty much kept up their productivity growth, but small firms have not. Small firms, nurtured by outsourcing, have been increasing their share of total output, but have been competing primarily by holding down wages and minimizing outlays on new equipment, worker training, and R&D.[5]

This pattern has probably gone furthest in the United States, where it has generated increasing criticism of corporate "short-termism," that is, the excessive focus on increasing stockholder value through financial speculation and downsizing maneuvers that raise share prices in the short term at the expense of other "stakeholders," notably the employees, and long-term productivity (Gordon, 1996; Shleifer and Vishny, 1990; Twentieth Century Fund, 1992). But under pressure from the globalized financial markets, corporatist arrangements in Japan and the continental European countries, such as long-term relational banking and sharing commitments to employees and the community, are reportedly giving way to short-termism, American style, with its exclusive focus on short-term maximizing of shareholder value (*The Economist*, July 13, 1996; Pozan, 1996).

Exchange-rate volatility as a trade-retarding factor

Under heightened exchange rate volatility and misalignment, exporters and importers betting wrong on the exchange rate swings can lose big, and when they bet right, import-competing firms can lose big. Hedging exchange rate risk has thus motivated much of the increasing Forex turnover. Hedging, however, adds to costs and can only partly transfer

[5] Analysis by a U.S. technology consulting institute of its 3,000-firm data set of small and large firms, primarily mechanical and metal working, with small defined as firms with under 500 employees, shows that (Luria, 1996):

1. Outsourcing by large firms has since the late 1970s been the major source of demand for the small firms.

2. Just-in-time inventory economizing by their outsourcing customers has forced these firms to hold more inventory, and to absorb wide swings of capacity utilization originating in cyclical demand fluctuations of their large customers.

3. This has pressured the small firms to minimize outlays on new equipment and to lower the wage bill through union busting and relocating in low-wage regions.

4. Productivity and nominal wages have been either flat or declining in "roughly half of the small shops on which we have data, and in about one-third of these they are falling far and fast."

risk, and the hedging instruments also facilitate speculation on foreign exchange and cross-currency interest rate movements. Multinational corporations and the financial institutions intermediating the hedging have thus become speculators, moving between hedging against rate movements and betting on them. Exchange rate volatility has tended, therefore, to be self-generating, promoting more intricate hedging instruments that become new vehicles for speculation, which in turn augments volatility. That the heightened volatility has been partly responsible for the slackened growth of the volume of world trade thus seems incontrovertible, although empirical studies disagree on the extent of the effect.

The dominance of the globalized financial markets over macroeconomic policy as a growth-retarding factor

The liberating of international capital movements has forced macroeconomic policy to react primarily to signals from the financial rather than from the job market. Walter Wriston, ex-CEO of Citicorp, chortles that the globalized financial markets now hold macroeconomic policy in a tighter grip than under the gold standard. Orthodox economists rationalize this dominance in more muted language, stressing that macroeconomic policies must now be "credible" to the financial markets.

The abrupt global increase of real interest rates after the 1970s is a concrete manifestation of this rise to dominance. Table 7 shows that the average real interest rate on ten-year government bonds of the G–7 in 1983–94 was over four times the 1971–82 average, and almost twice the 1959–70 average, with each of the G–7 experiencing the real rate increases.

Why the increase? Lenders reacting to rising inflation by demanding higher inflationary premia is an unsatisfactory explanation. It requires the belief that lenders had suffered from an extended money illusion and allowed real interest rates to fall toward zero in the 1970s when inflation was accelerating, from which they only awakened to demand higher inflationary premia in the 1980s when inflation was decelerating. A more reasonable explanation that does not denigrate the acuity of financiers is that the decontrol of financial markets in the 1980s unblocked channels for moving loanable funds around the world, which greatly weakened the power of national monetary authorities to influence real interest rates.

In the previous era of capital controls, holders of long bonds, when

Table 7
Annual real interest rates and volatility of G–7 ten-year government bonds 1959–94[a]

	Canada		France		Germany		Italy		Japan	
	Rate	CV	Rate	CV	Rate	CV	Rate	CV	Rate	CV
				I. Six-year averages						
1959–64	3.2	0.1	0.0	1.6	3.8	1.0	1.8	2.4	n.a	n.a
1965–70	2.9	0.4	2.3	0.8	4.5	0.7	2.8	1.1	n.a	n.a
1971–76	0.8	2.2	0.5	1.4	2.8	0.4	−2.7	4.3	−3.2	5.7
1977–82	1.8	1.1	0.8	1.8	3.3	0.6	0.1	3.2	2.7	2.0
1983–88	6.4	1.1	5.5	0.8	5.2	0.5	4.3	0.6	3.8	0.6
1989–94	6.1	1.4	5.7	0.6	4.3	1.2	6.3	1.2	3.2	0.5
1995	6.7		6.1		4.7		7.0		3.9	
				II. Twelve-year averages						
1959–70	3.0	0.7	1.1	1.7	4.2	0.9	2.3	1.9	n.a	n.a
1971–82	1.3	1.8	0.6	1.6	3.1	0.6	−1.3	4.0	−0.3	5.2
1983–94	6.3	1.3	5.6	0.7	4.7	1.1	5.3	1.4	3.5	0.8

	U.K.		U.S.		G–7 average	
	Rate	CV	Rate	CV	Rate	CV
				I. Six-year averages		
1959–64	3.2	1.1	2.8	0.5	2.5[a]	1.1[b]
1965–70	3.0	0.9	1.5	0.6	2.8[a]	0.7[b]
1971–76	−1.7	3.9	−0.2	2.3	−0.5	2.9
1977–82	−0.7	3.8	1.4	3.1	1.3	2.3
1983–88	5.5	0.7	6.4	1.4	5.3	0.8
1989–94	2.8	1.1	3.6	0.6	4.6	0.9
1995	5.4		5.0		5.4	
				II. Twelve-year averages		
1959–70	3.1	1.0	2.1	0.8	2.6[a]	1.2[b]
1971–82	−1.2	4.0	0.6	2.8	0.4	2.9
1983–94	4.2	1.6	5.0	1.8	4.9	1.2

[a] Deflated by respective national CPI.
[b] Excludes Japan.
Source: IMF, *International Financial Statistics*.

correctly or incorrectly anticipating higher inflation from a credit easing move, could only shift easily to domestic equities and shorter-term bonds. The reactions of long bond holders thus reinforced efforts of the monetary authorities to move output and employment nearer to capacity by lowering the real short-term rate. But with the generalizing of capital market decontrol in the 1980s, quick and easy movements by portfolio investors between domestic and foreign bonds and equities, and covered and uncovered interest arbitraging across currencies by banks and security houses, now counter government efforts to lower short-term rates. Table 8 shows that real short-term rates of the G–7 have also been far higher since 1982 than in the 1960s and 1970s, despite the higher unemployment rates and lower growth rates.

The monetary authorities have been forced to refocus monetary policy from countercyclical stabilizing to accommodating the appetite of the financial markets for high rates of return. And since financial globalization has rendered the manipulating of monetary aggregates as control instruments ineffective, the G–7 authorities have terminated their brief romance with monetarism and reverted to targeting short-term interest rates.[6] But that targeting is now mainly governed by the need to pacify financial market expectations. Thus, although the GDP growth rates of the G–7 in 1989–94 had dropped substantially from their 1983–88 average, there was only a slight fall of short- and long-term real interest rates (compare Table 2 with Tables 7 and 8).

Economists defending the position that liberalizing and globalizing financial markets has improved economic welfare now avert their eyes from the adverse real economic trends. They instead concentrate narrowly on financial data and build their positive welfare case on tautological interpretations of those data. Two recent OECD studies are illustrative. Neither refers to real economic trends in its welfare assessment. One of the studies has found econometrically that about half the increase of real interest rates between the 1970s and the 1980s was due to financial market liberalization but interprets the increase as simply a measure of the size of the prior allocative "distortion" that liberalization eliminated (Orr, Edey, and Kennedy, 1995). The companion study acknowledges that the declining cost of financial transacting and the increased size and diversity of financial services that has resulted from financial liberalization are not *per se* empirical proof of real economy benefits. Whether they are "depends on judgments about the value of the financial services being provided, in particular, the extent to which

---

[6] OECD economists, using a recursive VAR model, have found that, whereas changes in the G–7 monetary aggregates led nominal income changes during the 1970s, the "Granger causality" reversed after the early 1980s, with nominal income changes leading the monetary aggregates (Blundell-Wignall et al., 1990, pp. 9–12 and Tables 2 and 3). Using VAR analysis, "the other Friedman" has shown that the U.S. Federal Reserve's abandonment of monetary targeting in the 1980s was a sensible response to financial market reality (Friedman, 1996).

212   JOURNAL OF POST KEYNESIAN ECONOMICS

Table 8
Trends and variability of real short-term interest rates: G–7 countries, 1959–94

I. Real money market rates[a]

	France		Germany		Italy		Japan	
	Rate	CV	Rate	CV	Rate	CV	Rate	CV
			A. Six-year averages					
1959–64	−1.1	1.5	1.0	1.4	−0.1	19.6	2.7	1.0
1965–70	2.3	0.3	2.1	0.7	0.6	1.8	1.4	0.7
1971–76	−0.1	25.1	0.4	4.0	−3.0	0.7	−3.2	1.3
1977–82	0.1	36.6	2.6	0.7	−0.8	3.3	1.7	1.2
1983–88	4.4	0.2	3.2	0.3	6.1	0.2	4.0	0.2
1989–94	6.2	0.2	4.3	0.3	6.2	0.2	2.9	0.3
			B. Twelve-year averages					
1959–70	0.6	3.7	1.5	0.9	0.2	8.0	2.0	1.0
1971–82	0.0	103.0	1.5	1.4	−1.9	1.4	−0.7	0.3
1983–94	6.2	0.3	3.7	0.3	6.2	0.2	3.5	0.3

II. Treasury Bill Rates[a]

	Canada		U.K.		U.S.		G–7 average[b]	
	Rate	CV	Rate	CV	Rate	CV	Rate	CV
			A. Six-year averages					
1959–64	2.3	0.4	1.8	0.8	1.8	0.4	1.2	0.7
1965–70	1.8	0.4	1.9	0.5	1.5	0.4	1.6	0.3
1971–76	−1.3	1.4	−4.9	0.9	−1.0	1.7	−1.9	0.8
1977–82	2.1	1.0	−2.5	1.5	0.6	4.2	0.5	3.5
1983–88	5.0	0.2	5.3	0.2	3.0	0.3	4.6	0.1
1989–94	5.2	0.4	3.1	0.5	1.5	0.7	4.2	0.2
			B. Twelve-year averages					
1959–70	2.1	0.4	1.9	0.7	1.6	0.4	1.4	0.5
1971–82	0.4	6.4	−3.7	1.2	−0.2	12.7	−0.7	3.0
1983–94	5.1	0.3	4.2	0.5	2.7	0.6	4.4	0.2

[a] Deflated by each country's CPI.
[b] Simple averaging of the table's treasury bill and money market rates.
Source: IMF, *International Financial Statistics*.

the increased financial activity is viewed as being of economic benefit, rather than representing excessive or unecessary financial churning." But then, without citing any supporting real economy data, the study concludes that the benefits were indeed substantial. The lifting of interest rate controls and "regulation-driven credit rationing" must have improved allocative efficiency by "opening up opportunities for international portfolio diversification" and by removing a distortion, whose importance is indicated by the substantial increase of the margin between interbank and bank–customer lending rates in the OECD countries after 1980 (Edey and Hviding, 1995). To defend the orthodox case, premise must now also double as proof.

Liberalizing and globalizing financial markets has increased competition between lenders and augmented the supply of loanable funds. The sustained increase of real interest rates must therefore have been underpinned by a growth of global demand for loanable funds that more than matched the accelerated growth of supply. It appears, however, that the bulk of the demand increase has come from financial churning and other non-growth-generating uses. A global boom in real investment could not have motivated much of the demand increase, since, as Table 5 shows, there was no such boom. Nor has the financing of increased fiscal deficits been a major independent source of the rising demand for loanable funds. The ratio of overall fiscal deficits to GDP of the OECD countries averaged only slightly higher in 1983–94 than in the 1970s, while primary fiscal balances of the OECD countries improved after 1982. That is, the increased overall deficits mainly reflected higher debt service, to which the higher real interest rates contributed recursively (OECD, 1995a, appendix tables 30, 31, 32).

This leaves rising debt leveraging by households and businesses unrelated to the creation of new productive capacity as probably the most important single source of the accelerating demand for loanable funds. As percentages of household disposable income, both financial assets and liabilities of G–7 households have been rising since 1982, whereas both household savings and physical asset holdings have been falling (OECD, 1995b, 1996, annex table 58). That is, leveraging by G–7 households has been mainly for consumption and the acquisition of financial assets. As for business debt leveraging, it appears to have been related largely to debt financing of mergers and acquisitions, the purchase of privatized government assets, and the acquisition of equity shares for portfolio diversification and speculation.[7]

---

[7] U.S. outlays on mergers and acquisitions averaged $184 billion per year in 1984–89 compared to an $84 billion annual outlay on new productive facilities (Crotty and Goldstein, 1993).

214   JOURNAL OF POST KEYNESIAN ECONOMICS

Policy inferences

The Bretton Woods incompatibility thesis remains valid, but its policy solution is incompatible with today's changed political economy conditions. Building capital controls into the IMF Articles of Agreement was politically facile, since restrictive controls were already in place in most member countries as a result of the financial disorders of the 1930s and the disruptions of World War II.[8] A collective agreement to impose them now, while financial globalization is proceeding with a full head of steam and while an uncontrollable systemic breakdown is only a possibility, is politically infeasible.

But continuation of some of the trends produced by financial globalization is also economically and probably politically infeasible. Table 9 shows that, since 1982, real long-term interest rates have been exceeding the real growth rate by an increasing amount in each of the G–7, reaching nearly three times the group's GDP growth rate in 1995. By contrast, real interest rates of the G–7 averaged slightly less than the GDP growth rate during the gold standard era, which suggests that Wriston's celebrationist observation is not an overstatement.

Table 9, however, also offers a Belshazzar's Feast warning. The interwar period is the only other extended period during the past 115 years in which real long-term interest rates of the G–7 averaged substantially higher than real growth rates, yet the rising G–7 divergence since 1982 has now overtaken the interwar ratio. In conjunction with the rising debt/income ratios from increased debt leveraging, the rentier share of national income has therefore been rising persistently. Add the rising FIRE/GDP ratios and the diminished output and productivity growth and we have the essential elements of an unsustainable pyramid game in the making, in which, disguised by the increased capitalization and rising share prices of the equity markets, existing debt is being serviced increasingly by new debt rather than by rising real output. And since with liberalization the elements reflect mainly private-sector behavior, the $64 trillion dollar policy question is whether financial markets operate with an autopilot capable of bringing the trends to a halt gently, or whether the halting will come through systemic financial crises.

[8] However, Article 6 of the Articles of Agreement is a watered-down compromise of a tougher British draft proposal, initially favored by Harry D. White and the U.S. mission. Wall Street resistance forced White to pressure Keynes and the Bank of England into accepting a compromise draft that became Article 6 (Helleiner, 1994).

Table 9
Real long-term interest rates of the G–7 countries[a] divided by their real GDP growth rates, 1959–94

	Canada	France	Germany	Italy	Japan	U.K.	U.S.	All G–7
			A. Six-year average ratios					
1959–94	0.73	0.00	0.67	0.32	n.a.	0.86	0.78	0.50
1965–70	0.57	0.43	0.96	0.51	n.a.	1.25	0.42	0.61
1971–76	0.15	0.14	1.04	−0.79	−0.71	−0.81	−0.07	−0.15
1977–82	0.75	0.32	1.94	0.03	0.63	−0.64	0.78	0.52
1983–88	1.45	2.50	2.26	1.59	0.93	1.37	1.64	1.47
1989–94	4.69	3.35	1.43	4.85	1.28	2.80	1.71	2.19
1995	3.05	2.77	2.47	2.33	4.33	2.25	2.10	2.76
			B. Twelve-year average ratios					
1959–70	0.65	0.21	0.81	0.41	n.a.	1.05	0.60	0.55
1971–82	0.45	0.23	1.49	−0.38	−0.04	−0.72	0.35	0.18
1983–94	3.07	2.92	1.84	3.22	1.10	1.68	1.67	1.83
			C. Memorandum: pre-1959 G–7 average ratios					
1881–1913	0.97							
1919–39	2.40							
1946–58	0.36							

[a] Annual interest on 10-year government bonds deflated by national CPI.
Sources: 1959–94 data are from OECD *Economic Outlook*, annex tables, various issues, and IMF, *International Financial Statistics*, various issues. Pre-1959 data are from Bordo (1993), table 1, with real GDP per-capita growth rates in Bordo's table 1 multiplied by population growth rates.

Faith in the autopilot still burns brightly for some academic economists, but not for central bankers. The recent Mexican crisis is only one of a dozen instances since the end of Bretton Woods that evoked collective emergency intervention by the monetary authorities of the major financial centers to contain global repercussions from a financial crisis. Aware that the interventions, which often require rescuing large overexposed banks under the "too big to fail" doctrine, may sow the seeds of future crises by encouraging more risky bank behavior, the major central banks have also been trying collectively to tighten prudential supervision of their banks by a succession of Basle Accords.[9]

[9] Named after the Basle Committee on Banking Supervision, an adjunct of the Bank for International Settlements located in Basle, Switzerland. The committee is a consortium of twelve major central banks.

The accords have been unable, however, to keep up with the pace of financial innovating by the supervised banks. Reacting to interbank settlement breakdowns stemming from the failure of the Herrstatt Bank in 1974, the initial accords focused on clarifying the responsibility of headquarter banks for the liabilities of their offshore subsidiaries, and on coordinating international oversight responsibility over multinational banks. That did not prevent some multinational banks from a nearly fatal overloading with Third World loans relative to their equity capital. The subsequent debt crisis led to the 1988 Basle Accord, which classified bank assets into broad risk classes and set minimum bank capital standards for each class. But by the time this accord went into effect in 1992, the boom in customized derivatives, arranged by large international banks primarily for multinational corporations, was underway. The banks treated the derivative contracts as off-bank balance sheet items to which the capital standards did not apply. After an attempted agreement to close the loophole by imposing a uniform surcharge on derivative contracts was fought off by the banks, a new Basle accord was reached in 1996 that permits each bank to apply capital charges to its derivative contracts according to its own risk–return calculations, with regulators periodically checking the results against their prudential criteria. But in announcing the Federal Reserve's criteria, Chairman Greenspan observed, "We now know that a significant number of balance sheets are obsolete within a day. Thirty years ago it was quite adequate for regulators to look at financial statements on a periodic basis; today they must continuously up-date regulatory methods" (*Wall Street Journal*, August 8, 1996). Enforcing prudence on derivative dealing may require round-the-clock surveillance!

With the nominal value of customized derivative contracts in force globally totaling over $40 trillion in 1995 (Felix, 1996, Table A10), the risk that imprudent contracting might set off a systemic bank crisis is substantial. But prudence is not well defined in the case of customized derivatives. The contracts are complex, typically involving chains of financial commitments related to hedging by both sides of the contracts. A systemic breakdown can originate in three main sources. One is credit and settlement risk. In credit risk, one or more of the parties in the payment chain may not pay up. In settlement risk, the parties can make payment on schedule, but not in the requisite currency. In each case, prudent parties in the transaction chain are blindsided and the interrelated payment chain unravels. A second source is intellectual risk, meaning that the top management of transacting banks and/or firms lack an adequate grasp of the intricacies and riskiness of the contracts that their dealers and backroom "rocket scientists" are concocting, causing the enterprise to take on unplanned risks. Finally, there is the strong likelihood that the rocket scientists work with imperfect risk–return models.[10]

Concurrently, the ability of consortia of central banks, the IMF, and treasury ministers to make quick, adequate injections of liquidity to contain major crises is weakening. The dramatic decline of central bank reserves relative to the size of the globalized financial markets shown in Table 1 has created the need to cross into legislative territory in pursuit of emergency funding. In the Mexican crisis, the drawing down of an obscure U.S. Treasury reserve fund, established for a quite different purpose, was widely condemned in the U.S. Congress and media as an illicit use of taxpayer funds to bail out Wall Street and Mexico. Some of the G–7, resentful that the unusually large IMF contribution was engineered without consulting them, held back from contributing to the bailout fund. Circumscribed by legislative restrictions, international lender of last resort operations are losing scope and timeliness.

Soon after the Mexican crisis, the managing director of the IMF sketched out the road ahead for the IMF and the G–7 as follows: "In today's globalized markets, we must ensure that our ability to react approaches the instant decision making of investors if we want to have the ability to give confidence to markets and our members" (Camdessus, 1995). Which is a clear, if inadvertent, admission by a leading participant in the effort to reconcile crisis containment with unconstrained financial globalization that the strategy is intellectually bankrupt!

Alternative "market-friendly" policy adjustments

Two main policy approaches are gathering support among mainstream economists as they defect from the current orthodoxy about financial

---

[10] Tests presenting a given contract for pricing to backroom "rocket scientists" from different Wall Street banks have produced a range of prices differing by over 100 percent.

The risk/return models apparently suffer also from a fundamental flaw. They anchor their risk/return functions to a hypothetical fully balanced risk-free option strategy. A recent unpublished paper by Professor John Gilster (summarized in Lowenstein, 1996) shows, however, that the anchor point is an *ignis fatuus*. To maintain a risk-free position requires immediate recontracting when the price of the underlying volatile asset changes. Accumulating transaction costs therefore inexorably overtake the risk-free return, which means the risk/return model has no fixed point. To paraphrase Gertrude Stein, "there's no there there."

218 *JOURNAL OF POST KEYNESIAN ECONOMICS*

liberalization. Each goes half-way back to Bretton Woods. Each requires collective fiscal as well as monetary intervention to contain global financial volatility, but with measures that exclude direct capital controls.

One approach has the G–7 collectively set exchange rate targets and bands around the targeted rates. The rates would then be held within the bands by coordinated central bank interventions in the exchange markets, plus the coordinating of monetary-fiscal policies to keep the target rates in equilibrium. With Maastricht, the rates to be targeted reduce to the dollar/DM, dollar/yen, and dollar/sterling. The other approach would reduce financial volatility by "putting sand in the wheels" of the globalized financial markets; that is, by making international short-term capital flows more costly. As regards collective action, the leading "sand in the wheels" proposal is the Tobin tax, under which the major financial center governments would agree to impose a uniform tax on foreign exchange transactions.

The two approaches differ markedly in their assessment of the main source of global financial volatility. For the rate-targeting approach, the excessive volatility of the global financial markets is primarily a consequence of macroeconomic policy mismanagement. For the "sand in the wheels" approach, the volatility is mainly endogenously generated by the dynamics of liberated financial markets, which is what I have tried to show is the case. If valid, it means that, without accompanying "sand in the wheels" measures, the liberated financial markets are likely to destroy exchange targeting, as they did the ERM in 1992.

The ERM experience also casts serious doubt on the political realism of the fiscal-monetary coordination required by the exchange-targeting approach. The 1992 exchange crisis occurred despite four decades of economic and political institution building of the European Community, propelled ideologically by the trauma of World War II, and capped with the passage of the Maastricht Treaty, which gave the financial markets a clear statement of the medium-term macroeconomic policy intentions of the EC and its members. The globalized exchange-targeting approach would have to start without a comparable ideological push or institutional buildup. Some of its proponents see it as an evolutionary advance from the G–7 annual coordination meetings. But that is wishful thinking; the G–7 has been far more effective in coordinating rhetoric than policies.

Far less collective action is required to implement the Tobin tax approach. Indeed, implementation would give national governments greater autonomy over their macroeconomic policies. It would do this by partially divorcing interest and exchange rate movements from each other, and by substantially augmenting fiscal revenue.[11]

Nevertheless, its political feasibility is also problematic. The proposal is caviar for the general. The unemployed are unlikely to march on the presidential palace waving Tobin tax banners. On the other hand, the self-interested opposition from the financial markets is reinforced by opposition from conservatives who dislike the tax because they understand that it would make countercyclical and reformist policies more compatible with financial stability. Moreover, as a financial stabilizer, the tax would mainly help prevent buildups toward major financial crises but is inadequate as a crisis management tool. In a crisis, the pressure will sensibly be for stronger measures, such as direct capital controls, rather than a Tobin tax. Economists who see the virtue of the Tobin tax as a crisis preventer and as a necessary condition for making higher output and employment growth compatible with financial liberalization have a major educational task ahead if its collective adoption is to become politically feasible.

Should Latin America's economists join in the task? I think so. As minor participants in global forex trading, Latin American countries would collect little direct tax revenue, but would benefit considerably from the reduction in the volatility of global capital flows and the G–7 exchange rates. The ability of a developing economy independently to protect itself against adverse movements of portfolio funds is inversely related to its need to do so. When its export growth is strong and its foreign debt moderate, a developing country can safely risk the displeasure of the financial markets and limit disruptive portfolio inflows by discriminatory tax and interest rate measures, as most Asian countries and a few Latin American countries have done. Not so, however, when exports slow, the balance of payments is in deficit, foreign debts are high, and the need is to check portfolio capital outflows. Developing countries should, therefore, be pressing the G–7 to adopt a globalized Tobin tax and concurrently insist on a global sharing of the global tax revenue. A pressing task for Latin American economists ought to be to make this clear to the citizenry and governments.

---

[11] The interest–exchange rate divorce is because even a modest tax would widen the interest rate difference needed to make cross-currency interest rate arbitraging profitable. For example, an 0.25 percent tax rate would widen the interest rate divergence on 30-day paper by an additional 6 percent before triggering arbitrage flows. On revenue prospects, Ranjit Sau and I, using alternative elasticity and transaction cost assumptions, estimate that an 0.25 percent tax might raise annually between $200 and $300 billion globally in 1995 dollars (Felix and Sau, 1996).

REFERENCES

Bank for International Settlements. *Central Bank Survey of Foreign Exchange Market Activity in April 1992*. Basle: BIS, March 1993.

——. *Central Bank Survey of Foreign Exchange and Derivatives Market Activity 1995*. Basle, Switzerland: BIS, May 1996.

Blundell-Wignall, Adrian, and Browne, Frank. "Macroeconomic Consequences of Financial Liberalization: A Summary Report." Working Paper no. 98, OECD Department of Economics and Statistics, February 1991.

Blundell-Wignall, Adrian; Browne, Frank; and Manasse, Paolo. "Monetary Policy in the Wake of Financial Liberalization." Working Paper no. 77, OECD Department of Economics and Statistics, Paris, April 1990.

Bordo, Michael. "The Bretton Woods International Monetary System: An Historical Overview." In Michael Bordo and Barry Eichengreen (eds.), *A Retrospective on the Bretton Woods System*. Chicago: University of Chicago Press, 1993.

Camdessus, Michel. "The IMF in the Globalized World Economy." *IMF Survey*, June 19, 1995.

Crotty, James, and Goldstein, D. "Do U.S. Financial Markets Allocate Credit Efficiently? The Case of Corporate Restructuring in the 1980s." In G. Dymski, G. Epstein, and R. Pollin (eds.), *Transforming the U.S. Financial System*. Armonk, NY: M.E. Sharpe, 1993.

Devlin, Robert. *Debt and Crisis in Latin America: The Supply Side of the Story*. Princeton, NJ: Princeton University Press, 1989.

Diaz-Alejandro, Carlos. "Goodby Financial Repression, Hello Financial Crash." *Journal of Development Economics*, 1995, *19*, 1–24.

Dixit, Avinash. "Investment and Hysterisis." *Journal of Economic Perspectives*, Winter 1992, *6*, 107–132.

Dymski, Gary, and Pollin, Robert, eds. *New Perspectives in Monetary Macroeconomics: Explorations in the Tradition of Hyman P. Minsky*. Ann Arbor: University of Michigan Press, 1994.

The Economist. "Le Defi Americain Again," and "Showing Europe's Firms the Way." July 13, 1996.

Edey, Malcolm, and Hviding, Ketil. "An Assessment of Financial Reform in OECD Countries." *OECD Economic Studies*, 1995, *25*, 8–36.

Eichengreen, Barry, and Wyplosz, Charles. "The Unstable EMS." *Brookings Papers on Economic Activity*, 1993, *1* (1), 51–143.

Federal Reserve Bank of New York. *Summary of Results of the U.S. Foreign Exchange Market Turnover Conducted in April 1992*. New York, September 1992.

Feldstein, Martin. "Tax Policy and International Capital Flows." *Weltwirthschaftliches Archiv*, 1994, *130*, 675–697.

Felix, David. "Debt Crisis Adjustment in Latin America: Have the Hardships Been Necessary?" In Gary Dymski and Robert Pollin (eds.), *New Perspectives in Monetary Macroeconomics: Explorations in the Tradition of Hyman P. Minsky*. Ann Arbor: University of Michigan Press, 1994.

——. "Statistical Appendix." In Mahbub ul-Haq, Inge Kaul, and Isabelle Grunberg (eds.), *The Tobin Tax: Coping with Financial Volatility*. New York, Oxford University Press, 1996a.

——. "Financial Globalization vs. Free Trade: The Case for the Tobin Tax." *UNCTAD REVIEW 1996*. New York, Geneva: United Nations, 1996b.

Felix, David, and Sau, Ranjit. "On the Revenue Potential and Phasing in of the Tobin Tax." In Mahbub ul-Haq, Inge Kaul, and Isabelle Grunberg (eds.), *The Tobin Tax: Coping with Financial Volatility*. New York, Oxford University Press, 1996.

Friedman, Benjamin. "The Rise and Fall of Money Growth Targets as Guidelines for U.S. Monetary Policy." National Bureau of Economic Research Working Paper no. 5465, Cambridge, MA, February 1996.

Gordon, David M. *Fat and Mean: The Corporate Squeeze of Working Americans and the Myth of Managerial "Downsizing."* New York: Free Press, 1996.

Helleiner, Eric. *States and the Re-emergence of Global Finance: From Bretton Woods to the 1990s*. Ithaca, NY: Cornell University Press, 1994.

Lowenstein, Roger. "School Daze on Options . . . and Reality." *Wall Street Journal*, August 6, 1996.

Luria, Daniel. "Why Markets Tolerate Mediocre Manufacturing." *Challenge*, July–August 1996, 11–16.

Minsky, Hyman P. *John Maynard Keynes*. New York: Columbia University Press, 1975.

Obstfeld, Maurice. "Rational and Self-Fulfilling Balance of Payments Crises." *American Economic Review*, March 1986, 76, 72–81.

OECD. *Economic Outlook*. Paris: various years.

Orr, Adrian; Edey, Malcolm; and Kennedy, Michael. "Real Long-term Interest Rates: The Evidence from Pooled Time-Series." *OECD Economic Studies*, 1995, 25, 75–106.

Pozan, Robert C. "Foreign Investors and Corporate Governance: The Japanese Case." *Fidelity Focus*, Fall 1996.

Robinson, Joan. *The Accumulation of Capital*. Homewood, IL: Richard D. Irwin, 1956.

Shleifer, Andrei, and Vishny, Robert. "Equilibrium Short Horizons of Investors and Firms." *American Economic Review*, May 1990, 80, 148–153.

Twentieth Century Fund Task Force. *Report on Market Speculation and Corporate Governance*. New York: Twentieth Century Fund, 1992.

ul-Haq, Mahbub; Kaul, Inge; and Grunberg, Isabelle (eds.), *The Tobin Tax: Coping with Financial Volatility*. New York: Oxford University Press, 1996.

U.S. General Accounting Office. "Mexico's Financial Crisis: Origin, Awareness, Assistance and Initial Efforts to Recover." Report to the Chairman, Committee on Banking and Financial Services, House of Representatives, February 1996.

Wessel, David; Carroll, Paul; and Vogel, Thomas. "How Mexico's Crisis Ambushed Top Minds in Officialdom and Finance." *Wall Street Journal*, July 14, 1995.

[17]

EAST ASIA IS NOT MEXICO:
THE DIFFERENCE BETWEEN BALANCE OF
PAYMENTS CRISES AND DEBT DEFLATION

J.A. Kregel

What was different about the collapse of the Asian emerging markets in 1997? The free fall of the Mexican peso and the collapse of the Mexican Bolsa produced a 'Tequila effect' that spread through most of South America, but did not create a sell-off in the global financial markets similar to that which occurred on 27 October 1997. Normally, sharp declines in prices in emerging equity markets produce a 'flight to quality', in which international investors shift their funds back into developed country markets and local investors seek to protect their wealth by diversifying into developed country assets. Yet, the collapse in the Asian emerging markets, that started in Thailand, spread to the other second-tier newly industrialising economies (NIEs), and eventually extended to the first-tier NIEs produced the largest absolute declines ever experienced in the major developed country equity markets. If equity markets can suffer from what Alan Greenspan has called 'irrational exuberance', the Asian crisis suggests that they may also suffer from 'irrational pessimism'. Yet, there is much to indicate that in this case the financial markets in Japan, Europe and the US were quite rational in assessing the global implications of the financial crisis in Asia.

The developing countries in Asia have come to play a crucial role in global growth. In the 1990s, they accounted for roughly half of global expansion. The immediate implication of the Asian crises is that the collapse of growth in the region would produce a global deflation. This would make it more difficult for developed economies, particularly Europe and Japan, to expand at rates necessary to generate sufficient investment to produce reductions in unemployment. Recovery in the developed world outside the US and the UK is thus at risk as a result of declining Asian growth. Indeed, if the US cannot continue its current expansion, there is a clear risk of a global depression similar to that of the 1930s.

The stage for the decline in growth in the Asian region has been set by what may be called a series of competitive devaluations amongst the currencies in the region. The combination of globalisation of production and economic development in these countries has advanced to the point that a substantial proportion of their trade is now within the Asian region (including Japan), rather than with the developed economies.[1] It has been based on a progressive upgrading of the value added to production, as represented in the idea of the 'flying geese'. But, the logic of the 'flying geese' model is that progress to more advanced stages of development is determined by relative rates of increase in productivity, income per capita and real wages. Since much of the trade is linked to a division of labour within the region, with Japan and the more advanced NIEs exporting capital equipment and semi-finished goods to be assembled in Southeast Asia and then shipped on to others before final export to developed country markets, stable relative costs and prices have played an important part in regional integration and development. Currency instability is very disruptive to this process, causing random shifts in the relative position of individual countries and in their development plans. Thus, the entire logic of the Southeast Asian development process would be disrupted by volatile cross rates of exchange of the currencies of the countries in the area creating changes in relative competitiveness independent of changes in productivity and per capita income levels. If restrictive policies are necessary to restore the currency stability required to allow the 'flying geese' system of relative positions on the value-added ladder to function, then growth will fall and the demand for exports from the developed countries will decline.

While it is true that neither the US nor Europe depend on Asia for a substantial proportion of their exports (the US exports less than 20 per cent and Europe little over 5 per cent), it is an integral part of the process of globalisation; while the US may not export much to Asia, US companies do import to and export from their production facilities in Asia, so that the overall impact on US income will be much higher.[2] And these companies are primarily in the high technology area, that has been at the basis of the restructuring of the US economy and the performance of US equity markets. But how was it possible for one of the most successful development areas to suffer a virtually complete reversal of fortunes in less than a year?

An Interpretation of the Asian Crisis

The Asian crisis was not a typical balance of payments crisis, such as those experienced with such frequency under the Bretton Woods system, or the Mexican peso crisis of 1994/5. In Mexico, rapid liberalisation of domestic markets caused imports to grow much more rapidly than exports. Tight monetary policy to reduce inflation produced high interest rates, which attracted foreign capital inflows to deregulated and liberalised domestic financial markets which financed the trade gap, while it also caused real appreciation of the peso which further worsened the trade balance by turning relative prices against exports. The capital inflows also encouraged import growth as foreign borrowing allowed domestic banks to compete for domestic market share by lending to households to finance consumption and to arrange foreign exchange loans to domestic business at international interest rates. The result was a continually increasing Mexican payments deficit, along with record increases in banks' non-performing loans, a fall in private savings and low domestic investment, with slow growth and rising unemployment accompanying a fall in the rate of inflation and a government budget surplus.

Irrespective of the reversal of US interest rate policy, which was initiated in February 1994, the real appreciation of the peso would eventually have collided with the increasing external deficit, and Mexico would have experienced an exchange rate crisis that would have been aggravated by a domestic financial crisis due to bad bank loans to households and foreign currency exposure of business clients.[3]

The Asian crisis of 1997 has been very different. Most countries have been near surplus on their trade balance, if not on their current account balances, and have a long-term record of fiscal rectitude. Imports were not dominated by luxury consumption goods, savings ratios were extremely high and banks were not financing unsustainable consumption booms. Foreign exchange reserves were high and exchange rates had been stable throughout the 1990s. Yet, there was a discernible tendency towards deterioration in the foreign account caused by a fall-off in the rapid growth of exports in most countries. But, this was caused not by changes in what had until that time been successful internal stabilisation policy, but rather by changes in the external environment, over which they had little control and there were few policy responses available. This is a characteristic of the world of increased economic interdependence and free global capital flows.

External Balance

Current account balances had already started to show weakness throughout the region in 1994. This was, in part, due to the sharp fall-off in import growth in the developed countries. For the developed countries as a whole, the rate of increase in imports fell from 11.0 per cent in 1994 to 7.6 per cent in 1995 to 5.2 per cent per annum in 1996. In Japan, the rate of growth of imports fell from 13.6 per cent in 1994 to 3.5 per cent in 1996; in the US, the decline from 1994 to 1996 was from 12.0 per cent to 6.4 per cent; and in Europe, from 9.1 per cent to 5.3 per cent for the same period. As external positions deteriorated, most countries responded with restrictive policies and external imbalances had started to improve in 1997 (cf. UNCTAD 1997: Chapter 1).

By historical comparison, the trade deficits were not large. Ostrey (1997: 20-3) points out that they cannot be traced to 'excessive private consumption'. He further argues that there is 'relatively strong' evidence in favour of the long-term 'sustainability' of the deficits given the 'strength of savings and investment' — which 'implies that the resources needed to enlarge future productive capacity are in place and, therefore, that rapid economic growth... is likely to persist. In addition, the allocation of investment appears to be efficient, judging from the strong performance of total factor productivity and exports, as well as the absence of significant relative prices distortions in these economies.... In addition, both the absence of significant exchange rate misalignment together with relatively open trade and investment regimes have tended to foster diversification of the export base in the ASEAN countries, making the trade balance less sensitive to terms of trade shocks, and reducing the risks associated with terms of trade shocks.'[4] On this reasoning, the external account should not then have been a cause of crisis.

Capital Flows

The other side of the slowdown of developed country imports is an increase in capital flows from the developed economies into the Asian economies starting in 1993-4. This was further stimulated by the tightening in monetary policy to reduce the deterioration in the foreign balance and by the reaction of international investors to the Tequila crisis in Latin America. There was a sharp increase in the proportion of bank lending into the region, representing a radical change from past experience. In 1993, the banks in the Bank of International Settlements (BIS) reporting area listed US$14.8 billion of assets representing bank lending to Asia. In 1994, the figure jumped to US$47.8 billion and in 1995 nearly doubled to US$86.3 billion. The figure for 1996 was down slightly at US$72.3 billion.

Capital flows require both a borrower and a lender, but they are usually arranged by an intermediary. Thus, in addition to the fall in returns in developed countries that led to a search for higher returns in emerging markets, global investment banks were seeking alternative sources of revenue to help them emerge from their difficulties in the US in the 1980s. One of the ways that they could do this was by earning fee and commission income by arranging structured derivative packages which allowed emerging market borrowers access to funds at low interest rates prevailing in developed country markets, while offering assets earning high emerging market interest rates to developed country investors. A popular means of arranging lending was by means of equity swaps in which high-yielding debt issued by emerging market firms or banks was repackaged into investment trust vehicles which could be sold to institutional investors in developing countries as if they were investment-grade assets. Although the technical aspects of these packages are complicated, they almost all depend on the stability of exchange rates, since the exchange rate risk is borne not by the underwriting bank, but by the buyer or the seller.[5]

Financial liberalisation also made it possible for financial institutions in emerging economies to increase their role as intermediaries. The issue of bonds by Asian entities increased from US$25.3 billion in 1995 to US$43.1 billion in 1996. Korean entities alone accounted for US$16 billion, and Hong Kong, Indonesia and Thailand raised about US$4 billion each (IMF 1997c: 77). Many of these bonds served as the basis for derivatives contracts (discussed above) and were intermediated by offshore investment funds.[6] The result was a sharp increase in foreign exchange reserves, which further strengthened expectations of exchange rate stability.

The increase in capital inflows produced a sharp increase in foreign exchange reserves, which further strengthened expectations of exchange rate stability. However, as central banks attempted to keep their currencies from appreciating relative to the dollar, the rise in foreign exchange reserves was translated into increased liquidity for the domestic banking sector and in expanded domestic lending.

Exchange Rate Misalignments

However, this attempt to keep exchange rates stable to prevent loss of competitiveness was only partially successful since the dollar was itself on a strengthening path from the end of 1995, but this only started to become visible in real exchange rate appreciations in a number of countries from 1996. For example, the IMF's *Expanded Competitiveness Indicators System* (Turner and Golub 1997) reports that Indonesia's real effective exchange rate (the exchange rate of the rupiah corrected for changes in costs and prices in Indonesia relative to its trading partners, weighted by the amount of Indonesian trade with each trading partner), marginally depreciated in 1990-94, and only regained its 1990 level by 1995. In Thailand, the real effective exchange rate in 1994 was the same as in 1990, and rose only marginally in 1995. In Korea, the real effective exchange rate depreciated substantially in 1990-93, and remained at a roughly constant level until 1995. Malaysia and Singapore show marginal rises from 1990-92, and then stability thereafter. Only Hong Kong and the Philippines show substantial and sustained declines in competitiveness due to real exchange rate appreciation over the period 1990-95. This study supports the conclusion of the absence of substantial exchange rate readjustment cited above.[7]

Domestic Banks and Domestic Credit Expansion

Throughout this period, Asian countries were under pressure from both the IMF and the World Trade Organisation (WTO) to modernise, liberalise and deregulate their banking and financial systems. In 1993, Thailand created the Offshore International Banking Facility. The BIS notes that its existence 'was an important reason for the upsurge in cross-border inter-bank credit to Thailand' (BIS 1995: 19)[8] in 1994.[9] Ostrey (1997: 20-21) notes that 'in Thailand, risk-weighted capital-asset ratios were increased for both commercial banks and finance companies in order to comply with BIS standards, and now approach 10 per cent for local banks. In addition, required provisions for doubtful assets were increased, and limits on banks' net open foreign exchange positions were tightened. While banks have been successful in broadly matching the maturity structure of their assets and liabilities, rapid growth in foreign exchange lending has nevertheless created concerns of increased foreign exchange risk. In Malaysia, the position of the banking system has strengthened in recent years.' At the beginning of 1994, Korea initiated the conversion of short-term finance companies into investment banks, as part of an attempt to introduce features of developed countries' financial systems such as commercial paper markets and investment banking, such as the creation of offshore investment funds that were the major vehicles for the sale of derivative products of Korean banks and corporations. These effectively created a commercial paper market and provided new sources of foreign borrowing.

An IMF Working Paper (Montgomery 1997: 25, 19) notes the completion of the modernisation of the Indonesian banking system. It cautions that the basic problem is no longer the absence of appropriate regulation, but the supervision of the banks to ensure that regulations are respected, especially with regard to the rapid expansion of real estate lending, and to the reliability of the figures on bank capital adequacy. The paper also reports that the ratio of net foreign exchange liabilities to bank equity reached a high of 161 per cent in 1992/3, but had fallen back to little over 100 per cent in 1994/5.

These and other types of liberalisation throughout the region provided a fertile ground for the inflows of foreign investors' funds, which multilateral agencies such as the Organisation for Economic Cooperation and Development (OECD) and the IMF were actively encouraging. However, given the high savings rates in most Asian countries, and the preponderance of foreign direct investment (FDI, foreign companies' direct investments in productive capacity) flows in others, and the relative absence of demands for consumption finance, bank lending was directed primarily into two areas.[10] One was in providing loans to domestic firms, using the supply of cheaper foreign funds to offer interest rates below domestic rates. The other was to finance non-manufacturing initiatives, such as financial services, real-estate investments, and other types of infrastructure investment that previously had been rationed by government policies directing credit towards export-oriented manufacturing industries. With rates of growth averaging 8-10 per cent, and given the increasing importance of the globalisation of production in Asia, it was relatively easy for bankers to justify financing the rapidly expanding needs for new office space, leisure centres, golf courses and recreational residences. The exceptional returns that they expected on such investment could, of course, only be justified on the basis of continued global expansion. Unfortunately, it was coming to an end.

Asia is not Mexico

Thus, unlike Mexico, it is impossible to argue that excessive domestic bank lending and excessive real exchange rate appreciation led to a consumption and import boom which eventually created an expanding foreign deficit that speculators recognised as unsustainable since both the real exchange rate appreciations and the increased domestic bank lending occurred well after the beginning of the decline in trade balances and the increase in foreign bank lending. Rather, the process appears to have been the opposite. It was the rise in short-term bank inflows and the decline in developed country demand in the presence of liberalisation of domestic financial markets that led to the deterioration in the trade balance, which was then further aggravated by dollar appreciation and rapid domestic credit expansion. It is for this reason that the crisis was not a foreign exchange crisis caused by a payments imbalance, since there was no clear evidence that exchange rates were inappropriate. Reserves were extremely large,[11] external balances were moving in the right direction and official international agency assessments of country fundamentals suggested that the external positions were sustainable at existing exchange rates.

The Beginning of the Crisis

The crisis broke at the weakest link in the Asian economies, i.e. the recently liberalised and deregulated private domestic banking systems. Weakness in the financial sector in Indonesia was evidenced by its first private bank failure in 20 years in 1992, and the rescue of a major state bank in 1995 (Montgomery 1997: 13). In Thailand, where the expansion of the banking sector had been the most rapid,[12] the central bank had since 1996 been practising a policy of 'forbearance' (frequently used by developed country central banks, in particular the Federal Reserve), that is, central banks lending to support banks in difficulty in the hope that they can be rescued without public notice and without creating market panic. Given the degree to which Thai banks and finance companies had been financed through foreign currency lending to their new offshore banking centre, this meant using foreign exchange reserves for their internal function of lender of last resort. A similar process appears to have been at work in Korea from the spring of 1996. However, in Korea, the first signs of difficulty were in a run of bankruptcies starting with Hanbo steel in January 1997. But, despite increasing information of difficulties in Asian banks,[13] a Thai land development company failing to meet a foreign debt payment, and numerous bankruptcies in Korean corporations, foreign capital inflows into Asia continued unabated during the first half of 1997.

But the failure by the Bank of Thailand to arrange the rescue of the country's largest finance company, Finance One, in the Spring of 1997 concentrated the attention of international lenders and the feared reversal of short-term lending started. The failure took on special importance because it occurred against the background of increased uncertainty in international capital markets concerning the evolution of international interest rate differentials. At the beginning of May 1997, the view that the Japanese economy was engaged in a full-fledged recovery gained increasing support (although there was virtually no hard evidence to support this belief) and there was a sharp appreciation of the yen and a sudden rise in Japanese short-term interest rates on expectations that the Bank of Japan would move quickly to raise its discount rate.[14] As a result, funds that had been borrowed at low interest rates in Japan and Hong Kong, and invested at substantially higher rates in Asia, were quickly withdrawn and returned to Japan, supporting the appreciation of the yen and putting increasing pressure on Asian reserves and exchange rates.

The Thai financial crisis could not have avoided becoming an exchange rate crisis, given the degree to which foreign reserves had already been used to shore up banks through the 'lender of last resort' function and the fact that the reserves were not nearly sufficient to meet the liquidation of the entire amount of foreign lending while the foreign balance was continuing to deteriorate. A domestic banking crisis, which could have been handled by the central bank through creation of domestic currency in a relatively closed capital market, became a foreign exchange crisis because of the open capital market and the size of foreign capital inflows into the Thai banking system through the Bangkok International Banking Facility (BIBF). Since the Bank of Thailand could not print dollars, it could not act as lender of last resort for its own domestic banks' exposure in US dollars, while its use of its foreign exchange reserves to do so made it helpless to support the exchange rate.[15]

Thus, even though Thailand had a savings ratio of around 40 per cent, foreign exchange reserves that were three times the size of the 1996 current account deficit, slowing import growth as well as domestic consumption, and predominantly long-term capital inflows, the baht was floated on 2 July and the IMF called in at the end of the month to formulate a bail-out.

A Financial Crisis of International Capital Market Failure

The crisis could thus be explained as a case of 'market failure' of two different types. First, a failure of free, competitive international capital markets to produce the optimal allocation of capital. Funds continued to flow to Asian financial institutions after it was clear that financial instability was widespread. In the words of Alan Greenspan: 'In retrospect, it is clear that more investment monies flowed into these economies than could be profitably employed at modest risk' (Greenspan 1997: 1-2). Second, is a failure of privatised free-market 'banking systems, [that] were not up to the task of effectively absorbing and channelling to productive use large foreign capital inflows as well as the large amount of domestic savings of these economies.... Such weakness led to the misallocation of resources' (Hormats 1997: 1). On the other hand, Stanley Fischer notes that 'the maintenance of pegged exchange rate regimes for too long... encouraged external borrowing and led to excessive exposure to foreign exchange risk' (Fischer 1998: 2) — which suggests that international bankers and businessmen are incapable of identifying exchange rate misalignments.[16]

The rapid deterioration in conditions in Thailand — especially the change in exchange rate policy which led to substantial losses for foreign investors who had presumed that the probability of exchange depreciation was negligible — led to a reassessment of investors' expectations for exchange rate adjusted returns on their investments in the rest of the region. Speculators, having succeeded in Thailand, started to look for other possible candidates for depreciation.

The balance of payments deficit in the Philippines had been increasing for some years and attention quickly shifted to the exchange rate of the peso. The central bank responded with an increase in the overnight interest rate from 15 per cent to 24 per cent and the discount rate to 32 per cent, but under pressure, the peso was allowed to float within a fluctuation band on 11 July. Once the peso had fallen, it was clear that every country in the region was a potential target. Malaysia had the next worst balance of payments position, and its foreign borrowing from banks had been increasing rapidly. Although steps had already been taken in March 1997 to reduce exposure of financial institutions to real estate and financial investments, Malaysia quickly followed the Philippines and allowed the ringgit to float on 14 July. Singapore followed on 17 July, allowing a depreciation of the Singapore dollar, and although Indonesia had also tightened monetary policy in an attempt to support its currency, once Malaysia and Singapore had given up the dollar peg, Indonesia introduced enlarged fluctuation bands on 21 July. Thus, in the space of less than three weeks, Thailand, Philippines, Malaysia, Singapore and Indonesia gave up exchange rates that had been stable against the dollar for extended periods.

Had it been a typical Bretton Woods balance of payments crisis, it should have been over at this point; tight monetary and fiscal policy would have reduced imports and increased the demand for domestic assets, while the currency depreciations should have increased exports. The balance of falling imports, rising exports and increased demand for domestic assets — due to high interest rates and expectation of subsequent appreciation — should have brought equilibrium to the foreign currency markets and, following the Mexican example, growth and currency stability should have resumed after a period of high inflation. With an average of around 15 per cent of GDP in bad loans, it would have ranked on the high side of recent financial crises, but not out of the range of Mexico and Venezuela, and much lower than Chile. This was clearly the expectation of the IMF and most international observers. However, the move to floating exchange rates did not bring stability, but instead brought increased pressure. The reason, as noted above, was that this was not a typical balance of payments crisis, but a financial crisis.

Contagion and Capital Flows

As exchange rates continued to fall, it became clear that what had been a relatively stable process of adjusting trading patterns without sectoral adjustment crises would be permanently disrupted. As a result, Taiwan — even though it had a massive trade surplus, massive foreign exchange reserves, a budget surplus and no visible speculative pressure on its exchange rate — decided to recover its relative competitive position in the region and devalued its currency by 10 per cent on 17 October. This quickly extended the crisis from Southeast Asia to Northeast Asia and the first-tier newly industrialised countries (NICs). It suggested difficulty in even the strongest of the Asian economies. Given the pivotal role of Hong Kong between Taiwan and China and its recent change to special administrative region status under Chinese control, the result of the devaluation in Taiwan was to raise the possibility of a devaluation of the Hong Kong dollar, or even the Chinese renminbi.[17]

Given that the Hong Kong dollar was one of the few currencies in the region showing clear evidence of overvaluation and a deteriorating external balance, there was an instant flight of investors. The fact that the Special Province operated a currency board, in which domestic currency is 100 per cent backed by foreign exchange reserves, may have contributed to the panic. Investors in Hong Kong now ran the risk of a depreciation of the exchange rate or of a collapse of the prices of their financial assets, or both. The depreciation of virtually every other currency in the region suggested that there would be pressure on competitiveness and thus on the exchange rate. But, the operation of the currency board meant that even if the defence of the exchange rate was successful, this in itself would have negative impact on equity prices. Even if the board did not run out of US dollars, by selling dollars against Hong Kong dollars, it would sharply reduce the domestic money supply, producing a sharp increase in interest rates, and internal deflation, which would certainly create difficulty for domestic banks and property companies that were primarily involved in real estate lending and other financial ventures. Thus, even if the exchange rate held, in doing so, it would certainly bring about a collapse in the stock market. The obvious, safe course of action for a foreign investor facing this choice was to sell both Hong Kong stock and the Hong Kong dollar. The market was already under pressure in August and September, but fell 6 per cent on 22 October and another 10 per cent on 23 October, after the Taiwanese depreciation. As a result of sales of Hong Kong dollars, overnight interest rates rose from 7 per cent to 300 per cent and suggested that the domestic costs of exchange rate stability would be very large. Since a devaluation in Hong Kong would certainly have meant a devaluation of the Chinese currency, this would have ushered in a series of beggar-my-neighbour devaluations reminiscent of the currency instability of the 1920s and 1930s which led to the Great Depression. Faced with this prospect, the New York financial markets led the rest of the world's developed equity markets in a record absolute collapse on 27 October 1997.

Despite the bankruptcies of large manufacturing conglomerates (*chaebols*) and increasing concern for the Korean banks that had lent to these firms, given that many of the *chaebols* carried leverage ratios in excess of 500 per cent (i.e.

borrowed funds were five times owner's equity capital), markets continued to treat these as purely internal difficulties. Korean bank credit ratings were reduced in August, but it was only after the global equity market collapses at the end of October that markets focused on the viability of the Korean producers in conditions of global depression. Given the exchange rate changes in the region, the Korean currency was now clearly overvalued, its production was heavily concentrated in semiconductors (whose price had fallen from around US$50 per chip to US$5 in less than two years), and it was attempting to further expand in the international automobile market where excess capacity dominated. Finally, its current account had been deteriorating rapidly.

This would have been enough to raise the concerns of international investors, but at the same time, a series of Japanese bank bankruptcies occurred. Since the largest proportion of lending to Korea was from Japan, it was feared that they would recall their loans to Korean conglomerates, forcing more bankruptcies in Korea. Korea thus experienced the same withdrawal of foreign lending which had been occurring in the rest of the Asian region since the summer.

In November, it became clear that the Bank of Korea had for some time been using its foreign exchange reserves for lender of last resort lending to domestic banks unable to roll over their foreign borrowing. It also emerged that the level of short-term foreign lending was much higher than had been presumed. Thus, with around US$6 billion in foreign reserves and around US$100 billion of lending to be repaid to foreign lenders, the Bank of Korea allowed the won to float, and it went into free fall, much as the other currencies in the region, and the IMF was called in to provide support.

Given that Japanese banks were the largest lenders in the region, and had substantial exposure to increasingly shaky Korean companies, the collapse of the won created panic in Japan and the Bank of Japan had to inject some US$23 billion into the banking system on 29 November to keep the inter-bank money market from collapsing as Japanese banks withdrew credit, even from other Japanese banks. The rise in the yen which had started in the spring was thus reversed and it started to weaken against the dollar during November 1997.

This closed the first phase of the crisis, with Thailand, Indonesia and Korea accepting IMF conditional lending, and a number of other countries such as Malaysia, Hong Kong and Taiwan introducing similar policies independently of any international commitment of funds. Table 3.1 gives evidence of why these measures have been unable to reintroduce currency stability in the region. The withdrawal of commercial bank lending, plus current account financing and the sale of portfolio equity total US$58.9 billion, over two-thirds of the accumulation of reserves over the period 1990-96 of US$76.2 billion. In one year (in fact, since the outflows only started in earnest in July, the relevant period is closer to six months), the region was called upon to reimburse lending and make current payments equal to the accumulated reserves of the previous seven years. This is

Table 3.1
External Financing of Korea, Indonesia, Malaysia, Philippines and Thailand

Five Asian Economies: (US$ bn.)	1994	1995	1996	1997[a]	1998[b]
Current Account Balance	-24.6	-41.3	-54.9	-26.0	17.6
Net External Financing	47.4	80.9	92.8	15.2	15.2
– Direct Equity Flows	4.7	4.9	7.0	7.2	9.8
– Portfolio Flows	7.6	10.6	12.1	-11.6	-1.9
– Commercial Bank Lending	24.0	49.5	55.5	-21.3	-14.1
– Non-Bank Private Lending	4.2	12.4	18.4	13.7	-3.3
Net Official Flows	7.0	3.6	-0.2	27.2	24.6
Reserves (- = increase)	-5.4	-13.7	-18.3	22.7	-27.1

Notes: [a] estimate, [b] forecast.
Source: Institute of International Finance, 29 January 1998: 2.

Table 3.2
Asian Countries: Investment as Percentage of GDP, 1986-95

	1991-95	1986-90
Singapore	34.1	32.4
Malaysia	39.1	23.4
Indonesia	27.2	26.3
Thailand	41.1	33.0
Philippines	22.2	19.0
Korea	37.4	31.9
China	35.3	27.8

Source: Own calculations based on data from Asian Development Bank, *Key Indicators of Developing Asian and Pacific Countries*.

Table 3.3
Asian Countries: Current Account Balances as a Percentage of GDP, 1989-97

	1989	1990	1991	1992	1993	1994	1995	1996	1997
Hong Kong	11.5	8.5	6.6	5.3	7.0	2.1	-3.4	-1.0	-1.0
Singapore	9.6	8.3	11.2	11.4	7.3	15.9	17.7	15.0	13.7
South Korea	2.4	-0.9	-3.0	-1.5	0.1	-1.2	-2.0	-4.8	-3.9
Taiwan	7.6	6.9	6.7	3.8	3.0	2.6	1.9	3.8	3.1
China	-1.3	3.9	4.3	1.4	-2.7	1.3	0.2	0.9	1.2
India	-2.3	-2.2	-1.5	-1.5	-1.5	-0.9	-1.7	-1.2	-1.1
Indonesia	-1.2	-2.8	-3.7	-2.2	-1.3	-1.6	-3.4	-3.4	-3.6
Malaysia	0.8	-2.0	-8.9	-3.7	-4.4	-5.9	-8.5	-5.3	-5.9
Philippines	-3.4	-6.1	-2.3	-1.9	-5.5	-4.4	-4.4	-5.9	-4.5
Thailand	-3.5	-8.5	-7.7	-5.7	-5.6	-5.9	-8.0	-8.0	-4.6

Source: Asian Development Bank.

Table 3.4
Asian Countries: Fiscal Balances as a Percentage of GDP, 1988-97

	1988-93	1994	1995	1996	1997
Hong Kong	2.3	0.8	-0.3	0.1	1.4
Singapore	6.8	4.0	7.6	6.7	5.1
South Korea	0.5	0.6	0.5	-0.3	-0.5
Taiwan	-1.6	-6.3	-7.4	-8.0	-5.0
China	-2.6	-2.4	-1.3	-1.2	-1.3
India	-7.4	-6.5	-5.8	-5.1	-4.9
Indonesia	-0.6	-0.4	0.8	0.7	0.5
Malaysia	-3.7	-0.2	1.2	-0.7	1.6
Philippines	-3.3	0.7	0.5	0.3	0.4
Thailand	3.3	1.5	3.0	2.2	-0.7

Source: Asian Development Bank.

equivalent to a massive 'bank run' on the region, without any lender of last resort. Just as no bank can ever repay all its deposits at sight, no country which is open to international capital flows can repay virtually all of its short-term borrowing instantaneously without a collapse in the exchange rate and substantial disruption of the real economy. It is for this reason that the basic problem in the region was not mistaken domestic policy, or fundamental disequilibrium, or even lack of transparency in the banking sector, although there is no question that weakness in the banking sectors of many of the countries aggravated the crisis, but was primarily caused by the reversal of the excessively rapid rise in capital inflows and the fall in global demand.

Indeed, these are simply two sides of the same coin, excess saving on the part of the developing world outside the US, visible in the form of capital flows into the region, meant that domestic investment was increasingly substituted for export sales. This may be called an excess savings crisis. Alternatively, it may be termed an over-investment crisis, which, in a way similar to Japan, has caused massive over-investment and over-capacity which will produce downward pressure on the prices of traded goods and thus deterioration in the terms of trade of these countries. Indeed, it is ironic to recall that at the beginning of the 1990s, most official institutions were announcing that it would be a decade of savings shortage as the demand for capital by developing countries outstripped the supply of savings, and that high real interest rates would be the natural result. Less than half-way through the decade, there is instead massive excess capacity, a risk of a global glut of production. Yet, high real interest rates seem still to be considered the answer to the crisis.

Stage Two: The Cure is Worse than the Disease

The second stage of the crisis came in the policy response, largely based on the conditional lending by the IMF. The IMF also mistook the crisis for a traditional balance of payments crisis and applied the same measures that they had used with modest success in the Tequila crisis. These involved increasing interest rates to restore confidence in the currency, tightening government budgets to slow demand for imports, control of monetary aggregates to keep the rate of inflation from eroding the benefits to export competitiveness of devaluation and reform of the banking system. The idea was basically to put household and bank balance sheets back in equilibrium and to allow firms to create an export surplus. However, as noted above, the collapse of exchange rates had not been due to banks financing excess demand for imported consumption goods, but rather, financing imports of capital goods by firms. It was the firms' balance sheets that were generally at risk. And the IMF conditions only made their positions worse. First, the flight of foreign capital meant that they had to replace their short-term financing, but at sharply higher rates from domestic banks. Second, with falling global demand, firms became increasingly dependent on domestic demand, but fiscal policy was ensuring that demand would be falling. Thus, firms had rising short-term financing costs and falling income flows to meet them. Third, firms that had borrowed abroad had to repay foreign lenders. Given the long period of relatively stable exchange rates, much of this borrowing had not been hedged, and thus had to be repaid in foreign currency. But, export receipts were falling and the value in domestic currency was rising daily. All three of these factors meant that firms went from being in a position of illiquidity, i.e. of not being able to convert their assets into foreign currency quickly enough, to positions of insolvency, i.e. of having the value of their assets fall below their liabilities. That is, they were technically bankrupt. At the same time, domestic banks that had acted as intermediaries, borrowing foreign currency to lend to domestic firms, found themselves in the same position. But, their position was aggravated by the fact that if they charged higher interest rates, this simply made it more likely that their clients would go bankrupt and be unable to repay anything. The dispute with the IMF was thus over the impact of interest rate policy. The IMF wanted rates set at levels that were high enough to generate demand for domestic currency, while the firms and banks and most affected Asian governments wanted interest rates set low enough to allow firms and banks to make their payment commitments.

Given the fact that the only way that firms and banks could escape bankruptcy was by repaying their foreign currency loans as fast as possible, this set in train what Hyman Minsky, following Irving Fisher, has called a debt deflation process. In order to meet their current commitments, a firm is forced to sell assets, inventory, current output, anything that will prevent it from having to close its books as bankrupt. But this is a self-defeating process, for as they increase supply, they drive down the price of the assets they are trying to sell, reducing their ability to liquidate their assets for a value that will cover their commitments. For Asian firms, the proceeds of the sales reduced domestic asset prices, while their demand for foreign currency drove up its price, thus driving the terms of trade against them. In such conditions, there is no interest rate high enough to stop the sale of domestic investments and the sale of the domestic currency. Indeed, high interest rates only make the process worse. As firms and banks scrambled to save themselves from bankruptcy, they also drove down the value of the currency.

Indeed, the IMF seems incapable of accepting the idea that higher interest rates might increase the demand for foreign currency by more than it increases supply in a period of crisis and thus aggravate conditions. For example, Camdessus (1998: 2) notes that 'the key lesson of the "tequila crisis" [was] a timely and forceful tightening of interest rates... to make it more attractive to hold domestic currency'. Fischer (1998: 4) uses virtually identical language. But, they both refer to examples of the successful use of high interest rates to *defend* a fixed exchange rate, not to the success of the policy in conditions *after* the devaluation had already taken place.[18] In this regard, it is interesting to note that BIS (1997: 108) refers to 'the increases in (or continued high) real interest rates... in Indonesia and

Thailand... and in Malaysia' that had been put in place already during 1996 and early 1997.

After a substantial devaluation, for a company with foreign exposure, a higher interest rate only makes bankruptcy more probable. For a foreign lender seeking to recover funds, there is no increase in interest rates that can offset the bankruptcy of a creditor. Again, it is interesting to note that BIS (1997: 111) refers to the successful experience of both the US and Sweden of using low interest rate policies to resolve collapsing asset and real estate prices.

At the same time, the breakdown of the financial system made it impossible for firms to increase production or exports, so that while trade balances improved sharply, this was primarily the result of massive falls in imports, rather than increased exports. Thailand and Korea both showed surpluses by the end of 1997, but this had little positive impact on exchange rates. For the month of January 1998, imports in Korea fell at a 40 per cent annual rate, and in Thailand at a 30 per cent annual rate.

Since banks were also part of this process, the equivalent for a bank of the distress sale of assets is to call in loans, or to refuse to make loans. The result was that short-term inter-bank and commercial paper markets disappeared in many countries, and firms were unable to get financing for imports required for production, or even to obtain credit to finance exports. Further, the decision to reform the banking system by requiring rapid bank closures created widespread distrust in the remaining banks, and in many economies, including Hong Kong, there were large scale withdrawals of deposits from the banks, pushing even solid banks to difficulty and reducing even further their ability to lend to support production. Thus, the policies introduced created conditions of full-scale debt deflation in which banks and firms were forced to sell assets to make payments, driving down prices in both stock markets and foreign exchange markets. Thus, the second stage of the crisis involved the sustained meltdown of asset markets throughout December 1997 and January 1998. By the time the IMF had been convinced to introduce additional freedom (the conditions on all three lending agreements were reviewed and rewritten with more lenient conditions on fiscal positions and interest rates in the beginning of 1998), conditions had deteriorated to the point that it is unlikely that there will be positive growth in the region in 1998 and there is some question about 1999.

This phase of collapsing production and income in Asia is reflected in the sharp falls that have occurred in primary commodity prices and oil prices. Thus, the greatest negative impact from the crisis outside Asia has been in other developing countries and in the petroleum producing countries. It would not be surprising if a number of the former should have to apply to the IMF for balance of payments support as a result of the Asian crisis.

Clearly, a more reasoned response to the crisis would have been to attempt to slow the withdrawal of foreign lending and to ease the conditions of payment.

Low, rather than high interest rates would have been indicated, along with policies to stimulate growth. But, most important would have been rapid policies to reschedule foreign loans to stop the mad rush to sell assets and buy foreign currency. This has now started to occur in the case of Korea, which has reached agreement with international bank lenders to roll over the short-term debt owed by Korean banks.

The first step in the third phase of the crisis will then be to restore stability to asset markets, which means having both buyers and sellers, borrowers and lenders. This will allow producers to increase exports and the process of adjustment to begin. However, much of the productive capacity will in fact be closed by bankruptcy. And the fall in prices will be less than the change in exchange rates due to the fact that most Asian exports are import-intensive, so that import costs will be rising in dollar terms. Domestic costs will also be rising as the impact of depreciation on the domestic price level works through to domestic costs. It is also likely that capital flows will return, through foreign purchases of domestic productive capacity (to operate or to close, as occurred in East Germany). It is for this reason that it is difficult to determine appropriate exchange rates. At current exchange rates, this process should be extremely rapid, and will certainly bring calls from developed countries, swamped with imports, for protection measures. It would be ironic if the liberalisation of capital flows, which the IMF has now declared as its major objective, should lead to a deterioration in the free trade in goods and services, which was to be its original objective. The crisis suggests that the two are interdependent, and perhaps cannot be achieved simultaneously. Given that this is precisely the scenario which was the prelude to the global crisis of the 1930s, the collapse of global capital markets in response to the crisis was simply playing according to the script. It remains to be seen if policy can be crafted so as to avoid a repeat of the 1930s.

Notes

1. In 1994, the exports of the ASEAN-4 (Malaysia, Thailand, Indonesia, Philippines) plus the first-tier NIEs (Korea, Taiwan, Hong Kong, Singapore) to developing East Asia plus Japan was US$172 billion and to the other developed market economies US$168 billion, with another US$44 billion to the rest of the world (UNCTAD 1996: Table 24, p. 88).

2. For example, in 1997 the percentage of total imports into the US from affiliates of US companies was over 19 per cent from Thailand, over 18 per cent from Malaysia, and nearly 14 per cent from Indonesia. The share for Hong Kong was over 50 per cent and Singapore over 80 per cent. Korea was less than 3 per cent, while the Philippines was just over 5 per cent.

3. The Mexican crisis did differ from prior experience because of the large build up of foreign holdings of domestic financial assets, including government securities, such as Tesobonos that paid returns linked to the US dollar. The IMF bail-out package thus served primarily to provide an exit for foreign holders of peso-denominated Tesobonos while preserving currency convertibility. The IMF funding, rather than supporting current account convertibility, was thus used for the first time in history to ensure capital account

convertibility. The Mexican crisis might thus be said to be the mid-point between a standard Bretton Woods style exchange rate crisis caused by a current account deficit under restricted capital flows, and an exchange rate crisis caused by capital account outflows and a collapse of financial asset prices under free global movement of capital.

4. While Ostrey (1997) notes that any external deficit represents a potential risk in the case of external shocks, it points out that deficits in the 1980s had been much higher without generating difficulty.

5. It is for this reason that when the Thai baht devalued, it represented a major event, since all contracts which had been purchased on the high probability of exchange rate stability automatically changed in value, and frequently passed from positive to negative values, leading investors to sell them, which was the equivalent of withdrawing capital from the Asian economies.

6. For example, according to the Korean Securities Supervisory Board, 28 Korean securities houses operated over 100 funds with assets of nearly US$3 billion located in Malaysia, Ireland and France. Investment banks were also active in operating offshore funds. Roughly two-thirds of the assets of these funds were in Korean companies. The losses of these funds are estimated at over US$1 billion (cf. *Korean Times*, 19 February 1998).

7. Since the Mexican crisis the IMF has produced a number of studies attempting to identify indicators of future exchange rate and banking crises. The indicator which appears as significant in all of them is real appreciation of the exchange rate, which the IMF studies cited above suggest was not a major factor in Asia

8. The commentary refers to flows in 1994. The report also notes that 'tight monetary conditions help to explain the large banking inflows into South Korea'. An IMF Working Paper (Johnson, Darbar and Echeverria 1997: 38) notes that 'net private capital inflows were larger as a percentage of GDP in Thailand than in the other countries and a large part of these inflows through the international banking facility were short term in nature, which may have increased Thailand's vulnerability to a reversal of such flows.'

9. The *1996/97 Annual Report* (BIS 1997: 112-3) noted that 'the difficulties of Thailand's banking system can be traced in part to the creation... of the Bangkok International Banking Facilities (BIBF), which, as well as promoting Bangkok as an international financial centre, allowed local banks to borrow in dollars.... The Bank of Thailand has taken a number of measures to limit the growth of the BIBF on lending to the domestic market. From September 1995 local banks' net foreign exchange liabilities were made subject to ceilings (e.g. 20 per cent of assets). In addition, foreign deposits were excluded from the calculation of the statutory loan-to-deposit ratios that banks have to maintain.'

10. Composition of Bank Loans, 1993 (percentages)

East Asia	Home Mortgages	Consumer Credit	Enterprises	Government
Indonesia	4.1	6.9	70.7	2.2
Korea	12.7	11.7	74.5	1.1
Malaysia	13.9	11.2	30.1	0.5
Thailand	8.3	4.1	58.8	0.7

Source: BIS 1998b: 40.

11. According to the IMF (1997b: 64), emerging economies accumulated US$575 billion in reserves between 1990 and 1996, representing 49 per cent of the total flows; US$202.2 billion were to the Asian region, but only US$76.4 billion were to Asia excluding India and China (cf. IMF 1997b: 197-8). However, they are concentrated in China, Taiwan, Singapore and Hong Kong. Thailand's reserves increased by US$27 billion, and Singapore's by US$56 billion over the period.

12. Bank assets as a percentage of GDP for three Southeast Asian countries, 1989-94 (percentages)

Bank Assets/GDP	1989	1990	1991	1992	1993	1994
Indonesia	49.3	60.5	64.2	63.0	58.8	57.3
Malaysia	92.4	96.0	101.9	95.0	92.9	99.9
Thailand	72.7	79.2	82.2	85.0	94.6	109.5

Source: Montgomery 1997: Table 1, p. 7.

13. For example, both Korea First and Seoul Bank were known to be in difficulty as a result of corporate bankruptcies in early 1997. Figures for the end of 1996 showed 12.6 per cent of the loans of the eight nation-wide Korean commercial banks were impaired. International rating agencies had issued warnings on Thai banks and at least one international organisation had noted that the Southeast Asian economies were 'vulnerable to interruptions of capital inflows' (UNCTAD 1996: 102).

14. The move was all the more important because it 'was of a magnitude that market participants considered quite unlikely, even as late as 5 May. As the yen appreciated rapidly between 5 May and 9 May (the market) began to reflect a significant probability of large further appreciations' (IMF 1997c: 19).

15. However, it did operate actively in the forward market for baht, employing the technique of the bear squeeze (first employed in Berlin in the 19th century and by Poincaré in the famous stabilisation of the French franc, see Einzig 1937) to try to support the exchange rate. The Bank bought baht from speculators for exchange at a future date at an exchange rate determined by the relative interest costs of lending baht for the period. At the future expiry date of the contract the speculator had to sell baht to the Bank at the previously agreed price. If the baht had devalued by the future date, then the speculator could purchase in the market the baht he had to sell to the Bank at a lower dollar price than that he would receive, the difference representing speculative profit. In a bear squeeze the Bank makes it as difficult as possible for speculators to buy the baht that they have to deliver by restricting the Bank's sale of baht to speculators in the offshore markets. The speculators thus have to borrow the baht at extremely high rates (rates went as high as 1,300 per cent) to honour their contracts and take a loss. It is estimated (IMF 1997c: 35) that speculators lost as much as US$1.5 billion in the bear squeeze applied by the Bank of Thailand through the beginning of July. The problem with such a policy is that the central bank has to have enough foreign exchange to meet the forward sales of baht coming due until speculation is stemmed.

16. As, presumably, is part of the IMF Research Department, cf. Ostrey 1997, quoted above. See also IMF (1997c: 69): 'Among currencies not affected by the contagion was the Korean won, even though there were many parallels in economic circumstance with Thailand... observers have noted that this was perhaps because Korea's debt levels were lower, because the substantial depreciation of the won during the last year and a half had left it at a more appropriate level, or because the recent appreciations of the yen would have greater benefits for Korea than its neighbours. While these factors may have played a role, it should be noted that unlike... the Asian economies that were attacked, Korea restricts won credit to foreign residents, and the foreign exchange markets... are underdeveloped. Simply put, this makes it difficult for foreign investors to speculate against the won.'

17. Fred Bergsten (1997) has suggested that the Taiwanese move, which came on the eve of Jiang Zemin's visit to the US, was made in order to embarrass China.

18. Although the IMF has also criticised the Asian countries for the stability of their exchange rates, cf. Fischer (1998).

References

Bergsten, Fred (1997). 'The Asian Monetary Crisis: Proposed Remedies'. Testimony to the US House of Representatives Committee on Banking and Financial Services, 13 November.

BIS — Bank for International Settlements (1995). *International Banking and Financial Market Developments*, Basle, May.

BIS — Bank for International Settlements (1997). *67th Annual Report*, Basle, 9th June.

BIS — Bank for International Settlements (1998a). *The Maturity, Sectoral and Nationality Distribution of International Bank Lending, First Half 1997*, Basle, January.

BIS — Bank for International Settlements (1998b). *The Transmission of Monetary Policy in Emerging Market Economies*, Basle, January.

Camdessus, Michel (1998). 'The IMF and Its Programs in Asia', Remarks by the Managing Director of the IMF at the Council on Foreign Relations, New York, 6 February.

Einzig, Paul (1937). *The Theory of Forward Exchange*, London: Macmillan.

Fischer, Stanley (1997). 'IMF — The Right Stuff', *Financial Times*, 17 December.

Fischer, Stanley (1998). 'The Asian Crisis: A View from the IMF', address by the First Deputy Managing Director of the IMF to the Midwinter Conference of the Bankers' Association for Foreign Trade, Washington, D.C., 22 January.

Greenspan, Alan (1997). 'Statement Before the U.S. House of Representatives Committee on Banking and Financial Services', Washington D.C., 13 November.

Hormats, Robert D. (1997). 'Testimony Before the U.S. House of Representatives Committee on Banking and Financial Services', Washington D.C., 13 November.

IMF — International Monetary Fund (1997a). 'IMF Approves Stand-by Credit for Thailand', Press Release No. 97/37, 20 August.

IMF — International Monetary Fund (1997b). *World Economic Outlook*, Washington D.C., October.

IMF — International Monetary Fund (1997c). *International Capital Markets*, Washington, D.C., November.

IMF — International Monetary Fund (1997d). 'IMF Approves Stand-by Credit for Indonesia', Press Release No. 97/50, 5 November.

Johnson, R. Barry, Salim M. Darbar and Claudia Echeverria (1997). 'Sequencing Capital Account Liberalization: Lessons from the Experiences in Chile, Indonesia, Korea and Thailand', IMF Working Paper No. 97/157, November.

Minsky, H. (1982). *Inflation, Recession and Economic Policy*, Armonk, New York: Wheatsheaf.

Minsky, H. (1986). *Stabilizing an Unstable Economy*, New Haven: Yale University Press.

Montgomery, John (1997). 'The Indonesian Financial System: Its Contribution to Economic Performance and Key Policy Issues', IMF Working Paper 97/45, Washington D.C.: International Monetary Fund, April.

Ostrey, Jonathan D. (1997). 'Current Account Imbalances in ASEAN Countries: Are They a Problem?' IMF Working Paper No. 97/51, Washington D.C.: International Monetary Fund, April.

Turner, Anthony G. and Stephen S. Golub (1997). 'Towards a System of Multilateral Unit Labor Cost-based Competitiveness Indicators for Advanced, Developing and Transition Countries', IMF Working paper No. 97/151, Washington D.C.: International Monetary Fund, November.

UNCTAD (1996). *Trade and Development Report*, Geneva: United Nations.

UNCTAD (1997). *Trade and Development Report*, Geneva: United Nations.

[18]

Review of Pacific Basin Financial Markets and Policies, Vol. 3, No. 4 (2000) 557–564

Taiwan's Experience in Dealing with the Asian Financial Crisis and Examination of the Role of Short-term Capital Flows in the Emerging Market Economy

Paul C. H. Chiu
Former Minister of Finance, Taiwan, ROC

This paper is divided into three parts as follows. The first part explains why Taiwan was relatively unscathed by the Asian Financial Crisis, including the short term countermeasures that were taken. The second part examines the role of short-term capital flows in the emerging market economy, and the third part concludes the paper.

Reasons Why Taiwan Was Relatively Unscathed by the Asian Financial Crisis, Including Short Term Measures Taken

Taiwan underwent two severe tests during the Asian Financial Crisis: first in the area of trade, Taiwan's export with (the five member nations of) ASEAN dropped 29.7 percent during the Asian Financial Crisis. The annual growth rate of exports decreased from 5.3 percent in 1997 to negative 9.4 percent in 1998. Taiwan's growth rate was also affected, declining from 6.68 percent in 1997 to 4.57 percent in 1998. This was Taiwan's lowest growth rate since 1983.

Another area in which Taiwan underwent severe testing was the securities market. Taiwan's weighted stock price index stood at 8996 on July 2, 1997 and subsequently fell to 5474 by February 5, 1999.

Exports shrank, economic growth declined, the stock market fell, and the NT dollar depreciated. Taiwan, however, enjoyed a healthy economic structure, a comparatively sound financial system, large foreign reserves, low foreign debt, as well as energetic and flexible small and medium enterprises. These factors

558 • Paul C. H. Chiu

helped to keep the impact of the Asian Financial Crisis on Taiwan comparatively minor.

There are three major reasons for this. First, Taiwan has a free market economy and employs Industrial policies to promote long-term economic development. Second, Taiwan maintains a large foreign reserve and the capital adequacy of financial institutions. Third, Taiwan adopted effective foreign currency, economic, and financial crisis management policies during the Asian Financial Crisis.

1. Taiwan's Industrial and Macroeconomic Stabilization Policies

1. First, a discussion of the Industrial Structure and Balanced Fiscal Budget
   a) Small and medium enterprises or SME's, which constitute the basis of Taiwan's industrial structure, have increased individual spending power. Exports by SME's make up half of Taiwan's total exports. Exports continued to increase between 1986 and 1998. Furthermore, profits earned by SME's trickled down to the public as a whole, which kept the gap between the rich and the poor to a minimum while encouraging spending. The annual growth rate of consumer spending among Taiwan consumers, which hovered at 7.5 percent in 1998, helped maintain the stability of Taiwan's economy.
   b) Successfully upgrading industry and maintaining an appropriate economic growth rate. The newly emerging high-tech industries have drawn a great deal of investors from the private sector keeping the real average economic growth rate above six percent between 1990 and 1998.
   c) Maintaining a balanced fiscal budget in the central government. The government of Taiwan maintained small surpluses in the two fiscal years starting in July 1997 and ending at the end of June 1999.
2. Maintaining an Ample Foreign Reserves, Ensuring Adequate Capital Standard for the Banking System, and Stressing Greater Transparency in the Extension of Credit to Business
   a) During the Asian Financial Crisis, Taiwan had US$95 billion in foreign reserves, far exceeding the private sector's total foreign debt. Because of this, the exchange rate of the NT dollar was decided, for the most part, by market forces. In addition, regulations regarding foreign investment in the domestic stock market, allowed up to 50 percent of total market capitalization to be held by foreign investors. In reality, however, less than 4 percent of stocks were under foreign control. This was instrumental in helping Taiwan escaped the effects of highly volatile capital movements by short term foreign speculators.

b) When Taiwan began allowing the establishment of new private banks in 1991, it stipulated that each bank met a strict 8 percent capital adequacy floor ratio set forth by the Bank for International Settlements. Moreover, new banks were required to have NT$10 billion or about US$300 million in capital, effectively reducing the risk of the banking system. The debt to net value ratio among large Taiwanese businesses is approximately one while that for SME's is approximately two. Taiwan's relatively sound financial environment discourages banks and enterprises from engaging in excessive leverage in their operations.

c) The government established a credit information center to centralize the credit information of businesses for banking institutions and major insurance companies. Loan recipients are filed in accordance with their creditworthiness to effectively reduce the risks involved in granting loans and avoiding excessive extension of bank accommodations.

3. Short Term Countermeasures Adopted by Taiwan for Managing the Risks Arising from the Asian Financial Crisis

a) Expanding Domestic Demand. The 1998 and 1999 government budgets were expanded to increase public investment and subsidize the extension of low interest loans to encourage the purchase of housing by individuals. These supplements totaled NT$310 billion or roughly US$9.5 billion. In addition to this, the government introduced the Integrated Income Tax scheme, eliminating the double taxation of company dividends. The maximum ratio of tax burden of the highest personal income tax brackets for stockholders and individuals was reduced from 55 percentage points to 40 percentage points. The change of their tax liability was reduced by 27 percent. Common company shareholder tax liability was also reduced between 27 percent and 80 percent. This has been very conducive to economic stability.

b) Maintaining Foreign Exchange Market Stability. The Central Bank adopted a policy of floating exchange rates. As such, the NT dollar depreciated from 28.7 in July 1997 to 32.56 in February 1999. In addition, the Central Bank prohibited domestic non-bank entities from engaging in transactions of non-deliverable forward or NDF contracts in foreign exchange on May 25, 1998. The Central Bank did not close down the NDF market; rather it allowed Qualified Foreign Institutional Investors (QFII) access to the market. It also closely monitored the sources of funds of investors to avoid manipulation of the forex market by speculators. These measures have proven to be extremely effective in stabilizing the forex market and strengthening the soundness of the NT dollar.

560 • Paul C. H. Chiu

c) Maintaining Financial Stability.
   i) Preventing Bank Credit Contraction and Assisting Healthy Businesses Obtain Operational Capital. In November 1998, the government announced that firms experiencing short term financial shortages, but which were otherwise operating normally, could apply and have their loans extended by six months. In addition, the "Special Committee Providing Financial Aid to Enterprises" was established to prevent credit contraction and negative impact on securities dealers and securities finance firms ensuring sufficient funds for the securities market.
   ii) Acceleration of the Write-off of Non-Performing Loans. In February 1999, the government announced a reduction of the gross business receipts tax of the financial sector from 5 percent to 2 percent. Furthermore, the law stipulated that any increase In profits — roughly NT$132 billion — resulting from the business tax reduction was to be earmarked for writing off non-performing loans. These actions are expected to reduce the NPL rate from its current average level of 5 percent down to a much lower 2.5 percent within four years.
   iii) Prompt Corrective Action for Problem Financial Institutions. In the latter half of 1998, two short-term bills financing firms and one medium sized bank experienced substantial losses. The government took immediate action to quell any potential ripple effect and maintain market stability. Various methods were used, including the takeover of management of the problem bank by the central deposits insurance company and the purchasing of these firms by banking consortiums.
d) Vigorous Stabilization of the Securities Market
   i) The government set up the Stock Market Stabilization Task Force to coordinate the actions of semi-governmental institutional investors, including three government pension funds, the postal savings system, as well as banks and insurance companies, so that they can enter the stock market when needed to help stabilization.
   ii) In the latter half of 1998, 14 listed companies experienced substantial losses, leading the government to suspend trading for the stocks of these companies to maintain orderly market function.

After implementation of the aforementioned judicious policies, growth in bank loans and investment reached 7.56 percent at the end of 1998 and 6.38 percent at the end of March 1999. In addition, for 1998 the average return on net worth for the banking system reached 9.27 percent and no credit contracting took place thereby highlighting the soundness of the banking system. Moreover, there was a clear recovery of investor confidence in the domestic stock market. The TAIEX rose from a low of 5,474 in February 1999 to 8,488.84 at the end of December 1999, and in effect, the severe impact of the Asian Financial Crisis on Taiwan was resolved.

2. The Role of Short-term Capital Mobility in the Financial Architecture of Emerging Market Economy

There was one major difference between Taiwan's experience in dealing with the Asian Financial Crisis and that of some other Asian countries. Taiwan has a high savings rate and large foreign reserves. Taiwan's domestic investment relies mainly on domestic savings and foreign reserves as opposed to foreign capital. Taiwan is scheduled, however, to completely liberalize its capital market by the beginning of the year 2001. It behooves us, therefore, to assess how short-term capital flows affect a country's financial stability.

The financial architecture of the emerging economy is built upon two money multiplier or leverage effects. The first type of money multiplier or leverage effect is that which appears in monetary policy at the macroeconomic level. Foreign exchange (high-powered money) flowing into an economy can generate between five to 10 times the broadly-defined money supply or bank credit within this system. Through the influence of the velocity of money, both the level of real GDP and prices are affected. The second kind of multiplier or leverage effect is that which appears at the microeconomic level. The Bank for International Settlements requires that banks maintain a minimum capital adequacy ratio of 8 percent. This means that banks are allowed to undertake risky assets to some 12 times their capital. If banks, however, incur substantial capital outflows or sizable non-performing loans, a credit crunch will inevitably occur. It is believed that these two multiplier or leverage effects are two major building blocks of the financial system of emerging economies. Rapid mobility of international short-term capital flows can affect a high-powered money supply and the efficiency of bank resource allocation through these multiplier effects, which in turn exerts influence on the stability of an economy's financial environment.

In past years, the international community advocated free capital mobility. The basic reasoning behind this was that, by freeing up such movements of capital, funds would be allocated in the most efficient manner on the international front. This would not only promote technology transfer, but also bring more

562 • Paul C. H. Chiu

employment opportunities to recipient countries, shrink the gap between rich and poor countries, and ultimately stimulate global economic development.

Without doubt, inflows of short-term capital can provide more funds to import machinery, equipment, and raw materials, and is thus beneficial to capital formation. From a financial perspective, however, inflows of short-term foreign funds give rise to the expansion of high-powered money, and in turn have a five- to 10-fold multiplier effect in terms of expanding both bank credit and the broadly-defined money supply. It is worth noting that, among this five- to 10-fold multiplier effect, the four- to nine-fold increase in bank credit is generated by the monetary authorities through a partial reserve requirement ratio scheme in addition to the amount of the original increase in foreign exchange reserves. Although this additional liquidity may be partially absorbed by the increased demand for money through lower interest rates, there is a long lag time as it stimulates productivity. In the short run, this new liquidity gives rise to an excess supply of money. If short-term capital inflow is not sterilized in an appropriate manner or unlike Chile which transform short-term capital into long-term capital in accordance with a reserve requirement scheme, then it will certainly give rise to excess liquidity. Obviously, short-term capital inflow helps attract international finance techniques and modern corporate governance mechanisms to emerging economies, but sound financial architecture of this type takes a long time to set up. In the short run, emerging market countries may find it difficult to use it to counteract the impact that large fluctuations in short-term capital has on their economies. Excess short-term foreign capital will ultimately increase domestic money supply and bank credit, giving rise to excess liquidity and drawing money to stock markets and real estate. It is highly probable, therefore, that resources in emerging economies with excess inflow of short-term capital will be shifted to speculative financial activities, increasing the risk of the formation of bubble economies.

Foreign capital has a large influence on the financial stability of emerging economies. Turner (1991) and Reisen (1996) both observe that foreign short-term inter-bank lending is temporary and the most unstable in nature, followed by portfolio investment, and then foreign direct investment. The most stable is foreign long-term bank lending. This observation deserves our attention. Reisen proposes that the focus should be on gross capital flow, not just the net inflow and outflow.

The experience of Taiwan dealing with the liberalization of short-term capital movements attests to what these scholars have suggested. At present, short-term foreign funds borrowed by banks are used mainly to facilitate international trade financing. Furthermore, while the regulations regarding short-term inflows of foreign capital to invest in the securities and stock markets are lessened to a greater extent, to prevent excessive amounts of funds from flowing into banks, restrictions are also placed on institutional investors that may inwardly remit such funds. Specifically, at least 70 percent of the inwardly remitted funds must be invested in equities, and no more than 30 percent may be deposited with banks.

Furthermore, in addition to the necessary sterilization, to adequately regulate bank liquidity, Taiwan used to set ceilings on how much in terms of foreign liabilities banks could incur. This regulation has been rescinded. In 1999, a bill was passed stipulating that banks could borrow foreign capital on the condition that they first prepare a reserve. When necessary, it can be a tool used to protect against large inflows of short-term foreign capital.

Stated simply, the purpose of capital movement liberalization is to encourage transparency in emerging markets and to provide recipient nations with foreign capital for investment. But we must keep an eye on the stability of aggregate capital growth. Capital movement liberalization is a means to an end, not an end itself. The ultimate objective of any economic policy is to promote financial market efficiency and foster the stable growth of the economy. Any liberalization of capital movements should always serve those objectives.

The financial architecture of Asia today is not entirely based on the dollar-gold exchange standard regime. The US dollar, the Euro, and Japanese yen, however, are still important reserve assets, which serve in part as a base for the creation of monetary aggregates in many economies. For this reason, the increase or decrease in foreign exchange brought about by short-term capital movements significantly impact the changes in the monetary aggregates of the emerging market economies through the money multiplier. Under such circumstances, some economies will inevitably face a liquidity crisis when there are balance of payment deficits and sudden capital outflows, and will need to have their liquidity requirements met by other regional and global international organizations. Therefore, as financial globalization becomes a reality, economies will now need to cooperate more closely in order to resolve some common financial challenges that are currently facing us.

The way in which the Asian Financial Crisis spread from country to country illustrates just how important it is for the international community to get down to the business of reforming the international financial architecture. Steps are already being taken. For example, strengthening the economies of APEC members, including the interaction of international financial forums, including the forum for strengthening financial stability and the APEC G20 Meeting of Finance Ministers. In addition to these measures, maintaining order in emerging economies facing large inflows of short-term capital also remains an important policy.

564 • Paul C. H. Chiu

3. Closing Remarks

The successful introduction of the information technology industry into Taiwan, the gradual liberalization of capital movements, the accumulation of savings and foreign reserves, and judicious tax and macroeconomic measures have enabled Taiwan to escape from the Asian Financial Crisis relatively unscathed. As we look to the future, however, following full capital market liberalization in the year 2001, Taiwan, like many other Asian countries, will need to work to bolster macroeconomic management, enhance the transparency of financial institutions, and strengthen good corporate governance. We must also work together to create sound domestic financial and capital markets as well as continue to liberalize financial markets to attract foreign capital. This is to be done while maintaining monetary stability under the impact of short-term capital movements, so as to prevent the reoccurrence of financial crises. Furthermore, the financial and monetary authorities of countries around the world must strive to work more closely together.

References

Allen, Roy E. (1999), *Financial Crises and Recession in the Global Economy*, 2nd edition, Edward Elgar.

Corsetti, G., P. Presenti and N. Roubini (1998), "Paper Tigers? A Model of the Asian Financial Crisis", manuscript.

Eichengreen, B. (1999), "Taming Capital Flows", manuscript.

McKinnon, R. and H. Pill (1996), "Credible Liberalizations and International Capital Flows: The 'Overborrowing Syndrome'", in T. Ito and A. Kruger (eds.,) *Financial Deregulation and Integration in East Asia*, The University of Chicago Press.

Mishkin, F. (1997), "The Cause and Propagation of Financial Instability: Lessons for Policy Makers", in *Maintaining Financial Stability in a Global Economy*, The Federal Reserve Bank of Kansas City, pp. 55–96.

Obstfeld, M. (1994), "The Logic of Currency Crises", *NBER Working Paper* No. 4640, National Bureau of Economic Research.

Radelet, S. and J. D. Sachs (1998), "The East Asian Financial Crisis: Diagnosis, Remedies, Prospects", *Brookings Papers on Economic Activity* 1998:1, pp. 1–74, National Bureau of Economic Research.

Reisen, H. (1996), "Managing Volatile Capital Inflows: The Experience of the 1990s", *Asian Development Review* 14-1, p. 72–96.

Turner, P. (1991), "Capital Flows in the 1980s: A Survey of Major Trends", BIS Economic Papers No. 30. Bank for International Settlements, Basle.

[19]

Nd.

Revised, April 2001

MALAYSIA: WAS IT DIFFERENT?

Rudi Dornbusch
Massachusetts Institute of Technology

"Then the unexpected happened. The Asian miracle was shattered almost overnight and suddenly once fawning economists argued that all it really had been was a bubble, over-inflated by corruption, cronyism and bad loans. Asians were not only impoverished but were blamed for impoverishing themselves."

Mahathir Mohamad (1999, p.47)

The Asian crisis came as a big surprise to all: investors, credit rating agencies, international institutions, and not least of all, officials in the crisis countries. No question, the long run performance, hard work, high saving rates, seemingly competent officials collectively created a powerful presumption that all was well.[1] They gave assurance that problems, if any existed at all, would be isolated and manageable. And, since everybody held that belief, everyone reinforced everybody else in his or her unquestioned beliefs. No question either that once the weakness in balance sheets revealed itself, everybody's skepticism was profound and their willingness to remain invested was undermined. Preceding crises contained few surprises because they involved the usual suspects from Latin America. This time round it was miracle Asia, but the mechanics did not differ much.

What did differ in the case of Malaysia was the forceful reaction of the leadership and the departure from traditional post-crash responses. Dr. Mahathir staged a dramatic rejection not only of "speculators" and of the international capital market, but also of international officialdom. He took recourse to financial restrictions with quite a bit of grandstanding and, indeed, claimed that the country suffered less and recovered more quickly precisely because of these measures. He obviously and righteously delighted in sticking a finger in the eye of the IMF and G-6 treasuries.[2] It remains to explore whether that claim is indeed appropriate or whether it is primarily the domestic grand standing of a weakened and challenged leadership using the international issue to deflect attention from severe domestic political problems.[3]

The Malaysian case deserves attention not only on its own terms but also because the presumption of capital controls in response to crises – failing an early and gracious arrival of the IMF – has become far more of a concern. How after all can a finance

---

[1] Of course, there was a discussion about the productivity of Asian economies but that had to do with the sacrifice in achieving growth, not the vulnerability that made for the imminent crisis.

[2] G6 because Japan is not on record as questioning Malaysian policy responses. On the contrary, it participated and led the call for an Asian IMF and new and different policy responses to regional financial crises.

[3] See Haggard (2000) and Haggard and Low (2000) for the political setting and its link to capital controls.

minister stand up and assert that it is good policy for the country to experience meltdown, as a matter of principle, to accommodate departing investors? Moreover, if it could be demonstrated that it had an appreciably positive effect on dealing with a crisis, policy makers would even have to come around and welcome such a development. Of course, a presumption of capital controls would create a very trigger-happy international environment. It might be argued, with some merit, that the environment is already explosive and what is missing is a good response. Hence, no surprise, it is the *national solution* that countries lean toward and it does make for a good rhetoric.

In evaluating the Malaysian experience it must be understood that for this country two crises were unfolding simultaneously. One was the Asian financial crisis that brought down countries with vulnerable financial structures. The other one was the domestic political crisis arising from the challenge to Dr. Mahathir Mohamad by the deputy prime minister and finance minister, Anwar Ibrahim. The political crisis, in the eyes of the leadership, must have seemed at least as critical as the financial crisis; indeed, the financial crisis offered a means to sustain and reinforce political control by creating an economic state-of-siege situation and policy response. It surely is not a coincidence that capital controls were imposed one day, and Anwar was literally deposed the next.

If capital controls have not delivered clearly better economic results, that does not mean that they failed on the political side. The show-trial style attacks on speculators who were alleged to have undermined the Asian dream and the Malaysian model were a central move in the effort to ward off challenges to Mahathir's leadership. They were put in place to claim assertively that the economic development model, including the 20/20 vision and the ambitious public investment programs, were right and that the rest of the world was wrong. For the time being, they have been effective.[4]

Capital Controls

In the 1930s, Nazi Germany invented capital controls and soon, in an environment of capital flight and competitive depreciation, much of Europe moved to controls. The system become pervasive and accepted. Indeed, in the move to rules in the context of the IMF and the rebuilding of a more open world economy, capital account convertibility was not part of the story. That came much later, after 1958, when Europe gradually and unevenly shifted to full convertibility. The usual suspects, France and Italy, took until the late 1980s. Britain, for example, took until the Thatcher government to abolish exchange control, and in Japan and on the periphery it took even longer. Opening the capital account became the mantra of US financial policy in the late 1980s and, particularly, in the Rubin-Summers US Treasury with an agenda of opening financial services trade and domestic financial deregulation. Repressed finance gave way to an opening of domestic finance and to more substantial freedom for cross border flows.

The case for integrated international capital markets is just like that for open trade: a more efficient allocation of resources achieved by competition, diversification opportunities, and equalization of risk-adjusted returns. In addition, just as in the case of

---

[4] See Mohamad (1999) where Dr. Mahathir's presents the case.

2

open trade, overwhelming case can be made that restrictions to capital flows create a hotbed of privilege and corruption around exceptions and loopholes. Finally, the expectation is that an open capital market – and the accompanying international standards, regulation and supervision – will do a better job at allocating capital than politicized and corrupt local arrangements.

While there is a huge amount of work reporting on the costs of trade distortions, little is available on the issue of restricted capital accounts.[5] For example, there is no evidence that countries with open capital accounts grow faster (other things equal). Nor is there evidence of the converse. There is work showing that countries with high black market premia (meaning capital controls are binding) perform relatively poorly. But these premia certainly reflect not just controls but also macroeconomic instability and hence may not be conclusive.

We might approach the question of the effects of controls somewhat differently by asking what would we expect from a country imposing controls on capital flows. In the long run, in the absence of regulatory and tax distortions, we would expect controls to imply a less effective allocation of resources and hence less growth and/or less diversification. In the short term controls play a quite different role. If they are imposed in the midst of a crisis, unanticipated and temporary, they will work in the sense of stopping outflows, reduce pressure on the exchange rate/interest rate and hence avoid a state-of-siege situation with the resulting excess bankruptcy and disruption. They are quite analogous to a suspension of trading on the New York stock exchange or the Nasdaq or a bank moratorium – they stop the run and offer time to set things straight.[6] Economists' concern with ad hoc capital controls is less with the description offered here than with the feared implication that they will become a substitute for setting things straight. Malaysia is, of course, a case in point. The major question is whether the intention is to gain time or whether it is to lastingly change freedom of resource allocation. The former deserves much attention; the latter is politically attractive but has no economic support.

Moving now to the question of Malaysian controls, what might be argued? Supporters would no doubt claim that in the absence of controls the collapse would have been far deeper, the recovery much harder, and the lasting damage more profound. With this in mind, a capital control country – other things equal – would look much better than the other countries exposed to the same initial shocks but responding with orthodoxy rather than controls. Specifically, to make some progress on these issues, three questions might be answered:

---

[5] Even the evidence on trade is not unambiguous. See Brock and Durlauf (2000), Rodriguez and Rodrik (1999), and Doppelhofer, Miller and Sala-I-Martin (2000).
[6] In the aftermath of the 1987 stock market decline the Brady Commission reviewed the question of suspending trading and came out in support of circuit breakers as a means to restore markets. On the Nasdaq, trading is suspended for companies for which information is unavailable. These seem an interesting analogy for defensible limited-time capital flow suspensions. If on the New York stock exchange a circuit breaker lasts a half hour, perhaps the equivalent for an emerging market capital flow suspension is one month.

- On the eve of the crisis, was Malaysia appreciably different in its vulnerability from other crisis countries? If so, that is possibly the explanation for the claimed success in dealing with the problem.

- Did the policy measures – banking, stock market, capital controls, and business subsidies – make for a significantly better performance than in other economies? Better performance means higher growth, less pervasive bankruptcy without offsetting large increases in public debt, and less volatility.

- Is there an indication of lasting costs, or benefits, of the policy choices?

To anticipate the conclusion, the costs or benefits of capital controls remain ambiguous. Malaysia had more favorable preconditions, it did not do appreciably better, and the timing of controls coincided with the reversal of Yen appreciation, the end of the crisis elsewhere, and Fed rate cuts that put an end to the crisis atmosphere in world markets. However, because the costs are ambiguous, there is no evidence that the institution of capital controls or the failure to apply an explicit IMF program has yet resulted in any obvious detrimental effects.

THE BACKGROUND

It is helpful to place the Malaysian events within a broader timeline. The relevant time frame runs from the Thai problems starting in spring of 1997 to the interest rate cuts administered by the Fed in the aftermath of the LTCM problem and the Russian crisis. Various Asian economies joined the crisis progressively.

==

May-July 1997	Pressure on Thailand, exchange control, 2-tier market, Devaluation.
July	Philippines go to a float, Malaysia abandons support for the ringgit, Thailand goes to the IMF
August	Thailand suspends 42 banks, Indonesia abandons rupiah support, Malaysia restricts short selling, Indonesia restricts credit for rupiah trading
October	Indonesia goes to the IMF, Malaysia announces austerity budget, HK Dollar under attack
November	Korea abandons won support and goes to the IMF
December	Rescue package for Korea
January 1998	Malaysia announces full deposit guarantees
Jan.-Aug.	Asian IMF packages revised, financial restructuring, downgrading

4

May	Indonesia's Suharto steps down
August	Russian crisis, Yen peaks
September	LTCM crisis, Malaysia imposes capital controls, Deputy Prime Minister Anwar Ibrahim deposed
Sept.-Nov.	Fed cuts rates by 75 basis points

The background of the Asian crisis includes the large buildup of capital inflows in the first half of the 1990s, not FDI but rather bank loans and portfolio capital. The crisis involves, in 1997, the sudden drying up and reversal of these flows and the resulting macroeconomic pressures of currency depreciation, high interest rates, output decline and financial stress. This is shown in the accompanying figure for the Asian crisis economies as a group. The counterpart of the capital flows is a reserve loss and current account deficits in the crisis economies.

EXTERNAL CAPITAL FLOWS FOR CRISIS-ASIA (Bill $US)

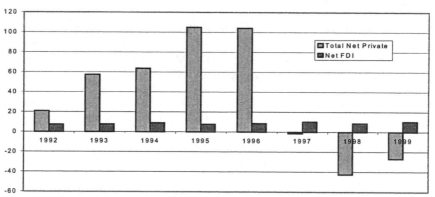

The pressure for outflows soon reached all economies. Within 6 months of the Thai debacle, Indonesia, Malaysia, the Philippines and Korea had all been hit and Hong Kong had come under attack.

One summary measure of events is the path of real GDP. From star performance through 1996, growth in 1997 was lower as the economies shifted toward crisis. The following year, 1998, involves an output decline everywhere and by 1999 recovery is underway. By 2000 per capita GDP is back above pre-crisis levels. Judged in that way, the crisis was as short as it was deep. But there are other measures that show more lasting damage, including an impaired banking system, significantly higher public debt everywhere, and a loss of growth momentum with the resulting temptation for government intervention.

5

MALAYSIA AND OTHER CRISIS COUNTRIES: GDP GROWTH

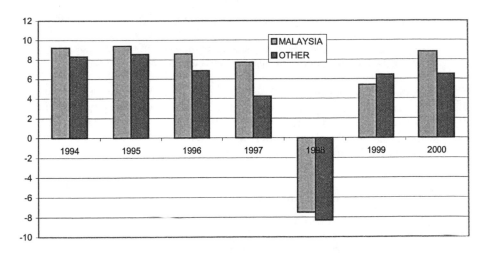

Another measure that might indicate differential performance is the real exchange rate. One might argue that, other things equal, in a capital outflow crisis countries with controls should suffer a less extreme real depreciation. However, that prediction is not born out in the accompanying figure.

REAL EXCHANGE RATE (Jan 1970=100)

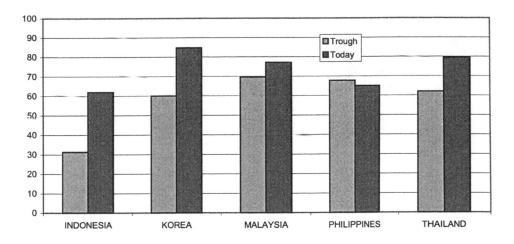

6

A CLOSER LOOK AT MALAYSIA

This paper does not address the immediate reason for the crisis. In Dornbusch (2001) there is a summary of the vulnerability factors: misaligned real exchange rates, nonperforming loans in the banking sector, funding risk of the national balance sheet due to excess debt or mismatches of maturity and currency denomination.

With the pressure of capital outflows and increases in interest rates (underway since early 1995), and poor export performance, growth declined and ultimately turned negative. Industrial production declined and resumed growth only in early 1999, investment as a share of GDP fell sharply to half its previous level, the stock market fell sharply, and the real exchange rate depreciated significantly.

Table 1 Malaysia: Economic Indicators							
	90-95	95	96	97	98	99	2000
Growth	8.9	9.8	10.0	7.5	-7.5	5.4	8.5
Inflation	3.7	3.2	3.3	2.9	5.3	2.8	1.5
Investment[a]	37.5	43.6	41.5	42.9	26.7	22.3	24.1
Budget Deficits[a]	-0.4	3.2	3.9	6.1	-0.9	0.2	-2.6
Current Account[a]	-5.8	-9.7	-4.4	-5.6	12.9	16.0	12.1
External Debt ($Bill)		34.3	39.7	47.2	42.6	43.6	45.0
% of GDP		38.7	39.3	47.1	58.8	55.2	50.4
% Short term [b]		19.1	27.9	25.3	17.8		
Reserves ($Bill)		23.8	27.0	21.7	26.2	30.9	33.2
[a]Percent of GDP [b]IMF (1999c) Source: Goldman Sachs, except as noted							

7

MALAYSIA: MONEY MARKET AND LENDING RATES

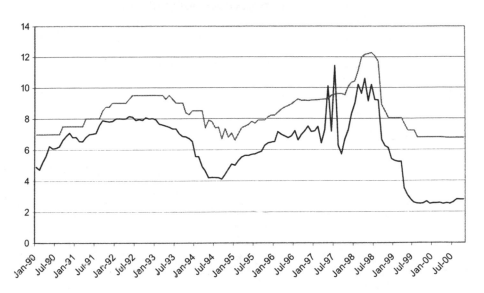

MALAYSIA: STOCK MARKET
(Index Jan 94=100, Source Datastream)

8

MALAYSIA: REAL EFFECTIVE EXCHANGE RATE
(JPMorgan Index 1990=100)

A large part of the macroeconomic scene involves problems with banks and firms with balance sheets unprepared for exchange rate movements, slowdown, or recession. The response in terms of restructuring, bailing out and subsidizing is certainly part of the controversial legacy. But this part is not really very different from the other economies where none of this happened promptly, decisively or successfully.

CAPITAL CONTROLS AND THEIR EFFECTIVENESS

One possibly critical difference between Malaysia and other crisis economies in the region was the imposition of stringent capital controls on September 1, 1998. This went further than the Thai measures (which had already been suspended) and it went further than the credit measures to avoid financing capital flight that had been used elsewhere. The Malaysian capital controls essentially involved the mandatory repatriation of offshore ringgit funds and their lockup with a one-year holding period, as well as restrictions on outflows.[7] These controls were partially relaxed in February 1999 to become a system of graduated exit taxes. FDI flows throughout were exempt and the exchange rate was fixed. The drastic attack on capital flows had the effect to stop capital flows, both ways, as shown in the accompanying diagram that uses portfolio flow data (made available by SSA.)

---

[7] See IMF (1999a) pp. 54-56. See, too, IMF (1999c).

9

By the canons of IMF policy and commitments, the imposition of capital controls was, of course, a radical measure. For whatever reason it was imposed, Dr. Mahathir justified it with a quote from Paul Krugman "extreme measures might be needed for extreme times." (See Mohamed (2000, p.106).) He might, in his justification for opting out of classical financial rules, have quoted Keynes, "in the Street it is better accepted to fail by traditional means than to succeed by unconventional ones."

Were controls decisive in producing the turn of events or was it happening anyway? It is readily seen from the graph above that the stock market recovery begins in September, 1998, as does the recovery of industrial production. The same is true for short-term interest rates. It is tempting therefore to see the imposition of capital controls as the turning point. However, as the IMF has rightly argued, at the time capital controls were imposed, markets had already settled in Asia, interest rates had been coming off and would soon do so everywhere under the impact of Fed rate cuts and a reduction in jitters. In fact, in Korea and Thailand rates had fallen by August to half their June levels. And the same was true in Malaysia.

MALAYSIAN OFFSHORE DAILY RATES (% p.a.)

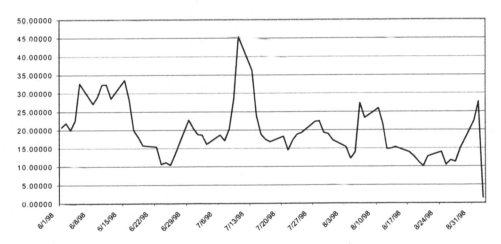

In fact, looking at *offshore* rates for Malaysia, and thus at the interest rates faced in the open market and a reflection of depreciation expectations, much of the pressure had subsided before the September 1 imposition of capital controls. By August, the offshore rates had, in fact, declined to around 10 percent, far below crisis levels. Interestingly, the spike in the graph, at the end is at the time the controls were put in place, reaching 28 percent on September 1! Thus, the claim that the pressure was continuing unabated is simply not borne out by offshore interest rates. On the contrary, it is the advent of

10

controls that raised rates. The political interpretation for the controls thus deserves more attention.

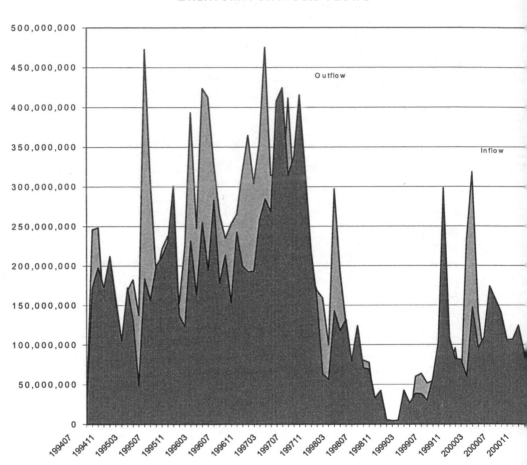

MALAYSIA: PORTFOLIO FLOWS

11

SHOULD MALAYSIA HAVE DONE BETTER?

Another way of looking at the question of non-IMF policies and the claim that Malaysia did well with this prescription is to ask how the country compared to others in terms of vulnerability. Two issues influence performance, initial conditions and policy responses. If performance was not substantially different, one might argue whether it should have been simply because initial conditions were significantly more favorable or unfavorable to start with. In particular, very bad balance sheets would imply more difficulty in dealing with the crisis and hence poorer performance. On the other side, better vulnerability indicators would mean less stress and hence better performance.

Table 3 Vulnerability Indicators: 1996				
	Stock Market Cap/GDP	Debt/Equity Ratio	Private Bank Credit/GDP	Short Term External. Debt/Reserves
Indonesia	40	310	55.4	177
Korea	28.6	518	57.6	193
Malaysia	310	150	89.8	41
Philippines	97.3	160	49	80
Thailand	55	250	100	100
Source: World Bank (2000) p. 70				

Tables 3 and 4 show a series of vulnerability indicators. In Table 3, Malaysia looks relatively good on the debt/equity ratio of the corporate sector and, more importantly, the ratio of short-term external debt to reserves. Both the stock market GDP ratio and the private credit GDP ratio are high. These were, indeed, Achilles heels since the high valuation reflected a vast share of GDP – 7 percent – of bank credit lent to stock purchases.

In Table 4, we look at the banking system by 1999. Malaysia looks relatively favorable in terms of nonperforming loans as a share of total loans. But as a ratio of GDP these numbers are high, reflecting the large share of private credit relative to GDP. In terms of the cleanup cost, Malaysia compares favorably, more so since the Korean numbers almost certainly understate the cost of restructuring the banking system and the corporate sector.

Table 4 Nonperforming Loans and Increased Public Debt: 1999			
	NPL/Total	NPL/GDP	Increase in Public Debt/GDP (% points)
Indonesia	55	22	68.6
Korea	16	23	20.7
Malaysia	24	35	16.0
Thailand	52	53	34.6
Source: IMF (1999a), World Bank (2000)			

Table 5 looks at statistics for debt and debt structure in the corporate sector. Again, in no way does Malaysia stand out unfavorably. Public debt in 1996 is higher than in Korea or Indonesia but certainly not alarming – the banking system and private investment (with or without cronyism) was financing the development strategy, unlike in Latin America. But Malaysia shows initially a better-rated banking system, lower debt/equity in corporations and a maturity of debt that is not substantially shorter than elsewhere.

Table 5 Public Debt, Bank Strength and Corporate Debt Structure in 1996				
	Public Debt/GDP	Bank Strength Rating	Debt/Equity Ratio (%)	Short Term Debt/Total Debt
Indonesia	22.9	D	188	54
Korea	8.8	D	355	57
Malaysia	36.0	C+	118	64
Philippines	105.1	D+	129	48
Thailand	15.7	D+	236	63
Source: IMF (1998) p. 36, Asian Development Bank (1999) p. 27, World Bank (2000) p. 70				

In summary, Malaysia was no more vulnerable than other crisis countries and, for that reason, should not have been doing worse. Accordingly, it cannot be argued that a situation that otherwise would have been much worse was contained by the effects of capital controls. Once again then, there is no evidence one way or another.

13

One more question is whether Malaysia enjoys lasting benefits from the continuing capital control regime (see Bank Negara Malaysia's website for the bureaucratic aspects of ongoing circulars modifying the regime). The answer here is surely that it is far too early to judge the impact, if any. In the ERM experience in Europe, the Netherlands paid a small but lasting price for a one-time devaluation that broke with the tradition of fixed rates on the DM. In emerging markets, differentials reflect ongoing control regimes, macroeconomic instability and, importantly, political uncertainties. To identify the capital control "misconduct" premium is overly ambitious.

14

REFERENCES

Ariyoshi, A. et al (2000) <u>Capital Controls: Country Experiences With Their Utilization</u>. IMF Occasional Paper No. 190.

Asian Development Bank (1999) <u>Asian Development Outlook</u>. Manila.

Brock,W. and S.Durlauf (2000) "Growth Economics and Reality." NBER Working Paper No. 8041.

Doppelhofer, G., R. Miller and X. Sala-I-Martin (2000) "Determinants of Long-term Growth: A Bayesian Averaging of Classical Estimates (BACE) Approach." NBER Working Paper No. 7750.

Dornbusch, R.(2001) "A Primer on Emerging Market Crises" <u>www.mit.edu/~rudi</u>.

Edison, H. and C. Reinhart (2000) "Capital Controls During Financial Crises: The Case of Malaysia and Thailand." International Finance Discussion Paper No. 662, Board of Governors of the Federal Reserve.

Haggard, S. and L. Low (2000) "The Political Economy of Malaysian Capital Controls." Unpublished manuscript, Harvard University.

----------- (2000) <u>The Political Economy of the Asian Financial Crisis.</u> Washington: Institute for International Economics.

IMF (1998) <u>International Capital Markets</u>. September.

IMF (1999a) <u>World Economic Outlook</u>. October.

IMF (1999b "Malaysia: Recent Economic Developments." IMF Staff Country Report No. 99/85.

----- (1999c) "Malaysia: Selected Issues." IMF Staff Country Report No. 99/86.

---- (2000) <u>International Capital Markets</u>. September.

Kaplan, E. and D. Rodrik (2000) "Did the Malaysian Capital Controls Work? " Unpublished manuscript, Harvard University.

Koay, S. (2000) Effectiveness of Capital Controls in Malaysia." Unpublished manuscript, December.

Mohamad, M. (1999) <u>A New Deal For Asia</u>. Malaysia: Pelanduk.

Rodriguez, F. and D. Rodrik (1999) "Trade Policy and Economic Growth: A Skeptics Guide to the Cross-National Evidence. " Unpublished manuscript, Harvard University.

Terence Gomez, E. and Jomo K. S. (1999) Malaysia's Political Economy. Cambridge: Cambridge University Press.

World Bank (1998) East Asia: The Road to Recovery. Washington, DC.

------------- (2000) East Asia: Recovery and Beyond. Washington, DC.

[20]

Journal of Development Economics 19 (1985) 1–24. North-Holland

GOOD-BYE FINANCIAL REPRESSION, HELLO FINANCIAL CRASH

Carlos DIAZ-ALEJANDRO*

Columbia University, New York, NY 10027, USA

Received December 1983, final version received March 1984

Some unintended consequences of financial liberalization in Latin America are analyzed in this paper. Intrinsic imperfections in financial markets, and the policy dilemmas they pose, are reviewed first. The stylized facts of Southern Cone experiments in financial liberization are then presented. Alternative ways of organizing domestic capital markets under Latin American conditions are discussed, and an eclectic, reform mongering program is proposed.

1. Introduction

This paper seeks to understand why financial reforms carried out in several Latin American countries during the 1970s, aimed at ending 'financial repression', as defined by Ronald McKinnon [see, for example, McKinnon (1980)], and generally seeking to free domestic capital markets from usury laws and other alleged government-induced distortions, yielded by 1983 domestic financial sectors characterized by widespread bankruptcies, massive government interventions or nationalizations of private institutions, and low domestic savings. The clearest example of this paradox is Chile, which has shown the world yet another road to a de facto socialized banking system. Argentina and Uruguay show similar trends, which can be detected less neatly in other developing countries, including Turkey. Indeed, even in the United States some worried observers have warned against the dangers of pell-mell deregulation of commercial banks [see Kareken (1981)].

*A version of this paper was first presented at a conference held in Bogota on November 22 and 23, 1982 — sponsored by the Universidad de Los Andes and the Banco de la República. Visits to CINVES, in Montevideo, and CIEPLAN, in Santiago de Chile, during March 1983, were very helpful for extending that early version. I am grateful to all these institutions and to numerous individuals who shared with me their views of the events narrated and of the issues discussed in the text. Among those who are unlikely to find embarrassing my acknowledgement of their help, I may mention José Pablo Arellano, Edmar L. Bacha, Guillermo Calvo, Jonathan Eaton, Richardo Ffrench-Davis, Arminio Fraga Netto, Jeff Frieden, Eduardo García d'Acuña, Jose Antonio Ocampo, Hugh Patrick, Gustav Ranis, Patricio Meller, Miguel Urrutia and Laurence M. Weiss. My gratitude is no less for the often extraordinarily generous cooperation of those not explicitly named.

The paper will first review dilemmas posed by intrinsic imperfections of any financial market, and will look at legal prerequisities for the reasonably efficient operation of those markets. Then it will examine the stylized facts of some Latin American experiments in financial liberalization, particularly those carried out in Southern Cone countries (Argentina, Chile and Uruguay). Finally, alternative ways of organizing domestic capital markets under Latin American conditions will be discussed; policies regarding the links between domestic and international financial markets will also be considered.

2. Peculiarities and dilemmas found in domestic financial markets

Are banks special, and really all that different from butcher shops? Neither type of firm is *exactly* like the textbook idealization of the atomistic firm operating in a perfectly competitive market, where spot prices summarize all information relevant for buyers and sellers of the product. Customers at a butcher shop will not only look at price , but will also attempt to ascertain quality; in some countries they will be aided by government-established quality categories and certifications. Breakdowns in the trust consumers have in their butchers or in government certification, say because of rumors regarding meat tainted by poisonous substances, could produce a kind of 'run' on butcher shops, and widespread failures among them.

The comparison is surely being forced. Few butcher shops will deliver meat of standard quality out of town to third parties on instruction from a customer. Few externalities could be expected from a 'run' on a butcher shop under suspicion. Furthermore, a butcher will seldom turn down a customer who wants to buy with cash everything in sight at the price announced by the butcher (he will just make sure the cash is not counterfeit); a banker will surely not lend all a customer wants to borrow at the going interest rate. The former is a spot transaction; the latter involves a promise to repay in the future which may or may not be sincere or wholly credible. Enforcing the loan contract or liquidating collateral property will involve costs, and even with speedy enforcement the bank may be unable to get all of its money back. The bank will incur costs to explore the credit-worthiness of borrowers; the butcher will not care much for the reputation of cash-carrying customers. There is no humanly possible way of devising a fail-proof system of finding out the true intentions of borrowers, so lenders are likely to end up rationing credit, i.e., putting a ceiling on what arms-length customers can borrow, regardless of their willingness to pay higher interest rates [see Stiglitz and Weiss (1981)]. Banks share with other financial intermediaries the problem of seeking reliable borrowers, but having liabilities that are payable on demand at par puts a premium on safe and fairly liquid loans for banks. Banks supply a service that is a very close substitute to the bulls and coins supplied by governments; such pretension imposes special limits on banks' portfolios.

Financial intermediaries, including banks, rely on borrowed funds; owners of those institutions typically invest their own capital only in amounts which are a small fraction of their total lending. A depositor in a bank will have preoccupations similar to those a lender has when eyeing a borrower: will I be able to get not only the promised yield but also my money back or delivered to a third party as specified in the legal contract? In a totally unregulated system the rational depositor will attempt to process a great deal of information regarding financial institutions, balancing expected returns versus risks of not being able to dispose of his funds as promised.

One can *imagine* a world in which all financial intermediation, including the payments system, is private and without any direct government regulation. The information imperfections may be partly offset by investments in information gathering by lenders and depositors; with the passing of time reputations would be built up. Balance sheets of financial intermediatries would be widely available and closely analyzed. It is even conceivable that possible economies of scale involved in the processing of information may not be so large as to impede large numbers of financial agents, assuring some competition among them. Unexpected shocks and informational failures in this economy could of course lead to bankrupticies of some financial intermediaries; an informed public presumably would know the source of such events, so there would be no ripple effects contaminating sounder institutions. One would expect to find a rich risk-return menu available to savers in this world, which would also generate an unregulated stock market for those preferring equity arrangements for obtaining or investing funds. Concentration of economic power, in the form of 'economic groups' and conglomerates, would presumably exist only if there are economies of scale to yield social benefits, with free entry checking monopoly behaviour. In this world, the market rate of interest would hover around the natural rate.

Note that even a purely laissez-faire financial system must count with some indirect government inputs in the form of an efficient and fair judiciary and police system to punish fraud and to handle the enforcement of contracts and the settlement of disputes and bankruptcy cases. And behind *that* one must presumably have a polity generating such a judicial and police system, and a body of contract, antitrust and bankruptcy laws which are regarded as fair, efficient and enforceable. Financial agents feeling a temptation to cheat on their contracts or give false information must know that such behavior will have very high costs; they must also know that even if they flee their country the long arm of the law is likely to reach them abroad. Governments in this world must be expected neither to change nor to corrupt these rules; domestic private citizens must not only believe in the stability of this system, but also believe that other citizens also have that

4   *C. Diaz-Alejandro, Consequences of financial liberalization*

belief. Foreign financial agents, when dealing with those of our country, must not expect to have these rules changed when things go wrong for them; foreign financial agents dealing within our economy would presumably be subject to the same rules of the game as our financial agents.

Even among those who find a predominatly laissez-faire financial system not only imaginable but also a desirable goal of policy, there are differences on how to organize the underlying monetary system. Some take for granted that the government will have a monopoly in the supply of cash and coins. Aware of the macroeconomic instability which could be generated by sudden changes in the public preferences between cash and the demand deposits supplied by banks subject to fractional reserves, as during the early 1930s in the United States, these observers would impose 100 percent reserves on banks supplying those deposits, while leaving the rest of the financial system unregulated. [See Friedman (1959).] In this view, a significant difference exists between money (cash plus demand deposits) and other financial assets. Other observers would carry a laissez-faire policy even into cash, eliminating the government monopoly, and leaving individual agents free to choose among all potential suppliers of cash, including foreign governments. In this approach there would be no need to impose reserve requirements on banks, which would be totally free of government regulations. The money supply would presumably adjust to real needs, while price and wage flexibility would maintain macroeconomic balance [see Hall (1982)].

The laissez-faire vision also has (at least) two variants regarding how the unregulated domestic economy should manage its exchange rate. If the country is large enough, those giving the government a monopoly over the money supply advocate a freely fluctuating exchange rate, with no restriction on international trade or on capital flows. If the country is small (with the borderline between large and small left fuzzy), even money monopolists favor some form of fixed exchange rate system. For politically turbulent nations, a variant of the liassez–faire vision in a small country would do away with the local central bank, i.e., no national could be trusted with the money monopoly, which would be turned over to a presumably benign and responsible foreign government, as in the cases of Panama and Puerto Rico.

No industrial country has come close to the laissez-faire vision, at least since the 1930s. The government monopoly over cash has been maintained, while banks have been regulated and subjected to fractional reserve requirements. In the United States, an explicit federal deposit insurance for accounts below a certain size was introduced during the 1930s and maintained since then, eliminating old-fashioned 'runs' on banks. Like any other insurance scheme, deposit insurance is vulnerable to moral hazard consequences, i.e., it induces depositors to think that 'one bank is as good as another', and leads bank managers to undertake riskier loans. To avoid such insurance-induced risk-taking, supervision over bank portfolios has accompanied deposit insurance. Indeed, the Federal Reserve holds impressive discretionary powers regarding the lending policies of commercial banks, and over their liquidation or merger, if banks are found to be in trouble. Those discretionary powers, however, are subject to review by the Treasury, Congress and the courts. Vigilance has been exerted by the Fedral Reserve to keep non-banking companies from owing or controlling banks.

While a trend towards bank deregulation has occured in the United States during the 1970s and early 1980s, removing some archaic populist controls, the view the 'banks are special' has been reaffirmed. The rescue of the Continental Illinois during 1984 in the face of a new type of run by uninsured international depositors, a rescue which extended de-facto insurance to all depositors, showed that *large* banks are quite special. This view is based on the externalities generated by the liquidity, mobility and acceptability of bank-issued transaction accounts, characteristics which take special significance in periods of financial stress [see Federal Reserve Bank of Minneapolis (1982)]. Only banks create and incur liabilities that are payable on demand at par and that are readily transferable to third parties. Your safe payments system is also my safe payments system; it is partly a public good, not only serving individuals, but also providing backup liquidity on which the whole of the financial system rests. The Federal Reserve Bank of Minneapolis concludes:

> '. . . the case for segregating *essential* banking functions into an identifiable class of institutions is every bit as powerful today as it was in the 1930s. If anything, concerns regarding financial concentration, conflicts of interest, and the fiduciary responsibilities associated with lending depositors' money may be more relevant today than they were 50 years ago' (p. 13).

Other industrial countries, such as Japan and those in Western Europe, are even farther away from the laissez-faire vision for the financial system than the United States. In several of those countries interest rates are also controlled or supervised by monetary authorities, and international capital flows are regulated. None relies on just price and wage flexibility to seek macroeconomic balance. (Note that those advocating a fixed-money-growth rule are typically as skeptical of the speedy workings of price and wage flexibility to maintain macroeconomic balance as Keynesian economists.)

Finally, it is difficult to find small and open countries which have *given up* monetary sovereignty after tasting it. Politically sovereign countries using other countries' moneys, or 'permanently' committed to a fixed exchange rate and unrestricted capital mobility with a monetary 'big brother', usually have come to those arrangements as part of a transition from a colonial status, and it is moot whether the arrangements are regarded as really permanent or

6   *C. Diaz-Alejandro, Consequences of financial liberalization*

only as a step in monetary learning by doing, a step which had to be accepted to placate special internal and external interests rather than taken after a thoughtful consideration of national welfare. During October 1983 there were reports that Israel was about to abandon its monetary sovereignty; the Minister responsible for the proposal resigned shortly afterwards.

3. Notes on the financial history of Latin American and Southern Cone experiments

While the financial history of Latin America remains to be written it appears that by 1920s most countries had succeeded in establishing commercial banks of the (then) traditional sort; several countries carried out banking reforms during those years following the advice of Professor E.W. Kemmerer, of Princeton University, and of visitors from the Bank of England. The banking system of South American countries already included institutions owned by national and provincial governments; Argentina, for example, had an important government-owned mortgage bank and several other public banks. The late 1920s were characterized in most Latin American countries by fixed exchange rates, convertibility and price stability; domestic interest rates were closely linked to those in New York and London. Although there was no 'financial repression', critics pointed to a lack of medium- and long-term credit, particularly to finance industry and non-export agriculture. Within agriculture, those without real estate collateral also complained about non-availability of credit. Domestic stock and bond markets were small; only Argentina seems to have had a promising formal domestic financial market, dominated by mortgage paper.

The 1930s brought exchange controls and the expansion of government financial institutions, which at the height of the crisis proved their usefulness in decreasing the incidence of panics and runs; the massive bank bankruptcies which occured in the United States during the early 1930s were not witnessed in the large Latin American countries, apparently thanks to the presence of state banks plus an activist policy of rescuing most private banks in trouble. By the 1940s many countries had development banks granting medium- and long-term credits to non-traditional agriculture, industry and construction. Those credits, at least during the 1930s and early 1940s, seemed to have been granted at interest rates still ahead of domestic inflation, or at least not too far behind it, and in most cases contributed to an upsurge in capital formation. Public development banks remained, often through the 1950s, relatively small and efficient, as in the case of the Brazilian BNDE. The drying-up of external sources of finance during the 1930s and 1940s encouraged these efforts to mobilize local savings.

By the 1950s, however, it was clear that in South American countries experiencing inflation the development banks created to solve one form of perceived market failure (lack of long-term credit for socially profitable non-traditional activities) had led to another, i.e., a segmented domestic financial market in which some obtained (rationed) credits at very negative real interest rates, while non-favored borrowers had to obtain funds in expensive and. unstable informal credit markets. Public controls over the banking system typically led to negative real interest rates for depositors. 'Financial repression' became an obstacle to domestic savings and their efficient allocation, and financial intermediation languished.

In inflation-prone countries, financial reforms were introduced during the 1960s in the form of indexing of some loans and deposits; those involving the housing market were a particularly popular field for these new policies. Post-1964 Brazil is the clearest example of a sustained effort to revive the domestic financial system and domestic savings using a number of indexing devices, but maintaining close government supervision of financial institutions and of interests rates charged in formal markets. The results of the Brazilian reforms have been mixed: domestic financial savings have been encouraged relative to the pre-1964 situation, in spite of continuing inflation, and the new policies supported impressive rates of capital formation. But attempts to encourage a significant stock market have failed, and the financial market remains heavily dominated by public securities. Private agents have shown reluctance to offer indexed securities. Credit to some sectors, such as agriculture, has been heavily subsidized for long periods of time. Brazil has also retained controls over the links between domestic and international financial markets, while following a passive crawling peg exchange rate policy, with sporadic jumps and other innovations.

In Central American countries, with a tradition of price stability and conservative macroeconomic management (before the 1970s), bank concentration and an association of a few private banks with dominant economic groups, historically raised concerns about monopoly power. Galbis (1979, p. 349) noted:

> 'The experience of El Salvador suggests that interest rate freedom cannot be expected to be a panacea and automatically produce interest rate equilibrium in countries that have a relatively concentrated and unsophisticated financial system, which is the typical case in small, less developed countries. Positive policy actions to avoid market distortions might be required.'

This type of concern led to the nationalization of the banking system in Costa Rica in the late 1940s and in El Salvador in 1979. Government regulation, including selective credit allocations, over such oligopolistic structures may make matters worse, consolidating access by a few favored businesses to subsidized credit; post-Second-World-War Greece is said to be an example of inefficient and inequitable regulation of concentrated banking sector.

Southern Cone countries, coming out of sundry populist experiences around the mid-1970s, undertook financial reforms going beyond those of Brazil in a laissez-faire direction. Post-1973 Chile provides the clearest example of this type of financial liberation [for a careful narrative, see Arellano (1983a,b)]. That experiment started with a fully nationalized banking sector; a first task was to return most banks to the private sector. This was done by auctioning them off, with generous credit arrangements, or by returning them to previous owners; apparently little effort was spent on investigating the banking credentials of new entrants. At an early stage interest rates were freed and 'financieras' were allowed to operate with practically no restrictions or supervision; early bankruptcies in December 1976 and January 1977 of the more adventurous and unregulated 'financieras' led to the establishment of minimum capital requirements for entry. Authorities repeatedly warned the public that deposits were *not* guaranteed, beyond very small deposits with banks, and that financial intermediaries, like any other private firm, could go bankrupt; it was explicitly stated that there would not be a 'bailing out' of banks and other financial intermediaries. Since 1974 multi-purpose banking was allowed, on the ground that the Chilean market is too small to sustain specialized financial institutions of efficient size. Reserve requirements were steadily reduced, reaching less than ten percent of deposits by 1980.

During 1977 it became apparent that an important bank (the Banco Osorno) was in serious trouble. The authorities, fearing that its bankruptcy would tarnish external and internal confidence in Chilean financial institutions, intervened, and rescued all depositors and the institution. Apparently, the fear that external loans would decrease if the Osorno had been allowed to go bankrupt was the crucial argument for intervention. Naturally, frech warnings were issued that, from then on, financial intermediaries would not be rescued. At that stage practically no inspection or supervision of bank portfolios existed; only in 1981 were significant regulatory powers given to the Superintendency of Banks. One may conjecture that after this event most depositors felt, de facto, fully insured and foreign lenders felt that their loans to the private Chilean sector were, in fact, guaranteed by the State. After 1977, banks, rather than 'financieras', became predominant in the financial system.

During 1979 the Chilean economic authorities started a process expected to culminate in a pseudo-exchange-rate union [see Corden (1972)] with the United States. The nominal exhange rate between the peso and the U.S. dollar was fixed in July 1979, and restrictions over convertibility and capital movements were relaxed; by 1981 those restrictions had been considerably weakened, and Chile witnessed a massive capital inflow. Presumably the hope was to make lending to Chile subject to no more currency risk than lending to Puerto Rico or Panama; the nominal exchange rate was supposed to last 'for many years'. Some of the economic authorities dreamed of doing away with the national currency altogether, but feared that the military might not wish to go that far.

The theoretical underpinnings of these policies included a special version of the monetary approach to the balance of payments, plus the hypothesis that financial markets, domestic and international, were no different from the market for apples and meat. Voluntary financial transactions between private agents were their own business, and presumably Pareto-optimal. Indeed, the nationality of those private agents was regarded most irrelevant. The then Director of the Western Hemishere Division of the International Monetary Fund put it this way at meeting held in Santiago de Chile during January 1980 [see Robichek (1981, p. 171)]:

'In the case of the private sector, I would argue that the difference between domestic and foreign debt is not significant — barring governmental interference with the transfer of service payments or other clearly inappropriate public policies — if it exists at all. The exchange risks associated with foreign borrowing are presumably taken into account as are the other risks associated with borrowing, whether it be from domestic or foreign sources. More generally, private firms can be expected to be careful in assessing the net return to be derived from borrowing funds as compared with the net cost since their survival as enterprises is at stake.'

The same author went on to argue that overborrowing by the private sector, even with official guarantees, was very unlikely, provided official guarantees were given on a selective basis; only public borrowing on international financial markets was regarded as posing more serious debt service risks [see Robichek (1981, p. 172)].

Convergence of domestic inflation and interest rates toward international ones proved to be a slow process, during which the fixed 'permanent' nominal exchange rate yielded great incentives for private capital inflows into Chile: during 1981 the current account deficit reached an astonishing 14 percent of Chilean Gross National Product, with international reserves holding their own, while domestic savings appeared to collapse. The process of financial liberation had also led to a widely noted (by opposition economists) concentration of potential economic power in the hands of a few conglomerates or economic groups, which combined financial and non-financial corporations. Before 1981, the official view seems to have been that those economic groups must reflect some economies of scale, and could be regarded as one special type of butcher shop, disciplined by free entry and other competitive pressures. Their allocation of credit resources, often heavily loaded in favor of companies associated with the group, was presumed to be more efficient than that which government bureaucrats could achieve.

As late as March 1981 international business publications were writing that 'Chile's free-enterprise banking environment' was proving to be a powerful magnet for foreign banks, and that more entrants into the thriving sector were lining up. (See *Business Latin America*, March 11, 1981, p. 79.) By June 1981 the same publications were noting with concern the cessation of payments on local credits by CRAV, a Chilean sugar company, as well as other blemishes on the economic miracle, but argued that 'the problem areas pose no immediate threat to growth' (*Business Latin America*, June 3, 1981, p. 173). Following the CRAV news, the Central Bank supported financial institutions to stem incipient 'runs'. By November 1981 the position of two important private Chilean banks and several 'financieras' became critical: they were 'intervened' by the Central Bank. Further interventions of financial intermediaries occurred during the first half of 1982; rather than harsh bankruptcy proceedings, these actions apparently involved a generous expansion of credit to the private sector. Between the end of December of 1981 and the end of June 1982, domestic credit in Chilean pesos expanded by 41 percent; of the net increase in domestic credit, 92 percent went to the private sector [see International Monetary Fund (1983, pp. 118–119, lines 32 and 32d)].

The massive use of Central Bank credit to 'bail out' private agent raises doubts about the validity of pre-1982 analyses of the fiscal position and debt of the Chilean public sector. The recorded public sector budget deficit was nonexistent or miniscule for several years through 1981, and moderate during 1982. [For evidence on the apparent Chilean fiscal performance, see McKinnon (1982).] The declining importance of ostensible public debt in the national balance sheet was celebrated by some observers; indeed it was argued that public sector assets, such as remaining public corporations, exceeded its liabilities. Ex post it turned out that the public sector, including the Central Bank, had been accumulating an explosive amount of contingent liabilities to both foreign and domestic agents, who held deposits in, or made loans to the rickety domestic financial sector. This hidden public debt could be turned into cash as the financial system threatened to collapse. Eminent students of fiscal and financial systems, who were involved in the Chilean reforms, apparently overlooked this potential debt bomb. (Present at the creation and early development of the new Chilean financial system were experts brought together by the Organization of American States Program for the Development of Capital Markets; together with the Chilean Central Bank, this program sponsored seminars on capital markets in Santiago during 1974, 1976 and 1977.)

By late 1981 and early 1982 Chile was also feeling the full force of the international economic crisis and discovering that it was not a 'small country' in international financial markets, in the sense of being able to borrow, in either public or private account, all it wished at a given interest rate, even including a generous spread. Pressures mounted on the already overvalued nominal exchange rate, fixed with respect to the U.S. dollar since July 1979; in June 1982 the unthinkable devaluation was carried out in haste, initiating a period of experimentation, which has included clean and dirty floating, a crawling peg, multiple rates, and a tightening up of exchange controls.

The official exchange rate rose rapidly from 39 pesos per U.S. dollar to a range of 74–80 pesos by January 1983; the free rate went substantially above official quotation. Those who had dollar debts were placed under stress; financial difficulties contributed to and were aggravated by a drop in real Gross National Product of about 14 percent during 1982. The Central Bank undertook rescue operations of banks and other financial intermediaries during the second half of 1982, to avoid a breakdown of the financial system. In January 1983 a controversial, massive intervention in five banks, the liquidation of another three, and the direct supervision of another two left the government in control of a good share of the Chilean corporate sector, as well as of its domestic and foreign debts. It has been estimated that non-performing assets of banks rose from 11 percent of their capital and reserves at the end of 1980, to 22 percent at the end of 1981, to 47 percent at the end of 1982, and to 113 percent in May 1983 [Arellano (1983a, p. 192)].

Many of those linked to the intervened banks and associated companies, including ex-Ministers of the Pinochet regime, charged that the January 1983 measures by the Central Bank and its now active superintendency of banks were unnecessary, arbitrary and politically motivated, hinting that rival economic groups stood to profit from the measures. General Pinochet himself took the lead in charging the troubled economic groups with a number of sins, including betrayal of the General's good faith. During 1983 and 1984 some well-known financiers and ex-Ministers were jailed, charged with fraud. Specifically, it has been charged that Banco de Chile and three other private Santiago banks set up a new bank in Panama, which was used to circumvent limits on how much a bank could loan to members of its own group, when those measures were belatedly (during 1981) imposed to control 'the conglomerates' rampant self-lending tactics' (*The Wall Street Journal*, March 6, 1984, p. 38)

Whatever the merits of these charges, it was clear that the domestic financial crisis in Chile had questioned not only the future of many existing banks and corporations but also the rules of the game as they had been understood during the years of the 'Chilean miracle'. The opaqueness of the intervention procedures, and of the announced processes to settle the tangled web of inter-company and bank debts even raised questions about the regime's respect for property rights or at least its willingness to provide effective mechanisms for the efficient exercise of those rights. On the other hand, only the depositors with the three liquidated banks underwent any direct losses (up to 30 percent of their deposits); all other depositors were assured that they could get their money back.

The 1982–83 breakdown of rules, and the reliance on discretion by Chilean officials, extended to the handling of private external debts. In contrast with other heavy borrowers, such as Brazil, a large share of the pre-1982 capital inflow into Chile went directly to private banks and corporations, borrowing abroad without government guarantees. Indeed, both private borrowers and lenders were warned by government officials that they were on their own, and that such debt could in no way be regarded as a Chilean *national* debt. In spite of these ex-ante announcements, during early 1983 external debts of private banks were taken over by the government, which announced its intention to continue servicing them. Those private debts have been included in debt rescheduling being negotiated between the Chilean state and the foreign bank advisory committee for Chile. Apparently the Chilean government caved in under pressure from the bank advisory committee, which argued that it would be extremely difficult for the international financial community to focus its attention on the pressing needs of Chile while an increasing number of companies and their associated Chilean banks were experiencing or approaching a suspension of their payments and subsequent bankruptcy. To make their viewpoint absolutely clear, foreign banks apparently tightened up their granting of very short term commercial credits to Chile during the first quarter of 1983, a technique reportedly used with some success ten years earlier vis-à-vis the same country. The International Monetary Fund, also active in the debt rescheduling exercise, has not publicly objected to this threat to the Robichek doctrine.

In sum, the ad hoc actions undertaken during 1982–83 in Chile to handle the domestic and external financial crisis carry with them an enormous potential for arbitrary wealth redistribution. The lessons private agents are likely to draw from these events are unlikely to be compatible with a reconstruction of a domestic financial sector relying on credible threats of bankruptcy to discipline borrowing and lending. In spite of the ex-post government guarantees to peso deposits, private individuals decreased their demand for peso-denominated assets, as domestic inflation picked up, and expectations grew that the clearing up of the domestic debt tangle would involve additional inflation, exchange-rate depreciation and arbitrary controls. Faith in orderly judicial proceedings to clear up debts and claims on assets appeared to be quite low; stories abounded of debtors fleeing the country, and of petty and grand financial chicanery going unpunished.

Argentine and Uruguayan domestic financial experiences offer a number of similarities and some contrasts to the narrated Chilean events [see Frenkel

(1984)]. In those countries domestic financial intermediation also flourished and then collapsed. Major comparative points are the following:

(1) Whether or not deposits are explicitly insured, the public expects governments to intervene to save most depositors from losses when financial intermediaries run into trouble. Warnings that intervention will not be forthcoming appear to be simply not believable. Fernandez (1983) has blamed explicit insurance for financial deposits by Central Bank authorities in explaining the Argentine financial crash of 1980–82. But, as we have seen, explicit insurance was much less used in Chile, where nevertheless many firms and households apparently felt that their deposits were implicitly guaranteed by the Central Bank [see Arellano (1983a,b)].

(2) The Central Banks, either because of a misguided belief that banks are like butcher shops, or because of lack of trained personnel, neglected prudential regulations over financial intermediaries. Not surprisingly, the assets held by Argentine and Chilean banks and 'financieras' around 1980-81 appeared to have substantially riskier relative to those held by similar institutions in the United States or in Western Europe, and relative to plausible counterfactuals of sensibly-regulated financial intermediaries in those countries. It has been argued that in Uruguay the presence of U.S. owned banks, regulated indirectly by the Federal Reserve, reduced the magnitude of risk-taking by banks.

(3) The new financial institutions in the Southern Cone attracted fresh entrepreneurs and stimulated the creation of new conglomerates and economic groups. While new entrepreneurial blood has an attractive aura, experience indicates that such venturesome animal spirits are better channeled toward non-financial endeavors, where the disciplining threat of bankruptcy could be more credible.

(4) In economies characterized by intractable market and informational imperfections, conglomerates and economic groups, even as they may correct government-induced financial repression imperfections, could exacerbate others, particularly via the creation of oligopolistic power. The close association of financial intermediaries with non-financial corporations, frowned upon by United States regulations, can indeed lead to distortions in the allocation of credit, as shown by the Argentine and Chilean experiences. Linkages in both countries between banks and firms, which were hardly arms' length, were responsible for the high use of debt by private firms. In Chile by late 1982 private firms were more indebted than state enterprises; within the private sector, extreme indebtedness was found among those that controlled banks (and that had acquired from CORFO those firms nationalized under the Allende Presidency). Between 1975 and 1982, Chile went from a financially shallow economy, where inflation had wiped out real value of debt, to an excessively financially deep economy where creditors

owned a very large share of real wealth, a clear case of 'too much debt and too little equity'. Interpenetration of economic and financial power appears to have reached extraordinary levels. The two largest business groups in Chile by late 1982 controlled the principal insurance companies, mutual funds, brokerage houses, the largest private company pension funds and the two largest private commercial banks; about half of all private external debt was channelled through the domestic banking system, so control of banks allowed ready access both to domestic and foreign credit. By late 1982 many banks had lent one quarter of more of their resources to affiliates.

(5) The freeing of interest rates and the relaxation of controls over financial intermediation will not necessarily encourage intermediation beyond short-term maturities. The flourishing of private financial intermediaries in the Southern Cone, even at the height of the boom, was limited to deposits and loans of less than six months' duration. Longer-term intermediation via banks or bonds, not to metion via active stock markets, remained very weak. Insofar as the new policies destroy pre-existing government-supported long-term intermediation arrangements, as in the case of the Chilean housing system, SINAP, financial liberation will reduce available long-term financial instruments. Stock markets may witness short booms, but will mobilize very few funds; charges of manipulation and fraud, plus lack of protection for minority stockholders, will reduce public interest in buying stocks in unregulated or badly regulated stock markets. It has been charged in the Chilean case that false stock transactions were an important component in the growth of financial intermediaries during 1977–81. It is argued that market prices of shares owned by large business groups were manipulated upwards, via phony transactions, to increase the value of collateral used to secure loans and to induce fresh inflows into captive mutual funds.

(6) The end of financial repression undoubtedly encouraged many types of financial savings; Arellano (1983a, b) documents the boom in Chilean financial savings and intermediation especially during 1977–82. Paradoxically, however, total domestic savings did *not* increase in the South American experiments in financial liberation, in spite of handsome returns to savings. Chilean Gross National Savings *fell* from an average of 16.3 percent of Gross National Produce during the decade of the 1960s, to 12.4 percent during 1975–81 [Arellano (1983b, p. 12)]. Arellano cogently argues that the expansion in Chilean financial savings came mainly from the foreign capital inflow, the recording on both sides of the ledger of accumulated interest and of capital gains, and a reorientation of saving flows from the public to the private sector [see also Harberger (1982) for a discussion of the poor performance of Chilean savings]. In 1980–81 reforms to the social security system gave a further boost to funds flowing into private financial institutions, by changing the pay-as-you-go government-managed system into a

capitalization scheme, in which pension funds were to be managed by private financial institutions.

(7) Aggregate investment performance showed no clear sign of either improving or becoming more efficient, in the South American countries undergoing financial liberation. In Chile gross fixed investment during the 1960s averaged 20.2 percent of Gross Domestic Product; during 1974–82 it reached only 15.5 percent of GDP [see Arellano (1983a, p. 226)]. Argentine and Uruguayan performance was better on the investment front, partly because public sector capital formation did not shrink as the Chilean case.

(8) Foreign lenders take govenment announcements that it will not rescue local private debtors, especially banks, with non-guaranteed external (or domestic) liabilities even less seriously than depositors take the threat of a loss of their money. The alleged Japanese attitude of not differentiating between the public and private external debt of a developing country appears to have been upheld ex-post as a sounder guide to action than the Robichek doctrine. Foreign banks lending to both the public and private sectors of a country have considerable leverage to convince governments to take over ex-post bad private debts, especially those of financial intermediaries. There appear to be no international referees to keep them from exercising such leverage. The substantive differences between the nationalization of Mexican private banks during 1982 and the intervention in Chilean private banks during 1983 may be less than one would think by reading the editorials of the international financial press. International banks, knowing they are regulated at home, where they also have close political connections with their governments, expect the same in borrowing countries.

While debts of private Chilean banks to foreign banks were fully assumed by the government, other operations by Southern Cone banks carried out abroad do not seem to have received the protective mantle of home-government support. For example, the Argentine authorities declined to accept responsibility for claims on the New York branch of the failing Banco Intercambio Regional, which was taken over by the New York State Banking Department [Johnson and Abrams (1983, p. 23)]. Given this experience, it is unlikely that Southern Cone banks will emerge as important competitiors in international banking in the near future.

(9) The combination of pre-announced or fixed nominal exchange rate, relatively free capital movements, and domestic and external financial systems characterized by the moral hazard and other imperfections discussed above set the stage not only for significant microeconomic misallocation of credit, but also for macroeconomic instability, including the explosive growth of external debt, most of which was incurred by private Chilean banks, followed by abrupt cessation of capital inflows. That macroeconomic instability would occur even assuming tranquil circumstances, but it is of course exacerbated by external shocks hitting economies made particularly

brittle and vulnerable by that combination of policies and institutions. Contrary to some old and new notions, the experiences of Argentina, Chile and Uruguay show that what happens to the *nominal* exchange rate does affect the *real* exchange rate, at least in the short and medium runs, and that changes in the exchange rate can be an important and efficient mechanism of adjusting the balance of payments. Faulty exchange rate policy appears much more important in explaining financial turbulence and the severity of the Chilean 1982–83 depression than the reduction in import barriers. The credibility of the latter was reduced by peso overvaluation, inducing an import binge and reducing local savings.

(10) Short-term real interest rates, plausibly defined, on the whole remained very high in Argentina, Chile and Uruguay, even during periods of massive capital inflow. A number of hypotheses have been offered to explain this phenomenon: macroeconomic policy; expectations of devaluation and inflation, which in the short run did not materialize; a change in the real productivity of capital; and even excessive spreads originating in Central Bank Reserve requirements. As in the case of explanations for the high, but less spectacular, real interest rates recorded in the United States during the early 1980s, none of the hypotheses are fully satisfactory [see Litterman and Weiss (1984)]. From the viewpoint of this paper, the most intriguing hypotheses for explaining extravagant Southern Cone real interest rates, which in Chile reached 32 percent per annum on the average during 1976–82 according to Arellano [Arellano (1983b, p. 31); this is the rate charged for short-term loans], focus on the nature of financial deregulation and imperfections in those markets. It was noted earlier that the high Chilean interest rates were reflected mainly in double-entry bookkeeping. It can be argued that firms and households borrowing at extravagant rates either expected them to last for very brief periods, or, if they did not, borrowers expected the government to bail them out, knowing as they did that many other borrowers were in a similar situation. Such expectations, of course, favored 'distress borrowing': either interest rates fell, or government would 'bail out' everyone. Whatever the validity of these arguments may be, it is clear from the Southern Cone experience that the type of deregulation experience by those countries gives no assurance of stable real interest rates hovering around reasonable estimates of the socially optimal shadow real interest rate. Some observers have argued that the main function of high real interest rates was to transfer the ownership of real enterprise wealth from debtors to creditors, a mechanism doomed to stop when no more share-holders' wealth was left.

(11) As elsewhere in Latin America, the decline in real Gross Domestic Product in Argentina (11 percent between 1980 and 1982), in Chile (15 percent between 1981 and 1983), and in Uruguay (14 percent between 1980 and 1983) may be said to be the reult of unfavorable external circumstances

during the early 1980s, combined with less than optimal domestic policies. As noted earlier, policy-induced stickiness in nominal exchange rates delayed adjustment to changes in external terms of trade and changes in capital flows. The brittle Southern Cone domestic sectors must also bear blame for first exaggerating the boom, then aggravating the recession and finally delaying recovery. The consequences of the Chilean financial crash have been the most spectacular, leading to a massive rearranging of the national balance sheet. Such a rearranging, however, has been a slow and opaque process, leaving many economic entities not knowing who owns what, or who owes what to whom, hardly ideal circumstances for encouraging a revival of private investment.

(12) As with international debt, the sorting out and allocation of losses and blame for 'mistakes' (only clear ex-post) by borrowers and lenders in the domestic financial markets present monumental conceptual and legal problems, especially when 'mistakes' are widespread. Since 1982 Argentina appears to have taken the time-honored route of washing out old financial mistakes via inflation (which is not allowed to be reflected in interest rates); this approach favors borrowers over lenders. As noted earlier, in the Chilean case the path out of the morass remains unclear; inflation accelerated, but 'only' to around 25–30 percent during 1983. There are few precedents and less accepted doctrine regarding financial processes as bizarre as those experienced by Chile during 1975–83. Bankruptcies, financial distress and confusion delay recovery beyond what would be necessary to achieve real adjustment to the new international terms of trade, capital market realities and expectations about growth in the international economy.

4. Options for Latin American domestic financial systems

Southern Cone domestic financial systems of the late 1970s and early 1980s ended up with a pessimum 'middle way': de facto public guarantees to depositors, lenders and borrowers, and no effective supervision and control (until it was too late) of the practices of financial intermediaries. Reform could logically head in two opposite directions: more laissez-faire with binding (constitutional?) commitments against future bail-outs, or toward more public controls, possibly culminating in nationalization of the banking system, as in Costa Rica, El Salvador, India and France. Other Latin American countries outside the Southern Cone, such as Brazil and Colombia, have domestic financial systems that, while showing signs of stress during the last few years, have not undergone Southern-Cone-type of crisis; their experiences (including their post-1981 troubles) could be useful in sketching desirable characteristics of domestic financial arrangements.

As noted earlier, the credibility of a government commitment to a truly laissez-faire domestic financial system is very low. Firstly, as illustrated in the recent Chilean experience, foreign financial agents will not accept a separation of private and public debts when a crisis arrives; financial laissez-faire in one peripheral country does not seem viable. Secondly 'public opinion', including generals and their aunts, simply does not believe that the state would (nor could) allow most depositors to be wiped out by the failure of banks and financial intermediaries. It may be that private financial agents, domestic and foreign, lenders, borrowers and intermediaries, whether or not related to generals, know that the domestic political and judicial systems are not compatible with laissez-faire commitments which a misguided Minister of Finance or Central Bank President may occasionally utter in a moment of dogmatic exaltation. When a crisis hits, agents will reason, bankrupcy courts will break down; when most everyone (who counts) is bankrupt, nobody is! Thus, even if one believed, à la Hayek, that the externalities and public good characteristics of the domestic monetary and financial system are negligible, one may conclude that the political, and social, infrastructure found in many developing (and developed?) countries conspires against the viability of such a pure laissez-faire financial system. The zealot may conclude that the nation does not measure up to the purity of the model.

So should one move back to good old 1950s style financial repression, extensive controls and perhaps full nationalization of the domestic financial system? It can be argued that a *believable* alternative system could be designed, avoiding many of the inefficiencies of financial repression while avoiding those of the Southern Cone experience, and blending both public and private financial agents. What follows sketches some features of that eclectic system.

Negative real rates of interest became common in Latin America during the 1940s and 1950s as inflation gained momentum and many monetary authorities maintained ceilings on nominal interest rates offered and charged by the banking and financial system. At that time most South American countries (but not Mexico, Venezuela, Central America and the Caribbean) also maintained extensive exchange controls. Limited international capital mobility buttressed the taxing of cash balances and financial repression; the then prevalent Keynesian orthodoxy also encouraged these developments. While persistently negative real rates of interest in the formal financial market occured only when the government imposed rate ceilings and exchange controls, it is not obvious that public regulation and participation in the domestic financial market necessarily had to lead to negative rates of interest. The Mexican financial system of the 1950s and 1960s, praised by development scholars, contained both public institutions and substantial government regulations. As already noted, the post-1964 Brazilian indexing and other financial reforms could hardly be described as involving a laissez-faire approach. The celebrated South Korean financial reforms of the 1960s were carried out with a high degree of public ownership and control of the formal financial sector [see Gurley et al. (1965, p. 45)].

Assuming that a country intends to maintain monetary sovereignty but that significant, yet not explosive, inflationary expectations persist, there is a strong case for making sure that firms and households have available a domestic liquid financial asset yielding a real interest rate which is not far below, nor much above, zero. The inflationary tax borne by currency balances may result from the inability of the fiscal system to find non-inflationary sources of revenues, or it may be simply a by-product of an inflationary spiral, whose inertial momentum could only be halted by a severe real contraction. Presumably the transactions convenience provided by domestic currency will be enough to generate some demand for it, even under moderate inflation, an assumption supported by South American experiences. But without a liquid and safe store of value denominated in domestic currency, which at least maintains its purchasing power, a national monetary and financial system will have little long-run credibility, short of draconian controls. It could also be argued that without such an asset the system would not meet the most elementrary tests of social equity.

It should be emphasized that introducing a 'zero-real-rate assets' next to a zero-nominal-rate asset involves a delicate trade-off, which may increase welfare only if the inflation tax on money remains 'reasonable'. The zero-real-rate asset will reduce the demand for money, but may also reduce the demand for assets denominated in foreign currencies. An inflation which accelerated sharply above historical norms, introducing massive currency substitution, could destroy the credibility of all domestic financial assets.

There are many possible ways to supply a zero-real-rate asset. The banking system, for example, could provide indexed savings accounts; depending on practical considerations, they could be used partly as checking accounts. At least that segment of the banking system would have explicit and full deposit insurance, perhaps only for accounts below a certain (generous) limit; insurance for larger accounts could partial. Naturally, the use by banks of funds coming from those accounts would be tightly regulated by a flinty-eyed superintendency of banks. Indeed, practical considerations could lead to the requirement of 100 percent reserves on that type of deposits, to be placed in very safe assets.

Enormous potential power is given by this scheme to the regulatory agencies: it could end up in the total control of credit by the Central Bank. Experiences in Latin America and elsewhere with a public monopoly of credit have not been so encouraging as to make one indifferent to this possibility. Safeguards against the monopoly scenario would include allowance for the supply of alternative financial assets, by either private agents or decentralized public ones, plus an active Congressional supervision of the regulatory agencies and the public banks. The latter point suggests

20   *C. Diaz-Alejandro, Consequences of financial liberalization*

that democracy, whatever its more fundamental virtues, is an important technical input for a healthy domestic financial system.

Suppliers of riskier financial assets would not have available public deposit insurance but would be subject to less regulation. Nevertheless, these would still include minimum capital requirements, strict 'transparency' information rules (regarding both assets and connections with other firms), and clear 'risk-may-be-hazardous-for-your-health' warnings to the general public. After recent experiences it is probably better to proceed cautiously in this segment of the domestic financial market, but not so cautiously as to make it an empty set. Interest rates offered and charged by these intermediaries would be expected to show significant real rates; at least on an experimental basis those rates would not be set by the monetary authorities, but spreads between rates paid to depositiors and those charged to borrowers would be subject to antitrust vigilance (as entry into this sector would not be completely free). Those spreads would depend, inter alia, on possible official reserve requirements; these could be presumed to be quite low for this segment of the market. Both foreign and private institutions would be expected to participate, but entry regulations and antitrust vigilance would be on guard against interlocking directorates among financial and non-financial firms and would lean against the creation of dominating economic groups and conglomerates. Prohibitions against the mingling of financial and non-financial firms, as in the Unites States's Glass–Steagall Act, appear particularly desirable where markets are relatively small.

Latin American experience, and indeed that of Continental Europe last century, makes one skeptical that private markets alone will generate a flow of financial intermediation high enough to support a rate of long-term fixed capital formation which fully exploits available high social rates of return to long-term investments. Private uncertainties and skepticism of all sorts, which will not disappear by freeing interest rates, reduce the scope for private long-term finance and for stock markets; the latter have continued to languish even when encouraged by various subsidies, as in Brazil. It will be recalled that this was the original motivation for the creation of public development banks in Latin America during the 1930s and 1940s. The need remains to close gaps left in long-term capital markets by acute uncertainties found in Latin American societies, and public development banks remain a plausible solution, in spite of the abuses and errors in their management registered over the last 50 years. Not all experiences have been negative; as noted earlier, public mortgage banks obtaining funds by issuing indexed obligations yielding modest real rates of interest and correspondingly pricing their mortgages, have registered important accomplishments in anumber of countries. The crucial lessons remain the avoidance of real interest rates too far from plausible estimates of the shadow opportunity cost of capital, plus political mechanisms to check potential abuses of those public agencies.

Decentralized, efficiently-run public financial intermediaries operating together with private intermediaries could play several important functions, besides merely plugging gaps in the long-term segment of the market. As recent Latin American experiences have shown, confirming the evidence of the early 1930s, during financial crises the public appears to turn to public banks for greater security. ('Flight to quality' in the Latin American context also benefits large, well-known banks.) Public banks could help focus market interst rates around the social opportunity cost of capital, decreasing instability in real interest rates. Those institutions could channel external funds, helping to keep tabs on the foreign debt and improve borrowing terms. Their operating costs would give evidence and provide a yardstick on reasonable spreads between interest rates paid to depositors and those charged to borrowers. By providing long-term credit to new, non-traditional activities, development banks would eliminate one of the excuses frequently given for extravagant protection against imports. Indeed, the valid cases for infant-industry protection or promotion are likely to be most efficiently handled under Latin American conditions using public credit instruments, suitably priced, rather than by barriers agains imports. Needless to say, public banks will not yield these results without a great deal of effort and pressure by those in charge of their management and supervision. Considerable experimentation is also likely to be needed, particularly regarding the establishment of a structure of interest rates compatible with both a vigorous rate of fixed capital formation and a matching flow of voluntary domestic savings.

The real exchange rate, no less than the real interest rate, remains a crucial price for Latin American economies. The southern Cone emphasis on exchange rate management as an instrument to achieve nominal targets, letting market forces settle the real exchange rate, emerges from recent experience as less successful than the Brazilian–Colombian crawling peg practice, which targets the real exchange rate as an explicit objective of policy. As with the real interest rate, the correct real exchange rate is not easy to define and calculate exactly, but grossly over- or under-valued real exchange rates, like giraffes, are not so difficult to recognize on sight. 'The correct real exchange rate' would be that compatible with expected current account deficits, output levels and long-term capital inflows, given commercial and other policies. These are *real* considerations; what about the role of the exchange rate (and of expected changes in *nominal* level) as a crucial link between domestic and international financial markets, and its impact on the capital account of the balance of payments?

Domestic policies targeting real interest rates and real exchange rates will not be compatible with free or untaxed capital movements and unrestricted convertibility, except by fluke (or short of extravagent average levels of reserves). This is not a pleasant conclusion for those familiar with past experiences with exchange controls over international flows in Latin America or elsewhere. Limitations on unconditional capital-account convertibility, however, may have greater or smaller inefficiencies and inequities depending on the context in which they are undertaken. A real exchange rate hovering around its long-run equilibrium level will do much to reduce pressure on convertibility limitation; it would be absolutely essential to avoid the temptation of manipulation convertibility restrictions to buttress overvalued exchange rates, as in the past. The heterodox tool of exchange controls must be managed with orthodox concern for real exchange rate. Note, incidentally, that even without convertibility restrictions overvalued exchange rates can be propped by manipulating the capital account of the balance of payments, i.e., high interest rates went along in the Southern Cone with overvaluation.

The prudential regulatory machinery could be used to discourage volatile international financial flows relying primarily on taxes or tax-like requirements, i.e., via special reserve requirements for certain types of unwanted international financial transactions, as is the practice in several Western European countries. Taxes would also be expected to capture arbitrage profits from borrowing abroad and lending domestically, under 'normal' circumstances. Persistent subsidies to encourage foreign borrowing would be a sign that either the real exchange rate or domestic real interest rates have drifted from their equilibrium levels.

Unrestrained convertibility in the capital account is in fact a luxury, desirable in itself, enjoyed only by a handful of countries which have either a very developped or a very underdeveloped domestic financial system. It is neither the ususal practice in OECD countries [see Bertrand (1981)], nor was it the expectation of at least some of the architects of the Bretton Woods system [see Crotty (1983)]. So long as domestic currency balances may be burdened by an inflation tax higher than those levied on foreign currencies, some limitations on convertibility are widely perceived as a necessary part of transitional policy package [see, for example, McKinnon and Mathieson (1981)].

The case for some limitations on free capital account movements rests partly on macroeconomic considerations, partly on the need to correct microeconomic imperfections on domestic and international financial markets. Events during 1982 must have put an end to the notion that there are small countries in international financial markets, in the sense that those countries could borrow all they want at a given interest rate. Currency and sovereign risks will inevitably tilt the supply schedule of foreign funds to any country in an upward-sloping direction, and may even give it a kinkier look, so that there will be a gap between private and social costs of borrowing [see Harberger (1981) for a clear, but apparently unheeded, exposition]. Moral-hazard considerations on both sides of the market, or expectations of bail-outs, reinforce the case for home-country supervision of international financial flows; if home countries do not undertake that supervision others will do it for them.

These considerations also cast doubt on the desirability of allowing the domestic financial system to offer deposits denominated in foreign currencies, either to domestic residents or to foreigners. Such deposits sharply curtail the freedom of maneuver of monetary authorities, for the sake of maintaining the credibility and reputation of the banks offering them. (The point is partly applicable to any contry whose banks have an international scope, even if deposits are denominated in home currency.) The Mexican and Uruguayan experiences suggest that deposits denominated in foreign currencies and insured by the home Central Bank enhance vulnerability to crises, introducing the likehood of sharp discontinuities in the rules of the game. At any rate, in general that type of deposit would not be compatible with limitations on capital account convertibility, limitations which would also rule out the feasibility of totally clean float for the exchange rate, including both spot and future quotations.

5. A final caveat

Recent Chilean experience shows that a balanced budget by itself will prevent neither a serious financial crisis nor acute macroeconomic turbulence. Yet previous Chilean experiences, and those of other Latin American countries, also show that fiscal extravagance is a sure way to bring about not only economic dislocation, but also the weakening and even collapse of fragile democratic institutions. This paper has discussed neither fiscal policy nor strategies on how to eliminate inflation. Implicity, it has assumed that Latin American inflations may be sustained by many sources, not just budgetary laxity, and that in most countries for the foreseeable future 'living with inflation' will be a more credible goal than eliminating it, and that this must be taken into account when designing desirable domestic financial policies, as well as other measure.

Nevertheless, there are inflations (and budget deficits) which no domestic financial system with a minimum of coherence could live with. Examples include inflations which accelerate for more than, say, three years in a row, reaching levels substantially above historical norms, or inflationary rates which fluctuate unpredictably from year to year. Under either circumstances relative prices will become very volatile, and real and financial calculations very difficult. In contrast, the Colombian experience of the last ten years or so provides an example of an inflation which is fairly predictable and relatively easy to live with. Finally, it would be nearly impossible to design reasonable financial systems, in a mixed-economy context, which could be

24   *C. Diaz-Alejandro, Consequences of financial liberalization*

compatible with sustained public expenditures and budget deficits of the magnitude of those registered in Chile during 1971–72, in Argentina during 1974–75, or in Mexico during 1981–82.

References

Arellano, José P., 1983a, El financiamiento del desarrollo, in: CIEPLAN, Reconstruccion economica para la democracia (Editorial Aconcagua, Santiago de Chile) 189–237.

Arellano, José P., 1983b, De la liberalizacion a la intervencion: El mercado de capitales en Chile: 1974-83, in: Estudios CIEPLAN, no. 11, Estudio no. 74. Dec., 5–49.

Bertrand, Raymond, 1981, The liberization of capital movements — An insight, The Three Banks Review, no. 132, Dec.

Corden, W. Max, 1972, Monetary integration, Princeton Essays in International Finance no. 93 (International Finance Section, Princeton University, Princeton, NJ) April.

Crotty, James R., 1983, On Keynes and capital flight, The Journal of Economic Literature XXI, no. 1, 59–65.

Federal Reserve Bank of Minneapolis, 1982, Are banks specials?, Annual report.

Fernandez, Roque B., 1983, La crisis financiera Argentina: 1980–1982, Desarrollo Economico 23, no. 89, 79–98.

Frenkel, Roberto, 1984, Notas para una investigacion sobre el sistema financiero en Argentina, processed (CEDES, Buenos Aires).

Friedman, Milton, 1959, A program for monetary stability (Fordham University Press, New York).

Galbis, Vicente, 1979, Inflation and interest rate policies in Latin America, 1967-76, International Monetary Fund Staff Papers 26, no. 2, 334–366.

Gurley, John G., Hugh T. Patrick and E. S. Shaw, 1965, The financial structure of Korea. Reprinted by Research Department, the Bank of Korea, Seoul.

Hall, Robert E., 1982, Monetary trends in the United States and the United Kingdom: A review from the perspective of new developments in monetary economics, Journal of Economic Literature 20, no. 4, 1552–1556.

Harberger, Arnold C., 1981, Comentarios, in: Banco Central de Chile, Alternativas de politicas financieras en economias pequenas y abiertas al exterior, Estudios Monetarios VII (Banco Central de Chile, Santiago de Chile) Dec., 1981–188.

Harberger, Arnold C., 1982, The Chilean economy in the 1970's: Crisis, stabilization, liberalization, reform, in: Karl Brunner and Allen H. Meltzer, eds., Economic policy in a world of change, Carnegie-Rochester Conference Series on Public Policy 17 (North-Holland, Amsterdam) 115–152.

International Monetary Fund, 1983, International financial statistics (Washington, DC) March.

Johnson, G.C. and Richard L. Abrams, 1983, Aspects of the international banking safety net, International Monetary Fund Occasional Paper no. 17, March.

Kareken, John H., 1981, Deregulating commercial banks: The watchword should be caution, Federal Reserve Bank of Minneapolis Quarterly Review, Spring/Summer, 1–5.

Litterman, Robert B. and Laurence Weiss, 1984, Money, real interest rates and output: A reinterpretation of postwar U.S. data, processed (Federal Reserve Bank of Minneapolis, Minneapolis, MN).

McKinnon, Ronald I., 1980, Financial policies, in: John Cody et al., eds., Policies for industrial progress in developing countries (Oxford University Press, New York) 93–120.

McKinnon, Ronald I., 1982, The order of economic liberalization: Lessons from Chile and Argentina, in: Karl Brunner and Allan H. Meltzer, eds., Economic policy in a world of change, Carnegie-Rochester Conference Series on Public Policy 17 (North-Holland, Amsterdam) 159–184.

McKinnon, Ronald I. and Donald J. Mathieson, 1981, How to manage a repressed economy, Princeton Essays in International Finance no. 145 (International Finance Section, Princeton University, Princeton, NJ) Dec.

Robichek, E. Walter, 1981, Some reflections about external public debt management, in: Banco Central de Chile, Alternativas de políticas financieras en economías pequeñas y abiertas al exterior, Estudios Monetarios VII (Banco Central de Chile, Santiago de Chile) Dec., 171–183.

Stiglitz, J. and A. Weiss, 1981, Credit rationing in markets with imperfect information, The American Economic Review 71, no. 3, 393–410.

Part IV
Instability and the Developed World

[21]

THE EURO: EXPECTATIONS AND PERFORMANCE

Dominick Salvatore
Fordham University

THE CREATION OF THE EURO

At the beginning of 1999, the member states of the European Monetary System (EMS) joined stage 3 of the Economic and Monetary Union (EMU) of Europe with the introduction of the euro and a common monetary policy by the European Central Bank (ECB). The euro was introduced on 1 January 1999 as the common currency of eleven European countries (Austria, Belgium, Germany, Finland, France, Ireland, Italy, Luxembourg, Spain, Portugal and the Netherlands). Britain, Denmark, Sweden, and Greece were not part of it (Britain and Denmark chose not to participate, Sweden was not eligible because it had not been part of the EMS, and Greece was not admitted because it was unable to meet four of the five Maastricht indicators; Greece was admitted on 1 January 2001). The official euro conversion rates for the participating currencies were decided in the fall of 1998 and are given in Table 1. The creation of the euro was certainly one of the most important events in postwar monetary history—never before had a large group of sovereign nations voluntarily given up their own currency for a common currency.

From 1 January 1999, the exchange rate of the euro fluctuated in terms of other currencies, such as the U.S. dollar, the British pound, the Japanese yen, and so on, but the value of each participating currency remained rigidly fixed in terms of euros. This meant that the exchange rate of the currencies participating in the euro fluctuate in relation to other currencies only to the extent that the euro fluctuated in relation to those other currencies.

BENEFITS OF THE EURO

Analyzing the benefits and costs of a common currency must inevitably start from the brilliant foresights of Mundell [1961] and McKinnon [1963], the originators of the theory of optimum currency areas. Using this theory, economists have analyzed and, on the whole, agree on the general benefits and costs from the establishment of the euro. The benefits are: (1) the elimination of the need to exchange currencies of EMU members (this has been estimated to save as much as $30 billion per year); (2) the elimination of excessive volatility among EMU currencies (fluctuations will only occur between the euro and the dollar, the yen, and the currencies of non-EMU nations); (3) more rapid economic and financial integration among EMU members; (4) a European Central Bank that may conduct a more expansionary monetary policy than

Dominick Salvatore: Department of Economics Fordham University Bronx, New York 10458 E-mail: salvatore@fordham.edu

Eastern Economic Journal, Vol. 28, No. 1, Winter 2002

TABLE 1
Official Currency Conversion Rates for the Euro

Country	National Currency	Currency Units per Euro
Austria	schilling	13.7603
Belgium	Belgian franc	40.3399
Finland	markka	5.94573
France	French franc	6.55957
Germany	Deutsche mark	1.95583
Ireland	punt	0.787564
Italy	Italian lira	1936.27
Luxembourg	Luxembourg franc	40.3399
Netherlands	guilder	2.20371
Portugal	escudo	200.482
Spain	peseta	166.386

The Launch of the Euro. *Federal Reserve Bulletin,* October 1999, 655-66.

the generally restrictive one practically imposed in the past by the Bundesbank on the other EMU members; and (5) greater economic discipline for countries, such as Italy and Greece, that seemed unwilling or unable to "put their house in order" without externally-imposed conditions.

Other benefits of the euro for the EMU members are (6) a seigniorage from the use of the euro as an international currency (the use of the dollar as an international currency confers about $8-10 billion in benefits to the United States, and the expectation is that the euro could provide similar seigniorage benefits to the euro area); (7) the reduced cost of borrowing in international financial markets (it has been estimated that U.S. cost of borrowing on international financial markets is about 25-50 basis points lower than it would have been if the dollar were not used as an international currency—for a total savings of about $10 billion, and the expectation is that the euro area could gain as much from the use of the euro as an international currency); and last but not least (8) the increased economic and political importance that the European Union (EU) will acquire in international affairs.

There is, however, a concern in the United States that the European Union will use this increased power to become more confrontational in transatlantic relations. To be sure, when there are real and important disagreements it is only proper and fair for the European Union to use its newly acquired clout to protect and foster its economic and political interests, but the hope is that it will not use it to pursue anti-American policies for their own sake and simply to assert its power or to strengthen internal cohesion. Similarly, the expected increased economic and political importance of the European Union in international affairs is likely to check American power now that the fear of communism has vanished and the Soviet Union has collapsed as a military superpower.

THE PROBLEM WITH THE EURO

The most serious unresolved problem that the establishment of a European Central Bank (ECB) and the euro may create is how a EMU member states will respond to asymmetric economic shocks. It is almost inevitable that a large and diverse single-currency-area such as the euro area will face periodic asymmetric shocks that will affect various member nations differently and drive their economies out of alignment [IMF, 2000, Ch. 6]. In such a case, there is practically nothing that a nation so adversely affected can do. The nation cannot change the value of its currency or use monetary policy to overcome its particular problem, and fiscal discipline will also prevent it from using this policy to deal with the problem, at least until the Growth and Stability Pact (GSP) is fully implemented and frees up the automatic stabilizers [Salvatore, 1997; 1998; 1999; Arestis, McCauley, and Sawyer, 2001; European Commission, 2001; Issing, 2001].

A single currency works well in the United States because if a region suffers an asymmetric shock, workers move quickly and in great numbers out of the region adversely affected by the shock and toward areas of the nation with greater employment opportunities. This escape hatch is not generally available in Europe to the same extent as in the United States. In fact, the Organization for Economic Cooperation and Development [1986] and the European Commission [1990] found that labor mobility among EMU members is from two to three times lower than among U.S. regions because of language barriers, inflexible housing markets, and labor markets that remain regulated.

In addition to much greater regional and occupational labor mobility, in the United States there is a great deal of federal fiscal redistribution in favor of the adversely affected region. In the euro area, on the other hand, fiscal redistribution cannot be of much help because the EMU budget is only about 1 percent of the EMU's GDP and more than half of it is devoted to its Common Agricultural Policy [Salvatore, 1997]. Furthermore, real wages are also somewhat more flexible downward in the United States than in the euro area. None of these "escape valves" are available to an EMU member adversely affected by a negative asymmetric shock. In fact, the difference in unemployment rates among EMU member nations is much higher than among U.S. regions.

Supporters of the single currency reply that the requirements for the establishment of single currency will necessarily increase labor market flexibility and, by promoting greater intra-euro area trade, a single currency will also dampen nationally differentiated business cycles. Furthermore, it is pointed out that highly integrated euro area capital markets can make up for low labor market mobility and provide an adequate automatic response to asymmetric shocks in the euro area. While these automatic responses to asymmetric shocks may in fact be present, they may not be adequate. It is true that meeting the Maastricht parameters will increase labor market flexibility, but this may be a slow process and may not be allowed to take place to a sufficient degree if euro area labor insists on retaining many of its present benefits (such as job security and high unemployment pay). Furthermore, "excessive" capital flows may also work perversely by reducing the incentive for fundamental adjustment measures and may even produce supply shocks of their own by pushing up the exchange rate of the EMU member adversely affected by an asymmetric shock.

A major asymmetric shock would result in unbearable pressure within the euro area because of limited labor mobility, grossly inadequate fiscal redistribution, and a European Central Bank that would probably want to keep monetary conditions tight in order to hold inflation at bay and to make the euro as strong as the dollar. Some indication of the type of problem that the euro area may be facing is given by the fact that in 2001 Ireland and the Netherlands were facing high growth and inflation while Germany and Italy were growing sluggishly. This meant that the ECB should have tightened monetary policy to cool off Ireland and the Netherlands and should have adopted an expansionary monetary policy to stimulate growth in Germany and Italy. A much larger asymmetric shock could create a much greater problem, and it is impossible to anticipate how the euro area would resolve and come out of it.

Whether increased economic integration within the EU reduces or increases the frequency and magnitude of asymmetric shocks is greatly debated. Frankel and Rose [1998] believe that greater economic integration dampens asymmetric shocks while Krugman [1993] believes the opposite. The available data are not sufficient to resolve the disagreement. Most economists, however, do believe that greater economic and financial integration enhances the effectiveness of the common monetary policy in member nations [Fratianni, Salvatore, and von Hagen, 1997; OECD, 1999; 2000b, Angeloni and Mojon, 2000]. There is also the question of the effectiveness of a euro-wide monetary policy on the various EMU members. Previous research by the IMF [1998] indicated that a rise in interest rates took twice as long to have a significant effect in Austria, Belgium, Finland, Germany, and the Netherlands than in France, Italy, Portugal, and Spain, but that the final impact was almost twice as large, on average, in the first group of countries than in the second because of their different financial structure. For example, the IMF found that Spanish banks passed an interest rate increase on to customers within three months, while German banks took one year or more because of their closer relationship with customers. Similarly, a country such as Italy, where adjustable-rate debt is common, responds faster to interest-rate changes than do countries such as Germany, where fixed-rate debt is more common. Although the euro will very likely lead to the narrowing of these country differences over time, they are likely to persist at least for several years to come.

THE MAJOR INTERNATIONAL CURRENCIES

An international currency is the currency of a nation (such as the U.S. dollar) that fulfills in the world economy the same basic functions that it performs in the nation's economy. That is, it serves as a unit of account, a medium of exchange, and a store of value. However, while the nation chooses its own currency, a national currency becomes an international currency as a result of market forces and by being able to perform the functions of money for both private and official transactions in the international economy [Cohen, 2000].

During the nineteenth and early twentieth centuries, the pound sterling was by far the dominant vehicle currency. Since then, the international use of the U.S. dollar

TABLE 2
Relative International Importance of Major Currencies in 1998
(in percentages)

	Official Use of Currencies		Currencies of Denomination in Private Transactions				
	(1)	(2)	(3)	(4)	(5)	(6)	(7)
	Foreign Exchange Reserves[a]	Pegging of Currencies[b]	Foreign Exchange Trading[c]	Euro-Currency Deposits[d]	Internat'l Bank Loans[e]	Internat'l Bond Issues[f]	Trade Invoicing[g]
U.S. dollar	65.7	30.8	49.8	50.8	69.8	45.7	47.6
Deutsche mark	12.1	4.6	17.2	14.8	3.3	10.1	15.3
Japanese yen	5.3	0.0	11.6	5.5	0.2	11.3	4.8
Pound sterling	3.8	0.0	6.1	8.0	15.6	7.9	5.7
French franc	1.3	23.1	2.9	4.0	5.3	5.1	6.3
Swiss franc	0.7	0.0	4.0	4.1	1.1	3.8	0.0
ECU	0.8	0.0	0.8	1.6	0.8	3.7	0.0
Other	9.9	49.8	7.6	11.2	3.9	12.4	20.3

Percentages may not add to 100 because of rounding. Sources: (a) IMF. *Annual Report*. Washington, D.C., IMF,2000, 111; (b) IMF. *Annual Report*. Washington, D.C., IMF, 1998, 18-19; (c) BIS. *Annual Report*. Basle. BIS, 1999, 117; (d) BIS. *Annual Report*. Basle. BIS, 1998, 116. Data are for 1997; (e) OECD. *Financial Market Trends*. February 1998, 69 ,82. Data are for 1997; (f) IMF. *International Capital Markets*. Washington, D.C., IMF, September 2000, 11, (g) Hartman [1999]. Data are for 1992. More recent data were not available.

increased in step with the increase in the relative economic and political importance of the United States. After World War II, the dollar became the dominant vehicle currency. The reasons for the decline of the pound sterling and rise of the U.S. dollar as a vehicle currency after World War II were (1) the high rate of inflation in the United Kingdom and sharp fluctuation in the value of the pound compared to the low inflation in the United States and stability of the U.S. dollar during the late 1940s and early 1950s, (2) the existence of exchange controls in England in contrast to the relative openness of the U.S. financial market, and (3) the decline in the sterling area's share of world exports in comparison to the rise in the U.S. share. Today, the pound sterling remains a vehicle currency (but to a much smaller extent than the U.S. dollar) because London remains a sophisticated international financial center [Tavlas, 1997]. One indication of the changed international role of the dollar and the pound sterling after World War II was the decision by OPEC (Organization of Petroleum Exporting Countries) in the mid-1970s to price petroleum in dollars instead of pound sterling.

Table 2 shows the relative importance of the dollar and other major currencies in international finance and trade in 1998 on the eve of the euro creation. The first column of the table shows that 65.7 percent of the international reserves held by central banks were held in dollars, 12.1 percent in Deutsche marks, 5.3 percent in yen, and smaller percentages for other currencies and the ECU (European Currency Unit). This is much greater than the U.S. share of world output and reflects the dominant international role of the dollar as a vehicle currency. On the other hand, the share of international reserves held in Japanese yen is much less (5.3 percent) than the share of Japan's output in world output (7.6 percent). It must be pointed out, however, that neither Japan nor Germany encouraged the use of their currencies as international reserves so as not to constrain their ability to conduct a domestic monetary policy. Being much larger than either Japan or Germany, the United States did not feel so constrained.

The second column of the table shows that 30.8 percent (20 of the 65 mostly-small countries) that pegged (i.e., defined their currency) in terms of an international currency pegged it to the dollar, 4.6 percent (3 countries) to the Deutsche mark, 23.1 percent (15 countries) to the French franc, and 41.5 percent (the remaining 27 countries) to other currencies, SDR (IMF's special drawing rights), or a basket of currencies. It was the strong appreciation of the U.S. dollar to which they pegged their currency that triggered the serious financial and economic crisis in some of the countries of Southeast Asia (Thailand, Malaysia, Indonesia, South Korea, and the Philippines) and Latin America (such as Mexico and Argentina) during the second half of the 1990s. The relatively large number of countries that pegged their currencies to the French franc were the France's former in West Africa and they, too, faced a financial crisis as a result of their inflation rate more rapid than France's during the last decade.

The third column of Table 2 shows that 49.8 percent of foreign exchange trading in world markets was in U.S. dollars, 17.2 percent in Deutsche marks, 11.6 percent in yen, and smaller percentages for other currencies. Once again the dollar dominated. It seems that once a currency becomes the leading currency, its domain will far exceed the share of its economy in the world economy because of the reduced costs and increased benefits that economic agents face when using the leading currency instead of other currencies. Columns (4) to (6) of the table show that dollars represented 50.8 percent of Euro currency deposits (that is, bank deposits in a currency other than the currency of the nation in which the deposit is made), 69.8 percent of international bank loans (that is, euro and foreign bank loans), and 45.7 percent of international bonds. Column (7) of the table shows the relative use of the various international currencies in trade invoicing. From the table, we can see that the U.S. dollar occupies a dominant position in international finance and trade—a position that is much greater than the U.S. share of world output, assets, and trade. Only in the number of nations pegging their currencies to another currency, does the French franc come close to the U.S. dollar (23.1 percent of the total for the French franc as compared with 30.8 percent for the U.S. dollar). In all other uses, the U.S. dollar is far more dominant with respect to the other international currencies.

Table 3 shows the currency composition of foreign-exchange reserves from 1990 to 1999. The table shows that the percentage of foreign exchange reserves held in U.S. dollars increased almost continuously from 50.6 percent at the end of 1990 to 66.2 percent at the end of 1999. This reflected the greater confidence in the U.S. dollar as a result of the superior performance of the U.S. economy in relation to Europe and Japan. The Deutsche mark's use declined from 16.8 percent of the total in 1990 to 12.1 percent at the end of 1998 (before its international reserve function was taken over by the euro, on 1 January 1999). Over the same period, the French franc declined from 2.4 percent to 1.3 percent, the Netherland guilder went from 1.1 percent to 0.3

THE EURO: EXPECTATIONS AND PERFORMANCE   127

TABLE 3

Share of Currencies in Official Holdings of Foreign Exchange Reserves, End of Year, 1990-1999 (in percentages)

	1990	1991	1992	1993	1994	1995	1996	1997	1998	1999
U.S. dollar	50.6	51.1	55.1	56.4	56.4	56.8	60.1	62.1	65.7	66.2
Euro										12.5[a]
Deutsche mark	16.8	15.1	13.0	13.4	14.0	13.5	12.8	12.6	12.1	
French franc	2.4	2.9	2.5	2.2	2.3	2.2	1.7	1.3	1.3	
Netherland guilder	1.1	1.1	0.7	0.6	0.5	0.4	0.3	0.4	0.3	
ECU	9.7	10.2	9.7	8.2	7.7	6.8	5.9	5.0	0.8	
Japanese yen	8.0	8.5	7.5	7.6	7.8	6.8	6.0	5.3	5.3	5.1
Pound sterling	3.0	3.2	3.0	2.9	3.2	3.1	3.4	3.6	3.8	4.0
Swiss franc	1.2	1.2	1.0	1.1	0.9	0.8	0.8	0.8	0.7	0.7
Unspecified currencies	7.1	6.9	7.4	7.4	7.1	9.6	9.0	9.0	9.9	11.6

Percentages may not add to 100 because of rounding. Source: IMF. *Annual Report*. Washington, D.C.: IMF, 2000, 111.

a. Not comparable with the combined share of euro legacy currencies in previous years, part of which reflected holdings of the Eurosystem that became domestic assets, and thus were no longer recorded as foreign currency holdings, upon conversion into euros on January 1, 1999 (for example, Germany's holdings of French francs became holdings of domestic assets after their conversion into euros).

percent, and the ECU from 9.7 percent to 0.8 percent. Again, we see that once a currency becomes the leading international currency, its dominance becomes far superior to the relative position of the nation in the world economy. On 1 January 1999, the euro took over the international reserve function of the euro-legacy currencies and by the end of 1999 it represented 12.5 percent of total world foreign exchange reserves. The euro represented a smaller percentage of foreign exchange reserves than the sum of the euro-legacy foreign exchange reserves at the end of 1998 because the portion of the international foreign exchange reserves that each euro-area country held in euro-legacy currencies became domestic assets upon the adoption of the euro on 1 January 1999.

Table 3 also shows that the Japanese yen represented 8.0 percent of total foreign exchange reserves in 1990 and declined almost continuously until the end of 1999, to 5.1 percent. Over the same period, the percentage of foreign exchange reserves held in British pounds (the United Kingdom was not part of the euro area) increased from 3.0 to 4.0 and those held in unspecified currencies increased from 7.1 to 11.6, while Swiss francs declined from 1.2 to 0.7. Thus, the relative importance of the dollar as an international reserve currency increased during the decade of the 1990 (after declining from 100 percent in the late 1940, to 85 percent in 1975, and 51 percent at the beginning of 1990) as a reflection of the higher growth and greater dynamism of the U.S. economy. As pointed out later in the paper, however, the relative share of the dollar is expected to decline in the future, while that of the euro is likely to increase.

THE EURO AS AN INTERNATIONAL CURRENCY

Expectation about the euro before its creation ranged from those, such as Feldstein [1991] and Dornbusch [1996], who did not believe that Europe needed or would succeed in introducing a common currency (or that if one were introduced, it would fail) to those, such Portes and Rey [1998], who not only believed that the euro would be created as scheduled and that it be very strong from the very beginning, but that it could also replace the dollar as the leading international currency in a very short time. In between these two positions were others (such as Frankel, [1995]) who were more cautious and believed that the euro would be created as a strong currency, but that it was not likely to replace the dollar as the leading international currency for a long time, if ever. My position [Salvatore 1996; 1997] at the time was that because Europe wanted the euro, it would get it, but the benefits would be more political than economic during the first years of its existence. Only afterwards was the European Union likely to receive major economic benefits.

An excellent framework for analyzing issues relating to the future role of the euro is that provided by Portes and Rey [1998]. The basic equation of their model is

$$V = f(B, E, T, I)$$

where, V = the volume of foreign-exchange transactions in euros
   B = cross-border bond flows in euros
   E = cross-border equity flows in euros
   T = volume of trade
   I = international use of the euro

In analyzing the future role of the euro, however, Portes and Rey concentrated on B and placed much less importance on the other variables in their model. Thus, they predicted that (1) creating a single financial market in the EMU would reduce transaction in the euro area so much as to make the euro a strong rival of the dollar (possibly even surpassing it as the leading international currency in a short time) and (2) the euro would appreciate sharply with respect to the dollar soon after its introduction. From a theoretical point of view, assigning much less importance to the other variables in the model (other than B) did not seem justified. Furthermore, the authors' justification for assuming that the supply of euros would increase at a later time than the increase in their demand, thus justifying a quick appreciation of the euro with respect to the dollar does not seem to be entirely justified. Indeed, because of these reasons their predictions did not turn out to be correct.

Despite its unexpected weakness in relation to the U.S. dollar and the Japanese yen since its introduction on 1 January 1999, the euro had been an important international currency from the very beginning and is bound to become even more important in the future. The reasons are that the EU: (1) is as large an economic and trading unit as the United States, (2) has a large, well-developed and growing financial market, which is increasingly free of controls, and (3) is expected to have a good inflation performance that will keep the value of the euro stable.

THE EURO: EXPECTATIONS AND PERFORMANCE 129

TABLE 4
Relative Economic Size of EU, USA and Japan in 1999 (in percentages)

	EU	USA	Japan
Relative Economic Size:			
Share of World GDP[a]	20.3	21.9	7.6
Share of World Merchandise Exports[b]			
(excluding intra-EU)	14.1	12.4	7.5
Financial Structure (in trillions of dollars)[c]			
Bank Deposits	4.9	5.1	5.5
Bank Loans	6.4	4.5	5.2
Outstanding Debt Securities	5.5	15.3	6.3
Issued by Corporations	0.2	2.7	0.7
Issued by Financial Institutions	1.9	4.3	0.9
Issued by the Public Sector	3.3	8.3	4.7
Stock Market Capitalization	5.5	16.5	7.3

Sources: (a) IMF *World Economic Outlook*, October 2000, 187, (b) WTO *Annual Report*, 2000, 168-171, (c) OECD *Financial Market Trends*. July, 2000, 111. Data for the EU refer to Euro Area.

As the data in Table 4 indicate, the 15-member EU (even though only 12 countries presently participate in the euro) has very similar shares of world GDP and exports as the United States, and the size of its financial sector is also similar. Thus, if the international use of the euro were to match its share of world GDP, exports, and financial sector, the euro would become as important as the dollar as an international or vehicle currency. This would mean that the relative international use of the dollar would fall to 40-45 percent of the total, with an equal share going to the euro, and the remainder going mostly to the yen and a few other smaller currencies, such as the Swiss franc, the Canadian dollar, and the Australian dollar—mostly the yen.

It is unlikely, however, that the international use of the euro will soon match the EU share of world GDP and exports (as some European economists believe). First of all, the absence of a federal government in the EU puts a ceiling on the integration process in the market for government securities, and so financial integration in the EU will inevitably fall short of that in the United States. Secondly, with a smaller and declining covariance among the assets of the various EU members, according to strict portfolio diversification motives, there is less of a reason for EU investors to increase their holding of euro-denominated assets, while there will be a greater reason for increasing their dollar—and yen—denominated assets, as long as the ECB pursues an independent monetary policy with respect to the U.S. central Bank (the Fed) and the Bank of Japan. Thirdly, a portfolio shift in favor of euro-denominated assets will occur only if the ECB will conduct a tighter monetary policy than the Fed, but with the need to reconcile the different monetary-policy requirements of the various EU members, this may be difficult to do.

It is unlikely that the euro will soon displace the dollar as the most important international currency for other reasons. These are: (1) most primary commodities are priced in dollars and this is likely to remain the case for some time to come; (2) non-EMU countries are likely to continue to use the dollar for most of their international transactions for the foreseeable future, with the exception of the former communist nations in central and eastern Europe and the former French colonies in Africa, which shifted from using the Deutsche mark or French franc, respectively, to using euros, and (3) of sheer inertia that favors the incumbent (the dollar).

Thus, it is more likely that about 50 percent of international transactions will be conducted in dollars in the future (down from the present 60 percent or so), 40 percent in euro, and the remaining 10 percent in yen and other smaller currencies [McCauley, 1997]. That is, the euro will very likely have more weight than the mark had up to 1998 but somewhat less than the relative weight that the EU has in international trade and finance in the world economy—at least during the first few years of its existence. This would involve a substitution of dollars for euros of about $500 billion to $1 trillion and lead to a depreciation of the dollar relative to the euro. But because this substitution is likely to occur gradually over time, it may not put undue pressure on the dollar. Furthermore, the increased financial integration resulting from the replacement of many currencies by a single one will also expand the supply of euro-denominated assets (as foreign borrowers tap into the expanded European financial system) thus dampening the tendency of the euro to appreciate with respect to the dollar.

To be noted is that with the euro, intra-euro area balance-of-payments deficits and surpluses will be netted out, and so the reserve needs for the euro area as a whole (to be held primarily in dollars) will be considerably less than the reserve needs of individual members without the euro. But it is what will happen in the much larger private international holdings of dollars (which depend primarily on expectations of future monetary and fiscal policies in the euro area) that will primarily determine the euro/dollar exchange rate. The emergence of the euro as a major international currency may also lead to a reduction in the international use of the yen, but this could be neutralized if Japan completes the planned deregulation of its financial sector and finally succeeds in resolving its serious decade-old banking and economic crisis.

THE EURO SINCE ITS CREATION

The euro was introduced on 1 January 1999 at the value of $1.17; it rose to $1.18 on 4 January (the first business day of the new year) but, defying almost all predictions, it declined almost continuously reaching near parity to the dollar at the end of 1999 and then falling to a low of $0.82 on 26 October 2000 (see Figure 1).

Just before its introduction, Portes and Rey [1998] and many others believed that the euro would appreciate with respect to the dollar to between $1.25 and $1.30 by the end of 1999 because of the important synergies that they believed would quickly develop between the use of the euro in foreign exchange transactions and in euro area financial asset markets. Instead, the euro depreciated by more than 30 percent by 26 October 2000, and so the question arises as to how could so many financial experts be so wrong. The major reason is that exchange rates, just as stock prices, are practically impossible to predict over short periods of time (days, weeks, or even months) because "news" and other unforeseen events usually overwhelm other more fundamental forces at work on which most experts rely to make their forecasts [OECD, 2000a]. One fundamental explanation for the depreciation of the euro during the first half of

FIGURE 1
Daily Exchange Rate U.S.$ /Euro

Federal Reserve Statistical Release - Foreign Exchange Rates Historical Data

its first year of existence was that the value chosen for its debut was set too high in the fall of 1998 (when the growth rate and the interest rate were expected to fall in the United State and rise in Europe). Because the opposite occurred, it was only natural for the euro to depreciate. Thus, aside for the embarrassment of some high-level euro area officials and European economists who had trumpeted the introduction of the euro with considerable fanfare and predictions of its appreciation, the depreciation that followed encouraged European exports and stimulated growth, which was anemic in most members of the euro area. As was the case for stocks, however, there was no shortage of forecasts as to the future euro/dollar exchange rate—and they were all over the place (for example, at the beginning of 2000, Deutsche Bank predicted that the euro would close the year at $1.12, as contrasted with the actual closing value of $0.94).

The euro continued to depreciate relative to the dollar during 1999 and 2000 for several reasons. First was the positive interest differential in favor of the United States, which attracted huge amounts of financial capital from Europe to the United States, and put upward pressure on the dollar and downward pressure on the euro. Second was the market perception that European countries were not restructuring as rapidly as necessary, and so growth and profitability were expected to be higher in the United States than in Europe. This attracted net direct investment from Europe to the United States and put further downward pressure on the euro. But even this does not tell the whole story—otherwise the euro should have appreciated with respect to the yen in view of the fact that growth and profitability were higher in Eu-

FIGURE 2
Daily Exchange Rate Japanese Yen /Euro

www.Oanda.com—Historical Currency Exchange Rate

rope than in Japan during 1999 and 2000. Instead, as Figure 2 shows, the euro depreciated even more with respect to the yen than with respect to the dollar.

The missing link was that financial markets viewed the lack of political unity in Europe as a sign of weakness. In short, the international value of a currency inevitably also reflects the political situation of the nation or economic area. As a result, the euro depreciated with respect to the dollar much more than justified by purely economic fundamentals. And the pronouncements by Schroeder, the German Prime Minister, in mid-2000 that he was not concerned about the weakness of the euro certainly did not help. Nor did Duisenberg's [1999] periodic exhortation to financial markets not to unduly punish the euro, followed by the half-hearted and weak intervention of the European Central Bank in support of the euro in mid-September 2000, lift the fate of the euro.

Although the EMU and the euro were not in danger of collapse in fall 2000, the continued weakness of the euro magnified the problems caused by the increase in petroleum prices for Europe (because petroleum is priced in dollars). The danger was that this would slow down growth and profitability in Europe more than in the United States and put even more pressure on the euro. It was for that reason that the European Central Bank in concert with the NY Fed (which executes international operations for the U.S. central bank) and the central banks of Japan, France, England and Canada, in a move that caught the markets by surprise, intervened in foreign exchange markets for the first time on Friday, 22 September 2000 in support of the euro, which had fallen in previous days to its all-time low of $0.82. By the end of the day the euro had risen to $0.88, but in the following days the euro fell back to its pre-intervention level.

THE EURO: EXPECTATIONS AND PERFORMANCE 133

Then on 28 September 2000, the euro received another blow by the clear rejection of Danish voters in the referendum to adopt the euro. This may influence the United Kingdom and Sweden to also refuse to join the single currency. By its vote, Denmark rejected the plan to create a "deep Europe"—the idea of eventually forging a federal European government and parliament with real authority—as wanted by France and Germany. That is, the Danish vote can be taken as a pure test of the political will to become part of the Franco-German vision of a large superstate. The Danes saw the euro as a way to compel Europe toward deep political integration and rejected the idea. Henceforth, if France, Germany, Italy, the Netherlands, and Belgium want a deep Europe rapidly, they will very likely have to go ahead alone. The Danish vote also underscored the daunting task facing the European Central Bank in forging confidence in a currency that has no single government and no unified fiscal policy behind it.

At the beginning of November 2000, the European Central Bank intervened again several times (but alone) in foreign exchange markets in support of the euro, but to no avail. Not even the uncertainty surrounding the election of the President of the United States was sufficient to lift the value of the euro. Only when it became evident, toward the end of November, that the growth rate of the United States had declined sharply and that, as a result, the European Union was expected to grow more rapidly than the United States in 2001, did the net capital outflow from Europe to the United States dry up, and the euro start to appreciate significantly with respect to the dollar. (It reached the value of $0.96 on Friday, 5 January 2001.) The trend was expected to continue with the euro reaching parity with the United States by mid-2001.

From February to June 2001, however, the euro fell and remained lower than $0.90 as markets anticipated that growth and profitability in the United States would resume in toward the end of 2000 or in early 2001, and thus that there was no reason for the euro to continue to appreciate relative to the dollar. Another possible explanation for the strength of the dollar relative to the euro was the continued higher growth of labor productivity in the United States compared to the European Union (despite the slowdown in the U.S. economy in the latter part of 2000 and first half of 2001). Only if the current U.S. slowdown kills the growth of its labor productivity, the argument goes, will the euro appreciate significantly with respect to the dollar. Still another possible reason for the continued strength of the dollar is that perhaps investors still see the United States as a "safe haven" in times (such as the present one) of economic turmoil (due to the financial crisis in Turkey and Argentina, the continued economic crisis in Japan, and danger of renewed financial instability in Brazil and Russia). As is clear from the above, there is no shortage of explanations for the current strength of the dollar and, as some older explanations are contradicted by emerging facts and evidence, new ones are confidently introduced. Of course, should the dollar begin to depreciate heavily with respect to the euro, all sorts of reasons will be advanced for that. In short, no economic model or theory can consistently and accurately predict exchange rate movements in the short run because fundamental forces at work are easily and frequently overwhelmed by transitory ones and "news".

THE EXCHANGE RATE BETWEEN THE EURO, THE DOLLAR, AND OTHER CURRENCIES

The introduction of the euro on 1 January 1999 proceeded smoothly and did not create problems for the working of the international monetary system [Danthine, Giavazzi, and Thadden, 2000]. What may create problems is the fact that with most trade and financial relations conducted within, rather than between, the three major trading blocks (the EU, NAFTA, and Asia centered on Japan), there will normally be less concern about the euro/dollar and euro/yen exchange rate, and less interest in intervening in foreign exchange markets to stabilize exchange rates (only with the deepening depreciation and undervaluation of the euro in 2000, did interest in the euro exchange rate came to the forefront). With less interest and less intervention, it is likely that the euro/dollar and euro/yen exchange rate will continue to be volatile in the future. This tendency also arises because the exchange rate is one of only a few market equilibrating mechanisms operating among the three major trading blocks. Exchange rates among the three leading currencies are likely to be especially volatile if and when the three blocks will face different cyclical conditions and shifting market perceptions about economic and financial prospects [Buiter, 2000].

Large exchange rate volatility, by adding to transaction costs, will affect the volume and pattern of international trade. These costs, however, are not very large and firms engaged in international trade and finance can easily and cheaply cover their foreign exchange risk. Potentially more damaging to the flow of international trade and investments than excessive exchange rate volatility are the wide and persistent exchange rate misalignments (as they seem to have developed in 2000 between the euro, on the one hand, and the dollar and the yen, on the other). An overvalued currency acts as an export tax and an import subsidy on the nation and, as such, reduces the international competitiveness of the nation or trading block and distorts the pattern of specialization, trade, and payments. A significant exchange rate misalignment that persists for years cannot possibly be hedged away and can impose significant real costs on the economy in the form of unemployment, idle capacity, bankruptcy, and protectionism, and these may lead to serious trade disputes. This is exactly what happened when the U.S. dollar became grossly overvalued in the mid-1980s.

Also important is the relationship between the euro and the currencies of the EMU countries that so far have not joined the euro (the British pound, the Swedish krona, and the Danish krone). The exchange rate between the euro and these other currencies is also likely to be subject to high volatility and misalignments without the establishment of an exchange rate mechanism similar to the ERM. But, as the experience with 1992-93 ERM crisis showed, such a system is unstable and crisis prone [Salvatore, 1996]. It is, however, in the interest of Britain, Sweden, and Denmark to enforce strong limits on the fluctuation of their currencies with respect to the euro in anticipation of their possible joining it in the future, and to avoid importing financial instability in the meantime. The only way to limit excessive exchange rate misalignment among the euro, the dollar and the yen is by greater macroeconomic policy coordination among the three major trading blocks than has hereto been possible.

Then there is the exchange rate between the euro and the currencies of the dozen or so former communist countries that are in line for admission into the European Monetary Union. These countries have opted for a wide variety of exchange rate arrangements from currency boards to flexible rates [Salvatore, 2001]. Important as they are, however, it is the exchange rate between the euro and the dollar and the euro and the yen that will determine for the most part how smoothly the entire international monetary system will operate in the future. The only way to limit excessive exchange rate misalignment among the euro, the dollar and the yen is by greater macroeconomic policy coordination among the three major trading blocks than has hereto been possible [Salvatore, 1999].

REFERENCES

Angeloni, I. and Mojon, B. After the Changeover: Three Conditions for a Successful Single Monetary Policy. *Euro*, 2000, 19-28.

Arestis P., McCauley, R. N., and Sawyer, M. The Future of the Euro: Is There an Alternative to the Stability and Growth Pact? Levy Institute Public Policy Brief, March 2001.

Board of Governors of the Federal Reserve. The Launch of the Euro. *Federal Reserve Bulletin, October* 1999, 655-66

Buiter, W. H. Optimal Currency Areas: Why Does the Exchange Rate Regime Matter? CEPR Discussion Paper No. 2366. London: CEPR, January 2000.

Cohen, B. J. Life at the Top: International Currencies in the Twenty-First Century. *Princeton Essay in International Economics*, December 2000.

Danthine, J. P., Giavazzi, F., and von Thadden, E. L. European Financial Markets After the EMU: A First Assessment. CEPR Discussion Paper No. 2413. London: CEPR, April 2000.

Dornbusch, R. Euro Fantasies. *Foreign Affairs*, September-October 1996, 25-37.

Duisenberg, W. F. Economic and Monetary Union in Europe—The Challenges Ahead, in *New Challenges for Monetary Policy*. Symposium sponsored by the Federal Reserve Bank of Kansas City. Kansas City, August 1999, 185-94.

European Commission. Is the Commitment to Sound Public Finances Robust Enough in Europe? IP/01/900, 27 June 2001.

_____. One Market, One Money. *European Economy*, 1990, 29-36.

Feldstein, M. Does One Market Require One Money? In *Symposium on Policy Implications of Trade and Currency Zones*, Kansas City: Federal Reserve Bank, 1991, 77-84.

Frankel, J. Still the Lingua Franca: The Exaggerated Death of the Dollar. *Foreign Affairs*, July-August 1995, 9-16.

Frankel, J. and Rose, A. The Endogeneity of Optimum Currency Criteria. *Economic Journal*, July 1998, 1009-25.

Fratianni, M., Salvatore, D., and Von Hagen, J., eds. *Handbook of Macroeconomic Policies in Open Economies*. Westport CT.: Greenwood Press, 1997.

Hartman, F. The Euro in the New Order of International Currencies. *Euro*, 1999.

IMF. The Real Effects of Monetary Policy in the European Union, Working Paper no. 160, Washington, D.C.: IMF, 1998.

_____. *World Economic Outlook Supporting Studies*. Washington, D.C.: IMF, 2000, Ch. 6.

Issing, O. The Euro Area and the Single Monetary Policy. Working Paper 44, Osterreichsche Nationalbank, Vienna, 1 May 2001.

Krugman, P. The International Role of the Dollar, in *Currencies and Crises,* edited by P. Krugman. Cambridge, MA: MIT Press, 1992, Ch. 10.

_____. Lessons of Massachusetts for the EMU, in *Adjustment and Growth in the European Monetary Union,* edited by F. Torres and F. Giavazzi. Cambridge and New York: Cambridge University Press, 1993, Ch. 7.

McCauley, R. N. The Euro and the Dollar. Essay in International Finance No. 205. Princeton: Princeton University Press, November 1997.

McKinnon, R. Optimum Currency Areas. *American Economic Review*, September 1963, 717-25.

Mundell, R. The Theory of Optimum Currency Areas. *American Economic Review*, September 1961, 657-65.

OECD. *Flexibility in the Labor Market.* Paris: OECD, 1986.

_____. *Facts, Challenges and Policies.* Paris: OECD, 1999.

_____. *Financial Market Trends.* Paris: OECD, February 2000a.

_____. *EMU: One Year On.* Paris: OECD, 2000b.

Portes, R. and Rey, H. The Emergence of the Euro as an International Currency, in *Prospects and Challenges for the Euro,* edited by D. Begg, J. von Hagen, C. Wyplosz, and K. Zimmermann. Oxford: Blackwell, 1998, 305-43.

Salvatore, D. The European Monetary System: Crisis and Future. *Open Economies Review*, December 1996, 593-615.

_____. The Unresolved Problem with the EMS and EMU. *American EconomicReview*, May 1997, 224-26.

_____. Europe's Structural and Competitiveness Problems. *The World Economy*, March 1998, 189-205.

_____. The Operation and Future of the International Monetary System, in *Ideas for the Future of the International Monetary System* edited by M. Fratianni, D. Salvatore, and P. Savona. Hingham, Massachusetts: Kluwer, 1999, 5-45.

_____. The EU Eastern Enlargement. *Empirica*, July 2001, 1-21.

Tavlas, G. S. The International Use of the U.S. Dollar: An Optimum Currency Area Perspective. *The World Economy*, November 1997, 709-47.

World Trade Organization. *Annual Report*, 2000, 168-171

[22]

STRATEGIC PROSPECTS AND POLICIES FOR THE U.S. ECONOMY

Wynne Godley and Alex Izurieta
The Levy Economics Institute of Bard College
NY, April 2002

INTRODUCTION

During the last three or four years several papers published by the Levy Institute have argued that, notwithstanding the great achievements of the U.S. economy, the growth of aggregate demand was being structured in a way which would eventually prove unsustainable. Chart 1 shows figures describing the 'structural' (cyclically adjusted) budget balance, expressed as a percentage of GDP, which have just been published by the Congressional Budget Office (CBO).

Chart 1: Standardized-Budget Surplus as Per Cent of Potential GDP

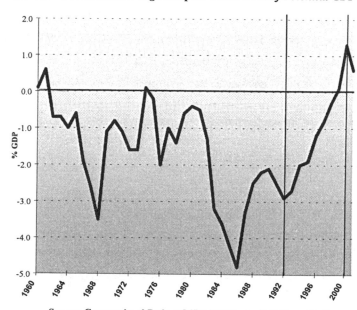

Source: Congressional Budget Office (CBO), April 2002, pp.11-12

As the chart shows, there was a tightening of the fiscal stance during the main period of economic expansion, between 1992 and 2000, which was much greater than in any previous period during the last forty years. In 2000 there was structural budget surplus equal to 1.3 per cent of (trend) GDP –the most restrictive fiscal stance for at least forty years; the budget had never previously been in structural surplus to any significant extent.

While the fiscal stance was tightening through the period of expansion, there was also a progressive deterioration in net export demand, so that the current balance of payments was a record 4.5 per cent of GDP in deficit in 2000. It followed that the expansion of demand in aggregate had been driven by a similarly unprecedented expansion of private expenditure *relative to income*; and that this had perforce been financed by growing injections of net credit which was causing the indebtedness of the private sector[1] to escalate to unprecedented levels.

Official projections always showed that the fiscal stance was set to go on tightening through each ensuing ten year period; and there was no reason to suppose, if growth were maintained and the dollar remained strong, that the balance of trade would not continue to worsen. Therefore, we argued, sustained growth in the future depended critically on there being a continued expansion of private expenditure relative to income, implying ever greater injections of net lending, and an ever increasing burden of servicing the debts.

The conclusion we drew was that this process must come to an end at some stage, and that when it did the entire stance of fiscal policy would have to be changed –in an expansionary direction. Moreover, if economic growth were to be sustained indefinitely, there would have to be a recovery in net export demand since otherwise the U.S.'s net international investment position would eventually spin out of control.

It is worth recalling the conventional view which was held, almost universally, until about a year ago. The consensus view was that the U.S. had acquired a *New Economy* which was

---

[1]   That is, the non-financial private sector.

immune to the business cycle and which, thanks to investment in new technology and labor market flexibility, had a much faster underlying growth rate than previously. So the good times were here to stay. But apart from faith in the New Economy, there was a widespread belief that the use of fiscal policy as a tool to manage the economy had been for ever discredited. Any attempt by governments to manage demand by fiscal measures would soon fail in its objective and do nothing but increase the rate of inflation. In particular, it would be counterproductive to attempt 'fine tuning', that is, to use fiscal policy to manage aggregate demand in the very short term. And underpinning all these views was the conviction that economies are self-righting organisms which governments will only mess up if they interfere.

But there has been a seismic shift during the last year. As to abolition of the business cycle, the latest figures show, in contrast with the consensus forecast at the end of 2000, that the GDP in the fourth quarter of 2001 was just 0.5 per cent higher than a year earlier. And, by the preliminary releases for the first quarter of 2002, GDP was 1.5 per cent higher than a year earlier. These are growth rates probably in the range of 3 to 1.5 percentage points (respectively) below that of productive potential. Unemployment rose 1.6 percentage points over the same period –by no means a record, but among the largest yearly increases during the post-war period.

But, in addition, there has been a large change in the stance of fiscal policy. In January 2001, the CBO was projecting budget surpluses of $313 billion and $359 billion for respectively 2002 and 2003. In March 2002, those figures had been revised to *deficits* of $46 and $40 billion –changes compared with what had been projected fifteen months previously which (using round numbers) totaled respectively $360 and $400 billion[2]. Downward revisions to the CBO's assumptions about economic growth appear to have reduced the

---

[2]   And that is before including anything for the President's Budgetary Proposals beyond what was in the Economic Stimulus Package enacted on March 9th.

surpluses originally forecasted by about $100 billion in each year[3], implying that there was a relaxation in the overall fiscal stance of, say, $260 and $300 billion in respectively 2002 and 2003 –that is, 2.5 - 3 per cent of GDP. This is an enormous change. True, the CBO's estimate of changes due to enacted legislation, $142 billion in 2002 and $204 billion in 2003, though very large, are rather lower than these figures, leaving around $100 billion in each year to be explained by what they call 'technical' factors. Yet from the outside analyst's point of view, there is little if any difference between a change to a budget estimate which is the result of enacted legislation and a change which is the result of technical factors; either way the analyst must conclude that the government is now proposing to inject into the economy the sums of money currently estimated by the CBO Whether the government has reached its fiscal stance on purpose or by default is beside the point.

We are not saying that these relaxations of fiscal policy should not have been made. On the contrary, the administration has swiftly moved in the right direction[4] and also in accordance with our own recommendations. The substantial relaxation of fiscal policy should now be counted, along with the huge reduction of interest rates, as an important reason why the slowdown has been partially checked. Yet this does not appear to have entered the public discussion very effectively. The brevity and moderate scale of the recent recession has been put down, not to a change in fiscal policy, but to the fall in interest rates combined with the natural resilience of the New Economy. And if policy did have anything to do with the recovery, it was monetary not fiscal policy which did the trick.

The sensible and pragmatic fiscal policy changes by the U.S. government stand in very sharp contrast to what has been happening in Europe, which was nearly treated to the rich spectacle of the German government receiving an official reprimand from the European Commission for failing to tighten fiscal policy at a time when unemployment was rising.

---

[3]   In its January 2002 report the CBO put changes due to economic assumptions at $148 billion in 2002 and $131 billion in 2003. But since then the CBO has revised its assumptions about GDP growth, raising the level by 1.2 per cent in 2002 and 0.4 per cent in 2003

A CLOSER LOOK AT RECENT DEVELOPMENTS

It was argued above that the growth of demand in aggregate between 1992 and 2000 could not have occurred unless there had been an unprecedented growth in private expenditure relative to income. The solid line in Chart 2 shows the private sector's financial balance, that is, the difference between total private disposable income and total private expenditure, over the last thirty years. During the main period of the recent expansion, between the second quarter of 1992 and the third quarter of 2000 (marked by vertical lines in the chart) the increase in private expenditure exceeded that of income by an amount equal to 12 per cent of GDP, driving the balance into substantial deficit. Nothing like that had ever happened before, at least during the last fifty years. The fall in this balance had, as its necessary counterpart, a rise in the net flow of credit to the private sector, which is shown by the broken line in Chart 2.

Chart 2: *Non-financial Private Sector: Financial Balance and Net Flow of Credit*

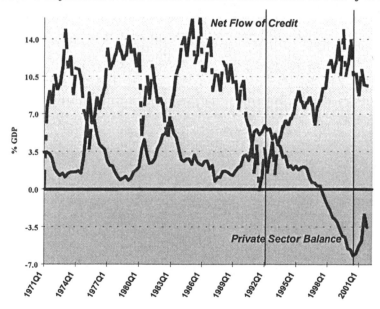

---

[4]   We only refer here to the scale of the changes, not to their composition.

Source: National Income and Production Accounts (NIPA); authors' calculations

The private deficit started to turn in the fourth quarter of 2000, that is, expenditure started to fall relative to income and it was this which was responsible for the slowdown. The slowdown, which as the chart shows was associated with a fall in expenditure relative to income, is a preliminary and partial vindication of the position we have been advocating for some time.

Chart 3: Private Debt Stock Relative to Disposable Income

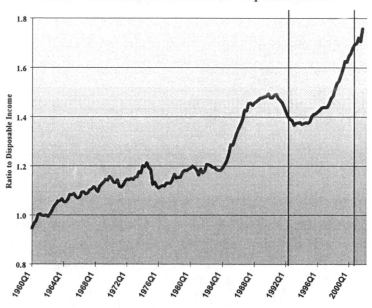

Source: NIPA and Flow-of-Funds; authors' calculations

But although the private balance started to revert, it did remain in deficit through 2001, and the net flow of credit continued at a rate far in excess of the growth of income. So, as Chart 3 shows, there was a continued rapid growth in the level of debt relative to income which continued through the whole of last year[5].

---

[5]   There was a growth blip in the third quarter of 2001 because of the one-time tax rebate, which temporarily raised disposable income relative to expenditure.

It is instructive to split the overall private financial balance into its two major components –the corporate and personal sectors. The solid line in Chart 4 shows the financial balance of the corporate sector which, unsurprisingly, is normally in deficit because investment is partly financed by externally generated funds. During most of the expansion, between 1992 and the first half of 2000, there was an increase in this deficit, but no more than during previous periods of expansion. The reversion towards zero in the second half of last year was the counterpart of the sharp fall in fixed investment and inventory accumulation. However, as the broken line in Chart 4 shows, the flow of net lending to the corporate sector continued at a relatively high level in part because corporations were still net purchasers of equity.

Chart 4: *Corporate Sector: Financial Balance and Net Flow of Credit*

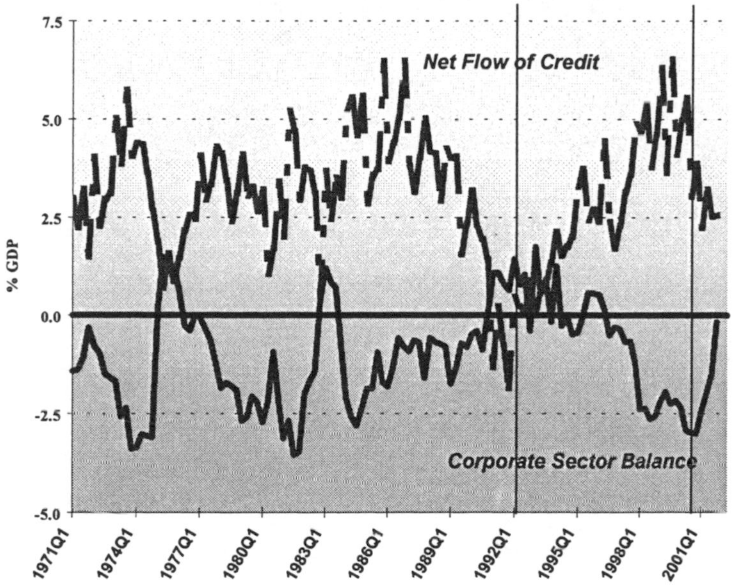

Source: NIPA; authors' calculations

So notwithstanding the sharp fall in investment, the level of corporate debt continued to rise rapidly through the year, reaching new records all the time. Chart 5 shows how corporate debt reached 8.5 times the flow of undistributed profits (gross of capital consumption) at the end of last year. Admittedly this ratio is swollen because profits had fallen a lot –but any way of scaling the debt (for instance by expressing it as a share of GDP) would tell the same story.

Chart 5:   *Corporate Debt Relative to Corporate Cash-flow Income*

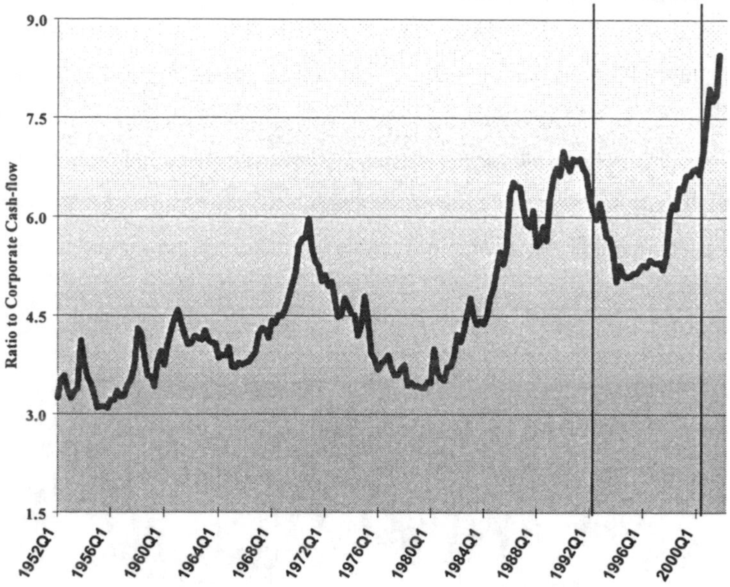

Source: NIPA and Flow-of-Funds; authors' calculations

It is, however, the behavior of personal sector which has been, and which remains, truly exceptional. The solid line in Chart 6 shows how personal expenditure (consumption and investment combined) rose relative to income throughout the main period of expansion. Since the third quarter of 2000, the growth of household expenditure has decelerated considerably, from about 5 per cent per annum to about 3 per cent; yet it continued to grow faster than income (once again, ignoring the third quarter blip). So although the economy slowed down, the personal sector's deficit[6] went on increasing. The broken line in Chart 6 shows how the

---

[6]   The concept of 'financial balance' is used in preference to the usual 'personal saving' because it includes capital consumption among receipts and investment among outlays. A financial deficit thus measures the extent to which the sector must be borrowing. The figures illustrated here have been derived, at the suggestion of Bill Martin of Phillips and Drew, as the difference between lines 10 and 12 in Table 100 of the Flow of Funds *plus* half the residual error (a negative number) in the NIPA.

net flow of credit to the personal sector increased steadily until the third quarter of 2000. And since then, although the growth of expenditure slowed down, the fact that it continued to exceed income meant that there was a continued injection of credit on a scale which supplemented income to the tune of about 10 per cent[7]. Doubtless it was the huge reduction in interest rates which caused, or at least facilitated, the credit-financed growth in consumption.

Chart 6: Personal Sector: Financial Balance and Net Flow of Credit

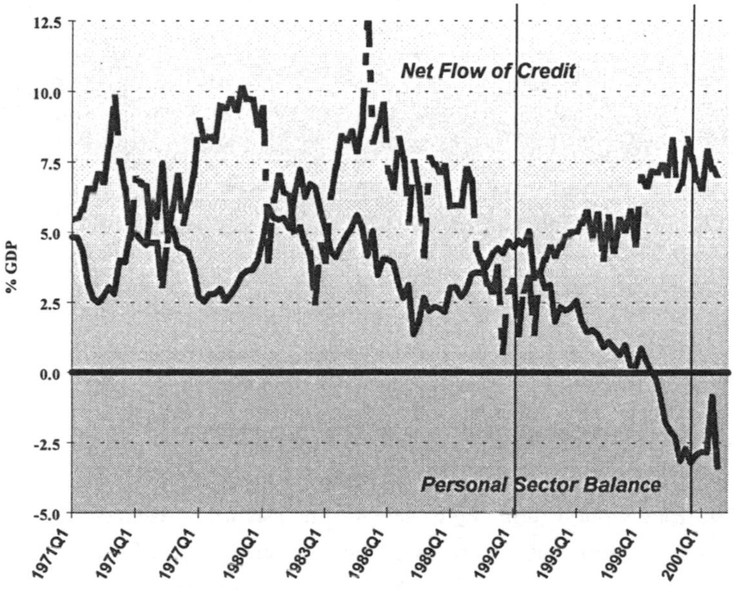

Source: NIPA; authors' calculations

The fact remains that as the flow of net lending was about double the growth of income during 2001, the ratio of personal debt to income, shown in Chart 7, had risen to another record by the end of the year.

---

[7]   The chart shows flows as a percentage of GDP (rather than personal income) for easy comparison with other charts.

Chart 7: *Personal Debt Relative to Personal Disposable Income*

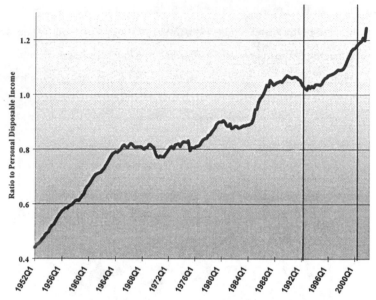

Source: NIPA and Flow-of-Funds; authors' calculations

SOME STRATEGIC SCENARIOS

The following sections bring up to date the analysis which we have presented at many previous Minsky conferences. As usual we begin by constructing a 'base run' *Scenario* based on the CBO's projections through the next five years. In order to derive their estimates of the Federal Budget in future years, the CBO made the assumption, which is not a forecast, that GDP will grow from now on a rate fast enough to keep unemployment at its present level; more precisely they projected a growth rate of 1.7 per cent between 2001 and 2002 followed by average growth at 3 per cent per annum during the subsequent five years. The CBO also assumed that inflation, measured by the GDP deflator, stays put at 2 per cent per annum. Our task in this section is to infer what has to be assumed about the rest of the economy if the CBO's economic assumptions are to be validated.

The immediately following section is divided into three parts dealing with, respectively, the budget, the balance of payments and private expenditure relative to income.

The Budget

Chart 8 below illustrates, with the solid line, the future course of the general government's budget[8] deficit expressed as a proportion of GDP, as projected by the CBO. As the chart shows, the general government's budget is now set to move from a small surplus in 2001 back into deficit this year and next. This is the relaxation of fiscal stance currently under way, which has undoubtedly helped to keep the US recession at bay. The *federal* budget is set, under existing policies, to achieve a surplus again in 2004 which rises to $185 billion in 2007 and grows further in subsequent years. The general government budget, shown in Chart 8, improves from 2002 onwards but only re-attains surplus in 2006.

Chart 8: Balances of Main Sectors: Historic & Simulated According CBO's Assumptions

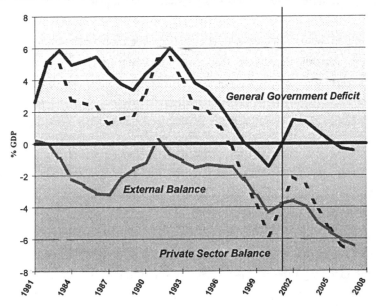

Source: NIPA, CBO, authors' model results

The Balance of Payments

The dashed line in Chart 8 shows our conditional forecast of the current balance of payments, on CBO's assumptions about growth and inflation, together with the assumption

---

[8]   The CBO's projection was adapted, using a scaling factor derived from the past relationship (which has been pretty stable) between the Federal Budget and the surplus or deficit of the general government.

that the dollar rate of exchange remains at its present level. We cannot justify these balance of payments projections at all scientifically, largely because recent figures both for exports and for imports are so far below what past experience would lead us to expect and we do not at present know how to interpret this. Yet it does seem uncontroversial to suppose, should output really grow fully as fast as productive potential from now on, and assuming that the rest of the world continues to be mired in relative stagnation, that the trade deficit will indeed resume its deteriorating path after the brief improvement which the slow-down has generated.

There are two reasons for supposing that, conditional on the assumptions being made, the current balance of payments could turn out to be even worse than our projection shows. The first question mark arises because it seems possible, at least, that the recent fall in imports is partly the consequence of extremely large negative inventory accumulation in the second half of last year; for there is a general presumption that the import content of inventory accumulation is considerably higher than that of final sales. If it turned out that the fall in imports had indeed been caused, to a significant extent, by negative inventory accumulation, we could well see a mighty surge in imports when inventories turn round –as they are bound to do at some stage. The jump in imports in February reported last week, though 'only one month's figures' is consistent with this interpretation.

A second puzzle concerns the future of net investment income, which has remained obstinately positive, though very small, although the net foreign asset position of the U.S. has deteriorated steadily, reaching some $2 .2 trillion (about 22 per cent of GDP) in the middle of last year. This is a phenomenon which raises a fundamentally important question, for the ultimate constraint on the extent to which any country can run a deficit in its external balance resides in the fact that, if the net foreign asset position continues to deteriorate, net interest payments must eventually accelerate out of hand. Yet so far from accelerating, net interest payments by the U.S. have remained obstinately close to zero.

Some light is shed on this phenomenon if the aggregate figures are broken down into net income from net foreign direct investment on the one hand and net income arising from financial assets –mainly equities and paper issued both by governments and by corporations.

Chart 9:   *Net Return from Direct and Financial Investment of the U.S.*

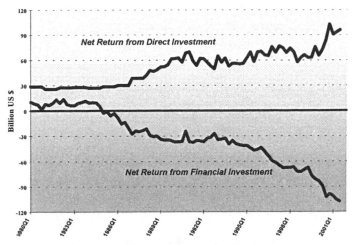

Source: Survey of Current Business (BEA); authors' calculation.

Chart 10: *Rates of Return on Financial Investment Compared with Treasury Rates*

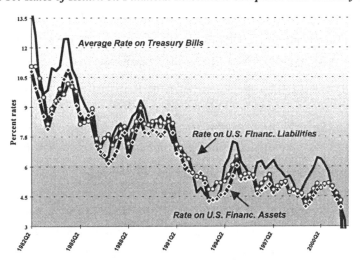

Source: Federal Reserve, BEA, authors' calculation.

As Chart 9 shows, there has been a growing deficit in net payments across the exchanges on financial assets, but this has been almost exactly offset by an increase in net receipts from direct investment. Net payments on financial assets have behaved in a rather orderly way. If the net flow is broken down into receipts on assets and payments on liabilities, and if each series is then expressed as a (messy) average rate of 'interest' on the relevant asset and liability stocks, it turns out, as Chart 10 shows, that each very roughly tracks the average of long term Treasury bill rates.

But no such coherence attends the figure for income from direct investment. The net stock of direct investment has been falling rather than growing and, measured at market prices, has actually been negative during the last three years. But for reasons which have never been satisfactorily explained, the rate of return to U.S. investors from their foreign direct investments remains obstinately –indeed increasingly– higher than the return to foreigners of making direct investments in the U.S.

The difficulty of interpreting data relating to all these property income flows is compounded by the fact that the income derived from financial investments, which are straightforward payments across the exchanges, are not *in pari materia* with income from direct investments, which measure the profits earned abroad whether they are distributed or not. Accordingly, income from direct investments do not, for the most part, describe transactions at all and may contribute little to the financing of the current account deficit.

In constructing the medium term simulation illustrated in Chart 8, we have so far assumed that the total net flow of income from all kinds of foreign investment remains close to zero, although the growing deficit in the current balance of payments implies that the negative net asset position doubles, from $2.2 trillion to about $4 trillion in 2007. But in reality the net outflow generated by financial assets could easily overtake the 'inflow' generated by direct investments. And it is at least arguable that income from direct investments, since it largely consists of undistributed profits, should be altogether ignored when considering whether or not a deficit can be financed. In sum, given our projected trade deficit, it is possible that a net outflow of investment income will add $100-200 billion per annum to the balance of payments deficit compared with that shown in the 'base run' of Chart 8.

Private Income and Expenditure

Given the CBO's assumptions about growth and inflation, together with their projections of the federal budget, and given also our projection of the balance of payments, it follows by accounting logic that the private sector's deficit[9], having fallen since the end of 2000, would have to start increasing once again, as depicted in Chart 8. Having reverted part of the way back towards its normal state of surplus during 2001, the growth of total private expenditure relative to disposable income would once again have to become the motor for expansion over the next five years. A growing excess of income over expenditure requires a growing flow of net lending relative to income.

Chart 11: Private Balance & Flow of Credit as Implied by CBO's Projections

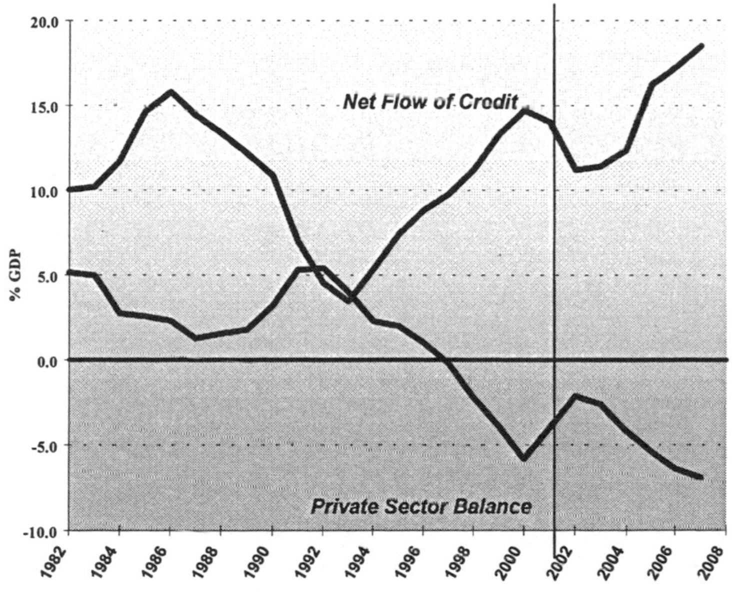

Source: NIPA, CBO, authors' model results

Chart 11 reproduces, from Chart 8, the necessary course of the private deficit if the CBO's projections are to be validated, alongside our own estimates of the flow of net lending which might then be required. And Chart 12 shows that the level of private indebtedness

---

[9]   The private financial balance expressed as a *surplus* is, of course, equal by definition to the government *deficit* plus the balance of balance of payments *surplus*.

implied by those net lending figures would be more than twice the level of disposable income in 2007.

Chart 12: Private Debt Relative to Income as Implied by CBO's Projections

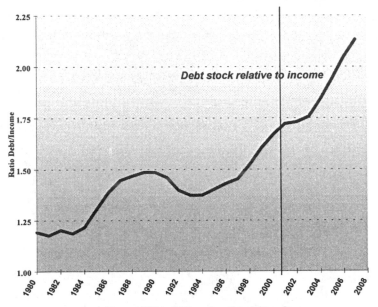

Source: NIPA, CBO, authors' model results

The projected flows of net lending and the stocks of debt shown in Charts 11 and 12 have been generated by a careful analysis of the past relationship between expenditure on the one hand and, on the other, disposable income, net lending and asset prices (houses as well as equities)[10]. Nobody knows better than ourselves how inaccurate these projections are likely to prove. Yet growth in output fast enough to keep unemployment constant, particularly when combined with a deteriorating balance of payments, could only be achieved if private expenditure were once again to rise continuously faster than income; and this would indeed require a resumption in the growth of net lending and the level of indebtedness. We are bound

---

[10]   For details see 'Seven Unsustainable Processes' by Wynne Godley, published by the Levy Institute in July 1999.

to conclude that our 'base run' tells a most implausible tale; existing household and corporate debt levels are already widely cited as a cause for concern. At the very least this base run forms an unwise and unsound basis for strategic thinking and fiscal planning.

CONTROVERSY

So far as we know, the main points which are habitually made by critics of the story we are telling are:

a) The burden on the personal sector of interest payments and repayments of debt, estimated by the Fed at 14.3 per cent of disposable income in the final quarter of 2001, is not particularly high.

b) It is inconsistent to count taxes on capital gains as a deduction from income without treating realizations of capital gains as part of income.

c) The recorded increase in personal indebtedness is of little consequence because it is usually, or often, a simple consequence of the fact that people use credit cards as a means of payment, paying off their liabilities at the end of each month.

d) The balance sheet of the personal sector taken as a whole remains very satisfactory, with assets far in excess of liabilities.

Taking these points in order:

a) At first glance the Fed's estimate of the burden of personal debt service may not look very high, although it is nearly at a record level –almost back to the previous peak just before the last credit crunch in the late eighties. However, the Fed's figures may be seriously misleading if judged as levels rather than changes. This is because there is a large discrepancy between the coverage of the numerator and denominator of the relevant fraction. The numerator refers only to servicing obligations generated by *household* mortgages and consumer credit, whereas the denominator, that is, *personal* disposable income, includes nonprofit organizations (churches, educational facilities etc.) and the entire *non-corporate business* sector. It is far from obvious how to correct for this difference of coverage, particularly because no figures seem to exist for *household* as opposed to *personal* income. What can easily be ascertained is that personal sector debt is 36 per cent higher than the household debt which the Fed uses in its calculation. A *pro rata* correction would raise the burden from 14.3 per cent to about 20 per cent –by any standard a 'large' figure.

In any case, as will be re-emphasized below, the point is not whether the existing burden is high but rather whether it can go on rising indefinitely. It may further be pointed out that the recorded burden has so far risen relatively slowly because of the fall in interest rates. As rates cannot fall much further, the rise in this ratio from now on is likely to track that of debt, while if interest rates rise the increase in the burden would accelerate.

b) The argument that *realized* capital gains should be counted as part of income –if we have stated it correctly– seems to be definitely incorrect. Compare two people who have equivalent conventional income, wealth, accumulated capital gains and spending intentions. One of them realizes capital gains to pay for expenditure in excess of income, the other borrows. At the end of the day on which the funds needed for spending are obtained, there is no difference whatever between the two transactors with respect to their net wealth. True, the realizing agent now has a liability to pay capital gains tax but that is not, on the day in question, different from the contingent liability for capital gains tax of the agent who borrows. The difference between the two agents resides solely in the structure, as opposed to the level, of their net wealth; all that has happened is that they have made different wealth allocation decisions and in no relevant sense is either the income or the net wealth of one higher than that of the other. Of course, if stock prices subsequently go up, the net wealth of the borrowing agent will improve relatively; if they fall, the realizing agent will be relatively wealthier. But that is part of a quite different story.

c) Ignoring the use of credit cards as a means of payment in the calculation of debt would not imply a significant difference to the growth of personal debt in total. Consumer credit accounted, during 2001, for circa 17 per cent of total borrowing by the personal sector.

Besides a high proportion of consumer credit must be accounted for by cars and consumer durables

d) Regarding the last point, i.e. the high level of net wealth relative to income, it should first be noted that although the collective balance sheet of the household sector was still in a healthy state at the end of 2001, it was very much less healthy than two years previously.

Chart 13: Household Net Worth Relative to Personal Disposable Income

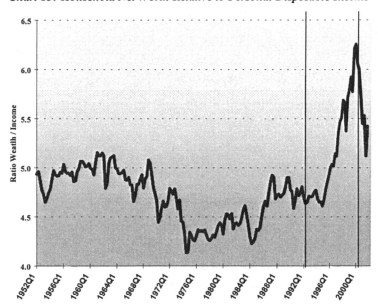

Source: NIPA & Flow-of-Funds, authors' calculation.

Chart 13 shows the net worth of households divided by personal disposable income. This ratio rose in a spectacular way in the late nineties, but since the end of 1999 wealth has fallen absolutely while incomes have continued to rise rapidly. So the wealth to income ratio has fallen back half of the way to what had previously been normal. A comparable story is told in Chart 14, which shows household debt as a share of household wealth[11].

---

[11]   That is, net wealth of households as recorded in the Flow of Funds gross of household debt.

Chart 14: Household Debt Relative to Household Wealth

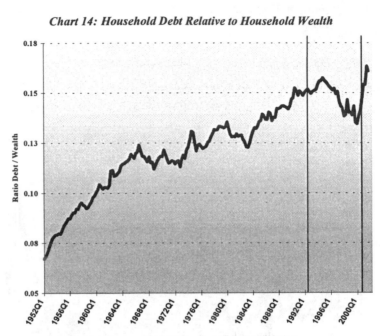

Source: Flow-of-Funds, authors' calculation.

There was a very sharp fall in the nineties as wealth rose much more than debt. But this has gone sharply into reverse during the last two years. Debt continued to rise rapidly while wealth fell –so the ratio rose rapidly, reaching record levels in the second half of 2001. It is worth mentioning finally that, as shown in Chart 15, the change in households' net worth, which some people prefer to the conventional measure of saving, has been negative since the end of 1999.

Chart 15: Change of Household Net Worth Relative to Personal Disposable Income

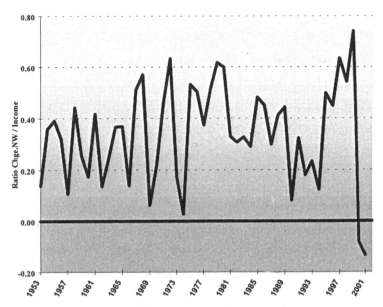

Source: Flow-of-Funds; authors' calculation.

Yet even if household balance sheets had not worsened dramatically during the last two years and even if the servicing burden were only 14.3 per cent of income, these arguments would not answer the central point which we have been making. We have at no stage argued that the *present* situation is necessarily unsustainable, although a very high level of indebtedness must make both households and businesses vulnerable to a fall in asset prices or incomes or to a rise in interest rates –the assets could lose half their value in an afternoon, yet the debts would remain. Our central contention, however, has always been a different one – that the *growth* of net lending (and of expenditure relative to income) which drove the economy between 1992 and 2000 cannot continue to fuel the *growth* of aggregate demand indefinitely in the future. In other words, while it is not impossible that the present *level* of debt may be OK, the flow of credit cannot be an abiding engine of growth. Eventually the cost of debt service must get to the point where, if there are to be sufficient funds to pay for expenditure in excess of income and also for debt service, recourse must be had to realization of assets. But while in normal times individuals can realize capital assets on any scale they wish, the same thing is not true for the personal sector taken as a whole. Sales by any whole sector can only take place to the extent that there are purchases by whole other sectors. It is not conceivable that the growth of personal consumption could be long financed by growing net purchases by the corporate sector or by foreigners. The personal sector as a whole cannot realize assets on a large, let alone growing, scale and any attempt to do so would cause a crash, eliminating the gains which people were trying to realize.

THREE STRATEGIC SCENARIOS

In conclusion we present three projections of the U.S. economy between now and 2007. These projections are not forecasts in the ordinary sense, most particularly they are not short term forecasts, although care has been exercised to ensure that they are consistent with recent developments and with the raft of indicators currently available; nor is there any pretense that our figures characterize future developments on a year by year basis. Our purpose in making these strictly conditional projections is to make a broad characterization of the major strategic problems which are likely to arise over the next five years; and to consider alternative strategies for dealing with them.

SCENARIO 1

We first retain all the assumptions about the fiscal stance made by the CBO. together with the assumptions about net export demand which we used to construct the 'base run' illustrated in Chart 8. *Scenario* 1 differs from the base run in that it makes what we believe to be more realistic assumptions about the private sector's indebtedness and the way in which its financial balance –the gap between income and expenditure– develops. Specifically we have assumed that the flow of net lending falls away during the next few years, causing the rise in indebtedness to taper off. The counterpart of such a fall in net lending would probably be a reduction in the private sector's deficit (that is, a fall in expenditure relative to income), on a scale such as that illustrated in Chart 16 below, which shows a reversion almost to zero.

Chart 16: Balances of Main Sectors: Simulated on Plausible Assumptions

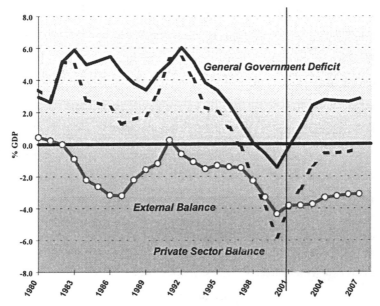

Source: NIPA, authors' model results.

The counterpart of such a fall in private expenditure relative to income would be to greatly reduce the annual average growth rate of GDP between now and 2007. The CBO assumed an average growth of 3 per cent; the simulation illustrated in Chart 16 implies an average growth rate of 1-1.5 per cent. This would at best be a '*growth recession*' for at this rate there would, by 2007, be a cumulative shortfall of GDP of more than 7 per cent compared with the base run, with unemployment rising to nearly 8 per cent. So far from moving into surplus, the general government would have a deficit equal to at least 2.5 per cent of GDP at the end of the period. The CBO's projection shows a Federal Budget *surplus* equal to 1.5 per cent of GDP; according to our *Scenario* 1 this would become a *deficit* of 1.5 per cent.

Things could turn out far worse than has been assumed in *Scenario* 1, always given that the fiscal stance does not change again. There has never, at least in the post-war period, been a period when the private sector was in deficit at all for any length of time, as we have assumed here. And on the few occasions when the private sectors of other countries have fallen into deficit on a scale like that which has occurred recently in the U.S. (e.g. in the UK and Scandinavia just over ten years ago) there was eventually a brisk reversion to surplus, which overshot what had previously been normal, in each case generating large and intractable recessions. In constructing these projections we assumed that equity and house prices would continue to rise moderately. But it is quite possible, given the other assumptions that we have made, that there will at some stage be another break in the stock market which would probably make matters very much worse, perhaps causing an outright recession at some stage.

SCENARIO 2

Seeing the ease with which the fiscal stance has been transformed since the beginning of last year, it is virtually inconceivable that things could turn out as depicted in *Scenario* 1 and Chart 16. If the fiscal stance can change once by $250 billion per annum with few people even noticing, it can do so again. In *Scenario* 2 we superimpose a fiscal relaxation on *Scenario* 1 such as to raise the growth of GDP back to that assumed by the CBO, that is, to about 3 per cent per annum, implying no significant change in unemployment. Chart 17 illustrates a possible outcome for the three financial balances under this assumption.

The main points to be made about this *Scenario* are, first, the relaxation in the fiscal stance (compared with what is now projected by the CBO) would have to be extremely large. At a minimum, all of the relaxation which is supposed to occur this next year and next ($250-300 billion in each year) which is at present due to be recouped in the following years would have to be reinstated. But if the private sector's financial deficit were to go on falling, as we have assumed, a far larger –and growing– relaxation would become necessary. By our reckoning, there would have to be a fiscal stimulus which would rise to about $600 billion per annum (at 1996 prices) by 2007. The general government deficit might have to rise to six per cent of GDP and the Federal deficit to perhaps five per cent.

Chart 17: Balances of Main Sectors when Growth is Achieved by Fiscal Expansion Alone

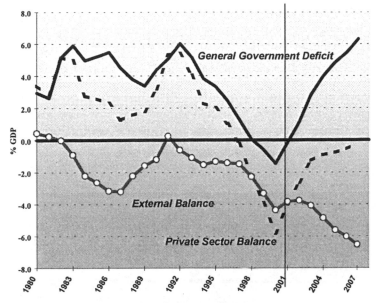

Source: NIPA, authors' model results

In *Scenario* 2 we ignore the difficulty of matching, on a year-by-year basis, the relative decline in private spending with the postulated fiscal expansion. In practice it is most unlikely that the two divergent processes could be so nicely matched throughout the period. In particular, should a break in the stock market cause a sudden collapse in private demand, it might be impossible to intervene effectively by changing fiscal policy. And with interest rates so low, it might also be difficult to check a major downturn with easier monetary policy.

The second important feature of *Scenario* 2 is that the balance of payments resumes its deterioration in exactly the same way as it did in the 'base run' illustrated in Chart 8. In the absence of new corrective measures, the external deficit would surely overtake the previous record, reaching perhaps 6 per cent of GDP, with no hint of recovery in sight. And this is a story of 'twin deficits' with a vengeance; for with the private balance close to zero and the external deficit about 6 per cent, the government deficit must (be found to be) about 6 per cent of GDP as well.

SCENARIO 3

Scenario 3, illustrated in Chart 18, is a 'dream' Scenario. An improvement in net export demand large enough to close the balance of payments deficit would generate sufficient growth combined with full employment without further fiscal expansion, thereby making all three balances converge towards zero over the next five years.

Chart 18: Balances of Main Sectors when Growth is Achieved by Net Export Demand

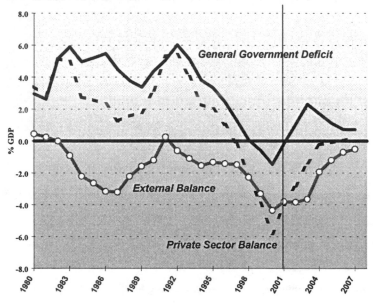

Source: NIPA, authors' model results

By our reckoning, this outcome could in principle be achieved if the trade-weighted dollar were to be devalued by 25 per cent[12] at the beginning of next year, if could be assumed that accelerated inflation did not whittle away the gains in competitiveness and also that world

---

[12]   The assumptions underlying this number are that import prices would rise by about 10 per cent and dollar export prices about 6 per cent, implying a fall in the foreign price of U.S exports of nearly 20 percent. The price elasticities of demand for exports and imports are assumed to be, respectively 0.9 and 0.7.

demand and output were not affected by the improvement in the U.S.'s balance of trade.

Scenario 3 possesses a certain beauty because it seems to solve all problems simultaneously. But its apparent simplicity and wholeness must not be allowed to mask the very strong assumptions which have to be made in order to make it come true. In the first place devaluation is no longer an instrument of policy. It is already clear that a large and growing balance of payments deficit cannot be counted on, in any degree whatever, to bring about an automatic and orderly depreciation of the dollar. Nor do changes in interest rates seem to have the slightest effect on exchange rates, whatever the textbooks may say. In short, in a world of free international capital markets it seems empty to recommend devaluation as a simple solution to the strategic problem.

Next, it is unclear how much domestic inflation would be generated by a 25 per cent devaluation. We incline to the view that this would not be a major problem although this is a highly controversial matter. The direct effect on prices would probably not be very large; the 10 per cent increase in import prices (which should probably result from a 25 per cent devaluation) should not, by itself, cause domestic prices to rise by more than 1-2 per cent. Furthermore, we know that there was a devaluation much larger than 25 per cent in the second half of the eighties without there being much acceleration in domestic inflation.

The problem of changed absorption, both in the U.S. and in the rest of the world, must be rated as extremely serious. There is no way of correcting the U.S.'s external deficit which does not imply a substantial (and equivalent) reduction in the country's absorption of goods and services. At present the U.S. is consuming about 4 per cent in excess of what it is producing, an amount which is larger than that by which the economy normally grows in a full year. This excess absorption would have, by the logic of accounting, to come to an end if the deficit were to be eliminated. Part of this, at least, would be brought about by the tightening fiscal stance –in accordance with the projections made by the CBO's assumptions– but however brought about the effect on living standards would be palpable.

But the necessary reduction in the U.S.'s absorption would also create a major problem for the rest of the world; it would mean a reduction of equivalent size in the net export demand for their goods and services. The U.S. would present the rest of the world with a nasty disinflationary shock since it would abruptly cease to be 'importer of last resort'. As already mentioned, in arriving at our figure of 25 per cent for the needed devaluation, the strong assumption was made that demand and output in the rest of the world does not alter. But this would only happen if the rest of the world were to take expansionary measures on whatever scale is necessary *to make it happen*. In sum, balanced growth and full employment in the U.S. may require a quite radical change in the way Europe, Japan and some other countries run their economies. Market forces are not good at counteracting financial imbalances. There may ultimately have to be active international co-ordination of trade and capital transactions as well as fiscal and monetary policy.

CONCLUSIONS

The main conclusions of this paper are:

a) Personal and corporate debt are both very high relative to income, and this makes the economy unusually vulnerable to shocks - for instance a fall in asset prices , a rise in oil prices or a rise in interest rates.

b) It is doubtful whether the government's fiscal stance, as projected by the CBO, is consistent with a growth rate fast enough to stop unemployment from rising after 2003. Such growth could only occur if private indebtedness, already a cause for concern, were to resume a rapid rate of growth relative to income.

c) A major relaxation of the fiscal stance after 2003 could generate an adequate growth rate, but only at the cost of a large and growing balance of payments deficit and also a large and growing budget deficit.

d) A rapid expansion of net export demand could, in principle, generate adequate growth while eliminating the other two imbalances - that is, the deficits both of the government and of the private sector. This could conceivably happen if there were a large (25 per cent?) devaluation of the dollar, so long as the competitive advantage is not offset by higher inflation. Such an outcome would require a substantial reduction (equal to at least 4 per cent of GDP) in U.S. absorption of goods and services; a further condition is that foreign countries offset the disinflationary shock which would be imparted by a large improvement in the U.S. balance of payments with expansionary measures of their own. But neither the institutions nor agreed principles which could carry out co-ordinated expansionary policies around the globe are at present in existence.

[23]

Economic
Policy
Institute

Briefing Paper

1660 L Street, NW • Suite 1200 • Washington, D.C. 20036 • 202/775-8810 • http://epinet.org

THE TICKING DEBT BOMB
Why the U.S. International Financial Position Is Not Sustainable

by Robert A. Blecker

For the last few years, most of the economic news in the United States has been glowing. The U.S. economy has grown at a healthy 4% average rate since 1997, with virtually full employment and almost negligible inflation, thus returning to macroeconomic conditions not experienced since the early 1960s. Two-and-a-half years after Federal Reserve Board Chairman Alan Greenspan warned of "irrational exuberance" on Wall Street, the New York stock market continues to climb to unparalleled heights. Meanwhile, more and more observers claim that we are now in a "new economy" that is immune to the forces that caused inflation and recessions in the past.

Yet in the midst of this celebratory environment, certain indicators regularly cast a pall over these otherwise sunny times. Month after month, year after year, the U.S. trade deficit sets new records. And as the United States borrows to cover the excess of its imports over its exports, the U.S. position as the world's largest debtor grows by leaps and bounds. Closely related to both of these trends is the drop in the U.S. private saving rate, which forces the country to continue borrowing from abroad in spite of the shift from a deficit to a surplus in the federal budget balance.

In fact, the U.S. economy's current prosperity rests on the fragile foundations of a consumer spending boom based on a domestic stock market bubble, combined with foreign bankrolling of the U.S. trade deficit. If present trends continue, the growth in U.S. international debt will not be sustainable in the long run. No country can continue to borrow so much from abroad without eventually triggering a depreciation of its currency and a contraction of its economy. The rising trade deficit and mushrooming foreign debt are thus warning signals of underlying problems that—if not corrected—could bring the U.S. economic boom crashing to a halt in the not-too-distant future.

Addressing the U.S. international debt situation will require action on two fronts: reducing the trade deficit and keeping interest rates low in order to reduce the burden of servicing the debt. Four specific policies that could help to avert a serious crisis over the next few years include: (1) promoting stimulus policies among U.S. trading partners with depressed economies in order to promote growth and to enable them to reduce their trade surpluses with the U.S.; (2) engineering a gradual depreciation of the dollar; (3) using a fiscal stimulus to keep the economy growing when the current consumption boom slows down; and (4) restructuring U.S. trade policy to promote more reciprocal market access and to stress the interests of U.S.-based producers exporting abroad.

The dimensions of the problem: trends and forecasts

Figure 1 shows the actual trends in the U.S. net international debt for 1983-97 along with baseline projections for 1998-2005, which are explained in more detail in the Appendix.[1] The United States was a

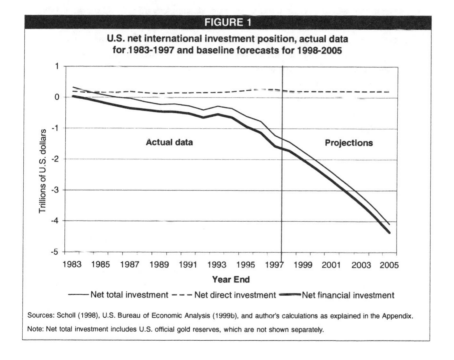

FIGURE 1

U.S. net international investment position, actual data for 1983-1997 and baseline forecasts for 1998-2005

Net total investment — — — Net direct investment ━━━ Net financial investment

Sources: Scholl (1998), U.S. Bureau of Economic Analysis (1999b), and author's calculations as explained in the Appendix.

Note: Net total investment includes U.S. official gold reserves, which are not shown separately.

2

net creditor country as recently as 1987 for total international investment, as it was for financial investment until 1983. But the borrowing required to cover chronic current account deficits since the 1980s has long since turned the United States from the world's largest creditor into the world's largest debtor (see Blecker 1991, 1998).[2]

As of the end of 1997, the total U.S. net international debt stood at $1.22 trillion.[3] Excluding official gold reserves held by the Treasury Department and direct foreign investment by multinational corporations, both of which are not liquid assets,[4] the net *financial* debt of the United States was $1.57 trillion at year-end 1997. This net financial debt represents the difference between the value of U.S. liquid financial assets (such as corporate stock, bank deposits, government securities, and other bonds) owned by foreigners and the value of similar foreign assets owned by Americans.

The U.S. still has a net positive (creditor) position in *direct* investment, since U.S. multinational corporations own more assets abroad than foreign multinationals own in the United States. However, this position has been relatively small and stable, and it is likely to stabilize at $200 billion starting in 1999. In contrast, the net *financial* investment position is negative (i.e., foreigners own more liquid financial assets in the U.S. than Americans own abroad), and this net financial debt is much larger and increasing rapidly.

According to the baseline forecast, the U.S. net financial debt increased to $1.72 trillion in 1998, and it will rise further to $2.02 trillion during 1999, $2.34 trillion in 2000, and a mammoth $4.36 trillion by 2005 (or an estimated 36.4% of gross domestic product at that time).[5] Adding back the positive net position in direct investment and the value of U.S. gold reserves, the total net debt is also projected to grow rapidly: from $1.22 trillion in 1997 to $1.43 trillion in 1998, $1.75 trillion in 1999, $2.07 trillion in 2000, and $4.09 trillion by 2005 (or an estimated 34.2% of GDP in that year).

The corresponding projections for U.S. net investment *income* balance—the difference between the inflows of profits, dividends, and interest received from U.S. investments abroad and the outflows of profits, dividends, and interest paid out on foreign investments in the U.S.—are shown in **Figure 2**. In spite of the U.S. turn to an overall net debtor position in the mid-1980s, total net investment income remained positive in the early 1990s because the rate of return on direct investment (in which the U.S. has a net creditor position) exceeded the rate of return on financial investments (in which the U.S. is a net debtor).[6] However, in the last few years the sheer volume of the net financial debt has begun to overwhelm the difference in rates of return, and the net investment income balance has been negative since 1997.[7]

In the baseline forecast, the net outflow of financial income (interest and dividends) jumps from an actual $77.1 billion in 1998 to an estimated $175.3 billion in 2005—a net outflow greater than the U.S. goods and services trade deficit in 1998. Including net direct investment income, which is assumed to remain positive (see Appendix for details), total net investment income jumps from an actual deficit of $22.5 billion in 1998 to a projected deficit of $111.3 billion by 2005. These deficits in investment income in turn worsen the overall current account balance, on top of the underlying deficit for trade in goods and services and net transfers[8] (which is assumed to be 3.0% of GDP in the baseline scenario). Thus, by 2005, the total current account deficit is projected to be 3.9% of GDP.

3

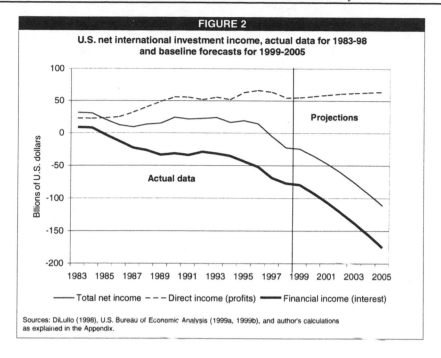

FIGURE 2

U.S. net international investment income, actual data for 1983-98 and baseline forecasts for 1999-2005

Sources: DiLullo (1998), U.S. Bureau of Economic Analysis (1999a, 1999b), and author's calculations as explained in the Appendix.

Like all economic forecasts, this baseline projection is conditioned on the assumptions that drive the analysis, in this case, the persistence of an underlying trade deficit of 3% of GDP and the continuation of moderate interest rates (averaging 4.25%)[9] through 2005. These are actually very conservative assumptions given that the Federal Reserve is now (as of June 1999) leaning toward raising interest rates and many analysts fear larger trade deficits in the next few years. Yet even these conservative assumptions show the net financial debt rising to $4.36 trillion (or 36.4% of GDP) and the current account deficit reaching $470.6 billion (or 3.9% of GDP) by 2005.

By altering these assumptions, we can make a series of alternative forecasts that illustrate a range of possible outcomes for the U.S. net foreign debt and net interest burden. **Table 1** summarizes the results of several alternative forecasts for 2005, the final year of the projections (the baseline scenario shown in this table corresponds to the forecasts depicted in Figures 1 and 2). Using these alternative forecasts, we can better assess the prospects for a hard or soft landing for the U.S. dollar and the U.S. economy.

The *improving trade balance* scenario assumes that the underlying trade deficit drops to 2.0% of GDP in 2000 and then falls gradually to 1.0% in 2005, perhaps because foreign economies recover from their current doldrums (and thus buy more U.S. exports) or because the dollar depreciates (i.e.,

TABLE 1
Alternative forecasts of U.S. net interest outflow,
current account deficit, and net international financial debt for 2005

Scenario	Net financial income (interest) inflow (+) or outflow (-)	Current account surplus (+) or deficit (-)	Net financial credit (+) or debt (-) position
	In billions of dollars		
Baseline (moderate trade deficit, 4.25% interest rate)*	-175.3	-470.6	-4,360.3
Improving trade balance**	-135.1	-190.8	-3,273.5
Worsening trade deficit***	-215.6	-750.3	-5,447.1
2% interest rate	-74.7	-370.0	-3,918.7
7% interest rate	-326.8	-622.1	-4,980.3
10% interest rate	-535.9	-831.2	-5,774.7
	In percent of GDP		
Baseline (moderate trade deficit, 4.25% interest rate)*	-1.5	-3.9	-36.4
Improving trade balance**	-1.1	-1.6	-27.3
Worsening trade deficit***	-1.8	-6.3	-45.5
2% interest rate	-0.6	-3.1	-32.7
7% interest rate	-2.7	-5.2	-41.6
10% interest rate	-4.5	-6.9	-48.2

*   The baseline assumes that the underlying trade deficit for goods and services plus net transfers remains at 3% of GDP from 2000 to 2005.
**   The improving trade balance scenario assumes that the underlying trade deficit falls to 2% of GDP in 2000 and then gradually declines to 1% of GDP in 2005.
*** The worsening trade deficit scenario assumes that the underlying trade deficit rises to 4% of GDP in 2000 and then gradually rises to 5% of GDP in 2005.

Note: Both alternative trade balance scenarios assume a 4.25% interest rate. All alternative interest rate scenarios assume the baseline underlying trade deficit of 3% of GDP.

See Appendix for more details.

foreign currencies recover, and U.S. products become more price competitive). In this optimistic scenario, the net financial debt grows more slowly to $3.27 trillion, or 27.3% of GDP, in 2005. The total current account deficit is also more moderate in this scenario, rising only to $190.8 billion in dollar terms, and falling to 1.6% of GDP in percentage terms. If this happens, the U.S. external debt and deficits would become sustainable and a soft landing for the economy would be assured.

    In contrast, the *worsening trade deficit* scenario assumes that the underlying trade deficit

5

jumps to 4.0% of GDP in 2000 and then rises gradually to 5.0% in 2005, perhaps because foreign economies (especially in Asia, Europe, and Latin America) become more depressed or because the dollar appreciates further (i.e., foreign currencies sink even more than they have in recent years, and U.S. products become even less price competitive than they are at present exchange rates). In this pessimistic scenario, the net financial debt explodes to $5.45 trillion or 45.5% of GDP by 2005, while the current account deficit hits $750.3 billion or 6.3% of GDP—levels that would almost guarantee the outbreak of a financial panic. These simulations reveal how strongly the U.S. external financial position depends on what happens to the underlying trade balance.

Table 1 also shows the results of varying the assumptions about interest rates.[10] If interest rates fall to an average of 2.00% from 2000 to 2005 (perhaps because of central bank efforts to prevent a global depression or deflation), the growth in the U.S. net financial debt is somewhat attenuated, but this debt still rises to $3.92 trillion or 32.7% of GDP by 2005. If interest rates are increased, however (perhaps because of renewed fears of inflation or efforts to prevent currency collapses), the U.S. net financial debt rises more sharply, to $4.98 trillion (41.6% of GDP) with a 7% interest rate and $5.77 trillion (48.2% of GDP) with a 10% rate.

The impact of alternative interest rates on U.S. international debt service payments is even more striking. At the low 2% interest rate, net financial income (interest) outflows fall to $74.7 billion in 2005, slightly lower than the actual level in 1998 ($77.1 billion), even though the foreign debt continues to rise in this scenario. On the other hand, higher interest rates generate alarming increases in net interest payments, reaching $326.8 billion in 2005 at a 7% interest rate and $535.9 billion with a 10% rate (accounting for 2.7% and 4.5% of GDP, respectively).[11] Financing such large net interest outflows would put a serious squeeze on U.S. income, as it has in debtor nations in the developing world.

Thus, these alternative forecasts forcefully demonstrate the importance of reducing the U.S. trade deficit and keeping interest rates down in order to prevent explosive growth of the nation's international debt position and debt service burden, and thereby lessen the risk of a hard landing. With a reduced trade deficit and/or a lower interest rate, the U.S. foreign debt could stabilize in relation to GDP and become sustainable with moderate continued borrowing. But with increased trade deficits and/or higher interest rates, the external debt could quickly reach a level that would be likely to spark a negative reaction from international investors, and hence be unsustainable.

How investors may react

The question of the sustainability of the U.S. international debt revolves around two closely related issues. First, will confidence in the U.S. economy remain strong enough for foreigners to continue to desire to invest hundreds of billions of dollars a year in U.S. financial assets, in order to cover our annual current account deficits? And second, will foreign creditors continue to be willing to hold the large portfolios of liquid U.S. financial assets that they have already accumulated? Note that these issues mainly concern the state of investors' psychology rather than economic models of whether a given debt trajectory is theoretically stable.[12]

6

If foreign investors cease to extend new loans to the United States, or if they sell off their existing portfolios of U.S. liquid assets, the debt growth projected in the baseline forecast (and in the more pessimistic alternative forecasts) could not occur. By refusing to extend new credits or selling off existing assets, foreign investors could force painful adjustments on the U.S. financial sector and the domestic real economy. Moreover, it is not only the reaction of foreign investors that matters. U.S. investors could also help to precipitate a financial crisis if they decided to move more of their assets offshore (what in developing countries is known as "capital flight").[13] Of course, a flight from U.S. assets requires other attractive locations to which investors could flee. While this may seem unlikely at present, an economic turnaround in Europe, Japan, or the emerging market nations over the next few years could create one or more alternative poles of attraction for international money managers.

The notion of an eventual U.S. financial crisis may seem far-fetched at a time when the U.S. economy is the envy of most of the world. Yet recent economic history is full of episodes in which confidence in a particular economy has changed dramatically and quickly—witness the 1994-95 crash in Mexico, which followed the pre-NAFTA euphoria about the booming Mexican economy, or the rash of crises in East and Southeast Asia in 1997-98, which followed many years of touting Asia's "miracle" economies and emerging financial markets. These experiences show that spending booms fueled by overly optimistic expectations can lead to the creation of unsustainable financial positions, including speculative bubbles in asset markets and real overvaluation of exchange rates, eventually leading to a revision of expectations and an inevitable crash (see Blecker 1998, 1999).

The United States has not been immune to losses of international confidence in the past. In 1978-79, confidence in the United States plummeted, forcing the dollar to depreciate and inducing the Fed to launch an infamous experiment with high interest rates to squelch inflation at the cost of high unemployment. (These high interest rates also led to an eventual dollar overvaluation in the early 1980s, which in turn contributed to the rise in the U.S. trade deficit and the shift to net debtor status later in that decade.) Earlier, the post-World War II Bretton Woods monetary system was brought down in large measure by fears of a "dollar overhang" in Europe, which led European governments to try to convert their dollar holdings to gold in the late 1960s. This in turn helped motivate the Nixon Administration to end the convertibility of dollars into gold, abandon pegged exchange rates, and let the dollar depreciate in the early 1970s.[14]

The problem in the late 1960s was an accumulation of large amounts of U.S. dollar reserves by foreign central banks, which engendered a fear of dollar depreciation that eventually became a self-fulfilling prophecy.[15] The problem in the late 1990s is an accumulation of large amounts of U.S. financial assets of all kinds—including private holdings of stocks and bonds as well as official central bank reserves (which are largely held in the form of U.S. Treasury securities). This situation runs the risk of creating a fear of dollar depreciation that could again become a self-fulfilling prophecy, only this time not so much through the actions of foreign central banks but through those of private international investors and banks (both domestic and foreign).

7

Possible triggers for a crisis

Although we can clearly see the risks of such a crisis of confidence developing in the future, there remains the question of what could be the "trigger" that would set it off. One possibility is that either the current account deficit or the net international debt will become so large as to create self-fulfilling expectations of an inevitable depreciation of the U.S. dollar. In recent crises (Mexico in 1994, Thailand in 1997), current account deficits that surpassed about 5% of GDP became seen as signals of a necessary currency devaluation. The U.S. current account deficit could easily become this large, as shown in some of the more pessimistic scenarios considered above (i.e., with a larger underlying trade deficit or a higher interest rate, compared with the baseline forecast). Alternatively, a growing net financial debt—reaching over 35% of GDP by 2005 in the baseline forecast, and between 40% and 50% of GDP in some of the more pessimistic forecasts—could ring alarm bells for international investors.

What matters for foreign investors is not just the *net* U.S. financial debt but also the *gross* amount of U.S. assets that they hold in their portfolios. **Figure 3** shows the dramatic surge in

FIGURE 3

Foreign holdings of U.S. securities, 1990-98

Sources: Scholl (1998), U.S. Board of Governors of the Federal Reserve System (1999), and author's calculations.

Note: Other U.S. securities for 1998 were estimated by the author, based on the net increase in foreign-owned securities other than U.S. Treasury securities (as reported in U.S. Bureau of Economic Analysis 1999b, Table 1) and the Standard & Poor's composite stock price index (as reported in U.S. Council of Economic Advisers 1999, Table B-95, 436). The December 1997-December 1998 percentage change in the S&P index was used to estimate the increase in the value of foreign stock holdings in the United States during 1998.

foreign ownership of U.S. securities since 1995. The series for U.S. Treasury securities includes both official holdings by foreign central banks and private holdings by other foreign investors, in roughly equal proportions. The series for other U.S. securities includes corporate and other bonds as well as corporate stocks, valued at current market prices. This surge in foreign security holdings has been driven in part by the speculative expectation that these assets will rise in price (especially the stock market boom), and in part by foreign investors searching for safe havens for their wealth while their own countries are in turmoil (especially U.S. Treasury securities). The foreign holdings of nearly $1.3 trillion of U.S. Treasury securities in 1998 account for fully 35% of all Treasury obligations outstanding at that time (about double the percentage in the early 1990s).[16]

Once foreigners own such large amounts of U.S. financial assets, they need to be concerned about their value—not only in dollar terms, but also in terms of foreign currencies. If investors begin to perceive that the assets themselves are overvalued and fear a collapse of U.S. stock or bond prices (e.g., due to a decline in the New York Stock Exchange), then they will move to sell off their U.S. stocks or bonds, which will push those markets down further and depreciate the dollar in the process. If investors perceive that the dollar is overvalued, they will fear a depreciation, with the same result.

There are no hard-and-fast rules for how big a current account deficit, net debtor position, or gross foreign asset ownership has to be in order to generate self-fulfilling expectations of a currency depreciation. But it is simply inconceivable that these variables could continue to increase indefinitely without engendering such an investor reaction at some point.

Indeed, there is one sign that international investors already expect a dollar depreciation sometime in the near future: the fact that money market interest rates are higher in the United States than in most other major industrialized countries. In the first quarter of 1999, U.S. money market interest rates averaged 4.73%, while the corresponding rates in the euro area averaged only 3.09% and in Japan a mere 0.15% (International Monetary Fund 1999a, 47). According to the theory of "uncovered interest arbitrage," when the interest rate on one country's bonds is lower than that on another's, investors will be willing to hold the first country's bonds only if the lower interest rate is compensated by an expected appreciation of that country's currency.[17] Thus, the persistence of lower interest rates in Europe and Japan compared with the United States suggests that international investors expect the European currencies and the Japanese yen eventually to appreciate relative to the U.S. dollar. This is not surprising, since both Europe and (to a much larger extent) Japan have trade surpluses with the U.S.

The trigger for a U.S. external financial crisis does not have to come from its international trade deficit or rising foreign debt, however. Any problems in domestic financial markets—such as a collapse of the New York stock market or a banking crisis resulting from overlending to consumers in an economic downturn—could precipitate a loss of confidence and drive international investors overseas. But even if the external debt is not the trigger, it makes the U.S. economy more vulnerable to a loss of confidence. If confidence is lost for any reason, foreign investors will react by selling off their portfolios of U.S. assets, which will exacerbate the decline in U.S. asset markets and put downward pressure on the value of the dollar. Moreover, if foreign investors refuse to lend more, they will force the U.S. to reduce its trade deficit, either through a massive depreciation of the dollar, a painful contraction of the domestic economy, or some combination of both.

9

1

How hard a landing—and what kind?

If there is a loss of confidence in the dollar in the near or medium term, there is still a question of whether the dollar will have a "hard landing" or a "soft landing." One factor that mitigates against a hard landing is that, unlike in Mexico in 1994 and various Asian economies (plus Russia and Brazil) in 1997-99, the U.S. dollar has a floating exchange rate. In contrast, the countries that underwent currency crises over the past several years all had some kind of pegged or fixed exchange rate, which their governments vainly tried to defend when investors lost confidence and began to pull their assets out. Especially in the original crisis countries (Mexico and Thailand), the governments spent billions of dollars of hard currency reserves in failed efforts to defend their pegs, and then eventually had to devalue anyway once they were virtually out of reserves.

Since the dollar has no official target value that the U.S. monetary authorities (the Treasury Department and the Federal Reserve) are obligated to uphold, it is possible that the dollar could decline gradually, essentially reversing its ascent since 1995 in a relatively smooth fashion. In an optimistic scenario, this could engender a soft landing for the real economy as well, by restoring the competitiveness of U.S. traded goods. This increased competitiveness would help lower the trade deficit and reduce the rate of increase in the net foreign debt (as in the optimistic scenario for an improving trade balance, discussed above). An improvement in the trade balance could then help the current economic expansion to continue, if the current sources of domestic stimulus (which are mainly related to consumer spending) begin to weaken, as most analysts expect. Something analogous occurred in the 1985-89 period, when a falling dollar helped the U.S. economy keep growing after the stimulus from the increased budget deficits of the early Reagan years had worn off.

But it is important not to be lulled into thinking that such a soft landing is assured. As we move into a situation where the country that issues the world's main reserve currency has such large foreign debts, we are moving into uncharted waters. The possibility of a dramatic reversal in confidence in the U.S. economy cannot be ruled out, especially in the case of a rupture in the stock market bubble. Moreover, floating exchange rates do not always depreciate gradually, but can collapse abruptly—as the dollar did in 1985-87 and numerous other currencies have since. If self-fulfilling expectations of a dollar depreciation do break out, investors could panic and try to sell off massive amounts of U.S. assets in a hurry, thus precipitating a sharp decline in the dollar's value.

Another factor often cited as precluding an Asian or Latin American-style crisis for the United States is the fact that this country can borrow in its own currency, while other countries generally have to borrow in foreign currencies such as Japanese yen or U.S. dollars. Thus, the U.S. does not have to worry about having adequate international currency reserves or export earnings to service its debts—and in a pinch, the Fed can always print more dollars to ensure adequate liquidity for debt service. Furthermore, the fact that the United States can service its debt in dollars means that a dollar depreciation would not force the U.S. to devote an increased proportion of its national income toward servicing its existing international debts, as other countries have to do when their currencies depreciate (essentially because it takes more of their own currency to meet debt service obligations that are fixed in foreign currency terms).

While there is some truth to this argument, the ability to borrow in its own currency does not completely insulate the U.S. economy from a possible currency collapse or other adverse consequences of a loss of confidence, especially in the long run. The world's willingness to lend to the U.S. in dollars is predicated on the expectation that the dollar will maintain its value (or, as noted above, that the U.S. will offer an interest rate high enough to compensate for any expected depreciation of the dollar). If there is a loss of confidence in either the U.S. as an investment location or the dollar's ability to hold its value, foreigners may become unwilling to continue lending to the U.S. in dollars—at least, not without a major hike in interest rates or some kind of indexing of debt service to the value of the dollar. In the extreme, the U.S. could someday be forced to borrow in euros or some other foreign currency.

Moreover, the Fed would be very reluctant to print dollars to satisfy external obligations. Increasing the dollar money supply in order to facilitate external debt service would be viewed as inflationary and would therefore be likely to engender precisely the kind of loss of confidence in the dollar that the Fed would be trying to avoid. Inflating away external debts, while always a possible strategy, would be the surest way to ensure that the dollar would lose its preeminent role in the international monetary system. Thus, if the U.S. ever tries to take undue advantage of its ability to service debts in dollars, it would undermine its power to do so in the future.

The current willingness of foreigners to lend to the U.S. in its own currency thus does not avoid, and in a sense only tightens, the constraints placed upon domestic monetary policy in order to maintain "confidence" in the dollar. While other countries are more free to let their currencies depreciate in order to improve their external competitiveness and solve their payments deficits, the United States cannot allow the dollar to depreciate too much if it wants to preserve the role of the dollar as the world's predominant international reserve currency and the primary vehicle for international lending activity. As a result, current international monetary arrangements can force the United States to keep the dollar at an exchange rate that is overvalued from the standpoint of balancing U.S. trade, and which therefore results in chronic large trade deficits and persistent foreign debt accumulation.

Even if the United States succeeds in avoiding a hard landing for the dollar, it may not be able to avoid one for the real economy. In fact, efforts to rescue the dollar could well backfire and make matters worse for domestic workers and firms. If the dollar starts to fall and the government wants to prevent a rapid collapse in the dollar's value, the most likely reaction would be an increase in interest rates by the Fed in order to reassure wary investors (just as the U.S. advised Mexico, Korea, Brazil, and other countries to raise their interest rates in the aftermath of their financial crises). High interest rates would be likely to slow the economy, especially by raising the costs of consumer and business borrowing and thus stemming the current rapid growth of consumption and investment spending.

If interest rates are increased, however, the existence of large debt burdens, both domestic and foreign, creates vulnerabilities that are generally ignored in standard economic models. With consumer debts rising to record levels in relation to household income,[18] a rise in interest rates would increase household debt service burdens[19] and could push financially strapped families over the edge into bankruptcy (especially if unemployment begins to rise as a result of higher interest rates). The same is true for corporations that have become highly leveraged—regardless of whether they borrowed for productive investments or for mergers, acquisitions, and buyouts. If interest rates spike upward while sales growth slackens and cash flow shrinks, highly indebted firms could become illiquid and the risk of corporate bankruptcy would increase. And if personal and business bankruptcies rise, banks that have lent heavily to consumers and corporations could be in serious trouble—as they were in the Asian crisis countries. Furthermore, the existence of complex derivative contracts and unregulated hedge funds has allowed investors to create highly leveraged financial positions that could be difficult to unwind without significant losses in the event of a general financial panic in the U.S.

Moreover, as shown earlier, higher interest rates would imply greatly increased net outflows of interest payments to foreign creditors, which would worsen the current account deficit and depress U.S. national income. Thus, the large domestic and foreign debts of the United States could potentially turn a soft landing into a hard one. This could happen if bankruptcies rise, banks fail, and domestic incomes have to be squeezed to permit greater outflows of net interest payments. Even the International Monetary Fund, while projecting a gradual slowdown of U.S. growth in its baseline forecast, and normally relatively optimistic in its outlook, warns ominously of the possibility of a hard landing for the U.S. economy:

> The willingness of foreign investors to continue financing the rapidly growing external deficit of the United States at current interest rates may not continue, in which case downward pressure on the dollar might be another cause of higher interest rates. All these factors could give rise to larger and more abrupt adjustments in private sector behavior, and a more abrupt economic slowdown, than envisaged in the baseline. (IMF 1999b, 26)

How big a "hit" could the U.S. economy take in the event of such a crisis? Some simple calculations reveal that a serious economic depression could easily result. Suppose that the U.S. was forced by a withdrawal of net foreign lending to balance its current account. Conservatively, this would require shrinking the current account deficit by 3% of GDP, or about $270 billion at current prices (given a GDP of approximately $9 trillion in 1999). Suppose further that the dollar falls only by enough to eliminate half of this gap. It can easily be estimated[20] that to close the rest of the gap (i.e., to reduce the trade deficit by $135 billion) via income adjustment, national income would have to fall by about 6% in real terms.[21] This would be an adjustment on the order of magnitude of what has been felt in crisis countries such as Brazil, Mexico, Korea, and Thailand in recent years, and much larger than the drop in output in any recent U.S. recession. That a depression of this magnitude would be needed to eliminate even half of the U.S. current account deficit via income reductions is a result of the U.S. economy's extreme openness to imports, which requires a major income squeeze to achieve a significant reduction in the volume of imports.

12

Is the U.S. borrowing to finance investment?

Some commentators have claimed that the growth in the U.S. foreign debt position is benign, because the United States has been borrowing to finance increased investment rather than to pay for a government budget deficit or a consumer spending boom.[22] But such a claim is mistaken on several counts. Of course, by definition U.S. international borrowing constitutes "net foreign investment" in the United States, but much of this "investment" is simply in paper assets such as stocks and bonds and does not necessarily translate into increases in productive investments in plant and equipment.

It is true that the government deficit has turned into a surplus in recent years, so that it can no longer be labeled a "twin" of the trade deficit (as it was rather misleadingly called in the 1980s— see Blecker 1992 and Morici 1997). Investment demand has been strong in the current economic expansion, but is not unusually high for this point in the business cycle. What *is* unusual about the current period is that *consumption* is abnormally high relative to national income (GDP).

As **Table 2** shows, productive investment spending (defined as gross private domestic investment in the national income and product accounts—essentially, business expenditures on plant and equipment plus new residential construction and inventory accumulation) was 16.1% of GDP in 1998, which is slightly higher than the 15.2% level recorded at the peak of the last business cycle (1989), but below the investment rates recorded at the peaks of the 1970s business cycles (17.6% of GDP in 1973 and 18.8% in 1979).[23] Consumption, on the other hand, accounted for 68.2% of GDP in 1998, and has been around 68% of GDP every year since 1993.

This is an unusually high proportion of consumption in GDP, as can be seen from the comparisons with the earlier years shown (and it is also high compared with the non-peak years omitted from the table). As a result, the private saving rate (which includes both personal and corporate saving) plummeted to 12.8% of GDP in 1998, down from 15.0% in 1989 and 17.5% in both 1979 and 1973. Indeed, as Godley (1999) notes, it is mainly the boom in consumer spending that has kept the U.S. economy growing so rapidly (and hence supported the increased demand for imports that has driven the increases in the trade deficit). At the same time, other traditional sources of economic stimulus, especially government spending and net exports, have been depressed.

As can be seen in Table 2, government expenditures on goods and services accounted for only 17.5% of GDP in 1998, the lowest level in many decades (and certainly in the 25 years covered by this table). The government budget surplus, by either of the definitions shown in Table 2, was a higher (positive) percentage of GDP in 1998 than at any time in the last 25 years.[24] Yet net exports (the trade balance in goods and services) remained in a deficit of -1.8% of GDP in 1998, while net foreign investment (the equivalent of the current account balance in the national income accounts) was -2.5% of GDP (a negative number indicating net U.S. borrowing from abroad).[25]

These data suggest the need for a serious rethinking of the conventional wisdom on the so-called "twin deficits." Back in the 1980s, it was argued that the government's increased fiscal deficit caused "crowding out" to some extent of both domestic investment and net exports (see, e.g., Branson 1985 or Dornbusch 1985). According to some proponents of the twin deficit hypothesis, mostly net exports were crowded out in the short run—due to the rise in the dollar (hence the run-

TABLE 2
Consumption, investment, government spending, the budget balance, the trade balance,
and saving rates as percentages of GDP, in business cycle peak years
since 1973 compared with 1998

	1973	1979	1981	1989	**1998**
Expenditures on:					
Personal consumption	61.6	62.3	62.3	66.1	**68.2**
Private domestic investment[a]	17.6	18.8	17.9	15.2	**16.1**
Government consumption and investment[b]	20.8	19.8	20.3	20.1	**17.5**
Government budget balance[b] as measured by:					
Surplus or deficit on current expenditures[c]	1.6	1.3	-0.1	-0.3	**2.6**
Government net lending or borrowing[d]	0.5	0.2	-1.1	-1.7	**1.7**
Trade balance as measured by:					
Net exports of goods and services	0.0	-0.9	-0.5	-1.5	**-1.8**
Net foreign investment in the U.S.	0.6	0.1	0.2	-1.7	**-2.5**
Saving rates:					
Private saving[a]	17.5	17.5	18.7	15.0	**12.8**
National saving[e]	17.9	17.8	17.6	13.3	**14.5**
Memorandum:					
Public investment[b]	3.5	3.3	3.3	3.4	**2.8**

Source: Author's calculations based on data from the U.S. Department of Commerce, Bureau of Economic Analysis, as published in U.S. Council of Economic Advisors (1999), and updated from the *Survey of Current Business*, various issues.

Notes: All variables are measured on a national income and product account basis in current dollars and expressed as percentages of gross domestic product (GDP).

[a]Investment and saving are measured on a gross basis, i.e., including depreciation ("consumption of fixed capital").
  Private investment includes business fixed investment, residential investment, and inventory accumulation.
  Private saving includes personal saving of households plus gross corporate saving.
[b]Includes federal, state, and local governments.
[c]Current government revenues minus government consumption expenditures.
[d]Includes the surplus or deficit on current expenditures plus government depreciation ("consumption of fixed capital") minus
  government investment.
[e]Equals the sum of private saving and the government budget surplus (net lending).

up in the trade deficit up to 1987)—while investment was crowded out in the long run (late 1980s and early 1990s; see Feldstein 1992). The implication was that, if the federal government balanced its budget, the trade deficit would disappear and private investment would boom. The data in Table 2 show that after the emergence of government budget surpluses in the late 1990s, the promised "crowding in" of domestic investment and net exports did not occur. The investment rate was slightly higher in 1998 compared with 1989, but the trade deficit was also larger, and the most notable change between these two years is the boom in consumption spending.

Of course, U.S. borrowing from abroad does allow us to *maintain* current levels of investment spending in spite of the decline in the private sector saving rate. However, these data show that U.S.

international borrowing has *not* financed a significant increase in the investment rate, but rather has permitted a striking increase in the *consumption* rate, contrary to what is claimed by those who view the U.S. trade deficit as benign.

However, even if the United States were borrowing more for investment and less for consumption, this would not necessarily preclude a future financial crisis. An investment boom that rested on excessive accumulation of foreign debt could still be unsustainable in the long run. Borrowing for investment purposes is no guarantee of future stability, as the Asian crisis amply demonstrated. Thus, the consumption-led boom is not a problem simply because it is consumption led, but rather because it rests on the fragile foundations of wealth effects (the stock market bubble) and increased borrowing (rising consumer debt at home and rising international debt to make up for the domestic saving shortfall), neither of which can persist indefinitely.

Policy implications

The rising trade deficit and international debt of the United States are sustainable only as long as foreign investors are willing to continue lending this country the hundreds of billions of dollars annually required to cover the underlying trade deficit and service the increasing foreign debt. This dependency on international borrowing makes U.S. policy making vulnerable to the decisions of both domestic and foreign investors about whether they want to keep their funds pouring into U.S. financial markets or prefer to send those funds elsewhere. Moreover, the projections in this paper show that in just a few years, under a range of plausible assumptions, the U.S. external debt burden could rise to a level that would be likely to alarm financial investors and cause a sudden withdrawal of funds from U.S. financial markets and dollars. In that event, confidence in the U.S. dollar would plummet, and the United States would be forced to accept a major dollar depreciation or to raise interest rates sharply to prevent one. Either way, the U.S. economy could be put through a painful economic contraction.

The issue, then, is not whether the U.S. can sustain large increases in its foreign debt position, but rather when and how the country will make the adjustments needed to correct the underlying problems. The worst-case, hard-landing scenarios do not have to happen if policy measures are taken soon to prevent them. Just as the Federal Reserve's interest rate cuts in the fall of 1998 helped to stabilize global financial markets and to prevent a U.S. recession, additional policy interventions both in the U.S. and abroad could help to slow down the growth of the U.S. foreign debt and prevent a future financial meltdown. But time is growing short, and—as recent experiences in Asia and elsewhere show—the longer action is delayed, the more difficult it can be to prevent a major economic downturn once a financial crisis erupts.

As the simulations in this paper reveal, alleviating the U.S. international debt burden requires action on two fronts: reducing the trade deficit in order to lessen the need for future borrowing, and keeping interest rates low in order to reduce the burden of servicing the debt. While there is no magic cure for U.S. indebtedness, there are several measures along these lines that could help to ensure a "soft landing" and avert a serious crisis over the next few years:

15

- First, the U.S. cannot act alone, and it cannot continue to serve as the world's "consumer of last resort" indefinitely. Thus, significant domestic stimulus policies are needed in our major trading partners with depressed economies: Europe, Japan, other Asian countries, and Latin America. This is a win-win strategy, which will benefit our trading partners and relieve trade tensions by boosting their growth and reducing their surpluses with the U.S. Without such foreign demand expansion, it will be much harder for the United States to reduce its trade deficit at a socially acceptable cost. The types of stimulus policies that are needed vary from country to country. In Europe and Latin America, standard monetary and fiscal stimuli would probably suffice (although in Latin America, debt relief would also help). In Japan and other Asian countries, structural reforms to increase consumption and liberalize imports are also necessary.

- Second, the dollar needs to come down gradually to a level that is more consistent with balanced trade. Engineering a gradual depreciation rather than a collapse will not be easy, but keeping interest rates low and cutting them further would be useful for this purpose as well as to mitigate the debt service burden. Recovery in Europe, Japan, and other areas would also help by boosting confidence in their economies, thus sparking appreciation of foreign currencies. In the long run, target zones with crawling bands should be used to stabilize the dollar's value at a lower level (Blecker 1999). Capital controls and foreign exchange restrictions (such as a "Tobin tax" on currency transactions) could be used to prevent speculators from pushing the dollar down too far, too fast. However, if there is a loss of confidence and the dollar falls—and especially if international cooperation has been lacking—it would be better to let the dollar drop than to raise interest rates through the roof and sacrifice jobs and incomes to maintain a strong currency. If a hard landing is unavoidable, it is better to have one for the dollar than for the real economy.[26]

- Third, raising the incomes of U.S. workers and reducing economic inequality could help by allowing families to finance their consumption expenditures more out of current income and with less borrowing, leading to a recovery of the personal saving rate. This in turn would require labor market policies such as strengthened minimum wage laws and union organizing rights, as well as a commitment by the Fed not to raise interest rates and slow the economy in response to workers' gains (see Palley 1998). In addition, when the consumption boom slows down, as it inevitably will, the U.S. government needs to be prepared to use a fiscal stimulus (such as an increase in public investment spending); trying to preserve a budget surplus in a slowing economy would be a recipe for turning a mild recession into a severe, 1930s-style depression. Tax cuts are less preferred than government investment spending, since they would probably only boost consumption and contribute to further shrinkage of the public sector in the future.

- Fourth, U.S. trade policies need to be reoriented to promote more reciprocal market access. These policies should stress the interests of U.S.-based producers exporting abroad rather than the rights of U.S. multinational firms investing abroad, especially when the latter are investing in

16

export platforms targeting the U.S. import market or in sales of goods produced in third countries. For example, U.S. trade negotiators should be more concerned about steel than bananas, and more concerned about labor rights than intellectual property rights. New and more effective methods of stemming import surges should be instituted, instead of relying on the time-consuming and legalistic anti-dumping laws. And the U.S. needs to stop signing trade agreements that do more to help U.S. businesses operating abroad than to help U.S. workers seeking good-paying jobs at home.

If these kinds of policies are not adopted by the U.S. and its trading partners, the debt bomb will keep ticking, eventually going off with unpredictable consequences both at home and abroad.

June 1999

Appendix

The projections of the U.S. net international investment position and net investment income in this paper are based on a simple dynamic model of the current account balance and net international borrowing or lending. The current account balance for each year t (CAB_t) is determined by

(A1) $CAB_t = TB_t*GDP_t + INVINC_t$

where TB_t is the (assumed) ratio of the "underlying" trade balance (for trade in goods and services plus net transfers) to GDP, GDP_t is the (projected) nominal gross domestic product, and $INVINC_t$ is the total net investment income balance of the country, for each year from 2000 through 2005 (the treatment of 1998 and 1999 is discussed separately below). The net financial investment position ($NETFIN_t$) for each year is assumed to change by the amount of the current account balance, i.e., the entire net borrowing required to cover the current account deficit is assumed to be done through the accumulation of financial debt. Thus,

(A2) $NETFIN_t = NETFIN_{t-1} + CAB_t$

Net financial income (interest and dividend) payments ($FININC_t$) are assumed to be paid at a given interest rate each year (INT_t) on the average level of net financial assets or debts for the year, which is simply the mean of the current and one-year lagged net financial position:

(A3) $FININC_t = INT_t*0.5*(NETFIN_t + NETFIN_{t-1})$

The total net investment position ($NETINV_t$) is determined by the identity:

(A4) $NETINV_t = NETFIN_t + NETDIR_t + GOLD_t$

where $NETDIR_t$ is the net direct investment position and $GOLD_t$ is the value of U.S. gold reserves. Finally, by another identity, total net investment income ($INVINC_t$) equals the sum of the financial net income ($FININC_t$) and direct net income ($DIRINC_t$):

(A5) $INVINC_t = FININC_t + DIRINC_t$

Using exogenously set forecasts for TB_t, GDP_t, INT_t, $NETDIR_t$, $GOLD_t$, and $DIRINC_t$, as well as an initial lagged

17

value of $NETFIN_{t-1}$, these five equations solve for the time paths of the five endogenous variables CAB_t, $NETFIN_t$, $NETINV_t$, $FININC_t$, and $INVINC_t$. Note that since each year's value for $NETFIN_t$ depends on itself (since $NETFIN_t$ depends partly on interest payments that are a function of current $NETFIN_t$), the model has to be solved using an iterative procedure (which was done using the Excel spreadsheet program).

The exogenously forecast variables are specified as follows. We assume that the underlying trade balance is a deficit of 3% of GDP for 2000-05 (i.e., $TB_t = -.03$) in the baseline scenario, and then vary this percentage for the alternative trade balance scenarios as discussed in the text. This baseline assumption is consistent with current predictions about the level of the U.S. trade deficit for the next few years. We assume that nominal GDP grows at a 5% annual rate each year, starting from the actual 1998 level (i.e., $GDP_t = 1.05 * GDP_{t-1}$), since the actual growth rate of nominal GDP has been approximately 5% in the last few years.

The interest rate is set at 4.25% in the baseline scenario ($INT_t = .0425$), which is approximately the mid-range of the implicit "interest rate" on U.S. international financial assets and liabilities over the past few years (actually, this "interest rate" includes both interest on bonds and bank deposits and dividends from corporate stock and other securities). This rate is determined by taking the gross inflows and outflows of financial investment income as proportions of the stocks of international financial assets and liabilities, respectively. This method yields the following implicit interest rates (in percent) for the last four years for which complete data are available:

Implicit interest rate on:	1994	1995	1996	1997
U.S. financial assets abroad	4.16	4.72	4.15	4.22
Foreign financial assets in the U.S. (U.S. liabilities)	4.48	4.70	4.27	4.28

Source: Author's calculations based on data in DiLullo (1998) and Scholl (1998).

A 4.25% interest rate is assumed in all scenarios for 1999; alternative interest rates are assumed for 2000-05 in the other interest rate scenarios as discussed in the text.

Since U.S. gold reserves are essentially constant in real terms at approximately 261.6 million fine troy ounces, their value varies only as a result of fluctuations in gold prices. We used the actual decrease in the market price of gold from $290.20 at year-end 1997 to $287.80 at year-end 1998 (International Monetary Fund 1999a, 42), to estimate the value of U.S. gold reserves at $75.3 billion for 1998. For 1999, based on a report in the *Financial Times* (June 9, 1999, 26), which forecast a price in the range of $250-$275 per ounce by the end of 1999, we used the mid-range forecast of $262.50 to estimate the value of U.S. gold reserves at $68.7 billion for this year, and then assumed that this value remains constant for 2000-05.

For the net direct investment position ($NETDIR_t$) and net direct investment income ($DIRINC_t$), we make *ad hoc* forecasts based on extrapolation from recent trends (see Figures 1 and 2). For the position, we start with the actual net direct investment position of +$272.0 billion at year-end 1997 and subtract the actual net direct investment inflow of $60.5 billion for 1998 (from U.S. Bureau of Economic Analysis 1999b) to get +$211.5 billion at year-end 1998 (ignoring valuation adjustments, which tend to be minimal for direct investment measured at current cost). Actual net direct investment flows have been quite variable in recent years, with net inflows in some years and net outflows in other years, and are hard to predict *ex ante*. We therefore assume that the net direct investment position levels off at +$200 billion in 1999 and remains constant at that level through 2005. Direct investment income also fluctuates, depending on levels of economic activity and rates of return at home and abroad and on the exchange rates at which U.S. investment income from abroad is converted into dollars. Actual net direct investment income fell from $63.7 billion in 1997 to $54.7 billion in 1998 as a result of the economic slowdown abroad and the fact that most other currencies depreciated against the dollar. We assume that net direct investment income is $55.0 billion in 1999, increases by $2 billion each year from 2000 to 2002, and then increases by $1 billion each year from 2003 to 2005, thus recovering to $64.0 billion (or approximately its 1997 level) by 2005.

The complete model as specified in equations (A1) to (A5) is used for the years 2000-05. For 1998 and 1999, the model is modified to take account of the additional information that is available for these years. For 1998, the actual level of net investment income (total, direct, and financial) is available from the balance of payments statistics. These actual data are therefore used for $INVINC_{98}$, $DIRINC_{98}$, and $FININC_{98}$, and equation (A3) is not used for 1998 (although it is used for 1999). Also, we do not use equations (A1) and (A2) for 1998 or 1999. For 1998, actual balance-of-payments data can be used to determine how much the net financial investment position in-

18

creased over the previous year. U.S. net financial inflows for 1998 were \$149.3 billion, including both official and other financial assets (but excluding direct investment).[27] Again ignoring valuation adjustments (since fluctuations in stock markets in the U.S. and abroad were highly correlated in 1998, and therefore changes in values of domestic and foreign stocks roughly cancel out, and the dollar did not substantially rise or fall in value between December 1997 and December 1998), we therefore compute the net financial position for year-end 1998 as $NETFIN_{98} = NETFIN_{97} - \$149.3$ billion. For 1999, we assume that net financial inflows are \$300 billion, i.e., $NETFIN_{99} = NETFIN_{98} - \$300$ billion.[28]

Endnotes

1.   The likely growth in the U.S. net international debt over the next several years is projected using currently available information about the U.S. balance of payments, the value of the dollar, and asset market conditions in 1998-99, as well as by extrapolating from current economic conditions and forecasts. The baseline scenario assumes that the underlying deficit for trade in goods and services plus net transfers equals 3% of the gross domestic product from 2000 through 2005. However, the total current account deficit (and thus the amount of net international borrowing) is larger than this underlying trade deficit because it also includes the net outflow of investment income (interest, dividends, etc.). The assumptions about the trade deficit and international borrowing for 1998 and 1999 are based on currently available data and forecasts and are discussed in detail in the Appendix. The baseline scenario also assumes that GDP grows by 5% per year in nominal terms and that the interest rate on international financial assets and liabilities stays at 4.25% from 1999 through 2005.

2.   The U.S. net debt increases by the amount of net borrowing from abroad during each year, which should in principle equal the current account deficit. However, in practice there are always "statistical discrepancies" in the actual balance-of-payments statistics. Also, adjustments are made each year for the effects of changes in asset values (especially stock market share prices) both at home and abroad, as well as for the effects of changes in foreign currency values on the dollar value of U.S. assets abroad.

3.   All U.S. international debt data used in this paper are taken from Scholl (1998). The net debt figure cited here includes direct foreign investment (DFI) valued at current cost, i.e., the replacement cost of the investment goods (plant and equipment) owned by U.S. firms abroad and by foreign firms in the United States. The Department of Commerce also reports a series that includes DFI valued at market value, i.e., the stock market value of corporate equity in each country. The latter measure fluctuates much more in the short run, due to the volatility of the stock market indexes used to measure the market value of DFI. Thus, we prefer to use the series with DFI valued at current (replacement) cost, which is more stable over time and better reflects a country's long-term DFI position. All data used in this paper include DFI at current cost where relevant.

4.   U.S. gold reserves, although technically included as an international asset for the United States, cannot legally be sold to service other U.S. obligations, and are therefore irrelevant to the ability of the U.S. to service its debts. DFI is usually based on long-term competitive strategies of multinational business firms and—as recent experiences in Latin America and East Asia have demonstrated—is usually not liquidated during a financial panic. Hence, DFI can also be regarded as illiquid and should be excluded in calculating the financial debts of the United States.

5.   All debt or credit figures cited are measured at the end of the year. In contrast, the figures for net investment income flows, discussed below, are measured for entire calendar years. These are standard procedures for measuring financial variables—stocks of assets or liabilities are measured at a point in time, while financial flows are measured over periods of time.

6.   Some analysts suspect that the magnitude of the net inflow of direct investment receipts may be exaggerated by the fact that foreign multinationals in the United States are more likely to take their profits out in the form of high transfer prices for inputs sourced from their home countries, while U.S. multinationals are more likely to bring their foreign profits home in the form of explicit accounting profits. If this suspicion is true, the upward bias this imparts to the investment income balance is exactly matched by a downward bias to the trade balance, with no net effect on the current account as a whole. See Godley and Milberg (1994).

7.   All balance-of-payments data used in this paper are taken from DiLullo (1998) and the Department of Commerce's international transactions statistical release of March 11, 1999 (U.S. Bureau of Economic Analysis 1999a), except as otherwise noted. Major revisions to the U.S. international transactions accounts for 1982-98, released on June 17, 1999 (in U.S. Bureau of Economic Analysis 1999b), were issued too late to be fully incorporated in this paper, but information from the latter release was used in the forecasts as cited in the Appendix.

19

8.　Net transfers are unrequited inflows and outflows of funds, such as foreign aid and private remittances (e.g., funds sent to relatives overseas by immigrants). In 1998, the United States had a net transfers deficit of $41.9 billion, in addition to a goods-and-services deficit of $169.1 billion and a net investment income deficit of $22.5 billion.

9.　An interest rate of 4.25% is assumed as the baseline because the implicit interest rates on U.S. international financial assets and liabilities have mostly been in the range of about 4.00% to 4.50% for the last several years (see Appendix), and thus this rate represents a continuation of current interest rate policies at home and abroad.

10.　All of the alternative interest rate scenarios assume that the interest rate is 4.25% in 1999; the scenarios differ in what they assume for 2000-05. All of these scenarios also assume the same underlying trade deficit for the United States (3% of GDP) as assumed in the baseline, although the total current account deficits are larger because they include the net outflow of investment income.

11.　Note that these forecasts ignore other effects of changes in interest rates (e.g., effects on demand and income) and their repercussions for the trade balance, effects that would have to be incorporated in a more complete model. In particular, high interest rates would probably stifle growth or cause a recession, which in turn would reduce the underlying trade deficit and thus ameliorate the increase in the debt.

12.　As discussed in more detail in Blecker (1999), new economic theories recognize that self-fulfilling expectations of investors can cause an economic situation to be unsustainable even if it would be sustainable under a different (i.e., more optimistic) set of expectations. These theories have been confirmed by recent experiences in the Asian financial crisis, in which "contagion effects" caused collapses of some currencies that did not otherwise have to be devalued (or which might have required more modest devaluations without the speculative attacks). Of course, when an economic situation is truly unsustainable, smart speculators will perceive this, often forcing sharp corrections in advance of when they would occur in the absence of the speculation.

13.　In recent financial crises, such as those in Mexico in 1994 and Thailand in 1997, it was often domestic investors who led the rush to the exits, since they were the most aware of their countries' problems.

14.　Another motive was the rise of U.S. merchandise trade deficits, which prompted a belief that the dollar was overvalued in the Bretton Woods system of adjustable exchange rate pegs.

15.　This problem was known as the "Triffin dilemma," after Triffin (1960), which has been described as follows in Caves et al. (1990):

> If the United States was allowed to continue running [overall] balance of payments deficits, eventually there would be a crisis of confidence, as foreigners all tried to cash in their dollars for gold before it was too late, and thereby exhausted the U.S. gold reserves. On the other hand, if steps were taken to end the U.S. deficit, then the rest of the world would be deprived of sufficient liquidity in the form of a steadily growing stock of [dollar] reserves. (480)

16.　Calculated by the author using data from U.S. Board of Governors of the Federal Reserve System (1999, Table L.209).

17.　Econometric evidence suggests that strict uncovered interest parity (interest rate premiums equal to expected rates of depreciation) does not generally hold (see Blecker 1998 for discussion and citations). However, the measurement of exchange rate expectations is a problem in all such studies, and there is still a presumption that interest rate differentials at least reflect the expected *direction* of exchange rate changes.

18.　According to Mishel et al. (1999, Table 5.12, 275), total household debt (both consumer and mortgage debt) as a percentage of personal income climbed from 57.6% in 1973 to 84.8% in preliminary data for 1997. At the same time, the household debt *service* burden rose only from 15.5% of disposable income in 1973 to 17.0% in 1997, due to low interest rates and more generous repayment terms (e.g., longer-term mortgages). See also International Monetary Fund (1999b, Figure 2.18, 103), which gives similar figures.

19.　This problem would be mitigated by the existence of long-term consumer debt with fixed interest rates, especially mortgage loans. Only consumers with flexible-rate loans or who take out new loans would be affected by the higher rates. However, if interest rates spike upward, the value of securitized fixed-rate mortgages could plummet, which could wreak havoc in financial markets.

20.　This estimate also assumes that foreign income stays constant, so that exports are unchanged, and that the income elasticity of import demand is approximately 2 (i.e., imports rise by 2% for every 1% increase in income). Many studies have found income elasticities of import demand for the U.S. over 2 (see Blecker 1996). However, most of these studies include only merchandise imports or some subset thereof (often, non-petroleum imports, and sometimes non-computer, non-petroleum imports). With imports of all goods and services included, the income elasticity is likely to be somewhat lower, and we use 2 as a ballpark figure.

20

21.   Using the advance gross domestic product estimates for the first quarter of 1999, the chain-type price index for imports of goods and services is 89.1 (=100 x (1,154.0/1,295.0), where nominal imports are $1,154.0 billion and "real" (1992 dollar) imports are $1,295.0 billion). Dividing $135 billion by 0.891 yields $151.5 billion in 1992 dollars, which is 11.7% of $1,295.0 billion. With an income elasticity of 2 (see previous note), real income needs to fall by ½ of 11.7%, or 5.9%, in order to reduce real imports by $151.2 billion. Data are from *Survey of Current Business* (May 1999, Tables 1.1-1.2, D-2).

22.   See, for example, the statements of Gary Hufbauer, Richard N. Cooper, Claude Barfield, Isaiah Frank, and Daniel T. Griswold in the *International Economy* (1999), who state slightly different versions of this proposition. However, other individuals in that symposium express views closer to those argued here (especially Martin Feldstein, Clyde Prestowitz, Ulrich Ramm, and Charles P. Kindleberger).

23.   Those who claim that investment has been unusually high in recent years generally cite data on "real" investment at chained 1992 prices, rather than the current price data used here (see, e.g., U.S. Council of Economic Advisers 1999, 69-73). The "real" data do show higher investment rates: in real terms, the share of gross private domestic investment in GDP rose to 17.6% in 1998, up from 14.2% in 1989 and 15.2% in 1973. But this appearance of an increased "real" investment rate is due entirely to the fact that prices of investment goods have been rising more slowly than prices of consumer goods (and some investment goods—especially computers and other electronic products—have fallen in price). While this increase shows that business firms spending on productive investment are getting relatively more bang for their bucks, compared with consumers, it does not gainsay the fact that such investment spending has not increased as a share of total domestic expenditures when measured at current prices.

24.   Note that this increase in public sector saving has not been matched by an increase in public investment; on the contrary, at only 2.8% of GDP in 1998 (see Table 2), public investment has shrunk to its lowest level in more than a generation. This dramatic contraction of the public sector's role in the economy is a direct result of the obsession with balancing the federal budget and shrinking the size of government, and is leading to emerging shortfalls of public investment in many areas (see Palley 1998).

25.   These were not the largest trade deficits in the period covered by Table 2; both peaked in 1987, when net exports were -3.0% of GDP and net foreign investment was -3.3% (not shown in the table, since 1987 was not a business cycle peak year).

26.   This is analogous to Jeffrey Sachs' argument (e.g., in Sachs 1999) that Russia, Brazil, and the East Asian countries should not have used high interest rates in efforts to keep their currencies from depreciating.

27.   In the newly revised balance-of-payments data in U.S. Bureau of Economic Analysis (1999b), what is now called the total "financial account" balance for 1998 was +$209.8 billion; subtracting net direct investment inflows of $60.5 billion yields net financial inflows (as defined in this paper, i.e., for liquid assets) of $149.3 billion.

28.   The total projected net capital inflow for 1999 is slightly larger due to the assumed net direct investment inflow of $11.5 billion, implying a total current account deficit of $311.5 billion or about 3.5% of GDP (which we project to be $8,936.6 billion). This is consistent with current projections that the U.S. current account deficit will be 3.5% of GDP in 1999 (IMF 1999b, Table 2.6, 67).

21

References

Blecker, Robert A. 1991. "Still a Debtor Nation: Interpreting the New U.S. International Investment Data." Washington, DC: Economic Policy Institute, Briefing Paper (July).

Blecker, Robert A. 1992. *Beyond the Twin Deficits: A Trade Strategy for the 1990s*. Armonk, NY: M. E. Sharpe, Inc., Economic Policy Institute Series.

Blecker, Robert A. 1996. "The Trade Deficit and U.S. Competitiveness," in Robert A. Blecker, editor, *U.S. Trade Policy and Global Growth: New Directions in the International Economy*. Armonk, NY: M. E. Sharpe.

Blecker, Robert A. 1998. "International Capital Mobility, Macroeconomic Imbalances, and the Risk of Global Contraction," New York: Center for Economic Policy Analysis, New School for Social Research, Working Paper Series III, No. 5 (June).

Blecker, Robert A. 1999. *Taming Global Finance: A Better Architecture for Growth and Equity*. Washington, DC: Economic Policy Institute.

Branson, William. 1985. "Causes of Appreciation and Volatility of the Dollar," in Federal Reserve Bank of Kansas City, *The U.S. Dollar—Recent Developments, Outlook, and Policy Options*. Kansas City, Mo.: Federal Reserve Bank of Kansas City.

Caves, Richard E., Jeffrey A. Frankel, and Ronald W. Jones. 1990. *World Trade and Payments*, fifth edition. Glenview, IL: Scott, Foresman/Little, Brown.

DiLullo, Anthony J. 1998. "U.S. International Transactions, First Quarter 1998," *Survey of Current Business* (July), pp. 59-103.

Dornbusch, Rudiger. 1985. *Dollars, Debts, and Deficits*. Cambridge, MA: MIT Press.

Feldstein, Martin. 1992. "The Budget and Trade Deficits Aren't Really Twins," *Challenge* (March-April), pp. 60-63.

Godley, Wynne. 1999. "Seven Unsustainable Processes: Medium Term Prospects and Policies for the U.S. and World." Photocopy, Jerome Levy Economics Institute, Bard College, Annandale-on-Hudson, NY, March.

Godley, Wynne, and William Milberg. 1994. "U.S. Trade Deficits: The Recovery's Dark Side?" *Challenge* (November-December), pp. 40-47.

International Economy. 1999. "Is America's Large and Growing Trade Deficit Economically Sustainable? A Symposium of Views," *International Economy*, May/June, pp. 10-17.

International Monetary Fund. 1999a. *International Financial Statistics*. Washington, DC: IMF, June.

International Monetary Fund. 1999b. *World Economic Outlook*. Washington, DC: IMF, April.

Morici, Peter. 1997. *The Trade Deficit: Where Does It Come From and What Does It Do?* Washington, DC: Economic Strategy Institute, October.

Palley, Thomas I. 1998. *Plenty of Nothing: The Downsizing of the American Dream and the Case for Structural Keynesianism*. Princeton, NJ: Princeton University Press.

Sachs, Jeffrey. 1999. "Brazil Fever: First, Do No Harm," *Milken Institute Review*, Second Quarter 1999, pp. 16-25.

Scholl, Russell B. 1998. "The International Investment Position of the United States in 1997," *Survey of Current Business* (July), pp. 24-34.

Triffin, Robert. 1960. *Gold and the Dollar Crisis*. New Haven: Yale University Press.

U.S. Board of Governors of the Federal Reserve System. 1999. *Flow of Funds Accounts of the United States*, Federal Reserve Statistical Release Z.1, March 12 and June 11, website www.bog.frb.fed.us/releases/.

U.S. Bureau of Economic Analysis. 1999a. "U.S. International Transactions: Fourth Quarter and Year 1998," BEA News Release of March 11.

U.S. Bureau of Economic Analysis. 1999b. "U.S. International Transactions: First Quarter 1999," BEA News Release of June 17.

U.S. Council of Economic Advisers. 1999. *Economic Report of the President, February 1999*. Washington, DC: Government Printing Office.

[24]

Is the U.S. Current Account Deficit Sustainable?

The U.S. current account deficit, driven by the United States' widening trade deficit, is the largest it has ever been, both as a share of the U.S. economy and in dollar terms. How much longer can the United States continue to spend more than it earns and support the resumption of global growth?

Catherine L. Mann

THE UNITED STATES is enjoying an economic boom that is fueling the growth of its trade deficit. At current exchange rates, the strength of the U.S. economy, combined with slow growth in demand in many other parts of the world, will lead to further widening of the U.S. trade deficit. How long can the trade deficit continue on that trajectory without disrupting the U.S. economy or the world economy?

Absent structural reforms in the United States and abroad, a large devaluation of the dollar, or significant changes in the business cycle, both the trade and the current account deficits will continue to widen until they become unsustainable, perhaps two or three years out. Changing the trajectory will be difficult. The U.S. trade deficit is now so large that even if world economic growth were to pick up and boost U.S. exports, U.S. imports would have to slow dramatically for the gap to narrow. To shrink the trade deficit significantly, say, over a two-year period, exports would have to grow twice as fast as they did in the 1990s, when growth averaged 7.5 percent a year, and the growth rate of imports would have to be halved, from 11 percent to

> ## "Absent structural reforms in the United States and abroad, a large devaluation of the dollar, or significant changes in the business cycle, both the trade and the current account deficits will continue to widen until they become unsustainable, perhaps two or three years out."

5¹/₂ percent a year. Moreover, following twenty years as a net recipient of capital inflows, the United States will soon be confronted with much larger service payments.

At some point, either the United States' negative net international investment position and the associated servicing costs will become too great a burden on the U.S. economy or, more likely, global investors will decide that U.S. assets account for a big enough share of their portfolios and so will stop acquiring more of them. At that point, asset prices, including interest rates and the exchange value of the dollar, will adjust, reflecting the change of sentiment in the markets. A change in the value of the dollar alone would narrow the trade gap for a while, but the deficit would soon begin to widen again. To put the U.S. current account and trade deficits back on a sustainable path will require structural reforms in the United States and its trading partners that encourage faster global growth, boost U.S. household saving rates, better prepare U.S. workers for technological changes in the global economy, and open up markets for U.S. exports, particularly of services.

The deficit is not now a problem

The underlying trend widening of the U.S. trade deficit in 1999 was exacerbated by the financial crisis in Asia and its spillover effects on Latin America and Europe. The dollar appreciated as capital seeking a safe haven flowed into the United States, while the U.S. Federal Reserve System lowered interest rates in response to global and local financial distress. The growth of U.S. GDP accelerated, fueling an increase in imports. At the same time, U.S. export growth collapsed—the result of the worldwide economic slowdown and the strong dollar.

The trade deficit has some positive features. One of the factors driving the U.S. economic expansion has been productivity growth, itself driven by rising investment rates, sound investment decisions, and globalization. As much as half of the recent increase in productivity growth may be due to globalization—which comes from growth in foreign markets, increased competition in domestic markets from foreign suppliers, and the breaking up of the value-chain of production and its relocation to facilities in other countries. Higher productivity growth increases the likelihood that foreign investors' expectations of high rewards from their investments will be realized.

Consequently, rapid productivity growth has made the United States extremely attractive to both domestic and international investors, reflected in a growing appetite for U.S.

assets. In 1998, 45 percent of international debt securities outstanding, and 57 percent of new security issues, were in dollars. U.S. government bonds accounted for about 30 percent of the entire global bond market—commercial and sovereign. If about 50 percent of the projected increase in the value of the global portfolio is invested in U.S. assets, the United States will, roughly, maintain its share of world asset markets.

The size and composition of foreign capital inflows enable the U.S. deficit to widen further. The United States' net external financial obligations, in terms of both the total stock outstanding (about $1.5 trillion) and net service payments ($25 billion), are small in relation to its $9 trillion economy. The United States borrows almost exclusively in domestic currency; more than 90 percent of its external debt to banks is in dollars. In addition, most of the private capital flowing into the United States consists of foreign direct investment and portfolio investment. If foreign investors sold off their holdings of U.S. equities and bonds, the prices of their assets would likely decline; they are therefore more motivated (compared with, say, bank lenders) to hold on to them. Finally, a large share of international transactions are denominated and carried out in dollars, which keeps demand for dollars high and demand for highly liquid U.S. government securities strong. All told, the United States can afford to carry a larger external deficit than a country whose obligations consist primarily of contractually fixed, short-term bank loans denominated in foreign currencies.

Sustainability requires structural changes

Nonetheless, the United States cannot live beyond its long-term means forever, nor will U.S. assets always be so favored by global investors. At current exchange rates and assuming a resumption of sustained growth in the world economy, by 2005 the current account deficit will be about $600 billion—more than 5 percent of GDP. This is both a large volume of assets, in dollar terms, that the United States is offering to international investors, as well as an unprecedented (for the United States) share of GDP. To avoid a sustainability episode in the future, it is critical that structural reforms start now. Never has the economic climate in the United States been so propitious for tackling these reforms—including raising U.S. household saving rates and preparing U.S. workers for change—and never have reforms been so necessary abroad—including liberalizing markets and lowering trade barriers, particularly in the service and professional sectors.

Fiscal discipline has been key to the U.S. economic expansion, but fiscal irresponsibility was replaced by excessive

household spending. When households spend more than they earn, it is difficult for government savings to make up the shortfall in savings because the import intensity of government output is about one-third the import intensity of consumer spending. So higher household consumption has a disproportionate effect on the trade deficit. Although the drop in measured household savings was particularly dramatic in 1999, a downward trend has been apparent for 15 years. Household spending in recent years has been driven by capital gains and unrealistic expectations that wealth will continue to increase at the same rate in the future as in the recent past. In the face of a downturn in the market, U.S. consumers would tend to borrow to maintain their current consumption patterns, making them vulnerable to higher interest rates and a prolonged economic slowdown.

Moreover, worker preparedness for the types of jobs that are emerging in the "new economy" is inadequate. A trade deficit can be good news—the trade deficit tends to widen when the U.S. economy is strong. But trade growth and technological change, which go hand in hand, can mean a difficult adjustment for workers in sectors that are contracting. However, trade growth and technological change will foster the development and expansion of other sectors, and the more flexible workers and firms are in their ability to adapt and to join the expanding sectors, the less likely is a backlash against globalization.

There is a limit to the role that investment capital can play in raising productivity; over the longer term, labor force preparation and performance are critical. The United States cannot keep its competitive edge, maintain rapid productivity growth, and raise living standards unless its workers are world class. High-technology services and goods have grown as shares of U.S. production, imports, and investments. Between 1996 and 1998, real net investment in computers and peripherals rose more than 40 percent a year; they now account for nearly half of the nominal nonresidential capital stock. High-tech capital requires highly skilled workers. Moreover, because skilled workers earn higher wages and are more likely to be employed, preparing workers for the jobs of the future might lessen the political tensions aroused by globalization and encourage higher household saving rates.

Studies by the McKinsey Global Institute of selected service sector industries suggest that labor productivity in the United States is greater than in France, Germany, Japan, and the United Kingdom by 30 percent in the airline industry, 30 to 40 percent in retail banking, 20 to 50 percent in telecommunications, and 10 to 50 percent in retail selling. In part because the U.S. domestic market for services is so well developed, the United States is the world's leading exporter of business and professional services. The service sector overall

Catherine L. Mann, Senior Fellow at the Institute for International Economics and Adjunct Professor at the Owen School of Management at Vanderbilt University, has held several posts at the U.S. Federal Reserve System and served as Senior Economist on the U.S. President's Council of Economic Advisers.

contributed a positive $76 billion to net trade in 1999, whereas goods trade was in deficit by about $345 billion.

The share of services in U.S. exports should increase further as the United States' trading partners grow and mature. For example, services account for about 35 percent of U.S. exports to the mature economies of Europe, where the share of services in GDP is about 70 percent; 25 percent of U.S. exports to South and Central America, where the service share of GDP is about 57 percent; but only 18 percent of U.S. exports to China and India, where the service share of GDP is 37 percent. Multilateral liberalization of services would help put the U.S. trade deficit on a sustainable path. As other countries open their markets to U.S. exports of services, contributing positively to the overall U.S. trade balance, U.S. imports of some services would also increase. Even more important, liberalization of services in markets abroad would spur much faster economic growth there—enough to raise global growth rates from 3.2 percent to 5 percent a year in the long run, according to the Organization for Economic Cooperation and Development.

A global policy challenge

The widening U.S. trade deficit is a reflection not only of policy problems in the United States but also of economic doldrums abroad, which pose an immediate challenge to policymakers there. Just as the U.S. trade deficit has both cyclical and structural aspects, so have the foreign economic doldrums. Japan's lost decade, tepid growth in many European economies, questions about the sustainability of Asia's rebound from the 1997 crisis, and Latin America's economic volatility—all make it difficult for the U.S. trade deficit to change direction based on U.S. actions alone.

A global expansion would benefit the U.S. economy; obviously, it would also be good for other countries. There, as in the United States, the key to raising long-term sustainable growth is faster productivity growth, which will come with increased market flexibility and globalization. This recipe would raise U.S. and global growth rates and put the U.S. trade and current account deficits on a sustainable trajectory. It is a win-win scenario.

Moreover, if structural reforms accompanied rising domestic demand in countries whose economies were growing, these countries would be able to offer higher returns to domestic and foreign investors. Investors would increase the share of non-U.S. assets in their portfolios, and the dollar would drift lower. Faster growth abroad and a modest drop in the dollar would stimulate the growth of U.S. exports and slow the growth of imports, and the U.S. current account gap would shrink. If such a shift occurred smoothly, the U.S.

economy could continue to expand for quite some time, amid robust and sustainable global growth.

If other economies continue to stagnate and needed structural reforms are postponed, however, U.S. investments will continue to yield higher returns than those in other countries; foreign investors will continue to acquire U.S. and dollar-denominated assets; and the current account deficit will grow wider. When a change in investor sentiment comes, it could be dramatic. What would happen if the dollar depreciated by a significant amount, say 25 percent?

Although such a depreciation would quickly close the current account deficit, U.S. consumers would shift from buying imported goods and services to buying those made domestically, and U.S. labor markets would tighten further. The combination of rising wages and a falling dollar likely would drive up prices. The U.S. Federal Reserve would probably raise interest rates, putting the brakes on the U.S. economy. A rapid change in the dollar's value and a raising of interest rates would likely disrupt financial markets, with knock-on effects on consumption and business investment in the United States and throughout the world.

Even though a sudden depreciation would be costly, it still would not put the current account on a sustainable trajectory. Absent structural changes in the U.S. and other economies, a sudden, significant depreciation would set off a dangerous cycle: the trade and current account deficits initially would narrow but they would soon widen again, as structural instabilities returned to the fore. Moreover, because a depreciation would affect only the trade component of the current account, its impact would wear off more quickly than did the impact of the depreciation of the dollar in the 1980s.

The United States' external deficits have widened dramatically during a period in which the U.S. economy has been robust, while stagnation and financial crisis have swept through much of the rest of the world. But, because globalization has enhanced productivity growth and because the United States is a central participant in international markets, the external situation is not yet unsustainable. Strong domestic demand in the United States can continue to support the transition to demand-led growth abroad for two or three more years. However, structural asymmetries in the components of the U.S. internal and external balances, as well as political and market sensitivities toward growing trade deficits, will unleash economic forces that ultimately could undermine the sustainability of the U.S. deficit. A failure to address policy and structural needs, in the United States and abroad, increases the likelihood that the resolution of the U.S. trade imbalance will be unpleasant and disruptive for the world economy. F&D

This article is based on the author's book, Is the U.S. Trade Deficit Sustainable? *(Washington: Institute for International Economics, 1999).*

[25]

Kiel Institute of World Economics
Duesternbrooker Weg 120
24105 Kiel (Germany)

Kiel Working Paper No. 978

Russia's Debt Crisis and the Unofficial Economy

by

Claudia M. Buch
Ralph P. Heinrich
Lusine Lusinyan
Mechthild Schrooten

April 2000

– 2 –

Russia's Debt Crisis and the Unofficial Economy*

Abstract:

Russia's foreign debt problems worsened substantially after the financial crisis of 1998. The paper focuses on the key role of the government in servicing foreign debt and promoting institution building by showing how foreign debt influences the choice between official and unofficial taxation. The enterprise sector is assumed to reallocate its resources between domestic investment and capital flight. It is discussed under which conditions debt rescheduling may create incentives for the government to promote institution building. The results of this paper shed light on the conditions under which the recent agreement with the London Club to write off substantial amounts of former Soviet debt can be successful.

Keywords: Foreign debt, debt restructuring, Russian Federation

JEL-classification: F34, H63

Dr. Claudia M. Buch
Ralph P. Heinrich
Lusine Lusinyan
Kiel Institute of World Economics
24100 Kiel, Germany
Telephone: +49-431-8814-332
Fax: +49-431-8814-525
E-mail: heinrich@ifw.uni-kiel.de

Dr. Mechthild Schrooten
German Institute for Economic Research,
Königin-Luise-Str. 5,
14191 Berlin, Germany
Telephone: +49-30-89789-344,
Fax: +49-30-89789-108,
E-mail: mschrooten@diw-berlin.de

---

* The authors would like to thank Hubert Strauß as well as participants of a seminar given at the *New Economic School* in Moscow in March 2000 for most helpful comments on an earlier draft. Remaining errors and inaccuracies are solely in the authors' own responsibility.

– 3 –

Table of Contents

1

1 Motivation

On the verge of the new millennium, the Russian economy faces a set of adverse conditions. Looking back to a decade of failed transformation characterized by an almost constant deterioration of gross domestic product (GDP), an even greater fall of investment, and a substantial decline in living standards, prospects for sustained economic recovery look dim. Although the devaluation of the ruble that accompanied the financial crisis of 1998, coupled with an increase in world commodity prices, has improved the price competitiveness of firms and has thus contributed to a recovery in industrial output and investment,[1] institutional re-forms have not been pushed ahead decisively as yet. This is one reason for the fact that capital flight remains prevalent. At the same time, Russia has virtually lost access to international capital markets after the crisis because of its default on parts of its foreign debt and because of a worsening of most of its traditional debt indicators. Mainly, Russia's foreign debt problem is a fiscal one. However, regaining access to foreign capital markets is a key issue for the Russian econ-omy as a whole.

This is the setting in which the on-going negotiations of Russia with its foreign creditors take place. Although, in August 1999, the sovereign debtors of the Paris Club agreed on an interim solution which foresees a quite substantial debt re-structuring, a final agreement is still pending. In February 2000, Russia and its private, London Club creditors eventually reached an agreement to write down about 36 percent of Russia's debt inherited from Soviet times. Debt relief granted by the Paris Club was still under discussion at the time of writing.

This paper discusses under which conditions debt relief will be successful. The restructuring of Russia's foreign debt is, of course, not unprecedented. For Rus-sia itself, creditors have earlier on agreed to reschedule Soviet-era debt. Like-wise, debt restructuring has been an issue for many developing countries and emerging markets, notably in Latin America.[2] At a risk of over-generalizing, some lessons can be drawn from these earlier experiences. On the borrower's side, successful fiscal adjustment was perhaps the most essential factor that con-tributed to an effective recovery from the debt problems. Also, implementation

---

[1]   For a review of recent economic developments in Russia see Russian Economic Trends (2000).

[2]   These experiences have been thoroughly reviewed in World Bank (1992-93), UNCTC (1989), Krugman (1989a,b), IMF (1993), Cline (1995), Bowe and Dean (1997).

2

of various debt-restructuring schemes, though an important vehicle in reducing the debt burden, was typically conditional upon improvements in the macro-economic situation and the institutional setup in the borrower countries.

These earlier episodes share many similarities with Russia but also differ in a number of important regards. Key characteristics of the Russian economy such as the dominance of public debt, and hence the importance of an internal transfer problems in debt performance, or the prevalence of capital flight, were also observed during the debt crises of the 1980s. Yet, Russia differs from other developing countries and emerging markets because the abolition of inherited and the creation of new institutional structures is a much more tedious process than in those economies where market-based institutions had already been in place. Socialist economies were not only branded by the coexistence of central planning and an informal sector, but also by non-cash payments and offsets between the enterprise sector and the government. While the implementation of market-oriented institutions takes time, the institutional framework of the Perestrojka era — an unsound mixture of the two systems — has still been in existence. Thus, Russia's unofficial economy is based on inherited structures for hidden, unreported transactions and old, but sophisticated networks of agents. The crisis of 1998 in itself has been a reflection of the deep crisis of the Russian state and an open manifestation of the weaknesses of the existing institutions.[3]

In addition to other forms of hidden and illegal economic transactions, such as corruption and shadow economy operations, non-cash payments are one of the major characteristics of the Russian unofficial economy (Table 1). Moreover, the legal framework itself actually allows for the existence of such a system of unreported payments, where the state is typically a major player.[4][5]

Not surprisingly, the institutional weaknesses most prevalently manifest themselves in the fiscal sphere. The inability of the government to institute a proper tax system, or, in other words, to replace implicit, unofficial means of taxation by official means, is thus a feature peculiar to the Russian economy. From the point of view of a potential investor, such an opaque tax burden increases uncertainty about future returns distorting incentives for productive investment activities.

---

[3] Generally, the Russian financial crisis shares elements both of a classical currency crisis characterized by tensions between the exchange rate regime and domestic policies (Flood and Garber 1984) and of a combination of banking and balance of payments crises, i.e. a "twin-crisis" (Goldfajn and Valdes 1997, Buch and Heinrich 1998).

[4] Additionally, it is necessary to distinguish between misreporting because of the technical inability to gather information or because of deliberate, hidden transactions.

[5] For a broader discussion on characteristics of the unofficial economy in the transition countries see Kaufman and Kaliberda (1996).

3

The purpose of this paper is to provide a framework for analyzing Russia's debt problem which takes the special role of the unofficial economy into account. In a first step, we give a brief account of Russia's foreign indebtedness as well as of Russia's external and fiscal developments (Section 2). We proceed by presenting a stylized model of the economics of debt restructuring which takes account of the trade-off between official and unofficial means of taxation for the Russian government (Section 3). The model shows that the share of official versus unofficial taxation is a key policy parameter in the hands of the government to affect the sustainability of its foreign debt. Section 4 concludes and summarizes the main lessons.

2 Russia's Debt Crisis

2.1 Foreign Debt Situation

Following a substantial devaluation of the ruble in the wake of the currency crisis of 1998, most foreign debt indicators of Russia have worsened significantly (Table 2). This effect has already been visible in 1998 but has become even more pronounced for more recent data. These show an increase in the ratio of debt-to-GDP from about 26 percent prior to the crisis to more than 100 percent.[6] Measured in relation to GDP, Russia's debt burden had thus been below the average of developing countries (33-35 percent) prior to the crisis but considerably exceeded the average afterwards. Other debt indicators have worsened as well. Foreign currency reserves, for example, are extremely low: the ratio of currency reserves to debt has fallen from 14 to 6.6 percent as compared to an average value of over 28 percent for developing countries.

The size of a country's foreign debt certainly has an important impact on its ability to service its liabilities. At the same time, the structure of the debt in terms debt instruments, the maturity, and the structure of the creditors matters as well. Hence, in the remainder of this section, an overview over the structure of Russia's foreign debt and the status of its debt negotiations is given.

2.1.1 *Structure of Foreign Debt*

---

[6] This figure uses data for the period June 1998 through May 1999.

4

Almost half of Russia's external debt obligations originates from Soviet time (Table 3). After the collapse of the Soviet Union in 1991, Russia, as the biggest successor country, assumed foreign liabilities and a substantial share of foreign assets of the former USSR. After several restructuring arrangements and repayments, the face value of these obligations as of the end of 1998 totaled around US-dollar 100 billion, or 55 percent of total foreign currency debt. New credits raised by the Russian government and non-sovereign borrowers amounted to 30 percent and 17 percent of total debt, respectively.[7] Through the debt restructuring agreement reached with the London Club in February 2000, Russia's foreign debt has been reduced by about 11 billion US-dollar (see Section 2.1.3).

Debt obligations against multilateral creditors (47 percent) and Eurobonds (29 percent) constituted the largest shares in the post-Soviet debt, whilst the debt against the Paris Club official lenders (40 percent) and against the London Club of private lenders were the major components of the Soviet-era debt. Credits of the Paris Club have not been securitized, while London Club claims have been restructured into tradable securities that correspond to the nominal value of the credits (PRINs – principal notes) and to the capitalized interest payments (IANs – interest arrears notes). In the group of non-sovereign debtors, Russian banks have had the largest share with almost two-thirds of total foreign debt.

The Russian Federal Government is the main debtor to foreigners. However, until the recent debt restructuring deal, London Club debt has been held by the state-owned Vnesheconombank.[8] In contrast to the government, Vnesheconombank can, in principle, be subject to a foreign jurisdiction. Particularly, part of the London Club debt has been contracted under British law. Creditors were thus not entitled to seize directly the assets of the Russian government, but only those of Vnesheconombank. Although Vnesheconombank has claims on the Russian Government, on former state-owned enterprises, for which investment credits had been raised from abroad, and on debtors of the former Soviet Union, the market price of its assets is very low. As of the end 1998, the face value of claims against countries such as Cuba, Syria, Mongolia, Afghanistan, Iraq or North-Korea amounted to around US-dollar 130 billion, of which US-dollar 93 billion were overdue (Vnesheconombank 1999).[9]

---

[7] The total does not sum up to 100 percent because resident Eurobonds and Minfins holdings are also included into the total debt, whereas non-resident holdings of GKOs/OFZs are excluded.

[8] According to an agreement with 17 Paris Club creditors signed in 1992, Vnesheconombank acts as a debt manager, but not the debtor, against the Paris Club.

[9] These claims give Russia a special role as it acts both as a creditor and debtor in the Paris Club.

5

2.1.2   Debt Repayment Schedule

In the years 1994-98, Russia paid US-dollar 30 billion in foreign debt service or 10 percent of debt-service due. As Table 4 shows, principal repayments have tended to decrease, whereas payments of interest have increased. Post-Soviet debt has been serviced timely, but Soviet-era debt has partly been repudiated. As of the end 1998, arrears totaled 11 percent of the Soviet-era obligations. In 1999, total debt service due amounted to US-dollar 17.5 billion (DIW et al. 1998). In the first half of the year, US-dollar 4.5 billion has been serviced, and further payments of US-dollar 4 billion had been projected by the end of 1999 (Finansovie Izvestia, 15.7.1999 and 29.7.1999). The major part of these payments has been made using foreign exchange reserves of the Central Bank as well as newly received IMF credits.

In the years 2001-2010, projected debt-service of the Russian Government amounts to around US-dollar 11 billion annually.[10] A sharp increase in payments to US-dollar 16 billion is expected in the year 2003 due to a redemption of Euro-bonds. Debt-service will be distributed relatively equally between principal re-payments and interest service, while the latter will exceed the former until 2002, and will fall short of principal repayments after 2003. A decrease in debt service is expected only after 2009. To this, foreign debt-service of US-dollar 5-6 billion annually by the private sector must be added. However, since these credits are mostly short term, their amount will decline relatively fast.

2.1.3 Debt Negotiations

Since the breakup of the former Soviet Union and Russia's acceptance of the Soviet external liabilities, both the Paris and London Club debts have been subject to a number of rescheduling arrangements (Table 5). However, those arrangements did not prove to be a sustainable and sound solution to Russia's external debt problem. In addition, the systemic financial crisis in mid-1998 showed the extreme vulnerability of Russia's external debt position and necessitated urgent resumption of debt restructuring negotiations with all its creditors. Negotiations between the Paris Club and Russia were stalled immediately after the crisis, however, because the IMF had suspended its programs with Russia. Since Paris Club negotiations are conducted only with those debtors that have credit arrangements with the IMF in place, the continuation of negotiations with

---

[10] This figure assumes that no new borrowing takes place but takes the debt rescheduling agreements reached with the London Club in February 2000 into account (Handelsblatt 22.2.2000). The figure does thus not correspond fully to those reported in Table 4.

6

Russia's official creditors depended upon Russia's successful conclusion of a new IMF credit arrangement, which eventually happened at the end of April 1999.

A temporary agreement with the Paris Club was reached in August 1999. According to the agreement, about US-dollar 8 billion of payments due between 1999 and 2000 will be repaid over 15-20 years. In 1999-2000, Russia will have to pay only some US-dollar 600 million (RFE/RL 2.8.1999). Russia expects to pursue further negotiations with the Paris Club in the second half of 2000 seeking terms for rescheduling its Soviet-era debt to Paris Club creditors similar to those most recently agreed with the London Club (RFE/RL 14.2.2000).

The agreement, eventually reached between Russia and the London Club in February 2000, entails a write-off of 37.5 percent of face-value the face value of PRINs and of 33 percent of those of IANs. The remainder will be restructured into a 30 year maturity eurobond with a seven year grace period. The eurobond will be a Russian sovereign one, *pari passu* with, and cross-defaultable into, other post-Soviet Eurobonds. The exchange is likely to be offered in the second quarter of the year 2000, whereas the total deal may be made into an official legal document at the end of May (Goldman Sachs 2000, RFE/RL 14.2.00). Such debt restructuring improves creditors' position by ensuring a higher seniority of their claims, and could serve as a strong impetus for Russia's renewed access to international capital markets.

In addition to the public sector, Russia's private borrowers have also experienced serious problems in their foreign debt servicing. As a response to the August 1998 financial crisis, temporary restrictions on capital account foreign exchange operations by Russian residents were imposed. This, first of all, included bank and corporate debt to foreign creditors estimated at US-dollar 40 billion at that time, and US-dollar forward contracts of about US-dollar 10 billion. However, private debt settlement has become even more complicated as Russia needs to initiate a large-scale restructuring of its banking system, a process which is likely to drag on for a considerable amount of time.[11]

2.2 Current Account Sustainability

Pursuant to the currency crisis of 1998, Russia's debt burden has increased not only in relation to GDP but also relative to its exports from about 120 to 200 percent after the crisis. Falling oil prices through 1998 are a major reason for this

---

[11] See Buch and Heinrich (1999) for a more detailed treatment.

7

decline. Still, the ratio remains below the threshold value beyond which the IMF considers the sustainability of foreign debt as critical (200–250 percent) (IMF 1997: 17). The ratio of debt service over exports has likewise increased from 6.5 to 8.8 percent, but remains below that of the average developing country (17.6 percent).

Russia's debt servicing capability depends crucially on the development of its current account surplus. This, in turn, is largely determined by the evolution of the real exchange rate and the world market prices of Russia's main export products, oil and gas. With the fall of oil prices in 1997 and 1998, Russia's trade account surplus dropped from about 20 billion US-dollar in 1995–96 to around 15 billion US-dollar in 1997–98. In 1999, data for the first nine months indicate an increase of the surplus over and above 25 billion US-dollar, reflecting both the real depreciation of the Ruble and the recovery of oil prices (RECEP 1999).

To show the link between the real exchange rate and the trade account more systematically, the following error-correction equation has been estimated:

(1) $$\Delta TA_t = c + (\alpha_0 - 1)\left[TA_{t-1} - \beta X_{t-1}\right] + \sum_{i=1}^{n-1}\alpha_i \, \Delta TA_{t-i} + \sum_{i=0}^{m-1}\beta_i \, \Delta X_{t-i} + \varepsilon_t$$

where TA = Russia's net exports (CIS *and* non-CIS) in US-dollars, deflated by US consumer prices. The index of Russia's industrial production (Y) and the real exchange rate index (Ruble versus US-dollar) (RER) were used as explanatory variables (X). We expect a real devaluation (i.e. an increase in RER) to improve the trade account surplus in the mid- to long-run whereas the short-run effect may be negative due to the slow adjustment of quantities (J-curve effect). An increase in domestic industrial production could, on the one hand, improve the trade account as part of the increase would be exported. On the other hand, increased industrial production may stimulate higher imports of inputs and may thus lower the trade account surplus.

All variables are taken in logs and are seasonally adjusted by the multiplicative technique implemented in EViews.[12] Specifying the model as an error-correction model implies that changes in the trade account surplus are determined both by deviations from long-run equilibrium (the error-correction-term in brackets) and by short-term changes in endogenous and exogenous variables. The model has been estimated for the period January 1994 through July 1999 (monthly data,

---

[12] The use of this technique has been possible because Russia's trade account has been in surplus during the period under review. Using the additive seasonal adjustment procedure instead, which can also be applied to negative data, left the main results unaffected.

8

67 observations). A general specification with four endogenous and exogenous variables has been chosen first, and insignificant lags have been eliminated subsequently (Table 6).

The second specification, including the oil price, explains roughly half of the variation in the trade account surplus and fulfills the assumptions of the linear regression model (normal distribution of the residuals, absence of heteroskedasticity and autocorrelation). The estimated long-run coefficients imply an improvement in the trade account by almost 3   percent following a 1-percent devaluation. Also, a 1 percent increase in the price for oil (Ural) improves the trade account by 2 percent. The adjustment with respect to the real exchange rate is somewhat less pronounced if the oil price is not included as an explanatory variable. Simulations show a J-type adjustment of the real external balance for both cases; a positive response starts very quickly, after 2-3 months, and the full adjustment is reached roughly one year after the devaluation (Graph 1).

As regards the impact of domestic industrial production, the demand effect dominates, i.e., the trade balance worsens if industrial production increases. Considering the importance of raw materials for Russia's foreign trade and the existence of long-run trade agreements, this result is hardly surprising. Yet, the extremely high long-run coefficient (−18 percent) should be interpreted with caution, and direct implications of economic growth on the development of the trade account should not be drawn.[13] It could be argued that the index of industrial production is determined also by export activities and can thus not be assumed as exogenous in the above specification. Testing for weak exogeneity by using the reverse specification showed no statistically significant cointegration relationship between the trade account and industrial production. In addition, the share of exports in total industrial production is relatively low in Russia.

Alternative model specifications have been tested to check the robustness of these results. Using the index of European or US industrial production as a proxy for foreign demand gave a negative coefficient while the remaining results were basically unchanged. Separate specifications of export and import equations showed that the positive response of net exports to a real devaluation is due mainly to the negative response of imports. A dummy variable capturing changes in the system of foreign trade regulations following the currency crisis such as

---

[13] Using domestic retail sales as a proxy of domestic demand instead gave a much lower long-run coefficient of about 4 percent. Yet, the explanatory power of the equation worsened substantially.

9

the introduction of a prepayment system for imports and a surrender requirement for exports, has been insignificant.

2.3 Fiscal Developments

The performance of Russia's trade account is one important factor behind the sustainability of the country's foreign debt situation. But, since foreign debt is owed primarily by the Russian government, sustainability also depends crucially on the solution to the internal transfer problem, i.e. on the ability of the government to tax efficiently the enterprise sector and thus to get access to hard currency earnings.

Efficient taxation and, more generally, a redefinition of the role of the state, however, have been one of the main weaknesses of the transformation process in Russia.[14] The official budgetary situation reflects not only the performance of the actual tax law but also the inefficiency of its implementation. Since the beginning of reforms, the Russian Federation has been confronted with low and, over a long period, even decreasing tax revenues. Important sources for the consolidated budget, which consists mainly of the federal and the regional budgets, have been the VAT and profit taxes (Table 7). During the first four years of transformation, revenues from both sources of taxation went down significantly. In the same period, severe cuts in expenditures were made related especially to the enterprise sector: official subsidies to the enterprise sector dropped from more than 10 percent of GDP in 1992 to around 2.5 percent in 1999. The sharpest decline in these official enterprise subsidies occurred in 1995 (–50 percent). Partly, these adjustments in the official fiscal sector have been a direct response to the requirements of the IMF, which has been monitoring, supervising and also to a certain degree financing Russia's macroeconomic policies. However, the expenditure cuts could not compensate for the declines in revenues. The budget has been running a chronic deficit,[15] which was financed not only by the domestic banking system but also by international creditors.

For a sustained period, it was symptomatic of the Russian economy that increases in the official deficit were accompanied by increases in tax arrears (Graphs 2 and 3). The dramatic increase in enterprise arrears against the budget was initiated by a presidential decree which came into force in 1996 and which

---

[14] See Aslund (1998) and Leijonhufvurd and Rühl (1997) for a similar conclusion.

[15] Data on the Russian fiscal situation are strongly infected by errors and revisions; here we use time series published by the Russian Economic Trends (various issues).

10

offered selected enterprises the postponement of tax payments (Ukaz 1996). This decision was nothing more than the implementation of an "unofficial" or hidden mechanism to bring additional liquidity to the enterprise sector, which was suffering from a restrictive monetary policy characterized by extremely high real interest rates (Schrooten 2000). Therefore, tax arrears can be considered a special kind of quasi-fiscal activity (QFA). In this sense, QFAs are simply unreported but voluntary governmental grants to the enterprise sector or even to selected enterprises.

At the same time, these subsidies usually have not come for free. Disaggregating the data on arrears by industry shows a quite interesting pattern: large industrial enterprises, especially those belonging to the energy sector, are the most important tax debtors. In return, these tax debtors have been expected to subsidize insolvent enterprises, industries, municipalities, and even some neighboring countries by offering products on the Russian market at prices below those prevailing on the world market (World Bank 1999b). Since the gap between the domestic and the international price level potentially creates losses for the energy sector, tolerating tax arrears can be a means to indirectly compensate firms for these losses. In this way, the government has used enterprises as a vehicle for conducting industrial, social, regional, and even foreign policies off-budget.

Subsidization and off-budget activities through tax arrears was not the only form of QFA in Russia. In the pre-crisis period, not only the inflation tax, but also the exchange rate policy functioned as a QFA. Especially the relatively fixed exchange rate of the ruble against the US dollar could be considered as a guarantee to the domestic enterprise sector, the banking sector and the government itself, ensuring a low real effective interest rate in the case of international borrowing. The nearly fixed exchange rate created a strong incentive for foreign borrowing and operated as a huge subsidy for doing so. While the inflation tax increased the tax burden on private economic activities for a relatively long period, the implicit exchange rate guarantee lowered the borrowing costs not only for the enterprise sector but also for the government.

Because property rights have not been implemented sufficiently, fiscal activities are often performed on a "non-cash-basis", and an opaque system of indirect subsidies and payments prevails. More recently, the forms of QFAs have changed as price controls and surrender requirements of foreign currency export earnings have been re-introduced (DIW et al. 2000). The government itself is often responsible for the postponement of wage and pension payments as well as for the non-payment for energy. This means that arrears appear not only on the

11

revenue side but also on the expenditure side of the budget. Since QFAs are developed and designed by the government itself, the Russian government seems to be able to switch between "official" and "unofficial" taxation.

Russia's QFAs are a matter of concern for several reasons. *First*, for a long period, the conventional or official report on the government's fiscal balance gave a misleading indication of the extent and role of governmental activities – and of the macroeconomic impact of the actual fiscal policy. The magnitude of governmental activities had been underestimated by a substantial margin. While the official budget figures nearly reached the given benchmarks for conditional credits by international financial organizations in regard to expenditure cuts and the size of the deficit, the scope of hidden governmental activities and the de facto deficit of the public sector were largely unknown.

Second, the patterns of QFAs implemented in the Russian Federation have distorted resource allocation. The Russian economy is not only characterized by a considerable degree of corruption and a large shadow economy, but also by a high share of non-cash payments or even non-payments, both of which are characteristic of the unofficial economy. While non-cash payments to the budget and tolerated tax arrears operate like an extensive subsidy system, the weak institutional framework functions as an unstable tax system. For entrepreneurs' investment decisions, not only the expected return but also the official corporate tax rate, the implemented deduction possibilities, and the (tax) burden arising from off-budgetary activities are important parameters. From the point of view of a potential entrepreneur, uncoordinated taxes and exemptions increase the uncertainty about future returns on investment. Moreover, the choice of where to invest, what to produce, and at what scale to operate will be distorted by considerations of which activities can best be shielded from unpredictable changes in the system. The unstable and opaque tax burden on investment activities is a symptom of the unstable institutional framework of Russia itself. However, the implicit tax rate arising from this unstable institutional framework is difficult to measure. Obtaining information about the tax burden which arises from the weak institutional environment is even more difficult than the calculation of non-payment against the budget sector. The prevalence of capital flight, however, can be seen as indirect evidence for the costs imposed on the enterprise sector through a weak institutional environment. In this sense, capital flight reflects the fact that enterprises are taxed in Russia through unofficial in addition to official means.

12

Third, QFAs often take the form of unfunded and even unanticipated liabilities either for the government or for the enterprises. Tolerated tax arrears and non-payments of the budget against the enterprise sector as well as a nearly fixed exchange rate in an inflationary environment or the newly introduced price controls for certain goods bring instability and tensions to the economy as a whole. In other words, in the short-run, it may be attractive to operate within the unofficial sector. In the long run, however, QFAs and the badly-developed legal and institutional framework appear to be very costly to the Russian economy.

The measurement of the size of the unofficial economy and of QFAs is difficult simply because of the hidden character of these transactions. Because in the Russian economy the "unofficial" economy and the implemented QFAs are very closely linked, we focus here on the non-cash payments and the non-payments between the enterprise and the state sector. The fact that tax arrears went up to 5 percent of GDP during the transition period (Goskomstat 1996) can be seen as one manifestation of this unofficial fiscal system.

Graph 2 shows the development of budget revenues and tax arrears since 1996. The sum of official tax revenues and arrears is used as a somewhat "fictive" measure of total revenue. Revenues defined in this sense increased markedly between 1996 and 1999. The sum of these "potential" revenues was much higher than the effective revenues. Although this fictive measure is certainly a very crude approximation of the importance of the unofficial economy, it nevertheless shows that the government can influence its official revenues to a certain degree by deciding to tolerate tax arrears of certain industries. At the federal level, only about 70 percent of the regular revenues have been collected in cash. At the regional level, barter and other forms of non-cash payment attained an even higher share of the budgetary revenues.

Since official budgetary revenues went down while tax arrears and international interest burdens increased since 1997, it was becoming increasingly likely that the Federation, as the most important Russian debtor on the international financial market, would fail to service post-Soviet debt. It has been argued above that the dominance of public debt is a distinguishing feature of the Russian debt problem. While public or publicly-guaranteed debt was important during earlier debt restructuring episodes as well, the current situation in Russia differs from these prior situations by virtue of the coexistence of an unofficial and an official fiscal sector. Hence, efficiently taxing the enterprise sector is one of the government's main tasks at present.

13

To this end, the government will have to invest into the institutions underpinning economic activity in a market economy. In a modern society — which should be created during the transition period — the state is responsible for the implementation and enforcement of most of the relevant rules of the economic game. The design of institutions has a key impact on overall economic development. Economic theory and empirical evidence show that efficient institutions bring down transaction costs by lowering search time and information costs or by correcting market failures. Inefficient institutions, in turn, cause higher transaction costs, negatively affect private sector activities, and therefore have a negative impact on output (Pagano 1993). In the present context, institution building implies *inter alia*

- creating a tax system with fewer taxes, fewer exemptions, and fewer contradictions,

- upgrading tax administration by training tax officials and raising salaries to levels that raise immunity against the temptations of corruption,

- reducing political discretion in tax enforcement by creating a truly independent judiciary which not only enforces the state's tax claims but also protects enterprises (and households) against transgressions by tax authorities,

- and increasing the supply of the public good "public security" in general by investing in uncorrupted police forces.

The Russian government also has to solve two major internal transfer problems. *First*, the enterprise sector has to be compelled to pay the outstanding taxes. *Second*, the tax-sharing system between the different levels of government has to be redesigned in such a way that the regions are forced to collect taxes only on a cash basis. Only cash revenues or revenues in US-Dollars make the repayment of foreign credits possible.

In the following section, a stylized model of Russian foreign debt is presented which analyzes this choice between official and unofficial taxation in a situation of high foreign debt stocks.

3   Foreign Debt and the Role of the Unofficial Economy

As regards the sustainability of Russia's foreign debt situation, it might be argued that the dependence of export revenues from the oil and gas sector and thus on the development of world market prices for these commodities leaves relatively

14

little room to maneuver for domestic policy. At the same time, Russia's situation is quite peculiar in the sense that public sector foreign debt dominates and that the economy has been characterized by chronic fiscal problems, coupled with a substantial role of the unofficial economy. The size of the unofficial economy, in turn, is to a large extent determined by economic policy making and can thus hardly be considered exogenous to the government's optimization problem.

These factors suggest that economic policy has an impact on Russia's ability to service its foreign debt, and that the situation cannot be analyzed without taking the interaction between public sector foreign debt and the unofficial economy into account. To our knowledge, links between these issues have not been treated in the literature so far. While there has been work on the resolution of foreign debt crises and on the economics of the unofficial economy,[16] these two strands of the literature have not been combined. In the following, we thus present a stylized model which allows us to analyze the choice of the Russian government between official and unofficial taxation in the face of its foreign debt burden. The framework is then used to model the decision of foreign creditors to restructure Russia's foreign debt.

3.1   Foreign Debt and the Choice Between Official and Unofficial Taxation

The model has two periods. We assume that Russia's enterprise sector is endowed with an initial amount of investible funds. In the first period, it allocates these funds between capital flight and investment into the domestic tradables sector in a way that maximizes second period profits after taxation, both official and unofficial (see Section 2.5 above).[17] The return to domestic investment inter alia depends on the development of the real exchange rate, with a depreciation raising the return in domestic currency. Considering the fact that Russia's exports are dominated by raw materials such as oil and gas which are denominated in US-dollar, this assumption can be motivated by the fact that costs of oil and gas producers are partly denominated in domestic currency. The government maximizes revenues by taxing the proceeds of domestic investment in the second period.

Assessing the actual tax burden Russian enterprises face is complicated by two factors. On the one hand, tax enforcement is very uneven, which results in sub-

---

[16] See Footnote 2 and Johnson et al. (1997), Kaufmann and Kaliberda (1996), Schneider and Enste (2000), respectively, for discussions of these issues.

[17] Given that what matters for the sustainability of foreign debt is the capacity to earn foreign exchange through exports, we ignore the non-tradables sector.

15

stantial tax arrears in the Russian economy. On the other hand, there are substantial off-budget activities which impose significant costs on the enterprise sector. As a result of these two factors, the actual tax burden differs from what is implied by the Russian tax code. We capture this phenomenon in our model by distinguish between "official" and "unofficial" taxation. For our purposes, "official taxation" is what generates government revenues as they appear in the budget, whereas "unofficial taxation" is anything that benefits the government and imposes a cost on the enterprise sector without showing up in the budget.[18]

The government has a stock of foreign liabilities on which interest is due in the first period, while interest plus principal are to be repaid in the second period. For the first period, the government is assumed to have a given stock of resources Y which are just sufficient to cover the contractual interest payment due. This means that the government is unable in the first period to undertake any investments into e.g. institution building. In the second period, the government uses proceeds from official taxation to service its foreign debt.

We assume that all proceeds from official taxation are allocated to this purpose until the contractual liability is fully paid; that is we do not assume that the government withholds tax revenues when it could use them to pay foreign creditors. However, the government is able to choose how much official tax revenues to collect and can thereby influence its ability to pay foreigners. If proceeds from official taxation exceed contractual debt service payments in the second period, the government can use the balance to consume rents.

We begin our analysis with the optimal investment decision of the enterprise sector. Subsequently we study the optimal tax policy of the government under the assumption that no debt relief occurs. Next, we derive conditions under which debt rescheduling benefits all parties. Finally, we discuss conditions under which debt write-downs would be called for.

In the following, all values are expressed in foreign currency terms. The enterprise sector takes the tax rates set by the government as data and chooses the fraction β of investible funds I to be allocated to domestic investment to maximize profits:

(1) $$\max_{\beta} \ (1-\beta)I(1+r_w)(1-\Delta) + X(\beta I, e)(1-t-b)$$

---

[18] Hence, the tax payments of the model must be understood as averages over profitable and loss-making enterprises (with the former paying taxes at higher rates and the latter paying no taxes and possibly receiving subsidies) and as actual payments made rather than as payments due. Accordingly, we are assuming that the enterprise sector as a whole is a net tax payer.

16

where r_w is the world interest rate, Δ is the inefficiency associated with capital flight (it reflects the costs of concealing illegal capital exports and concealing re-patriated profits from it), e is the real exchange rate defined as the ratio of foreign and Russian price levels divided by the foreign currency price of the ruble (i.e. an increase in e reflects a real depreciation), $X(\beta I, e)$ is the (strictly concave) re-turn to domestic investment, t is the official tax rate, and b is the unofficial tax rate (i.e. the unit cost imposed on the enterprise sector by the government's off-budget activities). The corresponding FOC of the enterprise sector's optimization problem yields

(2) $(1 - t - b) \dfrac{\partial X}{\partial \beta I} = (1 + r_w)(1 - \Delta)$.

The LHS and RHS of (2) give the marginal return to domestic and foreign in-vestment, respectively. From (2) the optimal share of domestic investment can be expressed as an implicit function of the exogenous parameters and the govern-ment's choice variables

(2') $\beta = \beta\left(\underset{-}{r_w}, \underset{+}{\Delta}, \underset{+}{e}; \underset{-}{t}, \underset{-}{b} \right)$,

where higher foreign interest rates, a lower inefficiency of capital flight, a real appreciation, and higher rates of official or unofficial taxation encourage capital flight. In particular, we have

(2") $\dfrac{\partial \beta}{\partial t} = \dfrac{\partial \beta}{\partial b} = \dfrac{\partial X / \partial \beta I}{\partial^2 X / \partial (\beta I)^2 I (1 - t - b)} < 0$.

The government maximizes its net revenues in the second period subject to the optimal allocation of investible resources by the enterprise sector:[19]

(3) $\underset{t,b}{\max}\ \Pi_G = X(\beta I, e)(1 - \bar{\gamma} t)t + X(\beta I, e)(1 - \delta)b - \tilde{F}$ s.t. $\beta = \beta\left(\underset{-}{r_w}, \underset{+}{\Delta}, \underset{+}{e}; \underset{-}{t}, \underset{-}{b} \right)$

where $\bar{\gamma} t$ is the inefficiency associated with a weak institutional environment (it might reflect the fact that the tax system per se is highly distortionary or that tax laws are enforced on a discretionary basis and thereby create distortions etc.), δ is the inefficiency associated with unofficial taxation (think of it as a cost of con-

---

[19] We are assuming here that no debt relief occurs. Hence, in the model, the government uses all its resources in the first period to service its foreign debt. This is why net government revenues in the first period are identically equal to zero and do not enter the maximization problem.

17

cealing bribes), and $\tilde{F}$ is second period debt service. Note that we assume that the efficiency loss due to official taxation is not constant at the margin but rather increases in the rate of taxation t. This takes account of the fact that at higher tax rates the deadweight loss and the incentives to evade taxation will be greater.

We assume that $\delta > \bar{\gamma} t$ for sufficiently low t, i.e. that there exists a threshold below which unofficial taxation is less efficient than official taxation, since otherwise it could never be optimal to use any official taxation at all.[20] Depending on the magnitude of the debt service relative to revenues from official taxation, we need to distinguish two cases for actual debt service $\tilde{F}$

$$\tilde{F} = \begin{cases} X(1-\bar{\gamma}\,t)t & \text{for } X(1-\bar{\gamma}\,t)t \le F(1+r_w) \\ F(1+r_w) & \text{otherwise} \end{cases}$$

where F is the principal of the contracted foreign debt. The former case reflects a situation where the government's official tax revenues are not sufficient to fully service the debt, while in the latter case the debt is serviced as contracted.

Consider first the case in which the government earns official tax revenue sufficient to service fully its foreign debt. Any tax receipts in excess of the debt payment are retained by the government. In this situation, the government is interested in choosing the most efficient form of taxation in order to maximize its revenues. Hence, the first order conditions for an optimum are:

(4)
$$\frac{\partial \Pi_G}{\partial t} = \frac{\partial \beta}{\partial t}\frac{\partial X}{\partial \beta I}I\big[(1-\bar{\gamma}\,t)t+(1-\delta)b\big]+(1-2\bar{\gamma}\,t)X = 0$$

$$\frac{\partial \Pi_G}{\partial b} = \frac{\partial \beta}{\partial b}\frac{\partial X}{\partial \beta I}I\big[(1-\bar{\gamma}\,t)t+(1-\delta)b\big]+(1-\delta)X = 0$$

Equations (4) reflect the fact that increases in the tax rates on the one hand lower the tax base by driving more domestic savings abroad (the first term in (4)), but on the other hand raise government revenue from a given tax base (the second term in (4)). Substitution of one of the two FOCs into the other yields the following expression for the optimal official tax rate[21]

(5) $\qquad t^* = \dfrac{\delta}{2\bar{\gamma}}.$

---

[20] For our argument to go through we require that the marginal deadweight loss of official taxation be an increasing function of the official tax rate. The above is the simplest functional form which satisfies this requirement.

[21] Assuming that $1-2\bar{\gamma}\,t \ne 0$ and $\delta \ne 1$.

18

The optimal official tax rate is an increasing function of the inefficiency of un-official taxation, and a decreasing function of the inefficiency of official taxation. After rearranging, we have

(5') $2\bar{\gamma}\,t^* = \delta$,

which says that, at the optimum, the deadweight losses from official and unof-ficial taxation are equalized at the margin, such that for a given aggregate tax rate $t+b$ facing the enterprise sector, a shift between official and unofficial taxation cannot reduce the aggregate deadweight loss.

Later on we will use the fact that official and unofficial taxation are substitutes, i.e.

(6)
$$\frac{\partial^2 \Pi_G}{\partial t \partial b} = \left[\frac{\partial^2 X}{\partial(\beta I)^2}I\left(\frac{\partial \beta}{\partial t}\right)^2 + \frac{\partial X}{\partial \beta I}\frac{\partial^2 \beta}{\partial t^2}\right]\left[(1-\bar{\gamma}\,t)t + (1-\delta)b\right]I$$
$$+\frac{\partial X}{\partial \beta I}I\frac{\partial \beta}{\partial t}(1-2\bar{\gamma}\,t+1-\delta) < 0$$
,

where we have used (2"). 22

Next, we consider the situation in which a solution with $X(1-\bar{\gamma}\,t^*)t^* > F(1+r_w)$ does not exist. In this case, any official tax revenues the government may collect ends up being paid out to foreign creditors and hence does not benefit the government. At the same time, official taxation discourages investment in the domestic economy and thereby reduces government revenue from unofficial taxation. Therefore, for $X(1-\bar{\gamma}\,t^*)t^* \leq F(1+r_w)$, it is optimal for the government not to subject any of the returns to domestic investment to official taxation, i.e. $t=0$. With no revenues from official taxation, the government is unable to service its foreign debt in the second period and hence defaults on its foreign debt; foreign creditors do not receive any payment in the second period in this case. The government instead maximizes

(7) $\Pi_G\big|_{t=0} = X(I\beta',e)b(1-\delta)$,

where β' indicates the enterprise sector's optimal response to unofficial taxation given that the official tax rate is zero. This yields the first order condition

(8) $\dfrac{\partial \Pi_G}{\partial b} = \dfrac{\partial \beta'}{\partial b}\dfrac{\partial X}{\partial \beta I}I(1-\delta)b + (1-\delta)X = 0$.

---

22 Assuming that the third derivative of the production function X is non-positive.

19

From (6), i.e. from the substitutability of official and unofficial taxation, we know that with official taxation constrained to zero, the optimal unofficial tax rate will be higher than with positive official taxation. Moreover, from (5') we know that the optimal unofficial tax rate will now be lower than the sum of official and unofficial tax rates before.[23] It follows that the aggregate tax rate facing the enterprise sector will be lower, capital flight will be lower, and export revenues (the tax base) will be higher. However, the government's gross revenues will still be lower than before, as these were at a maximum in the first scenario where the official tax rate was not constrained to zero.

Finally, it should be noted that even in the case where the government could generate funds sufficient to repay its foreign creditors, it may decide to default. This is because the tax base is larger under default. It may therefore be in the interest of the government to use only unofficial taxation even if the condition $X(1-\bar{\gamma}t^*)t^* > F(1+r_w)$ holds. I.e. even if by maximizing gross revenue, the government was able to fully service its foreign debt and to retain some official tax revenues, its net revenues may still be larger if it taxes only unofficially and defaults on its foreign debt. Thus the necessary and sufficient condition for default is:

$$(9) \qquad X(\beta^* \; 1)\left[(1-\bar{\gamma}\, t^*)t^* + (1-\delta)b^*\right] - F(1+r_w) \le X(\beta^{'} \; 1)(1-\delta)b',$$

where the asterixes indicate optimal solutions to (4) and (2), and the primes indicate optimal solutions to (8) and to (2) for $t = 0$.

If the situation is characterized by (9), debt service is not in the interest of the government. Hence foreign creditors will have to offer some incentive to the government in order to be able to recover their loans. One possible way of doing so is to create conditions that encourage the government to invest in institution building, so that official taxation becomes more efficient relative to unofficial taxation.

The following paragraphs show how debt restructuring can benefit both the government and the foreign creditors by encouraging institution building. Debt restructuring, in turn, can take two forms: rescheduling, i.e. a change in the time

---

23 Before, the positive effects of marginally raising the sum of the two tax rates were just compensated for by the negative effects. Hence, the net marginal effect on net government revenue was zero. Given that setting the unofficial tax rate at the previous sum of official and unofficial tax rates would result in a larger deadweight loss (since before the structure of official and unofficial tax rates minimized the deadweight loss for a given aggregate tax rate), the negative effects of raising the unofficial tax rates will start to dominate the positive effects before the previous level of aggregate taxation is reached.

20

structure of payments, and write-downs, i.e. reductions in the nominal value of the debt.

Debt rescheduling, i.e. allowing the government to pay part of its first period obligation only in the second period, can raise the overall amount received by foreign creditors if the government uses the additional liquidity available in the first period to invest into institution building. Institution building, in turn, results in domestic investment becoming more attractive for enterprises, and the tax base expanding for the second period, so that the government can pay more in the second period. From the point of view of the government, this can make sense as well, if institution building raises the tax base in the second period sufficiently for government revenues net of debt service to be higher than without institution building and debt rescheduling.

Debt write-offs can be structured such that they also provide liquidity relief and, in addition, reduce the amount to be repaid to creditors in the second period. They can also lead to higher revenues for both creditors and government by encouraging more official taxation of a given return stream.

21

3.2 Debt Restructuring and Debt Write-Off

As indicated above, we assume that the initial first period stock of government resources, Y, is just sufficient to cover the contractual value of first period debt service payments, $r_w F$, so that no resources are left for institution building.

Now suppose, it takes an investment of G to lower the inefficiency of domestic taxation from $\bar{\gamma}$ to γ. Then additional liquidity can be provided to the government in the first period by rescheduling foreign debt such that in the first period the government has to pay only $r_w F - G$ and in the second period its liability becomes $(1 + r_w)(F + G)$. This liquidity could be used to invest into institution building.

Debt rescheduling has two countervailing effects. On the one hand, it enables institution building in the first period and thereby provides the opportunity to reduce the deadweight loss of official taxation, thereby growing the 'pie' available to be shared between the government and foreign creditors. On the other hand, debt rescheduling raises the debt burden in the second period, thereby making default more attractive.

By assumption, investment into institution building would lower the deadweight loss from official taxation. This would have two effects. First, it would make official taxation more attractive relative to unofficial taxation (a "substitution effect"). Second, it would enable the government to raise a given amount of revenue with lower tax rates *provided the government does not rely exclusively on unofficial taxation*. This "income effect" translates into a lower tax burden for enterprises overall and thus reduces capital flight and increases the tax base. Given that in the default scenario, the government would not use official taxation without debt rescheduling, it is critical that the substitution effect be sufficiently large to induce the government to switch to official taxation.

Assuming that additional liquidity could alternatively be invested abroad on the same terms as the private sector can invest abroad, debt rescheduling will induce government investment into institution building and will induce a switch from unofficial to official taxation, iff

(10)
$$X^*(\gamma)\left[(1 - \underline{\gamma}\, t^*(\gamma))t^*(\gamma) + (1 - \delta)b^*(\gamma)\right] - (F + G)(1 + r_w)$$
$$> X'(1 - \delta)b' + G(1 + r_w)(1 - \Delta)$$

i.e. if the net revenue from raising both official and unofficial taxation and servicing the debt after investing into institution building exceeds the revenue

22

from not investing into institution building, sticking with unofficial taxation and defaulting on the debt. In view of the fact that the RHS of (10) exceeds the RHS of (9), debt rescheduling thus makes sense if the effect of the initial investment G on the deadweight loss of official taxation $\bar{\gamma} - \underline{\gamma}$ is sufficiently large, and/ or if the effect of the reduced official deadweight loss on the optimal tax rates is sufficiently large, and/ or if the effect of the change in tax rates on the tax base is sufficiently large.

The amount of liquidity relief to be granted by rescheduling is obviously limited at the amount due in the first period. If condition (10) above is not met, debt rescheduling is not a viable course of action. However, debt reduction might still lead to an improvement for both parties. If a debt write-down is granted in the first period (i.e. G and F is (partially) written off rather than being rolled over to the second period), then it does encourage institution building (which a write-down only in the second period would not). In addition, a write-down relaxes the above condition (10) because it not only provides liquidity relief but also reduced the amount of funds to be transferred in the second period which becomes $(1 + r_w)(F - d)$ where d is the amount of debt forgiven. Hence, if rescheduling is insufficient to satisfy the above condition, a partial write-down may be called for.

4   Which Way Out of the Crisis?

The severe real and financial crisis of 1998 has left Russia with a severely aggravated foreign debt problem. Traditional debt indicators have worsened, the country lacks access to international capital markets, negotiations with foreign creditors are protracted, the fiscal situation of the government has yet to improve, and capital flight continues. Finding a way out of this gridlock has seemed difficult: Russian firms are unwilling to invest domestically unless the government ensures property rights, foreign creditors are unwilling to lend new funds unless the government has proven its ability to reform, and the government procrastinates reforms as it fears their short-term costs.

As regards the sustainability of Russia's foreign debt situation, the paper has focused on the fact that the bulk of the foreign debt is owed by the government. At the same time, Russia's fiscal situation is plagued by the continued coexistence of an official system of taxation and a large, opaque system of unofficial taxation and subsidization. These unofficial fiscal activities both contribute to and reflect the deep-rooting institutional deficiencies of the Russian economy

23

which eventually are a heritage from central planning. Moreover, the importance of the unofficial fiscal system in an extremely weak institutional environment is the main distinguishing feature of Russia in comparison to earlier debt restructuring episodes.

This paper has presented a two-period model of the Russian debt problem, focusing in particular on the decision of the government to switch from unofficial to official means of taxation. For the government, the basic trade-off is between the efficiency losses due to unofficial taxation and the fact that unofficial tax revenues can be hidden away from foreign creditors. In other words, enhancing the efficiency of the official tax system can improve the incentives of the government to switch from unofficial to official taxation. One way to achieve a greater efficiency of the official tax system is to invest into institution building in the first period. Foreign creditors can contribute to this by rescheduling debt or even by granting debt relief.

Foreign creditors, in turn, face the trade-off that debt restructuring affords the government with additional resources that can be spent on institution building while, at the same time, current claims are forgone. The recent decision of the London Club to write off and restructure Russia's inherited debt will thus benefit the creditors only if investment into institution building is sufficiently efficient. Technical assistance might be used to achieve this goal. Additionally, foreign creditors can influence the decision of the government by making default more costly through, for instance, cross-default clauses on the renegotiated debt.

In this paper, the Russian enterprise sector has been modeled in a fairly stylized way. Most importantly, the tradables and the non-tradables sector have not been distinguished. Yet, an extension would be straight forward. In such a more realistic setting, the success of debt relief would also depend upon the incentives of the government to divert resources from the non-tradables to the tradables sector. Empirical estimates of Russia's trade account have shown the importance of oil price and real exchange rate developments for Russia's net exports and thus its debt servicing potential. Since the development of oil prices must be taken as exogenous by the Russian policymakers, ensuring the (price) competitiveness of domestic producers by an appropriate exchange rate policy thus enhanced Russia's ability to service its foreign debt. This requires, most importantly, a coordination of monetary, fiscal, and institutional reforms with exchange rate policies. If such a coordination is not achieved, competitiveness erodes, and a new crisis becomes all the more likely. In addition to institution building, sound and consistent macroeconomic policies are thus the key for successful debt restructuring.

24

5 References

Aslund, A. (1998) Russia's Financial Crises: Cuases and Possible Remedies. *Post-Soviet Geography and Economics* 39(6): 309-328.

Banerjee, A., J.J. Dolado, and R. Mestre (1992). On Some Simple Tests for Cointegration: The Cost of Simplicity. Discussion Paper of the Institute of Economics at Aarhus University. Aarhus.

Bowe, M., and J.W. Dean (1997). Has the Market Solved the Sovereign-Debt Crisis? *Princeton Studies in International Finance* 83. August. Princeton. New Jersey.

Brücker, H. (1996). Rußlands Auslandsverbindlichkeiten nach der langfristigen Umschuldung. Deutsches Institut für Wirtschaftsforschung. *Wochenbericht* 28/96: 470–478.

Buch, C.M., and R.P.Heinrich (1998). Twin Crises and the Intermediary Role of Banks. *International Journal of Finance and Economics* 4: 313–323.

— (1999). Handling Banking Crises — The Case of Russia. *Economic Systems* 23(4): 349–380.

Bureau of Economic Analysis Foundation (BEA) (1999). The Russian Economy at the Turn of the Millenium: Current Issues and Prospects of Development. *Information Bulletin* 15. June. Moscow.

Central Bank of the Russian Federation (CBR) (1999). Balance of Payments of the Russian Federation. http://www.cbr.ru. Stand: 4.10.1999. Moscow

Cline, W. (1995). International Debt Reexamined. Institute for International Economics. Washington DC.

Deutsches Institut für Wirtschaftsforschung (Berlin), Institut für Weltwirtschaft an der Universität Kiel und Institut für Wirtschaftsforschung (Halle) (DIW et al.) (1998). Die wirtschaftliche Lage Rußlands — Krise offenbart Fehler der Wirtschaftspolitik. Kieler Diskussionsbeiträge 330/331. Institut für Weltwirtschaft, Kiel. Published also as *Wochenbericht* 51(98) of the DIW and in Forschungsreihe 10/98 of the IWH.

Deutsches Institut für Wirtschaftsforschung, (DIW), Institut für Weltwirtschaft an der Universität Kiel (2000): Russische Wirtschaftspolitik setzt auf Investitionen. Kieler Diskussionsbeiträge 360. Institut für Weltwirtschaft, Kiel. Published also as Wochenbericht 15(00) of the DIW

Finansowie Izwestija. Various Issues. Moscow.

Flood, R.P., and P.M. Garber (1984). Collapsing Exchange-Rate Regimes. Some linear examples. *Journal of International Economics* 17: 1–13.

25

Goldfajn, I., and R.O. Valdés (1997). Capital Flows and the Twin Crises: The Role of Liquidity. International Monetary Fund. Working Paper 97/87. Washington DC.

Goldman Sachs Economics (2000). Daily News and Views – New European Markets, Middle East and South Africa. 14.2.2000. Moscow.

Goskomstat (1996). Social'no-ekonomiceskoe polozenie Rossii. Jan'var-avgust 1995g. Moscow. 1996.

— Social'no-ekonomicheskoe polozenie Rossii. Various issues. Moscow.

Handelsblatt (2000). Düsseldorf.

International Monetary Fund (IMF) (1993). Restructuring of Commercial Bank Debt by Developing Countries: Lessons from Recent Experience. Collyns, C., and M. El-Erian. IMF Paper on Policy Analysis and Assessment. PPAA/93/7. Washington DC.

— (1997). Debt Relief for Low-Income Countries and the HIPC Initiative. A.R. Boot, and K. Thugge. Working Paper WP/97/24. Washington DC.

— (1999a). International Financial Statistics. Washington DC.

— (1999b). Russia — Recent Economic Developments. Washington DC.

Johnson, S., D. Kaufmann, and A. Sljajfer (1997). The Unofficial Economy in Transition. *The Brookings Paper on Economic Activity*: 159-239.

Kaufmann, D., and A. Kaliberda (1996). Integrating the Unofficial Economy into the Dynamics of Post-Socialist Economies: A Framework of Analysis and Evidence. Policy Research Working Paper. 1691. The World Bank. Washington DC.

Krugman, P. (1989a). Private Capital Flows to Problem Debtors. In: Developing Country Debt and Economic Performance. Vol. I. ed. by J. Sachs. A NBER Project Report. Chicago: 299–330.

— (1989b). Market Based Debt Reduction Schemes. In: Frenkel J.A. et al.: *Analytical Issues in Debt*. Washington: 258–278.

Leijonhufvurd, A., and Rühl, C. (1997) Russian Dilemmas. EBRD Working Paper No. 21, European Bank for Reconstruction and Development, London.

Pagano, M. (1993). Financial Markets and Growth. *European Economic Review* 37(4): 613–622.

Russian-European Centre for Economic Policy (RECEP) (1999). Russian Economic Trends. Monthly Update. December. Moscow.

Russian-European Centre for Economic Policy (RECEP) (2000). Russian Economic Trends. Monthly Update. December. Moscow.

26

Radio Free Europe / Radio Liberty (RFE/RL). Newsline. Various Issues. Prague.

Schneider, F., and D. Enste (2000). Shadow Economies Around the World. Size, Causes and Consequences. International Monetary Fund. Working Paper. WP/00/26.

Schrooten, M. (2000). *Geld, Banken und Staat in Sozialismus und Transformation. Vom Zusammenbruch der Sowjetunion zur anhaltenden Finanzkrise in der Russischen Föderation.* Berlin.

United Nations Centre on Transnational Corporations (UNCTC) (1989). International Debt Restructuring: Substantive Issues and Techniques. Advisory Studies. Series B. No. 4. New York.

Ukaz Presidenta Rossijkoj Federacii (1996): O predostavlenii predprijatijam i organisacjam otcpocki po uplate zadolzenosti po nalogam, penjam i strafam za naruszenie nalogovo zakonodatel'stva, obrazovavszejcja do 1 janvarja 1996g. No. 65.

Voprosi Ekonomiki (1994). No. 1, Moscow.

Vnesheconombank (1999). Annual Report 1998. Moscow.

World Bank (1992-93). World Debt Tables 1992-93. External Finance for Developing Countries. Volume I. Analysis and Summary Table. Washington DC.

World Bank (1999a). Global Development Finance. Washington DC.

World Bank (1999b). Dismantling Russia's Nonpayment System: Creating Conditions for Growth. A Report by The World Bank. Washington D.C. September.

Table 1 — Types of Hidden Economic Activities

	Corruption	Shadow Economy	Unofficial Economy
Definition	Use of public power for private benefit	Unreported economic activities of the private sector on cash basis	Non-cash transactions in both, the private and the public sectors as well as between them
Typical forms	Bribes, unreported cash payments	Unreported income/wages on a cash basis	Barter trade, tax arrears, tax exemptions, non-payment of the budget sphere, the abuse of the legal framework for unreported fiscal activities
Incentive	Tax evasion Cost reduction	Tax evasion Tax compliance	Broadening of unreported budget revenues/fiscal activities; quasi-fiscal activities Economic activity within a non-cash payment system Tax reduction

28

Table 2 — *Debt Indicators: An International Comparison (in percents) 1992–1998*

	Debt / Exports	Debt / GNP	Debt service / Exports	Interest / Exports	Interest / GNP	International reserves / Debt	International reserves / Imports (months)	Short-term credits / Debt	Concessional credits / Debt	Multilateral credits / Debt
Russian Federation										
1992	143.0	18.6	2.5	0.6	0.1	..	..	16.7	1.3	0.7
1993	169.8	29.1	3.3	1.1	0.2	8.8	1.9	7.4	30.2	1.1
1994	156.7	37.9	4.4	1.6	0.4	5.9	1.3	8.1	27.2	1.3
1995	129.6	35.5	6.3	3.0	0.8	15.0	2.5	8.6	18.3	1.6
1996	119.5	29.7	6.7	3.9	1.0	13.0	2.0	9.7	19.8	2.2
1997	121.0	26.2	6.5	4.9	1.1	14.1	2.1	4.9	20.6	4.2
1998*	209.3	68.3	8.8	4.9	1.5	6.6	1.4	4.0		
Developing Countries										
1992	162.6	36.5	16.6	6.8	1.5	18.5	3.3	19.0	21.7	14.1
1993	167.2	38.4	16.4	6.4	1.5	20.6	3.7	19.0	22.6	13.8
1994	161.2	40.0	16.1	6.4	1.6	21.8	3.9	18.5	21.9	13.8
1995	142.7	38.2	16.0	6.7	1.8	25.1	4.0	19.8	20.2	13.4
1996	133.4	35.8	16.6	6.4	1.7	27.9	4.2	20.2	19.2	12.8
1997	129.0	34.9	17.0	6.1	1.6	28.1	4.1	20.0	17.2	12.5
1998*	146.2	37.3	17.6	7.4	1.9	28.4	4.6	16.7	17.0	12.9
Europe and Central Asia										
1992	138.0	25.3	12.1	5.0	0.9	11.6	1.8	16.8	9.0	7.6
1993	146.2	32.1	9.9	4.3	0.9	13.5	2.1	13.9	17.9	6.7
1994	136.0	38.8	12.0	4.2	1.2	15.2	2.5	11.6	16.5	7.2
1995	115.3	36.8	12.2	4.8	1.5	25.8	3.4	13.2	12.7	7.4
1996	108.7	34.7	11.5	4.7	1.5	25.3	3.1	14.9	12.6	7.3
1997	108.0	33.8	11.5	4.7	1.5	25.7	3.1	15.2	11.6	7.6
1998*	126.7	35.9	13.3	6.0	1.7	23.2	3.2	14.6	10.9	7.3

* Preliminary. Recent data on the Russian Federation are not exactly comparable with the previous ones and have been calculated based on the data from the IMF and the Central Bank of Russia. Instead of GNP, GDP has been used. The total debt - and interest service include only credits in foreign currency. Arrears on principal are included.

Sources: World Bank (1999a), IMF (1999a, 1999b), CBR (1999), own calculations.

Table 3 — Russian Federation: External Debt, 1994–1998 (in billions of U.S. dollars)[a]

	1994	1995	1996	1997	1998
I. Sovereign Debt					
A. *Russian-era foreign currency debt*	11.3	17.4	27.7	35.6	55.4
(post 1.1.1992)					
Medium and long term	...	...	...	...	55.4
Multilateral Creditors	5.4	11.4	15.3	18.7	26.0
IMF	4.2	9.6	12.5	13.2	19.4
World Bank	0.6	1.5	2.6	5.3	6.4
Other	0.6	0.3	0.2	0.2	0.2
Official creditors[b]	5.9	6.0	7.9	7.6	9.7
Eurobonds	0.0	0.0	1.0	4.5	16.0
Minfin Bonds (VI and VII)	0.0	0.0	3.5	3.5	3.5
Commercial Creditors (includes financial institutions)	0.0	0.0	0.0	1.3	0.2
Short term	...	...	...	...	0.0
B. *Soviet-era foreign currency debt*	116.2	110.6	108.4	99.0	102.8
(pre 1.1.1992)					
Medium and long term	...	...	...	...	102.8
Multilateral Creditors	0.0	0.0	0.0	0.0	0.0
Official creditors[b]	69.9	62.6	61.9	56.9	59.5
Paris Club	39.6	41.6	42.3	37.6	40.0
of which: arrears	...	...	...	...	0.8
COMECON	25.7	16.6	15.4	14.9	14.7
of which: arrears	...	...	...	...	0.0
Other, including non-Paris Club bilateral	4.6	4.4	4.2	4.4	4.7
of which: arrears	...	...	...	...	4.0
Commercial creditors	36.0	38.3	37.8	33.9	35.2
Financial institutions	31.1	33.0	32.5	29.7	31.2
of which: arrears	...	...	...	...	2.1
Other[c]	4.9	5.3	5.3	4.2	4.1
of which: arrears	...	...	...	...	4.1
Eurobonds	1.7	1.1	0.1	0.1	0.0
Credits contracted by entities other than VEB	1.0	1.0	1.0	0.5	0.5
Minfin Binds (Minfins III, IV, and V)	7.6	7.6	7.6	7.6	7.6
of which: arrears	0.0	0.0	0.0	0.0	0.0
Short term	...	...	...	...	0.0
C. *Total sovereign foreign currency debt*	127.5	128.0	136.1	134.6	158.2
(= A + B)					
D. *Total sovereign debt to nonresidents*	...	...	...	...	152.4
(= C - E - F + G)					
E. *Residents' Minfin bonds[d]*	...	...	...	...	7.3
F. *Residents' Eurobonds[e]*	...	...	...	...	3.7
G. *Nonresidents' GKOs/OFZs (ruble denominated)[f]*	...	...	...	...	5.2

Table 3 continues ...

30

Table 3 (continued)

	1994	1995	1996	1997	1998
II. Nonsovereign Debt					
Local governments	...	...	...	1.1	2.2
Medium and long term	...	...	...	1.1	1.9
of which: Eurobonds	0.0	0.0	0.0	0.9	1.4
Short term	...	...	...	...	0.3
Banks[g]	2.6	5.2	9.2	19.2	9.9
Medium and long term	...	...	...	...	2.8
Short term	...	...	...	...	7.1
Nonbank corporations (including arrears)	...	...	...	13.6	19.6
H. Total	...	...	...	...	*31.7*
III. Total External Debt (to nonresidents)	...	...	...	...	184.0
(= D + H)					
Memorandum items					
Sovereign arrears	...	...	...	...	10.9

a) Foreign currency values of outstanding external debt have been converted into U.S. dollars at the relevant market exchange rate prevailing at the respective date indicated. — b) Includes government to government creditors and official export credits. — c) Subject to reconciliation. — d) Estimated by the authorities at 60 percent of outstanding issues. e) — Applies only to Eurobonds issued in July 1998, in the context of the GKO-Eurobond exchange. Data on nonresident holdings of other Eurobond issues are not available. — f) Equivalent to Rub 76 billion, valued at the end-1998 exchange rate. The ruble amount is the discounted amount that resulted after the GKO/OFZ conversion. Also includes Rub 75 billion of OFZs not covered by the GKO/OFZ conversion. — g) Figures for 1994-97 include equity. At end-1998 such equity amounted to about US-dollar 0.5 billion.

Source: IMF (1999b).

31

Table 4 —   *Russian Federation: Foreign Currency Debt Service, 1994-1998
(in billions of U.S. dollars)*

	1994	1995	1996	1997	1998	1999	2000	2001	2002	2003	2004	2005
					Debt service due[a]							
Total	18.8	19.2	17.9	11.8	13.0	17.1	15.2	14.6	14.6	20.5	14.7	15.9
Principal	14.0	12.7	11.7	5.8	5.8	8.0	6.9	6.6	6.9	13.2	8.0	9.7
Russian-era debt	2.1	2.3	1.6	1.5	3.3	4.8	5.2	5.3	5.1	7.6	5.6	6.7
Soviet-era debt	11.9	10.4	10.1	4.3	2.5	3.2	1.7	1.3	1.8	5.6	2.4	3.0
Interest	4.8	6.5	6.3	5.9	7.3	9.0	8.3	8.0	7.7	7.3	6.7	6.3
Russian-era debt	0.7	0.9	1.0	1.4	2.3	3.3	3.2	2.9	2.6	2.3	2.0	1.7
Soviet-era debt	4.1	5.6	5.3	4.5	5.0	5.7	5.1	5.1	5.1	5.0	4.7	4.6
					Debt service paid							
Total	3.7	6.4	6.9	5.9	7.8	...	...	...	...	...	...	...
Principal	2.3	3.3	2.9	1.7	3.5	...	...	...	...	...	...	...
Russian-era debt	2.1	2.3	1.6	1.5	3.3	...	...	...	...	...	...	...
Soviet-era debt	0.2	1.0	1.3	0.1	0.2	...	...	...	...	...	...	...
Interest	1.4	3.1	4.1	4.2	4.3	...	...	...	...	...	...	...
Russian-era debt	0.7	0.9	1.0	1.4	2.2	...	...	...	...	...	...	...
Soviet-era debt	0.7	2.1	3.1	2.8	2.1	...	...	...	...	...	...	...
					Debt service paid (in percent of debt service due)							
Total	19.5	33.4	38.6	50.1	59.7	...	...	...	...	...	...	...
Principal	16.2	26.3	24.5	28.8	60.6	...	...	...	...	...	...	...
Interest	29.0	47.4	64.9	71.1	59.0	...	...	...	...	...	...	...

a) Does not take debt rescheduling agreements with the London Club of February 2000 into account.

Sources: IMF (1999b), BEA (1999), own calculations.

32

Table 5 —   Timetable of the Debt Rescheduling Agreements

28.10.1991	"Memorandum of Understanding on the Debt to Foreign Creditors of the Union of Soviet Socialist Republics and its Successors"
2.4.1993	Debt rescheduling agreement with the Paris Club: Rescheduling of the debts due by 31.12.1993 with a cutoff date 1.1.1991 and a repayment period of over one year. Repayment: 6 year grace period followed by ten semi-annual installments between 1999 and 2003; Extension for credit taken on after 1.1.1991 and for credit with a repayment period of under one year; Capitalization of 60% of interest due by 1993; Volume of rescheduled debt: ca. 14.5 billion US-dollar; Financial obligation for 1993: almost US-dollar 2 billion; Terms and conditions: Conclusion of an agreement with the IMF by 1.10.1993
	Declaration by the government of the Russian Federation on the acceptance of sole responsibility for the external liabilities and assets of the former USSR
4.6.1993	Debt rescheduling agreement with the London Club: Rescheduling of the debts contracted before 1.1.1991 of the amount of US-dollar 24 billion; Repayment: 15-year maturity including 5 year grace; Extension for credit taken on after 1.1.1991 and for credit with a repayment period of under one year; Capitalization of 40% of interest due by 1994 (along with interest payable from previous agreement); Financial obligation for 1994: ca. US-dollar 3 billion; Terms and conditions: Fulfillment of the conditions of the IMF agreement from 20.4.1994
3.6.1995	Debt rescheduling agreement with the Paris Club: Rescheduling of the debts due by 1994 with a repayment period of over one year. Repayment after 3 year grace period followed by 26 semi-annual installments from 1998 to 2011; Extension for credit taken on after 1.1.1991 and for credit with a repayment period of under one year; Capitalization of ca. 35% of the interest payable on the previous agreement; Volume of rescheduled debt: ca. 6.4 billion US-dollar; Financial obligation for 1995: ca. US-dollar 3.9 billion; Terms and conditions: Fulfillment of the conditions of the IMF agreement from 11.4.1994
16.11.1995	Agreement in principle with the London Club for a comprehensive rescheduling of the debt of the former Soviet Union: Rescheduling of debt of over ca. US-dollar 25.5 billion, repayment after 7 year grace period from 2002 to 2015; Payment of ca. US-dollar 2 billion in accrued interest of ca. US-dollar 7 billion; Capitalization of part of the interest due during the first six years; Volume of rescheduled debt: US-dollar 32.5 billion
15.4.1996	Long-term debt rescheduling agreement with the Paris Club: Rescheduling of debt due between 1996 and 1998 as well as the agreed repayment and interest payment from the previous agreements; Repayment of the main part in 20 years with 6 year grace period in gradually rising annuities, Repayment of the rest in 25 years with 6 years grace period; Capitalization of part of the interest due on 1996-1998 credit, no capitalization of the interest from the agreements Russia I-III; Volume of rescheduled debt: US-dollar 40.2 billion; Financial obligations for 1996: ca. US-dollar 9.5 billion; Terms and conditions: Fulfillment of the conditions of the agreement reached with the IMF on 27.3.1996

Table 5 continues ...

33

Table 5 (continued)

17.8.1998	Announcement by the government of the Russian Federation of a unilateral re-structuring of the ruble-denominated public debt (GKO/Offers); Restructuring of US-dollar 17.2 billion Treasury bills held by non-residents was proposed in November 1998; Introduction of temporary restrictions on capital account foreign exchange operations by the residents of the Russian Federation by proclaiming a 90-day moratorium (i) on repayment of financial credits extended by the nonresidents to residents, (ii) on insurance payments on the credits backed up with the pledged securities, (iii) on forward exchange contracts; by prohibiting the non-residents to invest in ruble assets with maturities of one year or less; and by proposing legislative changes to tighten control over the outflow of foreign exchange resources abroad. The moratorium did not apply to repayments on the service of the foreign government debt and to residents' current account operations; A switch to a floating exchange rate policy
1.8.1999	Agreement with the Paris Club: Rescheduling of ca. US-dollar 8 billion of payments due between 1999 and 2000 over 15-20 years; Financial obligation for 1999-2000: ca. US-dollar 600 million
11.2.2000	Agreement (verbal) with the London Club: A write-off of 37.5% of PRINs face-value, 33% of IANs restructured into a 30 year maturity eurobond with 7 year grace period, semi-annual coupons of 2.25% (annual) and 2.5% in year 1, 5% in years 2-7, 7.5% thereafter. The eurobond will be a Russian sovereign one, pari passu with, and cross-defaultable into, other post-Soviet era Eurobonds. The past due interest is to be restructured into a 10 year eurobond, with 9.5% initial payment, then a 6 year grace period and constant coupons of 8.25%; Exact amortization of principal on both bonds yet not released; The exchange is likely to be offered in the second quarter of 2000, and interest will be accrued on the old bonds till March 31, making that the likely start date of the new bond

Sources: Brücker (1996), World Bank (1992-93), World Bank (1999a), Goldman Sachs (2000), updated by the authors.

34

Table 6 — Determinants of Russia's Current Account

Explanatory variables	Dependent variable: Current account (CA_t)	
Constant	19.53***	38.10***
	(2.98)	(5.04)
	Error-correction term:	
Log CA (−1)	−0.39***	−0.59**
	(−5.16)	(−7.00)
Log IP (−1)	−12.65***	−17.53***
	(−3.19)	(−5.98)
Log RER (−1)	1.86***	2.87***
	(3.76)	(7.66)
Log $OILPRICE$ (−1)		2.01***
		(5.05)
	Short-run effects:	
Dlog IP (−1)		−4.95***
		(−2.89)
Dlog RER (−1)	−1.45	−2.84***
	(−1.45)	(−2.96)
Dlog RER (−2)	−1.27	−1.91**
	(−1.31)	(−2.17)
$\bar{R}^2$	0.35	0.48
White-test (prob.)	0.12	0.06*
Jarque Bera (prob.)	0.92	0.73
Time period	1994:1–99:9 (n = 69)	1994:1–99:9 (n = 69)

t-values in brackets, ***(**,*) = significant at the 1 (5, 10) percent level. For the long-run coefficients in the error-correction equation, *t*-values were obtained from the Bewley-transformed estimation of equation (1). t-value for the loading coefficient of the error-correction term were taken from Banerjee et al. (1992). A dummy variable (not reported) for January 1998 was used to ensure normal distribution of the residuals and to correct for heteroskedasticity. Tests on autocorrelation of a degree of up to the 12th order provided no evidence for autocorrelation in the residuals.

Sources: own calculations.

35

Table 7 — Consolidated Budget

	in % of total revenues/total expenditure								in % of GDP							
	1992[1]	1993	1994	1995	1996	1997	1998	1999	1992[1]	1993	1994	1995	1996	1997	1998	1999
Revenues, total	100	100	100	100	100	100	100	100	28.0	29.0	29.0	26.1	24.8	23.5	24.5	26.8
Profit taxes	29.4	33.8	27.5	27.0	17.3	15.8	14.7	18.4	8.2	9.8	8.0	7.0	4.3	3.7	3.6	4.9
Personal income taxes	8.1	8.8	9.9	8.4	10.1	11.6	10.8	9.8	2.3	2.6	2.9	2.2	2.5	2.7	2.7	2.6
Excises	4.0	3.6	4.2	5.6	9.6	10.3	10.3	9.1	1.1	1.0	1.2	1.5	2.4	2.4	2.5	2.4
VAT	37.5	22.5	21.0	22.0	25.8	26.5	23.8	24.0	10.5	6.5	6.1	5.7	6.4	6.2	5.8	6.4
Tax on international trade and transactions	8.8	4.7	10.8	4.6	3.0	1.1	2.4	2.9	2.5	1.4	3.1	1.2	0.7	0.3	0.6	0.8
Capital revenues	...	...	...	...	...	2.0	2.0	1.9	...	...	...	...	...	0.5	0.5	0.5
Privatization	...	...	...	...	...	1.8	2.7	...	...	...	...	...	...	0.4	0.7	...
Budgetary funds	...	...	...	...	...	...	...	8.1	...	...	...	...	...	...	...	2.2
Other	12.2	26.6	26.6	32.3	34.2	30.9	33.3	26.0	3.4	7.7	7.7	8.4	8.5	7.3	8.2	6.9
Expenditures, total	100	100	100	100	100	100	100	100	31.4	33.6	38.5	29.4	28.9	28.6	28.0	28.0
Economy	34.5	28.1	27.0	...	...	...	...	...	10.8	9.4	10.4	...	...	...	...	...
Industry, Energy, Construction																
Agriculture, fishing	...	...	...	7.4	6.0	4.6	2.9	2.5	...	...	...	2.2	1.7	1.3	0.8	0.7
Transport	...	...	...	4.2	3.9	3.4	2.6	2.9	...	...	...	1.2	1.1	3.4	0.7	0.8
Communication	...	...	...	2.7	...	2.8	2.5	2.1	...	...	...	0.8	...	0.8	0.7	0.6
Socio-cultural purposes	23.2	24.9	23.5	26.0	28.9	34.0	31.7	29.2	7.3	8.4	9.0	7.7	8.4	9.7	8.9	8.2
Education	...	...	...	11.6	...	...	...	...	...	...	...	3.4	...	...	...	...
Health	...	...	...	8.3	...	...	...	...	...	...	...	2.4	...	...	...	...
Social security	...	...	...	4.2	...	...	...	...	...	...	...	1.2	...	...	...	...
Defense	14.3	12.5	11.9	9.8	9.8	10.2	7.5	9.3	4.5	4.2	4.6	2.9	2.8	2.9	2.1	2.6
Administration, law enforcement	5.9	7.3	7.9	7.7	...	10.3	9.6	9.7	1.8	2.4	3.0	2.3	...	2.9	2.7	2.7
International trade	7.0	4.8	2.1	4.4	4.1	...	...	...	2.2	1.6	0.8	1.3	1.2	...	...	...
Debt service	...	...	...	5.1	6.6	6.2	14.2	13.0	...	...	...	1.5	1.9	1.8	4.0	3.6
Environment protection	...	...	...	...	...	0.5	0.4	0.4	...	...	...	...	...	0.2	0.1	0.1
Budgetary funds	...	...	...	...	...	...	...	7.4	...	...	...	...	...	...	...	2.1
Other	15.2	22.5	27.5	8.6	40.9	28.0	28.5	23.6	4.8	7.6	10.6	2.5	11.8	5.6	8.0	6.6
Overall balance in % of Expenditure/GDP	-10.8	-13.8	-24.5	-11.2	-14.4	-18.0	-14.0	-4.3	-3.4	-4.6	-9.4	-3.3	-4.2	-5.1	-3.5	-1.2

[1] In 1992 the volume of unreported fiscal activities was extraordinary high. Voprosy Ekonomiki (1994: 42).

Sources: Goskomstat (various issues), own calculations.

Graph 1 —   *Simulation of a 1-percent Real Devaluation*

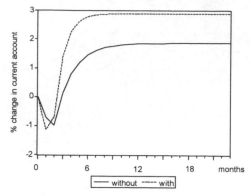

With (without) = estimation which takes (does not take) change of oil price into account.

37

Graph 2 —   Fiscal Policy Instruments at the Federal Level (percentage of GDP) 1993-1999

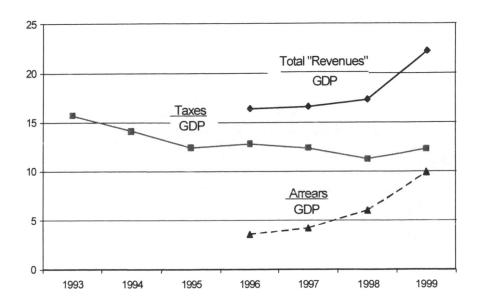

Source: Goskomstat; own calculations.

38

Graph 3 —   *Tax Arrears (percentage change on previous period)*
1996-2000

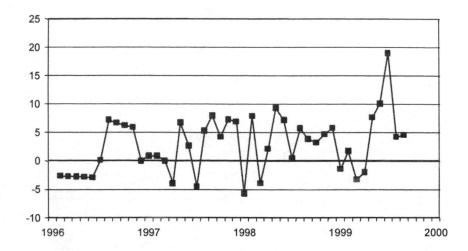

Sources: Goskomstat; own calculations.

Part V
Global Financial Instability

Reforming the Global Economic Architecture: Lessons from Recent Crises

JOSEPH E. STIGLITZ*

RECENT TURMOIL IN INTERNATIONAL financial markets has raised a set of fundamental questions for the global community: Is the set of international financial arrangements, established after the Great Depression and World War II and modified after the abandonment of the gold standard in 1973, up to the challenges of the twenty-first century? Are minor modifications (such as slight changes in the governance of the international financial institutions, increased transparency, or surveillance) all that is required to adapt these institutions to the needs of modern economies, or are more fundamental changes necessary? Today, although much has been proposed, discussed, and argued, no consensus on desirable changes has yet been reached. In the meantime, what can countries, especially the poor, the small, and the less-developed, do to protect themselves from the seeming ravages of storms brought on by international financial instability?

The subject is complicated, and in the time allotted to me, I cannot do it justice. Rather than endeavoring to provide a comprehensive treatment, I shall summarize my views in 10 basic points, followed by three important methodological observations.

We should keep in mind that the success of a development or stabilization program must be assessed by its impact on the livelihood of the concerned individuals, not by whether the exchange rate has stabilized! Our objective should be clear: the welfare of the citizens in the affected country, with due attention to distributional concerns. A program cannot be hailed a success if the exchange rate is stabilized, but the country falls into a deep and prolonged recession. One cannot count a program a success until unemployment has returned to normal levels and growth has resumed. Ascertaining success is made ever more problematic by hypothesizing on the counterfactual—that is, what would have happened in the absence of the program? Perhaps output would have fallen even more, and unemployment risen even more. But since the advent of modern macromanagement, governments in developed countries have been able to shorten downturns and to mitigate their severity by taking strong countercyclical measures.[1] Those advocating contractionary policies, for instance, in the event of a crisis that in any case would have dampened the economy's strength, bear a heavy burden of proof: They must either show that more expansionary

*Chief Economist, The World Bank.
[1] See, for example, Stiglitz (1997a, 1997b).

policies were not feasible or that the contractionary policies generated stronger long-term growth. Evidence on growth trajectories in general provides little evidence in favor of the latter hypothesis.

With these caveats in mind, let me turn to 10 key policy points.

1. *The international financial architecture has exhibited enormous fragility over the past quarter century.* Financial and currency crises have hit with increasing frequency, at high budgetary costs to the governments that inevitably try to resurrect their economies. But the cost is high; for years after the crisis, growth is slower and unemployment higher.[2] By one reckoning, 80 to 100 countries have faced a crisis since the mid-1970s.[3]

What inferences can we make from this experience? To introduce one of the two metaphors that I will use frequently in the subsequent discussion: If there is a single accident on a road, one is likely to look for a cause in the driver, his car, or the weather. But if there are hundreds of accidents at the same bend of the road, then questions need to be raised concerning the construction of the road itself. Roads need to be designed not for perfect drivers, nor for drivers trained to drive on race tracks, but for ordinary mortals. If average drivers repeatedly find the curves too difficult to navigate, it is time either to reengineer the design of the road or to impose regulations on the cars that drive on it.

2. *Capital and financial market liberalization are systemically related to this vulnerability.* Both theory and empirical studies confirm this conclusion. Premature financial market liberalization—for instance, before the appropriate regulatory structures are in place—frequently leads to excessively risky lending by banks. Empirical studies show that the probability of a financial crisis is particularly high in the five years following financial market liberalization.[4] The recent crisis in Asia followed this familiar pattern. Given the Asian countries' commitment to continue with financial market liberalization, there was no obvious way in which to manage the macroeconomic consequences of the surge of financial capital, which left even more suddenly than it entered.[5]

Advances in economic theory (e.g., Hellman, Murdock, and Stiglitz (1996)) show that reliance on capital adequacy standards, a common feature in countries that have engaged in financial market liberalization, is not Pareto effi-

---

[2] For the growth result, see Caprio (1997). Economic downturns leave a long-term adverse legacy, among other ways, through the attrition of human capital, which has been emphasized in the literature on the hysteresis effect and may be a factor in the sustained high levels of unemployment in Europe. See Blanchard and Summers (1986).

[3] Caprio and Klingebiel (1996) identify banking crises in 69 countries since the late 1970s, which only includes countries with sufficient data. They estimate that the inclusion of transition economies would add crises in at least 20 more countries.

[4] Kaminsky, Linzondo, and Reinhart (1998). See also the path-breaking study of Chile's 1982 crisis by Diaz-Alejandro (1985). In the context of the Scandinavian crises see Steigum (1992) and Kiander and Vartia (1996).

[5] For a more detailed discussion of the crises, see Furman and Stiglitz (1999).

cient. It is particularly problematic to rely on capital adequacy standards in economies with poor information systems and facing high risks. (Because of their smaller size, most LDCs are less diversified than larger economies and thus face greater risks.) The problems of regulation in the aftermath of liberalization are exacerbated by the drain on trained personnel, as the booming private financial sector is able to outbid the public sector. And the instabilities arising from excessive reliance on collateral lending, an important feature of the Asian economies, have long been known: Such lending practices reinforce a boom, but when collateral values collapse, defaults soar and credit is constrained, furthering the decline in asset prices. These natural instabilities are only reinforced by excessive reliance on capital adequacy standards, without the sophisticated reliance on forbearance-cum-tightened regulatory supervision associated with more advanced economies. The beginning of the downturn leads to a few bankruptcies, putting banks below the required capital adequacy standards. In a pessimistic environment, banks find it impossible to raise additional funds, thus forcing them to cut back on lending. But as they all do this, bankruptcies and the nonperforming loans soar, creating a vicious cycle.

Interestingly, many of the problems might not have arisen in the previous regulatory regimes. Thailand, for instance, before it felt pressure to liberalize, had imposed limitations on bank lending to speculative real estate. It had been aware that such lending is a major source of instability and, moreover, it was still under the impression that investing in employment—creating factories—provided better foundations for a growth strategy than building empty office buildings. But under pressure from those who pushed on it the doctrines of the liberalized market, it succumbed to the judgment of the market with disastrous consequences.[6]

There is a certain irony in this evidence of increased instability: One of the arguments *for* capital market liberalization is that it leads to increased diversification, which in turn makes the country less vulnerable. In fact, what diversification occurred was mainly within East Asia and, as it turned out, the shocks were highly correlated (with the correlation perhaps exacerbated by the policies undertaken). In any case, the increased vulnerability posed by liberalization far outweighed the benefits of diversification, a result also observed elsewhere in the world.

**3. *Although capital market liberalization clearly portends greater risks, it has not brought commensurate benefits in terms of economic growth.* **Again, both theory and evidence support this conclusion. Rodrik

---

[6] Another metaphor has become fashionable for small, less developed countries embarking on financial and capital market liberalization. It is likened to a small boat setting sail on a wild and rough ocean—even if well steered and solidly constructed, it is vulnerable to being hit broadside by a wave and capsizing. And if the captain has not had proper training and if holes have not been fully repaired (if capital market liberalization proceeds too fast after financial market regulation), then a speedy and disastrous outcome is even more likely. Indeed, a design to make the boat faster and sleeker at the same time makes it less stable. In Asia, there simply was no time to take advantage of the allegedly improved design before disaster struck.

(1998) shows that neither investment nor growth was associated with capital market liberalization using the same kind of cross country regressions that typically show significant gains from trade liberalization. And of all the regions in the world, East Asia was the least likely to gain from capital account liberalization; with its high savings rate, it was hardly in need of further capital infusions at the margin. The low returns that might be associated with these marginal investments made the expected returns low, and left the risks high.

There are a number of reasons more generally why the view that capital account liberalization gives rise to enhanced growth should be regarded with skepticism. Liberalization has, in general, focused on opening a country to short-term speculative flows; but precisely because of the volatility of such flows, it is hard to base productive long-term investments on these funds.

In assessing the various sources of vulnerability, one factor has received increasing attention: the ratio of short-term foreign debt to reserves. A large fraction of countries in which that variable exceeded unity experienced crises. This variable did not appear in earlier studies of crises because economists had pointed out that any domestic asset could be converted into foreign currency under a regime of complete convertibility, so *existing* short-term foreign liabilities did not really represent the magnitude of the potential "threat."[7] That the variable has recently attained prominence illustrates the potential *negative* effects of short-term borrowing. Consider a poor, small country in which a firm decides to borrow $100 million from an American bank at 18 percent interest. Prudent behavior on the part of the country then implies that it must increase its reserves by $100 million—likely held in the form of U.S. Treasury bills. In effect, the country is then borrowing from the United States at 18 percent and lending at 4 percent—hardly a strategy that is likely to engender domestic growth, though it may resoundingly benefit the United States, among the most ardent advocates of capital account liberalization.

The most important reason that capital and financial market liberalization may not be related to growth is that it enhances instability; instability, as we noted in lesson one, has significant adverse effects on growth.[8]

4. The adverse effects of financial and capital market liberalization can, in turn, be related to the fact that there are marked discrepancies between social and private returns and risks. East Asia's

---

[7] On the other hand, the result is consistent with multiple equilibria sunspot models: If everyone believes that a ratio is believed by everyone else to be associated with a crisis, then when they see the variable pass the threshold, they withdraw their funds, leading to a crisis. For early models of multiple equilibria (including sunspot equilibria), see Stiglitz (1972a) and Shell (1977).

[8] There are a variety of reasons for this: A pattern of instability implies greater riskiness for investment, discouraging one of the main sources of growth. In economic downturns, investments in R&D and other productivity enhancing expenditures, as important as they are for long-term growth, tend to be curtailed. See Greenwald and Stiglitz (1989).

crisis was related to private sector borrowing. Even Thailand's large borrowings should not have been a problem because the borrowing was being used to finance private investment, which presumably yielded a return in excess of the cost of borrowing. Only if one believed that there was a government subsidy (either explicit, or implicit, in the form of a presumed bailout) should one have been worried—that is, *if one believed in the efficiency of market allocations.* But the experience of East Asia has confirmed lessons from experiences elsewhere: There are large systemic risks imposed on the economy by financial sector weaknesses and the surges in capital flows associated with capital account liberalization. The costs of these disruptions are felt not only by the borrowers and lenders who engage in the transactions, but also by workers, small businessmen, and others throughout the economy.

5. *It is intellectually incoherent to argue for bailouts and highlight the importance of contagion and systemic risk but not to try to address the underlying source of the problem.* The previous point argued that there are externalities associated with private, international, short-term borrowing. If there were no such externalities, then it would be hard to defend bailouts, and there would be no worry about contagion. Just as we now recognize that the production of steel may give rise to an important externality—air pollution—and that the externality necessitates an important public role in trying to "force" (through price or other forms of regulation) less pollution, it is imperative to recognize the externalities associated with these short-term private capital flows. The consequence of internalizing this externality in the former case may well be less steel producing—essentially a redeployment of resources to better reflect the social costs and benefits of the activity rather than relying on the distorted market allocations in which important social costs are ignored. This, too, should be the case for the latter example. The widespread worry that interventions might reduce the flow of capital is as misguided as the worry that discouraging air pollution might discourage the production of steel.

6. *The thrust of the interventions should be to stabilize capital flows, for it is the instability of such flows which generates the high costs and which limits their benefits.* Again, let me analogize with a metaphor: Without a dam, the melting of the snows at the top of a mountain may give rise to disastrous floods, resulting in death and destruction. A well-designed dam will temper the flow of water, but it will not stop the movement of water from the mountaintop to the seaside. However, by stabilizing the flow, the dam serves to reduce and perhaps eliminate the deathly and destructive aspects of the torrent—indeed, the dam may convert the water into a powerful, productive force.

This has an important implication: A good dam does not have to stop all flows, even temporarily, to be of considerable value.

7. Frequently, the key to stabilization is a comprehensive program.
Elsewhere, I have outlined a three-pronged program.[9]

1. *Eliminating the government distortions that have encouraged short-term flows.* (Thailand had a facility that had the effect of directly facilitating those flows; Korea's restrictions on long-term flows indirectly encouraged short-term flows.)
2. *Strengthening financial institutions.* This in turn has a number of ingredients such as improved transparency; broad and effective bank regulation, including good, risk-adjusted capital adequacy standards (flexible and adapted to particular circumstances of each country); speed bumps, such as limiting the rate of increase of lending; and exposure limits, both direct and indirect (on the firms to which the banks lend)
3. *Direct interventions to stabilize the flows of capital not mediated through the banking system.*

It is important to recognize that the first two sets of measures, as important as they are, are both difficult—especially for less-developed countries—and are far from sufficient to inoculate countries against the kinds of instabilities that have been so prevalent in the last quarter of a century. Transparency in the form of mark-to-market accounting (requiring banks to record all assets at their current market value), for instance, is resisted today in the United States, even in the aftermath of the S&L crisis (which was in part attributed to poor regulation, including inadequately transparent information systems). There was no reform, even after it was recognized that failing to use marking to market practices not only reduced transparency but led to distorted investment policies that potentially and significantly increased the risk exposure of banks.[10] Even under the best of circumstances, obtaining the relevant data may be difficult—and is becoming increasingly so.

Note that in standard competitive theory (as articulated for instance by Arrow and Debreu (1954)), the basis of the belief in the efficacy of market processes assumes that all the relevant information is conveyed by prices. The kinds of quantitative information being called for would, under standard competitive assumptions, simply be irrelevant—no one is calling for steel firms to release their sales figures. This highlights the difference between markets for commodities such as steel and finance markets, and it undermines the oft-heard argument that free mobility of capital is just as welfare enhancing as free trade in goods. Financial markets are different. Similarly, even countries with advanced institutional structures cannot claim an impressive record in managing their banking systems—witness the recent financial crises in the United States, Scan-

---

[9] See Stiglitz (1998a, 1998b).

[10] Similarly, the well-known—and successful—opposition of U.S. government officials to FASB's proposals for more transparent accounting frameworks for stock options well illustrates the political problems that such proposals frequently encounter. See Stiglitz (1992).

dinavia, and Japan. No country has adequate risk adjustments for capital adequacy standards or deposit insurance premia. Similarly, the fact that the last major set of financial crises occurred in Scandinavia, countries noted for their transparency, suggests that transparency by itself is not sufficient.

The increased use of derivatives—the risk implications of which are often very difficult to assess—and their increasing complexity have further complicated attempts at transparency and improved regulation.[11]

Let me be clear: Improved regulation and increased transparency are clearly desirable. But we should not underestimate the difficulties or overestimate the effectiveness of these measures. Those who think that regulation and transparency are all that are needed are looking for cheap and easy solutions to a complex and serious international problem. Or, alternatively, they seek solutions that are ideologically compatible with the belief in "free markets"—in spite of the evidence of the importance of market failures described above (see point one).

That a comprehensive program needs to go beyond bank regulation is evidenced by the experience of Indonesia, where two-thirds of the domestic borrowing was undertaken by corporates. To return to the dam metaphor, stopping bank borrowing from abroad may be like putting your finger in a dike—it may plug up one hole, but the water will find a way around. If there are economic incentives (or misguided perceptions) that lead to a desire to borrow abroad, corporates that can will do so, even if banks cannot do so on their behalf.[12]

8. *Although a comprehensive program is essential, its features need to be adapted to the situation in each country.* In particular, the regulatory framework for LDCs may well differ markedly from those of more-developed countries because the risks are greater, the regulatory capacities are weaker, and information is poorer. Developed countries have been moving to monitoring banks' risk management systems, but direct controls should continue to play a more prominent role in LDCs. Thus LDCs may need to impose more stringent regulations on lending—for instance on speculative real estate. They may need to impose speed limits (restrictions on the rate at which loan portfolios can grow). They may need to limit the use of derivatives.

---

[11] In several instances, firms believed that they had a covered position, only to discover that the party providing the cover had gone bankrupt. Thus, bank regulators need not only to look at "exposure" but at the portfolio position of those providing cover, and the correlation between credit and market risks. The difficulties of doing so—and the disadvantaged position of regulators—should be apparent. The recent failure of bank regulators in the United States to prevent a lone hedge fund from borrowing sufficient amounts that its open positions posed systemic risk to the global financial system should make us less than sanguine about a strategy focusing on LDCs improving their transparency or regulatory capacities enough to prevent future crises.

[12] At the same time, strong bank regulation—including restrictions on exposure of firms to which the banks lend—can have a major impact on aggregate exposure. So too could appropriate risk adjustments for capital adequacy standards and deposit insurance, which presumably would induce banks to charge higher interest rates to firms that had high exposure. Current risk adjustments fall markedly short of the mark.

Modern bank regulation recognizes the inefficiencies—and even the dangers—of excessive reliance on capital adequacy standards, and the problems in doing so are particularly acute for LDCs. Matters become even worse if excessively stringent capital adequacy standards are imposed (too rapidly) in an economy in recession, where many banks will naturally fail to meet those standards. The systemic credit contraction to which that can give rise may be self-defeating for as banks contract credit to meet the capital adequacy standards (because in the midst of a recession, they are likely to find it difficult to raise new capital), more firms go bankrupt, only increasing the fraction of loans that are nonperforming. In a dramatic example of the fallacy of composition, a policy designed to ensure strong banks—when an isolated bank has problems—actually undermines the strength of the banking system when there are systemic weaknesses. Countries that have successfully managed financial crises and the accompanying recessions have engaged in "forbearance"—*temporarily* weakening (in effect) capital adequacy standards, while they have increased the intensity of supervision of transactions.

9. *A key part of the reforms to stabilize the international financial system is a fundamental reform of bankruptcy, including what I call a "super chapter 11."* The reform of bankruptcy law needs to recognize the difference between systemic bankruptcy, when a substantial fraction of the firms in an economy are bankrupt, and an individual bankruptcy, when an isolated firm cannot meet its obligations. The inferences that can be drawn concerning managerial competency are dramatically different in the two situations—few firms in any country could survive depreciations of currency and increases in interest rates of the magnitude that occurred in East Asia. The presumption should be that existing management continue in place; the burden of proof should be on creditors to establish that there was a persistent mismanagement of the firm's assets. This is much like chapter 11, in which management typically continues, with a simple rearrangement of claims (with creditors typically taking some equity shares, though the original equity owners are seldom fully wiped out). In a "super chapter 11" there would be an even greater burden of proof on creditors if they seek alternative arrangements, and perhaps even greater clarity in the specification of default options.

It is not only that the information conveyed by the two types of bankruptcy differs. The costs of the standard bankruptcy procedures can also be enormous when applied to systemic bankruptcy. When there is systemic bankruptcy, the frequent delays common in standard bankruptcy proceedings would impose huge social costs. A super chapter 11 should be structured so that corporate reorganizations could occur much faster and at much lower costs than even a standard chapter 11.

The bankruptcy would be a (decentralized, private sector) analogue to a standstill. And the bankruptcy law would act as a circuit breaker in the downward spiral that has characterized East Asia. Now, as the exchange rate falls, more firms become nonperforming in the loans, weakening the banking system, leading to a credit contraction, which reinforces the downward dynamics. With the bankruptcy standstill, the losses of domestic players are limited. (To be sure, a super chapter 11 might lead to higher interest rates—so that the cost of borrowing may more accurately reflect some of the true social costs. See point 4 above.)

But just as bank regulation needs to be adapted to the situation in each country, so too does bankruptcy law. Indeed, there is no single "Pareto dominating" bankruptcy law. There are trade-offs between the interests of lenders and borrowers, and even between domestic lenders and foreign lenders.

I have said nothing so far about grander changes, such as proposals for creating a "lender of last resort." Though this is not the place for a comprehensive treatment of what is, after all, a highly complicated subject, the following points do seem worth making:

- Having a lender of last resort is not sufficient to protect an economy. The Federal Reserve Bank was created as a lender of last resort, considerably prior to the Great Depression. It was only when the lender of last resort was accompanied by deposit insurance and tightened supervision that crises were prevented (and one without the other can actually make a crisis more likely, as the S&L debacle so clearly demonstrated). But in the international context, proposals for a lender of last resort are seldom accompanied by something that would pass as an analogue to deposit insurance, with a tax imposed on lenders to support the "bailout" fund.

- There are, moreover, questions concerning whether a lender of last resort is "necessary," if governments really permit flexible (market-determined) exchange rates and adopt adequate bankruptcy laws. Mutual funds do not need a lender of last resort simply because they do not have a "first-come, first-serve" repayment at "fixed rates." Countries are, in this sense, much more like mutual funds than they are like banks, assuming flexible exchange rates. The funds are needed to support the exchange rate—to give those few extremely wealthy individuals in Russia, for instance, time to take out their money at the high exchange rate. When one recognizes that billions and billions have been misspent by countries in the vain attempt to support their exchange rate—dollars that in the end come out of the pockets of the countries' taxpayers—the small sums lost in Harberger triangles and other forms of microinefficiencies (so often railed against) pale in comparison.

- The essential ingredient of a "lender of last resort" is that there should be a degree of automaticity in access to funds to countries that "qualify." But in our rapidly changing world, can that be assured? A government can gamble and lose its entire reserves overnight with derivatives. Should such a government be entitled to a bailout, simply because it had previously acted in prudential ways? In the end, judgment calls will be necessary. And how different will those judgment calls be from those currently being made?

- Moreover, the signal that a country does not qualify, or has changed from "qualified" to "nonqualified" status could itself set off a crisis. Concern about this has led to a shift from dichotomous policies to more continuous ones: Countries that are "more qualified" get access to funds "more easily" or on better terms. Can such a system be run in a transparent way? The less transparent, the less "rule bound," the less "automaticity" this system has, the less will the lender of last resort function be served. Remember, the principle behind the lender of last resort is that the knowledge that there is a large stock of funds available to support a currency deters an attack. But the greater the discretion, the less assurance there is that there is a large stock of funds available, and hence the greater the incentive for an attack.
- Moreover, we now recognize the central role capital flight plays in currency crises. Given the huge amounts that could leave a country under an open regime, there is a real question of whether any fund that is likely to be amassed will provide sufficient assurance to reduce substantially the likelihood of an attack.
- I noted earlier that central to the success of a lender of last resort is good supervision. Earlier, I detailed the problems LDCs face in bank supervision. How supervision is run is not, however, just a technical matter, which is why governments such as the United States have insisted that, while supervision should remain "independent," it also remain politically accountable. The U.S. Comptroller of the Currency reports directly to the Secretary of the Treasury. Historically, the United States and other countries that have managed their way through cyclical fluctuations well have engaged in a certain degree of forbearance, compensating for the forbearance in capital adequacy standards with tightened supervision of transactions. I doubt that the United States would be willing to delegate supervisory responsibility to a group of international bureaucrats, only remotely politically accountable. Will other countries be willing to do so? Perhaps, if in doing so they can purchase greater credibility for their banking systems and greater "automaticity" of funds in the event of a crisis. But the answer is by no means obvious. Note that financial crises are only one of many stimulants for a currency crisis (and hence the "need" for a bailout). How broad will the reach of supervision need to be? It takes an enormous amount of confidence in international institutions to cede the kind of authority that is required for a lender of last resort to work effectively. It is not clear that we are at that stage yet in the evolution of global economic governance.

10. *Most importantly, there needs to be a congruence between a country's exposure to risks, its ability to reduce (or its tendency to exacerbate) those risks, and the provisions it has made to insulate the most vulnerable from the consequences of those risks (including its safety nets).*

Earlier, I described small, less-developed countries in the international capital markets as small boats in a wild and rough sea: Even if well steered and strongly constructed, they are likely to be capsized by a sufficiently large wave. To be sure, if they are not well steered, and if there are holes in the boat, their survival is even more precarious. This metaphor suggests that strong precautions should be taken before going out to sea. Precisely the opposite has occurred. The boat has been redesigned to make it sleeker and faster (assuming it could survive!), which renders it more unstable, reducing survival chances further still. Worse still, it has been set out to sail in the roughest part of the sea, in the worst conditions, before safety vests have been put on board, and before the skipper has had a chance to be trained for the new design. The consequences have been all too predictable—and at great human costs.

Before concluding, I want to spend a minute on three methodological "lessons."

A. It is imperative that policymakers better integrate financial and real economics. As has been noted repeatedly, at the heart of the East Asia crisis were private capital flows and a worry about bankruptcy and default. If there were not such worries, Western banks would have been more than willing to roll over their loans, especially at the high interest rates being offered. Thus, not only is bankruptcy of a first-order importance, but policymakers need to focus on how policies being pursued affect the likelihood of bankruptcy—it is a key endogenous variable. What is remarkable is that more than 25 years after micromodels began emphasizing the key role that bankruptcy plays in modern capitalism (see, e.g., Stiglitz (1969, 1972b) and Greenwald and Stiglitz (1992)), more than 20 years after the link between interest rates and bankruptcy was clearly articulated (Stiglitz and Weiss (1981)), and 15 years after these ideas were embedded in macromodels (Greenwald and Stiglitz (1984, 1993) and Stiglitz and Weiss (1992)), standard macro-textbooks often do not even mention bankruptcy in the index.

Too often, the financial sector is summarized in a money demand equation. Doing so not only misses the complexity of the financial sector, but can also lead to misguided policies. Indeed, the standard reduced-form relationships between money and aggregate output, summarized in the LM curve, all too often are markedly altered in the event of a financial or currency crisis, even of the mild variety experienced in the U.S. S&L debacle.[13] If this is true for a relatively mild crisis, affecting a small fraction of the financial sector, how much more so is it likely to be the case for the kind of major upheaval experienced, for instance, by Indonesia?

B. One should be wary of anthropomorphizing the market and of the prognostications of armchair market psychologists. The market consists of many players, with different portfolios, risk preferences, and in-

---

[13] This is now recognized to be an important contributor to the Fed's failure to take appropriate actions to stave off the 1991 recession. See Stiglitz (1992).

formation. There is enormous heterogeneity of beliefs, so much so that a piece of information may at the same time make investments in a country more attractive to some and less attractive to others. In particular, economic downturns, while reassuring to foreign investors (though even this is questionable), would normally be expected to generate domestic capital outflows. Increased risk induces domestic residents to diversify. Although they cannot easily diversify their human capital, they can move out more of their physical wealth. Time after time, we have seen domestic capital flight as an important contributor to a crisis and its perpetuation.

One should be suspicious of anyone who says, "The market expects. . . ." I have never met "Mr. Market," and, as a former market participant, I can only say that frequently my expectations differ from those of the armchair market psychologists. Good analyses must take into account the diversity that makes a market, paying due attention to the differences between those in the country and those outside it.

C. We need to reach beyond anecdotes to construct coherent theoretical models and undertake empirical testing. Anecdotes are useful, both as teaching tools and in helping to guide our thinking. Journalists, who have to explain the world in simple terms, can be forgiven for relying on anecdotes in interpreting events. But economists and social scientists more generally should be held to a higher standard. Do higher interest rates lead to a stronger currency? Theoretical models can offer insights into the circumstances in which this might or might not be the case, and empirical work can cast light on whether these predictions are borne out in practice. The evidence is far from overwhelming in support of the "conventional wisdom" that higher interest rates are necessary, if not sufficient, for maintaining the strength of the currency.[14] The theoretical prediction that higher interest rates may so weaken an economy and increase the probability of bankruptcy that rather than attracting capital (net) they may induce capital to leave, seems to have been borne out in the data—and evidenced in the East Asia crisis.

Not only do anecdotes seldom support only one side—adherents of contrary positions can each proffer anecdotes in support of their opinions—but their interpretation is often elusive. In the East Asian context, the Mexican experience is often cited: it "stayed the course" and quickly recovered. But Mexico was smart; it chose as its neighbor and major trading partner a country with a booming economy and a strong financial system, with whom a major trade and investment treaty had just been signed. The countries of East Asia did not show as much wisdom, choosing as their trading partner a country going into its most severe recession in half a century and with a fragile financial system. To what extent should we credit "staying the course" and resolute action for the recovery? And to what extent should we credit "choosing one's neighbor"? My interpretation places a far greater weight on the latter; evidence for this can be gleaned by looking at the source of recovery—exports to U.S. firms. In-

[14] See Kraay (1998) and Furman and Stiglitz (1999).

deed, four years after the crisis, the domestic sector remains in weak shape. Considering one of the often reiterated lectures to the East Asian countries reinforces the point: Recovery will require addressing the weaknesses in the financial system. By contrast, there are repeated newspaper reports documenting the continuing deep weaknesses in the Mexican financial system, with nonperforming loans—four years after the crisis—still exceeding those in several of the East Asian crisis countries.

Every cloud has a silver lining, however thin: The disaster in East Asia, like the Great Depression, will prove a rich source of Ph.D. theses for decades to come. By examining such "extreme" events, we gather insights into the workings of the economy in more normal times. The story of East Asia (and the subsequent crises of 1998) is far from over, and it would be premature to reach any final verdicts. I suspect, however, that there will be a growing consensus in support of the basic lessons that I have outlined in this talk.

REFERENCES

Arrow, Kenneth J., and Gerard Debreu, 1954, Existence of an equilibrium for a competitive economy, *Econometrica* 22, 265–290.

Blanchard, Olivier J., and Lawrence H. Summers, 1986, Hysteresis and the European unemployment problem, *National Bureau of Economic Research Macroeconomics Manual* 1, 15–78.

Caprio, Gerard, 1997, Safe and sound banking in developing countries: We're not in Kansas anymore, *Research in Financial Services: Private and Public Policy* 9, 79–97.

Caprio, Gerard, and Daniela Klingebiel, 1996, Bank insolvencies: Cross-country experience, Policy research Working paper 1620, The World Bank.

Diaz-Alejandro, Carlos, 1985, Good-bye financial repression, hello financial crash, *Journal of Development Economics* 19, 1–24.

Furman, Jason, and Joseph E. Stiglitz, 1999, Economic crises: Evidence and insights from East Asia, *Brookings Papers on Economic Activity*, Washington, D.C.

Greenwald, Bruce, and Joseph E. Stiglitz, 1984, Informational imperfections in the capital markets and macroeconomic fluctuations, *American Economic Review* 74, 194–199.

Greenwald, Bruce, and Joseph E. Stiglitz, 1989, Financial market imperfections and productivity growth, National Bureau of Economic Research Working paper 2945.

Greenwald, Bruce, and Joseph E. Stiglitz, 1992, Towards a reformulation of monetary theory: Competitive banking, National Bureau of Economic Research Working paper 4117.

Greenwald, Bruce, and Joseph E. Stiglitz, 1993, Financial market imperfections and business cycles, *Quarterly Journal of Economics* 108, 77–114.

Hellman, Thomas, Kevin Murdock, and Joseph E. Stiglitz, 1996, Deposit mobilization through financial restraint; in Niels Hermes and Robert Lensink, eds.: *Financial Development and Economic Growth: Theory and Experiences from Developing Countries* (Routledge, London and New York).

Kaminsky, Graciela, Saul Linzondo, and Carmen M. Reinhart, 1998, Leading indicators of currency crises, *IMF Staff Papers* 45, 1–48.

Kiander, Jaakko, and Pentti Vartia, 1996, The great depression of the 1990s in Finland, *Finnish Economic Papers* 9, 72–88.

Kraay, Aart, 1998, Do high interest rates defend currencies against speculative attacks?, Unpublished paper, The World Bank.

Rodrik, Dani, 1998, Who needs capital-account convertibility?, *Essays in International Finance*, International Finance Section, Department of Economics, Princeton University, 207, 55–65.

Shell, Karl, 1977, Monnaie et allocation intertemporelle, Mimeo, Centre National de la Recherche Scientifique, Paris.

Panel on Global Financial Markets and Public Policy   1521

Steigum, Erling, 1992, Financial, credit boom and the banking crisis: The case of Norway, *Discussion paper 15/92*, Norwegian School of Economics and Business Administration.

Stiglitz, Joseph E., 1969, A re-examination of the Modigliani-Miller Theorem, *American Economic Review* 59, 784–793.

Stiglitz, Joseph E., 1972a, On the optimality of the stock market allocation of investment, *Quarterly Journal of Economics* 86, 25–60.

Stiglitz, Joseph E., 1972b, Some aspects of the pure theory of corporate finance: Bankruptcies and takeovers, *Bell Journal of Economics* 3, 458–482.

Stiglitz, Joseph E., 1992, S&L Bailout; in J. Barth and R. Brumbaugh, Jr., eds.: *The Reform of Federal Deposit Insurance: Disciplining the Government and Protecting Taxpayers* (Harper Collins Publishers, New York).

Stiglitz, Joseph E., 1994, Endogenous growth and cycles; in Y. Shionoya and M. Perlman, eds.: *Innovation in Technology, Industries, and Institution* (University of Michigan Press, Ann Arbor, Michigan).

Stiglitz, Joseph E., 1997a, The economic recovery of the 1990s: Restoring sustainable growth, Paper presented to the Georgetown University Macroeconomics Seminar, September 4, 1997.

Stiglitz, Joseph E., 1997b, The long boom? Business cycles in the 1980s and 1990s, Paper presented to the Center for Economic Policy Research, Stanford University, California, September 5, 1997.

Stiglitz, Joseph E., 1998a, Towards a new paradigm for development: Strategies, policies, and processes, Paper given as the Prebisch Lecture at UNCTAD, Geneva, October 19, 1998.

Stiglitz, Joseph E., 1998b, Beggar-thyself vs. Beggar-thy-neighbor policies: The dangers of intellectual incoherence in addressing the global financial crisis, Address to Annual Meetings of the Southern Economics Association, Baltimore, November 8, 1998 (forthcoming in *Southern Economics Journal*).

Stiglitz, Joseph E., and Andrew Weiss, 1981, Credit rationing in markets with imperfect information, *American Economic Review* 71, 393–410.

Stiglitz, Joseph E., and Andrew Weiss, 1992, Asymmetric information in credit markets and its implications for macroeconomics, *Oxford Economic Papers* 44, 694–724.

[27]

Financial Crises and Reform of the International Financial System

Stanley Fischer

Citigroup, New York

Abstract: Between December 1994 and March 1999, Mexico, Thailand, Indonesia, Korea, Malaysia, Russia and Brazil experienced major financial crises, which were associated with massive recessions and extreme movements of exchange rates. Similar crises have threatened Turkey and Argentina (2000 and 2001) and most recently Brazil (again). This article discusses the reform of the international financial system with a focus on the role of the IMF – reforms directed at crisis prevention, and those intended to improve the responses to crises. The article concludes with an appraisal of what has been achieved, and what remains to be done to make the international financial system safer.
JEL no. E5, E6, F3, F4, G1
Keywords: Financial crisis; reform of the international financial system; International Monetary Fund

1 Introduction

The topic of the reform of the international financial system, or of the international financial architecture, rose to prominence in the wake of the financial crisis in Mexico in 1994–95. Interest in it intensified as a result of the Asian financial crisis in 1997–98, and deepened following the Russian and Brazilian crises in 1998 and 1999.

The present debate is more narrow than that on the reform of the international monetary system in the decades of the nineteen sixties and seventies. Then the issue was how to replace the Bretton Woods system

Remark: This is a slightly revised version of the Harms Lecture delivered at the Kiel Institute for World Economics, June 29, 2002. I draw freely on Chapter 2 of my Robbins Lectures presented at the London School of Economics, October 29–31, 2001, *The International Financial System: Crises and Reform.* I am grateful to Prachi Mishra of Columbia University for assistance, and to my former colleagues at the International Monetary Fund for their direct assistance and for many discussions over the years that helped develop the views expressed in this lecture. Please address correspondence to Stanley Fischer, Citigroup, 399 Park Avenue, New York, NY 10022; e-mail: fischers@citigroup.com

2   Review of World Economics 2003, Vol. 139 (1)

of fixed but adjustable exchange rates among the major currencies, and the role of the International Monetary Fund within the system. Now the challenge is to reduce the frequency of crises among the emerging market countries, the mostly middle-income developing countries that are open to massive capital flows. In the last two years, Turkey, Argentina, and most recently Brazil (again) have joined the list of emerging market countries that have experienced major external crises.

In considering the reform of the international financial system, I will first discuss reforms directed at crisis prevention, and then those intended to improve the responses to crises. I will conclude by discussing what has been done to make capital account crises less likely in future, and the priorities for action.

2 Crisis Prevention

To reduce the probability of crises, changes are necessary in: first, country policies and institutions; second, the actions of the IMF and other official international financial institutions; and third, the operation of the international capital markets.

2.1 Country Policies and Institutions

Most crisis-prevention measures require improvements in a broad range of policies and the strengthening of institutions by countries seeking to participate in the international capital markets. I will focus on four issues: the choice of exchange rate system; fiscal policy and debt dynamics; capital account liberalization; and the adoption of codes and standards.

Exchange rate systems: Except for Ecuador in 1998–99 and Brazil at present, every emerging market country that suffered a capital account crisis in the last decade had some form of pegged exchange rate in place before the crisis. The pegs were formal in the cases of Mexico, Brazil, Russia, Turkey, and Argentina, and each was initially part of a policy package to reduce inflation. The pegs were informal in the three Asian countries, and were not the remnant of an inflation stabilization program.

These crises reinforced the conclusion that the impossible trinity makes a softly pegged exchange rate nonviable when the capital account is open (see Fischer 2001a). The normal statement of the impossible trinity is that an open capital account, a pegged exchange rate, and an independent monetary policy are not consistent. If the peg is hard, such as a currency board, then monetary policy is automatically dedicated to maintenance of the peg. But as we have seen recently in Argentina, even a currency board peg is not necessarily viable, for if fiscal policy goes off track, and/or the financial system is weak, monetary policy alone may well not be sufficient to hold the exchange rate.

A country may succeed for some time in living with the impossible trinity, particularly if the exchange rate is undervalued. But when the capital account is open, a pegged exchange rate is crisis-prone, vulnerable to a speculative attack, possibly producing a second generation crisis, in which the measures necessary to defend the peg are not politically viable.

In saying that a pegged exchange rate system is crisis-prone, I am *not* claiming that the only viable system is one in which the exchange rate floats freely. Official interventions in the foreign exchange market from time to time can be useful, *so long as they are not perceived as trying to defend a particular rate or narrow range of rates.*

Following a float, a country has to decide what nominal anchor to adopt, and what exchange rate policy to pursue. For a country with a reasonable rate of inflation – one in the low double digits – experience increasingly supports the use of inflation targeting as the basis for monetary policy. Such a regime has been successfully introduced in Brazil, Korea, South Africa, and several other emerging market countries – not all of them recent crisis countries.

Turning to exchange rate behavior: most of the countries forced to float have been very unhappy about the subsequent behavior of the exchange rate, and have sought a middle way that provides more predictability for the exchange rate. It is hard not to sympathize with this desire, both because exchange rates moved far more after the crises than had been expected, and because there are good reasons for a country to be concerned about the behavior of both nominal and real exchange rates.[1]

Thus, monetary policy in countries with floating exchange rate systems is likely to respond to movements of the exchange rate. While this

---

[1] Changes in the nominal exchange rate are likely to affect the inflation rate, and – especially in countries that are to some extent dollarized – also the health of the financial system and the distribution of wealth between debtors and creditors. Changes in the real exchange rate affect the current account of the balance of payments, often generating political pressures as a result.

is rarely if ever the case for the United States, it is more often so among other G-7 countries, and for smaller emerging market economies. In Canada, the use in the past of a monetary conditions index to guide monetary policy, based on movements in both the exchange rate and the interest rate, formalized the impact of exchange rate movements on monetary policy.[2] In countries that pursue an inflation-targeting approach to monetary policy, changes in the exchange rate will be taken into account in setting monetary policy, because the exchange rate affects price behavior.

In the reverse direction, there is an unresolved issue about whether monetary policy in a flexible rate system should be used in the short run to try to affect the exchange rate. In many respects, the issue is similar to that of how monetary policy in an inflation-targeting framework should respond to movements in output and unemployment. Although it has not received much empirical attention, there is almost certainly a short-run tradeoff between the real exchange rate and inflation, analogous to the Phillips curve.[3] This is an issue that deserves serious attention, for just as answers have been developed as to how to deal with the short-run Phillips curve in an inflation-targeting framework, so it remains necessary to answer the question of how in such a framework to deal with the short-run tradeoff between the real exchange rate and inflation.

Recognizing the difficulty for an emerging market country of defending a narrow range of exchange rates, Williamson (2000) proposes alternative regimes. Rudi Dornbusch has named these BBC arrangements: basket, band, and crawl. Williamson also recommends that countries, if necessary, allow the exchange rate to move temporarily outside the band, so that they do not provide speculators with one-way bets that lead to excessive reserve losses. In these circumstances, the band is serving as a weak nominal anchor for the exchange rate, and can perhaps be thought of as a supplement to an inflation-targeting framework.[4] Goldstein (2002) argues that the best regime choice for emerging economies

---

[2] Although the idea behind the monetary conditions index (MCI), that both the exchange rate and the interest rate affect aggregate demand, is correct, the MCI needs to be used with great caution, not least because the cause of any change in the exchange rate needs to be taken into account.

[3] Cushman and Zha (1997) contain VARs from which the implied tradeoff can be calculated in the Canadian case.

[4] Williamson himself believes that specifying a target exchange rate range may prevent markets from heading off on an errant exchange rate path. Another possibility is that by committing weakly to some range of exchange rates, the authorities make it more

is *managed floating plus*, where "plus" is shorthand for a framework that includes inflation targeting and aggressive measures to discourage currency mismatching.[5]

Although it is not clear that this type of intermediate regime will work for all emerging market countries, it is clear that floating exchange rates do fluctuate a great deal, and that it would be useful if it were possible to reduce the range of fluctuations. Some of the Asian crisis countries have been intervening regularly and apparently successfully in seeking to limit exchange rate fluctuations.

Outside the transition economies, countries have not succeeded in stabilizing from high (triple digit) inflation without the use of an exchange rate anchor. But doing so, without an exit mechanism, is very risky. And it is risky even if an exit mechanism is specified, as the case of Turkey in 2000–01 shows. So I conclude that while an exchange rate peg could be used in future to disinflate, the commitment would have to be quite short-lived.

I believe that of all the changes in the international financial system that have taken place since 1994, the shift towards flexible exchange rates by emerging market countries is the one that has most reduced the risk of future crises. However, while a flexible exchange rate regime precludes some types of crises, external financing crises can still occur in a flexible exchange rate regime, particularly a crisis that arises from the market's conclusion that a country's debt situation is not sustainable – as we see in the case of Brazil in 2002. Accordingly we turn next to fiscal policy.

Fiscal policy: The IMF's emphasis on the key role of fiscal policy in the macroeconomic policy mix is well known to the point of caricature.[6] The discussion usually turns on the need for fiscal contraction in the face of a variety of adverse external shocks. But sometimes, the IMF has recommended fiscal expansions, for instance in Japan in recent years, and after a short while, during the Asian crisis.

How should the required fiscal policy be calculated? In several programs, for instance those in Brazil, Argentina, and Turkey in the period

---

likely that fiscal policy will be brought into play if the real exchange rate moves too far from equilibrium.
[5] Goldstein (2002) argues that if managed floating were enhanced in this way, it would retain the desirable features of a flexible rate regime while addressing the nominal anchor and balance-sheet problems that have historically produced a "fear of floating" and handicapped the performance of managed floating in emerging economies.
[6] The focus here is on the macroeconomic aspects of fiscal policy.

6   Review of World Economics 2003, Vol. 139 (1)

since 1998, the agreed fiscal stance has been guided by the need to ensure that the debt-to-GDP ratio is put on a declining path. The well-known equation for debt dynamics is

$$\dot{d} = -x + (r - g)d,$$

where d is the debt-to-GDP ratio, x is the primary surplus (relative to GDP), r is the interest rate, and g the growth rate of GDP.

If a country is in an external funding crisis because the markets are concerned that the debt burden is nonsustainable, then the fiscal policy will have to be such as to persuade domestic and foreign investors that the debt-to-GDP ratio will at some point begin to decline. In a crisis, it is likely the real interest rate will be high and the growth rate will be low, tending to make for unsustainable debt dynamics – but also reinforcing the likelihood that if a credible change can be made in fiscal policy, then an apparently unstable debt dynamics will become stable.[7]

But theory has not provided a great deal of guidance about an optimal debt-to-GDP ratio. The issue was discussed in the United States during the period, not so long ago, when it was believed the government debt was about to disappear. The Maastricht upper limit of 60 percent of GDP seems to have gradually gained status as a norm. Whatever theory ultimately emerges, it is likely that if an optimal government debt-to-GDP ratio can be defined, it would be related to the private sector's saving behavior. It would also be related to the terms on which the government can borrow, and the variability of those terms, as well as the average rate of growth and its variability.

Interest rates paid by emerging market governments are not only higher but also vary a great deal more than those paid by industrialized country governments. For instance, over the period 1995–2000, during which the real interest rate paid by the United States and United Kingdom governments had a standard deviation of 0.86 percent per annum, the standard deviation for Korea was more than double that, and that for Mexico and Brazil – which averaged 4.2 percent per annum[8] – greater by a factor of five. This means that at any given debt-to-GDP ratio, the budget of an emerging market country is more vulnerable to interest

---

[7] This point is developed in Favero and Giavazzi (2002).

[8] The underlying data for standard deviations of real interest rates (quarterly data) are 0.88 for the United States, 0.92 for the United Kingdom, 1.88 for Korea, 3.66 for Mexico, and 4.71 for Brazil.

rate shocks than the budget of an industrialized country. Further, the costs of borrowing are likely to be highly nonlinear as a function of the debt-to-GDP ratio. We have also seen in recent years, in both Russia and Argentina, just how quickly a debt ratio can rise if the budget deficit is large and growth is slow or negative.

The conclusion is that if there is an optimal debt-to-GDP ratio, it must be smaller for an emerging market country than for an industrialized country – equivalently, that emerging market countries that become too dependent on the international capital markets, court great danger. Even if it is not possible to define an optimal debt-to-GDP ratio, it can safely be concluded that a 60 percent ratio for an emerging market country is too high, and that ratios nearer 30–40 percent are much safer.

Capital controls: The debate over capital controls has taken on an ideological cast that seems to have intensified during the most recent discussions. In principle, capital controls can enable a country to have the benefits of both a pegged exchange rate and an independent monetary policy, and also to control both capital outflows and inflows.[9]

As is well known, the founders of the Bretton Woods system, reflecting the prevailing interpretation of inter-war experience,[10] regarded short-term capital flows as being frequently destabilizing. The Articles of Agreement of the IMF do not make capital account liberalization a purpose of the Fund, and Article VI permits the Fund to ask a member to exercise capital controls to prevent the general resources of the Fund being used "to meet a large or sustained outflow of capital."

Most industrialized countries kept capital controls in place for most of the post-World War II period; even in the United Kingdom the last capital account restrictions were removed only in the late 1970s. China and India, both countries with capital controls, successfully avoided the Asian crisis, thereby providing an important element of stability in the regional and global economies at the time. Malaysia's imposition of capital controls and pegging of the exchange rate in September 1998 has attracted much attention, though evaluation of the ef-

---

[9] Capital controls are examined by De Gregorio et al. (2000), Eichengreen et al. (1999), and Williamson (2000); for more detailed discussion of experience with capital controls, see Ariyoshi et al. (2000).

[10] League of Nations, *International Currency Experience*, 1944, reprinted by Arno Press, 1978. Most of the volume was written by Ragnar Nurkse, to whom it is sometimes attributed.

fects of the controls has been difficult, since they were imposed after most of the turbulence of the first part of the Asian crisis was over, that is after most of the capital that wanted to leave had done so, and when regional currency values were close to their post-crisis minima.[11]

Nonetheless, support for capital controls is often seen as inconsistent with the Washington Consensus,[12] and a belief in free markets. In discussing capital controls, I shall assume that countries will in the course of their development want to liberalize the capital account and integrate into global capital markets. This view is based in part on the fact that the most advanced economies all have open capital accounts; it is also based on the conclusion that the potential benefits of well-phased integration into the global capital markets – and this includes the benefits obtained by allowing foreign competition in the financial sector – outweigh the costs.[13]

It is necessary to distinguish between controls on outflows and controls on inflows. For controls on capital outflows to succeed, they need to be quite extensive. As a country develops, these controls are likely to become both more distorting and less effective. They also cannot prevent a devaluation if domestic policies are fundamentally inconsistent with maintenance of the exchange rate.

When a country intends to liberalize capital controls on outflows, they should preferably be removed gradually, at a time when the exchange rate is not under pressure,[14] and as the necessary infrastructure – in the form of strong and efficient domestic financial institutions and markets, a market-based monetary policy, an effective foreign exchange market,

---

[11] See Kaplan and Rodrik (2001) for a relatively positive appraisal of the Malaysian controls.

[12] The original Washington Consensus list (Williamson 1990) did not include capital account liberalization, except for foreign direct investment.

[13] The argument is developed at greater length in Fischer (1998). The point has been much disputed, among others by Bhagwati (1998). With regard to empirical evidence on the benefits of capital account liberalization, I believe we are roughly now where we were in the 1980s on current account liberalization – that some evidence is coming in, but that it remains highly disputed. Reinhart and Tokatlidis (2002), Chari and Henry (2002), Bekaert et al. (2002), Galindo et al. (2002), Gourinchas and Jeanne (2002) provide empirical evidence and discuss whether financial liberalization spurs growth and through what channels.

[14] The removal of controls on outflows sometimes results in a capital *in*flow, a result of either foreigners and/or domestic residents bringing capital into the country in light of the greater assurance that it can be removed when desired.

and the information base necessary for the markets to operate efficiently – is being put in place. Unless the country intends to move to a hard peg, it would be desirable to begin allowing some flexibility of exchange rates as the controls are gradually eased. Prudential controls that have a similar effect to some capital controls, for instance limits on the open foreign exchange positions that domestic institutions can take, should also be put in place as direct controls are removed.

Some countries have attempted to impose controls on outflows once a foreign exchange crisis is already under way. This use of controls has generally been ineffective.[15] It has also to be considered that the imposition of controls for this purpose in a crisis is likely to have a longer-term effect on the country's access to international capital.

Several countries, among them Singapore, the three Asian crisis countries, and Malaysia, have taken steps to limit the offshore use of their currencies. In principle, this makes it possible to break the link between onshore and offshore interest rates, particularly by restricting the convertibility of the currency for nonresidents – who need access to the domestic banking system to complete their transactions.[16] Ishii et al. (2001) conclude that such restrictions have been more successful the more comprehensive they have been, and that they could provide the authorities with a breathing space in which to implement policy changes. But as with other capital controls, their effectiveness tends to erode over time. Further, the longer the measures are implemented, and the stronger they are, the higher the associated costs in terms of the efficiency of the financial system are likely to be.

Excessive indebtedness of domestic financial and nonfinancial institutions arises not from capital outflows, but from inflows, especially short-term inflows. The IMF has cautiously supported the use of market-based capital inflow controls, Chilean style. These could be helpful for a country seeking to avoid the difficulties posed for domestic policy by capital inflows. The typical instance occurs when a country is trying to reduce inflation using an exchange rate anchor, and for anti-inflationary purposes needs interest rates higher than those implied by the sum of the foreign interest rate and the expected rate of currency depreciation. A tax on capital inflows can help maintain a wedge between the two

---

[15] See Ariyoshi et al. (2000: 18–29) and Edwards (1999: 68–71).
[16] See Ishii et al. (2001). This paper describes three different mechanisms that are used to limit offshore currency trading.

interest rates. In addition, by taxing short-term capital inflows more than longer-term inflows, capital inflow controls can also in principle influence the composition of inflows.

Evidence from the Chilean experience implies that controls were for some time successful in allowing some monetary policy independence, and also in shifting the composition of capital inflows towards the long end. Empirical evidence presented by De Gregorio et al. (2000) suggests that the Chilean controls lost their effectiveness after 1998. They have recently been removed.

Thus, controls can be used to help limit capital outflows and maintain a pegged exchange rate, given domestic policies are consistent with maintenance of the exchange rate. However, such controls tend to lose their effectiveness and efficiency over time. Capital inflow controls may for a time be useful in enabling a country to run an independent monetary policy when the exchange rate is softly pegged, and may influence the composition of capital inflows, but their long-term effectiveness to those ends is doubtful. In a nutshell: capital controls may be useful, need to be exercised with care, are likely to be transitional – albeit possibly in use for a long time – and caution is necessary in removing them.

A capital account amendment to the Articles of Agreement of the IMF was on the agenda at the annual meetings of the IMF in Hong Kong in 1997.[17] Given recent controversies about capital flows, it is no longer on the agenda. But it should be. The Fund should have the *orderly* liberalization of the capital account as one of its purposes. Just as is the case with current account liberalization, countries could elect to maintain capital account restrictions (the equivalent of Article XIV of the Articles of Agreement), and, when ready and willing, could accept the obligations of an open capital account (the equivalent of Article VIII).

What benefits would this bring? For countries, it would provide a framework in which to think about their present capital controls, possibly to rationalize them, and eventually to undertake capital account liberalization. For the Fund, it would put center stage a set of issues that is critical to the operation of the international capital markets and the frequency of crises. And for the Fund and the economics profession, it would make it necessary to develop a body of knowledge about capital

---

[17] The Interim Committee agreed in April 1997 that there would be benefits to amending the Articles of Agreement to make capital account liberalization a purpose of the Fund, and to extend the Fund's jurisdiction to capital movements.

account restrictions and how best to remove them. It is striking that while accepted principles exist for current account liberalization – for instance, first replace quantitative restrictions by tariffs, then gradually reduce tariffs and their dispersion – we have few established principles about the removal of capital account restrictions. While many – myself included – believe that the capital account should be liberalized at the long end first, that there should be few restrictions on foreign direct investment, and that Chilean-style inflow controls can be useful, these views do not cover all capital account issues, and in any case need further substantiation and refinement.

The adoption of codes and standards: In considering systemic reforms after the Mexican crisis, the initial reaction was to emphasize the need to provide better information to the markets. The Special Data Dissemination Standard (SDDS), introduced in 1996, was developed in response. It describes a set of data, and information on procedures for their release, that subscribing countries have to meet. At present 50 countries have subscribed, including most emerging market countries. The General Data Dissemination System (GDDS) was developed subsequently for countries that do not yet aspire to meet the SDDS; it sets out procedures by which participating countries can gradually improve the quality of their data, with the assistance of the IMF.

Probably the most important improvement made under the SDDS is to bring uniformity to the release of information on reserves. The reserves template requires countries to make data on reserves available at least monthly, with no more than a one-month lag.[18, 19] Data on forward commitments have to be revealed. The requirement to provide external debt data is also extremely important – one of the main tasks the IMF found itself undertaking in its meetings with the private sector immediately following the outbreak of a crisis was trying to reconcile different external debt estimates.

If Thailand and Korea had been meeting the conditions on the release of reserves data before their crises, the markets would have known about the declining reserves much sooner, and Thailand would have been forced to reveal its forward interventions in the foreign exchange market.

[18] The IMF staff would have preferred weekly data, but some leading central banks objected. They argued that unless private sector participants were required to provide information on their positions, the central banks would be at a disadvantage if required to provide frequent and up-to-date information on their reserves.
[19] Many countries do better than this.

Each country would almost certainly have had to allow the exchange rate to move earlier, well before exhausting their reserves.[20] It is also possible that, if this information had been generally available, the political system in each country would have forced a policy adjustment on the central bank sooner.[21]

As this discussion suggests, transparency is important not only because it provides more information to the markets, but even more because it puts constraints on what policymakers can do. Subsequently the IMF developed Codes of Good Practices on Transparency in Monetary and Financial Policies, and on Fiscal Transparency, respectively. These set out standards against which countries can measure their own practices, and where necessary, seek to improve them. The Fund helps countries appraise their practices.

Countries' performance in meeting four standards in other areas – the Basle Committee's Core Principles for Effective Banking Supervision, and standards for securities regulation, insurance supervision, and payments systems – are assessed as part of the Financial Sector Assessment Program (FSAP), a joint effort of the IMF, the World Bank, and national supervisory agencies. The World Bank is taking the lead in assessing standards in four other areas: corporate governance (standard developed by the OECD); accounting (International Accounting Standards Board, IASB); auditing (International Federation of Accountants); and insolvency and creditor rights (principles developed by the World Bank).

Each standard provides a yardstick by which a country can appraise its performance in the relevant area, and seek to meet international standards. The key questions then are what are the incentives and obstacles to meeting the standards. The answers depend in part on how these systems are appraised, how and to whom the information is made public, what assistance is provided to help countries upgrade their performance, and how investors take country performance in these areas into account in making their investment decisions. Among the incen-

---

[20] The Mexican case is more complicated, since their reserves declined in two steps, first following the Colosio assassination in April and then in November. It is thus not obvious that adherence to the present reserves template would have produced an earlier exchange rate adjustment.

[21] The report of the Nukul Commission on the Thai crisis (*The Nation*, Bangkok, March 31, 1998) states that information on reserves was very tightly held within the Bank of Thailand.

tives should be the desire of policymakers to strengthen the economy and reduce the probability of crisis – an incentive that should always be present. Each country's performance in meeting a specific standard is monitored by the relevant body, and the results are summarized in a report on the observance of standards and codes (ROSC) that is posted on the Internet.[22]

Nothing would help improve standards more than if countries that met higher standards were rewarded with lower borrowing costs.[23] It is too early to tell whether spreads are lower for countries that meet relevant standards. However, anecdotal evidence and discussions with some market participants suggest that awareness of the contents of ROSCs is growing. If this awareness translates into lower spreads for those meeting higher standards, the standards initiative will begin to pay off both for individual countries and for the system as a whole.

2.2 Actions by the Fund

Much of what the IMF needs to do to prevent crises – the work on standards and codes, and the possibility of a capital account amendment to the Articles of Agreement – has already been discussed. In addition, the FSAP is an extremely important initiative, which is helping member countries strengthen their financial systems. I shall focus on three areas: improving surveillance, increasing transparency, and the possibility of prequalification for loans.

Improving surveillance: The Mexican crisis took the IMF by surprise, and it was easy to conclude that better surveillance would have helped prevent the crisis – particularly because at that time the IMF did not make much effort to monitor market and economic developments in real time. It was only after the Mexican crisis that news and financial data screens were widely installed in the Fund.

It is hard to quarrel with the notion that improved surveillance should help reduce the frequency of crises, and that Fund surveillance

---

[22] By the end of September 2001, 169 ROSC modules had been completed for 57 countries.

[23] One such incentive should have been provided by the fact that to qualify for the Contingent Credit Line (CCL) facility, a country has to be making satisfactory progress towards meeting international standards, particularly the SDDS, the Basle Committee's Core Principles for Effective Banking Supervision, and the Codes on Fiscal Transparency, and on Transparency in Monetary and Financial Policies, respectively. However, the CCL has had no takers.

through the annual Article IV report, along with more frequent interim interactions with member countries, should contribute to this end.[24] Fund surveillance has improved greatly since 1994.[25] The private dialog between the management and staff of the IMF and the officials of a country can be very frank indeed. Reporting to the Board is also typically very frank.[26]

A key question is whether the Fund should issue public warnings – a system of yellow and red cards – when it believes a country is heading for a crisis. In issuing warnings of potential trouble, whether in private or in public, the IMF has to be mindful of two types of error: the type-1 error of crises that were not predicted; and the type-2 error of a crisis that was predicted but did not happen. It has particularly to be concerned that its warnings may be self-justifying – and this is a difficult problem to deal with, one that member countries tend to emphasize. Members of the IMF Executive Board often repeat that they do not want the Fund to become a rating agency.[27]

The Fund has rarely issued a clear public warning of an impending crisis, but does express concerns that make the point. How would it have done if it had issued public warnings? Of the six major crises between 1994 and 1999, three were on the Fund's radar screen well before they happened – Thailand, Russia, and Brazil – and three were not, despite concerns having been expressed about some weaknesses in each of the Mexican, Indonesian, and Korean economies. During the crisis period, I predicted, within official circles, at least one crisis that didn't happen. Type-2 errors of this sort are especially worrisome.[28]

---

[24] Given the quantity of private sector research on industrialized and emerging market countries, the question arises whether the Fund has any advantage in undertaking surveillance of these countries. Part of the answer should be the quality of the Fund staff; in addition, Fund staff and management are likely to have a closer dialog with country officials, and may well have access to better information about policies and policy intentions.

[25] In 1999, a group of experts headed by John Crow, former Governor of the Bank of Canada, presented a report on Fund surveillance. See *External Evaluation of IMF Surveillance: Report by a Group of Independent Experts*, IMF, September 1999.

[26] I discuss below how such concerns are reflected in published reports.

[27] The Fund publishes each quarter a list of the about 40 countries whose currencies are usable for Fund lending; since the criterion for being on the list is to have a strong balance of payments and reserve position, this is a rating, albeit not a very refined one.

[28] If Fund warnings were self-justifying, there would not be any type-2 errors.

In addition to self-justifying predictions, it is necessary to consider warnings that may be self-negating – warnings of a potential crisis that induce a country to take action that averts the crisis. I have seen policy actions taken in some economies that in my view prevented crises. In such cases, success has many parents, and since it is the authorities within the country who have responsibility for policy decisions, they rightly tend to take the credit for averting the crisis.[29]

While I can envisage circumstances in which the Fund should issue public warnings – and in essence it did that a few weeks before the Thai devaluation – the quiet approach should be the norm. Public warnings are especially difficult when a country is in a program. If the Fund sees a problem coming, it warns the country, increasingly urgently, that the program is in danger. If the country does not respond, the Fund can cut off financing, or issue a public warning. But in these circumstances, the public warning is especially likely to be self-justifying. This dilemma is very real, and has arisen several times in recent years.

Why do countries fail to take action when warned? For one thing, as the late Herb Stein used to say, economists are very good at predicting that something cannot go on forever, but are less good at saying when it will end. (Stein's corollary is that if something cannot go on forever, it will end.) When warning a finance minister about the non-sustainability of the current situation, I was sometimes told that I or someone else said the same thing a year or more ago, and we were wrong. The response is to tell the story of the person on the way down after jumping out of a fortieth floor window, but that usually does not work – for it is rarely the case that those being warned are unaware of the dangers they run; rather there are usually reasons, good or bad (often political), for what they are doing. For another thing, policymakers embarked on a dangerous policy path tend to argue that there is something special about their economy that makes it immune to the normal rules of economics. Sometimes the officials concerned may believe that the trouble will come later, on someone else's watch. And sometimes they are right to ignore a warning, for it is wrong – but much less frequently than asserted by those being warned.

---

[29] I once took an informal poll inside the IMF asking for examples of crises averted; there were more than I expected, even after adjusting for multiple parentage. I am not aware of more scientific results on this issue.

16   Review of World Economics 2003, Vol. 139 (1)

It has sometimes been suggested that the Fund should refuse to lend to countries that get into a crisis after ignoring warnings. The idea of providing incentives to heed warnings is attractive, but this punishment may be too draconian. For not only are some warnings wrong, but also, in refusing to help a country that is willing to implement the needed policies, the IMF would be punishing the entire population because of the actions of a few policymakers who failed to respond to warnings – and who have probably been fired in the meantime. There is however a case for developing a procedure in which the terms of lending are adjusted depending on the country's previous behavior – though there is a delicate balance to be struck between providing incentives to heed warnings and providing disincentives to come to the Fund when trouble looms.

Beyond the standard traditional human intelligence aspects of surveillance, the Fund has invested in the statistical analysis of vulnerability indicators, as predictors of the probability of a crisis (see IMF 2000 and Goldstein et al. 2000). Similar exercises are undertaken in the private sector, and are published. While these efforts are interesting and the results worth close scrutiny, their forecasting record is not very good; further, to the extent that any one of these equations fits well and is used successfully to avert some crises, it may carry the seeds of its own destruction, in Goodhart's law or Lucas critique fashion (Berg et al. 1999).

The Fund is strengthening the vulnerability analyses it carries out for internal purposes: these bring together the statistical analyses with detailed country-by-country reports in seeking to identify countries that are vulnerable, and to recommend appropriate policy measures. While it should continue to strive to make surveillance ever better, we need also to keep reminding ourselves that no early warning system will be infallible.

Transparency: At the time of the Mexican crisis, the IMF published very little about its programs, its policy deliberations, and its surveillance activities – except for the *World Economic Outlook* and the *International Capital Markets Report*. If the Board agreed to support a program, an announcement of the amounts involved would be made. Program documents were not published; nor were Article IV reports.

Now the great majority of IMF members publish their Article IV conclusions (in the Public Information Notices (PINs)) and, more important, most agree to the publication of the Article IV reports themselves.[30] Most borrowers release the Letters of Intent that describe their IMF-supported programs. In addition, since the start of 2001, countries have been allowed to publish the staff reports on programs, and about half have been published since then. Staff papers on general policy issues are almost all published, sometimes also in preliminary form to solicit public comment. In addition, an Independent Evaluation Office, reporting to the Board, has been established and is beginning to operate.

All this marks a revolution in transparency, and a revolution within the Fund. At the time the changes were being debated within the Fund, some Board members feared that greater transparency would inhibit the frankness of the policy dialog between the Fund and its members, and the frankness of reporting to the Board. The objection was a serious one, even if it sometimes came from members with whom the policy dialog was not particularly frank. It was dealt with in part by allowing members to request the removal of market-sensitive information from reports that were later to be published.[31] On balance I do not believe the fears have turned out to be valid, though from time to time in clearing a report, I was mindful of the fact that the report would be made public.

The main argument for transparency put forward a few years ago was that it helps make markets more efficient. That it does, despite the difficulties skeptical markets frequently create for member countries and for the Fund. But transparency has many other benefits. As already mentioned, it improves policy, because policymakers operating in the light of day cannot do some of the things they can do in the dark of secrecy. It also improves the quality of the Fund's work, for Fund staff and management are bound to be even more careful to get it right when subject to scrutiny – and here the Independent Evaluation Office will also make an important difference.

But transparency does even more than that, in two regards. First, it promotes interactions with the outside world, for as the Fund puts information out, it has also to interact with the outside, listening to what outsiders are saying, and taking information in. This happens in a variety of ways: the posting of papers for comment on the web; the setting up of

---

[30] Publication rates of Article IV's are highest for the advanced countries, Central and Eastern Europe, and Western Hemisphere members.

[31] All changes made between Board presentation and publication of a report have to be reported in complete detail to the Board – this serves as a safeguard against changes that do not meet the market-sensitivity test.

Globalization and Economic and Financial Instability

the Capital Markets Consultative Group, a group of private sector capital market participants with whom general issues – but not the details of individual country cases – are discussed; and increased interactions with NGOs in both the industrialized and developing countries. In addition, transparency improves the depth and the quality of the interactions with the academic community. The Fund has to be careful in all these interactions not to betray the trust of its members by revealing privileged information, or by giving anyone favored access – and doing so requires real skill and tact.

Second, transparency strengthens the potential effectiveness of Fund surveillance over nonborrowing countries. In that regard, consider the United States. The US government used to ignore the annual Article IV report, and hardly anyone outside official circles got to see it. The Article IV report for the United States for 2001 was certainly not ignored: it was the subject of many news reports and of several op-ed columns in leading newspapers. And all the attention it received ensures the next Article IV consultation with the United States will be treated more seriously by the US authorities than in the past. Of course there is also a risk – namely that Fund surveillance fails to establish a track record. Which is to say, transparency strengthens the incentives for the Fund to do top-class work.

Let me confess also to a third argument that was sometimes on my mind – that transparency probably contributes a bit to democracy.

Looking back, I regard the transparency revolution as the most important change in the IMF during the seven years I was there. This is not simply a bureaucratic change; it is a culture change. It has some costs – but it is overwhelmingly a positive development.

Prequalification for loans: The Meltzer Commission recommended that the Fund move over five years towards a system in which countries would have to prequalify for loans, particularly by meeting strong standards for the health of the banking system.[32] Loans would be disbursed automatically if triggered. Other countries would not receive loans, except in cases of systemic risk.

Relying solely on prequalification for loans would set up the right incentives to meet the qualification conditions. However, automatic disbursement, independent of the country's macroeconomic policies,

---

[32] The report of the Meltzer Commission (the International Financial Institution Advisory Committee) is available at <http://www.house.gov/jec/imf/ifiac.htm>.

would not make sense, even if the country's overall policies had been good at the time the line of credit was negotiated, for macroeconomic conditions are almost bound to have changed at the time the country needs to draw on its line of credit. Further, while there should be incentives for prequalification, I do not believe the Fund should refuse to lend to nonprequalifying crisis countries – provided such countries are willing to adjust their policies to deal with the crisis. The discussion here parallels the discussion about the suggestion that the Fund not lend to countries that ignore warnings provided by the Fund – and we should note also that the Meltzer Commission's systemic risk contingency is one that discriminates against smaller countries.

Nonetheless, the notion of prequalifying for lending is an important one, which is embodied in the conditions for the Contingent Credit Line (CCL) facility. The basic idea is straightforward: the IMF offers a precautionary line of credit to countries that have demonstrably sound policies, but which nonetheless believe they may be vulnerable to contagion from crises elsewhere. In effect, it allows countries that have met certain preconditions to augment – at low cost – the foreign exchange reserves they can draw on in a crisis. The knowledge that these resources are available may in itself deter a speculative attack. By offering qualifying countries a seal of approval for their policies, it should also reduce contagion, by giving less reason for investors and creditors to pull their money out because of crises elsewhere.

The adoption of the CCL marked an important departure from the Fund's traditional lending activities. Rather than waiting to pick up the pieces after an accident has happened, the intent behind the introduction of the CCL was to use the Fund's lending capacity for crisis prevention, as well as crisis resolution. This obviously creates a risk of moral hazard. Countries have an incentive – in theory at least – to run weaker policies if they have an extra financial cushion in place. Perhaps more importantly, investors have an incentive to lend to countries with weaker policies if they believe that the presence of the credit line increases the chances that they will be repaid if things go wrong.

To counter this problem, the CCL was aimed explicitly at members with first-class policies, who would face a potential loss of access to international capital markets because of contagion rather than domestic policy weaknesses. But we do not live in a Manichaean world in which we can divide countries neatly between the righteous and the ungodly. So "first-class" should not be taken to mean "perfect." The eligibility criteria are demanding, but not so much so that they would disqualify any country that might benefit from signing up.[33]

Unfortunately, the CCL has not been adopted by any country, and as time goes by, it seems less likely that it will be adopted. In part this was because of a Groucho Marx-like concern that no country that was eligible would want to join the club. It is not clear whether a further reformulation of the facility would lead to its use, but as of now it seems that this important attempt to make the Fund's financial resources available for crisis prevention has failed.

2.3 Actions by Others

Almost every suggestion for change identified so far relates to the behavior of the emerging market economies or the IMF. But the behavior of the suppliers of international capital in the industrialized countries, particularly the financial institutions, also contributes to the excessive volatility of international capital flows, and thus to financial crises. This is the theme of Dobson and Hufbauer (2001), who argue (p.129) that "Changing the rules of the game in industrial countries is at least as important as strengthening the regulators and financial institutions in the emerging markets." This view was shared by the authorities in some Asian countries, who attributed the crises to the behavior of hedge funds.

Dobson and Hufbauer trace many of the capital flow reversals during crises to the behavior of short-term flows, intermediated in some way by banks (including, for instance, providing credit to hedge funds), subject to moral hazard caused by explicit and implicit insurance in the host countries. Their proposed solution is a set of measures for strengthening the new Basle Capital Accord, improving financial system regulation in part through increasing the accountability of supervisors, tightening the frameworks governing G-10 deposit insurance, and undertaking a review of the behavior of large portfolio investors with the goal of designing "disclosure rules and other incentives that would forestall large portfolio swings from becoming a future financial problem" (Dobson and Hufbauer 2001: 165). They also recommend creating a clear ex ante

---

[33] The key conditions are *(i)* at the time the credit line is agreed, the country is not expected to need to borrow from the Fund; *(ii)* the country's economy is in good shape, and it is making progress towards meeting relevant international standards; and *(iii)* the country must enjoy constructive relations with its private creditors, and be taking appropriate steps to limit its external vulnerability.

framework for private sector involvement in the resolution of international financial crises, a topic to which I will turn later.

The issue here is not the goals, which are admirable, but whether better rules and regulations can be designed. After all, the revised Basle Accord took a considerable amount of work and time, and is only now going into effect. With regard to hedge funds, an IMF study found that a wide range of financial institutions, including banks, had engaged in the same behavior as the hedge funds (Eichengreen et al. 1998). That conclusion could point two ways, but policymakers in the leading countries whose institutions supply funds took the view that the type of systemic risk that emerged in the Long Term Capital Management (LTCM) case could best be handled by greater diligence by the lenders to hedge funds. These conclusions left the authorities in some Asian and some European countries unconvinced, but a subsequent Financial Stability Forum study[34] was not able to push towards any consensus on the need for or possibility of greater disclosure of position-taking by financial institutions participating in emerging markets. Although it is doubtful that a different consensus will emerge anytime soon, this issue should remain on the agenda.

Dobson and Hufbauer also call for better coordination among G-10 supervisors and regulators. The Financial Stability Forum (FSF) was set up in 1999 to bring financial supervisors from the G-7 together with their finance ministry and central bank deputies, along with representatives of the major international regulatory agencies, and International Financial Institution (IFI) officials. As a forum, the FSF has a very small bureaucracy, but is able to draw on the institutions associated with it, and others, to prepare reports on major financial issues – and it has been active in this regard, producing several good reports. Its biannual meetings start with a surveillance discussion seeking to identify vulnerabilities in the international financial system, and in financial systems in individual countries. It is not clear yet to what extent the FSF has contributed to strengthening supervision in the international financial system.

The G-20 was also set up in the aftermath of the Asian crisis. Its membership is very similar to that of the International Monetary and Financial Committee (IMFC), the ministerial level body that in effect

---

[34] Financial Stability Forum, *Report of the Working Group on Highly Leveraged Institutions*, Basle, 2000.

22   Review of World Economics 2003, Vol. 139 (1)

governs the IMF. Given competing demands on the time of officials, rationalization of the proliferation of institutions in the international system would be desirable.

3 Crisis Response and Private Sector Involvement

While it is convenient to draw a distinction between crisis prevention and crisis response, the line cannot be clear-cut, for the way the Fund and the international system respond to crises also helps determine behavior before a crisis.

No issue in the debate over the reform of the system has generated more heat than that of private sector involvement (PSI). The term is used in several senses. The literal meaning is the contribution of the private sector to meeting a country's financing needs. In the debate over how the IMF should ensure PSI, the term is often used to mean non-business-as-usual ways to persuade the private sector to reduce net capital outflows from a country facing a capital account crisis. Some mean by PSI the losses or pain borne by foreign private investors during a crisis.

These different conceptions of PSI are relevant to distinct but related concerns about IMF lending. The first recognizes that given the scale of capital flows to emerging market countries, the public sector is unlikely to be able to fully offset swings in private capital flows, and that the private sector one way (voluntarily) or another (involuntarily) needs to provide some of the needed financing.[35] This leads to the second sense of PSI – that the IMF may on occasion need to find ways of helping ensure the private sector provides some of the financing.

The third – pain – sense is relevant to the efficiency of the operation of the capital markets, and to moral hazard. If markets are to operate efficiently, investors need to bear the real risks associated with their investments, and IMF programs should not shield them from that.[36] Oth-

---

[35] The question of the optimal size of the IMF and of individual programs could be analyzed using a cost-benefit analysis, in which at the margin the benefit to the global economy of an extra dollar provided to the IMF is equal to its marginal cost. There are of course formidable difficulties in quantifying the benefit to the global economy, including the need to weight the gains to different groups in the global system.

[36] A great deal lies behind this sentence: in particular, if optimal IMF operations can sustainably (in the stochastic equilibrium of the system) reduce the variability of output in emerging market economies, then the real risks facing investors are those in the equilibrium in which the IMF is acting optimally.

erwise moral hazard will lead investors to make decisions based on beliefs about extraordinary rescue packages rather than a careful appraisal of the real value of the investment. And if that happens, a successful rescue could contain the seeds of a future crisis.

Some emphasize fairness as much as efficiency, arguing that investors should not be bailed out by loans financed by advanced country taxpayers. In fact, IMF crisis loans have always been repaid[37] – often early – and the industrialized country taxpayers do not bear a burden.[38] Rather the loans are repaid by the taxpayers of the borrowing country – and accordingly many argue that investors are being bailed out by imposing a burden on domestic residents. To clinch this argument, it would be necessary to spell out what the alternative course of action for the crisis country would have been. There would surely have been substantial costs associated with any other course of action, such as defaulting on the debt.

For all three reasons – particularly because it does not have and should not have enough money to do otherwise – the IMF has to be concerned with private sector involvement in the resolution of financial crises. However, the issue has to be approached carefully, lest proposed solutions increase the frequency of crises. For instance, the formalization of a requirement that the banks, or any other set of creditors, always be forced to share in the financing of IMF programs, would be destabilizing for the international system. If such a condition were insisted on, the creditors would have a greater incentive to rush for the exits at the mere hint of a crisis. This is a real dilemma, one that suggests the need for a differentiated approach to involving the private sector, one that depends on the circumstances of each country: sometimes a formal approach may be necessary, as in Korea at Christmas in 1997; at other times, as in the case of Brazil in March 1999, when the commercial banks voluntarily agreed to maintain their lines of credit, less formal discussions could serve better; when financing needs are small, there may not be a need to approach the creditors; and in extreme and infrequent cases, an involuntary restructuring of the debt may be necessary.

---

[37] A few countries (among them Sudan, Democratic Republic of the Congo, Liberia) are in arrears to the IMF, but these are not countries that suffered capital account crises – rather they suffered from conflict and civil wars.

[38] I leave aside here the issue of whether the subsidy implicit in lending to crisis countries at IMF rates is a burden on the providers of funds.

The IMF's approach to private sector involvement is in a state of flux, but the framework in which it operates in practice is probably still best described by an agreement reached among the membership at the annual meetings in Prague in September 2000.[39] The approach emphasizes the need to rely as much as possible on market-oriented and voluntary solutions.

The basic principles of the framework are that official financing is limited; that debtors and their creditors should take responsibility for their decisions to borrow and lend; and that contracts should be honored, except *in extremis*. The approach taken in individual cases should be based on an assessment by the Fund of a member's underlying payment capacity and its prospects of regaining market access. Cases are expected to fall broadly into four categories:

(1) Those where policy adjustment and official financing should allow the member to regain full market access reasonably quickly. This is essentially the traditional catalytic approach. The framework specifies that extraordinary access to Fund resources should be exceptional, and that high levels of access to Fund resources require substantial justification, both in terms of its likely effectiveness and of the risks of alternative approaches.
(2) Those where official financing and policy adjustment need to be combined with encouragement to creditors to reach voluntary arrangements to overcome their coordination problems.
(3) Those where the early restoration of full market access on terms consistent with medium-term external sustainability is judged to be unrealistic, and further action by private creditors, possibly including comprehensive debt restructuring, may be needed in the context of a Fund-supported program to provide for an adequately financed program and a viable medium-term balance of payments.
(4) Those extreme cases where the member may have to resort to a temporary payments suspension or standstill pending action by its creditors to support the restoration of viability. In such cases, the Fund would be prepared to lend into arrears to private creditors, provided the country is seeking to work cooperatively and in good faith with those creditors and is meeting other program requirements.

---

[39] See the Annex for a full statement of the relevant paragraphs. I am grateful to Mark Allen of the IMF for allowing me to draw on material he has provided.

There are recent examples of programs in each category. The Brazilian program in March 2000 fell into the second category, and it was judged in the fall of 2000 that Turkey fell into that category too. The Argentine debt restructuring in the spring of 2001 was perhaps consistent with the third category, though full market access was not in the end restored. And Ecuador in 1998–99, in which the IMF did lend into arrears to private creditors, fell into the fourth category

Note that the framework does not use the words "liquidity" and "solvency" to categorize different cases. If the distinction were being used, cases 1 and 2 would be liquidity cases, and 4 would be a solvency case, with 3 not clear. The distinction is not used because, although analytically extremely helpful, it is difficult to apply to sovereign debtors. For them, the distinction is largely political, for solvency depends on the extent to which a government can or wants to reduce domestic demand in order to continue to service its debt. For instance, following the exchange rate crisis in February 2001, the Turkish government faced the choice of undertaking a massive fiscal adjustment in order to continue servicing its debt, or attempting a debt restructuring, which would probably have had to be involuntary. It chose the fiscal adjustment.

Nonetheless, four serious difficulties arise in applying this framework. The first became clear following the revised Turkey program in December 2000, after a voluntary agreement on a rollover of interbank lines had been reached with Turkey's commercial bank creditors. At that point the program looked likely to succeed, and the voluntary agreement by the banks could be seen as the solution to a collective action problem. But then during the next few months the markets' confidence in the Turkish program began to weaken, and the banks began to pull out their lines.[40] Given that the program was not going perfectly, it was difficult for the official sector to insist as strongly as before on the banks rolling over their lines.

The second difficulty lies in the enforcement of these voluntary agreements. In the 1980s, the authorities in the creditor countries exerted pressure on their banks, doing so to solve the collective action problem – namely, that if the banks agreed to provide the required amount of funding, each bank individually would be better off than it would have

---

[40] Part of the decline in interbank lines was a result of a decline in demand by Turkish banks.

been had it done what seemed best for it, acting alone, which was to attempt to withdraw its funds. Bank regulators have been much less enthusiastic about exerting such pressure in recent years, for they see a conflict between their regulatory role and their pressuring the banks to maintain portfolio positions against their will. Some industrial country regulators argued that it was up to the authorities in the crisis country to persuade the banks to hold their lines. But typically the crisis country has very little leverage in this situation. It is similarly difficult for the IMF to exert any leverage if the industrial country regulators are not also doing so. The key issue is whether by exerting pressure the industrial country regulators are indeed helping the banks reach a better equilibrium – and a judgment on that issue should be made case by case.

The third difficulty is in the notion of voluntary market-based re-structurings of the debt. To a first approximation, a purely voluntary market-based restructuring cannot reduce the present value of a coun-try's debt, for the country will simply be trading the debt up and down the term structure.[41] Thus not much should be expected from purely voluntary debt restructurings, though changes in the profile of debt payments – for instance pushing them out into later years – could be useful if the country has a temporary liquidity problem. The country *could* achieve a reduction in the debt burden by reducing the seniority and thus the value of existing claims in some way. And perhaps it could achieve some reduction in the debt burden by enhancing some new claims with the aid of financing or guarantees from the official sector, where the reduction in the value of the debt will be approximately equal to the reduction in the present value of interest payments implied by the substitution of lower interest official debt for higher interest market debt.

The fourth, most profound, difficulty occurs in the "extreme cases where the member may have to resort to a temporary payments sus-pension or standstill pending action by its creditors to support the restoration of viability." *The problem is that we have no accepted frame-work in which a country in extremis can impose a payments suspension or standstill pending agreement with its creditors to support the restoration of viability – and that accordingly any country contemplating a standstill faces enormous uncertainties about what will happen to the economy if it*

---

[41] The present value of the debt could change as a result of changes in the term struc-ture of interest.

does so. Those uncertainties are compounded by the absence of an accepted legal framework in which the debtor and its creditors can work to seek to restore viability.

Indeed it is striking that when governments face the decision on whether to seek to impose a standstill and/or restructure the debt in a nonvoluntary way, they are generally willing to go very far to avoid a default – especially so the countries that have adopted drastic solutions in the past, such as default, deposit freezes, and exchange controls.

A standstill could be appropriate and sufficient in a pure liquidity crisis, as a way of stopping a self-justifying run. However, a standstill might be the prelude to a restructuring. There is no way of knowing until after the dust has settled. Why are countries so reluctant to go down this road, especially given the frequency with which critics of IMF rescues argue that a default would be better for the international system and the country? The reasons are: that a debt restructuring will almost certainly involve a restructuring of the domestic financial system, where financial institutions – including banks and pension funds – hold government bonds as important parts of their portfolios; that it is impossible to know what interruptions there will be to the payments mechanism and to trade credit; and that it is impossible to know when domestic and foreign confidence in the government's ability to meet its promises will be restored, and for how long the country will be punished by the markets for having defaulted. Rightly or wrongly, probably rightly, debtor governments see the costs of a debt default as extremely large – and much larger than the critics of IMF loans typically imply.

The desire of countries to avoid default raises difficult issues for the official sector: the official sector should be on the side of those who want to honor contracts, and should not force default on countries that are willing to undertake the policies needed to avoid it – provided the country has a reasonable probability of doing so successfully. But there will be occasions when the probability of finding a way out of a crisis without a debt restructuring and write-down is low, and it is then that the official sector should not provide further assistance. It is the judgment of how far to go to help a country that seeks to avoid a default, and of what probability of success to require, that lies behind the controversies over recent IMF support for Turkey, its decision to support Argentina in August 2001, and not to provide further support in December 2001.

What can be done (Eichengreen 2000)? The most important suggested innovation is the creation of a legal procedure for sovereign bankruptcy, which would require finding legal mechanisms both to approve payments standstills by sovereigns, and for the restructuring and if necessary writing down of sovereign debts.[42,43] This is the SDRM or Sovereign Debt Restructuring Mechanism, which has been strongly supported and advanced by my successor at the IMF, and a previous Harms lecturer, Anne Krueger.

Should we make improvement in standstill and/or bankruptcy procedures for sovereigns a high priority? The costs of resorting to such measures have to be high if the credit mechanism is to work well. If creditors believe emerging market debtors will too easily use legal provisions to restructure debts, spreads will rise and capital flows to those countries will decline. That is why policymakers from emerging market countries generally oppose proposals to make it easier for them to restructure their payments, be it through collective action clauses or the creation of a sovereign bankruptcy procedure.

Nonetheless, the absence of procedures for dealing with situations where debts have a very high probability of becoming unsustainable distorts the behavior of the international system. Under present circumstances, when a country's debt burden is unsustainable, the international community – operating through the IMF – faces the choice of lending to it, or forcing it into a potentially extremely costly restructuring, whose outcome is unknown. I believe the official sector should go very far to help countries that are willing to take the necessary measures to avoid debt defaults, but debts will sometimes have to be written down. That should be costly for the country concerned, but not as costly as it is now.

Such a change in the international system would inevitably affect the nature and direction of capital flows, and we can be sure that if legal changes are made, the creditors will seek ways of restructuring

---

[42] National bankruptcy laws should apply to private sector debtors who cannot make payments; if debtors can pay in local currency, the stay could permit a delay in converting these payments into foreign currency.

[43] It is often argued that Article VIII-2b of the IMF Articles of Agreement could serve as the basis for international approval of a payments standstill imposed by a member of the Fund. However, this judgment is not shared by the IMF's lawyers, who point out that Article VIII-2b applies to exchange controls on exchange contracts, not to payments on debt contracts.

debt contracts to minimize the impact of the new framework. But we could also reasonably hope that such provisions would lead to more differentiation among countries, with flows increasing to those countries unlikely to need to use the bankruptcy mechanism, and relative spreads rising for those more likely to have to use it, thereby providing important incentives to strengthen the structure of the economy and economic policies.

So it is certainly desirable that the IMF continue its important work on this topic. But we should recognize that at best it will take many years to change the legal framework, and that it is quite possible that it will not in the end be possible to persuade the U.S. Congress on this issue. In any case, I believe the Executive Board of the IMF could make a contribution to this effort by describing in advance a set of procedures for how it will act if it concludes that countries have an unsustainable level of debt. This would help formalize the approach that has already been developed on an ad hoc basis in response to some of the recent crises. At the very least, it would provide more clarity on the question for debtors and creditors alike, which would be a good in itself.

The G-10 deputies' proposal for collective action clauses (CACs) in bond contracts, which should make them easier to restructure, is another possibility.[44] Ironically the Krueger proposal for an SDRM seems to have achieved one important result in persuading the private sector to support CACs. However, emerging market countries have resisted the suggestion, arguing it would raise spreads.[45] At present some emerging market countries are considering whether to include CACs in future bond contracts – and if they do, that will achieve many of the goals of a more complete SDRM.

There has been some fear that inclusion of CACs will create moral hazard on the part of borrowers, who will be too quick to seek to

---

[44] This proposal led to an Alphonse and Gaston act in which emerging country bond issuers announced they would be willing to follow industrialized countries in including such clauses, while the industrialized countries generally explained that they had no need for them. In 2000, the United Kingdom did include such a clause in a euro issue, in the hope that other countries would follow.

[45] The strong opposition to the initial (1996) proposal for CACs became less persuasive when it was realized that such clauses already existed in so-called British trust-deed bonds, and that no one had noticed. Subsequent empirical research by Eichengreen and Mody (2000) suggested that the inclusion of such clauses reduces spreads for high-quality borrowers and raises them for less sound borrowers – an appealing result, though one that is the subject of ongoing research.

30   Review of World Economics 2003, Vol. 139 (1)

restructure their debt obligations. I doubt this will happen, for the issuers have generally fought vigorously to avoid defaults. If there is a hazard in the adoption of CACs, it is that the official sector will become too quick to urge restructurings as an alternative to IMF lending. There is a balance to be struck, and it is important that the IMF not step back from the provision of financial resources to countries facing a liquidity crisis.

4 The Operation of the International Capital Markets

As the Mexican crisis developed, and as the Asian crisis intensified, it was easy to conclude that the capital markets were too powerful and too volatile, that contagion was excessive, and that they failed to discriminate appropriately among different levels of performance. And there were certainly occasions during the crisis when I felt that each of these charges was justified. It was less obvious what to do about them.

One response would have been for countries to close themselves off from the international capital markets. It is striking that despite the blandishments of events and some well-known economists, no country – including Malaysia, which removed almost all its controls within less than two years after imposing them – did that.[46] Emerging market country policymakers must have thought it useful to remain within the international financial system despite the problems that had caused for them.

Is there any way of establishing that the international capital markets are inefficient? As we know from the literature on the stock market, it is difficult to prove empirically that asset prices fluctuate excessively.[47] But let me mention a few pieces of evidence.

Larry Summers has argued that there is an inconsistency between the pricing of emerging market bonds and the frequency of defaults:

---

[46] To be sure, several countries did impose measures seeking to control or close access to offshore markets in their currency.

[47] It may be even more difficult to establish excess variability if there are multiple equilibria. Presumably the test of efficiency would then have seek to establish whether the system was in a good or a bad equilibrium at any given time. There have been several crises during which I was convinced we were in a multiple equilibrium situation, in which the government's policies would be fully viable if spreads were lower – the good equilibrium – but that the policies were not viable at actual spreads – the bad equilibrium. But I do not know how to establish that was the case.

specifically, that spreads are so high as to imply a substantial probability of default, but defaults have been few.[48]

Another striking fact has been the contagion that has been seen in the emerging markets – in the Mexican crisis, during the Asian crisis, and in the Russian crisis. However, I should add that I do not believe the difficulties in Brazil in the run-up to the 2002 election were primarily a result of contagion from Argentina; rather they mainly reflected political uncertainties in Brazil.

There are some good reasons for contagion among related markets, for instance, the stock prices of firms in the same industry tend to move together, but its extent in the Russian crisis was surely excessive. Further, the explanation that contagion spread to the stronger emerging markets in part because emerging market traders needed cash, which was most easily obtained in a relatively strong market, suggests a market inefficiency in which limited liquidity in the market as a whole distorts pricing relations among the different countries' bonds.[49]

During crises, the IMF sometimes heard suggestions that a particular course of action should be taken "for the good of the asset class." This is not a compelling basis for making a decision on an individual country, but it does support the view that treating emerging market bonds as a separate asset class distorts asset pricing among emerging market countries. Perhaps emerging market asset price determination would become more efficient if the bonds of the different emerging market countries were no longer treated as an asset class.

The data strongly suggest that the markets are doing a better job of discriminating among countries now than they did during the Asian and Russian crises. Spreads vary widely, no major anomalies in the ranking of spreads are immediately obvious, and despite current market tensions, several countries with good macroeconomic policies have spreads that appear relatively low by their historical standards, for instance Mexico, Poland, and South Africa.

Possibly we are in a period in which relative asset pricing among the bonds of the emerging market countries is becoming more efficient, and in which the countries with strong fundamentals, high transparency, and good investor relations programs are being rewarded by the markets.

---

[48] This argument is developed at greater length in Fischer (2001b).

[49] Some of the explanations for contagion in the Mexican crisis also relied on the rebalancing of dedicated emerging market funds.

32   Review of World Economics 2003, Vol. 139 (1)

But we should also remember that the overall flow of resources to the developing countries is highly variable, and that we are once again in a period in which gross flows are extremely low, and net flows are almost certainly negative.

In 1997 there was much talk about there being no need for the IFIs because the private markets were doing the job of financing the developing countries. That was never true for the smaller less developed countries, but the variability of private sector flows makes clear the need for the official sector to try to offset some of the fluctuations in private flows.[50]

5 Concluding Comments

Paul Volcker remarked during the debate over the international financial architecture that the proposals for reform were more like interior decorating than architecture. The proposals discussed in this lecture indeed lack the grandeur of the vision of the global economy that the wartime generation put in place, and the issues are less important for the behavior of the international system than those on the agenda of international monetary reform in the 1970s. But they are critical for the emerging market countries, and that is reason enough to treat them as matters of the highest priority.

Those who favor a more thoroughgoing reform of the system – including Paul Volcker – focus on the exchange rate system among the major currencies. There is no question that such fluctuations have been disruptive, and that changes in the yen-dollar rate contributed to the Asian crisis – given the peg of the Asian currencies to the U.S. dollar. But for now and the foreseeable future there is no prospect of changing the flexible exchange rate system among the major currencies.

Would emerging market countries be better off giving up their currencies and dollarizing or euro'izing? I believe that will ultimately happen, but that for a long time, most emerging market countries will and should continue to allow exchange rate flexibility. Had exchange rates been flexible, most of the famous crises of the last decade would either not have happened, or would not have taken the form they did. That is

---

[50] The argument that IMF lending creates moral hazard implies that spreads are on average too low. That point does not jump out of the data.

why the shift to flexible rates among the emerging market countries is the most important change in the international financial architecture during the past decade, which should greatly reduce the frequency of crises. But as we see in Brazil at present, the adoption of a flexible exchange rate regime does not prevent all external crises, for debt-sustainability crises will still occur.

What else needs to be done? All the measures we have discussed to prevent crises by strengthening individual economies – including lower debt-to-GDP ratios – will contribute to the better performance of those economies and the international system. So will lessons learned by the IMF from the recent crises. So too should better supervision by industrial country regulators over the financial institutions active in international markets, and more provision of information by those institutions.

The major unresolved issue is the framework for private sector involvement. Sometimes countries, like companies, need either a pause in their debt servicing (in a liquidity crisis) or a permanent reduction in the burden of debt servicing (in a solvency crisis). The international financial system will not work well unless the imposition of a standstill or debt reduction is extremely costly to a country, and very rare. But that cost is currently too high.

The introduction of collective action clauses in bond agreements will help reduce the costs of restructuring when that is necessary. But the balance between creditors and debtors could also be tilted by changing the legal framework for standstills and debt restructurings. What would happen to the international capital markets if the rules could be changed in this way? The initial reaction is to think that flows would decline, and spreads would rise. But there is another, more likely, possibility: that with more room for more orderly resolution of crises, and less risk of extreme crises, flows would soon rise and spreads would decline as the stability of emerging market economies grows.

What should we expect? Measures already in place or under way will increase the stability of the international capital markets, and as normalcy returns to the global economy, should also lead to greater flows to countries that are managing themselves well. Work on developing a better legal framework for standstills and sovereign debt restructuring should get under way, but will take time to complete and longer to agree. If the apparent improvements in the ability of the international capital markets to discriminate among countries continues, thereby helping provide incentives for good behavior, the system could be operating far better, with fewer crises, even before a new legal framework is in place.

Annex

From the Communiqué of the International Monetary and Financial Committee of the Board of Governors of the International Monetary Fund; September 24, 2000; Press Release No. 00/54

Private Sector Involvement

21. The Committee endorses the report by the Managing Director on the involvement of the private sector in crisis prevention and management. It welcomes the progress on developing a framework for involving private creditors in the resolution of crises. The Committee notes that this approach strikes a balance between the clarity needed to guide market expectations and the operational flexibility, anchored in clear principles, needed to allow the most effective response in each case. The Committee notes that Fund resources are limited and that extraordinary access should be exceptional; further, neither creditors nor debtors should expect to be protected from adverse outcomes by official action.

22. The Committee agrees that the operational framework for private sector involvement must rely as much as possible on market-oriented solutions and voluntary approaches. The approach adopted by the international community should be based on the IMF's assessment of a country's underlying payment capacity and prospects of regaining market access. In some cases, the combination of catalytic official financing and policy adjustment should allow the country to regain full market access quickly. The Committee agrees that reliance on the catalytic approach at high levels of access presumes substantial justification, both in terms of its likely effectiveness and of the risks of alternative approaches. In other cases, emphasis should be placed on encouraging voluntary approaches, as needed, to overcome creditor coordination problems. In yet other cases, the early restoration of full market access on terms consistent with medium-term external sustainability may be judged to be unrealistic, and a broader spectrum of actions by private creditors, including comprehensive debt restructuring, may be warranted to provide for an adequately financed program and a viable medium-term payments profile. This includes the possibility that, in certain extreme cases, a temporary payments suspension or standstill may be unavoidable. The Fund should continue to be prepared to provide financial support to a member's adjustment program despite arrears to private creditors, provided the country is seeking to work cooperatively and in good faith with its private creditors and is meeting other program

requirements. The Committee urges progress in the application of the framework agreed in April 2000, and in further work to refine the analytical basis for the required judgments, and it looks forward to a progress report by its next meeting.

References

Ariyoshi, A., K. Habermeier, B. Laurens, I. Oetker-Robe, J. Canales-Kriljenko, and A. Kirilenko (2000). Capital Controls: Country Experiences with Their Use and Liberalization. IMF Occasional Paper 190. International Monetary Fund, Washington, D.C.

Berg, A., E. Borensztein, G. Milesi-Ferretti, and C. Pattillo (1999). Anticipating Balance of Payments Crises: The Role of Early Warning Systems. IMF Working Paper 186. International Monetary Fund, Washington, D.C.

Bekaert, G., C. R. Harvey, and C. Lundblad (2002). Does Financial Liberalization Spur Growth? Paper presented at the World Bank Conference, Financial Globalization: A Blessing or a Curse? May 30–31, Washington, D.C. (http://www.worldbank.org/research/conferences/financial_globalization.htm)

Bhagwati, J. (1998). The Capital Myth: The Difference between Trade in Widgets and Dollars. *Foreign Affairs* 77 (3): 7–12.

Chari, A., and P. B. Henry (2002). Capital Account Liberalization: Allocative Efficiency or Animal Spirits? Paper presented at the World Bank Conference, Financial Globalization: A Blessing or a Curse? May 30–31, Washington, D.C.
(http://www.worldbank.org/research/conferences/financial_globalization.htm)

Cushman, D. O., and T. Zha (1997). Identifying Monetary Policy in a Small Open Economy under Flexible Exchange Rates. *Journal of Monetary Economics* 39 (3): 433–448.

Dobson, W., and G. C. Hufbauer (with the assistance of H. K. Choo) (2001). *World Capital Markets: A Challenge to the G-10.* Washington, D.C.: Institute for International Economics.

De Gregorio. J., S. Edwards, and R. Valdés (2000). Controls on Capital Inflows: Do They Work? *Journal of Development Economics* 63 (1): 59–83.

Edwards, S. (1999). How Effective Are Capital Controls? NBER Working Paper 7413. National Bureau of Economic Research, Cambridge, Mass.

Eichengreen, B. (2000). *Can the Moral Hazard Caused by IMF Bailouts Be Reduced?* Geneva: International Center for Monetary and Banking Studies, and London: Centre for Economic Policy Research.

Eichengreen, B., and A. Mody (2000). Would Collective Action Clauses Raise Borrowing Costs? NBER Working Paper 7458. National Bureau of Economic Research, Cambridge, Mass.

36 Review of World Economics 2003, Vol. 139 (1)

Eichengreen, B., D. Mathieson, B. Chadha, A. Jansen, L. Kodres, and S. Sharma (1998). Hedge Funds and Financial Market Dynamics. IMF Occasional Paper 166. International Monetary Fund, Washington, D.C.

Eichengreen, B., M. Mussa, G. Dell'Ariccia, E. Detragiache, G. Milesi-Ferretti, and A. Tweedie (1999). Liberalizing Capital Movements: Some Analytical Issues. Economic Issues 17. International Monetary Fund, Washington, D.C.

Favero, C. A., and F. Giavazzi (2002). Why Are Brazil's Interest Rates So High? Mimeo. Innocenzo Gasparini Institute for Economic Research. Bocconi University, Milan. July.

Fischer, S. (1998). Capital Account Liberalization and the Role of the IMF. In S. Fischer et al., Should the IMF Pursue Capital-Account Convertibility? Princeton University Essays in International Finance 207. Princeton.

Fischer, S. (2001a). Exchange Rate Regimes: Is the Bipolar View Correct? *Journal of Economic Perspectives* 15 (2): 3–24.

Fischer, S. (2001b). The International Financial System: Crises and Reform. *The Robbins Lectures*. October 29. (http://www.iie.com/fischer/sl.html)

Galindo, A., A. Micco, and G. Ordoñez (2002). Financial Liberalization and Growth: Empirical Evidence. Paper presented at the World Bank Conference, Financial Globalization: A Blessing or a Curse? May 30–31, Washington, D.C.
(http://www.worldbank.org/research/conferences/financial_globalization.htm)

Goldstein, M. (2002). *Managed Floating Plus*. Policy Analyses in International Economics 66. Washington, D.C.: Institute for International Economics.

Goldstein, M., G. L. Kaminsky, and C. M. Reinhart (2000). *Assessing Financial Vulnerability: An Early Warning System for Emerging Markets*. Washington, D.C.: Institute for International Economics.

Gourinchas, P., and O. Jeanne (2002). On the Benefits of Capital Account Liberalization for Emerging Economies. Paper presented at the World Bank Conference, Financial Globalization: A Blessing or a Curse? May 30–31, Washington, D.C.
(http://www.worldbank.org/research/conferences/financial_globalization.htm)

IMF (2000). Debt and Reserve-Related Indicators of External Vulnerability. (http://www.imf.org/external/np/pdr/debtres/): March 23.

Ishii, S., I. Oetker-Robe, and L. Cui (2001). Measures to Limit the Offshore Use of Currencies: Pros and Cons. IMF Working Paper 01/43. International Monetary Fund, Washington, D.C.

Kaplan, E., and D. Rodrik (2001). Did the Malaysian Capital Controls Work? Mimeo. Harvard, Kennedy School of Government, Cambridge, Mass.
(http://ksghome.harvard.edu/~.drodrik.academic.ksg/Malaysia%20controls.PDF)

Reinhart, C. M., and I. Tokatlidis (2002). Before and After Financial Liberalization. Paper presented at the World Bank Conference, Financial Globalization: A Blessing or a Curse? May 30–31, Washington, D.C.
(http://www.worldbank.org/research/conferences/financial_globalization.htm)

Williamson, J. (1990). What Washington Means by Policy Reform. In J. Williamson (ed.), *Latin American Adjustment: How Much Has Happened?* Washington, D.C.: Institute for International Economics.

Williamson, J. (2000). *Exchange Rate Regimes for Emerging Markets: Reviving the Intermediate Option.* Policy Analyses in International Economics 60. Washington, D.C.: Institute for International Economics.

[28]

Kiel Discussion Paper 350

Chilean-Type Capital Controls —
A Building Block of the New International Financial
Architecture?

Claudia M. Buch

June 1999

Contents

An earlier version of this paper has been presented at the 15th anniversary of the Advanced Studies Program of the Kiel Institute of World Economics. The author would like to thank Elke Hanschel, Stefan M. Golder, Susanne Lapp, Paola Monti, and Barbara Kowalczyk for a critical review and for most helpful comments on an earlier draft. All remaining errors and inaccuracies are solely in my own responsibility.

1.   The Policy Debate

The severe financial and economic crises which have beleaguered Asia, Russia, and Brazil recently and which have sent their shock waves not only through other emerging markets have left policymakers around the globe looking for possible remedies. Facing distortions such as asymmetries in information and price rigidities, the goal is to shield basically innocent bystanders from the adverse effects of external financial shocks and to provide countries with breathing space to correct policy mistakes. Taxes on short-term capital flows such as proposed in 1978 by James Tobin and as introduced in Chile in 1991 have entered policy discussions prominently. In his original proposal, Tobin (1978: 154f.) advocated throwing "some sand in the wheels of excessively efficient international money markets" by means of an "internationally uniform tax on all spot conversions of one currency into another."

A pure Tobin tax would cover all foreign exchange transactions and all traders. It would be collected by the national tax authorities at a low tax rate which is invariant to interest rates. Implementation must be world-wide, and the main intentions of the tax are to reduce financial market volatility and to expand the autonomy of national monetary policy. Yet, the implementation of such an instrument raises several issues, notably the coordination of national tax policies and the efficient use of the proceeds of the tax.[1]

Recent policy discussions have focused on unremunerated reserve requirements (URRs) of the type implemented in Chile since the early 1990s. Less attention than to Chile is usually paid to the case of Slovenia although the country has had a similar regime since 1995. URRs and other capital account restrictions which more than proportionally raise the costs of short-term capital are the focus of this paper: being expressed as constant percentage of the size of the financial flows, the tax rate per unit of time is larger for a short-term financial credit than for a loan with a longer maturity. Note,

however, that although URRs come closest to the original proposal of Tobin, URRs of the Slovene or Chilean type do not qualify as pure Tobin taxes. This is because they are not levied on all capital account items and because they are not imposed multilaterally.

Among the proponents of Chilean-type capital controls on inflows of foreign capital are a host of well-known economists and international institutions (cf. Eichengreen 1999; World Bank 1998).[2] A recent survey of financial liberalization episodes concluded that delaying and possibly limiting capital account convertibility might be a sensible strategy to deal with the risks of financial integration (Williamson and Mahar 1998: 65). On a policy level, various countries such as Malaysia, Russia, or Brazil have resorted to restrictions on the free flow of capital recently although most of these controls go substantially beyond the proposals from academia. These observations suggest that " [...], the abrupt reversals in economies that were hitherto deemed miraculous have challenged the conventional wisdom that it is a good thing to let capital move freely across borders."[3]

During the past two decades, various other variants of the Tobin tax have also been discussed. Eichengreen et al. (1995: 166), for example, proposed a tax or deposit requirement on all domestic-currency lending to nonresidents. Their proposal originally aimed at preventing speculation against EU currencies prior to the introduction of the euro and, more generally, to protect the domestic balance of payments. Garber and Taylor (1995) discussed zero-interest margin deposits or prudential bank capital requirements against net foreign exchange positions as options to limit the amount of foreign borrowing of commercial banks. Both restrictions would raise the effective costs of foreign loans and thus make borrowing from abroad less attractive. However, it can be shown that such regulations may have the perverse effect

---

[1]   For a discussion see also Frankel (1996).

[2]   For an overview, see the homepage of Nouriel Roubini via the homepage of the NYU Economics Department (http://www.stern.nyu.edu/Faculty/FacPict/Economics/index.htm).

[3]   *The Economist* (1/98) "Keeping the hot money out", downloaded from Roubini's homepage on Asia on April 21, 1999.

4

of speeding up the collapse of a fixed exchange rate regime rather than enhancing its sustainability precisely because they lower foreign borrowing (Buch and Heinrich 1999).

As the recent discussion has focused on Chilean-type capital controls, this paper will summarize the discussion to date and discuss whether URRs are an optimal response to increased financial risks. We start by giving a brief overview of global financial flows and capital account restrictions with a special focus on the experiences of Chile and Slovenia which have implemented Tobin-type capital controls (Chapter 2). Facing potentially adverse effects of foreign capital flows, policymakers essentially have two options. *First*, they can resort to measures that directly aim at reducing the volume and the volatility of capital flows by levying taxes on cross-border capital flows. The usefulness and effectiveness of such measures will be discussed in Chapter 3 of this paper. *Second*, policymakers can try to affect the structure of capital flows by an adjustment of domestic policies and by reforms of the international financial architecture.[4] The scope and the limitations of such approaches will be analyzed in Chapter 4. This chapter will particularly draw on the experiences of other transition economies of Central and Eastern Europe in dealing with the contagion effects of the Russian financial crisis in order to show the scope of domestic policy to shield a country from adverse external developments.

2. Capital Flows and Capital Controls

There is a common perception that capital flows have become more volatile in recent years and that a rise in short-term capital flows has promoted these developments. This chapter gives a brief account of the statistical evidence on the structure of capital flows, and it reviews the policies that countries have implemented to shield themselves from volatile capital flows.

---

4   For a recent contribution, see Eichengreen (1999).

2.1 Short-Term Capital Flows

Standard balance of payments statistics do give only insufficient account of the share of short-term capital flows in total international finance. Inflows of financial credits are often not classified according to their maturity, and portfolio capital flows are likewise not broken down by maturity. Data provided by the Bank for International Settlements (BIS) on the maturity structure of bank lending towards countries outside the BIS-reporting area can be used as an indicator, though (Figure 1). These data show that the share of short-term loans in total lending has shifted upward when comparing the 1990s to the 1980s. While in the 1980s roughly 40 percent of all foreign loans had a maturity of less than one year, this share increased to more than 50 percent in the 1990s. Recently, it has come down again. Interestingly, trends in developing countries have relatively closely tracked those in developed countries although the level of short-term loans has been somewhat higher for the group of developing countries in the 1990s.

Overall, Mussa et al. (1999) noted that there seemed not to have been a secular trend towards an increasing share of short-term foreign debt in recent decades. Yet, they confirmed the evidence presented in Figure 1: Remaining maturities tended to shorten during the boom phase of large capital flows between the late 1980s and mid-1990s while they lengthened afterwards.

2.2 Capital Account Restrictions

Despite the on-going liberalization of capital account transactions that has taken place over the past two decades, almost two-thirds of the countries surveyed regularly by the International Monetary Fund (IMF) had some restrictions on commercial or financial credits in place in 1998. At the same time, the share of countries imposing restrictions on capital account transactions seems to have fallen: in 1990, almost 80 percent of all countries surveyed had restricted

Figure 1: Short-Term Loans[a] as Percent of Total Foreign Loans, 1980–1998

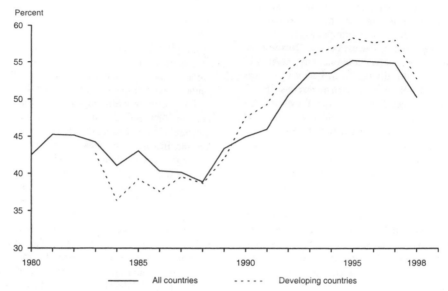

Percent

———— All countries   - - - - Developing countries

[a]Loans with a maturity of less than one year.

Source: BIS (1999b).

at least some capital account items, in 1998, it was merely two thirds of them (Table 1).

The motivations of countries to impose capital controls and the forms of controls that are actually being chosen have been the subject of various survey papers. In a recent study, Johnston and Tamirisa (1998) found that controls on capital *out*flows were more prevalent than controls on capital *in*flows. To improve balance of payment management, to address prudential considerations, and to overcome weaknesses in the state of development of the domestic economy are motivations to introduce capital controls.

The empirical literature tends to provide relatively little evidence to support the effectiveness of capital controls, particularly of controls on capital outflows. Dooley (1996) found that capital controls have been successful in driving a small gap between domestic and foreign interest rates but do not seem to have had the impact on economic welfare that economic theory might predict. Similar conclusions were reached by Grilli and Milesi-Ferretti (1995) who found capital controls to be correlated with higher inflation and lower real interest rates but not with economic growth.

Table 1: Capital Account Restrictions, 1970–1998

	1970	1980	1990	1998
Number of countries included	117	140	153	184
Share of countries with restrictions on capital account transactions (%)	79	75	78	66
Share of countries with restrictions on commercial credits (%)	...	...	...	60
Share of countries with restrictions on financial credits (%)	...	...	...	62

Source: IMF (1998b).

2.3   Taxes on Short-Term Capital Flows: The Cases of Chile and Slovenia

Since the focus of this paper is on the effects and the effectiveness of Tobin-type taxes on short-term capital flows, it is useful to review the experiences of Chile and Slovenia which

6

have implemented unremunerated reserve requirements (URRs).

Since 1991, foreign loans and deposits by nonresidents in Chile have generally been subject to a 20 % URR.[5] Instead of holding the reserves, the Bank of Chile has also offered investors to pay an up-front fee in an amount equivalent to the reserve requirement. The reserve rate was raised to 30 % in May 1992, and the deposit period was then fixed to one year. Also, a 1.2 percent stamp tax on local currency credits was at that time extended to all foreign loans, excluding trade credits. Although the exemption of this item has certainly created loopholes and has therefore reduced the effectiveness of the tax, Valdés-Prieto and Soto (1998) have argued that it would have been difficult politically to extend the coverage of the tax also to the export sector.

Valdés-Prieto and Soto have also calculated the tax equivalent (t) of the Chilean URR. Assume that an amount L invested in the international capital market yields the foreign interbank rate $i*$ plus an intermediation spread s. Then, the interest revenue foregone, when lending to an economy that imposes an URR, amounts to $(i*+s)rL$, where r = reserve requirement. This needs to be related to the total amount of funds lent, $(1-r)L$. Combining these terms, the tax equivalent of the reserve requirement is given by:

$$[1] \quad t = \left[\frac{(i*+s)r}{1-r} \right] \cdot \frac{holding\ period}{maturity}.$$

Hence, the effective tax rate increases in the foreign interest rate, in the intermediation spread, and in the reserve requirement. Moreover, the tax rate is lower (ceteris paribus), the longer the maturity of the loan. As the tax rate depends inter alia on the foreign interest rate, it is thus not fully controllable by the authorities (unless r is being adjusted continuously). Because only inflows of foreign capital are subject to the reserve requirement, the tax rate is zero for capital outflows, i.e., for loans granted abroad by Chilean residents. After rising gradually from zero to about 4 % between 1991 and mid-1992, the rate further increased to roughly 6 % in 1995 (Figure 2). In autumn 1998, the URR was set to zero, showing the intention of the authorities to flexibly adjust it to the cycle of international capital flows (Eichengreen 1999: 53).

At least in the beginning, the Chilean URR was considered as being relatively successful, and Labán et al. (1997: 21) concluded that "the case for the ineffectiveness of capital controls may have been overstated". Yet, because markets found ways to circumvent the reserve requirements by shifting activities into unregulated areas, the Chilean authorities successively had to expand the coverage of the controls (Labán and Larrain 1998). In 1995, the deposit requirement was extended to other financial investments, excluding foreign direct investment (FDI) and first issues of American Depository Receipts (ADRs). Since 1996, reserve requirements have also covered credits after their first rollover. Moreover, the maximum proportion of foreign investment projects that could be financed through debt was lowered from 70 to 50 percent, and the minimum amount of foreign direct investment exempted from the reserve requirement was raised. These adjustments became necessary because trades migrated to less regulated markets.

In addition, Chile's currency has come under pressure in the wake of the Asian crises to which Chile is heavily exposed due to its large exports to that region. In response, the government successively reduced the deposit requirement from 30 to zero percent in September 1998 (Laurens and Cardoso 1998: 10). The intention was to attract more capital in order to support the currency and to prevent a further devaluation which would hurt firms with open foreign exchange liabilities (Banco Central de Chile 1998). Thus, precisely at a time when currency turmoil elsewhere would suggest that a Tobin-type tax might prove particularly useful, the Chilean authorities apparently concluded that, whatever the benefits of the tax, they could no longer afford to turn away foreign capital. These developments need to be

---

5   This and the following information have been taken from Labán and Larrain (1998), Ffrench-Davis et al. (1995), and IMF (1998b). Chile's experience with capital controls in the 1980s is briefly reviewed in Edwards (1999).

Figure 2: Tax Equivalent of the Chilean Reserve Requirements, 1991–1996

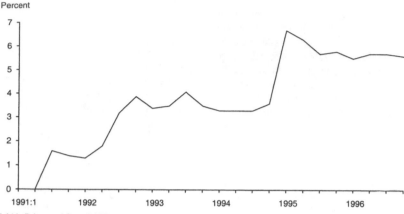

Source: Valdés-Prieto and Soto (1998).

taken into account when assessing whether Chile has been affected by the Asian financial crises.

Similar to Chile in the 1990s, Slovenia has introduced an URR on financial credits and has lowered the reserve rate to zero recently. In February 1995, the Bank of Slovenia (BoS) introduced a number of restrictions for regulating capital flows, among which a non-interest-bearing deposit in Slovene tolars for financial credits featured prominently: 40 percent of each financial credit from abroad had to be put in a non-interest-bearing account at the BoS for the period of two years if the financial credit had a maturity of less than seven years. For longer maturities, the deposit requirement was only 10 percent. Clearly, the Slovene capital control regime "punishes" short-term capital flows more severely than long-term flows, when one takes the annualized foregone interest rate into account. In January 1999, the BoS set the reserve requirement to zero, signaling that more foreign credits would be desired.[6] This move has followed a sharp drop in net capital inflows in 1998 (Buch and Hanschel 1999). As the system has not been abandoned entirely, the BoS in principle has retained the option to raise the reserve rate on short notice again.

3.   Effectiveness of Capital Controls

In a world without frictions and with perfectly competitive markets, there would be no scope for controls on the free flow of capital: differences in the rates of return on capital between two countries would trigger capital flows, rates of return would converge, and overall welfare would increase. Yet, as soon as more realistic features of markets such as asymmetric information and less-than-instantaneous adjustment processes are taken into account, the free flow of capital does not necessarily serve to achieve optimal welfare. Rather, a second-best equilibrium which features some form of capital controls may be the optimal solution.

The following chapter will look at the experiences of Chile and Slovenia with the reserve requirements more closely. It will be argued that the success of the regimes needs to be measured against the gain in monetary autonomy, the reduction in financial market volatility, and the impact on investment that is achieved.[7] Throughout the discussion, an im-

---

[6]   See BoS (1999).

[7]   We thus abstract from other motivations to have capital controls, such as the maintenance of the domestic tax base and the retention of domestic savings. See Grilli and Milesi-Ferretti (1995) for an overview.

8

portant caveat must be borne in mind: By focusing on the possible links between URRs and macroeconomic developments, influences of other important policy measures are often left out of account. This is a main reason why Nadal-De Simone and Sorsa (1999: 49) argued that "It seems premature to point out the Chilean experience as supportive of the effectiveness of controls on capital inflows [...]."[8] The Chilean authorities have, for instance, made substantial headway with regard to enhancing the stability of their banking system. Moreover, the choice of an exchange rate regime has implications for the structure of capital flows. In particular, pegged exchange rates tend to signal the belief to market participants that exchange rates will remain stable, thus encouraging borrowing from abroad.

3.1 Capital Controls and Monetary Autonomy

A main reason why capital controls are recommended and introduced, is their potential of affording the monetary authorities with greater autonomy. In the case of floating exchange rates, capital controls may help policymakers to dissolve the conflict between setting domestic interest rates and the resulting exchange rate (and thus trade) effects. In the case of fixed exchange rates, capital controls may give policymakers some autonomy over domestic interest rates without triggering capital inflows that may sacrifice a monetary target. Regardless of the exchange rate regime, monetary autonomy is thus the greater, the more effective capital controls are in influencing the *level* of capital inflows. In addition, the *volatility* of capital flows, which will be discussed below, has an impact on the degree of freedom of the monetary authorities, as a high volatility eventually requires frequent policy actions.

Whether capital controls are actually effective in achieving these goals, remains an empirical issue. Effectiveness depends, *first*, on the relevance of the controls. In Chile, the reserve

requirement was relevant in the sense that it yielded substantial tax revenue (Valdés-Prieto and Soto 1998). This is in contrast to the experiences of other, developing countries for which the evasion of capital account restrictions has been pervasive and which have raised little revenue from taxes on cross-border capital flows (Dooley 1996).

The *second* criterion is whether the controls have a dampening impact on overall inflows of capital. For Chile, this has not been the case (Laurens and Cardoso 1998: 12). While the composition of inflows has changed in favor of those flows exempted from the tax, the overall inflow of capital, and thus Chile's external debt, has, if anything, increased (Figure 3a).[9] This is a result of the strong fundamentals of the Chilean economy as well as of external factors which have increased the availability of financial funds. This is also reflected in a general increase in the foreign debt stocks of the Latin American countries, although Chilean foreign debt has been accumulating at a somewhat slower pace than the debt in the other two countries.

In relation to GDP, Chile's external debt has decreased in recent years (Figure 3b). This is in contrast to developments in Argentina or Mexico, where foreign debt has increased also in relative terms lately. Still, the decline in Chile is difficult to attribute to the imposition of the capital controls alone as it has started already in the mid-1980s and as a similar time pattern could be observed for a country like Brazil. Edwards (1998b) likewise gave evidence for an increase in capital inflows, and he found a change in the structure of capital flows towards longer-term instruments after the imposition of the URRs. Moreover, he showed the impact of the controls on the real exchange rate and on interest rate differentials to be limited and short-lived although some short-run influences were visible.

---

8   For a similar assessment, see Edwards (1999).

9   A theoretical argument explaining the increase in capital inflows after the imposition of URRs was provided by Cordella (1998). He argued that URRs served as a buffer against liquidity shocks. Hence, risk-averse agents which faced uncertainty about their liquidity needs would be more willing to provide funding in the presence of the URR. Note that this argument is essentially the same as for minimum reserve requirements in a domestic setting.

Figure 3: External Debt of Selected Latin American Countries, 1975–1996

a) Billions of current US dollars
   (index, 1975 = 100)

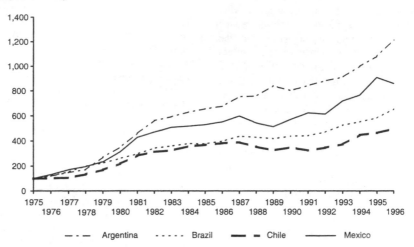

b) Percent of GDP

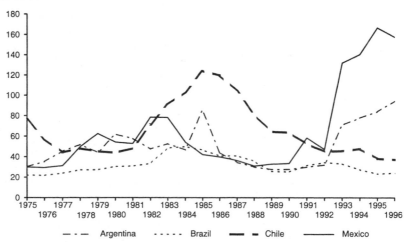

Source: World Bank (1999).

The evidence for Slovenia roughly supports the findings for Chile. Capital flows have increased in absolute terms after the imposition of the reserve requirement, and this has also transmitted into an increase of debt relative to GDP (World Bank 1999). Developments have been roughly in line with those in the Czech Repub-

lic or Estonia. Foreign debt of Hungary and Poland, in contrast, has declined in recent years, primarily as a result of the restructuring and repayment of old debt. For Slovenia, there is hardly any evidence for an impact of the controls on the overall composition of capital flows (Buch and Hanschel 1999). More specifically,

10

Slovenia has not received relatively more long-term capital inflows in the form of FDI or less financial credits than other comparable transition economies. In fact, as the BoS has been following an implicit exchange rate target, it has accumulated substantial foreign reserves and has in this sense failed to gain monetary autonomy.

Moreover, while (Chilean-type) capital controls may enhance monetary autonomy in tranquil periods, they are unable to prevent speculative attacks on overvalued currencies in general. Traditional speculative attack models indicate that inconsistencies between macroeconomic policies are at the heart of financial crises.[10] A speculative attack on the foreign exchange reserves of a central bank occurs if the (shadow) floating exchange rate, which is determined by market fundamentals, equals the fixed exchange rate, which the central bank tries to defend by selling its reserves. In such models, the probability of a speculative attack increases with the rate of monetary expansion. This, in turn, depends on the amount of deficit financing provided by the monetary authorities, on the interest sensitivity of money demand, and on the volume of foreign reserves of the central bank.

As the Asian financial crises have shown, fiscal and macroeconomic imbalances are not necessarily the sole causes of financial crises. Rather, institutional weaknesses, in particular in the banking sectors, have been identified as important causes of currency crises. Models that feature such microeconomic weaknesses have been labeled "third generation" speculative attack models, following the second generation models which have focused on self-fulfilling attacks (Obstfeld 1994).

Regardless of the crisis being caused by micro- or macroeconomic distortions, the issue has been raised that taxes on cross-border capital flows "buy time" for domestic policymakers to adjust to adverse external shocks. Essentially, this argument was supported by the analysis of Park and Sachs (1996) who showed that capital controls can delay the breakdown of a

fixed exchange rate system. In contrast to the present paper, the authors assumed fairly restrictive capital controls on both capital in- and outflows which fully prevent households from changing their foreign bond holdings. These controls thus shift the entire adjustment process to the current account. Yet, while the collapse of a fixed exchange rate can be postponed in this model, it cannot be prevented. Moreover, balance of payments crises are delayed only at the cost of lower consumption and of a greater jump in the exchange rate at the time of the collapse, if compared to a regime without capital controls. Hence, the time that policymakers can buy might be relatively short, and it will depend on how credible the public deems the adjustment to be. Moreover, the likelihood of a self-fulfilling speculative attack may be increased by the mere possibility that controls are introduced in the future (Dooley 1996: 669).

Overall, for the case of Chile, Laurens and Cardoso (1998: 16) rejected that the URR has helped the authorities to obtain breathing-space and to adjust domestic policies. Rather, the authors argued that the controls have tended to delay integration of the Chilean economy into global markets, have failed to reduce domestic interest rates, and have increased the degree of regulation in the Chilean economy. For Slovenia, the maintenance of the URR would be an obstacle to future EU and OECD membership and has consequently been critized by the EU.[11]

3.2 Capital Controls and Financial Market Volatility

The central intuition behind the proposal to introduce Chilean-type capital controls is the notion that financial markets react faster than goods markets, and that the interaction of traders on financial markets gives rise to herding behavior and noise trading. This, in turn, drives a wedge between the price of a financial

---

10 The literature on speculative attacks, which dates back to the seminal paper by Krugman (1979), is surveyed comprehensively by Agénor et al. (1992).

11 For a general discussion of capital account convertibility and OECD membership, see Quirk and Evans (1995). The opinion of the EU on Slovenia can be found in EU (1998).

Table 2: Share of Short-Term Foreign Bank Loans, 1992–1998[a] (Percent)

	1992	1993	1994	1995	1996	1997	1998
Asia	59.0	62.8	62.9	63.5	61.5	60.6	52.5
Eastern Europe	27.3	37.2	35.2	39.1	44.2	43.4	36.0
Czech Republic	...	...	40.4	48.6	49.3	50.0	58.8
Estonia	...	...	37.9	33.8	45.8	47.8	25.9
Hungary	23.8	26.9	30.7	34.6	39.2	34.2	34.7
Poland	31.4	33.1	23.2	29.6	33.2	38.1	40.7
Slovenia	...	...	39.8	30.9	17.8	21.2	22.9
Latin America	43.4	50.0	51.3	52.3	53.7	54.8	51.8
Argentina	47.6	52.6	53.4	56.5	44.8	61.4	54.8
Brazil	48.5	54.8	50.3	56.0	63.0	64.1	56.0
Chile	42.7	52.4	53.7	54.7	51.2	49.8	39.6
Mexico	42.4	47.1	51.3	45.4	60.1	61.3	44.9

[a]Liabilities vis-à-vis banks in the BIS-reporting area (maturity < 1 year).

Source: BIS (1999b).

instrument and its fundamental value, and thus causes excessive volatility in the price of financial variables. The fast and sudden changes in financial markets are in contrast to the delayed responses of the real sector. This might be suboptimal because physical investment and exports might be reduced and because resources might be misallocated. As a result, overall growth and welfare might suffer.

Using the standard sticky price model developed by Dornbusch (1976), it can in fact be shown that the imposition of a transaction tax reduces the degree of overshooting of exchange rates (Buch et al. 1998). Hence, domestic interest rate shocks have less of an impact on exchange rate volatility. The model shows at the same time, however, that there is no free lunch. Policymakers should take into account that the implementation of a transaction tax by itself is an exogenous shock which pushes the economy to a new steady state equilibrium. This is because, in essence, the imposition of a transaction tax has the same effect as a domestic interest rate shock. Hence, both the introduction and the subsequent elimination of transaction taxes cause an (overshooting) exchange rate adjustment. This must be considered when proposing the "temporary" introduction of capital controls in the event of an acute financial crisis. An additional case against temporary capital controls has been made by Reinhart and Smith (1997) who argued that, in order to be effective,

temporary controls on capital inflows would have to be very punitive.[12] Resulting welfare gains might thus be lost easily if the controls are not removed early enough.

One aim of Chilean-type taxes on capital flows is to change the structure of capital flows away from short-term (presumably more volatile) towards long-term (less volatile) capital flows, and in particular towards foreign direct investments. More specifically, as URRs increase the costs of short-term financial credits, one would suspect that they tilt the structure of foreign credits towards longer maturities.

Table 2 shows the shares of short-term bank credits in total bank credits received from abroad for selected countries. At the end of 1998, the share of short-term bank credits was in a similar range of about 52–53 percent in Asia and Latin America, and only 36 percent for the transition economies of Central and Eastern Europe. At least through 1996, developments in Chile tracked developments in Latin America as a whole quite closely. Since 1996, the share of short-term lending to Chile has been below-average and on a decline, reaching similar proportions as in the early 1990s. In contrast to the initial introduction of the URR in 1991, which seemed to have had relatively little

---

12 This argument is based on the observation that the intertemporal rate of substitution of consumption is low in developing countries. Hence, the current account effect of a small tax would be limited.

12

effect on the maturity structure of foreign bank lending, this might be attributable to the increase in the effective tax rate in 1996 (see Figure 2).

Looking at the composition of total capital flows, Laurens and Cardoso (1998: 14) reported mixed evidence on the effects of the URR. While some studies found a decline in the share of short-term inflows, others found the reverse or simply no effect. Mainly, these differences are due to different time frames and different definitions of capital flows being used. Generally, an important caveat that needs to be borne in mind is that net errors and omissions in the balance of payments have increased in Chile, and that statistics are suspected to have become less reliable after the introduction of the URR.

Evidence for Slovenia points much more clearly towards a change in the composition of bank lending towards longer maturities. Here, the share of short-term bank credits has been below the average for the region and has shown a clear downward trend throughout the period under study (1994–1998). Yet, as was already argued above, an impact of the URR on the overall structure of total capital flows, i.e., a decline of financial credits relative to FDI or

portfolio capital, could not be found (Buch and Hanschel 1999).

The results from the BIS data are confirmed by information on the structure of total foreign debt (Figure 4). In Chile, the share of short-term debt in total foreign debt has increased, if anything, between 1991 and 1994. More recently, the share of short-term debt has declined. Overall, the maturity structure of foreign debt has tended to follow a similar pattern for the four Latin American countries under review.

For Slovenia, the share of total short-term debt has declined between 1993 and 1996 from 6.5 to 1.4 percent, hereby following a similar trend as the debt structure of Poland (World Bank 1999). In the Czech Republic and Estonia, short-term debt reached values of almost 30 percent in 1996, showing an upward trend over time.

A priori though, data on the maturity structure of foreign debt provides little evidence on the volatility of capital flows. From an empirical point of view, one of the main problems in reducing the volatility of capital flows by means of a "tax" on selective flows is that standard classifications provide only limited evidence on the actual volatility of different capital account items (Claessens et al. 1995). Short-term capital

Figure 4: Short-Term Debt as Percentage of Total Foreign Debt, 1975–1996

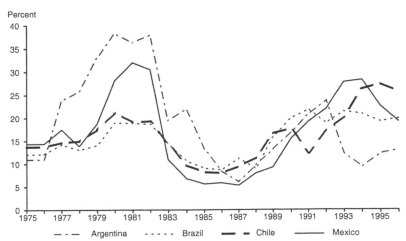

Source: World Bank (1999).

Table 3: Volatility of Capital Flows, 1969–1993[a]

	Foreign direct investment, net	Other long-term capital[b]	Portfolio investment	Short-term capital
Europe[c]	1.008	1.911	2.102	1.823
Latin America[c]	0.819	1.781	2.278	1.484
Japan	1.307	1.371	1.473	1.636
South-East Asia[c]	1.455	2.265	1.835	1.179
United States	1.302	1.469	1.188	1.297

[a]Volatility measures by the coefficient of variation = ratio of standard deviation to mean. — [b]Including long-term portfolio capital. — [c]Based on aggregate net flows to and from region.

Source: Lipsey (1999: Table 5).

flows are not necessarily the most volatile item in the capital account of the balance of payments, and the volatility of different capital flows varies from country to country.

This finding has been largely confirmed by recent evidence presented by Lipsey (1999, see also Table 3). His data support the view that foreign direct investment is stable relative to portfolio capital or financial credits. However, short-term capital is not necessarily the most volatile item in the capital account. In the transition economies of Central and Eastern Europe, for instance, the timing of the privatization process has often caused substantial volatility in foreign direct investment flows (Buch et al. 1998), i.e., in a capital account item which is typically considered relatively stable. In addition, it remains an open issue to what

Table 4: Volatility of Capital Flows and Exchange Rates before and after the Imposition of URRs[a]

	Mean of quarterly capital flows (millions of US dollars)			Standard deviation of quarterly capital flows (millions of US dollars)		
	before	after	probability[b]	before	after	probability[b]
	Slovenia					
FDI, net	29.6	47.9	0.07*	16.9	28.8	0.07*
Inflow	29.3	51.1	0.03**	16.6	29.6	0.05*
Outflow	0.3	−3.4	0.01**	3.5	3.2	0.78
Other investment, net	−23.4	60.7	0.23	91.2	220.2	0.00***
Inflow	41.5	91.2	0.29	78.4	140.6	0.05*
Outflow	−63.8	−30.4	0.55	101.9	169.5	0.08*
	Median of exchange rate to the US dollar[c]			Standard deviation of exchange rate to the US dollar[d]		
	before	after	probability[e]	before	after	probability[f]
	Slovenia					
Nominal	0.34	0.23	0.20	0.62	0.29	0.09*
Real	0.28	0.27	0.38	0.59	0.39	0.08*
	Chile					
Nominal	0.16	0.11	0.02**	0.21	0.19	0.12
Real	0.14	0.12	0.14	0.24	0.19	0.16

[a]Before imposition of capital controls = 1992:1–1994:4 for Slovenia (capital flows), 1992:1–1995:1 for Slovenia (exchange rates), 1983:1–1990:12 for Chile. After imposition of capital controls = 1995:1–1998:3 for Slovenia (capital flows), 1995:2–1997:12 for Slovenia (exchange rates), 1991:1–1998:12 for Chile.— [b]Results of t- and F-tests, respectively, on equality in means and variance (quarterly data). — [c]Median of absolute changes in exchange rates over previous month at an annual rate (monthly data). — [d]Standard deviation of change in exchange rates over previous month at an annual rate (monthly data). — [e]Results of Mann-Whitney U-tests on equality in the median. — [f]Results of Siegel-Tukey test on equality in the variance. — *, **, *** = significant at the 10, 5, 1 percent level, respectively.

Source: IMF (1999b); own calculations.

14

extent exchange rate volatility impinges upon the real sector.[13]

Evidence from Chile and Slovenia does not show a decline in the volatility of capital flows after the controls had been imposed. As for Chile, there was a relatively strong increase in the standard deviation of capital inflows subject to controls after the controls had been introduced. In the four years prior to the introduction of the URR, the coefficient of variation (standard deviation/mean) was 1.52, and it increased to 4.22 in the four subsequent years.[14] At the same time, there is support for a reduction in exchange rate volatility pursuant to the introduction of the URR. Yet, as Laurens and Cardoso noted (1998: 14), the effects of capital controls and of foreign exchange market intervention of the monetary authorities can hardly be isolated.

The results for Slovenia look similar: While the URR has not shielded the economy from an increase in financial market volatility as evidenced by increased volatility of capital flows, real and nominal exchange rates tended to be less volatile in the period following the introduction of the URR (Table 4). Mainly, this is the result of the exchange rate policy that the Slovene authorities have pursued: By defending an implicit exchange rate target vis-à-vis the D-mark, exchange market interventions have apparently been used to prevent an increased volatility of capital flows to transmit into increased exchange rate volatility.

3.3 Capital Controls and the Sequence of Financial Liberalization

Increased volatility in financial markets is a concern because inter alia it threatens the stability of banking systems. Recent episodes of banking and balance of payments crises, so-called "twin crises"[15], have thus shifted interest away from capital controls as a means of affording domestic policy with a greater degree of autonomy towards capital controls as a means of preventing banking crises. Hence, the debate on the optimal sequencing of external and internal financial liberalization has been revived (Eichengreen et al. 1999).

If distortions in the domestic banking system cannot be eliminated at short notice, McKinnon and Pill (1995) proposed to restrict short-term capital flows and to limit consumer borrowing and mortgage finance while liberalizing FDI flows as a second-best strategy. They argued that in the presence of an implicit deposit insurance system and of insufficient banking supervision, external financial liberalization exposes commercial banks to a variety of risks, including foreign exchange risks. Because of asymmetries in information about domestic fundamentals, market participants rely on the information that is provided by domestic banks. Yet, banks which operate in a distorted environment fail to take the downside risks of their activities into account and might thus signal overly optimistic beliefs about the domestic economy. If investor sentiment changes, foreign capital is suddenly withdrawn.

The optimal sequencing of internal and external financial liberalization has been an issue not only since the recent financial crisis. It has rather been discussed in the context of reforms in developing countries before. Blejer and Sagari (1987), for instance, argued that external financial liberalization should follow internal liberalization in order to shield temporarily domestic banks from competition from abroad. Focusing on the role of banks in reducing information asymmetries in financial markets, Aizenman (1998) showed that external financial liberalization by lowering deposit interest rates might increase banks' willingness to take risks and thus reduce their incentives to monitor firms. Hence, overall welfare might decline.

---

13 Döpke and Pierdzioch (1999) reviewed the relevant empirical literature and found no evidence for a link between financial market volatility and the real sector in Germany.

14 These data were calculated from Labán et al. (1997: Table 1). In the *International Financial Statistics* of the IMF (IMF 1999b), on which the calculations of Table 4 are based, quarterly data for the Chilean balance of payments were available only from 1991 onwards.

15 See Buch and Heinrich (1999) for an overview and a theoretical discussion.

This would hold in particular if distortions such as an automatic deposit insurance system made banks prone to take risks, and if domestic banking supervision was weak. Consequently, it might be argued that by using a reserve requirement to drive a wedge between domestic and foreign interest rates, the resulting welfare loss might be reduced.

However, the case for a sequencing of domestic and external financial liberalization becomes less evident if two additional factors are taken into account. *First*, the ability to cover insufficient supervision of the domestic banking system and other distortions by means of capital controls must be questioned. As Valdés-Prieto and Soto (1998) argued, countries which lack the means to monitor the domestic banking system efficiently typically also lack the means to administer a system of capital controls efficiently. Evidence surveyed by Dooley (1996: 675) supports this argument, as in industrialized countries (with more efficient supervisory systems) capital controls tend to have a greater impact on the volume and the composition of capital flows than in developing countries (with less efficient supervisory systems). This led Laurens and Cardoso (1998: 21) to conclude that "such [Chilean-type] measures should not be recommended in countries whose institutions, in particular the central bank, do not have the expertise and resources to enforce them." Yet, these are precisely those countries for which the imposition of controls seems particularly warranted.

Second, opening up for foreign capital and granting market access to foreign banks can help to improve the efficiency of domestic financial intermediation. All too often, countries with financial systems that had been shielded from foreign competition previously found that they had little alternative to opening up for foreign banks after financial crises had hit. In those Asian economies which fell victim to financial market turbulences, market access of foreign banks has been liberalized recently. In the case of Russia, the central bank has stated its intention to drop existing entry restrictions for foreign banks, and foreign capital is hoped

to play a role in the recapitalization of Russia's banking system.

In summary, these considerations show that the case for internal-before-external financial liberalization is less evident than the conventional wisdom might suggest. This holds in particular if limited external financial liberalization includes limited market access of foreign banks. In fact, those countries that have opened up for foreign competition in the financial services sector decisively have typically fared better than those that have taken a more cautious approach. Rather than trying to fine-tune liberalization steps, it seems that progressing simultaneously on internal and external financial liberalization is the preferable option. At the time of opening up for foreign capital, minimum prudential standards should be in place which might be established with the help of foreign technical assistance. At the same time, distortions such as automatic deposit insurance systems should be abolished as these may send false signals to foreign and domestic investors.

Again, evidence from Eastern Europe can serve as a useful reference.[16] In Estonia, for instance, most restrictions on the free flow of foreign capital were relaxed at the beginning of the reforms in 1992/93, and capital flows (including the market access of foreign banks) were fully liberalized in 1994. At the same time, the Estonian authorities have made clear that they would not bail out insolvent banks unconditionally and have closed down a fair number of banks in early 1993. Although the Estonian economy has been showing signs of overheating and has been running large current account deficits recently, it is not evident that the capital account regime has contributed negatively to these developments. Hungary presents another interesting case as the country has opened up its banking sector more rapidly for competition from abroad than the Czech Republic or Poland (*The Banker* 1999). If anything, this has enhanced the efficiency of the Hungarian banking system without jeopardizing the survival of the incumbent banks.

[16] For a more detailed analysis of the advanced transition economies and for an overview of the relevant literature see Buch et al. (1999a).

16

3.4   Capital Controls and Uncertainty

When discussing the welfare implications of capital controls, not only direct effects on the volatility of financial markets and on monetary autonomy but also more indirect effects on investment should be taken into account. Generally, empirical support has been found for the hypothesis that growth and investment, on the one hand, and the development of the financial sector, on the other hand, are positively related.[17] Williamson and Mahar (1998) reported evidence which looked directly at the implications of capital account liberalization for the access of firms to external credits and the efficiency of investment. On balance, the available evidence points to a positive link between liberalization and investment efficiency.

In contrast to earlier work on the links between external financial liberalization and growth, which were based on standard investment functions, recent theoretical contributions have employed models which feature investment under uncertainty.[18] Uncertainty about the course of domestic policies, and irreversibility of investment increase the willingness of investors to postpone their projects (Dixit and Pindyck 1994). This has implications for the volume and structure of capital inflows as well as for the sequencing of capital account liberalization. In the presence of uncertainty and irreversibility of investment, capital inflows will be biased towards relatively liquid, short-term investments (Buch et al. 1999b). Hence, measures that increase uncertainty and irreversibility (such as the imposition of capital controls) might have the unintended effect of tilting the structure capital flows towards short-term funds.

Bartolini and Drazen (1997) have used a framework of investment under uncertainty to show that, if foreign investors are incompletely informed about the actual intentions of a government, the introduction of capital controls can have negative effects on total investment as it sends negative signals about future policies. In their model, information about the type of a government is distributed asymmetrically between investors and governments. Governments can raise revenue by taxing the capital stock in their country, and they differ with respect to the alternative sources of income to which they have access. The imposition of capital controls sends a negative signal to investors that governments lack alternative sources of income and are thus likely to impose controls in the future. Conversely, abolishing controls on capital outflows sends a positive signal and increases net capital inflows.[19]

Using a similar framework, Labán and Larrain (1997) have taken issue with the common practice to be more liberal with the liberalization of capital inflows rather than outflows.[20] They show that a relaxation of controls on capital outflows, aimed at reducing the scope for a real appreciation of the domestic currency, may actually increase net capital inflows rather than lowering them. In the presence of capital controls, the option to defer the investment decision has a positive value to investors. This option value of waiting is positive if uncertainty about the future prevails, if the current investment opportunity is available also in future periods, and if capital controls make investment irreversible. Conversely, policy measures that reduce the option value and thus increase investment are those which either reduce the irreversibility of investment (for example, by lowering controls on capital outflows) or that reduce uncertainty about future investment conditions.

---

17   See Levine (1997) and Rajan and Zingales (1998) for surveys of the relevant literature.

18   See Fry (1995) for a survey of the traditional literature.

19   This argument, however, does not apply necessarily if economic agents believe that an abolition of capital controls will be reversed in the future. Van Wijnbergen (1985) showed that if in the aftermath of trade liberalization uncertainty regarding a future reversal of economic policy remains, investors may postpone investments.

20   See Johnston and Tamirisa (1998) for the empirical evidence.

4. What Are the Alternatives?

The analysis so far has suggested that policy-makers better expect little help from the imposition of URRs when trying to shield their economies from the adverse effects of fast-moving (short-term) capital flows. The imposition of capital controls, if orchestrated faultily, may even have the unintended effect of sending negative signals to both foreign and domestic investors about future policies and therefore may affect investment negatively. In short, capital controls cannot substitute for sound domestic policies, in particular in the banking sector. At the same time, structural policies cannot be adjusted quickly. Hence, implementing sound policies must be a long-term strategy and cannot be resorted to in the acute case of a financial crisis. In addition, negative spillover and contagion effects might affect also those countries which have already implemented sound policies. Hence, safeguard measures to shield otherwise sound countries from the adverse effects of international financial crises might have to be devised.

This section briefly discusses alternatives that are available to policymakers both at a national and at an international level to mitigate potentially negative effects of international capital flows. We start with a discussion of the links between domestic policies and contagion effects, using the response of the transition economies of Central and Eastern Europe to the recent economic and financial crisis of Russia as an example. In addition, recent proposals to reform the international financial system are reviewed.

4.1 Domestic Policies and Contagion: The Case of Eastern Europe

Although the literature tends to find little evidence for the effectiveness of Tobin-type capital controls on volatility or the volume of capital flows, the controls might nevertheless have had an effect in shielding countries such as Chile or Slovenia from adverse effects of acute financial crises elsewhere. Ultimately, the importance of spillover effects is an empirical issue. Edwards (1998a) assessed the contagion effects of the Mexican financial crisis of 1995 on Argentina and Chile. He found that nominal interest rates were more volatile in Argentina than in Chile in response to the crisis and that interest rate differentials in Chile adjusted less quickly after the imposition of capital controls. At the same time, it is difficult to argue that Chile was infected by the spillovers from Mexico to a lesser extent than, for instance, Argentina *because of* the controls, as other relevant policies might have differed as well.

This section discusses briefly the experience of the transition economies of Central and Eastern Europe with the Russian financial crisis. In contrast to Slovenia, these economies have opened up their capital accounts relatively quickly for foreign capital. This raises the issue of whether, by liberalizing their capital accounts, countries such as the Czech Republic, Hungary, and Poland have unduly exposed themselves to contagion from Russia. If contagion can sweep away countries whose major fault was to prematurely open their capital accounts and subject themselves to the whims of international financial markets, then the Russian crisis should be the litmus test.

In August 1998, the Russian ruble succumbed to a successful speculative attack which turned Russia into a severe economic and financial crisis. By the end of March 1999, the value of the ruble had plummeted to less than 75 percent of its pre-crisis value. Recent developments in Russia have undeniably taken their toll on these countries (Figures 5 and 6). Stock markets have fallen, currencies have at least temporarily been under pressure, and foreign financing has become more difficult to obtain. The question is whether these contagion effects would go beyond the direct effects, working through, for instance, trade links, and would thus lower longer-run growth prospects.

The first important observation is that the decline in stock prices and the increase in risk premia on bonds after the Russian crisis parallels developments on Western markets. The German stock index, for example, likewise declined, and

Globalization and Economic and Financial Instability   *597*

18

Figure 5: Stock Market Indices, 1997–1999[a]

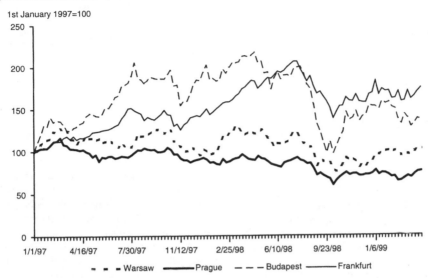

1st January 1997=100

[a]Price indices in local currency, 1997: 1 = 100.

Source: Datastream.

Figure 6: Exchange Rates to the US Dollar, 1997–1999

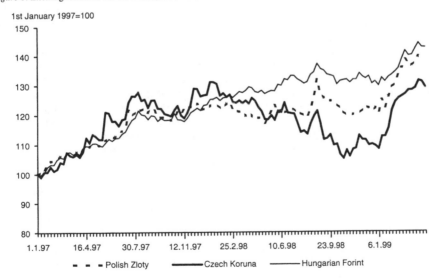

1st January 1997=100

Source: Datastream.

Table 5: Changes in Bank Claims on Transition Economies, 1996–1998[a] (in millions of US dollars)

	1996	1997			1998		
		Year	Q3	Q4	Year	Q3	Q4
Eastern Europe	10,756	18,536	8,279	2,680	−461	−10,420	−961
Czech Republic	1,963	1,583	−81	973	−105	699	233
Hungary	784	2,057	801	866	2,074	−34	−66
Poland	−596	2,223	1,370	−301	2,861	220	307
Slovenia	770	147	−265	−10	174	76	−81
Russia	6,798	9,830	4,136	1,469	−6,333	−10,715	−1,604
[a]Estimated exchange rate adjusted changes.							

Source: BIS (1999a).

spreads on corporate bonds issued by medium-sized borrowers from industrialized countries have increased in the wake of the crisis. Hence, it is difficult to argue that the Russian crisis has had particular spillover effects on the countries under study over and above the general trends in international equity and bond markets in the second half of 1998. Rather, contagion effects of the Russian financial crisis in the stock market seem to have been a European phenomenon whereas the effects of the Asian crises have had a decidedly more global dimension (Linne 1998).

Moreover, the temporary pressure on the currencies has not unduly constrained domestic economic policies. There have not been any forced devaluations, central banks have not lost reserves over a longer period, nor were they forced to raise interest rates significantly. At the end of 1998, Poland and the Czech Republic even lowered key interest rates. Finally, possible adverse effects on the ability of these countries to access the international capital market seem to have been short-lived (Papi 1998). In the third quarter of 1998, claims of foreign banks on Russia plummeted (Table 5), and the contraction continued through the fourth quarter. In the same period, claims on other transition economies, notably the Czech Republic and Poland, increased while claims on Hungary decreased only slightly. Likewise, claims on Slovenia declined in the fourth quarter of the year. This may have been one of the reasons why the Bank of Slovenia eventually set the reserve requirement for foreign financial credits to zero in early 1999.

A number of explanations for this outcome can be found. One is that direct trade links with Russia are relatively small. The immediate impact of reduced demand from Russia on these countries' real economies has therefore been limited. This may have helped steady the nerves of international investors who were wondering whether it was time, after pulling out of Russia, to pull out of the Czech Republic, Hungary, or Poland. Hence, the substantial trade re-orientation and diversification that has taken place during transformation has made the countries less vulnerable to negative shocks spilling over from Russia. As regards financial linkages, macroeconomic implications also seem relatively minor as exposure to countries in the former Soviet Union is confined to individual banks from the region (Turtelboom 1998). Moreover, the prospect of EU membership may have provided added stability to the advanced reform states, essentially because the EU has conditioned entry talks on progress in reforms.

The key factor that emerges from the experience of the accession states is that, in contrast to Russia, the countries have backed up their integration into international capital markets by deep-reaching reforms in other relevant areas. International capital markets have so far rewarded their reform efforts by clearly discriminating between these countries and Russia.[21] Overall, the impact of the Russian crisis on those countries has been limited thus far, and average growth and inflation forecasts

---

[21] A similar conclusion was reached in the most recent transition report of the EBRD (1998). See also Fries et al. (1998).

20

for 1999 are only somewhat less favorable than those for 1998 (EBRD 1998).

Evidence from Asia likewise suggests that structural reforms at the domestic level can reduce the exposure of emerging market economies to volatile capital flows. In Asia, a major factor behind changes in the composition of capital inflows away from long-term FDI towards short-term flows have been sterilization policies which held domestic interest rates at high levels (Kaminsky and Reinhart 1998). Moreover, exchange rate policies must be sufficiently flexible to adjust to external shocks.

Perhaps the most important policy implication apart from the need for sound structural reforms is the crucial need to disseminate transparent, timely, and reliable information to the international investment community. Better information policies would substantially reduce the costs of obtaining information for market participants and thus stimulate long-term investment. Although this would not eliminate financial market volatility, improved availability of information is likely to increase the stability of capital flows and the importance of market fundamentals for international investment decisions.

4.2. Reforming the International Financial Architecture

Apart from adjustments of domestic policies, institutional changes in the international financial architecture can potentially help to reduce the probability that basically innocent bystanders are hit by financial crises in other countries. As the relevant contributions to the on-going debate have been discussed and comprehensively summarized elsewhere (Eichengreen 1999), only two proposals will be sketched here. The first relates to an adjustment in the lending policies of the IMF by providing Contingent Credit Lines (CCLs) to its member countries. The second proposal is representative for a class of suggestions which intends to rely more heavily on market mechanisms to alter the structure of foreign debt. More specifically, we will discuss briefly the Universal Debt Rollover

Option with a Penalty (UDROP) which has been suggested by Buiter and Sibert (1999).

Essentially, all proposals for reforming the international financial architecture are based on the notion that asymmetries in information and uncertainty prevent financial markets from telling insolvent and merely illiquid borrowers (or countries, for that matter) apart. Under perfect information, markets would be able to distinguish illiquid from insolvent borrowers. They would extend additional finance to the former, but would deny fresh finance to the latter.[22] Under imperfect information, such a separating equilibrium is not reached necessarily. Rather, borrowers are likely to be pooled together, and finance might be denied to all applicants. Should a financial crisis strike somewhere, markets would reassess the probability that other countries might be affected. In this situation, the inability of a borrower to service its external debt would be taken as a negative signal about solvency.

Recently, the IMF has decided to provide a Contingent Credit Line to its member countries.[23] The CCL aims at assisting those countries which are fundamentally sound but which are exposed to the risk of contagion effects from financial crises elsewhere. Hence, it precisely aims at granting liquidity to illiquid countries which might otherwise be pooled together with insolvent countries. Obviously, in order to mitigate significantly moral hazard in financial markets, at least three issues need to be resolved. *First*, the decision which countries qualify for assistance under such program has to be made ex ante, i.e., prior to the emergence of a crisis. Essentially, access to the CCL would thus be on a case-by-case basis. As quick action is typically required when a financial crisis hits, this requires relatively efficient decision mechanisms. *Second*, the discretionary nature of the process potentially opens the field for political

---

[22] Note that in a national context, refinancing for illiquid borrowers (banks) is provided via the lender-of-last-resort facility of the central bank. However, such facility does not exist in an international context, i.e., for foreign-currency-denominated debt (Buiter and Sibert 1999).

[23] This paragraph draws on Golder (1999).

lobbying and for a renegotiation of initial terms. *Third*, defining clear access criteria will be difficult, and the actual refinancing needs are still an open issue.

In parallel to this new lending facility, market-based schemes which are based on an adjustment of international bond terms are thus under discussion. One of these proposals has been advanced by Buiter and Sibert (1999). They have suggested to attach a mandatory roll-over option (UDROP) to any cross-border financial contract. Should a borrower have insufficient funds to cover its foreign liabilities, it would be granted the option to roll over its external debt at a penalty rate. This would give merely illiquid borrowers the opportunity to raise additional finance. As borrowers would decide unilaterally whether to exercise this option, there would be no need to assess the borrower status externally. Hence, the asymmetric information problem would be mitigated. The option would be priced on the market, i.e., the costs of foreign borrowing would rise.

The authors discussed several objections to their proposal. Most importantly, adverse selection and moral hazard problems would arise because both illiquid and insolvent borrowers could make use of the option. Therefore, Buiter and Sibert proposed to grant the right to roll over a loan only once, i.e., a potential insolvency would eventually come to the surface after an additional period has elapsed. Also, UDROP should be mandatory for all financial contracts in order to prevent bad risks to mimic good risks (which would not make use of the option were it voluntary). Obviously, even with these modifications, UDROP would not solve the problems on international financial markets entirely. Under asymmetric information, the fair pricing of the roll-over option would remain an open issue. Also, effective supervising whether all contracts actually have the option attached to them would need to be ensured. Yet, the proposal shows that it is feasible to invent new contract designs which might be superior to non-market based solutions.

5.   Concluding Remarks

The main result of this paper is that (Chilean-type) capital controls are no panacea. This, by itself, should not be very surprising as there is no economic policy measure which, seen in isolation, has beneficial effects always and everywhere. In fact, proponents of capital controls and in particular of taxes and reserve requirements on short-term capital flows would argue that these instruments should be part of a consistent overall reform program. Without safeguards against volatile capital flows, otherwise sound economic policies may be derailed, and financial crises elsewhere may hit innocent bystanders.

Essentially, the case for Chilean- or Tobin-type capital controls is based on the notion that financial markets react faster than goods markets. This market imperfection may cause fluctuations in the real economy which are not linked to fundamentals and, hence, a corrective tax may enhance welfare. This argument has hardly been challenged by the present paper. Yet, the introduction of restrictions on short-term capital flows will be welfare-enhancing only under a set of special conditions. These, in turn, are hardly found in reality.

On a rather practical level, the actual design and enforcement of the tax is an open issue. If current and capital account transactions have been liberalized in general, various mechanisms to evade the tax can be devised. While these do not erode completely the effectiveness of the tax, they still reduce its impact. Moreover, as additional (scarce) resources must be freed to supervise the enforcement of the scheme, other policy areas might suffer.

In addition, Chilean-type capital controls and other taxes on cross-border financial flows have the potential of reducing the overshooting of exchange rates. Yet, the imposition of these taxes by itself can lead to an overshooting process because it is conceptually identical with a negative shock to the domestic interest rate. This mechanism cautions particularly against the imposition of temporary controls.

22

Even though Chile's and Slovenia's URRs might have lowered inflows of short-term financial credits, this has not necessarily reduced the volatility of capital flows. One reason for this finding is that there is no clear evidence as to which type of capital flows is the most volatile and how volatility changes after the imposition of controls. In contrast to the conventional wisdom, short-term capital flows are not necessarily the most volatile capital account item. Exchange rate volatility, in contrast, has tended to come down in the period following the imposition of URRs. Yet, the extent to which this decline is a result of exchange market intervention of the monetary authorities rather than the capital control regime, remains an open issue.

The ability of URRs to provide both the monetary authorities with greater autonomy and leeway to implement structural reforms must be questioned. In Chile and Slovenia, the controls have not halted an increased inflow of foreign capital. Generally, URRs cannot prevent speculative attacks on misaligned currencies but may at best delay the timing of a speculative attack. Proponents of a tax would argue that it is precisely this additional breathing time that governments gain which makes the tax attractive. Yet, this window of opportunity may fail to deliver what it promises if domestic authorities are not willing or able to act quickly and to tackle structural problems.

It is often argued that capital controls could be used to shield banking systems that are poorly supervised from adverse effects of external

financial liberalization. Yet, the administrative capacity to enforce such regulations is typically poor precisely in those countries for which the controls would seem most desirable. This paper has argued that internal and external financial liberalization could proceed in parallel if the authorities are willing to implement basic banking standards (possibly with the help of foreign technical assistance), to withdraw implicit deposit insurance schemes, and to open up for foreign banks.

Alternatives to taxes on cross-border capital flows suited to reduce exposure to volatile capital flows and to contain contagion in financial markets have been discussed. Evidence from Eastern Europe has shown that countries with relatively open capital accounts and, in principle, sound policies could handle contagion effects from the Russian financial crisis relatively well. This suggests that domestic policy has room to maneuver even in globalized financial markets. Sufficiently flexible exchange rate policies and reforms of the banking sector have helped the successful transition economies to stave off adverse external shocks. Hence, by pursuing structural reforms, by disseminating clear and transparent information, and by using market mechanisms to alter the structure of foreign debt, governments can significantly reduce exposure to external shocks and can most efficiently use scarce administrative resources. Hereby, international institutions have an important role to play in designing and enforcing an institutional framework in which such mechanisms can be implemented.

23

References

Agénor, P.-R., J.S. Bhandari, and R.P. Flood (1992). Speculative Attacks and Models of Balance of Payment Crises. *IMF Staff Papers* 39 (2): 357–394.

Aizenman, J. (1998). Capital Mobility in a Second Best World: Moral Hazard with Costly Financial Intermediation. NBER Working Paper 6703. National Bureau of Economic Research, Cambridge, Mass.

Banco Central de Chile (1998). Nueva información proporcionada por el Banco Central de Chile. Downloaded from http://www.bcentral.cl/Informacion/informacion.htm on June 25.

The Banker (1999). Falling Barriers. 149 (April): 40.

Bartolini, L., and A. Drazen (1997). Capital-Account Liberalization as a Signal. *American Economic Review* 87 (1): 138–154.

BIS (Bank for International Settlements) (1997). *BIS Quarterly Review. International Banking and Financial Market Developments*. (November). Basle.

— (1999a). *BIS Quarterly Review. International Banking and Financial Market Developments*. (June). Basle.

— (1999b). *BIS consolidated international banking statistics* (formerly: *Maturity, Sectoral and Nationality Distribution of International Bank Lending*). (various issues). Basle.

Blejer, M., and S. Sagari (1987). The Structure of the Banking System and the Sequence of Financial Liberalization. In M. Connolly and C. Gonzaléz (eds.), *Economic Reform and Stabilization in Latin America*. New York: Praeger.

BoS (Bank of Slovenia) (1999). Foreign Exchange Regime in Slovenia. Downloaded from http://www.bsi.si/html/eng/laws_regulations/foreign_exchange.html on March 19.

Buch, C.M., and E. Hanschel (1999). The Effectiveness of Capital Controls: The Case of Slovenia. Kiel Working Paper 933. Institut für Weltwirtschaft, Kiel.

Buch, C.M., and R.P. Heinrich (1999). Twin Crises and the Intermediary Role of Banks. *International Journal of Finance and Economics* (forthcoming).

Buch, C.M., R.P. Heinrich, and C. Pierdzioch (1998). Taxing Short-Term Capital Flows: An Option for Transition Economies? Kiel Discussion Papers 321. Institut für Weltwirtschaft, Kiel.

— (1999a). *Foreign Capital and Economic Transformation: Risks and Benefits of Free Capital Flows*. Kieler Studien 295. Tübingen.

— (1999b). The Value of Waiting: Russia's Integration into the International Capital Markets. *Journal of Comparative Economics* (forthcoming).

Buiter, W.H., and A.C. Sibert (1999). UDROP: A Small Contribution to the New International Financial Architecture. *International Finance* (July, forthcoming).

Claessens, S., M.P. Dooley, and A. Warner (1995). Portfolio Capital Flows: Hot or Cold? Development Discussion Paper 501. Harvard Institute for International Development, Cambridge, Mass.

Cordella, T. (1998). Can Short-Term Capital Controls Promote Capital Inflows? IMF Working Paper 131. International Monetary Fund, Washington, D.C.

Dixit, A.K., and R.S. Pindyck (1994). *Investment under Uncertainty*. Princeton, N.J.: Princeton University Press.

Döpke, J., and C. Pierdzioch (1999). Brokers and Business Cycles: Does Financial Market Volatility Cause Real Fluctuations? Kiel Working Papers 899. Institut für Weltwirtschaft, Kiel.

Dooley, M.P. (1996). A Survey of Literature on Controls over International Capital Transactions. *IMF Staff Papers* 43 (4): 639–687.

Dornbusch, R. (1976). Expectations and Exchange Rate Dynamics. *Journal of Political Economy* 84: 1116–1176.

EBRD (European Bank for Reconstruction and Development) (1998). *Transition Report 1998: Financial Sector in Transition*. London.

24

Edwards, S. (1998a). Interest Rate Volatility, Capital Controls, and Contagion. NBER Working Paper 6756. National Bureau of Economic Research, Cambridge, Mass.

— (1998b). Capital Flows, Real Exchange Rates, and Capital Controls: Some Latin American Experiences. NBER Working Paper 6800. National Bureau of Economic Research, Cambridge, Mass.

— (1999). A Capital Idea? — Reconsidering a Financial Quick Fix. Foreign Affairs 78 (3): 18–22.

Eichengreen, B. (1999). *Toward a New International Financial Architecture: A Practical Post-Asia Agenda*. Institute for International Economics, Washington, D.C.

Eichengreen, B., J. Tobin, and C. Wyplosz (1995). Two Cases for Sand in the Wheels of International Finance. *Economic Journal* 105 (428): 162–172.

Eichengreen, B., M. Mussa, G. Dell'Ariccia, E. Detragiache, G.M. Milesi-Ferretti, and A. Tweedie (1999). Liberalizing Capital Movements: Some Analytical Issues. Economic Issues 17. International Monetary Fund, Washington, D.C.

EU (European Commission) (1998). *Regular Report from the Commission on Slovenia's Progress Towards Accession*. Downloaded from http://europa.eu.int/comm/dg1a/enlarge/report_11_98_en/index.htm on June 29, 1999.

Ffrench-Davis, R., M. Agosin, and A. Uthoff (1995). Capital Movements, Export Strategy, and Macroeconomic Stability in Chile. In R. Ffrench-Davis and S. Griffith-Jones (eds.), *Coping with Capital Surges*. Boulder, Col.: Rienner.

Frankel, J.A. (1996). How Well Do Foreign Exchange Markets Work: Might a Tobin Tax Help? In Mahbub-ul-Haq, I. Kaul, and I. Grunberg (eds.), *The Tobin Tax: Coping with Financial Volatility*. New York: Oxford University Press.

Fries, S., M. Raiser, and N. Stern (1998). Macroeconomic and Financial Stability: Transition and East Asia "Contagion". EBRD Working Paper 27. European Bank for Reconstruction and Development, London.

Fry, M.J. (1995). *Money, Interest, and Banking in Economic Development*. Baltimore: Johns Hopkins University Press.

Garber, P.M., and M.P. Taylor (1995). Sand in the Wheels of Foreign Exchange Markets: A Sceptical Note. *Economic Journal* 105 (428): 173–180.

Golder, S. (1999). Precautionary Credit Lines: A Means to Contain Contagion in Financial Markets? Kiel Discussion Papers 341. Institut für Weltwirtschaft, Kiel.

Grilli, V.U., and G.M. Milesi-Ferretti (1995). Economic Effects and Structural Determinants of Capital Controls. *IMF Staff Papers* 42 (3): 517–551.

IMF (International Monetary Fund) (1998a). *Balance of Payments Statistics Yearbook*. (January). Washington, D.C.

— (1998b). *Annual Report on Exchange Arrangements and Exchange Restrictions 1998* (and various earlier issues). Washington, D.C.

— (1998c). Chile: Selected Issues. IMF Staff Country Reports 26. Washington, D.C.

— (1999). *International Financial Statistics (IFS)*. CD-ROM. Washington, D.C.

Johnston, B.R., and N.T. Tamirisa (1998). Why Do Countries Use Capital Controls? IMF Working Paper 181. Internatioal Monetary Fund, Washington, D.C.

Kaminsky, G.L., and C.M. Reinhart (1998). Financial Crises in Asia and Latin Amercia: Then and Now. *Amercian Economic Review* 88 (2): 444–448.

Krugman, P.R. (1979). A Model of Balance-of-Payment Crises. *Journal of Money, Credit, and Banking* 11: 311–325.

Labán, R.M., and F.B. Larrain (1997). Can a Liberalization of Capital Outflows Increase Net Capital Inflows? *Journal of International Money and Finance* 16 (3): 415–431.

Labán, R.M., and F.B. Larrain (1998). The Return of Private Capital to Chile in the 1990s: Causes, Effects, and Policy Reactions. Faculty Research Working Paper 2. John F. Kennedy School of Government, Harvard University, Cambridge, Mass.

Labán, R.M., F.B. Larrain, and R.A. Chumacero (1997). What Determines Capital Inflows? An Empirical Analysis for Chile. Development Discussion Paper 590. Harvard Institute for International Development, Cambridge, Mass.

Laurens, B., and J. Cardoso (1998). Managing Capital Flows. Lessons from the Experience of Chile. IMF Working Paper 168. International Monetary Fund, Washington, D.C.

Levine, R. (1997). Financial Development and Economic Growth: Views and Agenda. *Journal of Economic Literature* 3 (2): 688–726.

Linne, T. (1998). Ansteckungseffekte von Aktienmärkten durch Währungskrisen. Mimeo. (December). Institut für Wirtschaftsforschung, Halle.

Lipsey, R.E. (1999). The Role of Foreign Direct Investment in International Capital Flows. NBER Working Paper 7094. National Bureau of Economic Research, Cambridge, Mass.

McKinnon, R.I., and H. Pill (1995). Credible Liberalizations and International Capital Flows: The "Over-Borrowing Syndrome". CEPR Discussion Paper 437. Center for Economic Policy Research, Stanford, Calif.

Mussa, M., A. Swoboda, J. Zettelmeyer, and O. Jeanne (1999). Moderating Fluctuations in Capital Flows to Emerging Market Economies. Paper presented at the Conference on Key Issues in Reform of the International Monetary and Financial System, May 28–29, Washington, D.C.

Nadal-De Simone, F., and P. Sorsa (1999). A Review of Capital Restrictions in Chile in the 1990s. IMF Working Paper 52. International Monetary Fund, Washington, D.C.

Obstfeld, M. (1994). The Logic of Currency Crises. NBER Working Paper 4640. National Bureau of Economic Research, Cambridge, Mass.

Papi, L. (1998). Capital Still Flowing into Emerging Europe. Deutsche Bank Research. *Emerging Europe Weekly,* December 11, London.

Park, D., and J.D. Sachs (1996). The Timing of Exchange Regime Collapse under Capital Controls. *International Economic Journal* 10 (4): 123–141.

Quirk, P.J., and O. Evans (1995). Capital Account Convertibility: Review of Experience and Implications for IMF Policies. IMF Occasional Paper 131. International Monetary Fund, Washington, D.C.

Rajan, R.G., and L. Zingales (1998). Financial Dependence and Growth. *American Economic Review* 88 (3): 558–586.

Reinhart, C.M., and R.T. Smith (1997). Temporary Capital Controls. University of Maryland and International Monetary Fund. Mimeo. Downloaded from http://www.stern.nyu.edu/Faculty/FacPict/Economics/index.htm on April 21, 1999.

Tobin, J. (1978). A Proposal for International Monetary Reform. *Eastern Economic Journal* 4 (3/4): 153–159.

Turtelboom, B. (1998). Emerging Europe after Russia. Deutsche Bank Research. *Emerging Markets Research: Global Emerging Markets 1998.* (October): 40–51.

Valdés-Prieto, S., and M. Soto (1998). The Effectiveness of Capital Controls: Theory and Evidence from Chile. *Empirica* 25: 133–164.

van Wijnbergen, S. (1985). Trade Reform, Aggregate Investment, and Capital Flight: On Credibility and the Value of Information. *Economics Letters* 19 (4): 369–372.

Williamson, J., and M. Mahar (1998). A Survey of Financial Liberalization. *Essays in International Finance* 211. Princeton, N.J.: Princeton University Press.

World Bank (1998). Foreword to "Global Economic Prospects and the Developing Countries 1998/99: Beyond Financial Crisis". Downloaded from http://www.worldbank.org/prospects/gep98-99/foreword.htm on April 15, 1999.

— (1999). *World Development Indicators.* CD-ROM. Washington, D.C.: World Bank.

[29]

What Should the World Bank Think about the Washington Consensus?

John Williamson

The phrase "Washington Consensus" has become a familiar term in development policy circles in recent years, but it is now used in several different senses, causing a great deal of confusion. In this article the author distinguishes between his original meaning as a summary of the lowest common denominator of policy advice addressed by the Washington-based institutions (including the World Bank) and subsequent use of the term to signify neoliberal or market-fundamentalist policies. He argues that the latter policies could not be expected to provide an effective framework for combating poverty but that the original advice is still broadly valid. The article discusses alternative ways of addressing the confusion. It argues that any policy manifesto designed to eliminate poverty needs to go beyond the original version but concludes by cautioning that no consensus on a wider agenda currently exists.

Ten years ago I invented the term "Washington Consensus" to refer to the lowest common denominator of policy advice being addressed by the Washington-based institutions to Latin American countries as of 1989 (Williamson 1990). While it is jolly to become famous for coining a term that reverberates around the world, I have long been doubtful about whether my phrase served to advance the cause of rational economic policymaking. My initial concern was that the phrase invited the interpretation that the liberalizing economic reforms of the past two decades were imposed by Washington-based institutions (for example, see Stewart 1997) rather than having resulted from the process of intellectual convergence that I believe underlies the reforms.[1] Richard Feinberg's "universal convergence" (in Williamson 1990) or Jean Waelbroeck's "one-world consensus" (Waelbroeck 1998) would have been a much better term for the intellectual convergence that I had in mind.

I have gradually developed a second and more significant concern, however. I find that the term has been invested with a meaning that is significantly different from that which I had intended and is now used as a synonym for what is often called

The World Bank Research Observer, vol. 15, no. 2 (August 2000), pp. 251–64.
© 2000 The International Bank for Reconstruction and Development / THE WORLD BANK

"neoliberalism" in Latin America, or what Geeorge Soros (1998) has called "market fundamentalism." When I first came across this usage, I asserted that it was a misuse of my intended meaning. I had naïvely imagined that just because I had invented the expression, I had some sort of intellectual property rights that entitled me to dictate its meaning, but in fact the concept had become public property.

The battle of economic ideas, as McCloskey (1998) has argued, is fought to a significant extent with rhetoric. The use of a term with dual meanings and strong ideological overtones can therefore pose serious dangers not only of misunderstanding but also of inadvertently prejudicing policy objectives. Specifically, there is a real danger that many of the economic reforms favored by international development institutions—notably macroeconomic discipline, trade openness, and market-friendly microeconomic policies—will be discredited in the eyes of many observers, simply because these institutions are inevitably implicated in views that command a consensus in Washington and the term "Washington Consensus" has come to be used to describe an extreme and dogmatic commitment to the belief that markets can handle everything.

The objective of this article is to consider what should be done to minimize the damage to the cause of intellectual understanding, and therefore of rational economic reform, that is being wrought by the current widespread use of the term "Washington Consensus" in a sense different from that originally intended. Would it be productive, for example, to insist that the original usage is the correct one? Or should one simply refuse to debate in these terms? Is it possible to escape by declaring fidelity to some "post–Washington Consensus"? The first stage in answering these questions is a careful examination of the semantic issues involved.

The Original Version

My original paper (Williamson 1990) argued that the set of policy reforms that most of official Washington thought would be good for Latin American countries could be summarized in 10 propositions:

- Fiscal discipline
- A redirection of public expenditure priorities toward fields offering both high economic returns and the potential to improve income distribution, such as primary health care, primary education, and infrastructure
- Tax reform (to lower marginal rates and broaden the tax base)
- Interest rate liberalization
- A competitive exchange rate
- Trade liberalization
- Liberalization of inflows of foreign direct investment

- Privatization
- Deregulation (to abolish barriers to entry and exit)
- Secure property rights.

The need for the first three reforms is, so far as I am aware, widely accepted among economists. Nevertheless, when I reviewed the progress that Latin American countries had made in implementing the recommended set of policies several years later (Williamson 1996), it appeared that the least progress had come in redirecting public expenditure priorities. The other seven reforms have stimulated a measure of controversy and therefore merit comment.

In my original paper I specified interest rate liberalization as the fourth reform. I am now well aware that many economists have reservations about that formulation. As a matter of fact, I have such reservations myself: in Williamson and Mahar (1998) interest rate liberalization is identified as merely one of six dimensions of financial liberalization. Moreover, Stiglitz (1994) has argued that interest rate liberalization should come toward the end of the process of financial liberalization, inasmuch as a ceiling on the deposit interest rate (equal to the Treasury bill rate, he suggests) might provide a constraint on gambling for redemption. I find this argument persuasive and long ago changed my description of the fourth element of the Washington Consensus to financial liberalization. More recently Stiglitz (1998) has expressed a much more basic objection to financial liberalization, arguing that the success of some East Asian countries stemmed importantly from their policy of directing credit to particular industries rather than allowing the market to determine the allocation of credit. That argument is highly contentious, especially in the aftermath of the East Asian economic crisis of 1997–98.

My fifth choice—a competitive exchange rate—was not, I have concluded, an accurate report of Washington opinion. I suspect that by 1989 a majority of economists, in Washington as elsewhere, were already in favor of either firmly fixed or freely floating exchange rates and hostile to the sort of intermediate regime that in my judgment gives the best promise of maintaining a competitive exchange rate in the medium term. (My own preference remains an intermediate regime of limited flexibility, provided that excludes an old-fashioned adjustable peg, even if such a regime is more likely to spawn speculative pressures than a floating rate.) But note that the East Asian countries did by and large achieve and maintain competitive exchange rates, at least before about 1996 (and even after 1996 only Thailand failed to do so).[2]

My sixth reform was trade liberalization. Here I see little reason to doubt that I reported accurately on opinions in the international financial institutions and the central economic agencies of the U.S. government (although parts of Congress and the Department of Commerce are not noted for their dedication to liberal trade). But this is another area where critics can rightly claim that the policies that nurtured the East Asian miracle were, at least in some countries, at odds with the policies endorsed in the Washington Consensus. Much the same is true of foreign direct investment, except that the East Asian economies were less hostile to a policy of openness; only the Republic of Korea rejected most foreign direct investment during the years of the miracle.

Privatization commanded a lot of support in Washington, where it had been put on the international agenda by James Baker when he was secretary of the U.S. Treasury, in his speech to the World Bank–International Monetary Fund Annual Meetings in Seoul in 1985. Privatization was controversial in much of the rest of the world, where one's attitude to public versus private ownership had long been the litmus test for qualifying as left-wing or right-wing. Deregulation was rather less politically polarizing: it had been initiated by the centrist Carter administration in the United States, rather than by the right-wing Thatcher government that pioneered privatization in the United Kingdom. Deregulation, however, was not a policy that reverberated in East Asia, where the industrial policies pursued in some (though not all) countries ran very much in the opposite direction. The notion of the importance of secure property rights had come both from Chicago's law and economics school and from the work of Hernando de Soto in Peru. The concept was presumably offensive to those who resisted the advance of the market economy, but this breed was extinct in Washington by 1989 (if, indeed, it had ever existed there). My impression is that the institution of private property was somewhat more securely entrenched in East Asia than in most of the rest of the developing world.

So much for the content of my version of the Washington Consensus. What inspired it? In an immediate sense, it originated from an attempt to answer a question posed to me by Hans Singer during a seminar at the Institute for Development Studies: what were these "sensible" policies that were being pursued in Latin America (and that I was arguing justified approval of the Brady Plan to provide these countries with debt relief)? In a more profound sense, my effort was an attempt to distill which of the policy initiatives that had emanated from Washington during the years of conservative ideology had won inclusion in the intellectual mainstream rather than being cast aside once Ronald Reagan was no longer on the political scene.[3] Taking an even longer perspective, my version of the Washington Consensus can be seen as an attempt to summarize the policies that were widely viewed as supportive of development at the end of the two decades when economists had become convinced that the key to rapid economic development lay not in a country's natural resources or even in its physical or human capital but, rather, in the set of economic policies that it pursued.

Let me emphasize that the Washington Consensus as I conceived it was in principle geographically and historically specific, a lowest common denominator of the reforms that I judged "Washington" could agree were needed in Latin America as of 1989. But in practice there would probably not have been a lot of difference if I had undertaken a similar exercise for Africa or Asia, and that still seemed to be the case when I revisited the topic (with regard to Latin America) in 1996 (Williamson 1997). This doubtless made it easier for some to interpret the Washington Consensus as a policy manifesto that its adherents supposedly believed to be valid for all places and at all times.

Current Usage

The following is a selection of recent definitions of the Washington Consensus that I happened to stumble across. (I have undertaken no bibliographic research to compile this list.)

"A die-hard liberalization advocate (or a Washington-consensus believer). . . . " (Ito 1999)

". . . the self-confident advice of the 'Washington consensus'—free-up trade, practice sound money, and go home early. . . ." (Vines 1999)

" . . . the Washington Consensus: policy prescriptions based on free market principles and monetary discipline." (Hamada 1998)

"The Washington Consensus had the following message: 'Liberalize as much as you can, privatize as fast as you can, and be tough in monetary and fiscal matters.' " (Kolodko 1998)

"The bashing of the state that characterized the policy thrust of the Washington Consensus. . . ." (United Nations 1998)

"This new imperialism, codified in the 'Washington Consensus'. . . ." (Alam 1999)

"The Brazilian crisis has reignited the debate over the so-called Washington Consensus on the creation of a laissez-faire global economy." (Rajan 1999)

In none of these examples is my phrase used in the sense that I originally intended. On the contrary, when I coined the term in 1989, the market fundamentalism of Reagan's first term had already been superseded by the return of rational economic policymaking, and one could discern which ideas were going to survive and which were not (monetary discipline but not monetarism; tax reform but not tax-slashing; trade liberalization but maybe not complete freedom of capital movements; deregulation of entry and exit barriers but not the suppression of regulations designed to protect the environment).

How is it that a term intended to describe a technocratic policy agenda that survived the demise of Reaganomics came to be used to describe an ideology embracing the most extreme version of Reaganomics? The closest I can come to understanding this is to note that my version of the Washington Consensus did indeed focus principally on policy reforms that reduced the role of government, such as privatization and the liberalization of trade, finance, foreign direct investment, and entry and exit. It did this because the orthodoxy of the generation whose ideas were embodied in the practices being challenged in 1989 had been much more statist than was by then regarded as advisable, and hence the policy reforms that were needed at that time were all in the direction of liberalization. This need for liberalization did not neces-sarily imply a swing to the opposite extreme of market fundamentalism and a minimalist role for government, but such boring possibilities were repressed in the ideological debates of the 1990s. For it is certainly true that the Washington Con-sensus came to be used to describe an ideological position, a development that Naim (2000) argues resulted from the world's acute need for a new ideology to provide a focus for debate in place of the god that had failed. My qualifications about the Washington Consensus being an agenda for a specific part of the world at a particu-lar moment of history were quickly forgotten, as the search for a new ideology, to endorse or to hate, was perceived to have succeeded. Ravi Kanbur argues that the staffs of the Bretton Woods institutions perceived themselves as storming the cita-dels of statism, which led them as a negotiating ploy to demand more in the way of liberalizing reforms than they really expected to achieve—a tactic that led citizens in the World Bank's client countries to identify these institutions with something closer to market fundamentalism than the institutions really believed in.

The term's use as a synonym for market fundamentalism appears to be the domi-nant, but not the only, current usage. Many Bank staff members, including those who wrote *Beyond the Washington Consensus: Institutions Matter* (Burki and Perry 1998), still use the term in the way that I intended, and I think most of them would endorse the reform agenda to which I had applied the term as a reasonably accurate and appropriate summary of what the Bank and other agencies concerned with the promotion of development were, and should have been, advising countries to do.

Joseph Stiglitz, formerly the World Bank's chief economist, recently used the term in the alternative, neoliberal, sense (1999b). This at least makes it clear that he was not attacking his colleagues when he spoke of reviewing "the major ways in which . . . the 'Washington Consensus' doctrines of transition, failed. . ." (Stiglitz 1999a:4). He proceeded to question the priority given to rapid privatization and the lack of attention to establishing competition or building social and organizational capital, and later he spoke of "the standard form of voucher privatization promoted by the Washington Consensus. . . ." I am not aware that Washington has ever displayed any particular preference for voucher privatization; certainly this was not a theme of the 1996 *World Development Report* (World Bank 1996), which dealt with the tran-sition. I agree with Stiglitz on the substantive questions he raises: one can put too much emphasis on rapid privatization, and it is more important to do it right than to do it quickly; I agree that the great merit of privatization is that it can be used to further competition; I am skeptical about voucher privatization; and I think I agree about the importance of social and organizational capital, if I understand what the words mean. (I would describe them as social cohesion and good institutions, re-spectively.) What I do not understand is what is gained by describing these sensible ideas as refuting a doctrine described by a term that many people in the Bank regard as providing a useful summary of the advice the Bank dispenses.

Do Washington Consensus Policies Promote Poverty Reduction?

The answer, quite obviously, depends on which interpretation of the Washington Consensus one is referring to. The popular, or populist, interpretation of the Washington Consensus, meaning market fundamentalism or neoliberalism, refers to laissez-faire Reaganomics—let's bash the state, the markets will resolve everything. I would not subscribe to the view that such policies offer an effective agenda for reducing poverty. We know that poverty reduction demands efforts to build the human capital of the poor, but the populist interpretation fails to address that issue. We know that an active policy to supervise financial institutions is needed if financial liberalization is not to lead to financial collapse, which invariably ends up using tax revenues to write off bank loans that were made to the relatively rich. And some measure of income redistribution would be recommended by any policy that was primarily directed at reducing poverty rather than simply maximizing growth, but market fundamentalists rule out all income redistribution as plunder.

A plausible alternative concept would be that the Washington Consensus consists of the set of policies endorsed by the principal economic institutions located in Washington: the U.S. Treasury, the Federal Reserve Board, the International Monetary Fund, and the World Bank. I would argue that the policies these institutions advocated in the 1990s were inimical to the cause of poverty reduction in emerging markets in at least one respect: their advocacy of capital account liberalization. This was, in my view, the main cause of the contagion that caused the East Asian crisis to spread beyond Thailand and that resulted in a tragic interruption of the poverty reduction those countries had achieved (Williamson 1999). (I did not include full capital account liberalization in my version of the Washington Consensus because I did not believe it commanded a consensus, if only because I could not believe I was the only person in Washington who feared that capital account liberalization could precipitate a tragedy such as that which occurred in East Asia.)

My version of the Washington Consensus began with the proposition that the inflation caused by lack of fiscal discipline is bad for income distribution. The second reform specifically involved redirecting public expenditure toward primary health and education, that is, toward building the human capital of the poor. Tax reform can be distributionally neutral or even progressive. A competitive exchange rate is key to nurturing export-led and crisis-free growth and is hence in the general interest, including that of the poor. Trade liberalization, certainly in low-income, resource-poor countries, tends to be pro-poor because it increases the demand for unskilled labor and decreases the subsidies directed to import-competing industries that use large volumes of capital and employ small numbers of workers, many of them highly skilled. Foreign direct investment helps raise growth and spread technology, provided that import protection is not excessive, so that the case of immiserizing growth does not arise (Brecher and Diaz-Alejandro 1977).[4] The impact of privatization depends very much on how it is done: the sort of insider-voucher privatization that occurred in Russia allows the plunder of state assets for the benefit of an elite, but a well-conducted privatization with competitive bidding can raise efficiency and improve the public finances with benefits to all, including the poor. Deregulation in general involves the dismantling of barriers that protect privileged elites (even if some of them, like trade unionists, have difficulty thinking of themselves as an elite), and hence there is a strong presumption that it will be pro-poor. Private property rights are certainly a defense primarily for those who have private property, but the improvement of such rights is nonetheless very likely to be pro-poor because these are the people who find themselves unable to defend their property when property rights are ill-defined (for example, Hernando de Soto's squatters on the periphery of Lima).

I have omitted one of the ten reforms from the preceding list: financial and interest rate liberalization. This is the primary focus of Stiglitz's criticisms when he refers to something that I can recognize as akin to my version of the Washington Consensus. I have realized for some time (see Williamson 1996) that my first formulation was flawed in that it neglected financial supervision, without which financial liberalization seems all too likely to lead to improper lending and eventually to a crisis that requires the taxpayers to pick up the losses from making bad loans (Williamson and Mahar 1998). But should economists therefore endorse the view that directed lending as pursued in some—though not all—East Asian countries is pro-growth and thus ultimately pro-poor? On this issue, at least, I would have thought that the East Asian crisis, especially in Korea, should have tempered economists' enthusiasm for the practice. The high debt-equity ratios that resulted from directed lending were certainly among the causes of the financial fragility that deepened the impact of the crisis.

Thus most of the reforms embodied in my version of the Washington Consensus are at least potentially pro-poor. In some cases this conclusion is sensitive to the way in which reform is implemented: that is certainly true of tax reform, privatization, and, above all, financial liberalization. But I see no reason why the World Bank should back away from endorsing my version of the Washington Consensus in view of its reaffirmation of poverty reduction as its overarching mission. That is not to claim that the Washington Consensus, in any version, constituted a policy manifesto adequate for addressing poverty. My version quite consciously eschewed redistributive policies, taking the view that Washington had not reached a consensus on their desirability. But time has moved on, and we are now looking to *World Development Report 2000/01* for an outline of the policies needed to supplement my version of the Washington Consensus in a world that takes poverty reduction seriously.

The Semantic Dilemma

One can react to the semantic dilemma posed by the different definitions currently in use in three possible ways. Consider these alternatives:

- *Insist on the original usage.* Insist that my version of the Washington Consensus is the only correct and legitimate interpretation, as a corollary of which the term will (with the qualifications noted above) be recognized as pro-poor. This alternative strikes me as both presumptuous and unrealistic: once a term has escaped into the public domain, one cannot dictate the reestablishment of a common usage. The likely result would be a perpetuation of the public confusion that I am attempting to address.
- *Abandon the term.* Refuse to debate in the terms that have been so compromised by the widespread adoption of the "populist" definition. I cannot imagine that this approach would end the populist use of the term; it would simply be a cop-out.
- *Endorse a post–Washington Consensus.* A more promising strategy has been adopted at least twice within the Bank. In 1998 the Latin America Regional Office of the World Bank issued a policy document that favored going beyond the Washington Consensus (Burki and Perry 1998). Stiglitz did almost the same, semantically at least, in urging a post–Washington Consensus in his lecture to the World Institute for Development Economics Research in January 1998.

When I first came across this approach, I thought it implied that the reforms included in the Washington Consensus were necessary but not sufficient for promoting development, an idea that seemed eminently reasonable. Clearly the Bank today would want to go further and endorse a wider array of antipoverty instruments than was able to command a consensus in 1989, when the most I thought I could legitimately include was the promotion of public expenditure on primary health and education.[5]

In their book, Burki and Perry (1998) explicitly refer to my version of the Washington Consensus and assert that the widespread implementation of the "first-generation" reforms it prescribed was paying off in Latin America in resumed growth and an end to high inflation. They noted that the reforms had not been equally effective in reducing poverty and inequality, which they argued demonstrated a "need to focus on improving the quality of investments in human development, promoting the development of sound and efficient financial markets, enhancing the legal and regulatory environments (in particular, deregulating labor markets and improving regulations for private investment in infrastructure and social services), [and] improving the quality of the public sector (including the judiciary) . . ." (p. 4). This is an agenda dominated by institutional reform, which is indeed what has become known in Latin America as the second-generation reform agenda (Naim 1995).

It is not equally obvious why Stiglitz would want to propagate a post–Washington Consensus that implied endorsing and extending the original version, given his interpretation of what was included in it. In fact, the Stiglitz version of a post–Washington Consensus does not endorse any version of the original. He is advocating a policy package that is intended to supersede the Washington Consensus altogether. His new policy package is asserted to differ from the original in two dimensions.

First, he argues that the implicit policy objective underlying the Washington Consensus is inadequate. In addition to pursuing economic growth, the objectives should include "sustainable development, egalitarian development, and democratic development." In other words, he believes that policy objectives should include the state of the environment, income distribution, and democracy, as well as per capita gross national product. I find those objectives much more congenial than a single-minded preoccupation with economic growth, although I am not sure that the World Bank could formally endorse the pursuit of democracy (its Articles do, after all, forbid its involvement in politics).[6] Second, in addition to expanding the objectives, Stiglitz argues that it is necessary to pursue "sound financial regulation, competition policy, and policies to facilitate the transfer of technology and transparency" to make markets work in a way that will support development.

I have a somewhat different view of what should be added to the Washington Consensus to make it a policy manifesto supportive of egalitarian, environmentally sensitive development. I agree that financial regulation (prudential supervision) is crucial and that transparency is a useful complement to supervision in achieving appropriate conduct of financial institutions. Moreover, competition is a natural complement to deregulation in promoting a well-functioning market economy (although a liberal import regime is the most effective competition policy in tradables, as Srinivasan argues in his comment in this volume). I would not have included technology transfer in such a manifesto, although I would have no objection to including institutional changes that seemed likely to promote technology transfer if I were reasonably confident that I knew what these changes were (besides accepting foreign direct investment). Similarly, I would consider it desirable to include policies focused on improved environmental conditions, although I am not sure that I would know how to select policy measures at a comparable level of generality to my 10 original points. But my emphasis would have been different; I would have focused much more generally on institutions. To explain why, let me offer a brief history of postwar development thinking.

In the first wave of theorizing about economic development, from the 1940s to the early 1960s, economists saw the accumulation of physical capital as the key to development (as reflected in the Harrod-Domar model, the Lewis model, and the two-gap model). The second phase recognized that human capital provided another and more inelastic constraint on development, a constraint that explained why Europe and Japan had recovered from World War II so rapidly, when growth in developing countries had been lagging despite the adoption of development policies and the beginning of large-scale aid. The third phase, which started about 1970 with the work of Little, Scitovsky, and Scott (1970) and Balassa (1970), emphasized that the policy environment influenced the level and dominated the productivity of investment. The Washington Consensus attempted to summarize the outcome of this debate on the policies that were conducive to economic development. The major advance of the 1990s stemmed from recognition that the central task of the transition from communist to market-based economies involved building the institutional infrastructure of a market economy. This realization was complemented by a growing recognition that bad institutions can sabotage good policies. This viewpoint was reflected in Stiglitz's (1999a) remarks on the transition, in Naim's (1995) work on supplementing the Washington Consensus, in Burki and Perry (1998), in the *World Development Reports* of 1997 and 1998, and in the World Bank's decision to launch a crusade against corruption.

What should one make of the idea of launching a post–Washington Consensus? I would not be happy at such a move if it were interpreted to imply a rejection of "the" Washington Consensus, although I would have no problem if it involved rejection of the populist, or market-fundamentalist, version. But it seems a somewhat odd crusade. The time of the original consensus, 1989, was an unusual period in that the ideological battles of the Reagan era, not to mention the cold war battle between capitalism and communism, were passing into history, leaving in their wake an unusually wide measure of agreement that several rather basic ideas of good economics were not only desirable but of key importance in the current policy agenda of at least one region—Latin America. Currently, there is no similar coalescing of views, certainly not on the wider agenda that Stiglitz has laid out. (Consensus on egalitarianism? With aid fatigue threatening the future of the International Development Association? On environmental sustainability? In a world where the U.S. Senate refuses even to consider ratifying the Kyoto Protocol?) I agree, rather, with Tim Geithner (1999:8): "I don't think anyone believes there is some universal model that can or should be imposed on the world—Washington consensus, post Washington consensus, or not."

Resolving the Dilemma

Let me conclude by laying out my own ideas on how to resolve the dilemma.

- There is little merit in attacking abstract, undefined concepts that are interpreted to mean whatever the author momentarily decides they mean. It is better to spell out those concepts that are being criticized and debate policies on the basis of their merits.
- The World Bank should recognize that the term Washington Consensus has been used in very different ways. One summarizes policies that are pro-poor; another describes a policy stance that offers the poor very little and warrants no support.
- It is appropriate to go beyond the Washington Consensus by emphasizing the importance of the institutional dimension as well as of the sort of policies embodied in the original version of the Washington Consensus—policies that will promote an equitable distribution of income as well as a rapid growth of income.
- The hopeless quest to identify a consensus where there is none should be abandoned in favor of a debate on the policy changes needed to achieve a rounded set of objectives encompassing at least the level, growth, and distribution of income, as well as preservation of a decent environment.

The Bank will do the cause of economic development a great service if it can frame future debate in these terms. Admittedly my suggestions do not answer the pleas for a new ideology that would more adequately reflect the goals of the multilateral development banks and that might thus increase the chance of establishing local ownership of the sort of economic policy stance conducive to rapid and equitable growth. Let me plead in defense that I am not a suitable person to launch an ideology, inasmuch as Naim (2000) characterizes an ideology as a thought-economizing device and I actually believe that thinking is more desirable than economizing on thought.

Notes

John Williamson is senior fellow at the Institute for International Economics. This article was written as a background paper for *World Development Report 2000/01*. The author is indebted to the participants in a session at which an early version of the paper was discussed, notably Ravi Kanbur and Moisés Naím.

1. This intellectual convergence was the result of the collapse of communism, which resulted not from machinations of the Bretton Woods institutions, or even of the U.S. Central Intelligence Agency, but because socialism does not work except in a simple economy, and even then it seems to have worked reasonably well only when large numbers of people were inspired with revolutionary zeal.

2. Exchange rate policy is the one topic on which I have a serious difference of view with T. N. Srinivasan's comment that accompanies this paper. The term "competitive exchange rate" originated with Bela Balassa and signifies a rate that is either at, or undervalued relative to, its long-run equilibrium. I do not regard measuring the latter as an exercise in futility; see Hinkle and Montiel (1999) for evidence that other people in the Bank do not either. I dissent from the consensus Srinivasan proclaims that holds that only currency boards and freely floating rates offer viable regimes. For further details, see Williamson (forthcoming).

3. In trying to identify policies from the Reagan-Thatcher era that had not won consensus support, I wrote in 1996: "it [the Washington Consensus] did not declare that the only legitimate way to restore fiscal discipline was to slash government expenditure; it did not identify fiscal discipline with a balanced budget; it did not call for overall tax cuts; it did not treat as plunder the taxes raised to redistribute income; it did not say that exchange rates had to be either firmly fixed or freely floating; it did not call for the proscription of capital controls; it did not advocate competitive moneys or argue that the money supply should grow at a fixed rate" (Williamson 1997:50).

4. Growth of output of a heavily protected product can immiserize a country if the resources used in production exceed the social value of the output.

5. However, in commenting on my paper, Stanley Fischer (then the Bank's chief economist) argued that I could and should have gone further: "Emphasis on poverty reduction has increased in recent years and will continue to do so. [A good forecast.] The concern with poverty reduction goes beyond the belief that economic growth will reduce poverty, to the view that targeted food subsidies as well as the medical and educational programs to which Williamson refers, can reduce the number of poor people . . . and should be used for that purpose" (Williamson 1990:27).

6. Some people might wish to add nation-building to the noneconomic objectives to be pursued by development policy (as was common in the 1960s).

References

The word "processed" refers to informally reproduced works that may not be commonly available through library systems.

Alam, M. Shahid. 1999. "Does Sovereignty Matter for Economic Growth?" In John Adams and Francesco Pigliaru, eds., *Economic Growth and Change*. Cheltenham, U.K.: Edward Elgar.

Balassa, Bela. 1970. "Growth Strategies in Semi-Industrial Countries." *Quarterly Journal of Economics* 84(1):24–47.

Brecher, Richard, and Carlos Diaz-Alejandro. 1977. "Tariffs, Foreign Capital, and Immiserizing Growth." *Journal of International Economics* 7(4):317–22.

Burki, Javed, and Guillermo E. Perry. 1998. *Beyond the Washington Consensus: Institutions Matter*. Washington, D.C.: World Bank.

Geithner, Timothy F. 1999. "The World Bank and the Frontier of Development Challenges." Remarks delivered to a conference on "Reinventing the World Bank: Challenges and Opportunities for the 21st Century," Northwestern University, May 14. Processed.

Hamada, Koichi. 1998. "IMF Special: Keeping Alive the Asian Monetary Fund." *Capital Trends* 3(September).

Hinkle, Lawrence E., and Peter J. Montiel, eds. 1999. *Exchange Rate Misalignment: Concepts and Measurement for Developing Countries*. New York: Oxford University Press.

Ito, Takatoshi. 1999. "The Role of IMF Advice." Paper presented to International Monetary Fund conference on "Key Issues in Reform of the International Monetary and Financial System," Washington, D.C., May 29. Processed.

Kolodko, Gregorz. 1998. *Transition.* World Bank Development Economic Research Group newsletter, June.

Little, Ian, Tibor Scitovsky, and Maurice Scott. 1970. *The Structure of Protection in Developing Countries: A Comparative Study.* Baltimore, Md.: Johns Hopkins University Press.

McCloskey, Deirdre N. 1998. *The Rhetoric of Economics.* 2d ed. Madison, Wis.: University of Wisconsin Press.

Naím, Moisés. 1995. "Latin America: The Morning After." *Foreign Affairs* 74(July–August):45–61.

———. 2000. "Washington Consensus or Washington Confusion?" *Foreign Policy* (spring):86–103.

Rajan, Ramkishen S. 1999. "The Brazilian and Other Currency Crises of the 1990s." *Claremont Policy Brief.* Claremont College, Claremont, Calif. May.

Soros, George. 1998. *The Crisis of Global Capitalism.* New York: Public Affairs.

Stewart, Frances. 1997. "Williamson and the Washington Consensus Revisited." In Louis Emmerij, ed., *Economic and Social Development into the XXI Century.* Washington, D.C.: Inter-American Development Bank.

Stiglitz, Joseph E. 1994. "The Role of the State in Financial Markets." In Michael Bruno and Boris Pleskovic, eds., *Proceedings of the World Bank Conference on Development Economics 1993.* Washington, D.C.: World Bank.

———. 1998. "More Instruments and Broader Goals: Moving toward the Post–Washington Consensus." United Nations University/World Institute for Development Economics Research, Helsinki.

———. 1999a. "Whither Reform? Ten Years of the Transition." In Boris Plesovic and Joseph E. Stiglitz, eds., *World Bank Annual Conference on Development Economics.* Washington, D.C.: World Bank.

———. 1999b. "The World Bank at the Millennium." *Economic Journal* 109(459):F577–97.

United Nations. 1998. *Annual Report of the United Nations University.* Tokyo.

Vines, David. 1999. In an obituary for Susan Strange. Newsletter no 9. Economic and Social Research Council Programme on Global Economic Institutions, Swindon, U.K. Processed.

Waelbroeck, Jean. 1998. "Half a Century of Development Economics: A Review Based on the *Handbook of Development Economics.*" *The World Bank Economic Review* 12(May):323–52.

Williamson, John. 1990. "What Washington Means by Policy Reform." In John Williamson, ed., *Latin American Adjustment: How Much Has Happened?* Washington, D.C.: Institute for International Economics.

———. 1996. "Are the Latin American Reforms Sustainable?" In Hermann Sautter and Rolf Schinke, eds., *Stabilization and Reforms in Latin America: Where Do We Stand?* Frankfurt: Vervuert Verlag.

———. 1997. "The Washington Consensus Revisited." In Louis Emmerij, ed., *Economic and Social Development into the XXI Century.* Washington, D.C.: Inter-American Development Bank.

———. 1999. "Implications of the East Asian Crisis for Debt Management." In A. Vasudevan, ed., *External Debt Management: Issues, Lessons, and Preventive Measures.* Mumbai: Reserve Bank of India.

———. Forthcoming. *Exchange Rate Regimes for Emerging Economies: Reviving the Intermediate Option.* Washington, D.C.: Institute for International Economics.

Williamson, John, and Molly Mahar. 1998. "A Survey of Financial Liberalization." Princeton Essays in International Finance 211. Princeton University, Princeton, N.J.

World Bank. 1993. *The East Asian Miracle: Economic Growth and Public Policy.* New York. Oxford University Press.

———. 1996. *World Development Report: From Plan to Market.* New York: Oxford University Press.

[30]

The Washington Consensus a Decade Later: Ideology and the Art and Science of Policy Advice

T. N. Srinivasan

In 1990 Williamson coined the term "Washington Consensus" to describe "the lowest common denominator of policy advice being addressed by the Washington institutions to Latin American countries as of 1989." He now protests in an article in this volume that the phrase has "become a synonym for 'neoliberalism' or what George Soros (1998) has called 'market fundamentalism'. . . . " This development should have caused no surprise, given the visceral hatred in many parts of the world for free markets. Because they view the U.S. government and its "lackeys"—the World Bank, the International Monetary Fund, and to a lesser extent, the Inter-American Development Bank—as the chief advocates of free markets, these opponents of free markets would have attacked anything called the "Washington Consensus." Had he instead called it the "Williamson synthesis," perhaps the package would have been a less inviting target for attack, although one cannot be sure: given the author's association with the hated Washington institutions, he could not have credibly absolved them from responsibility for the synthesis.

More than a decade has passed since Williamson proffered the consensus package. It is tempting (following the advice of the late Senator George Aiken of Vermont, who suggested that the United States simply declare victory and withdraw from the then-raging Vietnam War) to announce that the policy prescriptions contained in the consensus package have been successful and are no longer contentious! Even though there is considerable evidence of the success of many elements of the package where appropriately implemented, unfortunately the top echelon of at least one of the institutions celebrated in the consensus—the World Bank—seems to be misinformed and confused about the contents of the policy package. Others doubt the appropriateness of some of the recommended policies and argue that other elements of the package never commanded a consensus. It is useful, therefore, to reexamine

The World Bank Research Observer, vol. 15, no. 2 (August 2000), pp. 265–70.
© 2000 The International Bank for Reconstruction and Development / THE WORLD BANK

the package for its contemporary relevance, taking into account the experience of the 1990s.

At the outset, let me say that I regard the policy package less as a consensus and more as a reflection of the author's synthesis of lessons from four decades of development experience. Indeed, Williamson's phrase "common denominator of policy advice" can mean only one thing: that the advice is based on policy implications that emerged not only from a number of studies of certain Latin American countries but also, more generally, from experience in many developing countries. In this sense, trade liberalization as a sensible policy was supported by studies published in the 1970s by the Organisation for Economic Co-operation and Development (Little, Scitovsky, and Scott 1970), the National Bureau of Economic Research (Bhagwati 1978; Krueger 1978), and the World Bank (Balassa 1970). (A later World Bank study, Papageorgiou, Michaely, and Choksi 1991, lent similar support.) But only the utterly naive would interpret this advice as unqualified in the sense of being appropriate regardless of the specific circumstances of an economy or the time horizon involved. Yet the studies covered many countries with varying socio-political-economic institutions and many different time periods, and almost all of them still found possible benefits from trade liberalization—a fact that testifies to the robustness of the policy advice. Be that as it may, it is common knowledge among economists that the response to any policy change, such as trade liberalization, that operates through price incentives depends both on nonprice factors and on the time horizon. For example, if domestic supply constraints (other than price received) are severe in the short and medium run, removing all price distortions would have only a limited favorable response. And, to the extent that tax revenues are largely derived from trade taxes, the government may be constrained as to how far it can liberalize trade by reducing trade taxes without compromising fiscal discipline. This constraint may not be binding, however, if the actual applied tariffs exceed revenue-maximizing levels, as is often claimed. In any case, one can enumerate many nuances and caveats to each of the recommended policies in the package. But only an ideologue or the utterly ignorant would conclude that because caveats apply, any attempt to change the status quo through the implementation of the recommended policies is undesirable.

Similarly, the advice to liberalize interest rates was a common conclusion from several studies of financial repression in developing countries. Williamson now concedes that it could be costly to liberalize interest rates before other elements of financial liberalization, such as prudential supervision of banks by capable and knowledgeable central bank authorities, are in place. Although this point is obviously valid, the scope of its applicability is arguable. For example, in many developing countries, most banks are publicly owned, and whether they would or could gamble for redemption if deposit interest rates were to be liberalized is open to question. At any rate, as in the case of trade liberalization, the case for interest rate liberalization is likely to remain intact for many developing countries.

The advice on fiscal discipline was also based on the experience of many developing countries, particularly Latin American countries, that had previously undergone episodes of hyperinflation and stop-and-go sequences of stagnation and growth. India's experience in the 1980s, when it abandoned fiscal discipline to run deficits financed by costly borrowing at home and abroad, is instructive. The spurt in growth following the reckless fiscal expansionism proved unsustainable and ended inevitably in a macroeconomic-cum-balance of payments crisis in 1991. The fact that India did not experience Latin-style inflation before or after the abandonment of fiscal discipline is beside the point: because most of India's poor workers, particularly those in agriculture and informal service sectors, are not protected against inflation, even moderate inflation by Latin standards has serious consequences for the welfare of the poor in India.

The advice to redirect public expenditure toward health care, primary education, and infrastructure has long been part of conventional wisdom. A point that is not part of the conventional wisdom (and one that leading advocates of redirection such as Amartya Sen and his acolytes do not emphasize) is that failure to liberalize trade, to privatize inefficient public enterprises of dubious social value (such as airlines, hotels, and steel mills), and to reform the tax system eats away public resources that could otherwise be directed to the social sectors. Thus trade liberalization, privatization, and tax reform, which constitute three of the ten policies in the consensus package, are important not only in and of themselves but also because they make more resources available for social sectors.

The package called for "a competitive exchange rate," an unfortunate choice of words. An exchange rate is the price of one currency in terms of another currency or a basket of currencies. The word "competitive" used in the context of an exchange rate evokes painful memories of competitive devaluations by many countries in the interwar era. Under the classic Bretton Woods system of fixed exchange rates, one could interpret an "uncompetitive" exchange rate to mean one that is overvalued relative to its long-run equilibrium value. The operational significance of the interpretation is vastly diminished, however, by the fact that the long-run equilibrium rate is hard to define, that it was not defined in the Articles of Agreement of the International Monetary Fund, and that it is not simple to compute from available data in any case. Perhaps by a competitive exchange rate Williamson meant an undervalued exchange rate and that in fact Japan and the East Asian economies following Japan maintained competitive exchange rates in this sense.

Edwards and Savastano (1999) recently surveyed the empirical studies on exchange rate regimes in developing countries. They identified two camps: one group ascribes a key role to the exchange rate as a nominal anchor; the other stresses the perils of relying on an asset price and therefore sees the exchange rate as a nominal anchor in a world of integrated global capital markets. In their view

> ... the differences between the two broad camps identified lie in their differing views regarding three key features of exchange rate policy in a context of high capital mobility: (1) the scope for (and effectiveness of) sterilized and unsterilized intervention as a means for attaining (and preserving) a degree of nominal exchange rate stability; (2) the costs that "excessive" fluctuations of the nominal exchange rate may impose on the economy's performance; and (3) the *time dimension* of their analysis—i.e., the horizon over which monetary policy, the exchange rate, capital flows and the rest of the economy are assumed to interplay. All of these are empirical issues for which little, if anything, is known for the case of developing countries—not even for the relatively advanced ones. (Edwards and Savastano 1999:22)

Since the Asian financial crisis, a consensus seems to be emerging that the only two viable exchange rate regimes are either a system of rigidly fixed exchange rates implemented through a currency board arrangement or its opposite, a regime of freely floating exchange rates. Williamson, however, now prefers an intermediate regime between the two with limited flexibility. He does not explain why and how the limited flexibility of the regime could be credibly signaled to distinguish it, on the one hand, from the old-fashioned and now discredited crawling peg and, on the other hand, from a regime of transition to a free float. The advice to keep the exchange rate "competitive" has no operational content even if a competitive exchange rate could be defined in conceptual terms. Of course, allowing the rate to float freely obviates this problem.

The recommendation to liberalize flows of foreign direct investment grew in part out of the need to have capital inflows that did not create debt and in part from the desire for other benefits such as technology transfers, which were believed to be associated with such investments. Such investment flows are not likely to be as volatile as short-term capital flows because a decision to invest in another country is probably based on the long-term fundamentals of the recipient economy. Even as late as 1989, private capital flows, including foreign direct investment, had not accelerated as much as they did in the 1990s. The financial crises starting with Mexico in December 1994 and ending with the most recent one in Brazil in 1998 have exposed several weaknesses in the domestic financial sectors of developing countries and in the international financial architecture. The crises have, if anything, reinforced the advice to liberalize foreign direct investment flows.

The advice to deregulate, in the sense of abolishing barriers to entry and, equally important, to exit, continues to be pertinent because it is based on age-old and proven virtues of competition. Indeed, benefits from removing price distortions will be limited if firms not strong enough to compete in an undistorted market are not allowed to exit and if more efficient firms are denied entry.

The obverse side of deregulation is the need to ensure competition to firms that are privatized. For internationally traded goods and services (except possibly in wide-body passenger jet aircraft!), the world market is far larger than the minimum efficient scale of production, so that opening to trade is adequate to generate competition. In nontraded sectors where considerations of scale economies or network externalities preclude the possibility of more than a handful of firms operating on an efficient scale, a regulatory authority needs to be established and an appropriate set of regulations promulgated so that the few private firms operate in a socially desirable manner. Interestingly, technological developments have vastly eroded scale economies in electricity generation, telecommunications, and other nontraded goods and services that were once deemed natural monopolies.

In 1990, when Williamson published his consensus, regulation and privatization in developing countries were scarce, and there was none in Russia and the Eastern European countries, which were still part of the disintegrating Soviet Union. In the decade since then, privatization has taken off, particularly in the transition economies. It is fair to say, however, that the state of knowledge about appropriate mechanisms for privatization and regulatory frameworks (particularly for private financial intermediaries) is still in a state of flux. Nonetheless, the advice to privatize remains relevant, with a cautionary note about the need to ensure sufficient competition for privatized enterprises.

My brief evaluation of the Washington Consensus 10 years after its promulgation strongly suggests that its policy advice remains largely intact. In general, sound policy advice, while undoubtedly based on received theory and empirical evidence, necessarily has to involve judgment. Economic theorizing involves simplification and abstraction of complex reality; econometric analysis of empirical evidence often imposes restrictions on theory such as, for example, specific functional forms for utility and production functions, the nature of heterogeneity among firms and consumers, and distributional assumptions about stochastic terms. Simple and abstract theory (which in its "second-best" version could amount to saying that almost anything is possible!) and its highly restrictive econometric specification cannot deliver policy conclusions that can be directly applied to the situation of any given economy at a particular time. To advise on policy requires sound judgment on the part of the advisor—judgment that goes beyond findings for theoretical and econometric models. Such judgment will incorporate knowledge about history, particularly economic history, and about the specific socio-political-cultural features and institutions of the country involved. For example, cross-country regressions, even if they are not mindless, cannot deliver policy conclusions about the desirability of trade liberalization or capital inflows or about the effect of openness on growth. At best, such regressions are an efficient means for discovering patterns in the data from which capable researchers can draw inferences after bringing to bear their knowledge about the economies involved while firmly eschewing attribution of causality. To say that judgment based on the specifics of the case is needed is not to argue either that there can be no robust policy conclusions of wide applicability or that only discretion, rather than rules, should govern policy choice. What it means is that formal analysis has to be supplemented by informally allowing for factors that by necessity have been excluded from the formal analysis. There is art as well as science in policy advising! An honest policy advisor will clearly indicate where his judgment enters and where theory and econometrics stop. It is not hard to isolate the theoretical and econometric bases and the astute judgment of Williamson in the Washington Consensus.

Note

T. N. Srinivasan is Samuel C. Park Jr. Professor of Economics at Yale University.

References

The word "processed" describes informally reproduced works that may not be commonly available through library systems.

Balassa, Bela. 1970. "Growth Strategies in Semi-Industrial Countries." *Quarterly Journal of Economics* 84(1):24–47.

Bhagwati, Jagdish. 1978. *Foreign Trade Regimes and Economic Development: Anatomy and Consequences of Exchange Control Regimes.* Cambridge, Mass.: Ballinger.

Edwards, Sebastian, and Miguel A. Savastano. 1999. "Exchange Rates in Emerging Economies: What Do We Know? What Do We Need to Know?" Revised version of a paper presented at a Stanford University conference on "Economic Policy Reform: What We Know and What We Need to Know," September 17–19, 1998. Processed.

Krueger, Anne. 1978. *Foreign Trade Regimes and Economic Development: Liberalization Attempts and Consequences.* Cambridge, Mass.: Ballinger.

Little, Ian, Tibor Scitovsky, and Maurice Scott. 1970. *The Structure of Protection in Developing Countries: A Comparative Study.* Baltimore, Md.: Johns Hopkins University Press.

Papageorgiou, Demetris, Michael Michaely, and Armeane M. Choksi, eds. 1991. *Liberalizing Foreign Trade.* Oxford, U.K.: Basil Blackwell.

Soros, George. 1998. *The Crisis of Global Capitalism.* New York: Public Affairs.

Name Index